European Societies in the Bronze Age

The European Bronze Age, roughly 2500 to 750 BC, was the last fully prehistoric period and crucially important for the formation of the Europe that emerged in the later first millennium BC. This book provides a detailed account of its material culture, and focuses on the findings of the past twenty years, when a large amount of data was collected, necessitating a revision of received views on many aspects of the period. By comparing and contrasting evidence from different geographical and cultural zones of Europe, it draws out the essential characteristics of the Bronze Age. Arranged thematically, it reviews the evidence on settlement, burial, economy, technology, trade and transport, warfare, and social and religious life, and describes the main theoretical models that have been developed to interpret these new materials. The result is a comprehensive study that will be of value to specialists and students, and accessible to non-specialists.

ANTHONY F. HARDING is Professor of Archaeology at the University of Durham. He has worked on sites in many countries of Europe, directing excavations in Britain, Poland and the Czech Republic, and has published widely on Bronze Age archaeology. His publications include *The Bronze Age in Europe*, with John Coles (1979); *The Mycenaeans and Europe* (1984) and *Die Schwerter im ehemaligen Jugoslawien* (1995).

CAMBRIDGE WORLD ARCHAEOLOGY

EUROPEAN SOCIETIES IN THE BRONZE AGE

A. F. HARDING

Department of Archaeology
University of Durham

CAMBRIDGE
UNIVERSITY PRESS

PUBLISHED BY THE PRESS SYNDICATE OF THE UNIVERSITY OF CAMBRIDGE
The Pitt Building, Trumpington Street, Cambridge, United Kingdom

CAMBRIDGE UNIVERSITY PRESS
The Edinburgh Building, Cambridge CB2 2RU, UK
  http://www.cup.cam.ac.uk
40 West 20th Street, New York, NY 10011-4211, USA
  http://www.cup.org
10 Stamford Road, Oakleigh, Melbourne 3166, Australia

First published 2000

Printed in the United Kingdom at the University Press, Cambridge

Typeset in Trump Medieval 10/13 [wv]

A catalogue record for this book is available from the British Library

Library of Congress cataloguing in publication data

Harding, A. F.
European societies in the Bronze Age / A. F. Harding.
   p.   cm. – (Cambridge world archaeology)
Includes bibliographical references and index.
ISBN 0 521 36477 9 (hc.)
1. Bronze Age–Europe.   2. Europe–Antiquities.   I. Title.
II. Series.
GN778.2.A1H38 2000
936–dc21 99–28849 CIP

ISBN 0 521 36477 9 hardback
ISBN 0 521 36729 8 paperback

For Jan Bouzek, teacher and friend

CONTENTS

FIGURES

TABLES

PREFACE

The origin of this book lies in the publication and reception of an earlier work on the Bronze Age, *The Bronze Age in Europe* (1979), which J. M. Coles and I wrote in the mid-1970s. The work represented the first attempt to give a continent-wide (if necessarily superficial) account of a complicated set of materials, and remains the only such work. Though the critical reception was on the whole favourable, it rapidly became evident that as a tool for *understanding* the Bronze Age it was of limited use, framed as it was around a descriptive approach to the culture sequence in each area of Europe. In spite of this, many people continue to ask whether a revised edition of *The Bronze Age in Europe* will be produced. The answer is that, though it may be needed, the enormous amount of work which would be necessary to bring it up to date would be quite beyond the powers and wishes of its authors, who have other tasks to fulfil and interests to pursue.

Instead, I have felt for a number of years that what would be of much more use would be a work which sought to analyse different aspects of the Bronze Age on a thematic basis. Other commitments prevented me from starting it until 1994, and as I have proceeded I have often felt that the enterprise was a rash one. For a start, the sheer volume of material that has been produced in the last twenty years, and continues to pour out, is staggering. The reader will note from the References that the great majority of items listed date from the period since 1979 (which is not to say that works before this date are superseded; some of the more important can be found referenced in Coles and Harding 1979). Had I known prior to starting work how vast the literature would prove to be, I might have thought again.

But this is just a question of quantity. What has given me far more pause for thought is the question of coverage, and the value of generalisation. I used to think that many processes and phenomena present in the Bronze Age were much the same across all of Europe, and that therefore one could write a story for the period that would give a satisfactory and satisfying account valid for most areas. Such an assumption was, of course, ridiculously naive and hopelessly ignorant. As I have read, visited sites, and talked to practitioners, I have come to realise how complex the situation really was, and how difficult – invalid, indeed – generalisation is.

Nevertheless, I do attempt in what follows to discern common patterns in what people were creating and doing in the Bronze Age. Dissimilarities are just as important as similarities in this respect. Why did people in Britain react to much the same environment so differently from people in France? How did it come about that identical bronze forms were adopted from one end of Europe to the other at the start of the Late Bronze Age? While I cannot promise to answer such questions, I do at least feel it is worth asking them.

The book attempts to cover the whole of Europe, but inevitably it deals more with some areas than others. In part these reflect my own biases and knowledge, but they do also stem from the fact that better and more recent work has been done in some areas than others. It will rapidly become evident that Britain, Scandinavia and central Europe are the areas most often cited for examples, though I have tried to use appropriate examples from every part of the continent. I confess to almost total failure as far as the more eastern areas are concerned, but this is not entirely through lack of knowledge (see chapters 3 and 8 in *The Bronze Age in Europe*); I have found little sign of recent high-quality work in, for instance, Russia which would merit significant inclusion here. The relative shortage of Mediterranean examples is a failing all my own, which I admit in the full realisation that much excellent work has been carried out in Iberia and Italy in recent years. But just to have given the island of Sardinia the attention it deserves would have greatly extended this book, as Webster's recent synthesis (1996) makes clear. I do not expect to escape censure for such failings, though I would plead in mitigation that there is a limited number of case studies which it is practical to introduce into a book of this length, and since my concern has been, among other things, to discern the presence or absence of patterning in the data available, it would not have been appropriate to use isolated and disparate examples from all over Europe. The reader will judge whether or not I have been successful in this enterprise, but I hope she/he will not feel the enterprise to have been worthless in the first place. Though both 'Europe' and 'the Bronze Age' are constructs, they serve a purpose in communication (as I explain on p. 4), and I would contest the importance of this particular period of time in this particular continent against all comers.

It is my pleasurable duty to record the names of the many people who have helped me during the arduous process of writing this book. The unstinting generosity of fellow-students of the Bronze Age never ceases to amaze me, offered out of pure altruism (as far as I can tell) and leading me to think that, contrary to popular belief, there *is* such a thing as a free lunch. My duties at work in recent years, and other academic and family commitments, have not permitted me the time to undertake extensive museum and site tours of the sort that preceded the writing of *The Bronze Age in Europe*, but regular contact with leading scholars has done much to fill the gap.

I am extremely grateful to Kristian Kristiansen for lending me a manuscript of his book *Europe before History* (1998) considerably before publication. I have read and profited from this work, and its general ideas have without doubt influenced me; but I have refrained from making detailed use of it, and quoting it, because its approach to the same material is very different from mine, and I wanted to be sure to avoid any suspicion of plagiarism – or even copying of the same sources (most of which were, of course, already familiar to me). Kristiansen has a particular view of the period to present, and he has selected his material to suit that view; my concern has been to paint some sort of whole picture, using theoretical ideas while still mostly dealing with the artefactual data. Just before submission of this book to the press, I saw Marisa Ruiz-Gálvez Priego's book *La Europa atlántica en la edad del bronce* (Barcelona, Crítica, 1998). This work will clearly be an invaluable guide to the western end of Europe in the Bronze Age, and it covers many of the same topics as does the present book, with many fascinating insights of an anthropological and sociological nature. I have not, however, made use of it to modify the present work.

For reading and commenting on chapters or sections in draft I am greatly indebted to my colleagues and friends John Chapman, Colin Haselgrove, Pippa Henry, Simon James, Matthew Johnson, Janet Levy, Billy O'Brien, Peter Rowley-Conwy and Jo Wood; Elizabeth Donnan read the entire typescript. Bob Chapman provided many helpful comments and advised me on matters Iberian. The kindness of all of them has saved me from many errors, but I alone am responsible for those that remain.

Many scholars have generously provided me with books, offprints, and illustrative material, sometimes knowing that I would use them to quarry material for this book, more often not. Others have discussed Bronze Age issues with me over longer or shorter periods. Among them I would particularly like to mention (in alphabetical order): David Anthony, Lawrence Barfield, Graeme Barker, Niels Björhem, Zbigniew Bukowski, Colin Burgess, Alessandro Canci, Andrea Cardarelli, Anne Carlie, Neritan Ceka, Horia Ciugudean, Janusz Czebreszuk, Philippe Della Casa, Margarita Díaz-Andreu, Marta Dočkalová, Caroline Earwood, George Eogan, M. Fansa, Vacláv Furmánek, Sabine Gerloff, Alex Gibson, Ilirian Gjipali, Alessandro Guidi, Bernhard Hänsel, Alexander Häusler, Richard Harrison, the late Fritz Horst, Jiří Hrala, Albrecht Jockenhövel, Sławomir Kadrow, Anita Knape, Tibor Kovács, Rüdiger Krause, Wolf Kubach, Andreas Lippert, David Liversage, Raffaele de Marinis, Dragi Mitrevski, Ignacio Montero, Stuart Needham, Johannes-Wolfgang Neugebauer, Peter Northover, Billy O'Brien, Debbie Olausson, Janusz Ostoja-Zagórski, Aleksandar Palavestra, Chris Pare, Sebastian Payne, Renato Perini, Renato Peroni, Mauro Perra, Neil Price, Margarita Primas, Klavs Randsborg, Peter Romsauer, Nico Roymans, Emily Schalk, R. Schneider, Stephen Shennan, Biba Teržan, Henrik Thrane, Peter Turk, Lucia Vagnetti, Helle Vandkilde, Rastko Vasić, Magdi Vicze, John Waddell, Eugène Warmenbol and

Peter Wells. Many others, too numerous to mention individually, have provided help in other ways.

I thank my Durham colleagues who have patiently listened to assurances that the manuscript was 'almost ready' for several years, and for putting up with my periodic absences while library and site visits were in progress; Yvonne Beadnell and Sandra Rowntree for their professional and speedy execution of the illustrations; Trevor Woods for photographic reproductions; and Jessica Kuper of Cambridge University Press for her patience over a manuscript that took such a long time to appear. Finally, a special word of thanks to my family for their forbearance during the long hours and days that the writing of this book has entailed.

A. F. HARDING

Durham, December 1998

CHAPTER I

INTRODUCTION

This book is concerned with the history of human societies and the course of human interactions in Europe during the period that is traditionally called the Bronze Age, that is to say in absolute years the period of time between about 2500 and 800 BC. During this time, Europe changed from a continent settled by small farming and pastoral groups, strongly linked at the local level but only weakly linked, if at all, at broader levels, to one where it is possible to discern the existence of quasi-political groupings on a relatively large scale; from a society where individuals were powerful but did little to express that power in their material remains to one where the expression of status and power was extremely important; and from a society where the use of metal was rather rare and its circulation highly restricted to one where metals were a commonplace and vast quantities were produced.

The progress of these aspects of life and death was not, however, even across time or space. Nor were the processes outlined uniform in their manifestation. Europe is a large and geographically complex area (fig. 1.1), and the variety of its landscapes inevitably finds reflections in the patterns of activity of its inhabitants. It has also traditionally been seen as a melting-pot for the creation of 'peoples', that is to say ethnic identities. Although perspectives on both these aspects have shifted in recent years, it is undeniable that people reacted differently in different places and at different times to stimuli that from today's perspective look to have been similar or identical. In other words, one can identify groups of people, that is to say common groupings of material culture remains, whom it is convenient to lump together, naming them 'groups' or 'cultures'. It is this diversity of human reactions that is explored in this book.

Since people were different and reacted differently, the inevitable temptation is to write a book that merely lists or describes those reactions, in the form of material manifestations. It is in truth hard to escape this tendency altogether, since one is forced to relay some of the details of the more significant finds and sites that constitute the remains of any period of the prehistoric past, and the reader will find plenty of such descriptions in this work. These are, however, accompanied by an attempt to view the finds in a wider perspective, to arrive at some understanding of a common approach to particular aspects of life or death. The advantage of this approach is the

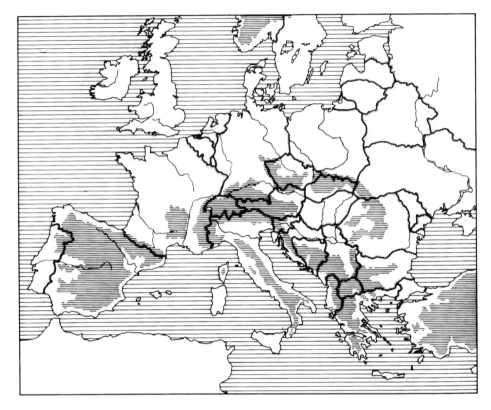

Fig. 1.1. Political and physical divisions of Europe.

possibility it offers of taking a wide view of problems common to everyone at particular periods of the Bronze Age. The disadvantage, and sometimes it is a crucial one, is that any attempt at discerning a common pattern becomes an imposition on the data, because it is clear there *was* no common pattern – things really were different in different parts of Europe.

An appreciation of this diversity is vital, particularly when one is concerned with mental processes that led to superstructural developments in the field of ideology and beliefs. With purely technological matters one is on safer ground, since there were only a limited number of ways of solving particular problems, such as extracting and smelting copper, working timber, or building houses. Even here, though, there are aspects which can be regarded as having had an ideological component, for example the form of houses, or attitudes to wood or stone that were more than merely utilitarian. This interplay between daily needs and expressions of the psyche finds its commonest expression in the treatment of the dead: the dead must be disposed of, but the way it is done can take on an enormous variety of forms, not merely in terms of the mechanics of disposal, but as regards the funeral service itself.

One can no more suppose that the last rites as practised in Ireland were the same as those in Romania than suppose that the Bronze Age Irish were ethnically the same as the Bronze Age Romanians.

Nevertheless, the attempt at discerning common patterns has been thought worthwhile in enough cases to justify the writing of a book with this broad geographical scope. The alternative, that of writing many smaller books about the Bronze Age of particular regions (and at what scale? that of the county? the state? the geographically defined region?), has often been done, and to this author at least has little appeal, tending as it does to create divisions where there are none. Thus general books on the Bronze Age in Hungary,[1] or Slovakia,[2] or eastern Austria[3] or the British Isles,[4] serve a useful local purpose but do little to further the understanding of the period on a wider level.[5]

The themes presented here therefore explore the extent to which general trends may be discerned, while endeavouring to avoid imposing such trends on the data. Although by today's standards the Bronze Age was a long period (around 1700 years in most of barbarian Europe, equivalent to all the time that has elapsed since the adoption of Christianity under Constantine), by comparison with anything which had gone before it was a time of rapid development and change, particularly so in the later stages. Furthermore, it was a time when contact between different parts of the European continent became common, so that major innovations in one area were adopted almost simultaneously in others; this is particularly true of technological change, but could apply as well to other, more 'psychological' developments such as burial modes. This means that it could be perfectly reasonable for common trends to have developed across much of the continent, and for archaeologists to attempt to spot them. Since the object of study is human beings and their responses, however, it would be unrealistic to expect such similarities to go beyond the most superficial of levels.

As well as dealing in the general, therefore, it will be necessary to look at the particular. In this, the study of local context is especially important. It has become a commonplace that sites and finds must be contextualised in order for any understanding of their meaning and form to be developed. The aim is laudable, but the results presented for public digestion so far, though bold and imaginative, have seemed less than impressive when it comes to convincing the sceptical that the particular interpretation presented has to be the correct one.

---

[1] Kovács 1977.
[2] Furmánek *et al.* 1991.
[3] Neugebauer 1994.
[4] Burgess 1974; 1980a.
[5] One of the criticisms levelled at *The Bronze Age in Europe* was that the authors did not have an adequate knowledge of the period in given countries, so that multi-author volumes using local specialists were said to be the way forward e.g. V. Trbuhović, *Starinar* 30, 1979, 137–8.

A word is necessary about the use of the terms 'Europe' and 'Bronze Age' in this book. 'Europe' is intended purely as a geographical description, meaning that part of the globe that lies between Connemara and the Urals, Malta and the North Cape; for purely practical reasons, I do not include Greece and the Aegean area in the present work except in order to introduce the occasional comparison.[6] I do not believe that any other significance can or should be assigned to the term in a rather remote period of the past, least of all that there was any special 'Europeanness' about Bronze Age Europe. By the same token, the 'Bronze Age' merely represents that chunk of time, roughly 2500 to 800 BC, that is traditionally called the Bronze Age. On the other hand, I believe that the phenomena encountered in this area and period are intrinsically interesting and that at certain times it is possible to illustrate the existence of trends and processes that were common to large parts of the territory, and were different from those occurring elsewhere on the globe. In this sense, I intend to show that 'Bronze Age Europe' is a worthwhile subject of study.

The Bronze Age is a much-studied period, and since the last century many authors have trodden the ground that underpins the present work. On the other hand, there have been astonishingly few books written that deal with the period as a whole and with Europe at large. Exceptions from the older literature are the works on chronology by Montelius and Åberg,[7] while Childe wrote a very general brief account, drawing in the East Mediterranean as well as 'barbarian' Europe.[8] The huge volume by Gimbutas, dealing with central and eastern Europe, represented a milestone in Bronze Age studies, bringing a vast quantity of little-known and inaccessible data before a wider public, and presenting a daring if controversial picture of the period in ethnogenetic terms.[9] Some of these matters were picked up by Coles and Harding in an attempt at treating the whole period over the whole continent; a more recent survey based primarily on radiocarbon dating is that by González Marcén, Lull and Risch.[10] A brief but extremely useful summary is provided by Müller-Karpe, who also gives a wide range of illustrative material from all parts of Europe,[11] while a short general account was provided by Bergmann.[12]

The problems faced by the generalist attempting to write a synthesis of a long period over a wide geographical area are compounded by political and linguistic difficulties, which create artificial divisions in the cultural story

[6] No disrespect is thereby intended to Greece and its archaeology, which are of course fully 'European' in a geographical sense; but the cultural manifestations are so different, and so extensive, that only a full-length book (of which many already exist) could do justice to the situation.
[7] Åberg 1930–5.
[8] Childe 1930.
[9] Gimbutas 1965.
[10] Coles and Harding 1979; González Marcén, Lull and Risch 1992.
[11] Müller-Karpe 1974; 1981.
[12] Bergmann 1987.

and render much literature inaccessible to many people, especially to Anglophones. With the changes that have occurred in Europe since 1989, however, much more is being written in the major world languages, especially English. Several countries have made one or more of their vehicles of archaeological publication into foreign-language journals (e.g. *Archaeologia Polona*, *Památky Archeologické*); in others this was the case already (e.g. *Acta Archaeologica* (Budapest)). While there are some areas where this trend is not yet apparent (Russia is a notable example), there is no doubt that it is now much easier to acquire and read the literature than it used to be. Of course English speakers are in a particularly privileged position in this respect. Unfortunately, the trend mentioned will do nothing to encourage them to widen their linguistic horizons, reinforcing many in their present view that what is not written in English is not worth reading. This form of cultural imperialism and isolationism is particularly sad at a time when many barriers in Europe are in other respects being broken down.

While the literature is more accessible than it was, this fact does bring other problems in its wake. During the period over which this book was written, a glut of publication on Bronze Age archaeology has occurred, stimulated among other things by the designation of 1994 as the 'Year of the Bronze Age' by the Council of Europe, part of a campaign to raise awareness of Bronze Age sites and monuments, for both touristic and conservation reasons. Conferences and exhibitions have been held in more than a dozen countries, and books or exhibition catalogues have been produced to accompany them, often lavish in scale. It is still too early to assess the longer-term benefits of this awareness-raising action, but the publication of many hitherto unknown sites and artefacts has certainly been of benefit to the scholarly world, even though this frequently involves sifting through great masses of semi-popular writing to extract a small number of pearls.

This cannot be the only reason, however. The designation of the 'Year of the Bronze Age' was really a symptom, not a cause. Scholarly interest in the period had been on the increase for years prior to 1994; there has been a vast outpouring of publication on Bronze Age matters in the last twenty years. It is not altogether easy to explain the reasons for this. In part it stems from the hugely increased level of activity within archaeology generally. But it must also reflect the fact that people have come to realise that the Bronze Age contains material for study of a kind and quantity that cannot be found in other prehistoric periods. A comparison with the Neolithic is instructive. In the Neolithic, very large numbers of sites are now known in many parts of Europe – settlements in central Europe, graves in north and west Europe, various combinations of these in other areas – and during the 1970s a great deal of attention was focused on these cultural manifestations. To the dispassionate observer, however, there is no doubt that there is a certain sameness, a lack of variety, about the material remains of the Neolithic; this is perhaps one of the features that were attractive to those of a positivist persuasion in earlier decades. Where this is not the case, the opposite is often true: the remains are so bafflingly enigmatic that it is hard to see how one can make much progress with understanding them, other than through post-processual approaches. A good example of this would be the study of megalithic tombs, where detailed typological study is a quick route to insanity. This is not to say that these problems do not also afflict Bronze Age studies in some part. It is rare to find a student – at least in the Anglo-Saxon world – who finds bronze implement typology fascinating, and stone circles are just as resistant to typological study as are megalithic tombs. But the range and quantity of material available for study is very much larger in the Bronze Age, particularly as modern survey and analytical techniques have demonstrated the richness of the source materials. Maybe too there has been a feeling that it is now the turn of the Bronze Age, that it has been understudied in the past and now offers possibilities for fruitful study. Whichever of these is correct, the problem remains. Anyone wanting to embark on serious study of the Bronze Age faces an enormous task in assimilating the literature. It is hoped that this book will make such a task somewhat easier.

The Bronze Age and its students

The course of Bronze Age studies over the last century, and especially over the last half century, has been determined by, but has also determined the work of, the scholars who have engaged in it. This observation is not, of course, peculiar to the Bronze Age; it applies to the study of any period or any subject. The Bronze Age differs from preceding periods, however, in that it produced very large quantities of specialised artefacts, which it has seemed natural to study in great detail; at the same time, it has lacked the great fortified sites and proto-urban centres that characterise the Iron Age. Its subjects of study have been conditioned accordingly.

To some extent these preoccupations have been those of their age. Morris has indicated how the nature of Bronze Age studies has changed with successive generations of archaeologists, at least in a British context;[13] similar effects have been felt in other countries. For many years, artefact studies and funerary monuments were the principal objects of study. Artefacts were long ago appreciated as the key to Bronze Age chronology. In the nineteenth century, the work of Montelius or of Reinecke showed the way to the development of a sound chronological basis, by means of a sophisticated analysis of artefact types and associations. Workers in other areas, such as Déchelette in France or John Evans in Britain, also used artefacts for chronological purposes, even though their schemes did not have the same permanency.

---

[13] Morris 1992.

Funerary studies were extremely popular in earlier years, especially in the last century but also in this. Funerary monuments, particularly tumuli or barrow mounds, are conspicuous and usually produce finds. In many instances, the foundations of our knowledge of the period are the work of early barrow excavators: F. X. Franc in western Bohemia or Sir Richard Colt Hoare and William Cunnington in Wessex are good examples. The excavation of Bronze Age funerary monuments was not, however, confined to the last century. Many excavators have dug large numbers of funerary monuments in recent times, for instance P. Ashbee in Britain or Zh. Andrea in Albania.[14]

Given these preoccupations, it is not surprising that other aspects of the archaeological record and its interpretation were left out of consideration. Settlement studies, for instance, made barely any impact for many years, with the notable exception of the Swiss lake sites (in many ways the Swiss equivalent to Victorian barrow digging in Britain). But even the recovery of vast quantities of material from both the west and the east Swiss sites did not lead to any significant attempt at understanding the sites other than in terms of their situation and building method. In other parts of Europe, settlement studies relating to the Bronze Age hardly existed; even where settlement sites were dug, such as the southern English sites excavated by General Pitt Rivers, the Argaric settlements of south-east Spain dug by the Siret brothers, the Sicilian sites dug by P. Orsi,[15] or the *nuraghi* dug by Taramelli, no real attempt was made to set them in an overall context of a Bronze Age living system. Even fewer efforts were made to understand the nature of the Bronze Age economy, or the society that gave rise to it, except in the most general terms.

Few works that aimed to set the Bronze Age in an overall context emanate from these earlier years. One exception is Gordon Childe's book *The Bronze Age* (1930), an early work, but one that built on the foundations for European Bronze Age studies laid in *The Danube in Prehistory* of the preceding year. In this work, Childe foreshadowed many of the debates that concern Bronze Age scholars today: the economic and social significance of metalworking, the status and role of the smith, the effects of metalworking on small communities, and the longer-term effects on human society more generally. The work differs from all others written on the Bronze Age at this period by its willingness to engage in speculation about matters that some considered unknowable, and its insistence on a social and economic role for technological matters; in view of Childe's personal and political beliefs, this is perhaps not surprising, but it was for its day unusual, and finds few parallels until the very recent past.

Not surprisingly, major trends in archaeology generally have found their reflection in Bronze Age studies. Thus the fashion for environmental

[14] Ashbee 1960; Andrea 1985.
[15] Leighton 1986.

examination and explanation that was prevalent in Britain in the 1970s under the influence of E. Higgs spawned a series of articles that considered sites in their environmental setting, examined the economic foundations for their existence, and catalogued their biological debris in exemplary detail. While one could not pretend that the 'New Archaeology' had a big influence on mainstream Bronze Age studies, there was a certain spin-off: the number of quantitative analyses increased markedly, and the influence of new modes of thought can be gauged from, for instance, the work of J. Levy or K. Kristiansen. This last author has also been one of those responsible for the application of World Systems Theory to European Bronze Age studies, while his contributions to various volumes that have applied models of various kinds to the archaeological record have seen Marxist, structuralist and other approaches tried out on selected Bronze Age evidence. The stimulus this provided has not, however, translated itself – at least in the Anglo-Saxon world – into large numbers of students entering the field for research purposes, though in Germany, Spain and Italy Bronze Age studies have always attracted plenty of them. Through the 1980s and 1990s, the mood has been characterised more by uncertainty than anything else. On the one hand, many Bronze Age workers continue to adopt a positivist attitude to their subjects of study, and to believe that definite answers to specific questions can be obtained from the rich data sources at their disposal, if only enough analysis can be done; on the other, there is a trend to more subjective approaches to the Bronze Age, as to other periods of the past, under the influence of the post-modern movement. An extreme example of this is perhaps C. Tilley's 1991 book on Norwegian rock-art,[16] but glimmerings of the same thing can be seen in a number of articles that have appeared since the mid-1980s.

A fully post-modern approach to the Bronze Age is yet to come. The contextualisation of the study of the Bronze Age is a task that is already under way, though few mainstream Bronze Age scholars would consider the task either legitimate or necessary. Yet for the study of a society and an economy where exchange mechanisms, industrial production and personal display were key elements, it clearly is necessary to specify one's personal context before any attempt at interpretation is made. The nature of archaeological facts in a Bronze Age context is also something to which little – if any – attention has been paid; it will become apparent that for this author the equation of 'archaeological facts' and 'artefacts' is still valid, and that artefacts constitute the source material with which the Bronze Age is to be studied.

[16] Tilley 1991.

Frameworks of study: chronology

In order to set the developments that are the subject of this book in correct perspective, an appreciation of the time-scale over which they occurred is essential. The relative chronology of most parts of the European Bronze Age is well understood, though the details still give rise to debate and discussion in the literature. On the other hand, the absolute chronology has long been a matter of considerable uncertainty, stemming from the fact that the available sources were incapable until recently of giving a definitive answer to the question being asked. Traditionally, absolute chronology in the Bronze Age depended on the time-scale established in Egypt and Mesopotamia, to which that of the Aegean could be related, and that of Europe in turn to the Aegean (the cross-dating method). This produced results that were broadly acceptable, but did not command unanimous support.

From the 1960s, radiocarbon dating has been available to provide an independent chronology, but the progress of research on Bronze Age chronologies for most areas of Europe has been patchy and faltering. Earlier attempts to use radiocarbon dates to derive chronologies for central Europe were often decried as unreliable because they enforced a rethink of the traditional position. Added to this were numerous problems of context with many of the dated samples, for the most part isolated dates from poorly stratified or inadequately excavated sites. In recent years, however, the situation has changed with the advent of dendrochronologically dated sequences. These are only available in certain areas, notably the Alpine zone and Ireland, but since it is usually possible to link cultures, sites and objects to those areas with dendro dates the results are still of good quality. Added to this is the vast improvement in the quality of radiocarbon dates. Laboratories are extremely careful to date only those samples whose context is good; long stratified sequences are preferred; high-precision dating, using the results of dendrochronological calibration of the radiocarbon age, is possible; and the advent of accelerator mass spectrometry (AMS) dating has enabled the carbon-14 atoms to be measured directly in samples, rather than by counting the emission of beta-particles as happens in conventional dating. As a consequence, it is now possible to place absolute dates on many of the important transitions between different periods of the Bronze Age in much of central, southern and western Europe. This is not to say that problems do not remain, for instance in the East Mediterranean, where a major event such as the eruption of Thera in the Late Bronze Age is still the subject of controversy.

Relative chronologies

In broad terms, it is usual to divide the Bronze Age into three parts, Early, Middle and Late. In practice, the progress of knowledge in many areas means that these divisions are barely meaningful any more; in Germany, for instance, a series of phase labels based on representative finds has largely displaced the Early/Middle/Late system, which was in any case hard to apply because of the subtle meanings attached to German or French versions of such terminology (e.g. Spät-, Jung-, Jüngere- Jüngst- and End-Bronzezeit, or Bronze tardive and Bronze final, all loosely translatable as 'Late Bronze Age'). Similar trends are visible in other areas, for instance in the British Isles.

It is necessary, however, to have an understanding of the principal chronological schemes that are in use in continental Europe, above all those devised long ago by Reinecke for southern Germany and by Montelius for Scandinavia, because they are still in everyday use. These two schemes have been successively applied to larger and larger areas of Europe, and continue to exert a major influence.

Reinecke

Paul Reinecke (1872–1958), working with closed find groups (graves and hoards) in Bavaria, developed over a period of decades a system of phase labels for the 'Bronze Age' (Bronzezeit) and 'Hallstatt Age' (Hallstattzeit), each of them being assigned four stages labelled A, B, C and D. The Hallstattzeit was based on the finds from the great cemetery of Hallstatt in central Austria, which included finds of iron and were therefore attributable in broad terms to the Iron Age. Subsequently it became clear that phases A and B of the Hallstattzeit actually belonged to the period that came to be called the Urnfield period (Urnenfelderzeit) because of the characteristic burial mode of depositing cremated bone in a funerary urn, and the urns in a defined burial place or 'urnfield'. Accordingly the practice grew up of assigning Bronzezeit A–D and Hallstattzeit A–B to the Bronze Age (in its general sense), and Hallstattzeit C–D to the Iron Age (the abbreviations Br or Bz and Ha are commonly used).

In broad terms, Br A represents the Early Bronze Age, Br B–C the Middle Bronze Age (or Tumulus Bronze Age, after the characteristic burial form of the period), and Br D with Ha A–B the Late Bronze Age or Urnfield period. All of these phases have at various times been subdivided, but the precise meaning attached to the divisions has not been constant from scholar to scholar. I cannot here enter into the complex debates which have attended these exercises. Instead, a brief indication of the more important aspects of the subdivisions is necessary.

Br A is divided into A1, representing the earliest full bronze industries, and characterised by inhumation cemeteries such as Singen (Konstanz) or Straubing, and hoards with flanged axes and metal-hilted daggers such as Bresinchen (Guben),[17] and A2, to which a different range of specific types such as the pin with perforated spherical head or the socketed spearhead are

[17] Breddin 1969.

assigned.[18] There is also good evidence for the existence of a third Early Bronze Age phase, sometimes called A3, sometimes A2/B1, containing material that is clearly later than classic A2 but not yet fully developed into the full Tumulus Bronze Age material; this phase is represented at the recently excavated Austrian cemetery of Franzhausen II.

Phases B and C, the Middle Bronze Age, have both been subdivided at various times, but in general terms all that is relevant for present purposes is that they represent the sequence of the 'Tumulus cultures'. On the other hand, the divisions of the Urnfield period (Br D, Ha A and B) are extremely important. All three phases have been divided, but the divisions established by H. Müller-Karpe in 1959 have proved most influential. Building on the foundations of earlier scholars, he codified a system which divided Ha A into A1 and A2, and Ha B into B1, B2 and B3. This has not proved uncontroversial. A number of authors denied that they could recognise the separate existence of phase B2 as defined by Müller-Karpe on the basis of the cemetery of Kelheim near Munich. Nevertheless, the usage has continued in Germany, at least; in Switzerland, where the second phase is not generally discernible, Ha B2 is sometimes used in more or less the same sense as Ha B3 in Bavaria.[19] Each of the phases is characterised by a range of artefact types known from graves and hoards (settlement material is not always easy to slot into this sequence), and in general the range of material is extremely well known and easily recognised, though debates continue over the details. Thus the relative chronological sequence is not in doubt (fig. 1.2).

Montelius

Oscar Montelius (1843–1921) lived and worked in Stockholm but had a vast knowledge of the archaeology of all parts of Europe. The chronological scheme for which he is justly famous was developed by him in order to understand the phasing of the Scandinavian Bronze Age, but his panoramic knowledge meant that it had ramifications far beyond Scandinavia.[20] Working from closed find groups, Montelius distinguished six periods, I–VI, of which I–III are referred to as Early Bronze Age, IV–V as Late Bronze Age, and VI falls at the transition to the Iron Age. In Period I local metal production was still slight, and significant numbers of objects were imported from central Europe and the Carpathian Basin. Period II is the main *floruit* of the earlier northern Bronze Age, with many richly furnished barrow graves and large quantities of metal. In Period III, cremation started to become common, and by Period IV it was absolutely dominant. In terms of the central European chronology, I corresponds to the Early Bronze Age, II and part of III to the Tumulus period, and IV and V to the Urnfield period.

[18] e.g. the Langquaid hoard: Hachmann 1957, table 54.
[19] Though recently it has become evident that there is indeed funerary material that falls between Ha B1 and B3: Matter 1992, 312ff.
[20] Montelius 1986.

France	N. Europe (Montelius)	C. Europe (Reinecke, Müller-Karpe)
Ha Final		Ha D
Ha moyen		Ha C
Ha ancien	Period VI	
		Gündlingen
Br. Final IIIb	Period V	Ha B2/3
Br. Final IIIa	Period IV	Ha B1
Br. Final IIb		Ha A2
Br. Final IIa	Period III	Ha A1
Br. Final I		Br D
Br. moyen	Period II	Asenkofen 2 / Br C / Göggenhofen {1 2}
Br. ancien	Period I	Br B / Lochham 1
Campaniformes (Beakers)	Late Neolithic	Langquaid 2 / Br A / Singen Nitra 1

(C. Europe vertical labels: URNFELDER; TUMULUS BRONZE AGE / BRONZEZEIT)

Fig. 1.2. Cultural sequence, west-central and northern Europe.

The Montelian periodisation is still in common use, though the phase definitions have been refined or modified. In addition to Scandinavia, the scheme is used in northern Germany and Poland, and in part in the Low Countries. Between Reinecke and Montelius, therefore, the larger part of the European continent is covered, or at least can be cross-referenced.

For other areas there are other schemes in use (fig. 1.3). A. Mozsolics developed a special phasing for the bronze hoards of the Carpathian Basin,[21] which has not, however, been adopted by all students of the period, even in Hungary.

---

[21] Mozsolics 1967; 1973; 1985.

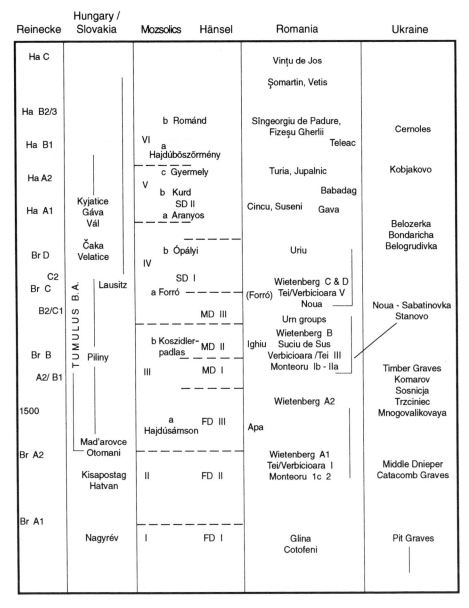

Fig. 1.3. Cultural sequence, east-central and eastern Europe.

More widely used in recent years is the scheme of B. Hänsel for the same area, but resting on a wider range of sites and artefacts than Mozsolics's scheme.[22] This uses the terms Early, Middle and Late Danubian Bronze Age (frühe/mittlere/späte Danubische Bronzezeit, or FD I–III, MD I–III, and SD

---

[22] Hänsel 1968.

I–II); it has come to be widely adopted, not least because of the prolific writings of Hänsel's pupils on the Carpathian Basin and neighbouring areas.

A cultural sequence of great importance that must also be introduced is that named after the cemetery of Únětice (German 'Aunjetitz') near Prague. The characteristic material culture from this and similar inhumation cemeteries, including the famous 'hour-glass' cups, is found over a wide area of central Europe, centred on the Czech Republic but also occurring in eastern Germany, central and southern Poland and northern Austria. Although it can be equated with Br A1 and A2 in the Reinecke system, a local five-stage sequence of development has been distinguished for the pottery.[23]

In most other areas of Europe, either the Early/Middle/Late scheme is in use, or a sequence of culture names is preferred. This is the case in Britain and France, Italy and Spain (figs. 1.4 and 1.5), and the Balkans. One area that has its own distinctive sequence is south Russia and Ukraine, where it has been usual to refer to culture names based on grave form – Pit Grave (Russian *jamnaya kultura*), Catacomb Grave (*katakombnaja kultura*) and Timber Grave (*srubnaja kultura*).[24] In other parts of Russia a sequence of local culture names is used.

Absolute chronology

Had this book been written thirty, or even twenty, years ago, it would probably have been considered necessary to devote many pages to a consideration of the absolute dating of the phases and cultures which would have been enumerated. This dating would have been derived largely from cross-dating via the Aegean to Egypt, and the links between the Aegean Bronze Age civilisations and the 'barbarian' world.[25] As it is, the progress of development of independent dating frameworks has been so rapid and so successful that for much of the period discussion is no longer necessary: the time-spans involved are now clear in outline. This optimistic statement needs to be qualified in a number of respects. First, dendro dates come mainly from settlement sites, and are largely concentrated in those areas where there is good preservation of organic remains (dates for oak coffins of northern Europe are the exception). In practice this means the Alpine area, southern Germany and Ireland, with some material now becoming available from elsewhere (e.g. Poland).

---

[23] Moucha 1961; 1963.
[24] Both Russian and translated versions may be found in the literature. Gimbutas (1965), Sulimirski (1970) and Coles and Harding (1979) use the translated form, as did Piggott and others; Mallory (e.g. 1989) and Anthony (e.g. 1996) use the Russian form. In this work the translated form is used, because I believe it aids comprehension and is more consistent: in Britain the term 'Schnurkeramik' is not used, let alone 'šnurová keramika', but 'Corded Ware'. Complete consistency is impossible since it is commonplace for Anglophones to refer to the Linearbandkeramik or LBK, and the TRB, rather than their English translations.
[25] e.g. Renfrew 1968; Harding 1980; Randsborg 1991; Gerloff 1993; 1996.

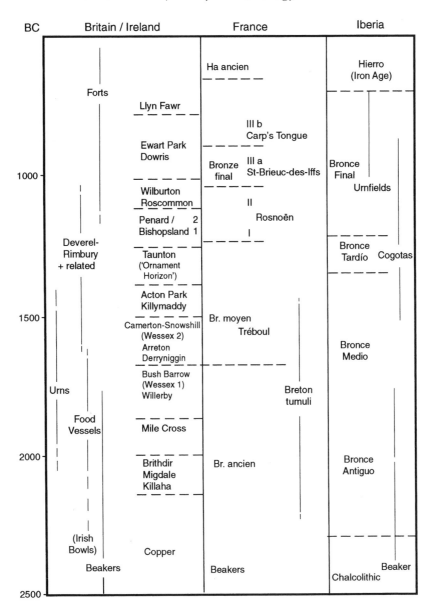

Fig. 1.4. Cultural sequence, western Europe.

Thus the dates for the felling of trees used on a site such as Zürich-Mozartstrasse (below, p. 42) are known to the exact year; what is more difficult is to relate the material culture used on the site to the established phases as known from graves and hoards. Second, sizeable parts of Europe still have no adequate radiocarbon chronology, certainly not one based on series of carefully contexted samples subjected to high-precision dating. All too often the

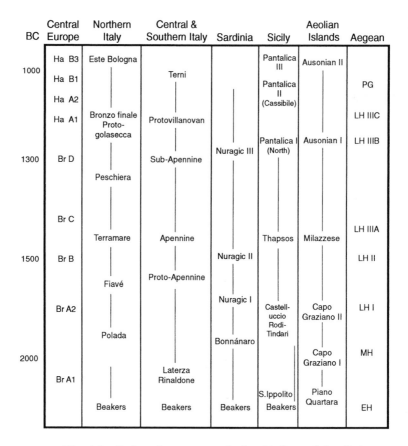

Fig. 1.5. Cultural sequence, Italy, Sicily and Sardinia.

association of samples with events on sites is vague or absent altogether, and the dates are isolated. Still rarer are programmes of dating on organic materials that are integral parts of bronze implements, such as has been carried out by the British Museum in recent years.[26] Admittedly one cannot be sure in these cases that the organic element dates to the time of manufacture and original hafting of the bronze object, but given enough objects to date in this way patterns become clear. Third, the establishment of an independent chronology in one area need not necessarily give a precise chronology to another, though it is likely to act as a good general guide. Fourth, radiocarbon dates have to be calibrated against the curve derived from samples of known age in order to obtain true calendrical dates, and the calibration curve does not affect all periods equally. In some centuries (most notably in the mid-first millennium BC) there is a plateau in the curve which means that a wide range of calendrical dates is possible for a given radiocarbon age. This

[26] Needham *et al.* 1997.

problem affects the latest dates for the Bronze Age, though it is more acute in the Iron Age.

In spite of these difficulties, little – except the availability of finance to procure datings – stands in the way of establishing a sound chronological framework for all parts of Europe throughout the Bronze Age. The procedures are routine; subject to the availability of suitable material, cultural sequences should be accurately dated everywhere within a couple of decades.

A good example of the way in which traditional dating methods (cross-dating) are modified by new independently derived dates is given by the oak coffin graves of north Germany and Denmark. The famous 'princely' burial sites of Helmsdorf and Leubingen belong to the classic phase of the Únětice culture, equivalent to the earlier part of Br A2, and were assigned to the middle of the second millennium BC, in accordance with the standard view that Br A2 and its congeners in the Carpathian Basin were to be placed parallel with the Shaft Graves of Mycenae (c. 1650–1450 BC on the traditional chronology). Dendro dates on the grave constructions of these two graves in fact gave the dates 1942 ± 10 BC (Leubingen) and 1840 ± 10 BC (Helmsdorf).[27] Even allowing for a period of time represented by the outermost (absent) rings of the timbers involved, the gap between the two sets of dates is at least two centuries, probably three, and cannot be bridged by special pleading alone. A radical revision of traditional chronologies became necessary.

Less dramatic in its effects, but equally important as a rather precise indicator of deposition date, is the series of dendro dates obtained on Danish coffin graves. Those that were datable belong to Period II.[28] The latest rings on these coffins all fall in the period 1425–1350 BC, and with an allowance of 20 additional years for the absent sapwood they span the period 1396–1330 BC. In this case, the dates are in accord with the expectations of traditional chronology – one implication of which is that the Early and Middle Bronze Ages must have lasted considerably longer than previously thought.

Dendro dates have also had a marked effect in the dating of the Urnfield period, introducing a general tendency to heighten the start and finish dates of each period.[29] The problems of relating settlement materials to grave and hoard finds reappear here, and the discrepancies between the dendro-dated sequence and the 'historical' chronology laid down by Müller-Karpe have not yet been resolved.

Table 1.1 illustrates current best estimates for absolute ages in each area, on the basis of radiocarbon dates.[30]

---

[27] Becker, Jäger *et al.* 1989; Becker, Krause and Kromer 1989.
[28] Randsborg 1991.
[29] Sperber 1987.
[30] These are derived from a variety of recent sources, but above all from the proceedings of a conference held in Verona in 1995 (Randsborg 1996), and selected other works e.g. Chronologie 1986; Skeates and Whitehouse 1994; Needham *et al.* 1997; Sperber 1987.

Table 1.1. *Radiocarbon chronology for Bronze Age Europe*

Britain	Start	End
Beakers	2450	1700
Early Copper (MA I–II)	2400	2150
Migdale (MA III)	2200	1950
Food Vessels, Collared Urns (MA IV–V)	2100	1500
Acton Park, Taunton	1770–1350	1380–1210
Penard	1380–1210	1220–1080
Wilburton	1220–1080	1100–960
Blackmoor	1100–960	1000–860
Ewart Park	1000–860	880–750
Llyn Fawr	880–750	
France		
Early Bronze Age	2300/2200	1600/1500
Middle Bronze Age	?1800/1700	1500/1400
Bronze final I–II	1400	1200
Bronze final III	1300	800/700
North and central Italy		
Beakers	2550	1800
Polada	2400	1400
Apennine	1690	660
Late Bronze Age	1500	1140
Protovillanovan	1430	660
Spain		
Argaric Bronze Age, motillas	2300/2250	1600/1500
Middle–Late Bronze Age	1600/1500	1300
Bronce Final I	1250	1100
Bronce Final II	1100	940
Bronce Final III	940	750
Iron Age (Hierro)	800	
Central Europe		
Bell Beaker/Corded Ware		2000
Singen (Br A1)	2200	2000/1950
Bodman/Schachen, Zürich-Mozartstrasse (Br A2)	2000/1950	1600/1500
Tumulus Bronze Age (Br B–C)	1500	1300
Br D	1400	1200
Ha A1–A2	1250	1050
Ha B1	1100	1000
Ha B2/3	1050	750
Ha C	750	
Scandinavia		
Late Neolithic II	1920	1730
Period I	1730	1510
Period II	1500	1250
Period III	1440	1040
Period V	850	760

Climate and environment

A detailed discussion of the natural environment in Bronze Age Europe is beyond the scope of this book. The availability of relevant source materials is extremely variable, though pollen sequences have been studied in almost all areas and other types of proxy data are also available.[31]

The Bronze Age falls within the climatic period called the Sub-boreal, which is sandwiched between the Atlantic and Sub-atlantic periods. In general, this was a warm and dry period, in contrast to the warm wet Atlantic and the cool wet Sub-atlantic. But such a bland general statement conceals a mass of small variations, both spatial and temporal. Fine-resolution pollen sampling shows that within the broader picture obtained by traditional pollen analysis there is a similar detailed set of fluctuations happening in the pollen record, which as a proxy climate indicator reflects changes in air temperature, precipitation and so on. Lake-level fluctuations and the movement of the tree-line in the Alps similarly indicate a constantly changing pattern. In peat bogs there are indications that peat growth was periodically halted, and soil profiles in some central European sites suggest that markedly dry conditions prevailed at some points in the Urnfield period. At other times, these were replaced by catastrophically wet conditions, which were responsible for the abandonment of many lakeside sites that lay close to normal lake water level. Indeed, it has been suggested that the pattern of climate change can be followed through the study of lakeside settlement: at the times when it is absent, water levels were high; when present, water levels were relatively low. There are problems with this approach as the importance of cultural factors is almost totally ignored, but it is certainly puzzling that many sites were completely abandoned after major flooding episodes and never, or only centuries later, reoccupied.

On British moors and heaths, there is extensive evidence for the deterioration of soils during the course of the Bronze Age.[32] The examination of buried soils beneath Early Bronze Age barrows has sometimes shown that mixed oak forest lay not far away, while the presence of cereal pollen is a clear sign that parts of the landscape were cleared and cultivated. But examination of some 'cairnfields' (below, p. 158) has found that soils were already podsolised and the clearance of stone that they represent has even been seen as a strategy for maintaining yields in the face of catastrophic environmental deterioration.

One of the problems in determining the nature and importance of environmental conditions in the Bronze Age is that both human and natural agencies were at work. Specifically, clearance of forests that may never have been

---

[31] Coles and Harding (1979) include brief discussion of environmental conditions in each area of Europe. The general picture may be obtained from works such as Tinsley in Simmons and Tooley 1981, Harding 1983a, and other syntheses.

[32] Dimbleby 1962.

touched since the global warming after the Ice Age must have proceeded apace. Molluscan evidence in southern England has sometimes shown an extensively cleared landscape in the Late Neolithic and Early Bronze Age (for instance at Stonehenge); pollen diagrams on moorlands suggest a recurring attack on the woodlands, probably in the form of numerous small-scale clearances rather than the extensive clearance of large tracts.[33] Similar patterns can be seen in the lowland areas of much of the rest of Europe.

Much has been written in recent years about the possible impact of major natural catastrophes and other events, notably volcanoes,[34] and, most recently, comet or asteroid impacts. The only active volcanoes in Europe are in Iceland and the central and eastern Mediterranean (Vesuvius, Etna, the Aeolian Islands and Thera), but Thera at least is known to have undergone a massive eruption in the Bronze Age. Such eruptions eject huge clouds of debris into the atmosphere, and the finer particles can linger at high altitudes for months or years, where they may block solar radiation. As a consequence, vegetation on the earth's surface can be severely affected. Short-lived plants will leave no permanent trace in the fossil record, but trees can show stunted growth in their annual rings. This phenomenon is visible in Irish bog oaks in the 1620s BC.[35] There are other grounds for believing that this pattern is to be associated with the eruption of Thera (though the date of the eruption has been the subject of controversy and is still not definitively settled). Whether or not this was the case, growing trees suffered a severe setback at that date, which must reflect the sudden onset of markedly colder conditions worldwide. If the impact on trees was so strong, it would also have had dramatic effects on growing crops and grassland. The effects on human life must have been correspondingly significant; various marked changes in the archaeological record have been attributed to the aftermath of such events.

But for most of the time life was not rocked by calamities on such a grand scale. Climatic and environmental conditions fluctuated, so that the observer on the ground will have suffered bad years for crop production along with the good ones, as has always been the case. The extent to which human groups buffered themselves against such effects is a cultural matter; there is some evidence that in the Late Bronze Age, for instance, specific strategies were adopted for this precise purpose (p. 145). Given the small scale of most Bronze Age communities, however, responses to the natural environment were probably palliative rather than prophylactic.

[33] e.g. Balaam et al. 1982.
[34] Baillie 1989; 1995; Burgess 1989; Gross-Klee and Maise 1997.
[35] Baillie 1995, 75ff.

Conclusion

In an age where relativist approaches are becoming the norm and there is a tendency to deny the relevance of constructs such as 'the Bronze Age', it might be thought a risky enterprise to devote a book to the topic. Yet, as I hope to show, the geographical area known today as Europe in the time-span 2500–800 BC was host to a mass of technical and conceptual developments that make it legitimate to describe and analyse it, and appropriate to treat it as an entity with its own character and trajectory that was different from those of other continents.

In contrast to most previous approaches to the period, however, this book does not deal much with artefact typology or chronological analysis, and it attempts to avoid straight description of sites and artefacts. An inclusive approach is adopted to Bronze Age studies, though it will become evident that I believe some are more useful than others. The 'Year of the Bronze Age' was a celebration of 'Europe's first Golden Age', concentrating on the spectacular end of the range of monuments and artefacts that emanate from the period. This book is intended no less as a celebration of the period, which represents a crucially formative phase in the human past, constituting the change from Neolithic farming villages, in many ways little altered since the arrival of the first farmers, to Iron Age proto-states on the verge of literacy and written history. The people who created the archaeological record studied here were in all likelihood biologically the same throughout, and enter history with particular ethnic labels attached to them. One of the tasks of this book is to chart the ways in which the complexity that is visible then was achieved, what were its roots, and what its constituents.

CHAPTER 2

THE BRONZE AGE HOUSE AND VILLAGE

Bronze Age life was for the most part a life based in agricultural villages.[1] Few of these villages possessed houses of special size or elaboration. In most parts of Bronze Age Europe they are unspectacular affairs, no more than clusters of pits and post-holes, or cooking places marked by accumulations of fired stones, discovered by chance during development work or the excavation of sites of a different period. The study of Bronze Age settlements is possible to differing degrees in different parts of Europe, as a result of differential survival and differential success at extracting the necessary information from the archaeological record. Spectacular discoveries in a few areas are balanced by an almost complete absence of known sites in others.

That the fugitive traces of Bronze Age house sites can reflect stable and long-lived settlement has been apparent since the work of Strömberg and Stjernquist on the settlement sites of Scania.[2] Settlement traces which on the basis of a few good plans can be reconstructed to something much bigger can be found in many areas, and emanate from all parts of the Bronze Age.[3] The remains of hearths, ovens and cooking places are often found; some were originally inside buildings, others outside. Analysis of the internal structure of Bronze Age settlements defined only by pits identified clusters that might correspond to original activity foci, probably houses and their associated activities (a cluster being a grouping of potentially contemporary features which represent a non-coincidental agglomeration).[4] Such groupings of features could sometimes be seen to occupy a roughly oval area up to 25 × 40 m across, interpreted as the remains of single socio-economic units, in other words

[1] An excellent general study of Bronze and Iron Age settlement in barbarian ('Celtic') Europe has appeared quite recently, to which the reader is referred for fuller discussion of some of these matters, in particular the nature of house construction and the internal arrangements of houses in the late second and first millennia BC: Audouze and Büchsenschütz 1991.

[2] Strömberg 1954, 1973–4; Stjernquist 1969.

[3] The 26 pits containing Únětice pottery and bone, stone and antler tools from Sundhausen in Thuringia provide an example from the Early Bronze Age (Walter 1990a); the large site, at least 500 × 300 m in extent yet with only one recognisable house plan, at Graben near Augsburg in Bavaria, is a Late Bronze Age Urnfield case (Dietrich and Sorge 1991). In the lower Pegnitz valley in eastern Bavaria a series of small sites, or sites investigated only in small areas, produced domestic debris (pottery, bones, loom-weights, hearths or oven floors) from scattered pits and post-holes, which allow no possibility of reconstruction (Reisenhauer 1976); these are isolated examples among many that could be cited.

[4] Turková and Kuna 1987.

house sites. The distance between the central points of feature groups varied between 20 and 50 m.[5] In the Únĕtice culture area, isolated pits containing domestic pottery, sometimes with surrounding post-holes, were the norm. At Grossmugl (Stockerau) attempts were made by the excavators to interpret large pits with stake-holes around as semi-sunken dwellings, but these were never very convincing, either in form or in structural detail, and it is much more likely that such pits were for storage than anything else.[6] Smaller pits for domestic purposes can be seen at many sites, for instance Döbeln-Masten in Saxony,[7] or Bruszczewo in western Poland.[8] At Iwanowice in south-east Poland,[9] a dynamic model of change in the creation of building complexes ('house clusters'), as defined by 'T-features' (trapeze-shaped pits), was created. A ridge 8 ha in area ('Babia Góra') saw the movement over time of individual buildings or groups of buildings, as detected by the detailed and sophisticated analysis of pottery sets, with varying density and extent of settlement.

Especially pervasive and liable to good preservation are the heaps of stones, exhibiting signs of heating, which were used for cooking in clay-lined pits, and survive to archaeologists as 'burnt mounds'. Known in Ireland as *fulachta fiadh*, they occur in most areas of Europe where there has been extensive survey work, and though dating is hard, many examples have been shown to belong to the Bronze Age.[10] Examples are known not only from Britain and Ireland, but also from Sweden,[11] from Switzerland,[12] and many other places. Recent interpretations suggest that some of the burnt mounds of Scandinavia might be the remains of cremation pyres rather than cooking places,[13] or that they were saunas or hot baths.[14] It would not be right to impose an identical interpretation on all sites; I favour the traditional explanation for most burnt mounds, without ruling out other explanations for some of them. Contextual study is therefore essential.

Many different specific settlement types and modes developed in different areas and parts of the Bronze Age. Tell sites in south-east Europe, glacial mounds and valley-side sites in Alpine valleys, hut platforms on north-western moors, extensive settlement areas on central European loess lands: all had somewhat different requirements and possibilities, but the form of the houses on them was much the same in terms of shape, size and building

---

[5] At Dobromĕřice, which was completely excavated, the number of individual groupings was between five and ten, with two to three storage pits per grouping.

[6] Beninger 1941.

[7] Coblenz 1973.

[8] Pieczyński 1969.

[9] Kadrow 1991a; 1991b.

[10] Hedges 1986; Buckley 1990; Hodder and Barfield 1991.

[11] 'Heaps of fire-cracked stones' are very common: Hyenstrand 1967–8; Larsson 1986, 150ff.; 1990; Lundqvist 1991.

[12] For instance at the site of Uf Wigg at Zeiningen in the Aargau: Brogli 1980.

[13] Kaliff 1994.

[14] T. Laurie, pers. comm.

materials, though not necessarily in internal arrangements. Where information is lacking, widely differing environmental and social conditions make it extremely dangerous to impose the pattern of one area on another. The analyses are therefore site- or area-specific, but nonetheless certain general points are applicable to Europe as a whole.

One of these, worth stressing at the outset, is that settlement traces as recovered may represent palimpsests, that is, the remains of reoccupation on the same site over and over again. Thus an apparently bewildering array of pits and post-holes will need to be 'dissected' if the true pattern of any one phase is to be analysed, and this may not be possible where there is no independent means of assigning dates to features. The 'palimpsest problem' means that more than one solution may be possible to the question of settlement size and complexity. This has implications for the size of sites and therefore communities. One cannot assume that the settlement unit remained the same throughout the period or across the whole of the European landmass, either in absolute size or in terms of social complexity. In this chapter I will be looking at sites on which houses or domestic debris have been found. These were farmsteads (single buildings), hamlets (small groups of buildings) or villages (larger groups of buildings), in other words settlement sites of different size.

The house

The basic unit of residence, the house, is recorded patchily across Europe. Even in those parts where excavation and survey have uncovered plentiful house foundations, little is known about superstructure or internal fittings. For these one is often dependent on models and depictions, which are, however, rarer than in the Neolithic. An exception is a painted clay urn from Stora Hammar in Scania (fig. 2.1, 1), in the form of a sub-rectangular tub with rounded ends and almost conical roof. The painted elements show vertical posts and thatch, and a doorway.[15] A series of triangular or trapezoidal shapes on Hallstatt period vases from Schirndorf in Bavaria have been taken to be huts or tents.[16] Rock-art depictions from the Nordic area are all extremely uncertain and ambiguous; but the Val Camonica art portrays a variety of post-built structures shown in elevation view, some apparently with outside stairs and more than one storey, and all with pointed, i.e. ridged, roofs (fig. 2.1, 2). Some, for instance on the Bedolina rock, are on stilts and may represent pile dwellings.[17]

The usual extent of evidence on the ground consists of holes for upright

---

[15] Capelle 1991.
[16] Stroh 1988.
[17] Anati 1961, 106, 137–8, 239–41.

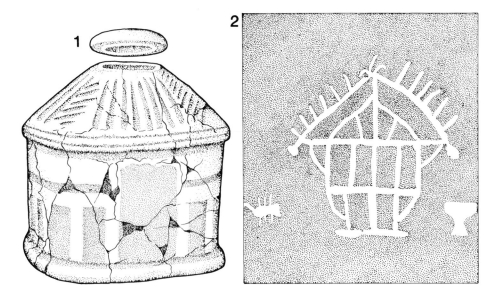

Fig. 2.1. Depictions of Bronze Age buildings. 1. House urn from Stora Hammar, Scania (after Capelle 1991). 2. Detail from a rock-art panel in the Val Camonica, apparently showing a wood-framed construction with purlins and sloping roof (after Anati 1961).

posts, slots for sleeper beams, or low stone banks which represent wall foundations. Imagination and analogy has to construct the rest. In this, there is naturally a bias in visibility towards those areas that utilised stone, as against those which made use of wood, wattle and daub. Nevertheless, excavation techniques are now fully capable of recovering the remains of post-built houses, provided only that they can be identified on the surface. Survival of sub-surface features is often surprisingly good, and where such features were cut into the subsoil, it is often the case that related aspects such as storage facilities are also preserved.

Bronze Age houses, like those of other periods, were either round or rectangular.[18] This is an important distinction for more than merely typological reasons. Round-houses were often very small, whilst rectangular houses often reached substantial dimensions, implying that activities other than eating or sleeping took place in them, or that residence groups were larger. Here not only the absolute size of houses is important, but also the often fugitive evidence of function in different parts of the same house, or in different houses.

A number of theoretical works in sociology, anthropology and architecture

[18] This is not quite true, as a series of U-shaped houses on the coast of southern Norway, associated predominantly with fishing and hunting, demonstrates: Løken 1989.

have discussed the question of how space in settlements is organised according to behavioural criteria, and specifically social needs. The use of space is
a social matter: 'each society constructs an "ethnic domain" by arranging
space according to certain principles. By retrieving the abstract description of
these principles, we intuitively grasp an aspect of the social for that society';[19]
'spatial organisation is a function of the form of social solidarity';[20] 'human
groups create orderly patterns of space and structures'.[21]

Much has been written on this topic, but relatively little is of direct application to archaeology.[22] Kent has demonstrated in a range of ethnographic examples that as societies become more complex (in terms of stratification,
specialisation and division of labour) their architecture and use of space become
more segmented. Of the five levels or categories of complexity that she
describes, European Bronze Age societies would fall in the middle three. Her
'category III' societies are characterised by chiefdoms, political confederacies,
ranking in age grades or sets, with economic and socio-political specialisation
and emphasis on gender differences; categories II and IV are respectively less
and more developed in these terms. In terms of architecture, category III
societies make frequent use of wealth and gender divisions, and separation for
activity areas. To what extent European Bronze Age societies fit these categories requires discussion, but there is a *prima facie* case for seeing second- and
first-millennium BC Europe as falling in this general area (see chapter 12).

One of the most controversial methods of analysis of these matters has
been the development of a spatial syntax with which to describe and understand the 'social logic of space'.[23] Proceeding from the premise that 'human
spatial organization . . . is the establishment of patterns of relationships composed essentially of boundaries and permeabilities of various kinds', and that
there is a finite number of ways in which space can be organised, Hillier and
Hanson have developed ways of categorising the plans of both individual
buildings and collections of buildings (e.g. villages or farmsteads). Buildings,
according to them, 'by the way in which they are collected together, create
a system of open space',[24] the form and shape of the open space constituting
one's experience of the settlement; hence their development of 'alpha-
analysis', a method for analysing settlement layouts in terms of the space
created by, in other words between, the buildings. Different layouts will

[19] Hillier and Hanson 1984, 48.
[20] Ibid. 142.
[21] Fletcher 1981, 118.
[22] Exceptions in this respect are the work of Fletcher (1977; 1981; 1984; 1995), who has developed models for understanding the relationship between population size, density and settlement area; Chapman (1989/1991); Grøn (1991), who has made a number of specific suggestions
for understanding the relationship between social organisation and settlement layout, in the
context both of the Maglemosian of the Mesolithic and Iron Age settlements such as Feddersen
Wierde; and Kent (e.g. 1990).
[23] Hillier and Hanson 1984.
[24] Ibid. 89.

then promote different internal logics, depending on whether inhabitants are members of the same spatial or 'transpatial' group, and thus whether boundaries are strongly defined or not. This approach has been predictably criticised for its lack of attention to context and its prior assumption of knowledge about social structure, but there are aspects of it which are of value to archaeology.

One of these is 'access analysis', the study of access to the interiors of buildings, which will differ according to whether those involved are inhabitants or visitors. Since 'buildings transmit social information through their interior structures', and embody knowledge of social relations, their analysis should – theoretically, at any rate – reflect those relations. Specifically, analysis of the number of levels of access in buildings can indicate how open a structure was, or how far access to the innermost parts (in terms of defined steps or stages from the entrance) was allowed. For archaeologists, the method might help in revealing aspects of social relations that would otherwise be lost.

Access analysis has been applied to the study of Iron Age houses, though it is debatable to what extent understanding of them has been heightened as a result.[25] As far as the structures of Bronze Age Europe are concerned, in most instances there is no indication that access was restricted, at least by means of archaeologically retrievable features. The vast majority of Bronze Age houses were in structural terms one-cell affairs, though this is not to say that internal divisions, archaeologically invisible, were not present. In the case of the three-aisled houses of the north and north-west of Europe, it may be that not all parts of the building were accessible to all, and in particular not to visitors. This is also true for the houses of Early Iron Age Biskupin, where it appears that the sleeping quarters were in a raised loft above the animal stalls, and would not have been entered by visitors. Even potentially complex structures such as the long halls of Lovčičky (fig. 2.12) cannot realistically be subjected to access analysis in the absence of full information about internal arrangements.

Perhaps more profitable has been the analysis of internal space in terms of a structuring approach to architecture, which sees the house as a cosmos, an entity that expresses its occupants' beliefs about the world they live in. Thus orientation, sidedness, constructional elements and the positioning of functional features all represent aspects of that 'cosmology'.[26] Special attention is paid to distinctions between food-processing areas, areas for rubbish disposal, activity areas, and so on.[27] The problem from the point of view of a

[25] Foster 1989.
[26] Parker Pearson and Richards 1994a.
[27] e.g. by Parker Pearson and Richards (1994b) on Orcadian Neolithic houses, or Barrett (1994) on southern English round-houses of the Late Bronze and Early Iron Ages. Much attention is there accorded the supposed binary oppositions (light:dark; front:back; clean:dirty) that are present, though this approach has recently come in for criticism (Haselgrove and Gwilt 1998).

generalising approach is that it is hard to define any wider context within which to situate such work.

An indication of how post-processual interpretations of house plans might be moving can be seen from a recent analysis of a pair of houses in the Late Bronze Age settlement of Apalle, near the north side of Lake Mälaren in central Sweden (fig. 2.2).[28] Both are essentially of the three-aisled variety (see below), but the earlier has evidence for separation of a find-free hearth area from an area with a clay and lime floor and pits, while along the side where the entrance lay were sheep and ox jaw-bones. By contrast, in the later house there was no lime and no room divisions; all the floor was of clay and the hearth was centrally placed. Fire-cracked stones and daub, probably from the early phase, are incorporated into the walls and refuse areas of the later. The interpretation dwells on the relative isolation of the first-phase hearth area ('more private, anonymous'), the hearth being used for heating and not for cooking, whereas in the second phase the central hearth suggests cooking and the area outside the house is more structured and 'private'; 'the later settlement put more emphasis on the individual household ... contact between the house as a building and the midden was now reinforced'. Furthermore, the deposition of animal bones, including those of wild animals, might indicate a desire to bring the wild into the domestic sphere. These interesting ideas require confirmation from other sites if widespread acceptance is to be achieved, but the study is commendable in seeking to understand the curious placing of animal bones and fire-cracked stones.

Round-houses

Simple round huts are known from several parts of the Bronze Age world, of which Britain and southern Italy are the most notable; rare examples are known in continental Europe. The use of the round-house developed spontaneously in these two areas; there was no general tradition of round-house building in Europe which linked them. Round-houses may have been preferred for two main reasons. In functional terms, they present identical features and thus problems to be solved in all parts of the structure with the exception of the doorway; there are no corners, angles or ends to complicate matters. In fact the only decisions to be taken, once a location for building was agreed, was the orientation of the entrance (probably determined by the direction of the prevailing wind), and the angle and method of roofing. The other reason might be psychological. The standard burial site of north-western Europe in the first half of the Bronze Age was the round mound, often containing circles of posts or stakes. Like Neolithic long barrows and long-houses, round-houses and round barrows may have been viewed as two aspects of the

[28] Ullén 1994.

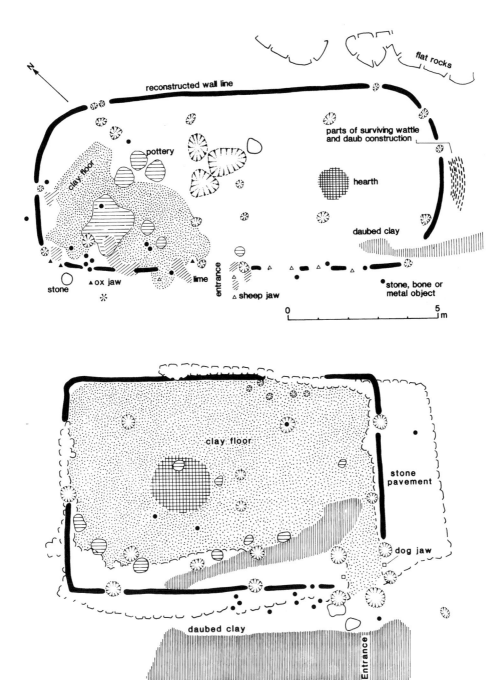

Fig. 2.2. Apalle, central Sweden. Outline plans of House 13 from the earlier settlement (*upper*) and House 2 from the later settlement (*lower*) (after Ullén 1994).

same thing – houses for the living and houses for the dead. It seems less likely that notions of equality, such as one associates with the Arthurian legend, have a role to play, as the internal arrangements of well-excavated houses were highly structured. One suggestion is that the round-house acted as a microcosm of the universe, the entrance to the east relating to sunrise and the daily rebirth of the cycle of light and darkness, revolving round the house; in other words, a reflection of the prevailing cosmology, not the prevailing wind.[29]

An obvious way of differentiating round-houses was through size, which no doubt relates to function: increasing diameter rapidly increases floor area in a round-house (a hut of diameter 4 m has floor area 12.6 m²; one of diameter 7 m has floor area 38.5 m²). Size alone is not necessarily a good guide to function or importance, however; the precise nature of the fittings and furniture, and the disposition of artefacts, are probably more reliable. For practical purposes, the space enclosed by the post ring (typically 5–6 m across, thus around 20–30 m² in area) was the usable area of the house. Taking into account the various activities that can be demonstrated for some Bronze Age houses (flint-knapping, weaving, leather-working), and assuming that they took place indoors at least some of the time, it would be quite reasonable to allocate at least 6 m² to each adult. A round-house of area 24 m² (diameter c. 5.50 m) would allow four persons that amount of space. Such space could be allocated simply in quadrants, or (more likely) people's space would overlap so that particular activities would be placed according to the need for light, elbow room, and so on.

Nothing certain is known about the superstructure of round-houses. In many, including some stone-built examples, there is a ring of post-holes which must have supported the roof. It is likely, however, that the roof continued outwards beyond the post ring, probably sloping downwards to the ground.

Britain

In most parts of Bronze Age Britain, the standard house-type was round, usually with a ring of posts to support the roof (fig. 2.3). In upland areas where stone was available, a ring-bank served as the foundation for a wall of brushwood or wattle, sometimes with daub. In lower-lying situations, such as on southern British downlands or river gravels, the houses could be formed of post rings with additional strengthening elements such as ring-grooves or stake-rings. Though they frequently appear alongside other activity indicators, such as field boundaries, isolated huts occur quite commonly in many areas.[30]

---

[29] Parker Pearson 1996.
[30] e.g. the South Dorset Ridgeway: Woodward 1991, 150; Marlborough Downs: Gingell 1992.

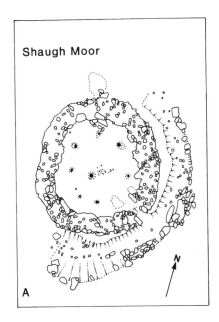
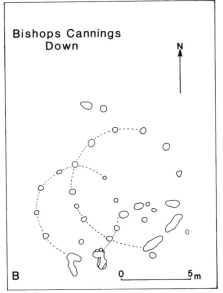
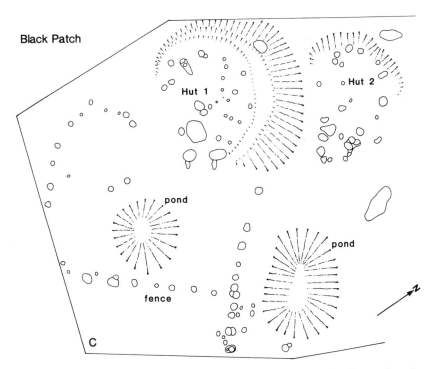

Fig. 2.3. Round hut plans from southern England: A: Shaugh Moor, Enclosure 15, House 67 (after Wainwright and Smith 1980), B: Bishops Cannings Down (after Gingell 1992), C: Black Patch, Hut Platform 4, south-western part (after Drewett 1982).

Settlements with round-houses have long been known in the upland zone in the British Isles, but only extensively investigated in the last twenty years.[31] Such a site on Dartmoor is Shaugh Moor, where a Bronze Age date is assured.[32] Enclosure 15 contained five ring-houses and a variety of less obvious post-built structures. They were marked by broad stone foundations broken by entrances that faced south-east or south-west. The largest house, 67, was around 6.5 m in diameter internally (fig. 2.3, A); the smallest, 18, only 3.7 m. Both had massive walls not less than 1.5 m thick and in places considerably more than this. Internally, the houses had a post-hole ring and some indication of other features, formed by clusters of post- or stake-holes in conjunction with pits; flagstones were provided in the later of the two phases of building.[33] The house at Bracken Rigg, Co. Durham (fig. 2.4, lower), was 8.8 × 8.2 m in diameter, and consisted of a low stone ring-bank with single entrance paved with stone slabs facing south.[34] A ring of six post-holes in the interior must have supported the roof; there was a roughly central hearth. Here the single house must have been occupied by a family or extended family group. Bearing in mind that in summer some members of the family may have been out on the moors away from base, and that in winter they may have sought necessary resources or even lived in lower-lying, perhaps coastal, locations, the living quarters may have sufficed for up to ten people; even so they seem cramped and the demographic unit dangerously small.

The site at Houseledge, Black Law, Northumberland (fig. 2.4, upper), consists of a linear arrangement of hut circles with field banks and clearance cairns adjoining the house plots.[35] The houses are irregularly circular; at the first to be investigated a stone bank overlay a ring-groove either from an earlier structure or the internal structural arrangement for the stone house (there is no ring of post-holes). This house was c. 9 m in internal diameter, the floor partly cobbled. The entrance of this house faces south-east and leads directly to a field bank; that of the adjacent house appears to face north.

These upland examples are complemented by those from the southern English downlands. It has long been known that simple round post-built houses were the norm in sites of the Early and Middle Bronze Age, such as Thorny Down, Wiltshire.[36] While it used to be considered that these were simple post rings, sometimes with a central post, the more elaborate double-ring structures seen on Early Iron Age sites were not recognised until

---

[31] Sites such as Grimspound or Rider's Rings on Dartmoor (Devon) were long thought to be of Iron Age or even later date, and in the absence of excavation this was understandable; even now they cannot be dated directly: Pattison and Fletcher 1994.
[32] Wainwright and Smith 1980.
[33] Similar round-house sites, but not enclosed, may be seen at a variety of other upland sites, for instance Stannon Down on Bodmin Moor, Cornwall: Mercer 1970.
[34] Coggins and Fairless 1984.
[35] Burgess 1980b.
[36] Stone 1941.

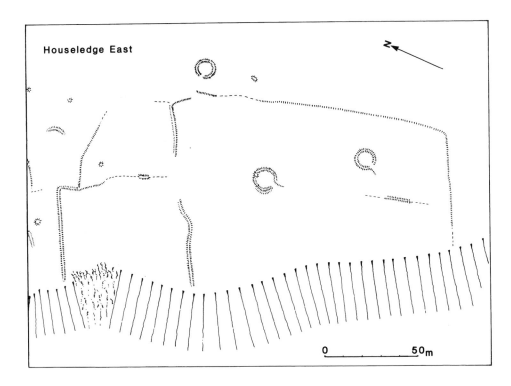

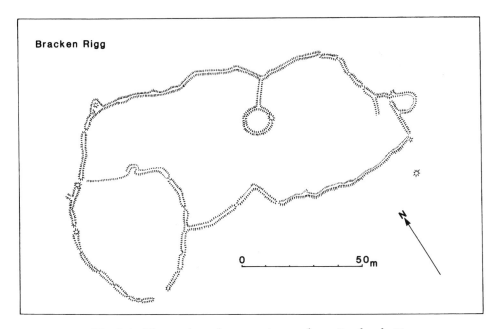

Fig. 2.4. Plans of settlements in northern England. *Upper*: Houseledge, Northumberland (after Burgess 1984); *lower*: Bracken Rigg, Co. Durham (after Coggins and Fairless 1984).

relatively recently.[37] Other sites with round-houses of this type include Black Patch[38] and Itford Hill.[39]

Round-houses also appear in the Late Bronze Age in fortified sites and on crannógs. At Rams Hill, Berkshire, a considerable number of post-holes, which were grouped by the excavators into round or oval houses and four-post structures, were found.[40] At Paddock Hill, Thwing, a large round-house lay at the centre of the site in the Late Bronze Age, the only such structure on the site; the timbers of the outer wall were placed in a bedding trench 25 m in diameter, with a ring of massive post-holes inside this on a diameter of 16 m.[41] Similarly, at Lofts Farm, Essex, a single roundish house 11 × 10 m across lay in the middle of a roughly square enclosure,[42] while at the North Rings, Mucking, Essex, three circular post-built houses 5–5.5 m in diameter lay in the western half of a large round, ditched enclosure.[43]

There is extensive and increasing evidence for lakeland occupation in the Bronze Age, in the form of crannógs.[44] At Clonfinlough, in the centre of Ireland near the Shannon, an oval enclosure formed by a palisade was around 50 × 40 m in extent, and contained two large round-houses on platforms, a smaller round hut, and a working area (fig. 2.5).[45] The main platforms were around 7 to 9 m in diameter, with wicker walls and floors formed of brushwood matting on a support of stone flags and a roundwood substructure. The upper level of the platform was made of superimposed layers of split oak planks, laid in a roughly circular arrangement around a central hearth area. The entrances faced north-east, away from the prevailing south-west wind. If, as is assumed, these platforms were houses, then they would have been roofed, probably with a reed thatch. At Ballinderry II, two construction types were present: small round constructions of wicker lay at the eastern side of the

---

[37] e.g. Shearplace Hill, Dorset: Rahtz and ApSimon 1962; Avery and Close-Brooks 1969.
[38] Drewett 1982.
[39] Burstow and Holleyman 1957.
[40] Bradley and Ellison 1975, 52ff. These were assumed to belong to a phase of Bronze Age fortified enclosure, but recent redating has shown that the developmental sequence of the defences occurred within a relatively short period at the start of the Late Bronze Age, and that the internal structures, where datable at all, could fall before the period of enclosure (Needham and Ambers 1994).
[41] Manby 1980.
[42] Brown 1988.
[43] Bond 1988.
[44] Morrison 1985; Wood-Martin 1886. These structures of brushwood and stones, resting on shallow lake beds, were traditionally thought to belong to the post-Roman period, and it is probably true that crannógs proper, situated on small islands in lakes, such as Lagore, are an Early Christian development. Lake-side settlements, on the other hand, go back to the Bronze Age (Lynn 1983). Irish examples include Knocknalappa, Co. Clare (Raftery 1942), Ballinderry II, Co. Offaly (Hencken 1942), Cullyhanna, Co. Armagh (Hodges 1958) and Clonfinlough, Co. Offaly (Moloney 1993b); in Scotland sites such as Milton Loch, Kirkudbrightshire, or Oakbank, Loch Tay, start in the middle of the first millennium BC (C. M. Piggott 1952–3; Morrison 1985, 24). A new consideration of the dating of Scottish sites, illustrating their preponderance in the first millennium BC: Henderson 1998.
[45] Moloney 1993b.

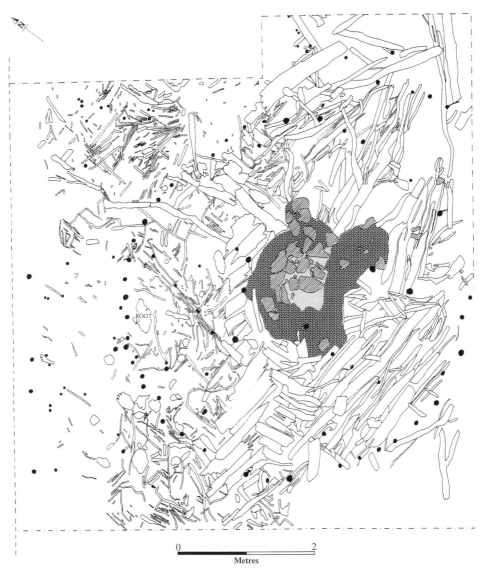

Fig. 2.5. Plan of Hut 3 at Clonfinlough, Co. Offaly, Ireland The oval ring of dark circles marks the line of uprights forming the house wall; the stippled and hatched area is the central stone hearth surrounded by charcoal and crushed stone. Source: Moloney 1993b.

platform, while at the western end were the perforated oak planks of a roughly square building, apparently built in the technique known as *Ständerbau*, whereby a framework of wooden posts sits on sill-beams, the spaces in between the posts being infilled with wattle and daub, and additional load-bearing posts being present in the house interior.[46] Unfortunately nothing is known of the superstructure of either type.

In continental Europe, the round-house is hardly known. An exception is provided by the lines of post-holes that form a round structure at Nijnsel, North Brabant, the Netherlands, and at a few other similar sites.[47] The plan thus formed is highly ambiguous, however, and in any case seen by its excavators as relating to British round-houses rather than as a manifestation of a Dutch round-house tradition.

From this it can be seen that the diameter of houses is very variable. Mostly they fall between 4 and 7 m in diameter, in other words within the range discussed above, but the houses at Bracken Rigg and Houseledge are larger than this, and those at Lofts Farm and especially Thwing very much larger. Completely different patterns of residential organisation probably obtained in the sites with large houses, plausibly related to the desire or need to include under one roof all family members as well as all the activities that would normally be performed indoors; by contrast, groups of small houses would have seen the division of both sleeping and activity functions.

Italy and Sicily

The other main area where round or oval stone-founded houses appear is south Italy and Sicily, notably the Aeolian Islands and Sardinia. Sites such as Montagnola di Capo Graziano on Filicudi, of the Early Bronze Age,[48] Milazzese on Panarea of the Middle Bronze Age[49] or the acropolis of Lipari (multiperiod)[50] contain numerous oval stone house outlines, though there is little available information on inter-house variation.[51] At Porto Perone, Leporano, near Taranto (Apulia), round post-built huts were present throughout the Bronze Age levels, but only in the later, Middle Apennine layers, was a group excavated.[52] Post-holes formed rings up to 4 m in diameter, with clay floors and hearths surrounded by stone settings inside them.

At La Muculufa in central southern Sicily, houses of the Early Bronze Age Castelluccio culture were round, and in the case of hut 2 of a characteristic

---

46 Hencken 1942.
47 Beex and Hulst 1968.
48 Bernabò Brea and Cavalier 1966.
49 Bernabò Brea and Cavalier 1968.
50 Bernabò Brea and Cavalier 1980.
51 A comparison of house size and occurrence of special finds at Milazzese shows little correlation between the two, though finds were differentially abundant and one house (XI) is marked not only by plentiful local pottery but also by imported Mycenaean vessels, clay hooks, miniature vessels, and by two moulds for the casting of bronze strips or bands. Indeed this southern part of the site, along the cliff edge, seems to have been richest in finds overall, though since the whole site is on a rocky promontory one would want to be sure that post-depositional factors were not to blame.
52 Lo Porto 1963.

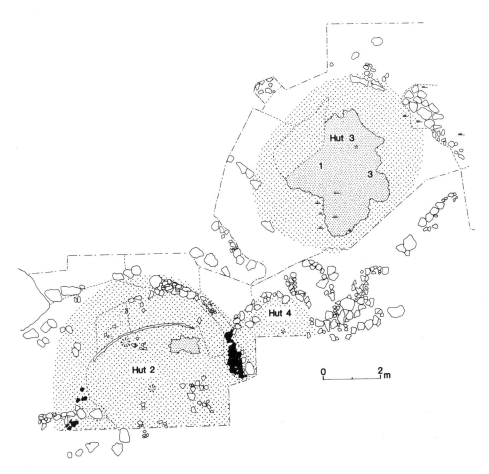

Fig. 2.6. Plan of Early Bronze Age houses at La Muculufa, Sicily (after McConnell 1992).

type, with stone foundations and superstructure of wattle and daub resting on four posts, and a bench of earth running round the inside of the stone wall; the hut measured 8 m in external diameter, and 4.8 × 4.5 m internally (fig. 2.6).[53] This is larger than most houses of the Castelluccio culture, as for instance at Manfria.[54] The appearance of round huts in Early and Middle Bronze Age contexts in Sicily and the Aeolian Islands is standard but their form and precise method of construction are somewhat varied. In other words, although there was a clear expression of a residential mode in these villages, the way in which it was achieved varied, perhaps indicating relative isolation and consequently local architectural autonomy. This must also be the

[53] McConnell 1992.
[54] Orsi 1911; 1926; Orlandini 1962.

case for the round or oval houses in the settlements surrounding *nuraghi* in Sardinia (see p. 300).[55]

Round-houses were thus highly restricted in occurrence, and frequently associated with building in stone. In part this reflects the technology of building in this material, but in part it must be connected with specific forms of residence pattern, perhaps involving the occupation of multiple buildings by a single family.

Rectangular houses

Many more rectangular houses are known than round ones in Bronze Age Europe. The best examples come mainly from the Low Countries and south Scandinavia from the Early Bronze Age onwards, from Alpine lake sites, and from the Urnfield world. In most other areas they were present, but survive poorly.

At Březno (Louny) a number of Únětice houses have been found, with settlement traces stretching for some distance along a river terrace.[56] In this case, two distinct settlement areas some 200 m apart were found beside the river Ohře; there were six long-houses in the western area and five in the eastern. All the houses are long rectangular post-built constructions with only slight traces of internal subdivisions or roof supports. House 32 is the largest building known from the entire Únětice culture area, and measures 32 × 6.5 m; other houses at Březno may have been equally large, but are not completely preserved. Presumably the walls of these houses, formed of posts set up to 1 m apart, were supplemented by an infill of reeds and daub. Since they are the only visible support for the roof, which must have been ridged, it is likely that purlins and cross-beams were used to spread the load. A broadly similar situation is likely to have applied at the less well-preserved settlements at Postoloprty[57] and Blšany[58] (both Louny, Czech Republic); at the latter, part of a house, similar to those at Březno, was preserved to a length of over 16 m.

More or less well-preserved house plans are present in various parts of Early and Middle Bronze Age central Europe. At Cham-Oberwil on the Zug Lake in central Switzerland, for example, the excavators recognised several house types: four-post structures, the posts 2–2.5 m apart; larger rectangular houses with stone-packed post-holes (three rows of five posts, giving a construction 13 × 8 m); and one even larger structure measuring 18 × 8 m.[59] The variety of constructions, with four-posters being present as well as rectangular build-

[55] e.g. Barumini: Lilliu 1962.
[56] Pleinerová 1966, 359ff.; 1990.
[57] Soudský 1953.
[58] Pleinerová 1960b.
[59] Gnepf *et al.* 1996.

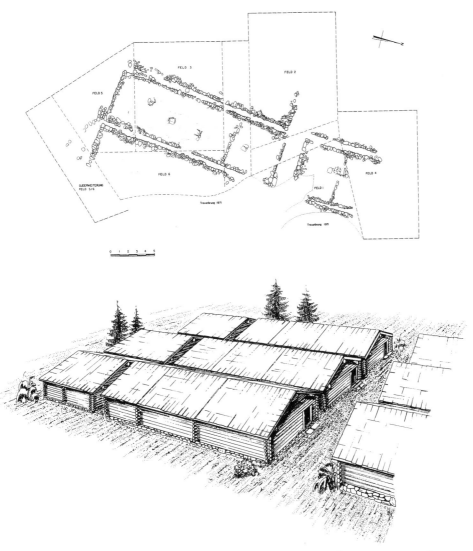

Fig. 2.7. Plan and reconstruction of houses of Horizon B at the Padnal near Savognin, Engadin, Switzerland. Source: Rageth 1986.

ings of various sizes, can be seen at many other sites.[60] Not dissimilar are the results from the extensive excavations on the glacial mound of the Padnal at Savognin (Engadin, Graubünden, Switzerland),[61] one of a number of such settlements in the inner Alpine valleys (fig. 2.7). In the earliest phase (Horizon

---

[60] For instance the otherwise scanty remains at Hörbing-Forstgarten (Deutschlandsberg, Steiermark, south-east Austria) (Hebert 1991) or at Schöningen-Esbeck (Helmstedt, eastern Lower Saxony) (Maier 1996).
[61] Rageth 1986.

E) the houses were post-and-plank-built, sometimes with a stone foundation, in one case with a floor of wooden planks; they were squarish or rectangular and around 4–5 m in each dimension. In subsequent phases, they were invariably stone-founded, with wooden walls, sometimes with stone-paved floors; in Horizons D and C the houses were long (up to 9 m in length), with internal divisions into separate rooms, hearths and storage areas. In Horizon D there was a rectangular wooden construction interpreted as a cistern, 4.8 × 3 m in extent, built of larch-wood posts and planks and sunk into a pit. Whether such arrangements were typical for other Alpine settlements is harder to say, because the extent of excavation and preservation is rarely so good as at the Padnal;[62] but at other sites in the Alpine valleys remains of post-built houses are commonly found.[63]

Not surprisingly, it is in waterlogged sites that the most spectacular remains of wooden houses are preserved, above all in the lake sites of the Alpine area.[64] Most Alpine lake-side sites produce abundant wood, usually piles, but little evidence for house form. One example of this is Fiavé,[65] where, in spite of the many hundreds of piles that supported structures, the form of individual houses is not known. In general, houses on wet ground were formed of horizontal members stabilised by vertical posts and 'post-shoes' or sole-plates (short perforated planks for stabilising vertical posts) at the corners. The horizontal timbers, which are usually all that survive archaeologically, were the lowest element of the walls, and on them were placed either further horizontal timbers, to produce a log cabin (*Blockbau*), or a vertical framework of posts, the gaps filled in with hurdles, wattle and daub, or similar materials. It is often hard to tell from the archaeological remains which technique was in use, unless remains of the wattling are preserved.

Knowledge of Early Bronze Age settlements has been radically transformed by the discovery of well-preserved lake-side sites at Zürich-Mozartstrasse[66] or Bodman-Schachen (phase I) on Lake Constance, and the Forschner site in Upper Swabia,[67] and a number of other sites that cover this period, for instance

---

[62] St Veit-Klinglberg: Shennan 1995, 85ff.

[63] Wyss 1971a. A systematic presentation of these Alpine house types has been possible following the excavation of Munt Baselgia at Scuol (Schuls-Kirchhügel) in the Engadin (Graubünden) (Stauffer-Isenring 1983). A whole series of house floors was found here, with posts marked by stone settings, stone wall foundations, and on occasion wooden floors and sill-beams. Most houses were post-built, the walls being constructed either of simple wooden members lying on the earth, or of the same resting on stones, or of wattle-and-daub. An inner line of posts in some houses supported a ridge roof.

[64] Summary presentations of house types in these areas have been produced by Wyss (1971a) and Audouze and Büchsenschütz (1989/1991), building on the pioneering work of Vogt (1954, 132ff.).

[65] Perini 1984.

[66] Gross *et al.* 1987.

[67] Billamboz *et al.* 1989; Keefer 1990; Torke 1990.

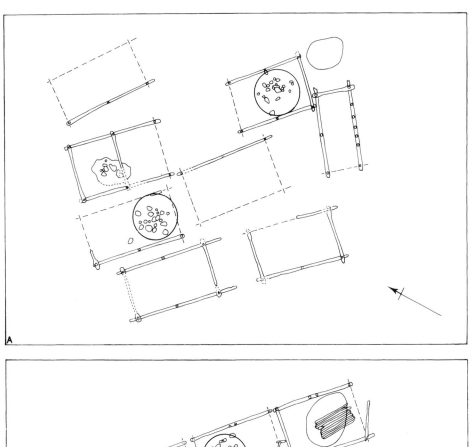

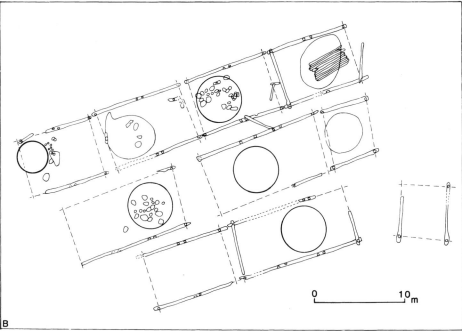

Fig. 2.8. Zürich-Mozartstrasse, plans of Early Bronze Age villages, phases A (*upper*) and B (*lower*) (after Gross 1987).

Meilen-Schellen.[68] The Mozartstrasse settlement in Zürich (fig. 2.8) produced two successive groups of Early Bronze Age structures, mainly sleeper-beam buildings, rectangular in shape, with the wall outline consisting of sleepers laid directly on the ground and perforated by mortise holes; posts were then passed through the holes and rammed into the ground. The dimensions were usually 3–4 m wide and 5.5 to 6.6 m long. The construction method did not differ significantly between the two phases. They were overlain by a wooden floor or platform covering some 200 m², which may have served as a foundation for further constructions; numerous sole-plates were found on and around the platform. Dendro-dating enabled the excavators to place the sleeper-beam houses at or before 1607 BC, the platform before 1545 BC and the sole-plate houses after that; sole-plates of alder and posts of ash east and south of the platform date to around 1545, while an oak palisade and houses formed of beech sole-plates and oak posts have a felling date of 1503/4 BC. The Forschner site on the Federsee in Baden-Württemberg saw two main phases of occupation, the first in the eighteenth century BC, the second from 1508 BC on. Rectangular houses were first erected in 1764 BC, though details of their construction methods are not yet available. At Meilen-Schellen on Lake Zürich traces of several phases of house-building were recovered, of which the clearest saw the construction of a long rectangular building, marked by sole-plates, at least 11.5 m long and 4 m broad, erected in the 1640s BC. The nature of the superstructure is not known, but is unlikely to have consisted of large timbers, probably being wattle and daub instead.

Houses on tells

The excavation of tell sites in Hungary and Bulgaria has produced a series of house plans of varying types and methods of construction (fig. 2.9). The recent spate of tell excavations in Hungary[69] has shown that every site dug can produce house plans in addition to stratigraphic sequences. The commonest building material was wattle and daub on a light framework of upright posts, not dissimilar to what had been used since far back in the Neolithic, especially in Bulgaria. Excavations at Tószeg (Szolnok) have recovered small parts of such buildings since the last century,[70] but systematic work in the 1970s showed that houses of this type belonged to the lowest, Nagyrév, levels, and were variable in size, some having three and others two internal rooms, with beaten earth floors and open square or circular hearths beside one of the

---

[68] Ruoff 1987; see also Becker *et al.* 1985. From earlier discoveries one may mention the site of the Bleiche at Arbon, also on Lake Constance, though the structures there were more difficult to interpret (Fischer 1971).
[69] e.g. Máthé 1988; Bronzezeit in Ungarn 1992.
[70] Mozsolics 1952; Banner *et al.* 1957.

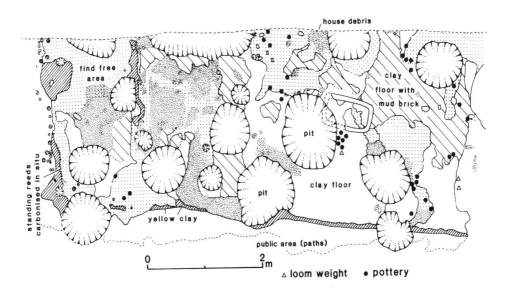

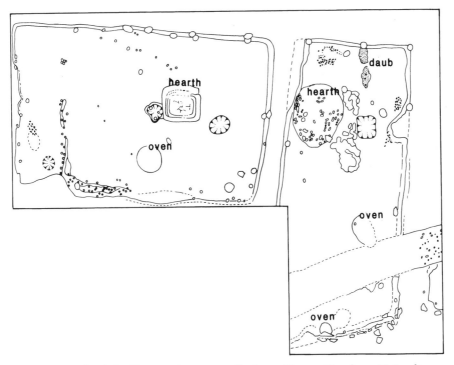

Fig. 2.9. House plans on tell sites. *Upper:* Feudvar, Vojvodina, Trench E, level 13, western house, schematic representation of excavated elements (after Hänsel and Medović 1991); *lower:* Jászdózsa-Kápolnahalom, house plans of level 6 (after Stanczik and Tárnoki 1992).

walls.[71] In the succeeding Hatvan layers, the *Blockbau* (log cabin) technique was sometimes used. This information was confirmed by other recent excavations on Hungarian tells, for instance Tiszaug-Kéménytető,[72] where the rectangular houses were between 7 and 9 m long and 3.5 and 5 m wide; or Jászdózsa-Kápolnahalom (fig. 2.9, lower).[73] The *Blockbau* technique is also found, for instance at Törökszentmiklós-Terehalom[74] and Békés-Várdomb in south-east Hungary, where it occurs side by side with post-building; it is not known for sure why one technique was used in some instances and the other in others.[75]

In a series of excavations in the Berettyó valley, all tells investigated produced a succession of house plans, usually with post-framed outline and plastered floor, or in some cases wooden plank floor.[76] Sometimes sleeper-beams, or halved beams laid horizontally, were pierced by upright members to produce these post-holes, but in other sites true sleepers were used, leaving no post traces. At Szilhalom there was a large house of Gyulavarsand date with wattle and daub walls and an inner post row. Floors were sometimes replastered (three times at Herpály), but the excavators believe that wood was in general preferred to clay for floors, by contrast with the Neolithic. House outlines with hearths and pits were recovered at Aszod,[77] but excavation has not so far enabled dimensions to be established.

Houses on the extensively excavated tell at Feudvar in the Vojvodina were typically post-framed with reed and daub infilling and clay floors (fig. 2.9, upper).[78] Houses were on average 5–6 m wide and 10–12 m long and probably had a raised bench in one corner and a loom in another, in addition to the eccentrically placed hearth.

The situation on Bulgarian tells in the Bronze Age is harder to understand because of the vicissitudes of excavation and publication. But in general it appears that post-framed wattle-and-daub constructions continued throughout the Bronze Age wherever tells themselves continued (bearing in mind that many sites appear to come to an end with the Early Bronze Age). Houses of this sort are present at Ezero in this early period,[79] but also later at sites such as Nova Zagora[80] and Ognyanovo.[81]

The situation on the *terramara* sites of northern Italy is essentially similar. These sites, often deeply stratified, are in essence tells, and consist largely

[71] Stanczik 1980; Bóna 1992.
[72] Csányi and Stanczik 1992.
[73] Stanczik and Tárnoki 1992.
[74] Tárnoki 1992.
[75] Banner and Bóna 1974.
[76] Máthé 1988.
[77] Tárnoki 1988.
[78] Hänsel and Medović 1991, 73ff.
[79] Georgiev *et al.* 1979.
[80] Katinčarov 1972.
[81] Detev and Macanova 1977.

of occupation debris. Excavation has usually consisted of deep soundings through them, recovering a stratigraphic succession but not exposing any great horizontal area; as a consequence, house plans are barely known. Recent work has, however, concentrated much more on area excavation, so that it is now clear that rectangular or trapezoidal post-built houses were the norm, as one can see at Ca' de' Cessi (Sabbioneta, Mantova)[82] or Santa Rosa (Fodico di Poviglio, Reggio Emilia).[83] Earlier work had suggested that round huts were present, or in the case of Castione dei Marchesi (Borgo San Donnino, Parma) solid wooden constructions of *Blockbau* type.[84]

Scandinavia, Holland and France

Although house plans have been recovered in Scandinavia over many years,[85] a series of excavations in northern Europe in the last 15 years has transformed knowledge of Bronze Age houses in that part of the world, demonstrating the existence of a rather specific tradition.[86]

At Egehøj in north-east Jutland the remains of three houses dated to Period I consisted of post-framed walls forming sub-rectangular areas, with a central row of load-bearing posts, with pits containing weaving equipment, heaps of fired stones, and whole pots sunk into the floors.[87] This simple rectangular plan appears to represent the earliest house type, and is also seen at Hemmed Church house III in eastern Jutland,[88] or in the series of houses at Hesel (Leer, Lower Saxony) (fig. 2.10).[89] Subsequently, the single row of roof supports gave place to two rows, presumably supporting a 'trestle' arrangement and thus forming three 'aisles'. This change took place by Period II, as can be seen at Hyllerup in western Zealand;[90] this three-aisled form then became the norm, though other variations are also found.[91] The addition of the third aisle has been seen in connection with the need to stall animals indoors,[92] under the eaves, though why this should have changed between Periods I and II is not

[82] de Marinis *et al.* 1992–3, 50ff.
[83] Bernabò Brea and Cremaschi 1990; 1996.
[84] Säflund 1939, 96ff., 219.
[85] e.g. the settlements at Broby/Börje in Uppland, or Ivetofta/Bromölla on Lake Ivö in southern Sweden: Schönbäck 1952; Stenberger 1977, 226.
[86] Thrane 1985; Tesch 1992; Rasmussen and Adamsen 1993; Karlenby 1994; the lengthy discussion by Tesch is fundamental to the study of Bronze Age houses in general, and Scandinavian houses in particular.
[87] Boas 1983.
[88] Boas 1989.
[89] Schwarz 1996.
[90] Pedersen 1986.
[91] In addition to the many examples in south Scandinavia, comparable constructions were apparently present at Ullunda in central Sweden, where a single three-aisled long-house of the Early Bronze Age was reconstructed in the Middle Bronze Age over added gravel levelling material, and in Rogaland, southern Norway, where houses at Forsandmoen, Forsand, were also of this type: Price 1995; Løken 1989.
[92] Tesch 1992, 290; Rasmussen and Adamsen 1993, 138.

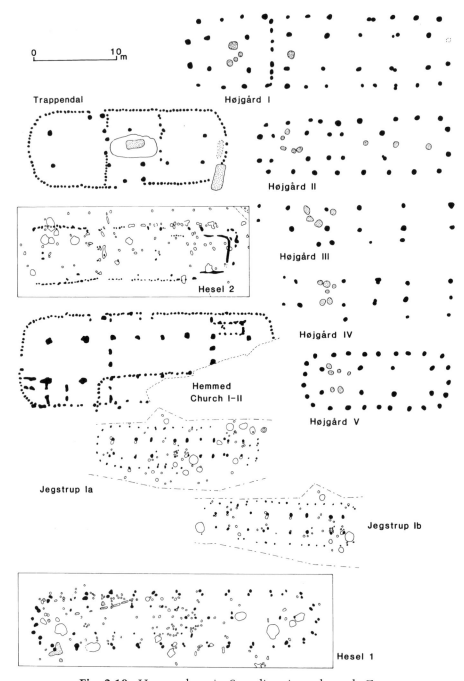

Fig. 2.10. House plans in Scandinavia and north Germany.
Højgård I–V (after Ethelberg 1986); Trappendal, Kolding
(after Boysen and Andersen 1983); Hesel 1–2, Lower Saxony
(after Schwarz 1996); Hemmed Church, Jutland (after Boas 1983);
Jegstrup Ia–Ib (after Davidsen 1982).

clear. Tesch also suggests that the trestle arrangement involved less use of stout timbers, indicating a possible shortage of wood and thus major landscape changes.

At Trappendal (Kolding) a post-built long-house with rounded ends, 23.5 m long, was found under a barrow (fig. 2.10).[93] The house was divided into three internal rooms by transverse walls, and had a hearth at either end. The size of this house – much smaller than the 50 m long building at Store Tyrrestrup – and the use of misshapen timbers at Bjerre have again been taken to indicate local wood shortages, but this is hard to believe for such a substantial building.[94] Quite why the house should have been overlain by a barrow is mysterious, but it suggests a close connection between the two; perhaps even that the Trappendal house was not purely domestic in function. A comparable case is to be seen at Hyllerup, and at Handewitt (Schleswig-Flensburg) in northern Germany;[95] such a situation recalls the connection between houses and burial sites in the Neolithic,[96] while the affinity between Early Bronze Age round-houses and round barrows in Britain has already been mentioned.

Variation in the form and construction method of houses is apparent at various sites, for instance at Højgård (Gram, southern Jutland), where of 11 houses, two were supposed sunken-floor houses, two were post-frame houses and seven three-aisled long-houses (fig. 2.10),[97] and at Vadgård in northern Jutland,[98] where five houses have thick turf walls; some are totally enclosed by turf walls, while others have them only on the south side. There are no internal roof-bearing constructions and few hearths. It has been suggested that these turf constructions have a quite different function from the more normal post-built structures,[99] though determining what it was is more difficult since they seem less than ideal either for ordinary occupation or for storage. The variation in house form is also evident in the Köpinge area of southern Sweden, where in addition to long-houses with or without internal divisions there are small, roughly square houses with only two pairs of trestle posts, and sunken-floor huts, probably outbuildings.[100]

This remarkable set of discoveries in Denmark continued into the Middle and Late Bronze Age as with the houses of the three-aisled variety at Hemmed Church on the Djursland peninsula in north-east Jutland[101] and Jegstrup (Skive) in central Jutland (fig. 2.10).[102] Traces of painting on the surface of

[93] Boysen and Andersen 1983.
[94] Rasmussen and Adamsen 1993, 137.
[95] Bokelmann 1977.
[96] For example the house beneath the court tomb at Ballyglass, Co. Mayo, western Ireland (Ó Nuailláin 1972) or the segmented building at Barkær in eastern Jutland (Madsen 1979).
[97] Ethelberg 1986.
[98] Lomborg 1976.
[99] Rasmussen 1992–3.
[100] Tesch 1992, 300.
[101] Boas 1989.
[102] Davidsen 1982.

daub are known at Voldtofte. Recent excavations in central Sweden have been taken as suggesting that a further change took place around 1000 BC: the length of houses decreased markedly, from well over 20 m before that time to less than 20 m afterwards, though what might have caused such a change remains mysterious.[103]

Such aisled long-houses of post-built construction are also widely known in north-west Europe, most notably in the Low Countries. The sites of Elp and Nijnsel have been known for some time, but more recently a large number of excavations in both Holland and Belgium, allied to good-quality recovery techniques, has produced settlements ranging in date from Middle Bronze Age to Early Iron Age where post-framed houses are present, and the majority of these are three-aisled;[104] this information can be taken as replacing that known previously from sites such as Zwaagdijk (Wervershoof, North Holland).[105] Such houses continue through the Late Bronze Age and into the Early Iron Age.[106] In Lorraine, the fragmentary remains of rather similar houses have been recovered in recent excavations.[107]

The houses can reach considerable lengths, as with the 27 m inner length at Zijderveld and Dodewaard, and have a number of internal partitions, quite apart from the inner rows of posts whose main function was of course to support the roof. Apart from rows of large posts, one also finds smaller posts in pairs forming the wall; there is some debate as to what filled the space in between the post pairs. It is likely that a double wattle wall is represented, perhaps with reed or straw between to add to the insulation of the wall, which was very likely coated with daub inside and out. In some cases a clear porch arrangement is present.

Central Europe in the Late Bronze Age

The Late Bronze Age villages of central Europe differed significantly from those of the west. In recent years improved excavation technique has enabled the recovery of a number of Urnfield settlements complete with house plans; of many possible examples, two are here singled out for detailed attention: Zedau (Osterburg) in the Altmark (part of Sachsen-Anhalt),[108] and Lovčičky near Vyškov in Moravia.[109] Both were excavated initially as rescue projects

---

[103] Karlenby 1994.
[104] Fokkens and Roymans 1991.
[105] Modderman 1964. Of numerous cases which could be quoted, those from Wijk bij Duurstede (Utrecht), Zijderveld (South Holland) and Dodewaard (Gelderland) or Nijnsel (St Oedenrode, North Brabant) serve as good examples: Hessing 1991; Hulst 1973; 1991; Beex and Hulst 1968.
[106] As seen at Den Burg on the island of Texel (North Holland) or Oss-Ussen, Mikkeldonk (North Brabant): Woltering 1991; Fokkens 1991.
[107] Blouet, Koenig and Vanmoerkerke 1996.
[108] Horst 1985; the plan shown in simplified form by A. Jockenhövel's review of this work, *Germania* 68/1, 1990, 272.
[109] Říhovský 1982.

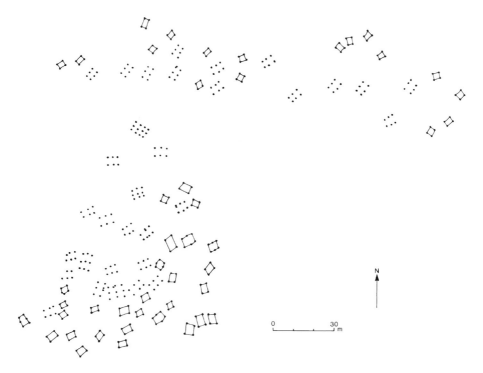

Fig. 2.11. Zedau, Ostmark: simplified plan of the Late Bronze Age settlement (after Jockenhövel, *Germania* 68/1, 1990, 272, and Horst 1985).

in advance of sand extraction, and in neither case is the entire settlement preserved. Nevertheless, few other sites – other than enclosed or fortified ones – come near in terms of fullness of plan. Examples of what might be comparable is represented by the site found by chance under the Roman fort at Künzing (Deggendorf) on the Danube in Lower Bavaria,[110] or the very large site at Unterhaching near Munich.[111]

At Zedau, around 400 post-holes were assigned to 78 separate houses, of various kinds (fig. 2.11). Thirty-two of them were post structures on level ground, and 28 of these were small rectangular structures, consisting of two parallel rows of three posts, enclosing an area of 24–36 m². There were no internal divisions, and in only five instances could the remains of a hearth be detected. The excavator called this house type the 'Buch type', after the suburb of Berlin where a very similar settlement was excavated before the Second World War.[112] The other four houses were rather larger, having three

---

[110] Herrmann 1975.
[111] Keller 1980. A catalogue of these Late Bronze Age house sites has been published by Müller (1986).
[112] Kiekebusch 1923.

rows of posts; in two houses these were four posts long, and in the other two
three posts long; the internal area thus reaches up towards 40 m^2, though the
positioning of the interior posts meant that not all this area could be effectively utilised. Only one produced a hearth. Besides these 32 houses on level
ground, there were a further 46 structures that were partially sunk into the
ground, with posts placed at the corners outside the depression. Some were
extremely small, while others were almost as big as the level-ground structures. No hearths were found in them. The excavator saw these as being
connected with economic activities such as storage, grain-processing and
the like, as opposed to the level-ground structures, which he thought to
have been dwelling houses. It certainly appears that at Zedau there were no
large installations either for extended family occupation or for communal
activities. Even the largest of the post structures, at 40 m^2, pales into insignif-
icance beside the Dutch or Danish examples, which commonly reached
150 m^2 and sometimes more. Why should residence patterns have changed
so markedly around the line of the river Elbe?

At Lovčičky the differences between houses are even more marked (fig.
2.12). Of 48 reconstructable house plans, all are post-built (just one has a
trench foundation on three sides). Forty of the 48 have large post-holes set
apart some distance from each other (average 2.25 m), and a mere four have
close-set post-holes, while only three are constructed of small posts. The
majority are relatively small houses of predominantly rectangular plan, with
two or three rows of posts, covering an area from as small as 7 m^2 to as large
as 35 m^2. Clearly buildings of such different size were intended for radically
different purposes. Then there are a few houses with a central row of posts,
presumed to be for supporting the roof. Two of these are much larger than
the rest, House E with closely spaced posts having a length of over 21 m and
a ground area of 144 m^2, and House AS with quite small, widely spaced posts,
a length of around 35 m and an area of 187 m^2. In the case of this last example, examination of the plan might suggest that more than one building is
involved, particularly as there are slight but definite changes in orientation
and post size along the walls.[113]

The difficulty of identifying with certainty the extent and nature of houses
in this period can be seen from numerous examples.[114] At Lovčičky, the nature
of the excavation (scraping the topsoil off by machine to expose the loess subsoil) means that only those features which penetrated deep enough into the
ground to leave a significant trace below topsoil level will have been recorded.

---

[113] More recent methods of computer analysis of post-hole distribution might well come up with
   different configurations of house plans.
[114] e.g. the Elchinger Kreuz site at the intersection of the A7 and A8 motorways near Ulm, dug
   as a rescue excavation in 1975–6: Pressmar 1979. Some post-holes lie in a row, but parallel
   rows such as one would expect from rectangular houses are harder to identify, and the seven
   hearths found do not clearly fall inside such tentative outlines as one can make out.

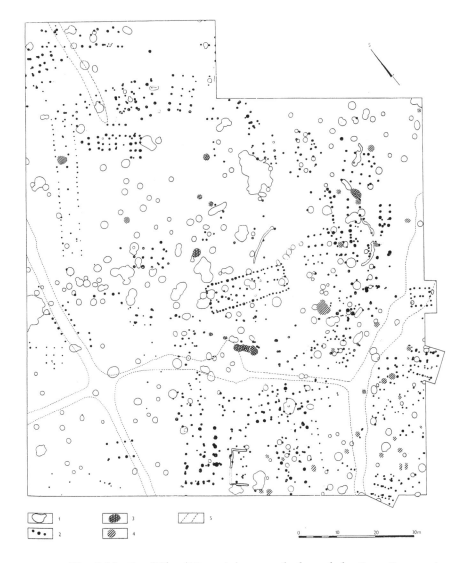

Fig. 2.12. Lovčičky (Moravia): general plan of the Late Bronze Age settlement. Source: Říhovský 1982. Key: 1. Velatice culture pits. 2. Post-holes. 3. Eneolithic pits. 4. Únětice culture pits and graves. 5. Rust-brown stripes.

This is the case with most wood-built houses, but it is often accorded too little importance in the literature; puzzling gaps in the distribution of features across a site must sometimes be attributable to this factor, since it is entirely possible that at least some posts did not go down deeper than the 30 cm of modern ploughsoil. Such an explanation may in part account for the poor preservation of a plan such as that of the Knovíz-period settlement of Březno (Louny) in north-west Bohemia.[115] There, an extensive area of pits was found, but post-holes occurred in only some five spots, and of them only in one case could a complete house-plan be reconstructed (a rectangular structure measuring 15 × 5.5 m, with a central hearth and one end more or less free of structural timbers, the other – probably divided by a screen or partition – with numerous post subdivisions that must relate to function rather than construction).[116]

Numerous other Late Bronze Age settlement sites are known from central Europe, but in most cases the information is a reduced and repetitive version of what has already been seen. Most Lausitz houses, for instance, were simple post-built one-room affairs.[117] A notable exception is the long-house at Książek (Wałbrzych), apparently with five rooms; but the plan invites the suspicion that a two-room building was rebuilt, probably more than once, on the same alignment but shifted axially. At Hascherkeller in Bavaria, a double ditch system, with a palisade in the inner one, surrounded a series of enclosures which contained pits, many of them full of daub; no post-structures were found.[118]

On the Alpine lakes, Late Bronze Age structures are more numerous than Early Bronze Age ones.[119] At Greifensee-Böschen a series of square house outlines constructed in 1047/6 BC was recovered, formed by timbers resting on sole-plates at the corners and presumed to have supported a wall of horizontally laid beams in the log cabin or *Blockbau* technique. One of the houses, however, produced a hurdle that had fallen outwards from the wall, and such fabrications, sealed with daub, would represent a more likely form of wall construction. These log cabins were also present at Zug-Sumpf, and strongly recall the structures of the first phase of the Wasserburg at Bad Buchau,[120] where corduroy-style wooden floors were also sometimes present (see p. 60). At Auvernier-Nord excavations in the 1970s produced no less than 24 rectangular house plans, each formed of three lines of wall-posts.[121] Floors are partly of clay, on which fires were lit; on or beside these clay features, which show as lenses in section, querns and fire-dogs (crescentic clay objects) were often found, indicating that they were houses and not barns or granaries. A similar situation applied at Cortaillod-Est, where a remarkable picture has been built up through dendrochronology and timber analysis.[122]

---

[115] Pleinerová and Hrala 1988.
[116] Similar information, from a somewhat different cultural milieu, comes from Sobčice (Jičín, north-east Bohemia); in addition to pits and post-holes, the rectangular outline of a bedding trench forming a potential house some 6 m wide and at least 25 m long was found: Motyková 1973.
[117] Buck 1986; Bukowski 1990.
[118] Wells 1983.
[119] Sites with extensive evidence for houses include Auvernier-Nord (Arnold 1977; 1983), Zug-Sumpf (Speck 1954; Ruoff 1984), Greifensee-Böschen (Ruoff 1984; Eberschweiler *et al.* 1987) and Cortaillod-Est (Arnold 1984; 1990).
[120] Reinerth 1928; Kimmig 1992.
[121] Arnold 1983.
[122] Arnold 1984; 1990.

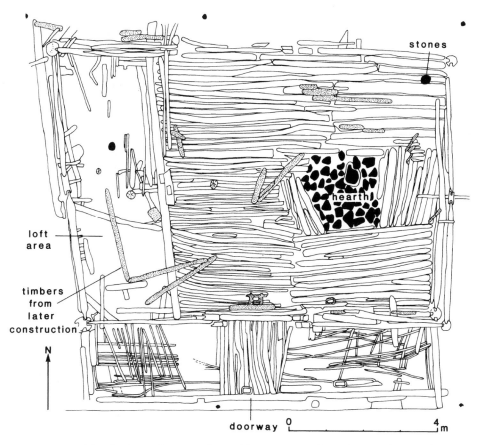

Fig. 2.13. Biskupin, plan of house 3, earlier phase (after Rajewski 1950).

Other waterlogged sites with good information on house form include the Polish stockades of the late Lausitz culture (Early Iron Age), the most famous being Biskupin (Żnin). Here the houses were large, 9 by 8 m, with an ante-room leading to a main room with hearth, loom and other facilities; the floor was of wooden poles and beams, corduroy-style.[123] A ladder led to an upper floor, probably a hay-loft, doubling as sleeping-quarters (fig. 2.13). Dry-land sites of the same period are inevitably less informative: at Sobiejuchy there was evidence of dense occupation, as represented by daub lines, hearths or ovens, and pits, but individual houses could barely be distinguished.[124]

The only southern British sites with extensive evidence for waterlogged wooden structures that are presently known and excavated are Runnymede

---

[123] Rajewski 1950.
[124] Harding and Ostoja-Zagórski 1989.

on the Thames[125] and Flag Fen near Peterborough.[126] Behind a palisade of posts
that served as the waterfront at Runnymede were the substantial posts of a
large rectilinear building. Other structures may be presumed to have lain
nearby, and other waterside sites, such as Wallingford, Oxfordshire, were probably similar.[127] At Flag Fen a platform supported buildings, but the excavator
has argued for a ritual rather than a domestic function for the site.

Caves

It is commonly supposed that the occupation of caves must relate to cult
activities rather than domestic activity, and in some cases this is certainly
true (see below, chapter 9). In others, however, the character of the occupation does not necessarily permit such an interpretation, and caves may rather
have represented an easy way of obtaining shelter, at least at certain times –
perhaps on a seasonal basis, perhaps at times when for other reasons there
were difficulties in the way of erecting permanent buildings.

A sizeable number of caves were occupied in the Bronze Age in continental Europe, without any particular evidence that cult activities were involved.
This may apply to some of the caves of central Europe discussed in chapter
9. Cave sites were used in Bulgaria throughout the Bronze Age and into the
Iron Age, as at Devetaki, Emen, Magura and Muselievo;[128] in some cases the
remains of wattle-and-daub house constructions were found in them. Caves
were also used in Romania.[129]

In south-west Germany cave sites with pottery were especially common in
the Middle Bronze Age,[130] a fact that compares interestingly with the apparent reduction in lake-side settlement a little further south in Switzerland in
this period, and the contemporaneous increase in hill settlement (as also at
the end of the Bronze Age). The move to hills and caves must betoken a reluctance or inability to maintain settlement on the lowlands, but interest in
these caves may rather have been of a symbolic than a utilitarian nature.

Many French caves that are best known for their Stone Age occupation
were also utilised in the Bronze Age; this is certainly true of many southern
French sites such as the Grotte Murée[131] and many others,[132] and is also found

---

[125] Longley 1980; Needham 1991, 114ff.
[126] Pryor 1991.
[127] Thomas *et al.* 1986.
[128] Mikov and Džambazov 1960; Nikolova and Angelov 1961; Džambazov and Katinčarov 1974;
Gergov 1979.
[129] As with the Cioclovina cave (Hunedoara), or a number of others in south-west Transylvania;
see recent excavations of a long stratified sequence at Peştera Cauce (also Hunedoara) by
S. A. Luca (University of Sibiu) to whom thanks are due for the information.
[130] Biel 1987, 51ff., 82f.
[131] Courtin 1976, 27.
[132] Sandars 1957, 283ff., 329f.; Guilaine 1976, 443ff.

in neighbouring Aragon and Catalonia and adjacent parts of Spain.[133] A number of caves in the south and east of France have Late Bronze Age occupation and burial, for instance the Grotte du Hasard at Tharaux (Gard),[134] the Grotte des Planches at Arbois (Jura)[135] and many others (see pp. 317ff.). It may also be the case in British sites such as those in Somerset (Wookey Hole, Soldier's Hole, Sun Hole; all Cheddar), south Wales (Lesser Garth Cave, Glamorgan; Ogof yr Esgyrn, Brecknock) or the Peak District and Yorkshire Pennines (Elbolton cave, Wharfedale).[136] The character of the occupation was much the same as it had been in previous millennia, representing everyday domestic activity rather than any special utilisation for cult or ritual – though such aspects may well have merged imperceptibly with more mundane ones.

In the Apennines of Italy, caves in the higher areas were frequently used in the Bronze Age, as in earlier periods, and have been seen as part of a wider system of transhumant exploitation.[137] Examples of these are the Grotta a Male and the Grotta dei Piccioni (see p. 142). Caves are common in many other parts of Italy, and they were utilised in many periods of prehistory; it is thus not surprising to find that in north-eastern Sicily, for instance, cave occupation is found during the Early Bronze Age.[138]

The village

Individual houses are not entities that can be completely understood on their own, because they are part of a larger set of relations, the settlement as a whole. Just as the positioning of houses, both mentally and physically, was a crucial element of Lévi-Strauss's structuralist analysis of ethnographic settlement, so the layout of villages recovered by archaeology must relate to the mental and social processes that underlay the workings of those villages. The disposition of buildings, in other words the disposition of the spaces in between the buildings, is a statement about how the inhabitants viewed and interacted with each other; it represents the possibilities for circulation within the settlement. It also has a functional character. Tightly clustered settlements depended on fields and garden plots that were located outside the built-up area. These could have been disposed in a radial fashion, so that each house had the shortest journey to its dependent fields; or (more likely) they could have extended in other patterns, with proprietorial rights to them determined by factors other than proximity. Dispersed settlements, on the other

---

[133] Eiroa 1979; Arqueología en Catalunya 1983, 74ff.; Rodanés Vicente 1992; Maya 1992; Alcalde *et al.* 1994.
[134] Roudil and Soulier 1976.
[135] Pétrequin 1985; Audouze and Büchsenschütz 1991, 125.
[136] Burgess 1980a, 227; Mason 1968; Gilks 1973.
[137] Barker 1975.
[138] Pellegrini 1992, 479.

hand, could have had garden plots between the buildings, suitable for some cultivation of vegetables and the grazing of a few animals, though not for more extensive grain-crop production which would still have been located outside the built-up area altogether. These functional and interactional elements must have cross-cut each other. It is not enough to say that the need for horticulture determined the dispersed pattern of settlement in individual cases, since this pattern results in a level of inter-neighbour interaction that must be lower than that experienced by the inhabitants of closely spaced houses; in just the same way as those who live in detached houses today have a greater interactional distance from their neighbours than those who live in terraces. This is partly because of the physical distance between the buildings, but interactional distance is not simply a matter of physical distance; it depends crucially on such matters as the position of doorways relative to each other and to common space, and how easy it is for visitors to penetrate the space of their neighbours, for instance whether fences or hedges are erected between garden plots, whether access to and through the main door is unrestricted, and similar matters. Neighbours in terrace houses can make access very difficult for each other by such means; equally, neighbours in houses detached from each other by considerable distances can keep 'open house'.

This concept of interactional distance is an important one for trying to understand the form and layout of both houses and settlements. At the same time, it has to be admitted that there are few guidelines for achieving such an understanding; much of what can be said about Bronze Age settlements has to be based on ethnocentric notions, derived from present-day experience or recent ethnographic evidence. More practically, it is also the case that the majority of settlement sites in this as in other periods are extremely incomplete, whether through destruction or through partial excavation; statements about the use of space on them are therefore necessarily circumscribed. This is the case for the majority of Early Bronze Age sites in central Europe. In many of the dry-land sites mentioned above a single house is present, so that little can be said about the overall form of the settlement. Even in more extensive cases, uncertainties about the nature of the evidence means that the location of buildings is at best speculative.

Fletcher has suggested that the size and density of populations and the area occupied by their settlements are correlated,[139] and specifically that small-scale agricultural settlements (such as one imagines existed in the Bronze Age) have populations between 100 and several thousand, and densities between 2–3 persons and over 100 persons per acre. The settlements of Bronze Age Europe would clearly fall at the lower end of this scale as far as population size was concerned, but would vary considerably in terms of density,

[139] Fletcher 1981, 100.

from the isolated farmstead to the densely occupied fortified site. Fletcher further suggests that there are cycles of spatial arrangement in settlements, going from a situation where there is a lack of pattern towards one where spatial order develops.[140] With repeated rebuildings this order disintegrates, and the settlement order breaks down, as characteristically in failing communities. Whether one could go further and see lack of order in settlements as signifying the disintegration of community life is more debatable; there is no doubt that, historically speaking, communities have adopted many approaches to the ordering of space, not all of them obvious in terms of 'rational' explanation.

As with the analysis of house form, approaches have been suggested based on methods of formal analysis. Hillier and Hanson utilised a variety of transformations of the crude locational data in order to develop a spatial syntax, or 'morphic language', concentrating especially on the ways in which the positioning of buildings enabled or prevented access to various parts of the settlement; the 'permeabilities', or ways in which space could be crossed, are key to this approach.[141] It is not entirely clear how this can be applied to archaeological plans in such a way as to produce information on social organisation that was not evident beforehand. On the other hand, there are some sets of variables in settlement form that can profitably be examined. Chapman looked at site size, building size, ratio of built to unbuilt space, and minimum inter-building distance, in order to explore the 'dimensional order' of Balkan Neolithic and Copper Age sites.[142] Tells and flat sites could by this means be seen to have different spatial approaches: on tells the ratio of built to unbuilt space varies between 2:1 and 1:3, whereas on open sites it varies typically from 1:7 to 1:15 or more; the inter-building distance on tells is as little as 2–3 m but on open sites it is typically 5–15 m. Another relevant factor is orientation of the long axis of buildings: on tells this tends to be similar, but on open sites it can be extremely variable, even if doorways tended to face the same way (commonly 180° from the prevailing wind). These measures are a convenient way to describe and map the differences between different types of site, though of course they do not explain those differences; they are a symptom, not a cause.

A further factor to be taken into account is the presence or absence of enclosing features, such as palisades, or ditches and ramparts. One can question whether the form of open settlements can be compared directly with those that are enclosed or defended. The very presence of enclosing features gives a settlement a quite different feel, as one can appreciate from fortified medieval towns, though in functional terms the way that houses interacted

[140] Fletcher 1984.
[141] Hillier and Hanson 1984.
[142] Chapman 1989/1991.

may have been much the same. In terms of the inhabitant–stranger relationship, of course, fortified sites were quite different from open ones. In what follows, however, settlement plans are considered and compared without differentiating between the enclosed and the unenclosed.

The Bronze Age village

As well as the presence of enclosing features, a number of other basic distinctions are apparent on Bronze Age settlement layouts. Chief among these are the degree of agglomeration or dispersion, for which the built:unbuilt ratio acts as a good measure, and the ease of accessibility, as discussed above. Enclosing ditches or palisades were present from the Early Bronze Age, as can be seen from sites in Slovakia and some Hungarian tells.[143]

Clustered, or agglomerated, village sites occur frequently across much of Europe and throughout the Bronze Age. The internal structure that they exhibit is, however, varied. At Early Bronze Age Zürich-Mozartstrasse, for instance, rows of box-like rectangular buildings were found, each one barely large enough to contain a family unit (fig. 2.8). Each construction looks very similar to all the others, which suggests that there was a building template or 'module' in operation; but the buildings had different functions (for instance, not all had hearths, several different sizes were present).[144] In phase a, the eight rectangular buildings were 1–2 m apart and with one exception aligned the same way, but their disposition appears somewhat random. By contrast, in phase b nine of the ten buildings are aligned in three lines with narrow passages between them only 1 m across, a change that indicates increasing structuring and spatial order in the settlement. Since the positions of doorways are not known, it is impossible to carry out a proper access analysis, nor can one securely tie in individual buildings with specific functions (apart from the outliers interpreted as granaries or stores). The ratio of built to unbuilt space is around 1:5.3 in phase b, indicating that there was an apparently unbuilt area around the houses up to the surrounding palisade; in the built-up area the figure is much higher, as the inhabitants lived cheek by jowl. The Forschner settlement on the Federsee in Baden-Württemberg is comparable.[145] Clusters of single-cell houses are present in the south-west part of the site in its first phase, with individual buildings elsewhere within the enclosure (fig. 2.14, upper). Animals could have been corralled here, but the major areas of economic exploitation must have been situated well away from the swampy ground on which the settlement lies.

A rather similar situation existed in the Late Bronze Age in this area. At

[143] Furmánek *et al.* 1991, 179ff.; Tárnoki 1988.
[144] Gross 1987, 62ff.
[145] Torke 1990.

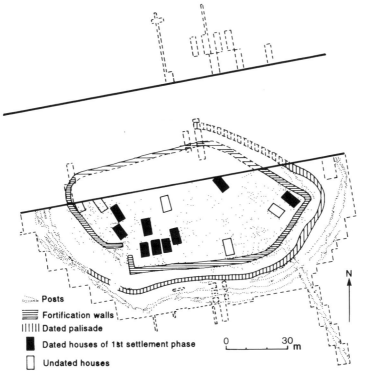

Posts
Fortification walls
Dated palisade
Dated houses of 1st settlement phase
Undated houses

N

0   30 m

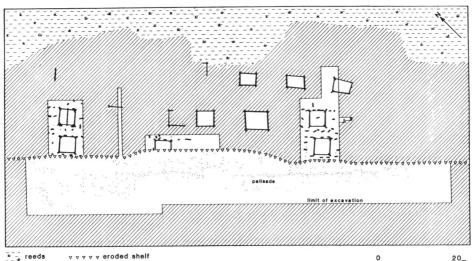

reeds   ᵛ ᵛ ᵛ ᵛ eroded shelf

palisade

limit of excavation

0   20 m

Fig. 2.14. *Upper*: Forschner settlement I (Early Bronze Age), south-west Germany, showing houses and other dated features (after Torke 1990); *lower*: Greifensee-Böschen, plan of Late Bronze Age settlement showing buildings and palisade (after Eberschweiler *et al.* 1987).

Bad Buchau (Wasserburg) the first-phase plan resembles that of Forschner quite strikingly, but in the second phase it was different; in neither is there space for other than modest animal corralling, and certainly not for horticulture.[146] Neither in the first phase, with 38 small buildings, nor in the second, with nine larger ones, is there a clear impression of systematic planning; the built:unbuilt ratio remains at around 1:6 in each case. The change of plan is more remarkable. Most commentators have assumed that the move from one-celled buildings, dispersed widely across the enclosed space, to multi-celled, concentrated around the edges, reflects a social change, from a small quasi-egalitarian community to one based on power vested in major families. In practice the change may not be so great as has been thought, since the buildings of the first phase form a series of natural clusters which may represent grouped residential units or modules. The main change in the second phase is to link these units into a single building.

At Greifensee-Böschen the simple square or rectangular structures were more or less regularly spread out over the excavated area (fig. 2.14, lower).[147] At Auvernier-Nord a dense pattern of rectangular buildings was present, with minimal space between, very much in the same manner as at Zürich-Mozartstrasse, and the same was true at Cortaillod-Est.[148] Indeed, along the shores of Lake Neuchâtel there was a series of Late Bronze Age sites similar to Cortaillod and Auvernier, varying mainly in size: from over 1.5 ha at Cortaillod-Les Esserts, around 1 ha at Auvernier-Nord and Concise, to as small as 0.25 ha at Cortaillod-Plage.[149]

Little is known about the overall disposition of houses on tell sites because of the relatively small areas excavated, but where there is suitable information all the indications are that occupation covered the entire tell surface, with minimal free space in between. The excavation of Feudvar in the Vojvodina, for instance, showed a shifting pattern of rectangular houses separated by streets, the houses many times renewed but never with more than a few metres of space between them. There was certainly no room for animal grazing or plant cultivation in the village; as with other tells, this must have taken place in the surrounding countryside.[150] Though little is known about individual houses, the layout of Italian *terramara* sites is comparable. In the lowest of the three cultural layers at Santa Rosa near Poviglio (Reggio Emilia), the extensive post-holes of houses and other buildings were dug into the subsoil, lying in straight parallel rows, and among them were ash mounds, sherd scatters and hearths, resting on what is thought

[146] Reinerth 1928; Kimmig 1992.
[147] Eberschweiler *et al.* 1987.
[148] Arnold 1983; 1990.
[149] Arnold 1990, 138f.
[150] Hänsel and Medović 1991; cf. Chapman 1989/1991.

to have been a wooden structure.[151] In the upper layer are the remains of plaster walls, but no post-holes, indicating that structures probably lay on sleeper-beams.[152]

The villages of small round-houses in a number of Mediterranean situations, for instance in the Early Bronze Age sites of southern Iberia, the Aeolian Islands, or around Sardinian *nuraghi*, represent clustered settlement in much the same way. There is little sign of detailed planning on these sites: houses appear to have been built adventitiously on the next available piece of land. Although the building methods and house types were quite different, sites such as El Argar, El Oficio, Ifre[153], Peñalosa (fig. 2.15)[154] and Cerro de la Encina[155] clearly exhibit the centripetal tendency which is such a feature of Bronze Age settlement, especially in the Early Bronze Age.

Although houses in Bronze Age sites in southern England usually appear in a dispersed form, there are cases where a degree of clustering is present. At Black Patch, Sussex, for instance, Hut Platform 4 (the most extensively preserved and recovered part) has been reconstructed in terms of an occupation by an extended family, with sleeping only in larger houses that contained hearths, and individual huts being assigned to individual family members, on the analogy of various ethnographic examples.[156] Since, however, little trace of hearths survived, even in huts that contained charcoal and fire-cracked flints, the case for thinking that only some houses were heated is unproven. Taken purely in terms of available space, it would be possible to imagine that Hut Platform 4, with its five houses, could have housed 20 people or more, and the whole settlement, with its four hut platforms, considerably more than that, but not all hut platforms were necessarily contemporary: a case has been made, for instance, that Hut Platform 4 was a two-phase affair, huts

---

[151] Bernabò Brea and Cremaschi 1990; 1996. Discovered initially in the last century but remaining relatively undamaged because the cultural layers were too thin to be worth carting away as fertiliser, large-scale excavations since 1984 have uncovered much of the plan of the site. A small occupation area, 1800 m² in extent, lay to the north, with a larger annexe extending southwards, and covering some 7 ha. In the first phase, a ditch and bank surrounded the settlement area; in the second, a thick layer of earth is present, interpreted as having been brought on to the site, presumably to level it.

[152] Angelucci and Medici 1994. The sequence at other sites, for instance Cavazzoli (Reggio Emilia) (De Marinis *et al.* 1992–3) or Ca' de' Cessi appears to be very similar, though at the latter the excavator has interpreted the post-holes of the lowest layer as indicating the presence of a raised platform, a dry-land *palafitta*; this interpretation harks back to that of Pigorini in the last century, and are not widely accepted, but it must be admitted that the size and depth of the post-holes are very considerable, recalling the massive piles of Fiavé. Indications on other *terramara* sites from air photography and surface survey suggest that comparable results are to be found elsewhere (e.g. Baggiovara: Modena 1989, II, 167; Colombare di Bersano: Bruzzi *et al.* 1989). In general, studies on *terramare* have shown that they tend to cover 1–1.5 ha in the earlier phase of their existence (initial phase of the Middle Bronze Age), but expanded greatly thereafter (Bernabò Brea *et al.* 1991–2).

[153] Siret and Siret 1887.

[154] Contreras Cortés *et al.* 1995.

[155] Arribas Palau *et al.* 1974.

[156] Drewett 1982.

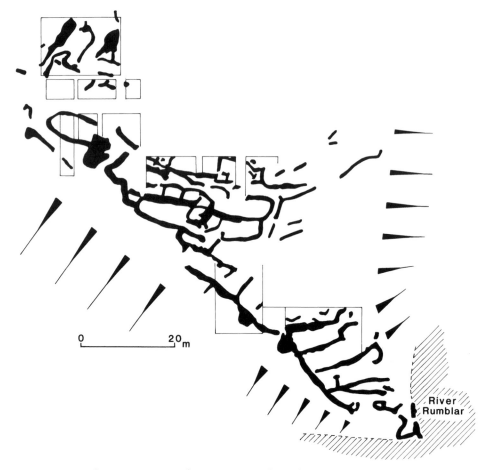

Fig. 2.15. General excavation plan of the settlement at Peñalosa, southern Spain, showing 'habitation units' and structural complexes (after Contreras Cortés *et al.* 1995).

2 and 4 being replaced by huts 1 and 3, with hut 5 possibly an animal shelter.[157] Similar considerations apply to the nearby site of Itford Hill,[158] with around ten huts in the main area and a further two in the separate enclosure IX; here, as at Black Patch, indications of differential function were present in that only certain huts contained pits, and two huts produced nine out of the 13 loom-weights found (for comparison, ten loom-weights from Black Patch were all from Hut Platform 4, hut 3).

On the enclosed site of Barca near Košice in eastern Slovakia, 23 house floors in four rows were recovered, some of them rebuilt several times.[159]

---

[157] Russell 1996.
[158] Burstow and Holleyman 1957.
[159] Kabát 1955; Hajek 1958 (1961); Vladár 1973a, 277ff.; Točík 1994 for a revision of the sequence.

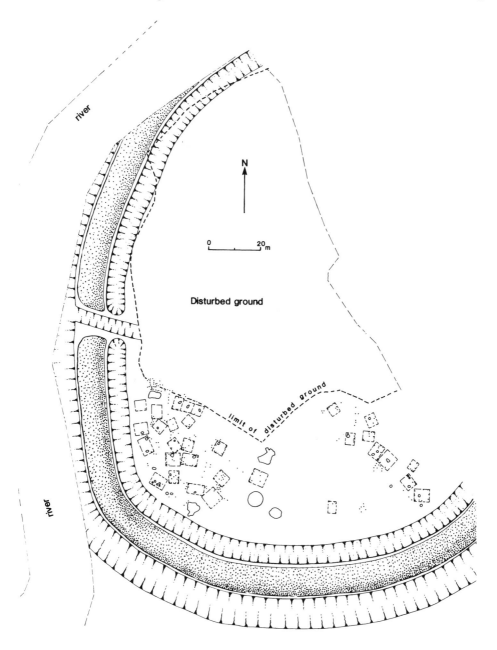

Fig. 2.16. Nitriansky Hrádok, reconstructed plan of the Early Bronze Age fortified settlement showing post structures inside the bank and double ditches (after Točík 1981).

Streets ran between these rows, with the narrow ends of the houses fronting them; only very small distances (60 cm or less) separated individual pairs of houses. The houses were reconstructed as one-, two- or three-room buildings, with the latter dominant and often having two hearths.[160] Another extensively excavated site of this type is at Nitriansky Hrádok (fig. 2.16), where numerous square or rectangular house-plans were recovered, though little evidence of ordered layout was apparent.[161] The most recent work on these Slovakian fortified Early Bronze Age sites is at Nižná Myšľa, a few kilometres south-east of Barca.[162] House foundations, separated by streets, were found in the (admittedly rather narrow) trenches dug, though traces were slight because of the intensive cultivation of the area. Remains of domestic activity extended over a large area. The built:unbuilt ratio at Barca is around 1:1 (more precise figures are not possible), and the inter-building distance apparently about 1 m; there is no known open space inside the enclosing ditch and rampart. Even if not all houses were actually contemporary, the intensity of occupation is still high.

Of the Late Bronze Age hillforts, the best example from the point of view of internal arrangement has usually been considered the Wittnauer Horn in Aargau canton in northern Switzerland.[163] According to the excavator, two rows of houses faced each other, suggesting a highly ordered approach to the organisation of the site interior; detailed examination of the site report, however, does not bear out his assertions, and recent work has not confirmed the presence of such regularly disposed houses.[164] Rather similar to the claimed layout of the Wittnauer Horn is the site of Cabezo de Monleón (Caspe, Zaragoza) in the Ebro valley of north-east Spain, where on a narrow flat-topped hill complete excavation has uncovered no fewer than 57 rooms or huts in three series of continuous buildings, fronting on to an open area (fig. 2.17).[165] Different rooms served different functions (cult, weaving, flint-working, bronze-casting) but there is no indication of social division in the elaboration of the buildings or of their status as residential and economic units.[166]

---

[160] These buildings were apparently defined by daub spreads and by post-holes, with narrow slots marking the wall-bases; but because the site archive was lost no final report was ever published, and no detailed house plan is available.

[161] Točík 1981.

[162] Olexa 1982; 1992. Excavation here since 1977 has shown that the mound of Várhegy, rising 45 m above the plain of the river Hornád, was occupied by an extensive settlement with fortification, and a cemetery. The fortified site started as a small area, around 1 ha in extent, with a ditch cutting it off around the north and east sides. In the second phase, belonging to the beginning of the Middle Bronze Age, the site seems to have extended to around 7 ha, with a cemetery lying over part of the site.

[163] Bersu 1945.

[164] Berger *et al.* 1996.

[165] Beltran Martinez 1984.

[166] Hilltop sites, sometimes with added fortification circuits, occur in many parts of Spain, as in the Granada uplands, or the Mediterranean hinterland in Valencia province: Fernández Castro 1995, 79, 102.

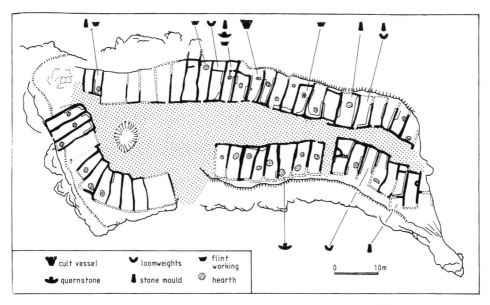

Fig. 2.17. Cabezo de Monleón (Zaragoza): plan of the Late Bronze Age hilltop site. Source: Harrison 1988 (after Beltran Martinez 1984).

Agglomerated plans are also seen at the rather later sites in north-east Germany and on the Polish lakes, of which much the best known is Biskupin.[167] What is most remarkable about many of these agglomerated village plans is the small amount of space left free between the buildings. At Biskupin and Auvernier-Nord this lack of space must have amounted to a critical shortage. Although the houses probably allowed for one or two animals to be stabled, and for a range of domestic activities to be practised, all other agricultural functions must have occurred outside. Such sites raise fundamental questions about how their internal organisation and structure might have functioned. Although there are no signs of specially equipped houses which might have served as the seat of authority (in the sense of a chief's dwelling), it is hardly conceivable that the process of decision-making did not function without such authority. Elites may not be visible in dwelling sites, but the evidence of prestige production in metalwork leaves little doubt that there were those present who were able to direct craft production to their own ends. The lack of conspicuous construction on dwelling sites does not imply a lack of leadership or ranked social organisation.

There were thus three general forms of agglomerated settlement. In one, simple huts were placed near each other without any specific evidence of intentional placing; this is the form usually seen in the Mediterranean. In the

---

[167] Rajewski 1950; cf. Buck 1986.

second, huts were still small and simple but were disposed in a structured manner that indicates a detailed concern with interaction between the different buildings. Examples of this are the Swiss and German lake-side sites, and the house platforms on British agricultural settlements. In the third, buildings are tailored to specific needs of enclosure and defence and placed in a regular, and apparently intentional, set of alignments. This group includes hillforts and stockades such as the Wittnauer Horn and Biskupin. Inevitably, the precise way in which Bronze Age builders created buildings and layouts reflects local concerns and conditions; detailed study of such layouts must take these contextual concerns into account.

Dispersed layouts

Sites with a high degree of clustering were the norm only in certain places and at certain times. It is more usual in most areas and periods to find a more dispersed form of layout, though even here some sites appear to have been planned while on others the positioning of individual elements was a matter of coincidence or personal choice. The latter seems to apply to the form of villages like Zedau or Lovčičky, but closer inspection reveals more structuring than initially appears. The situation of the large hall-house E at Lovčičky, with its large timbers closely set together, appears to be central to the whole village (fig. 2.12), and it is bordered by mainly open space on north and south (there are hardly any certain houses to the north, though pits cover the entire area). The house seems likely, both from size and construction and from its position, to have served a purpose as a communal facility. On the other hand, some of the small square structures are likely to have served storage or other economic functions rather than as dwellings. Slightly differing orientations in the other post-structures, and overlaps between houses, bespeak differences in period of construction. At any one moment around six to eight houses existed, in addition to the central communal hall, arranged roughly in a circle around it. The plan thus demonstrates an interplay between private and communal space. It also indicates the continuing use of a settlement area over many decades or centuries, with houses being rebuilt on somewhat different spots.

By contrast, at Zedau the impression is one of unplanned development (fig. 2.11). Here too the houses were no doubt erected over a period of time so that not all pits and post-holes should be seen in conjunction, especially where structures cut or are placed close beside one another. It is notable that the four-post pit structures tend to congregate in particular parts of the site, to the south-west lying in an arc around the southern post structures, and to the north and north-east outside the northern post houses. This reinforces the view that they represent facilities for storage or other non-habitation purposes. Each post house at Zedau possessed at least one four-post store-room;

this seems reasonable when one considers that the floor area of the houses did not exceed 40 m², leaving little room for occupants and their activities. This fact, combined with the rather regular orientation of the houses, gives the lie to any idea of a totally unregulated treatment of space at Zedau. Admittedly the orientation of the houses may reflect a desire to keep entrances away from north-east winds, but even so the degree of conformity to a norm is remarkable.[168]

A not dissimilar situation pertained on sites in the Low Countries, where extensive area excavations in recent years have uncovered complete or nearly complete village plans of the Bronze and Early Iron Ages. Clusters of houses on the Everse Akkers at St-Oedenrode in North Brabant, for instance, suggest that a 'village' (actually a farmstead) consisted of a main farmhouse and a number of outbuildings and pits (fig. 2.18).[169] Some clusters may have been somewhat more elaborate than this: cluster 3, for instance, had a major farmhouse of rectangular plan outlined by sleeper-trenches, a series of four-post structures that are probably granaries or hay-lofts, but a number of long rectangular post-built structures that in central Europe would be interpreted as houses. The overall pattern of the settlement area is one of shifting buildings.[170]

In Scandinavia, some villages are weakly clustered, while others consist of isolated buildings.[171] A plan such as that of Bjerg in the Nr Omme area of western Jutland has numerous long-houses, aligned on much the same axis, but in many cases overlapping with each other. This phenomenon, repeated in many similar sites, indicates something of the time depth represented in such plans, and has usually been taken to reflect a long-term occupation of a given territory, with repeated rebuildings of structures within a broad zone of settlement, movement taking place every two or three generations.[172] The consistent orientation indicates both the continuity of plan, but also the conservative approach to the placing and layout of buildings. The assumption is that each building housed a family group, and that a collection of family groups formed a village; each family created a home in the same form as all the others, and only its position at any one time varied. Most such villages probably contained between two and ten buildings at one time, though there appear to be plenty of examples where a single farmstead represented the norm for settlement.[173]

---

[168] To this, the statements of the excavator – to the effect that most of the features on the site were contemporary, and that there is little definite plan – run contrary; but the lack of a systematic analysis of all features discovered renders the point debatable: Horst 1985, 64–5.

[169] van Bodegraven 1991.

[170] A similar situation is seen at Den Burg, Texel (Woltering 1991), Bovenkarspel (Ijzereef and van Regteren Altena 1991) and other sites.

[171] Rasmussen and Adamsen 1993.

[172] Olausson 1992, 273 with refs.

[173] e.g. near Ystad: Olausson 1992, 273.

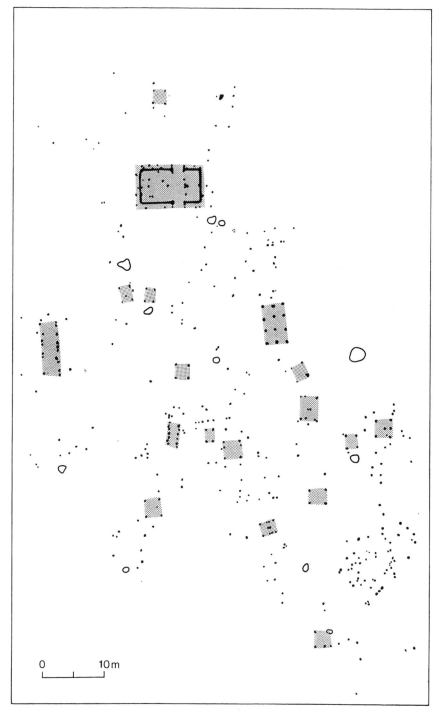

Fig. 2.18. St-Oedenrode (North Brabant): general plan of house cluster 3. Source: van Bodegraven 1991.

Do the small agricultural settlements seen in southern England, for instance on the Wessex downlands or on Dartmoor, represent something very different from this Scandinavian model in terms of population size and social complexity? The houses are rather simpler in construction, but the range of outbuildings, and the interpretation as a family-sized farmstead, is much the same. Shaugh Moor Enclosure 15, for instance, has five houses disposed around the inside of the enclosure wall, a central circular post structure, and a number of indistinct stone features in other parts of the interior (see above). The Grimspound enclosure contains over 20 hut circles, as well as walled areas next to the inside of the enclosure wall, probably for stock,[174] and Rider's Rings has some 15 hut circles, rather more spaced out, with a larger stock-maintenance area.[175] In spite of the excavator's belief to the contrary, it seems likely that animals were corralled inside the Shaugh Moor enclosure, since it could hardly have been used for defence.

In settlements of the Deverel–Rimbury phase, different structures have been shown to have differential patterning in terms of layout and finds, some serving as living quarters with areas for food consumption, tool manufacture and craft production, others being used for food storage and preparation, and other activities.[176] A group of such structures might form a unit or module, an element which recurs regularly on southern English sites of the period and which might succeed one another on the same spot, giving rise to complicated palimpsest plans. Middle Bronze Age enclosures in southern England commonly contained one or more houses, the rest of the space presumably being left free for animals.[177] Many of these were quite small in extent, and some apparently held no houses, but there were also larger enclosures that may have stood at the top of the pile in hierarchical terms.[178] Not all areas possess such enclosures, even in central southern England, which may be a result of shifting patterns of control and authority.

Villages in their surroundings

In a period when the economy was based on subsistence farming, most sites in lowland areas of the temperate zone were situated with regard to the needs of that mode of life, most obviously that of water. Some wetland areas of the British Isles, notably the west of Ireland, have produced good evidence on the

---

[174] Pattison and Fletcher 1994.
[175] Burgess 1980a, 210.
[176] Ellison 1981, 417ff.; 1987. Well-known sites for which this has been suggested include Itford Hill, Sussex and Thorny Down, Wiltshire: Burstow and Holleyman 1957; Stone 1941; Ellison 1987.
[177] Such enclosures have been tested by excavation in a number of instances, in Cranborne Chase (South Lodge and Down Farm): Barrett *et al.* 1991, 144ff.; in north Wiltshire: Gingell 1992, 7ff.; and in south Dorset: Woodward 1991, 39ff.
[178] The enclosure at Hog Cliff Hill, Maiden Newton, Dorset, is one such (Ellison and Rahtz 1987), and Rams Hill, Berkshire, and Norton Fitzwarren, Somerset, are others (Ellis 1989).

siting of settlements. Along the Shannon and Fergus estuaries, for instance, structures are strung out along the shoreline, in areas that were partly carr woodland, partly reedswamp, saltmarsh and mudflat.[179] In north-west Bohemia six situations were standard for the Late Bronze Age Knovíz sites: on river and stream terraces, seasonal stream banks, near springs, on lake margins, or on hilltops.[180] The first three accounted for the great majority of sites (over 70%), but the distribution of the last (hilltop sites) was the most uniform, perhaps reflecting the more territorial nature of defensive sites. Over the whole area studied, around 2000 km², the density of sites was broadly similar; sites are regularly spaced along river courses, with inter-site distances of between 1 and 3 km. At Iwanowice in south-east Poland, settlements occupy terraces above the floodplain of the Dłubnia river (a tributary of the Vistula), and are situated at distances of 0.5–1.5 km from each other, with cemeteries filling in some of the intermediate zones (including those on higher ground).[181] Study of Lausitz culture settlements showed their intimate relationship to features of natural and economic importance (see below, p. 232).[182]

In the investigation of agricultural landscapes, a special role is played by those parts of Europe where the remains of tillage survives. In southern England, a number of landscape survey projects have taken place in recent years.[183] On the Marlborough Downs, archaeologists had long been aware both of the extensive field systems, and of a group of enclosures named after the sites on Ogbourne Down: 'Ogbourne enclosures'.[184] A series of small-scale excavations, both on open settlements and on enclosures, showed that, rather than stock enclosures, these were proper settlement sites, lying in the middle of an intensively worked landscape (fig. 4.11). Scatters of Bronze Age pottery at intervals through this landscape confirm the presence of house sites. Settlements lie in or beside field systems that are typically 5–10 ha in extent, the inter-site distance between settlements being between 0.5 and 1.5 km. Areas of what one may assume were unenclosed pasture lay between the field systems. Further south, on the South Dorset Ridgeway, another extensive survey and excavation programme has shown the development of the area from one dominated by Late Neolithic ritual monuments (henges) to one with an extensive barrow landscape, and then to a series of field systems with accom-

---

[179] O'Sullivan 1995.
[180] Bouzek *et al.* 1966.
[181] Kadrow 1991a; 1991b.
[182] Buck 1986.
[183] The work of the Marlborough Downs project is particularly impressive (Gingell 1992), and also that of the South Dorset Ridgeway survey (Woodward 1991), the Cranborne Chase project (Barrett *et al.* 1991), and on the Berkshire Downs the Maddle Farm project (Gaffney and Tingle 1989).
[184] Piggott 1942.

panying settlement enclosures.[185] In northern England, too, survey work over the last 30 years has transformed knowledge of prehistoric agricultural landscapes. In Northumberland, for example, the foothills of the Cheviot Hills have produced large numbers of excellently preserved sites, for instance at Snear Hill and Todlaw Pike (fig. 4.14), or Linhope Burn, where hut platforms are situated in the middle of an extensive agricultural landscape.[186] Extensive landscapes with settlement occur in many other parts of northern, western and upland Britain and Ireland.[187]

Emerging urbanism?

Some authors have considered that the trend towards clustered settlement, so evident from many of the areas considered above, along with the creation of surrounding features (fences, palisades, ditches, ramparts) that marked the edge of the settlement, indicate that settlement in some parts of the Bronze Age can be called 'urban' or at least 'proto-urban'.[188] It has, for instance, been asked whether the Early Bronze Age enclosed sites (chapter 8) represent 'forts', 'fortified settlements' or some other form of enclosure,[189] and the same question applies to Late Bronze Age hillforts. Unfortunately there is little agreement on what constitutes a 'town' as opposed to a 'village', other than that it should have certain administrative, political and commercial functions. Whether such functions could be identified archaeologically in a period prior to the use of writing is a moot point.

What is certain is that during the earlier first millennium BC there were marked trends towards settlement aggregation. Over the course of the Bronze Age as a whole, social divisions seem to have become more marked, 'industrialisation' (in the form of on-site metallurgy) developed, and quasi-political territorial units were created. Few would doubt that during the course of the Iron Age one can discern the start of truly urban entities; the processes that led to their development were also at work during the Bronze Age. In this sense, the term 'proto-urban' has meaning. But it would be false to suggest that sites such as Barca or Nitriansky Hrádok were urban or 'proto-urban' in any sense other than that they were agglomerated settlements. Little or

[185] At South Lodge in Cranborne Chase, the enclosure was created in a landscape already subdivided into fields, as lynchets pre-dated the enclosure which therefore came relatively late in the sequence of events (Barrett *et al.* 1991, 146, 181ff.).

[186] Burgess 1984, 145ff.; Gates 1983, 143; Topping 1990–1.

[187] North York Moors: Spratt 1993; Harding 1994. Derbyshire: Barnatt 1987; 1991. Rhossili Down, south Wales: Ward 1987; see Ward 1989 for Dyfed. Ffridd Brynhelen (Clwyd): Manley 1985. Denbigh Moors: Manley 1990. Scottish borders: Jobey 1978, 1978–80, 1983, 1985; Halliday 1985. Perthshire: Thorneycroft 1932–3. Caithness: Mercer 1985. Monavullagh Mountains of Co. Waterford: Moore 1995.

[188] Examples of this tendency can be found from the Adriatic area (Ceka 1985; 1986), central Europe (Vladár 1973a) and Iberia (review in R. W. Chapman 1995).

[189] Zeitler 1993.

nothing in the rest of the archaeological record would suggest that political organisation was as developed as social organisation, that interdependencies of territories and central places were on the same scale as interdependencies of individuals within single places. This is certainly true for the Early Bronze Age, where Barca falls. Only towards the end of the Bronze Age can one imagine that hillforts and certain other sites achieved the degree of centrality and internal organisation that would merit the term 'proto-urban' (see chapter 13).

Summary: the village

The Bronze Age village was in general terms neither very large nor very elaborate in physical space and organisation. The great majority of sites were small agricultural hamlets; as the period progressed, there was a tendency – at least in central Europe – for sites to become larger and for defences to be erected, though there were also some early, short-lived, manifestations of this phenomenon. There remains no convincing evidence for social division in the construction of these villages; what organisation can be seen relates rather to the need for individual households to have access both to storage facilities and to the means of reaching the outside world.

A basic distinction between dispersed and agglomerated villages is apparent. Various factors must have influenced those who created the houses and villages, some of them functional such as the needs of agriculture, horticulture and stock-breeding, some social and demographic such as patterns of kinship and community interaction, and others ideological such as the means of expressing power relations within and between communities. Deciding which factors were most important is partly a matter of personal preference, but partly something to be assessed in each individual case.

Although generalisation is dangerous when one is dealing with such a wide span of time and space, certain patterns do emerge. Most inhabitants of Bronze Age Europe were peasant farmers, and usually their settlements consisted of small hamlets or isolated farmsteads. In the north and north-west, these hamlets almost invariably consisted of dispersed houses or house clusters, but in the centre, south and east they were agglomerated, sometimes strongly so. This basic distinction finds a reflection in the large cemetery sites of the period. It cannot, however, be related in any simple fashion to environmental conditions. The agglomerated villages of Germany are only a few hundred kilometres from the dispersed settlements of Denmark or the Low Countries, in a similar environment. One should therefore look to the social and the ideological for explanations, or at least correlations, in trying to understand these distinctions.

CHAPTER 3

BURIAL

Since no elixir of life has yet been discovered, all humankind continues to end up as dust, ashes and bones, to the great advantage of archaeology. Bronze Age people were no more successful than anyone else at discovering the secret of eternal life, and consequently there are a lot of them available for study in skeletal or combusted form. Estimates of their numbers are necessarily little more than guesses, but there is no doubt that the surviving buried population of the Bronze Age is much greater than that of the Neolithic, and probably on a par with that of the pre-Roman Iron Age. It is a huge resource for study.

Traditionally, the study of burials has been a popular activity for Bronze Age scholars, but over the years their preoccupations have changed. Originally the quest for grave-goods was all-important; these were then catalogued and divided into types. Later, this information was combined with that on age and sex, and with statistics on orientation and grave form, to produce 'combination tables' which aimed to show the associations of each object. This led directly to the production of chronological charts through the use of seriation techniques. *En route*, many individual studies of artefact types were possible, especially for unusual or well-represented types. Such studies have also led to the study of social status, intra- and extra-societal relationships, the evolution of social and political systems, and the relationship between archaeological artefacts and kinship structures.

General studies of burial have usually been concerned with the information potential of the evidence, and specifically with what burial can say about social organisation in the society from which the dead came.[1] In spite of the difficulties involved, many writers believe that regularities linking living societies and their procedures for the disposal of the dead do exist, particularly as concerns the patterning of mortuary differentiation, the consistency of differentiation according to social position, and the way that complexity of mortuary differentiation increases with the complexity of societies themselves. In O'Shea's analysis, four basic principles reflect the 'minimum level of constraint operating on mortuary variability in archaeological contexts': all societies employ regular procedures for the disposal of the dead; the

---

[1] Chapman, Kinnes and Randsborg 1981; Pader 1982; O'Shea 1984.

mortuary population exhibits demographic and physiological characteristics that reflect the living population; each burial represents a systematic application of a series of prescriptive and proscriptive directives relating to the individual; and all the elements in a burial context were originally contemporaneous in the living society at the time of burial.[2] This relatively optimistic view of the potential of mortuary data corresponds closely to the view adopted in the present work.

A different stance is taken by Barrett, who argues that if mortuary analyses are to have any power they must 'observe the way mortuary practices intervened in an overall cycle of social reproduction', that is the 'entire system in both its material and its human aspects'.[3] Specifically, Barrett advocates distinguishing between funerary rituals and ancestor rituals – the former concerning the rites of passage that are observed at the time a person dies, the latter concerned to bring ancestors symbolically into the present. Drawing on the work of Turner and Van Gennep, he seeks to establish in what ways the structuring of the archaeological record in Neolithic and Bronze Age Dorset could reflect the actions of the mourners at funerals, and specifically (in a Bronze Age context) how the developmental sequence of barrow construction in Wessex cemeteries might indicate the nature of the ritual. The element of continuity in the use of burial sites, whether flat or mounded, rightly emphasises the importance of 'the ancestors', whose burial places could have played a major role in the social structuring of behaviour.[4]

This concern with the actions carried out at funerals as part of a mortuary 'field of discourse', rather than merely with the form of disposal of the dead, is a recurring theme in recent treatments of the subject of death and burial, and has considerable attraction as a subtle and sophisticated way of interpreting the finer details of grave form and body disposition. For instance, Mizoguchi has suggested that structuration theory, applied to the material culture remains of funerary sites, can be used to interpret the 'mortuary field of discourse', which can be treated as one aspect of social reproduction, in other words the way humans reproduce the social forms and actions of the environment in which they live.[5] In the specific instance studied, that of the barrow cemetery at Shrewton, Wiltshire, it was suggested that the use of space was successively elaborated by the erection of stake-circles in the creation of an alignment of barrows, and that new practices were introduced whereby bodies were cremated elsewhere and the remains brought back to the graves.[6] Both features are interpreted as suggesting that the physical movement of people was controlled, so that the authority of individuals and groups came

---

[2] O'Shea 1984.
[3] Barrett 1988a; Barrett, Bradley and Green 1991, 120ff.
[4] Olausson 1993.
[5] Mizoguchi 1992.
[6] Green and Rollo-Smith 1984.

to play a crucial part in structuring the 'mortuary field of discourse'. A somewhat comparable analysis is that offered by Garwood, in which a discussion of the reproduction of the principles structuring Late Neolithic and Early Bronze Age society is coupled with the analysis of barrow and cemetery development in Wessex, descent being stressed – reflecting the importance of ancestors – rather than any simplistic interpretation of 'ranking' based on the possession of goods.[7] The complexities of the funerary ritual, and their relationship to living society, are also explored by Kaliff.[8]

Disposal of the dead, a basic and universal rule of hygiene, took as many forms in the Bronze Age as in other periods. A basic dichotomy between inhumation and cremation is perhaps the most obvious form of variability, and one to which I shall return by virtue of its profound implications for belief systems and spiritual life; but there are others which may have seemed equally important to those involved, such as burial in a simple pit or under a mound; burial on one side or the other or on the back, with head pointing in one direction or another, the knees bent or straight, the ashes deposited in an urn or not – there are numerous possibilities. The interplay between these sets of variables – it is not necessarily accurate to define them as opposites, as some have done – makes the burial record of the Bronze Age exceptionally rich, but also exceptionally complicated. In many ways the story of Bronze Age burial is the story of that interplay.

A dichotomy that operates on an altogether different level is that relating to the representation of burial evidence in the ground. A good many areas and periods of the European Bronze Age have few known burial sites; an example close to home is the Late Bronze Age of Britain. The progress and chances of discovery and survival have an influence on such matters, but there are archaeologically well-researched areas, with good survival of material from other periods, which have nevertheless failed to produce burials, and in such cases it is hard to avoid the conclusion that their absence is not merely coincidental but the result of specific patterns of deposition, or its converse.

This chapter, therefore, deals with the patterning of burial itself, not with social reconstruction from the burials. It will examine cemetery patterning and burial mode through time and space, and certain special ways of treating the dead, in particular the use of barrows (tumuli), pyres, coffins and mortuary houses, and the interplay between inhumation and cremation as disposal modes.

Cemetery patterning and grave patterning

Across the vast area of Europe, there are clear traditions of burial in each area and period. Broadly speaking they may all be defined as one of three

[7] Garwood 1991.
[8] Kaliff 1997.

variations on the general theme of body disposal: cremation, flat inhumation and mounded inhumation. Within this broad grouping, much detailed variation is present. One can view this variation on two levels: that of broad distinctions between areas and that of detailed distinctions within each area and site.

On the broad, macroscopic level, it is necessary first to make the distinction between different stages of the Bronze Age. Each stage saw a rather different pattern of burial mode across Europe, though generalisation is dangerous. In the Early and Middle Bronze Age, burial was usually by inhumation, whereas in the Late Bronze Age it was by cremation. The earlier inhumations could be either under a mound (barrow, tumulus, cairn, kurgan) or placed in a pit or built grave (cist, shaft) with no covering mound. In general, the practice of mounded burial increased during the Middle Bronze Age, certainly in central and western Europe. The advent of cremation leads to the burial rite lending its name to the period. Cremated remains were placed either in pits or in pottery containers (urns), and the urns placed in a defined deposition area, an 'urnfield'. Hence the Late Bronze Age in continental Europe is also called the Urnfield period, when cremation was dominant, if not universal (depending on area).

For the Early Bronze Age, a number of studies by A. Häusler has set out the main variables (see table 3.1).[9] Two main traditions are present: tumulus burial, found in the east, parts of the Balkans, the north and the west; and flat inhumations, found throughout central Europe and in Italy and Spain (fig. 3.1). Cremation is, with rare exceptions, restricted to the Hungarian plain and adjacent regions. These distinctions are in themselves interesting, but the fact that within them it is possible to discern sex-dependent orientation, distinctions in the precise treatment of the body, and different principles in the utilisation of space under tumuli, is also of importance. At the most basic level, differences in treatment of the dead are presumed to reflect different attitudes to the dead and death, and potentially therefore spiritual and cultural preferences; perhaps also ethnic and linguistic affinities.

Flat inhumation burial

Flat inhumation was the standard rite through much of central Europe in the Early Bronze Age, and particularly between the Rhine and the Vistula, in Germany, the former Czechoslovakia, Austria and Poland.[10] In this vast area, large numbers of multiple inhumation cemeteries are to be found, usually arranged according to specific principles of interment. The dead were usually laid in the grave with the legs somewhat bent, though sometimes they could

[9] Häusler 1977; 1994; 1996.
[10] Primas 1977a; Ruckdeschel 1978.

Table 3.1. *Main Bronze Age burial traditions by area*

Tumulus burial	Flat inhumation	Cremation
Early Bronze Age		
S. Russia	C. Europe	Hungary
S. Scandinavia	Italy	
N. Germany	C. Russia	
Netherlands	N. Russia	
Britain (both rites)		
Brittany		
E. Hungary		
W. Serbia		
Albania		
Middle Bronze Age		
C. Europe		
N. Europe		
Pontic zone		
Parts of Balkans		
Late Bronze Age		
C. Europe (few)	C. Europe (few)	C. Europe (dominant)
Parts of Balkans		Italy
Steppe zone		N. Europe
		France and Spain
		Most of Balkans
		?British Isles

be placed flat on their backs. The different parts of this burial province can be distinguished according to the specifics of the practice utilised in them, in particular the 'sexually differentiated bipolar deposition mode', the practice of placing males lying in one direction, and females in the polar opposite, the face looking in the same direction in each case because of the side on which the body was laid (fig. 3.2). This practice occurs in various parts of continental Europe, though the sexual differentiation was not always of exactly this type: for instance, it could be expressed merely by placing the bodies on different sides, the heads always placed to the same compass direction. In this, orientation towards sun positions may have been important.

Cemeteries such as these are those in eastern Austria and in Slovakia, for instance those of the Nitra, Unterwölbling and Košt'any groups. The cemetery at Gemeinlebarn (St Pölten, Lower Austria) is the best known of them, and has been the subject of many studies.[11] All graves were oriented approximately north–south, but in one group the head is to the south, in another to the north. The early excavators did not carry out biological determination

[11] Christlein 1964; Stein 1968; Ruckdeschel 1968; Gallay 1972; Bertemes 1989; Neugebauer 1991.

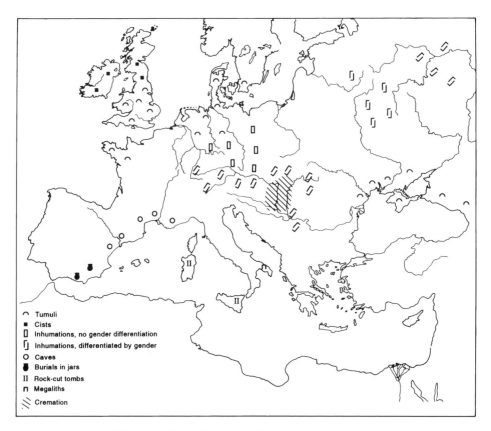

Fig. 3.1. Burial traditions in Early Bronze Age Europe (after Häusler 1977).

of sex, relying instead on the occurrence of ornaments in the first group and weapons in the second to identify them as female and male respectively. The more recent excavations, which did sex the skeletons, provide confirmation of this.[12] At Mokrin in the Yugoslav Banat, the 312 graves were arranged in similar manner.[13] At BrANČ in western Slovakia, the orientation and position of the body was strongly differentiated according to sex.[14] Here the principal orientation was from east–west to NE–SW, the males having the head to the west and the face looking south, the females having the head to the east and the face also looking south. Similar arrangements applied in Bavaria in graves of the Straubing group.

The cemetery at Singen (Konstanz) contained 95 excavated graves arranged

---

[12] Heinrich and Teschler-Nicola, in Neugebauer 1991.
[13] Girić 1971, 193ff.
[14] Vladár 1973b.

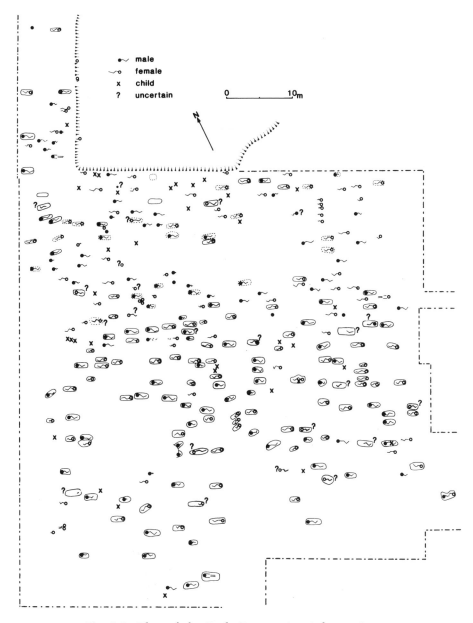

Fig. 3.2. Plan of the Early Bronze Age inhumation cemetery at Výčapy-Opatovce, Slovakia, showing 'sex-differentiated' burial position, the sex determined from the skeletal remains by an anthropologist and not by orientation or grave-goods (after Točík 1979). Males are oriented west–east, and lie on their right side, females east–west and lying on their left side; in both cases the head looks to the south. The few exceptions to this rule, where a skeleton was identified as one sex but buried with the rite for the other, are indicated by query marks.

in four (or possibly more) groups, with two outliers that may form a fifth; the areas in between were excavated or watched during development so that the fact of grouping is not in doubt.[15] The cemetery extends over an area roughly 200 × 100 m (fig. 3.3). The graves are mostly formed of stone settings, with inhumation burials – some in coffins – laid in them. Bodies are laid north–south or close to it, females with head to the south, males with head to the north. Two graves do not fit this pattern: a male grave lying on the right side, head to the south-west, and a female grave (a young adult) on the left side, head to the NNE. The male had no grave-goods, but the female conformed to expectation with an arm-spiral and a disc-headed pin. The association tables show that grave-goods are strongly sex-specific, though it is notable that only 15 graves could be attributed with any degree of certainty to a given sex. Of these, daggers occurred in six of the eight male graves, the only find to recur in association with men. Women, by contrast, usually had one or more pins, sometimes a neckring or armring, more rarely foot spirals and other ornaments. All identified females lay on their right side and had the head to the south; it is thus a reasonable assumption that other graves with this disposition are also female. Defined like this, there was also a strong association between female graves and awls, a tool probably used for leather-working; while there is no inherent reason why it should be women who were equipped with these tools, the evidence that this was in fact the case at Singen is very strong. Unusually, pots of any kind are virtually absent in the Singen graves.

In spite of this impression of regularity there are a number of discrepant features, for instance north–south-oriented graves, the body lying on the left side, with pins (i.e. male grave form, female grave-goods); a male grave with dagger but also jet pendant, silver wire ring, spiral wire and arm-spiral; and two female graves with daggers. The placing of these was unusual: in the neck and shoulder area rather than by the waist or arms as with male graves; in neither case were the rest of the grave-goods remarkable. How are these divergences to be explained?

In certain instances, it may be that individuals were being specially marked out because of social characteristics or other special circumstances. The provision of daggers to two women – one young, the other old – may be a case in point, and the daggers were worn in a different manner from that adopted by men. In the case of the 'males' possessing pins, it is noteworthy that none was anthropologically sexed, the determination depending solely on the north–south orientation of the grave. While grave-goods are concentrated in female graves (those with head to the south), daggers are almost all in those with head to the north. The division of society through funerary rites was

---

[15] Krause 1988. A similar arrangement was observed at Grossbrembach (Sömmerda) in Thuringia, there based primarily on anthropologically observed traits (Ullrich 1972).

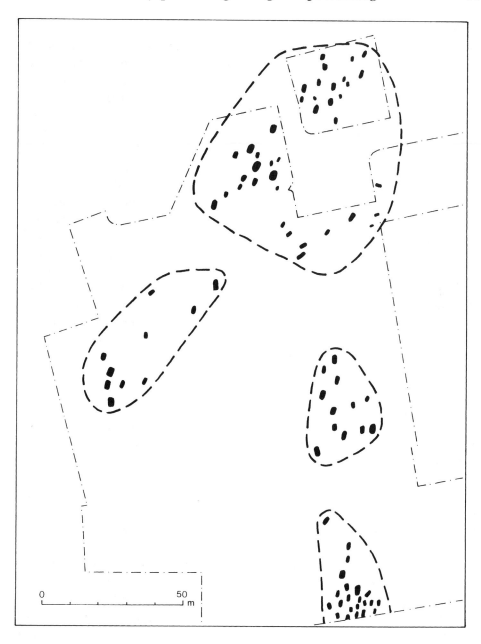

Fig. 3.3. Plan of the inhumation cemetery at Singen (Konstanz) (after Krause 1988). The dot-and-dash line indicates the limit of archaeological observation; the heavy dashed line the boundaries of suggested grave groupings.

thus almost complete, but not quite. Did women who were left as head of a family, perhaps through being widowed, assume male roles? Could such women be regarded as 'foreign' to the main Singen population, perhaps originally members of a different community and brought in through marriage?

In contrast to these sex-dependent grave rites, in the cemeteries of the Únětice culture in Bohemia and adjacent areas grave form was not usually dependent on sex – though grave-good provision might be. A general study of the early Únětice grave rite has highlighted the main features.[16] Flat inhumations predominate, and only two examples from 377 studied had mounded coverings. The dead were usually placed in rectangular or oval pits, the majority on their right side, the head to the south. A certain number were multiple graves. The graves could be laid out in irregular rows, with some evidence of grouping within the cemeteries. Study of individual cemeteries, however, quickly shows that other forms may occur: in double-grave 19 at Moravská Nová Ves-Hrušky, for instance, the grave-pit had large post-holes at the four corners, which the excavators interpreted as the remains of a roofed building covering the burial.[17]

A recent publication is that of the cemetery at Těšetice-Vinohrady in south Moravia, excavated in 1956–8.[18] Forty-one Early Bronze Age graves were investigated, 37 in a central group and 4 somewhat removed. At least 45 individuals were represented. In 2 graves there were 2 individuals, in one 3 (male, female, child). Only 20 of the graves were intact: 18 had been robbed and 3 disturbed by cultivation, though in fact this seems to have made little difference to what objects are found in the graves, and several graves with no goods were intact. Wooden coffins were found in 14 graves with 3 further possible examples; wooden box flooring was found in a further 4.

The distribution of grave-goods by age and sex shows that adult males have most pots, an average of 3.0 per grave (excluding multiple graves), adult females have 2.08 per grave, but children only 1.56 per grave. When it comes to bronzes, however, the pattern is quite different: male graves have only three daggers and three ornaments in total, females only a single dagger but 29 ornaments; 2 of these graves contain large numbers. Surprisingly, children's graves contain 5 daggers and 26 ornaments. In other words, pottery apart, male graves were poorly provided for, while women and children sometimes received significant numbers of goods. This may well be connected with the practice of male or family wealth being exhibited in the women and children;[19] the larger number of pots in male graves may be a reflection of

---

[16] Matoušek 1982.
[17] Comparable instances occur elsewhere in central Europe from Corded Ware times onwards: Stuchlík and Stuchlíková 1996, 76ff.
[18] Lorencová, Beneš and Podborský 1987.
[19] Cf. Shennan 1975.

Fig. 3.4. Reconstructions of 'mortuary houses' in barrows:
1. Ridge roof construction at Etteln, Kr. Paderborn, Westphalia.
Source: Bérenger 1996; drawing by K.-D. Braun; 2. Mortuary construction at Grünhof-Tesperhude. Source: Kersten 1936.

larger numbers of mourners (family members or others with obligations of kinship or status) present at the funeral.

Table 3.2. *Grave-goods at Těšetice-Vinohrady*

	Number	Pots	Daggers	Ornaments	Other	Total
Male	12	32	3	6	3	44
Female	15	28	1	34	6	69
Child	18	27	5	31	6	69

Tumulus burial

Logically, disposal of the dead must be undertaken in one of a very limited number of ways. The body can be burnt, if sufficient wood is available; it can be disposed of in water or exposed; but if it is to be buried as an inhumation, there are only two basic possibilities: a pit can be dug to receive the body (as for instance with much of Christian burial at the present day), or the body can be laid on the ground and material heaped up over it (a chamber can be created around it, or a mound can be heaped up over a pit). The latter demands more labour, and a supply of earth, turves or stone, but it has the advantage that it creates a highly visible monument, which in a pre-literate society without the use of monumental stone served as eloquent testimony to the identity of the deceased. The enhanced visibility of burials under tumuli, along with the presumptively special social circumstances that led to their erection, make them natural objects of study wherever they occur.[20]

Tumulus burial appears in many parts of the Bronze Age world (table 3.1), being the standard burial rite in much of the earlier part of the period in the east, the north and the north-west. There were also other areas where it was used, but sparingly. This applies to the barrows of the Early Bronze Age of central Europe and of the Middle Bronze Age outside the Tumulus culture area (as in early Lausitz cemeteries). In parts of the Urnfield world, too, tumuli appear sporadically, but where they are present they are a well-defined phenomenon. It cannot be assumed that either the causes or the method of expression are the same in each case. There are, however, certain considerations which are common to all manifestations of tumulus burial, regardless of area and period.

- To judge from the numbers of graves recovered in tumuli, they cannot have been provided for more than a minority of the population, even in those areas where large numbers are present, though Atkinson argued that those interred in the barrows of England and

[20] It is no accident that a conference in Lund in 1991 was concerned specifically with the phenomenon and its implications (Larsson 1993a).

Wales represent almost the entire original Beaker and Early Bronze Age population (a view that few share).[21]

- The visible mound represents the final phase of the creation of the burial place. Prior to its heaping up, a variety of actions took place, and various permanent or impermanent features were created – pits, grave chambers, post circles, stone rings or other settings, pyre burning, and so on.
- Tumuli have attracted the attention of tomb-robbers and early antiquarians over the centuries. Many are robbed – in some areas almost every mound that survives – and it is often difficult to demonstrate with certainty that the contents of a given grave are complete, let alone those of a whole cemetery.
- Tumuli involve the heaping up of turf, earth, stones or a mixture of any two or all three. In cases where turf is used, there is a significant area of land where cultivation may be impeded.
- Conditions of preservation are similar in widely separated areas of Europe. The finds of organic materials such as items of clothing are exceptional and stem from waterlogging (it is recorded in a number of instances that water poured out of the oak coffins when they were disturbed) or other means of excluding oxygen, such as ultraeffective stone and clay sealing layers. Normally even tree-trunk coffins are reduced to no more than stains in the soil.
- Once built, tumuli acted as magnets for further burial and ritual activity. Late Bronze and Iron Age mounds are often added to Neolithic and Early Bronze Age tumulus cemeteries. By the same token, Bronze Age graves were often added to Neolithic and Copper Age tumuli.
- Many more tumuli may once have been present than now appears to be the case. Agricultural and related activities have frequently removed the mounds, leaving them to be recognised – usually from the air, from survey and fieldwalking, or from chance discoveries – by their grave-pits or ring-ditches.
- Ring-ditches may often represent the remains of tumuli, but equally they may have been used as the defining lines of funerary or ritual enclosures. This was especially the case in the Late Bronze Age, in the Low Countries, or the Aisne valley of north-east France, for example.
- Analysis of tumulus cemeteries is invariably hindered by the incompleteness of the artefactual record. It has, nevertheless, been possible in some instances to attempt a reconstruction of the living population and depositional activities from which the tumuli emanate.

North-west Europe

Although no one knows for sure how many barrows are present in Britain, Brittany and the Low Countries, the lists published by Grinsell for Britain,

---

[21] Atkinson 1972.

and by other authors, provide some guidance.[22] In the standard typology of British barrows, a basic distinction is drawn between those barrows with relatively large mounds surrounded by a ditch, and those with very small mounds, the ditch encircling them at some distance ('disc barrows').[23] The large mounds are further divided into those with a marked gap or 'berm' between the mound and the ditch ('bell'), and those without ('bowl'), though in practice this difference seems less significant than it does on the printed page, and Grinsell was forced to use various combination descriptors ('bell-disc') to encompass the variability encountered.

Grinsell enumerated 5935 round barrows in 'Wessex', from East Somerset to West Sussex; the numbers have increased since then. Comparable lists for the roughly comparable area of East Anglia produced over one thousand barrows and nearly 3800 ring-ditches (table 3.3).[24] The number of barrows recorded in Brittany and north-west France is much smaller. In Belgium and Holland there is a higher density than in France, probably comparable with those in East Anglia and neighbouring parts of Germany.[25]

Table 3.3. *Barrows in East Anglia*

	Barrows	Ring-ditches
Cambridgeshire	262	1207
Essex	49	1542
Norfolk	625	549
Suffolk	249	474
Total	1185	3772

Absolute frequency of barrows in different areas is an important indicator. Even within one geographical area different zones were differentially provided with barrows. Thus in Wessex the chalklands were much more densely populated with barrows than heavier soils nearby. On the Isle of Wight, for instance, the ridges of chalk appear to act as magnets for barrows, which are much less common off the chalk.[26] At the same time, barrows cluster for other reasons as well, and in Wessex this phenomenon is most obvious around the major ceremonial monuments of Stonehenge and Avebury.

Alongside variations in density, barrow disposition and topography also have important information to yield. Fleming distinguished linear, nucleated

[22] These were used by Atkinson (1972) to plot total numbers of barrows on the map of England and Wales.
[23] Grinsell 1941a.
[24] Lawson, Martin and Priddy 1981.
[25] Ampe *et al.* (1996, 62) give a minimum figure of 650 for East and West Flanders, on the basis of recent aerial photography campaigns.
[26] Grinsell 1941a.

and dispersed cemeteries in Wessex.[27] The linear cemeteries (also seen in Denmark) are visually the most striking, suggesting a level of planning that lasted over centuries. This can be appreciated especially in those instances where a Neolithic long-barrow formed the initial focus for a linear cemetery, as is the case with the Winterbourne Stoke crossroads group.[28] But the separation of cemeteries one from another is equally striking, illustrating how the landscape around Stonehenge was humanly constructed, with open space or woodland between the cemeteries, and perhaps differential rights of access according to kinship or other affiliations. It is not only the immediately visible form of the cemeteries that is striking. The landscape was structured on a wider scale as well: for instance, concentric rings of barrows encircle Stonehenge and Avebury.[29] On the South Dorset Ridgeway there is evidence for the structuring of barrow placing, but it is a linear arrangement relating to major territorial units.

Of great importance, to judge from the frequency with which it was employed, was the custom of placing the grave within settings of stones or posts. Sometimes these are no more than a ring-bank of stone cobbles, or a small cairn heaped up over the grave-pit within the body of the mound; but on other occasions they are much more elaborate. The variations are very numerous. Most common in the Low Countries and the British Isles are the varieties of post and stake ring which surrounded the central burial.[30] These can be single, double or treble, and closely or widely spaced (fig. 3.5). The concept of circular structures is presumably akin to that of the circular burial monument, itself part of a wider ritual scene, as evidenced by henge monuments and stone circles. In the case of barrow circles, it is important to know whether the post rings were a structural part of the monument or only connected with whatever activities preceded the heaping up of the mound. The evidence is not altogether consistent. Ashbee states that 'most of the internal circles were of a temporary nature, the stakes being withdrawn before the erection of the barrow',[31] and it was certainly true that in some British examples the wooden posts were replaced by stone structures for the final form of the monument. In other cases, for instance in Holland, the posts are substantial and do not give the impression of being temporary. The post rings seem to have defined the *temenos* or enclosed area in a semi-permanent way before the truly permanent elements were erected, as can be seen from the evidence for feasting and other ceremonial activities – even without the deposition of a body – on certain sites.[32]

---

[27] Fleming 1971.
[28] Grinsell n.d., 18.
[29] Woodward and Woodward 1996.
[30] Glasbergen 1954a; 1954b; Ashbee 1960, 60ff.; Ampe *et al.* 1996, 60ff.
[31] Ashbee 1960, 65.
[32] Allen *et al.* 1995.

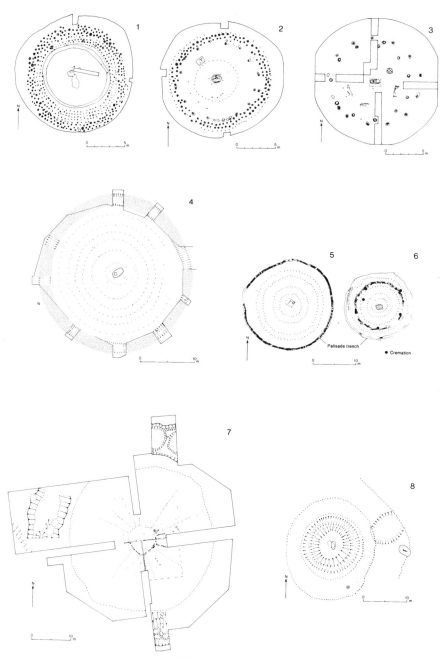

Fig. 3.5. Barrows with post rings of various types. 1–3. Toterfout-Halve Mijl barrows 22, 8 and 5 (after Glasbergen 1954a). 4. Four Crosses, Llandysilio, Powys (after Warrilow *et al.* 1986).
5–6. Brenig, Denbighshire, barrows 40 and 45 (after Lynch 1993).
7. North Mains, Perthshire (after Barclay 1983). 8. Tallington, Lincolnshire, site 16 (after Simpson 1976).

What is clear is that the heaping up of the mound was the final act of the primary use of the site (the subsequent addition of secondary burials in the body of the mound is an ancillary matter). All the actions that involved disturbance of the original ground surface – pit-digging, post erection, stone settings – cannot have been carried out while there was a mound in place. Furthermore, the mound could not have been erected if there were significant numbers of posts. With the proviso only that some or all of the posts must have been removed when the time came to take this step, there are several possibilities for the order of events. The burials in the centre of the enclosure, with or without a 'mortuary house', may have preceded the post rings or vice versa; maybe there was very little difference in time between them. Some barrows remained open as post-defined enclosures for some considerable time, since burial pits cut into the subsoil are not confined to the centre of the barrow, and in some cases the grave-goods show different pottery styles, suggesting a long period of development.

One may compare these post rings, which Ashbee interprets as the remains of mortuary houses, to those sites which clearly did contain structures in the form of a chamber or 'house'. Such structures are found in barrows in many parts of the distribution; but only rarely is their form unambiguously known (fig. 3.4). Such a case is the site of Grünhof-Tesperhude in Lower Saxony,[33] and of other sites in the same area,[34] and most recently of a remarkable wooden structure in barrow 24 at Etteln (Borchen, Paderborn).[35] These consisted of large roughly rectangular buildings made of large posts, sometimes containing wooden coffins, and burnt down prior to the erection of the barrow. Something of the same sort is present under some Dutch barrows, as at Toterfout-Halve Mijl, though the scale of these constructions is much smaller, usually with rather small posts at the four corners of an assumed building that straddled the burial.[36] They resemble such British examples as have been found, as at Beaulieu barrows II and IX in the New Forest, Hampshire, and a few others.[37]

It is not known how these mortuary structures operated; it seems that they were intentionally fired once the burials had been made and before the barrow was erected. The term 'mortuary house' seems to be something of a misnomer; these were chambers not unlike those in some Neolithic barrows but, unlike them, they were used for individual, not collective burial. Unlike the post rings, the chambers did not have to be removed for the erection of the barrow but were an integral part of it.

The majority of barrows are unexceptional, in terms of both construction

---

[33] Kersten 1936.
[34] Wegewitz 1941; Ehrich 1949.
[35] Bérenger 1996, 133ff.
[36] Glasbergen 1954b, 142ff.
[37] C. M. Piggott 1943, 7f., 24f.; Ashbee 1960, 52f.

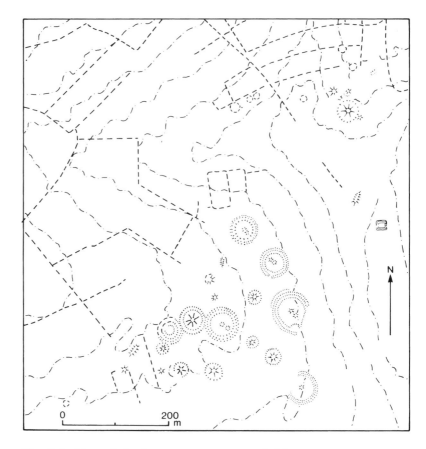

Fig. 3.6. Plan of the barrow cemetery at Oakley Down, Dorset. Dot-and-dash lines are contours, dashed lines are ancient field boundaries (after RCHME 1975).

and contents. Constructional features may be only pits or stone settings, with mounds of turf and earth; the primary graves may contain a Copper Age vessel (Bell Beaker, Corded Beaker), or an Early Bronze Age vessel, or nothing at all. Attention has therefore focused on those graves which contain material that is unusual in quality or quantity or both – most notably the Armorican First Series graves in Brittany and those of the 'Wessex culture' in Britain.[38] Unfortunately, the great majority of these have suffered greatly from incompetent or unrecorded excavation, which makes it very hard to have any confidence in theories that depend on fine detail in the finds record. Even correlations with the size or form of barrows are not always easy to establish since many of the published accounts do not include that information. There are, however, some correlations that have validity. It is certainly true

[38] Piggott 1938; 1973.

that disc barrows are mainly found in Wessex and have an association with material of the 'Wessex culture', though perhaps not as strongly as Grinsell made out since on his own figures only 15 of the surviving 145 disc barrows in Wessex produced Wessex culture grave-goods.[39] This is admittedly more impressive than the 16 out of 250 bell barrows, and far more so than the 69 out of some 3600 bowl barrows, but it hardly constitutes a secure basis on which to categorise the whole of the southern British Early Bronze Age.

Piggott listed one hundred graves that he attributed to a 'Wessex culture', but since many of these contained nothing more diagnostic than beads of shale, amber or faience, the definition has been criticised. The distribution of dagger graves, for instance, extends far beyond the boundaries of Wessex,[40] and the same is true of faience beads[41] and amber.[42] Ironically, in the same number of the same journal where Piggott published his original paper, Grimes published the material from a rich grave in Glamorgan at Breach Farm, Llanbeddian, comprising a pygmy cup, a flanged axe, a tanged chisel, a small flat dagger, two 'arrowshaft smoothers' and a group of fine flint objects: convex scraper, leaf-shaped point, three triangular and three discoidal knives and 13 fine arrowheads of the Conygar Hill type.[43] There are many other instances of rich graves: those in north Britain containing jet crescentic neck-laces,[44] or that from Mold, north Wales, containing a male inhumation, a splendid gold cape, 200–300 amber beads, sheet-bronze fragments and gold 'straps', are the most notable.[45] Some authors have referred to the 'air of provincialism about even the richest of the non-Wessex material, examples of local interpretations of Wessex ideas',[46] but such subjective judgements do little to further the argument. What is important about Wessex is the *relative* density of 'rich' graves in the area.

To take the example of one Wessex cemetery: that from Oakley Down, parish of Wimborne St Giles, Dorset.[47] The cemetery (group of tumuli) contains 30 barrows, disposed in an apparently irregular manner, an example of what Fleming calls a nucleated cemetery (fig. 3.6). The 30 consist of 23 bowl barrows, 2 bell barrows, and 5 disc barrows; mean inter-barrow distance is only a few paces. Material usually considered typical of the Wessex culture, including 4 daggers, was found in barrows 4 (bell), 6, 7, 8 (discs), 9, 10 (bowls), 13 (disc), 20 and 22 (bowls). The richest graves (according to the surviving

[39] Grinsell 1974, 87f.
[40] Gerloff 1975: 236 daggers and a further 110 knife-daggers are listed, excluding 19 tanged cop-per daggers and 4 knife-daggers of Beaker date, and a few exotic pieces.
[41] Harding 1984a, 311ff. with refs.
[42] Beck and Shennan 1991, 72 fig. 6.1.
[43] Grimes 1938; good recent illustration in Clarke *et al.* 1985, 161 ill. 4.98, 297–8 no. 138; Green 1980, 334 no. 186.
[44] Morrison 1979.
[45] Powell 1953.
[46] Clarke *et al.* 1985, 107.
[47] Grinsell 1959, 143ff.; 1982, 53f.

material) were in barrow 8, where the western mound contained 100 amber beads and spacer-plates, a bronze awl and a flat riveted knife-dagger.[48] There is no evidence here that any of the primary graves belong to anything other than the period of the 'Wessex culture', even though not all qualified for either Piggott or Gerloff to include them as members of that group. In this respect they differ from the situation of those cemeteries that can be seen to have begun life in the Beaker period, or even in the Neolithic, such as the Shrewton cemetery,[49] or a number of the cemeteries around Stonehenge such as the Cursus group, where at least two barrows started with Beaker burials.[50]

In endeavouring to interpret this cemetery one is notably hampered by the lack of information about age and sex. It has generally been assumed that daggers occur in male graves and beads in female,[51] but there are virtually no studies on skeletal material to support this. For comparison, it is true that at Singen almost all the male graves contained daggers and all the dagger graves where the sex could not be determined from the bones were on other grounds (e.g. orientation) assumed to be male.[52] Accepting this correlation for Oakley Down leads to the conclusion that males were not, as a rule, provided with rich grave-goods (Bush Barrow is exceptional in this respect). More usual was the situation in Oakley Down barrow G.9, or Amesbury G.85, where an Armorico-British B dagger was found with a knife-dagger, bone pins, arrow-straighteners and antler implements.[53] By contrast, female graves could be marked with significant numbers of goods, as at Oakley Down barrow 8, or many other famous Wessex graves. This still leaves the great majority of graves with few, if any, marks of distinction, other than the fact of burial in a tumulus cemetery in a central part of Wessex. *Mutatis mutandis*, this situation is not so different from that obtaining in central European flat cemeteries. As in them, wealth was more commonly displayed with females than with males: many of the gold ornaments and trinkets of Wessex are believed to have come from female graves.

France and the Low Countries

The Early Bronze Age tumuli of Brittany present many of the same problems.[54] The number of burials is similar to that in the Wessex area: perhaps 380 burials are attributable to the Armorican Barrow culture.[55] Since they

---

[48] Gerloff 1975, 165 no. 281; Annable and Simpson 1964, 58 nos. 407–13.
[49] Green and Rollo-Smith 1984.
[50] Grinsell n.d.
[51] Gerloff 1975, 197.
[52] Krause 1988, 103ff.
[53] Gerloff 1975, 76 no. 137; Newall 1930–2.
[54] Briard 1984c.
[55] Briard 1975.

were divided into two 'series',[56] one having arrowheads and generally considered 'rich', the other only pottery, a number of further excavations have reinforced the division without altogether solving the question of the relative date and significance of the phenomenon, though a powerful body of opinion holds that the Second Series is in fact later than the First, being of Middle Bronze Age date (i.e. the distinction is chronological, not social).[57] The First Series consists of only 31 barrows, the Second of 72; in addition a further 103 were too poorly provided to be assigned to either series (fig. 3.7). Barrows from the 50 or more that have been discovered or excavated since 1951 do not fall exactly into the two series; there is, for instance, a class of barrows with stone cists ('tumulus à coffres') that can contain both flintwork and pottery,[58] and a considerable number of secondary burials that have few or no grave-goods.[59] The cist barrows must be seen in relation to the numerous free-standing cists that are present in Brittany, a situation resembling that in northern Britain where cists were commoner than mounds. It is also clear that even within the Second Series, there is considerable variation in grave form and accompanying grave-goods.[60] The crude interpretation of the First Series graves as an intrusive princely stratum overlying the lower social classes (represented by the Second Series and the unclassifiable graves) is thus an oversimplified picture.

Early Bronze Age tumuli elsewhere in France are rather rare, though there is a large Middle Bronze Age group in the forest of Haguenau in Alsace.[61] Some parts of coastal Normandy have large numbers of barrows,[62] but France north of this is virtually devoid of known examples;[63] occasional examples occur elsewhere. Were the Early Bronze Age in France as a whole better known, it might be possible to assess the position of tumulus burial more accurately. As it is, the somewhat anomalous position of Brittany and Normandy might suggest that the creation of a burial tradition under barrows followed the same course as in southern England.

In the Netherlands, barrows are found throughout the central part of the country but are especially common in the north in Drenthe, and in the south in North Brabant. Glasbergen's fundamental study estimates that between 1500 and 2000 barrows were extant in the Netherlands at the start of this century, of which 500 had been excavated by the time he wrote.[64] Since that time, aerial photography has found more sites, as with recent studies in

---

[56] Cogné and Giot 1951.
[57] Gallay 1981, 110ff., 117.
[58] e.g. Kergoglay barrow, Plouhinec: Briard *et al.* 1979.
[59] e.g. Saint-Jude 1, Bourbriac, Côtes-du-Nord: Briard and Giot 1963.
[60] Briard 1983.
[61] Schaeffer 1926; Bonnet *et al.* 1981.
[62] Verron 1976.
[63] Gaucher 1976.
[64] Glasbergen 1954b, 11.

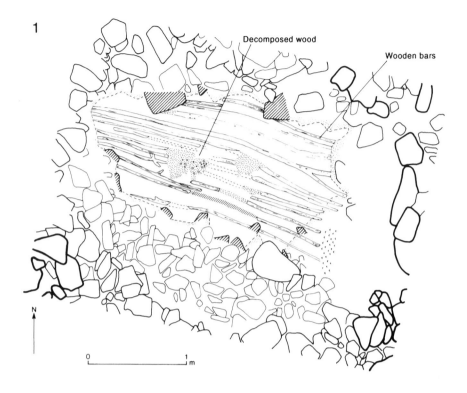

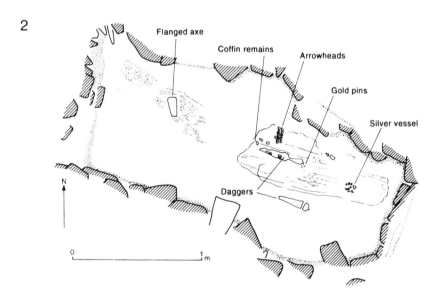

Fig. 3.7. Burial cists in Breton First Series barrows. 1. Saint-Jude en Bourbriac, Côtes-du-Nord; 2. Saint-Adrien, Côtes-du-Nord (after Briard 1984c).

Belgium,[65] and a number of others have been excavated or published,[66] so that the true density of barrows in the Netherlands is probably no lower than for comparable areas of southern England or Denmark. Unlike those areas, however, datable finds are rather rare, especially those clearly attributable to the Early Bronze Age: dagger graves, for instance, are absent. What is more, it is clear that barrow burial, including that in coffins, continued into the Middle Bronze Age just as it did in Denmark; at Hooghalen, this was the richest period of grave deposition, and at Toterfout-Halve Mijl the presence of urn burials indicates continuing interest beyond the Early Bronze Age. The continuing use of barrows in late parts of the Bronze Age, and beyond, is attested not only by urn burials in major mounds erected earlier in the period, but by cemeteries of small barrows containing cremations along much of the course of the lower Rhine.[67]

Northern Europe

Mound or cairn building was extremely popular in many parts of northern Europe at various stages of the Bronze Age. Especially in Jutland and adjacent parts of north Germany large mounds litter the countryside in certain areas; many tens of thousands of barrows survive or are recorded, sometimes in cemeteries of remarkable density, as can be seen from the entries in the great corpus of Aner and Kersten, in which over 43,000 barrows are attested in Denmark (excluding north-east Jutland) and the western part of Schleswig-Holstein.[68] Admittedly, some of these belong to the Viking period, and only a relatively small number are known to have produced finds of Late Neolithic or Early Bronze Age date, but it is likely that the vast majority are prehistoric. Some began life in the Copper Age and were used again in the Early Bronze Age, while others were only built in the latter period. In Sweden, some areas are conspicuous for the large numbers of cairns and mounds that are visible: in parts of Scania and on the west coast where they are found on promontories and islets, sometimes visible from the sea and perhaps indicating the connection of the dead person with territories that included stretches of water. Near Göteborg, for instance, the study of barrows and cairns, coupled with the reconstruction of shorelines given a 10 m relative rise in sea level, has enabled scholars to work out the line of the Bronze Age 'strait', lined with islets bearing such mounds.[69] Estimates for the west coast of Sweden are of 2800 cairns and 1100 barrows,[70] including a certain number of large sites (greater than 20 m in diameter).

[65] Ampe *et al.* 1996.
[66] e.g. Hooghalen near Hijken: van der Veen and Lanting 1989.
[67] Kersten 1948.
[68] Aner and Kersten 1973–95.
[69] Sandberg 1973.
[70] Bertilsson 1981.

Barrows usually contained pits, stone settings or coffins, and seem to have been regarded as discrete containers for the resting-place of the dead. At Löderup 15 in Scania, however, a group of four barrows served as a focal point for cemetery growth over a long period, apparently from the Late Neolithic right through to the Roman Iron Age.[71] In this case, burials were placed both in and around the barrows, so that it is not even possible to determine which burials were primary to the barrows. This site also raises questions about continuity of burial tradition and, though it is perhaps an extreme example, illustrates the point that major barrows of whatever period attracted attention from later generations.

Much attention inevitably focuses on the spectacular finds of textiles, wooden objects, leather, bark and other organic materials from certain Danish (and to a lesser extent German) barrows, and the information from them is indeed unrivalled in scope and scale. Particularly the barrows at Skrydstrup, Egtved, Muldbjerg, Trindhøj, Lofthøj and Borum Eshøj – all in Jutland, except Lofthøj, which is on Zealand – produced the finds which help to make the Prehistoric Department of the National Museum in Copenhagen one of the richest and most important in all Europe. These finds have been described many times.[72] It is important to realise that there is no reason to believe them to have been exceptional at the time they were deposited. The barrows were much like many others, and the tree-trunk coffins which characterise many of them are repeated hundreds of times over (see below). What is exceptional is the degree of preservation.

It is uncertain from this how many and what sort of people were buried in barrows in Scandinavia. As with many areas, there are a significant number of burials with few or no grave-goods, for which only the fact of barrow burial is distinctive. But there are also a significant number of people buried with swords and other prestige objects. Even with the large numbers of barrow burials known, the total number cannot account for more than a small minority of those who lived in the periods covered. Therefore access to barrow burial was restricted, and the rest of the population are not archaeologically visible.

The existence of grave distinctions is evident from both the size of monuments and the type of construction used: for instance stone or earth for the body of the mound (though this may have been rather a question of available materials than conscious choice). Within both traditions, certain sites were marked out by extra size, reflecting enhanced status.[73] The size and elaboration of the great mound of Bredarör at Kivik in south-east Scania, at 75 m in diameter, is exceptional and presumed to indicate extraordinary status in its occupant(s); the decorated slabs of the grave chamber confirm the impres-

---

[71] Strömberg 1975.
[72] e.g. Glob 1974.
[73] Bertilsson 1981.

sion.[74] What Thrane has termed 'mini-mounds' can be seen where good excavation has taken place and preservation conditions are favourable; some of these developed into major tumuli, as at Lusehøj, while others became part of tumulus cemeteries.[75]

A case has been made for seeing the orientation of graves within mounds of Periods II and III (tending towards east–west) as related to the position of sunrise or sunset.[76] It has been argued in the case of Merovingian and Anglo-Saxon cemeteries that the precise orientation of a grave indicates the part of the year in which the grave was dug, on the assumption that an exact alignment was intended and achieved. The fact that in some Bronze Age instances the axis of pre-mound ploughing was also that of the grave-pits lends credence to the idea of an intentionally constructed and maintained orientation.

Central Europe

In the Middle Bronze Age in central Europe the practice of burial deposition under mounds was standard over much of the region, particularly the areas identified with the 'Tumulus culture' (principally Germany and Bohemia, with adjacent territories such as Alsace, parts of Austria, even parts of the middle Danube basin). Tumuli also appear quite frequently at this time in the area of the Lausitz culture (mainly Poland, the north of the Czech lands and easternmost Germany). Since the Tumulus Bronze Age overlapped the main period of Bronze Age tumulus burial in the north and west of Europe, and the continuation of the 'kurgan culture' in the east, some scholars have been tempted to discern higher order affinities – for instance Gimbutas's theory that such mounds are the hallmark of racially homogeneous people whom she called the 'kurgan people' and identified with the Indo-Europeans.[77] By contrast, some areas maintained quite different rites – for instance parts of France, Britain and Ireland, Italy and large parts of south-east Europe.

When one looks at central Europe prior to the Tumulus period, the commonest tradition is, as discussed above, that of the flat inhumation cemetery. But interspersed with these flat cemeteries are barrow burials, a few of which have attracted an inordinate amount of attention. Most famous are the pair of barrows in Sachsen-Anhalt at Helmsdorf and Leubingen, and the cemetery of barrows at Łęki Małe in western Poland.[78] Several of these had rich grave-goods, and the two German barrows had elaborately constructed timber grave-chambers, with ridge roofs; one of the Polish barrows had a deep shaft under a burial chamber. In terms of size and elaboration, the tumulus at

---

[74] Moberg 1975; L. Larsson 1993b.
[75] Thrane 1993.
[76] Randsborg and Nybo 1984.
[77] e.g. Gimbutas 1965.
[78] Coles and Harding 1979, 40ff. with refs.

Szczepankowice (Wrocław) is just as impressive as Łęki Małe, though relatively few of the grave-goods survived.[79] One large mound was excavated, and another possible example lay nearby. An initial stone setting was enclosed in a primary mound, into which a woman's and a child's grave had been inserted. The mound was later enlarged. The stone setting, 8 × 6 m in extent, was initially defined by wooden elements; three post-holes and other traces of wood lay under the perimeter. The mound itself had a substantial turf stack over the stone setting, while the main mound was of earth. The central grave had been robbed, so little idea can be obtained of the original state or richness of the burial, but at 5 m high and 25 m across, this mound was a construction of considerable size, comparable with the Łęki Małe barrows (respectively 24, 30, 30 and 45 m in diameter and 4.6, 3.9, 3.1 and 4.4 m high).

The really remarkable thing about Helmsdorf and Leubingen is the timber structures, which are not known from other sites in central Europe (though something similar is present at Pustopolje in Bosnia: see below). It is quite evident that, if other tumuli had comparably good survival, timber chambers might have been shown to be present. In other words, it is a matter of preservation rather than original rarity.

There is a long tradition of Copper Age barrow burial throughout the eastern half of Europe, where the graves are associated with the provision of ochre and sometimes with cord-decorated pottery, but this early tradition stops with the beginning of the Bronze Age proper.[80] Early Bronze Age barrows can occur in cemeteries of a score or more,[81] but relatively few have been tested by excavation, and where they have, there are frequently poorly furnished graves which cannot be attributed to a specific date. The standard work on the Únětice cemeteries of Poland lists 13 localities with Early Bronze Age finds and mounds apart from Łęki Małe.[82] In Saxony, Billig listed a number of sites with barrows, though admittedly only that at Gaussig, Kr. Bautzen, contained typical Early Bronze Age finds.[83] In Moravia, Lower Austria, the Burgenland and western Slovakia Early Bronze Age barrows are known from a number of places.[84] In Thuringia, Walter has listed a number of sites where barrows were present, ranging in date from the full Early Bronze Age to the transition to the Middle Bronze Age.[85] Neugebauer has made a case for seeing the presence of small tumuli in the later phases of the cemetery at Gemeinlebarn F, given the greater distance between graves compared to the earlier phases.[86] These

[79] Sarnowska 1969, 289ff.
[80] Budinský-Krička 1967 (Slovakia), Ecsedy 1979 (Hungary), Panayotov and Dergachev 1984 (Bulgaria), Jovanović 1975 (Serbia; also in Hügelbestattung 1987), Sulimirski 1968 (southeastern Poland) and Ciugudean 1995 (Transylvania).
[81] There are 14 barrows at Łęki Małe, for instance.
[82] Sarnowska 1969, 30ff, 359ff.
[83] Billig 1958.
[84] Tihelka 1953, 236, 297, 307; Chleborád 1963; Benkovský-Pivovarová 1987.
[85] Walter 1990b.
[86] Neugebauer 1991, 64.

sites indicate that barrow burial was far from uncommon in the Early Bronze Age in central Europe, but treating them all as high-status graves is problematic. Apart from anything else, it leaves open the question of what happened to high-status individuals in areas where there are no barrows.

Barrow burial really came into its own during the Middle Bronze Age, when much of continental Europe saw the prevalence of this burial form. Many studies of individual culture areas have appeared, though an appreciation of the true significance of the phenomenon seems some way off.[87] At the community level, this has led to important advances in understanding. At the level of cultures and culture groups (the terminology of D. L. Clarke), however, the significance of the dominance of barrow burial across Europe in the Middle Bronze Age remains obscure. Even if Gimbutas's hypothesis about the spread of Indo-European speakers were to be accepted, much remains uncertain about the relationship between Early and Middle Bronze Age burial traditions, and that of both to the Copper Age barrow horizon. Few systematic studies have been carried out on the relationship between barrow size, artefact wealth and the age and sex of the deceased – not least because so few sites provide the possibility of carrying out such analyses, having been excavated prior to the advent of adequate recording techniques. Yet such studies remain crucial if an understanding of the Tumulus phenomenon is to be advanced.

In the Urnfield period, cremation in pits or urns was the norm over vast areas. But here too, barrows are found: not just very large ones in selected areas but small ones as well in many parts of Europe. At cemeteries such as those near Milavče in western Bohemia, several large tumuli belong to the Middle Bronze Age, and many smaller ones to the Late Bronze Age.[88] An extensive cemetery of small barrows at Solberg in Thuringia is of just this type,[89] and much of what Kersten and others termed the 'niederrheinische Grabhügelkultur' essentially consisted of similar cemeteries of small barrows, found in western Germany and the Low Countries.[90] Comparable instances may be found on many early Lausitz cemeteries, for instance in Moravia,[91] or at Trenčianské Teplice in Slovakia.[92] Groups of barrows (in other words cemeteries) can be seen in western Hungary where in the early Urnfield period they are quite common along with flat cemeteries; for instance, 80–100 mounds were noted at Zirc-Alsómajer, and in some cases small chambers made out of limestone slabs containing the burial urns were present.[93] A

---

[87] e.g. Čujanová-Jílková 1970; Ziegert 1963; Feustel 1958; Točík 1964; Willvonseder 1937.
[88] Čujanová-Jílková 1984.
[89] Speitel 1991.
[90] Kersten 1948.
[91] Nekvasil 1978, with references for other areas.
[92] Pivovarová 1965, 112ff.
[93] Patek 1968, 81ff.

recently excavated tumulus at Sávoly-Babócsa (Somogy county, near the western end of Lake Balaton) was 25 m across but had developed from a small
mounded grave in the centre, burials being added to the enlarged mound over
time.[94] Cremation was the standard rite both in barrows and in flat graves.
In other words, barrows were actually rather common in the Late Bronze Age,
and by no means restricted to graves with rich goods.

The other side of this coin is that there are a certain number of 'special'
barrows. Best known is a small number of very rich sites in Germany and
Scandinavia, for instance the 'King's Grave' at Seddin,[95] the mound at Lusehøj
on Funen,[96] and 'King Björn's mound' at Håga near Uppsala;[97] these belong to
an advanced phase of the Bronze Age. But from a much earlier part of the
Late Bronze Age there are a number of famous barrows in Moravia and western Slovakia, notably Velatice, Očkov, Dedinka, Kolta and Čaka, and a smaller
number, less well-known, from north-west Hungary,[98] which date to the earliest part of the Urnfield period and which contain goods that look to be
unmistakably part of a warrior's accoutrements.[99] There are other grounds for
inferring high rank for the occupants of these burials: not only the presence
of fine pottery and bronzes, even body armour and weapons, but also the presence of a pyre.

Barrow burial thus appeared in many different phases of the Late Bronze
Age in central Europe, though it was seldom the norm. Where it does occur,
one can plausibly regard it as having held a special significance in social terms,
which seems not to be the case in the Middle Bronze Age. Indeed, the regular recurrence of the tumulus rite at intervals through the central European
Bronze Age implies that it maintained a role, at times dominant, at others
submerged, through much of the period.

The Balkans

The appearance of tumulus burial in the Balkan peninsula can be traced back
to the Copper Age, equivalent to its first appearance in east-central Europe
(see above); good examples are the Bulgarian site of Tărnava (Vraca)[100] and a
few large mounds on the Dalmatian coast with exotic finds including gold
and silver, as at Mala Gruda[101] and Velika Gruda.[102] In the Early Bronze Age
finds of tumuli are rare: a certain number appear in western Serbia and east-

---

[94] Honti 1996.
[95] Kiekebusch 1928.
[96] Thrane 1984.
[97] Almgren 1905.
[98] Paulík 1960, 414ff.
[99] Říhovský 1958; Paulík 1962; 1966; 1974; 1983; 1984; Točík and Paulík 1960.
[100] Nikolov 1976.
[101] Parović-Pešikan and Trbuhović 1971.
[102] Primas 1992; 1996b; Della Casa 1996b; cf. too Parović-Pešikan 1977–8.

ern Bosnia, notably those at Belotić and Bela Crkva,[103] but also a group around
Titovo Užice.[104] There are many tumulus cemeteries in the hilly plateaux of
southern Croatia and Bosnia, but the scarcity of finds makes it hard in many
cases to know to which period they belong; they were certainly being built
in the Early Bronze Age.[105] By the Late Bronze Age there are significant numbers of barrows being built on the Glasinac plateau east of Sarajevo, a tradition that continued unbroken deep into the Iron Age.[106] Because this area is
both elevated and remote, the material culture reflects in only a limited way
what is known in more favoured parts of the peninsula, for instance in the
Sava plain or on the two sides of the Adriatic. Most of the grave-goods are
ornaments, but nothing is known of correlation with age and sex. This curious funerary culture finds little reflection in settlements. It has for this reason been suggested that Glasinac must have acted as a special burial area to
which people came specifically for the purpose of burying the dead.

Still more remarkable is the situation of the group of tumuli in the
Kupreško polje (upland basin) in southern Bosnia, and specifically the tumuli
at Pustopolje.[107] Although these mounds were poor in finds, wood was well
preserved, so that details of the coffin or chamber in which the dead person
was laid were recovered: an unusual construction consisting of a box-like
chamber fastened down with cross-bars that fitted into wedges at the sides,
one of the cross-bars being a reused sledge runner (fig. 7.3). The body lay in
a woven woollen rug or cloak but was otherwise naked. This find serves as
a reminder that most of the most striking elements of burials have perished.

Also contemporary with the Glasinac tumuli are those in Albania, mostly
in the east of the country, on the middle and upper river valleys (fig. 3.8).[108]
They are especially common in the valley of the Mat, but also the Shkumbi,
Devoll and others; there are a number of sizeable cemeteries in inland regions
around the upper Drin and its tributaries. Most of these tumuli date to the
Iron Age, but a few start earlier, certainly in the Late Bronze Age and possibly in some cases in the Middle Bronze Age. Such tumuli contain grave-goods
that mirror what is found in flat graves on and near the Dalmatian coast in
cemeteries like those at Nin or Prozor[109] and are therefore commonly attributed to tribes of Illyrian affinity. The number of certain Late Bronze Age
graves is not large, and the dating of a number of artefact types – both metal
and ceramic – is debatable; it was noteworthy that in a few cases imported
Greek material found its way into local Albanian graves, an important sign
of status-related accumulation.

[103] M. and D. Garašanin 1956.
[104] Zotović 1985.
[105] e.g. Marović 1991; Kosorić 1976 and many other similar reports.
[106] Benac and Čović 1956.
[107] Benac 1986; 1990.
[108] e.g. Andrea 1985.
[109] Batović 1983; Drechsler-Bižić 1983.

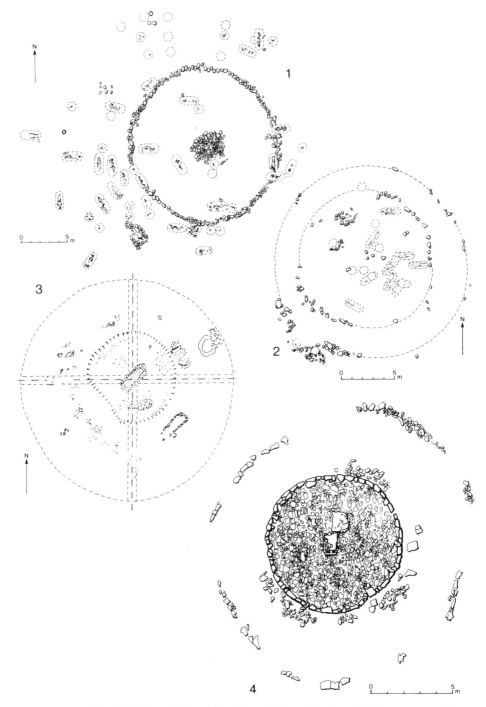

Fig. 3.8. Tumuli in Albania and Yugoslavia. 1–2. Barç, tumuli 1 and 2 (after Andrea 1985). 3. Arilje, Davidovića Ćair (after Zotović 1985). 4. Orah, tumulus 1 (after Govedarica 1987).

A case has been made for seeing these Balkan tumuli as an element of Indo-European material culture spreading through the peninsula along with Indo-European language, including Greek.[110] This theory depends on the belief that tumulus burial is a characteristically Indo-European trait, and was mainly propounded by M. Gimbutas. While it may be legitimate to identify certain items of culture as characteristically Indo-European, that does not mean that they automatically indicate the presence of such peoples. The fact of barrow burial in itself seems far too general a trait to be capable of indicating the source and direction of movement of such influences. The Balkan tumuli go back to the Copper Age tradition which was indeed introduced some time around 3000 BC. After that, the idea seems to have maintained its own momentum, popping up here and there in the peninsula at regular intervals, and in some areas (e.g. Bosnia) lasting throughout the Bronze Age. By the Late Bronze Age tumuli were valued as a means of creating monumental markers that indicated both the position and the status of the deceased, a development wholly fitting in the context of the social and political development taking place at the period.

Coffin burials

Burial in a coffin was used in various parts of the Bronze Age world. In the absence of a systematic study of this phenomenon, one is forced to rely on rather impressionistic statements based on the more accessible sources. Lists of coffin burials have been created for Bohemia,[111] Moravia[112] and Britain;[113] elsewhere the coverage is more haphazard.[114] Coffins are usually thought of as having been hollowed-out tree trunks, and this is indeed a frequently found form. But it is by no means the only type of wooden container for the dead. At least as common as tree-trunk coffins in the Nordic area were wooden containers of a different, unspecified and usually unreconstructable, kind; a small number are known to have been plank-built.

Coffins were commonest in the Nordic area (fig. 3.9). Statistics can hardly be regarded as reliable, in view of the likelihood that many early excavators failed to recognise the existence of coffins unless they actually survived as preserved wood; but Broholm states that more than one-third of the 1060 grave finds of the Early Bronze Age emanate from oak coffins, and his detailed catalogue lists 455 coffins from 1100 graves of Period II and coffins in 282 of the 1300 graves of Period III.[115] A tabulation is presented in table 3.4. These

---

[110] Hammond 1967; Early Bronze Age tumuli in Levkas are seen as indicating this spread into Greece: Hammond 1974.

[111] Pleinerová 1960a.

[112] Tihelka 1960.

[113] Grinsell 1941a, 103ff.; Elgee and Elgee 1949, 105f.

[114] Jockenhövel 1969–70, 61.

[115] Broholm and Hald 1935/1940, 8; Broholm 1952–3. These statistics appear to be confirmed by the great catalogue publication of Aner and Kersten (1973–95).

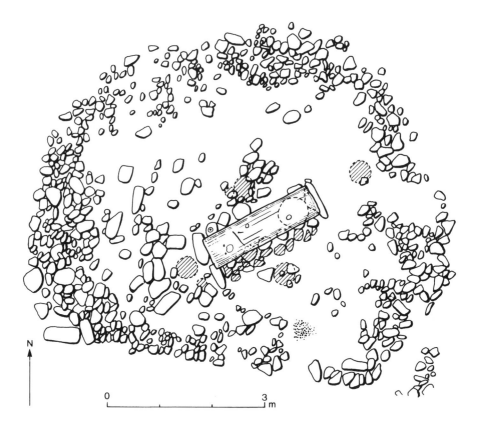

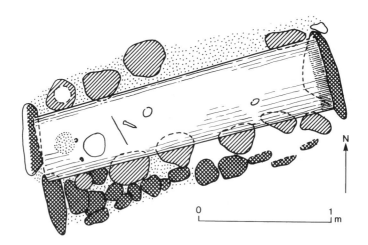

Fig. 3.9. Barrow with coffin burial, Beckdorf, Kr. Stade, Lower Saxony (after Wegewitz 1949). *Upper*: general plan of the excavated barrow; *lower*: detail of the coffin with finds.

figures show first that there is considerable variability in barrow numbers in the different provinces of Denmark and northern Germany (over 7600 barrows are known in Aner and Kersten's area X, the Ringkøbing district of western Jutland, compared with only 829 in area XVIII, Kreis Rendsburg); and within these figures there is variability in the frequency with which tree-trunk coffins are found; less than 10% of barrows with known Late Neolithic to Early Bronze Age finds in west and south Zealand (Area II) have them as compared with over 40% in south Schleswig east (Area IV). An example where systematic modern excavation revealed large numbers of coffins is that of Löderup 15 in south-east Scania.[116] Of 43 graves of the Late Neolithic-Early Bronze Age on this site, no less than 35 contained wooden coffins, either tree-trunk or plank. Clearly at this site coffin burial was the norm; this was apparently not the case for other sites in southern Scania.

Further south, there are many Early Bronze Age examples in Lower Saxony,[117] and the Urnfield cemetery at Vollmarshausen near Kassel also had a couple of instances of burnt coffins.[118] The cemetery at Wahlitz, Kr. Burg near Magdeburg in eastern Germany, had coffins in seven of nine large grave-pits and others in small pits;[119] they were present in all four graves at Hofheim near Frankfurt;[120] wedging stones at grave head and foot have been interpreted as packing for coffins at Singen.[121] For the Low Countries, where no exact figures are available, reference to the classic work reveals a number of examples in Holland.[122]

In central Europe, coffins occur in many Únětice cemeteries, such as Rebešovice;[123] recent examples include those from Mušov,[124] Těšetice-Vinohrady (fig. 3.10),[125] Przecławice[126] and Moravská Nová Ves-Hrušky.[127] A curiosity of some Únětice graves at Březno (north-west Bohemia) is that of multiple burials in coffins, in some cases with evidence for the removal or collecting up of skulls and other bones.[128] In several of these cemeteries coffin graves accounted for a sizeable proportion of the total (62.5% at Rebešovice, 40% at Mušov, 37.2% at Przecławice). In the case of Rebešovice the excavator gave good reasons for believing that the original number would have been still higher. At Gemeinlebarn F, there were 4 tree-trunk

[116] Strömberg 1975.
[117] Wegewitz 1949, 152ff.
[118] Bergmann 1982, 139f.
[119] Voigt 1955.
[120] Jockenhövel 1969–70.
[121] Krause 1988, 36f.
[122] For instance at Noordsche Veld, Zeijen; Kamperschie, Weerdinge; Wessinghuizen barrow 1; Drouwen and a number of others: van Giffen 1930.
[123] Ondráček 1962.
[124] Stuchlík 1987.
[125] Lorencová *et al.* 1987.
[126] Lasak 1982; 1988, 51.
[127] Stuchlík and Stuchlíková 1996.
[128] Pleinerová 1981.

Table 3.4. *Coffins in Nordic barrows*[1]

Area (vol. no.)	Total barrows	Barrows with Neo-EBA finds	Tree-trunk		Planks		Wood		Total coffin burials
			barrows	finds	barrow	finds	barrow	finds	
I	2935	362	51	65	5	5	51	65	107
II	4700	392	31	44	5	5	35	42	71
III	4774	313	36	42	2	5	40	53	78
IV	3722	218	89	160	3	3	33	51	125
V	1738	231	47	78	5	6	48	59	100
VI	3678	321	51	68	6	7	40	49	97
VII	2926	300	61	87	8	10	40	55	109
VIII	6561	361	37	58	3	3	35	52	75
IX	4386	258	34	48	3	3	23	25	60
X	7639	246	30	35	5	5	41	50	76
XVIII	829	137	17	27	1	1	34	49	52
Total	43888	3139	484	712	46	53	420	550	950

Note: [1]Coffins are recorded as of tree-trunk, plank and wood construction. Separate figures are given for barrows and finds, as there are frequently several coffins in a single barrow.
Source: Statistics taken from Aner and Kersten 1973–95.

coffins and 103 definite and 35 probable wood coffins (fig. 3.10);[129] at Unterhautzenthal there were 4 wood coffins and a tree-trunk one.[130] The high percentage of coffins at Gemeinlebarn, provision ranging from infants to the elderly, speaks against coffins having been provided for a specially privileged class of people. On the other hand, those without coffins are generally 'poor': the adults come from the poorer wealth clusters, and the rest are children.

In Britain, coffins survive very rarely; usually it is only the outlines that can be traced. Exceptions are those from Wydon Eals, Haltwhistle, Northumberland,[131] or Loose Howe, Yorkshire.[132] On the other hand, recent excavations have produced plenty of coffin traces (though no actual wood), which strongly suggests that they were actually quite common in British barrow burials. By contrast, no examples appear to be known from Ireland.[133] Admittedly, the burial rite there depends mostly on cists and pits, sometimes under or within tumuli, and the stone-walled cist probably fulfilled the function of the coffin. In Brittany, traces of wood have been reported in some of the First Series barrows, but these seem more likely to have been part of 'mortuary houses' or wooden chambers than movable coffins. Such wooden constructions occur in certain well-publicised examples, such as Helmsdorf and Leubingen, but were probably quite common. In a few cases traces of

[129] Neugebauer 1991, 72ff.
[130] Lauermann 1995.
[131] Snagge 1873.
[132] Elgee and Elgee 1949.
[133] Waddell n.d. [1990].

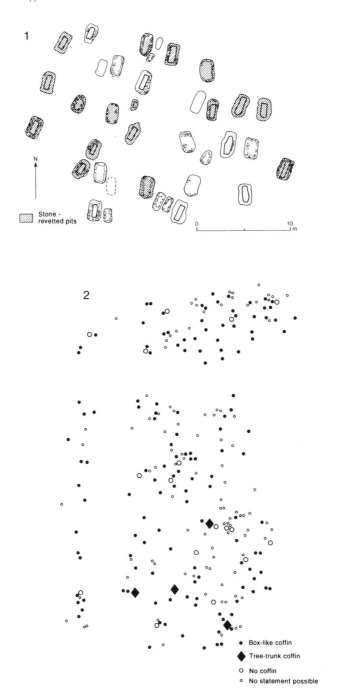

Fig. 3.10. *Upper*: Plan of the cemetery at Těšetice-Vinohrady, Moravia, showing coffin graves, some in stone-revetted pits (after Lorencová *et al.* 1987); *lower*: Gemeinlebarn F, plan of the cemetery showing coffin graves (after Neugebauer 1991).

wood have been recorded, as with Eneolithic tumuli of the Banat,[134] and wooden planking is sometimes mentioned. It is likely that excavation technique has frequently not been adequate for the recognition of poorly preserved wooden constructions or coffins.

Two distinct burial traditions utilising coffins seem to be discernible. One, the better known, is that of north and north-west Europe, where a significant proportion – perhaps a majority – of burials were deposited in tree-trunk or other coffins, at least in certain areas and at certain periods. The other is that of the flat inhumation cemeteries of central Europe, as typified by the sites of Rebešovice or Těšetice-Vinohrady. From the analysis of Těšetice-Vinohrady coffins were not especially associated with rich graves or with those of a particular age or sex. Some coffin burials in Britain were marked by prestige grave-goods: the Gristhorpe burial contained a bone pin, a bronze dagger with a pommel of whale-bone, a wooden knife or spatula, a bone ornament, a bark basket, a flint arrowhead and two flint flakes.[135] The Hove barrow contained the famous amber cup, a bronze dagger of Camerton type, a whetstone pendant and a little battle-axe.[136] Another 'rich' coffin burial was that at Winterbourne Stoke G.5.[137] But equally, some coffin burials had few or no grave-goods, for instance the unaccompanied cremation at Rushmore barrow 9,[138] or the coffin burial in the barrow at Poor's Heath, Risby, Suffolk.[139]

Little attention has been paid to the environmental implications of the provision of oak coffins or to their symbolic significance. Large numbers of mature oaks, of diameter typically one metre or more and therefore scores or hundreds of years old, were felled during the Early Bronze Age. Given that originally the number of coffins must have been much greater than the present total, and that tens of thousands of barrows of potentially Bronze Age date cover the landscape of northern Europe, the potential effect on the oak population would have been marked. Equally important was the symbolic significance of burial in a massive oak tree-trunk coffin, and the connection with oak-built domestic structures. Houses of the Bronze Age in temperate Europe were often predominantly of oak. The relationship between houses and tombs has often been commented on in a Neolithic context, and it is probably no coincidence that a number of house plans have been found underneath Bronze Age burial mounds.[140] There is a strong and recurrent symbolism in the motif of the tree, not necessarily the oak, in Nordic myth and legend. Thus 'the world ash-tree' (Yggdrasil) is one of the main cosmological

---

[134] Girić 1987.
[135] Williamson 1872.
[136] Gerloff 1975, 105.
[137] Piggott 1938, 37.
[138] Pitt Rivers 1888, 32, 40 pl. 87,4.
[139] Vatcher and Vatcher 1976.
[140] Trappendal: Boysen and Andersen 1983; Hyllerup: Pedersen 1986.

symbols of the Teutonic North representing the universe;[141] Hunding's house accordingly has a mighty ash rising in its middle and spreading out all over the roof. Askr (ash-tree) was one of the first two people in the world. The concept of the Tree of Life is important in the Judaeo-Christian tradition, as with the story of the Garden of Eden (Genesis 2); the tree was guarded by cherubim and by a sword whirling and flashing. In Greek mythology, the human race grew from tree seeds, ash according to Hesiod, oak in Homer; trees are also associated with the dwellings of gods and with longevity or immortality. The association of yews with graveyards probably expresses this notion, as may the great evergreen tree at Old Uppsala recorded by Adam of Bremen. Trees are frequently anthropomorphised in world mythology; thus Daphne (the laurel tree). Burial in a tree-trunk coffin, as it were inside a tree, thus carries with it obvious connotations of the return to the source of life, a re-enclosing within the womb from which all humans sprang.

Boats and death

The close similarity between tree-trunk coffins and dug-out canoes can also be seen as more than a coincidence of the same materials used for similarly shaped objects; the 'boat of death' is a recurring theme in antiquity.[142] The Loose Howe and Shap burials actually involved canoes used as or with burials, as does a find from Disgwylfa Fawr, Ceredigion, west Wales;[143] none is close to significant stretches of water (Loose Howe lies high on the central watershed of the North York Moors, Shap on the Cumbrian Fells). It is possible that these canoes were used because they had finished their useful sailing life and were available for reuse, but the labour involved in transporting them to their resting-place must have been considerable.

One of the principal motifs of Urnfield symbolism was the boat, usually drawn by birds (see chapter 9).[144] The pre-echoes of the disposal of Arthur's body in later mythology are striking, though no funerary boats are actually known in Bronze Age Europe (unlike Old Kingdom Egypt). Whether any of the ship depictions in Scandinavian rock art are connected with rituals of death, as has been suggested for some other motifs, is a moot point. What is not in doubt, however, is the connection of boat-shaped settings of stones with graves. Such 'ship-settings' are known from many parts of Scandinavia and north Germany, especially in Småland and on Gotland (fig. 3.11).[145] Many are of Iron Age and Viking date, but some have been shown by excavation to belong to the Bronze Age. Of the 300–350 whole or fragmentary settings on

[141] Simek 1993, 375.
[142] Grinsell 1941b.
[143] Green 1987.
[144] Kossack 1954b.
[145] Strömberg 1961; Müller-Wille 1968–9; Capelle 1986; 1995.

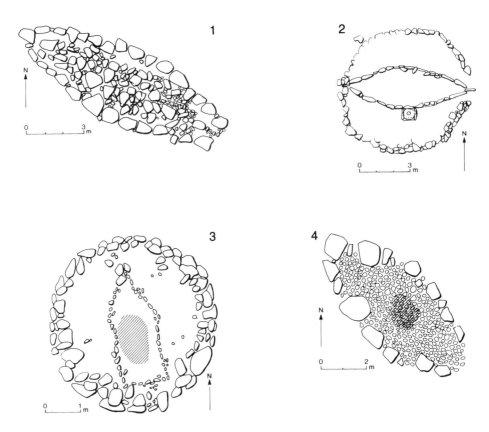

Fig. 3.11. Ship settings from Germany and Sweden. 1. Slätteröd 6, Västra Karup (after Strömberg 1961). 2. Lugnaro, Halland (after Capelle 1995). 3. Thumby, Schleswig-Holstein (after Capelle 1995; Aner and Kersten 1973–95). 4. Hjortekrug, Törnsfall, Småland (after Strömberg 1961).

Gotland, only around 30 have been investigated, the earliest belonging to the end of the Middle Bronze Age, the latest to the Late Bronze–Iron Age transition (some 10 of the 30 excavated examples on Gotland had Late Bronze Age finds). Most are less than 20 m long, but the examples from Gnisvärd on Gotland are 33 and 45 m in length. A well-investigated example is that at Slätteröd (V. Karup, western Scania), excavated in 1959–60.[146] Measuring 11.5 × 4 m, and oriented WNW–ESE, it consisted of 30 blocks of granite, the interior filled with stones; under them was a charcoal layer, and in it a cremation pit. Finds, not numerous, included flint arrowheads and other objects, potsherds and animal bones, the latter indicating feasting in connection with the deposition rituals.

[146] Strömberg 1961.

Who was eligible for burial in a ship setting in the Bronze Age is unknown to us, but the continuing popularity of the rite is important for the study not only of religion but also of entire belief systems and ethnic affinities. The continuity evident through nearly 2000 years, and even the possible connection with rock-art depictions that may stretch back considerably further, makes the ship burial one of the most important aspects of symbolism in northern prehistory.[147] One may again turn to Nordic mythology, where medieval sources make mention of the custom, sometimes with the boat being burned, sometimes not; in the case of Beowulf and some other legends, the burning boat was sent out to sea with the corpse in it,[148] as was also the case with the Norse god Balder.

Inhumation and cremation

Although cremation burial is inevitably associated above all with the Urnfield rite in the Late Bronze Age, it had appeared in a number of areas long before this. In the Early Bronze Age of Hungary it was the standard rite in the cemeteries of the Nagyrév and Kisapostag groups,[149] and in the Middle Bronze Age in those of the Vatya group (see. fig. 3.1).[150] As mentioned above, cremation also occurs in the Early Bronze Age in north-west Europe. In Britain, cremation was widely practised in the Early Bronze Age, and was dominant in the north; it occurs with regularity in Wessex, Yorkshire and other areas.[151] During the course of the Middle Bronze Age, it became the commonest rite practised in Britain, as is seen in the Deverel–Rimbury barrows and related sites in various parts of England.[152]

Cemeteries usually practised the same rite during a single period, suggesting some stability of practice and therefore of belief. There are, however, plenty of examples of sites where both inhumation and cremation were practised, sometimes simultaneously (as far as one can tell). Thus while one may not be sure in British or Irish mounds whether separate burials by different traditions in a single mound were contemporaneous,[153] in some of the 'biritual' cemeteries of central Europe the practice is assured. The Tumulus-period cemetery of Dolný Peter (Komarno) in south-west Slovakia contained 50 inhumations, five cremations and one grave with both inhumation and cremation.[154] There was no indication from the grave-goods that there was any large difference in time between the graves, though in general the cre-

---

[147] Müller-Wille 1968–9.
[148] Simek 1993, 39.
[149] Patay 1938; Mozsolics 1942; Butler and Schalk 1984.
[150] Bóna 1975.
[151] Petersen 1972; Burgess 1980a, 295ff.
[152] Petersen 1981; White 1982; Allen *et al.* 1987.
[153] Waddell n.d. [1990], 20.
[154] Dušek 1969.

mations were less well provided for than the inhumations (for instance, they do not possess the long dress-pins so typical of the Tumulus cultures). The cemetery at Streda nad Bodrogom (Král'ovsky Chlmec) contained 67 Bronze Age graves, of which 24 were inhumations, 34 cremations, and 9 'symbolic graves' (i.e. graves with grave-goods but no sign of a body).[155] The largest and most important cemetery of the Middle Bronze Age in central Europe, at Pitten in Lower Austria, had 221 excavated graves, of which 74 were inhumations and 147 cremations; there was a slight tendency for males to be inhumed and females to be cremated, though the numbers are too small to be statistically valid (table 3.5).[156] At Gemeinlebarn F, a single cremation was found among the 258 graves, presumably indicating an exceptional individual or circumstance of death.

Table 3.5. *Burial rite by sex at Pitten*[157]

	Inhumed	Cremated
Male	23	3.5[1]
Female	12	25.5[1]

Note: [1]These numbers are not integers because of uncertainties over assigning sub-adult individuals to sex.

With the Late Bronze Age Urnfields, cremation becomes absolutely dominant, but 'bi-ritual' cemeteries are also found. At Przeczyce in Silesia there were 727 inhumations and 132 cremations;[158] at Grundfeld in Franconia roughly equal numbers of each.[159] On the other hand, there are very many large Urnfield cemeteries which utilised exclusively cremation – for instance Moravičany (Mohelnice, Moravia), which had 1260 registered graves, only one of them definitely not a cremation,[160] or Vollmarshausen (Kassel), with 252 recovered graves, all by cremation.[161] This is a standard pattern for much of central Europe in the Late Bronze Age, as well as for large parts of the Mediterranean areas, Scandinavia, France and elsewhere. Not surprisingly, the change to cremation as standard burial rite has been seen as a reflection of profound changes in attitudes to death, with preservation of the body after death no longer being seen as important. For this reason, some authorities have sought to place major ethnogenetic changes at the start of the Urnfield period, new beliefs representing the arrival of new peoples.

[155] Polla 1960.
[156] Hampl *et al.* 1981/1985; Benkovsky-Pivovarová 1985; Teschler-Nicola 1982–5.
[157] Teschler-Nicola 1982–5, 201.
[158] Szydłowska 1968–72.
[159] Feger and Nadler 1985.
[160] Nekvasil 1982.
[161] Bergmann 1982.

The interplay between inhumation and cremation achieves a curiously paradoxical culmination in the fact that grave forms originally created for the inhumation rite came to be provided with cremations. The most striking examples are perhaps the coffins and cists of Denmark, which in Period III frequently contained cremations,[162] but another case is the pit graves of Champagne, large enough for an inhumation but actually containing a cremation.[163] A curious combination of coffin and cremation is to be seen at an Únětice burial with 'indirect cremation' at Jessnitz, Kr. Bautzen, where fire was applied to a body already lying in a plank coffin; this deduction was made because the ash all lay in the upper part of the burial, and was not present lower down.[164] If the grave itself was a symbol of one sort and the treatment of the body another, this situation represents a kind of conflict of symbols. Although commonly regarded as indicating a major shift in beliefs, the maintenance of the grave forms of an earlier period may suggest that the symbolism of container was stronger than that of the treatment. There are many possibilities for interpreting this phenomenon in terms of competing ideologies; the desire to place the deceased within the tree, interpreted above as the source of life or the womb, here remained dominant.

In view of the very abundant evidence for the Urnfield rite throughout Late Bronze Age Europe, one might wonder whether differences between particular cemeteries are significant. The number of sites is so large, and the time over which the rite was utilised so extensive, that it seems only to be expected that one site will differ markedly from the next. In fact, many sites are remarkably similar, and within a given area the repetitious nature of the evidence lends the phenomenon a leaden quality from which all but the hardiest have retreated. Nevertheless, inter-site comparisons can be instructive. Olausson, for instance, looked at Piledal and Svarte near Ystad on the south Scanian coast and found that, though they were broadly contemporary (mainly Period V), there were marked differences between them that could not altogether be accounted for by taphonomic factors, important though these were.[165] Urn burials, for instance, were commoner earlier at Svarte, only becoming the norm in the late period of use at Piledal; there were generally more bronze objects at Svarte, including two graves with an unusually high number and several bronzes exhibiting fine workmanship. The Svarte cemetery was larger, reflecting a population consisting of an estimated two extended families as opposed to one at Piledal. Yet both sites seem to have served as burial places for contemporary populations within a short distance (*c.* 20 km) of each other. The suggestion has been advanced therefore that the apparent wealth of the

---

[162] Broholm 1944, 138ff., 291.
[163] Chertier 1976, 55.
[164] Wilhelm *et al.* 1990.
[165] Olausson 1986.

Svarte cemetery reflects groups who controlled both coastal and inland resources, including coastal trade.

The differences between contemporary cremation cemeteries in the same area have also been explored.[166] Larsson showed the existence of five hierarchical strata in the cemetery of Fiskeby near Norrköping in south-eastern Sweden, with the degree of differentiation increasing through time into the Iron Age; various factors such as population increase, changed economic relations and conflicts of interest were suggested as being responsible. Skjöldebrand looked at the differences between Fiskeby, Klinga and Ringeby, all in the same area. On all sites, the commonest burial type was the cremation pit with urn and pyre debris, but whereas at Fiskeby and Klinga this accounted for well over half the burials, at Ringeby it was a much smaller proportion, other special burial types making up the remainder; stone constructions were also much commoner there, and pots found in many more graves. The cremated bone also appears to have been treated differently. These differences are taken to reflect differing social conditions on Ringeby as opposed to Fiskeby and Klinga, it being suggested that elites maintained a stronger dominance at the latter compared with the former.

In view of the large number of graves on Urnfield cemeteries, one might expect there to be significant evidence for spatial ordering of the graves. In some instances this has been reported, but in general little interest has been evinced in this aspect. At Vollmarshausen six discrete deposition areas were identified, separated by unused space (fig. 3.12); these areas were interpreted as family burial zones, each with a somewhat different burial history and particular traits of burial practice – for instance the provision of lids to the urns, commoner in some areas than others. Given a total use period of some 500 years, family sizes of three to seven individuals can be reconstructed from these burial zones.[167] At Gemeinlebarn F three deposition zones were identified, which it is suggested could represent the burial places of three contemporaneous family groups (fig. 3.13).[168]

Pyres

Cremation burial usually implies that the body was burnt on a pyre.[169] The reconstruction of such elements is almost entirely conjectural: there are no surviving pyres, only the possible spots where they once stood, in the form of blackened or reddened stretches of ground, usually surviving where they have been protected by the heaped-up earth of a mound. Some have thought that the 'heaps of fire-cracked stones' so common in Scandinavian archaeology

[166] Skjöldebrand 1995; Larsson 1985.
[167] Bergmann 1982, 106.
[168] Neugebauer 1991, 131.
[169] McKinley 1997 for a full discussion of cremation, pyres and pyre debris under barrows.

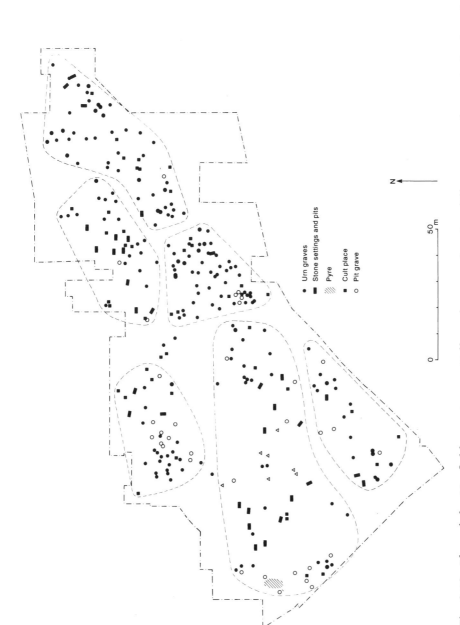

zFig. 3.12. Plan of the Urnfield cemetery at Vollmarshausen, showing different grave forms, 'cult places' and pyre (burnt area) (after Bergmann 1982). The dashed lines separate areas interpreted as the burial zones of individual families.

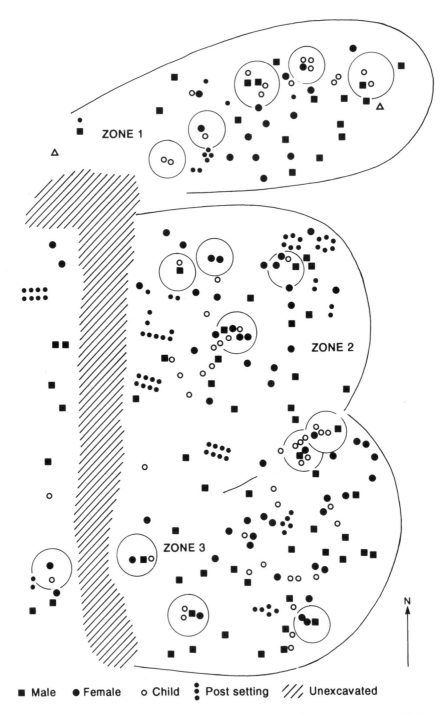

ZONE 1

ZONE 2

ZONE 3

N

■ Male ● Female ○ Child ⦂ Post setting /// Unexcavated

Fig. 3.13. Gemeinlebarn F. Hypothetical reconstruction of three contemporary burying communities. Circles indicate possible family groups (after Neugebauer 1991).

are in fact the remains of cremation pyres, and experimental evidence shows that this is possible, if not likely in every case.[170] Pyre traces have been recorded in a number of sites. At Dolný Peter, some of the inhumation graves with ring-ditches also possessed 'hearths', which were perhaps pyres where the cremations that also occurred on the site took place.[171] A late Urnfield barrow at Illingen in Baden-Württemberg contained a wooden chamber that lay in a charcoal spread interpreted as a pyre, a phenomenon more usually found with flat graves;[172] one example of such a pyre can be seen at Haunstetten in Bavaria[173] and another at Melbeck tumulus 3 (Lüneburg), where the molten remains of both female and male bronze objects were scattered through a substantial burnt area.[174] In Scandinavia, pyre debris was incorporated into burials from Period V on, in the form of charcoal and sooty earth mixed in with the cremated bone.[175] Structures interpreted as the remains of cremation installations, in other words pyres, are seen at the Moulin cemetery at Mailhac in southern France.[176] Some Wessex barrows had burnt areas underneath with the remains of burnt bone in them;[177] these traces vary in size and shape. The case of Bulford G.49 is remarkable: a rectangular space was defined by stakes, timber was laid in it lengthwise, and the whole thing fired.[178] At Poor's Heath, Risby, the blackened area in and under the barrow was nearly 8 × 7 m in extent and had apparently been hollowed out of the mound rather than pre-dating it.[179] At Snail Down site III, Wiltshire, a pyre of substantial timbers, about 2 m square, was built on the grass surface and fired, prior to the interment of the ashes in an urn over which a turf stack was erected.[180] Traces of a pyre were found at Cloghskelt, Co. Down, Ireland, and possibly at other sites on that island.[181]

Cemetery enclosures

The concept of enclosure in connection with burial finds an expression in other forms too; it is not merely the substantial barrows of the Early Bronze Age that made use of such features. In the Urnfield period, for instance, the cemeteries of western Europe – western Germany, the Low Countries, France – made frequent use of the *enclos funéraire* to define individual deposition

---

[170] Kaliff 1994; 1997.
[171] Dušek 1969.
[172] Quast 1992.
[173] Wirth 1991.
[174] Laux 1996, 161.
[175] Stjernquist 1961, 100ff.
[176] Janin 1996, 26f.
[177] Grinsell 1941a, 92f.
[178] Hawley 1909–10, 619.
[179] Vatcher and Vatcher 1976, 271f.
[180] Thomas and Thomas 1955.
[181] Waddell n.d. [1990], 20.

areas. An air photograph of a Late Bronze Age cemetery in these areas would show a mass of small ditched features, the ditches usually round (*Kreisgraben*) or in some cases in the northern half of the Low Countries and in Westphalia keyhole-shaped; less frequently oval or sub-rectangular.[182] The small round ditched enclosures were mostly small barrows such as were common in many parts of the Urnfield distribution. The larger features seem genuinely to have defined 'funerary enclosures', which in some cases in the Netherlands contained wooden post structures.[183] At Broussy-le-Grand (Marne) a rather slight penannular ditch defined an area 13–14 m across and contained a number of bone groups as well as pottery, stone, burnt chalk and charcoal.[184] This site recalls the penannular cremation enclosures in Britain such as Catfoss, Whitestanes Moor and Loanhead of Daviot,[185] while southern English cremation cemeteries such as Simons Ground show obvious similarities.[186] The sub-rectangular enclosures are less common, but they are seen at Aulnay-aux-Planches (Marne), for instance, where they contain cremations;[187] on the same site was found a long rectangular enclosure that is interpreted as cultic (see chapter 9). At Telgte, Kr. Warendorf, Westphalia, a cemetery extended over some 2 ha and in the investigated part 73 ditches of various shapes and 131 cremations were recovered, including 9 long ditches, 16 round ditches, and 35 keyhole ditches, 16 of them with complex wooden constructions (fig. 3.14).[188]

These enclosure ditches defined special areas. The keyhole shape cannot have any such functional significance as is the case with mounds, and even the sub-rectangular enclosures cannot realistically have been covered by barrow mounds. One can compare the shape with that of pendants of late Urnfield and Hallstatt date in central Europe, notably the East Alpine zone, often seen as anthropomorphic, perhaps copying a skirted human figure.[189] What is important is the recognition of their symbolic import and their variability, which contrasts with the otherwise uniform funerary rite, with poor grave-goods.

Other special treatment of the dead

Because I have been concentrating on temperate Europe so far, the existence of special forms of burial in the Mediterranean has gone unmentioned. While the rock-cut tombs of Castelluccio, Thapsos, Pantalica and elsewhere in Sicily

[182] Verwers 1966, 1972, 13ff.; Wilhelmi 1974; Chertier 1976, 57ff.; Kooi 1979; 1982.
[183] Kooi 1982, 6f., fig. 2.
[184] Chertier 1976, 64f.
[185] Burgess 1980a, 317ff.
[186] White 1982.
[187] Brisson and Hatt 1953.
[188] Wilhelmi 1981.
[189] Kossack 1954b, pls. 15, 17.

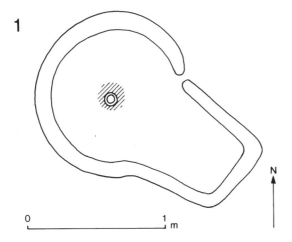

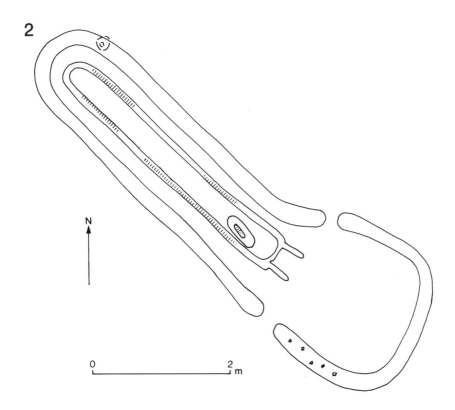

Fig. 3.14. Telgte, Kr. Warendorf, Westphalia. 1. 'Keyhole grave'. 2. Long grave with inner ditch and cremation, and sherd scatter in the outer ditch (after Wilhelmi 1981).

were a local phenomenon and do not necessarily imply special treatment of the dead, the provision of imported Greek pottery at Thapsos reflects the ability of local elites to acquire exchange goods by virtue of their inherited or achieved status. Still more remarkable are the monumental constructions of some Mediterranean islands: the 'giants' graves' of Sardinia and the *navetas* of the Balearics, to name but two forms. Giants' graves (*tombe di giganti*), essentially long megalithic tombs with elaborate carved stone facades and semi-circular forecourts formed by projecting hornworks, belong mostly in the Early Bronze Age, though some go on later.[190] *Navetas* are also elongated monumental stone structures with an interior chamber, the dating of which is concentrated in the second millennium BC.[191] Both forms present many of the same problems and interpretative possibilities as megalithic tombs of the Neolithic, since they are collective tombs where individuals could not be identified once defleshing had occurred. It is certainly arguable, however, that there were special requirements to qualify for burial in one of these tombs, in other words that they represent aspects of power exercised within the communities that erected them.[192]

In many instances the accompanying goods may indicate the craft or occupation of the occupant, notably through metalworking tools and other comparable equipment. The Catacomb Grave burial in kurgan 4 at Novaya Kvasnikova (Volgograd), accompanied by a sledge with wooden runners and items of equipment suggesting that the deceased specialised in arrow production, is more unusual (fig. 3.15).[193] But none of these cases involves special treatment of the corpse, as far as one can tell. On the other hand, the faces of the bodies at Sergeevka (Kherson, Crimea) were covered with what appeared to be masks – the eyes with balls of ochre, clay and black soil, the mouths with soil, and the nostrils with soot and powdered shell.[194] This may not have been a mask in the usual sense of the word, but it is certainly striking, as the excavators point out, that these sense organs were closed up. This may have been connected with the common practice of plugging orifices at death, but equally it may have been intended symbolically, providing the dead with a special persona for the grave. The use of ochre is another special feature, going back to the Copper Age;[195] its red or yellow colour must have been part of its special significance.

Another special form of burial took place in caves. Caves used for burials are especially common in France and Belgium, as with the Grotte des Duffaits

---

[190] Webster 1996, 78ff., 104ff.
[191] Pericot García 1972, 59ff.; Veny 1974; Castro Martínez *et al.* 1997, 60ff.
[192] See Webster 1996, 81ff.
[193] Yudin and Lopatin 1989.
[194] Novikova and Shilov 1989.
[195] Häusler 1974; 1976.

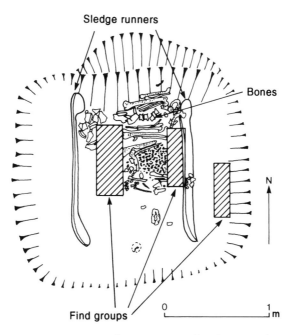

Fig. 3.15. Novaya Kvasnikova, Staropoltavkino, Volgograd, kurgan 4, burial 5. Burial of a craftsman, with sledge runners (after Yudin and Lopatin 1989).

in Charente,[196] the Trou de l'Ambre and other sites in upland Belgium,[197] the Grotte du Hasard in Gard,[198] and many other sites. It is difficult, and probably misleading, to separate these caves from those which are regarded as having had a cultic significance (see below, pp. 317ff).

Grave-robbing

The disturbance of graves in antiquity is frequently attested on Bronze Age burial sites. This is especially true of tumuli, where, however, much of the digging is of relatively recent date; but it is also very common on flat inhumation cemeteries.[199] At Gemeinlebarn F, only 14 of 258 graves were undisturbed; most were disturbed to a greater (113) or lesser (92) degree. Sometimes the grave-robbers confined their activities to the removal of objects (presumably metal); sometimes the bones were disordered; in extreme cases the whole skeleton was removed.[200] Inevitably there is less evidence for the disturbance

---

[196] Gomez 1973.
[197] Warmenbol 1988.
[198] Roudil and Soulier 1976.
[199] Raddatz 1978; Rittershofer 1987.
[200] Neugebauer 1991, 112ff.

of cremations, since they did not usually contain such a quantity of metal goods. Grave-robbing concentrated on particular classes of object, especially ornaments and especially objects from adult graves.[201] At Pitten near Vienna there was a tendency for daggers to be robbed from male graves, and earlier rather than later graves – presumably by the population that was responsible for the later graves; for unless sizeable amounts of valuable metal were deposited, the objects in question were only of interest to those for whom they were still current, usable items.

This evidence for extensive disturbance is an important consideration when one comes to look at questions of social organisation, since it means that one cannot be sure to what extent one really has a true picture of which buried individuals were rich and which were not. It also carries with it a strong implication that graves were marked on the surface by posts, stones or mounds. Since the graves of the rich and powerful might be more likely to be so marked, these would be the ones most likely to attract attention from robbers, and accordingly inferences on social organisation should be drawn with extreme circumspection.

Epilogue

Burials of the Bronze Age, as of any period, serve a special purpose in the study of the past because of their ubiquity. In the specific context of the Bronze Age, two related studies interact: the relative treatment of individuals within a single site or group of sites; and the relationship between different groups of sites across wider territories. In other words, there is a *macro level* on which to view the evidence (distinctions between different regions of Europe, perhaps corresponding to major ethnic divisions), and a *micro level* (distinctions between individuals or groups of individuals, corresponding to families, moieties or – at most – tribal units).

Much here depends on the specific interpretation adopted for the relationship between contrasting modes of funerary practice – barrows/flat graves, cremation/inhumation, abundant provision of grave-goods/slight provision. The prevailing view has been that systematic differences between regions and phases are significant for the reconstruction of social and political life, and that major shifts of practice in the same region reflect changes in belief systems, which in turn could reflect changing ethnic or linguistic affinity. On the other hand, since many burial forms and accoutrements are largely symbolic in nature and one cannot understand what the symbolism means, it is impossible to predict what the social and personal correlates of such features are. The heaping up of a mound into a barrow was a symbolic act (since all that was needed in functional terms was enough earth to prevent the decay

---

[201] Rittershofer 1987.

of the body causing smells and infection), and one may speculate on whether a return to the womb of 'mother' earth, or another similar metaphor, was envisaged. The connection with wooden grave furniture and tree-trunks is a further aspect of this funerary symbolism.

The contrasting modes of deposition, with their differing approaches to grave-good provision, hinder appreciation of social organisation but do not prevent it altogether. The relative scarcity of 'rich' graves (those with abundant goods) has been interpreted as largely accidental, the result of post-depositional factors. But there are plenty of grounds for thinking that they were always scarce; the predominance of flat cemeteries in central Europe with relatively poor provision does not appear to mask a system of differentiation that would originally have seen some graves (individuals) as exceptionally marked out. Systematic differences between different areas are likely to reflect in part the availability of materials and craft skills, and in part the regional traditions of funerary practice.

Although one might expect from an analysis of other cultural elements that through time Bronze Age burial practice would exhibit increasing complexity and differentiation, this is not in general the case. In those areas where large inhumation cemeteries gave way to large cremation cemeteries, there is little indication that any such structural change occurred, while in the north and west, where barrow burial was replaced by a more mixed rite, including abundant cremation, the change was rather in the reverse direction. Since elaborate metalwork increased in quantity and quality, and other indicators imply an expansion of available means of displaying prestige, the interpretation of the phenomenon comes back to one of practice. Yet it would be wrong to despair of obtaining meaningful information from burial sites. In cases where integration of cemetery data with settlement and other evidence has been possible, a picture of unrivalled clarity has been obtained of Bronze Age living systems. It must be the goal of Bronze Age archaeology to extend and enlarge such analyses to include wider and more diverse areas of Europe.

CHAPTER 4

THE DOMESTIC ECONOMY

While trade and craft production played an important part in the overall structure of economic life in Bronze Age Europe, for most people most of the time what mattered was the procurement of food and the production of commodities in the home. Smiths, traders, even warriors and heroes had to eat and be protected from the elements; and if they did not produce and process their foodstuffs themselves, others in their homes and villages must have done. Yet the study of this aspect of Bronze Age life is curiously underdeveloped. Perhaps because the remains of economic activities are mundane in nature they have attracted little attention, and a narrative account of the domestic economy is still barely possible. Only by supposing that the many gaps in the evidence can be filled in from similar evidence elsewhere, by building a composite picture, can a more rounded account be attempted.

Agriculture and food production

Peasant farming was the mainstay of Bronze Age life. The study of Bronze Age agriculture is based on a number of sources: artefacts, cultivation traces, field outlines and the remains of the exploited materials, plant and animal.[1]

Artefacts

The tools that the prehistoric farmer needed were analogous to those needed by modern farmers, and revolve around the main processes of agriculture: tools to break the ground, remove weeds and bring up nutrients from the subsoil (spades, hoes, digging sticks and ards or ploughs); and tools to bring in and process the harvest (sickles or reaping knives, threshing and winnowing devices).

In a Bronze Age context, the first category is extremely rare. From some wet sites come wooden objects whose function can be reconstructed as being for ground-breaking, principally mattock-like instruments, more rarely ards. The various wetland sites investigated in recent decades have been a prolific source of information in this respect. A unique double digging-stick from

---

[1] Recent works have covered most of this ground in general outline: Fowler 1983; Thrane 1990.

Døstrup (Aalborg) is radiocarbon-dated to 2700 ± 85 and 2620 ± 85 BP.[2] Spades or shovels are very uncommon.[3] The marks of a rounded spade were found at Gwithian, Cornwall, in close proximity to the marks of ard ploughing.[4] Double-paddle spades, as known from Jutland, seem to have started in the Bronze Age, though more are later in date,[5] and many peat spades are known from late prehistoric Denmark.[6] Spades may have played a major part in ground preparation, and are not necessarily inferior to ards in this respect, especially for intensive garden-type cultivation. Indeed, since Bronze Age ards could only scratch a furrow, spades would have been better for creating a tilth since they could actually turn the soil over and bring up the nutrients from lower levels, as well as killing shallow-rooting weeds through light and oxygen starvation.

A suggestion made some years ago, to account for the perhaps surprising lack of tools available for ground-breaking in Bronze Age contexts, was that some of the very numerous bronze axes might have been used for the purpose.[7] They occur commonly in hoards along with sickles, and their numbers might be thought to be grossly disproportionate to the relative needs of carpenter and farmer. In fact Bronze Age hoes, spades, mattocks and ards must almost always have been made of wood, and few have survived.

Ethnographically, there are records of ground preparation by means of trampling and grubbing by pigs, especially on wet ground where plough teams could not operate. Herodotus[8] records this technique for Egypt, and Pliny the Elder also mentions it.[9] Such a technique, which would leave no archaeological trace, could well have been used in the many areas where no tillage tools survive.

What can be well attested is the practice of ploughing with a simple scratch ard. Not only do a few examples survive; there are also depictions on rock art and, most commonly, the surviving traces of ard-marks on preserved soil surfaces, usually beneath barrow mounds. These are commonly in two directions, at right-angles to each other; this was also the case at Gwithian, where the ploughing could be seen to lie within areas defined by banks, that is, in fields. There has been much debate over the years about the function and significance of the ard-marks beneath barrows, of which scores of examples are now known from north and north-west Europe. Some have thought that the marks were found beneath barrows simply because the mound chanced to

---

[2] *Tools and Tillage* 4/1, 1980, 57. Implements from Ukraine also deserve mention: Shramko 1992.

[3] There are some Neolithic finds, e.g. a shovel-like implement found in the Cortaillod levels at Twann: Wesselkamp 1980, 17 pls. 8, 23.

[4] Thomas 1970; Harding 1976.

[5] Lerche 1977; that from Aalestrup (Viborg) radiocarbon dated to 2720 ± 75 BP (*Tools and Tillage* 4/1, 1980, 58).

[6] That from Nørre Omme, Ringkøbing, dated 2450 ± 75 BP.

[7] Harding 1976.

[8] *Histories* II, 14.

[9] *Natural History* XVIII, 47, 168. Tákacs (1982) gives various ethnographic examples.

preserve that part of a much larger ploughed area; others that the area destined to be covered with a barrow mound was specially ploughed in advance
of barrow construction to clear it of weeds.[10] Those who support this theory
point to the fact that grave-pits were often aligned along the axis of the ploughing,[11] though this need not indicate a sacred character to the ploughing, nor
are grave pits invariably so aligned. Given the evidence of the Gwithian
ploughed fields, and the survival of plough-marks under later monuments of
clearly non-ritual character,[12] it seems greatly preferable to view the traces
under mounds as merely part of a larger ploughed field and therefore an indication of how such activities were normally carried out.

The ards that made these marks are somewhat mysterious.[13] Those that
survive archaeologically are light wooden constructions, made from one or
two component pieces, consisting of a main pole or beam, with the actual
ard-share, or sole, pointing back at an angle of around 30 degrees (fig. 4.1).
The one-piece examples, such as those from Vebbestrup and Hvorslev in
Jutland and depicted also on the rock-art panel at Litsleby,[14] were constructed
from a piece of wood, sometimes the bole of a tree, that gave maximum
strength to the implement, but even so the damage and fracture rate must
have been very high.[15] The two-piece ards probably represent an attempt to
make life easier by having a replaceable share, but in practice it must have
been very difficult to keep the share firmly fastened in position as it was
dragged through the soil. The same would be true for the stone shares that
are found in the Northern Isles of Scotland, perhaps Neolithic in date,[16]
Sweden and Finland,[17] and Ireland.[18] These show the expected degree of wear
and battering, but the method of fastening to the beam is not known. Two-
piece ards are also known from the Balkans, as shown by the finding of a
bronze shoe-like share from the Gava layers of the Neolithic and Bronze Age
settlement of Bordjoš in the Banat (fig. 4.1, 7),[19] and a recent find from Eton
in southern England was probably also a two-piece ard;[20] this is arrow-shaped
and radiocarbon-dated to 900–760 BC.

As well as the crook ard, there are a number of examples of the so-called

[10] Pätzold 1960.
[11] Randsborg and Nybo 1984; Rowley-Conwy 1987.
[12] As at the Roman forts of Carrawburgh (Breeze 1974) or Rudchester, and under Bronze Age
house remains at Sumburgh, Shetland: Lamb and Rees 1981.
[13] Shramko 1964; 1971 (Ukraine); Glob 1951 (Denmark); Perini 1983; 1987, 352 fig. 172 pl. 61.309;
Rageth 1974, 196 (Italy).
[14] Glob 1951, 25ff.
[15] Forerunners for such objects can be seen in the 'Furchenstock' and similar implements at
Twann and elsewhere: Wesselkamp 1980, 20f., pls. 14–16.
[16] More than 400 examples are known: Rees 1979a; 1979b.
[17] Damell 1981; Brady 1990a.
[18] Brady 1990b.
[19] Medović 1993.
[20] *British Archaeology*, July 1997, 5.

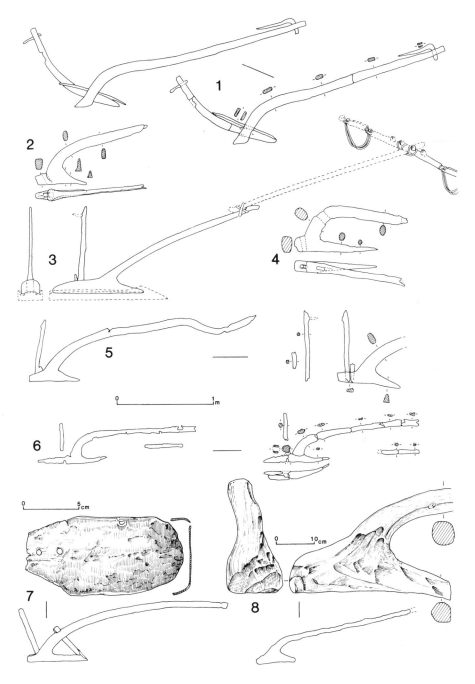

Fig. 4.1. Ards (wood except no. 7). 1. Døstrup (after Glob 1951). 2. Sergeevsk (after Shramko 1964). 3. Lavagnone (after Perini 1983). 4. Tokary (after Shramko 1971). 5. Polesje (after Shramko 1971). 6. Vebbestrup (after Glob 1951). 7. Bordjoš, bronze ard-share (?) (after Medović 1993). 8. Fiavé (after Perini 1987).

bow ard, that from Donnerupland being the best known;[21] the radiocarbon date of 2560 ± 100 BP for the piece from Døstrup (fig. 4.1, 1) indicates a long ancestry for the type.[22]

These ards were rather light, and must have had considerable difficulty operating in heavier soils, though from the distribution of ard-marks it is known that heavy clay soils were ploughed. Reynolds found in experiments that crook and bow ards do not actually make 'ard-marks' in the subsoil, and while bow or beam ards created some disturbance in the soil, crook ards do very little in this respect, being inferior to both beam ards and mattock-hoes.[23] He suggested, therefore, that crook ards were used specifically to create a seed drill rather than to break the ground. To take the place vacated by the crook and bow ards, he has hypothesised that there must have been a 'rip ard' that would actually be capable of creating the marks, perhaps like some of the beam ards seen on Swedish rock art, with a powerful main beam and a substantial ard-share coming down into the ground. Especially at the start of cultivation, after clearance of trees and other vegetation, breaking the ground must have been a major undertaking. The mat of roots that survives a surface fire would have been a major obstacle to tillage by any means; it may not even have been possible to draw an ard through such ground. Initially, therefore, painstaking and laborious digging using sticks, mattocks and spades would have been necessary; but once roots were removed, regular treatment with an ard would have been the major element in keeping weeds down and preventing the regeneration of shrubby plants. There is no evidence that heavier ploughs, 'sod-busters' to use the terminology of Reynolds, were in use in the Bronze Age, though this may reflect only the chances of discovery.

According to the rock-art depictions, ards were pulled by paired animals, probably oxen. The yokes used were presumably similar to those known from other comparable situations, for instance with vehicles or from contexts of Neolithic and other dates.[24] A double yoke from Vinelz (Bern) may belong to the Late Neolithic or Corded Ware layers, though a Bronze Age date is also possible; it is of the type known as a 'neck yoke'. Better dated yokes, probably of the neck type, were found at both Lavagnone and Fiavé, belonging to the Early and Middle Bronze Age,[25] and a yoke from near Loch Nell, Argyll, Scotland, has given a radiocarbon date range of 1950–1525 cal BC (fig. 4.2).[26]

Following the initial preparation of the ground, sowing – by hand – would have taken place, after which there followed a long period when the seedlings and young plants would need to be protected from disturbance by animals or

[21] Glob 1951, 29ff.
[22] Ibid., 36ff.
[23] Reynolds 1981.
[24] Fenton 1972/86; Rees 1979a, 72ff.
[25] Perini 1987, 200, 350f., figs. 170–1, pls. 40, 89; Perini 1988b, 88ff. figs. 40–3.
[26] Sheridan 1996.

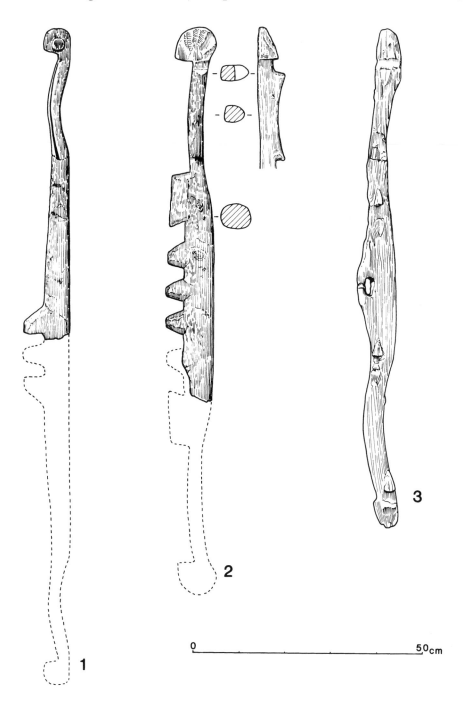

Fig. 4.2. Wooden yokes. 1. Lavagnone (after Perini 1988b).
2. Fiavé (after Perini 1987). 3. Loch Nell, Argyll (after Sheridan
1996).

competition from the more vigorous growth of other, unwanted, plants ('weeds'). Such protection would have taken the form of fences or walls (see below), and the weeding would be by wooden hoes and sticks. The next stage which is visible archaeologically is therefore the harvesting, using sickles that were initially of flint and wood, as in the Neolithic, and then of bronze (fig. 4.3). Enormous numbers of these tools are known; from relatively early in the Bronze Age they appear in hoards, which sometimes consisted of nothing but sickles, but more often appeared along with other tool types. A number of sickle forms have been identified, the commonest being that with flattish tang-like grip and curving blade – the *Griffzungensichel* of German writers, also referred to as a harvesting knife (*Erntemesser*).[27] It is of some interest that this form, though extremely common in continental Europe, was not adopted everywhere. In Britain, for example, there are relatively few bronze sickles, and those that do appear are mostly of the socketed type.[28] Many sickles were probably of wood, or wood with flint inserts, as known from various Alpine lake-side sites.[29] It is also possible that uprooting was practised, but such a practice is unlikely to have been much used.[30] Uprooting is more suited to producing straw, whereas it was the grain that the harvester was seeking; it is only suitable on very light soils where plants can be easily pulled up, otherwise the effort expended is disproportionate and labour excessively time-consuming. In the Mediterranean areas, the arable component of the economy may have been more restricted but was hardly absent altogether. Other tools, such as knives, may have been used for the purpose.

In terms of the processes that followed on from harvesting, such as threshing, winnowing and various forms of cleaning, there are no tools that can with certainty be assigned to such purposes. This is not surprising since in ethnographic situations they are invariably of wicker or similar materials. Here the state of the crop, as represented in carbonised grain finds, can sometimes be of assistance. Recent work has added remarkably to knowledge in this respect,[31] since it is frequently possible to indicate what stage in the processing a given sample had reached, and therefore what processes were being carried out. Parching and pounding must have been carried out after initial cleaning in the case of the glume wheats, such as emmer and spelt, in order to assist in detaching the seed from the husk, and ovens that are found on archaeological sites may in some cases have been for this purpose.

[27] Primas 1981.
[28] Fox 1939; 1941; 87 socketed sickles from the British Isles, 35 unsocketed from Britain, almost all from southern England.
[29] Ledro: Rageth 1974, 193f., quoting also Polada and Lucone; Fiavé: Perini 1987, 306ff., figs. 136–9; Perini 1988b, 90ff. figs. 45–6.
[30] Steensberg 1943.
[31] By Hillman, Jones and most recently van der Veen (1992) with references to earlier work.

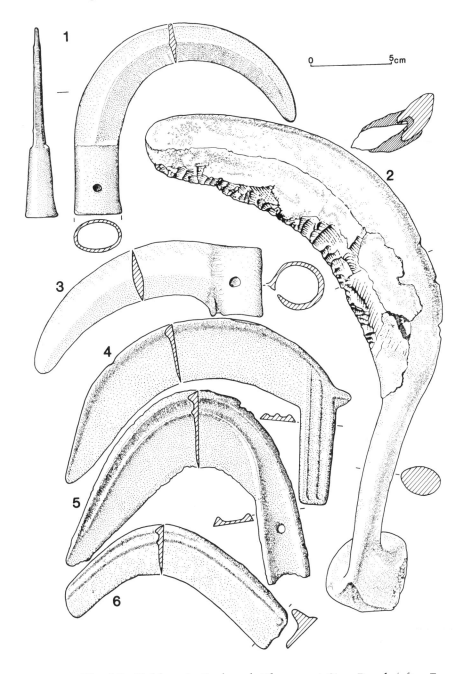

Fig. 4.3. Sickles. 1. Socketed: Thames at Sion Reach (after Fox 1939). 2. Composite (wood and stone): Fiavé (after Perini 1987). 3. Ring-grip: Castle Dawson, Co. Derry (after Fox 1941). 4–5. Flanged (grip-tongue): Grossetzenberg-Polzhausen and Herrnbaumgarten (after Primas 1986). 6. Knob: Neuchâtel (after Primas 1986).

After cleaning, grain would have been used or stored. In many parts of Europe, storage pits were the normal means of effecting this, though not commonly in Bronze Age Britain until the later stages, when practices best known from Iron Age contexts took hold. In continental Europe, such pits were the norm, though relatively little is known about how they functioned. On Knovíz sites in northern Bohemia, pits of various shapes are found, sometimes with the remains of stored grain or acorns.[32] The variability has been shown to be a function of soil type and destruction processes. The frequent occurrence of pits on sites, especially Late Bronze Age sites, in many parts of continental Europe reflects this storage practice; very similar observations have been made in many areas.[33]

On sites built on wet foundations, wooden granaries were provided, as on Swiss sites or at the Wasserburg at Bad Buchau.[34] In these buildings, large storage vases would be placed; such vessels also occur on dry-land sites, and were clearly preferred in situations where for whatever reason pits were not considered suitable, or the technology was found wanting. Sometimes inverted vases are found in pits, as at the Early Bronze Age site of Döbeln-Masten[35] or the Late Bronze/Early Iron Age site of Sobiejuchy.[36] A further suggestion is that grain was stored in the attics of wooden houses, which would account for the frequent presence of burnt grain in house remains.[37] A find from Twisk in North Holland of a circle of pits, with abundant carbonised grain, is interpreted as a corn-stack (fig. 4.4).[38]

The final stage in the process was to convert the gathered material, from whatever source, into food for the table. Inevitably the information on this process is very limited. Finds from the North Italian lake sites have indicated both bread and possibly *gnocchi*; bread and porridge were present at Twann in the third millennium, and bread occurs in graves of the Late Bronze and Early Iron Age in the Münster region,[39] and in a grave at Bellenberg (Neu-Ulm) in southern Germany.[40] Acorns are present in various sites in the Alpine region and elsewhere.[41] What is known about Bronze Age food and cookery represents a series of tiny windows on what must have been a huge fund of knowledge. The crust of *Camelina sativa* seeds on the bread from the Aggtelek cave in north-east Hungary,[42] or the porridge in a pot at Hascherkeller (Landshut, Bavaria),[43] merely indicate the extent of our ignorance.

---

[32] Bouzek and Koutecký 1964; Bouzek, Koutecký and Neustupný 1966, 80ff.
[33] e.g. Zedau: Horst 1985, 32ff.
[34] Stocker 1976, 31f.
[35] Coblenz 1973.
[36] Harding and Ostoja-Zagórski 1984.
[37] P. Rowley-Conwy, pers. comm.
[38] Buurman 1987.
[39] Währen 1984; 1987.
[40] Währen 1989a; cf. Währen 1989b.
[41] e.g. Pascalone, Fimon: Barfield 1971, 72.
[42] Schultze-Motel 1979, 269.
[43] Benefit in Wells 1983, 87f. fig. 77.

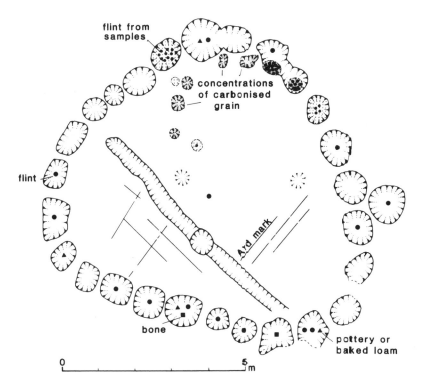

Fig. 4.4. Twisk, North Holland. Middle Bronze Age circular structure, with ard-marks and finds indicated, interpreted as a cornstack (after Buurman 1987).

Plants and animals

It is astonishing how many reports on well-preserved and clearly important sites still include little or no mention of economic and environmental matters, let alone a full specialist report. With honourable exceptions, some to be described and discussed below, it is still hard to find adequate data on the Bronze Age economy from excavated sites in much of Europe. Plant remains tend to have been better treated than animal bones, perhaps because they seem to excavators to be more unusual, and are only spotted in the trench when in considerable quantity, often in a storage pit or vessel. Bone, on the other hand, is both easy to see and abundant, and since the majority is usually unworked (though it may commonly be fragmented by human action) it is often regarded as unglamorous by comparison with artefacts that stem directly from productive activities.

Animals
Although it is abundantly clear that Bronze Age farmers practised a mixed agricultural strategy, at least in temperate lowland Europe (and probably in

other areas as well), the surviving evidence for animal exploitation is very variable, and the study of the evidence differentially developed. In Britain, for instance, where the field evidence for land use is extensive and well preserved, there are very few large assemblages of animal bone available for study. By contrast, in stratified sites in central Europe, such as on Hungarian tells, there are large assemblages of bone but little or no indication from the land about how it was utilised.

Broadly speaking, Bronze Age economies were cattle-based in temperate Europe and caprid-based in Mediterranean Europe, a conclusion confirmed by a recent comparative study of Early Bronze Age animal exploitation.[44] But since caprids and pigs were also important in the north, and cattle in the south, it might be fairer to say that in all areas the animal economy was mixed, with variations of emphasis depending on the local environment. Even in each broad environmental zone there is evidence for variability between sites, probably reflecting either local preferences or a response to environmental differences at the local level. Thus the arid areas of southern Navarra in north-east Spain have produced many Bronze Age sites with hardly any horses on them, while in the adjacent better-watered Zaragoza province horses are present.[45]

Even where the generalisations presented above apply, it is evident that the picture was not a static one, and changes occurred over time. Bökönyi was of the opinion that there was no uniform system of animal-keeping in Hungary during the Bronze Age – or, no doubt, in the rest of Europe.[46] Nevertheless, his account and contributions by other scholars since[47] point to a number of recurring features. Cattle remained the dominant species, but ovicaprids and pigs increased somewhat in numbers, the pig especially towards the end of the period. In Britain, where cattle normally predominate, it has been considered likely that during the course of the Bronze Age sheep became significantly more important and that wild animals decreased as forest was cleared.[48] The increase in importance of caprines is interpreted by some as evidence of the increasing importance of wool products, perhaps in response to a cooler climate. At Runnymede, one of the samples showed a preponderance of pig bones (fig. 4.5). It has been suggested that pigs would suffer less acutely from liver fluke than cattle and sheep, and since evidence for the presence of this parasitical worm was found on the site, this may be a reasonable explanation. Whether a shift towards pigs really represents a move from pasture to arable is harder to say. Other authorities, for instance in central Europe, have believed that climatic changes were the major motive

[44] Chaix 1996.
[45] As at Moncín: R. Harrison, pers. comm.
[46] Bökönyi 1974, 33.
[47] e.g. Bartosiewicz 1996.
[48] Clark 1947; Tinsley and Grigson 1981.

Major animal species: Britain & Netherlands

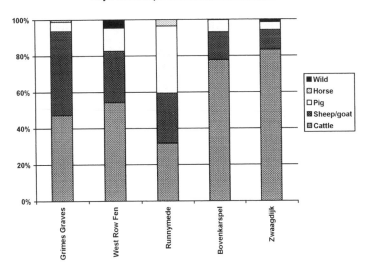

Major animal species: Lausitz

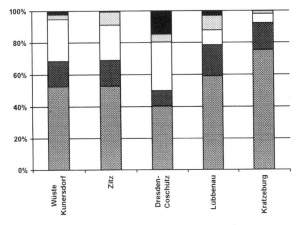

Fig. 4.5. Animal species at sites in north-west Europe (*upper*); Germany (Lausitz culture) (*lower*). Note the importance of pig at Runnymede and Dresden-Coschütz, and the importance of caprines at Grimes Graves.

force in changing exploitation patterns; Bökönyi, for instance, interpreted the increase in pig numbers towards the end of the period as evidence that pigs could adapt more easily to the cooler, damper climatic conditions than other species.

The position of the horse is of great importance and interest, because of the special status commonly accorded this animal in peasant societies. In

Hungary, the evidence for the arrival of the horse is particularly good; at the Bell Beaker site of Csepel-Háros it was the most abundant species, and though it declined in overall importance on sites after this date, it does appear as a regular feature of Bronze Age sites (fig. 4.6).[49] A study of Bronze Age horses in central Europe makes clear that the horse is usually present in bone assemblages from Bronze Age sites; of the larger samples studied, only Zwaagdijk in the Netherlands and Dvory nad Žitavou in Slovakia lacked horses.[50] They are, however, never numerous, typically accounting for less than 5% of the bones recovered. From an analysis of a dozen more or less complete skeletons it could be shown that these horses were small to medium-sized, rather bigger in Slovakia, and that there were no signs of any special selection according to breed in the cases where intentional burials or sacrificial animals are involved.

It is curious, in view of the importance of the horse in other respects, that it is so little represented on Bronze Age sites. In this context the finding of horse hoof-prints sealed beneath gravel used as levelling material in the reconstruction of an Early Bronze Age house at Ullunda in central Sweden is significant (fig. 4.13, lower); domesticated horses are not otherwise known in Sweden until the final phase of the Late Bronze Age.[51] The horses were not pulling a load but may have been carrying a burden, perhaps the gravel in question, in panniers on their backs. While oxen were probably used for pulling the agricultural carts whose remains survive, the light chariot would surely have been drawn by a horse. The finding of harness elements from the Early Bronze Age onwards seems indisputable evidence for the use of horses for draught purposes and perhaps for riding too. New horse harness items in eastern Europe in the earlier first millennium BC appear to show that the horse was by that time used in battle for rapid mobility, probably being ridden.[52]

The virtual disappearance of wild animals in many faunal spectra is in general a characteristic element of Bronze Age sites. There are exceptions to this statement, and the exploitation of wild species never disappeared altogether as long as there were fish to fish and game to hunt. Their presence at a mere 1% at Bovenkarspel does indicate, however, the drastic decline in their importance – perhaps through progressive removal of woodland and other areas where wild animals could shelter, as well as through shifts in cultural preferences. In some areas, however, wild species maintained an important place in the faunal spectrum. Even in developed stages of the Bronze Age, not only red and roe deer but also aurochsen were still being hunted on the Hungarian plain. It comes as some surprise to find that the aurochs was still lumbering

[49] Bartosiewicz 1996.
[50] Müller 1993a; 1993b.
[51] Price 1995.
[52] Gallus and Horváth 1939; Kossack 1954a.

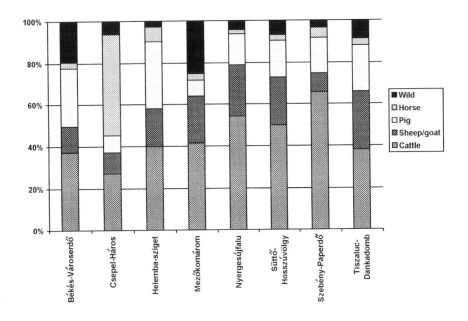

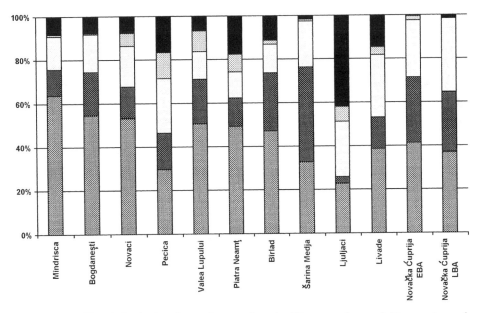

Fig. 4.6. Animal species at sites in Hungary (*upper*); Romania and Serbia (*lower*). At Csepel-Háros (a Beaker period site) the horse is dominant, but at no other site. The proportion of wild animals fluctuates considerably, and at Ljuljaci they constitute the single most important element. At most sites cattle are the dominant species.

about central Europe at a time when much of the landscape was assumed to have been brought into cultivation. Obviously there were still areas where such animals could live, perhaps intentionally maintained areas such as forest and seasonal marshland. Since no field systems survive from this part of Europe, one cannot know to what extent the landscape was utilised as a whole – whether, for instance, the fields that must have been attached to major tell sites extended all the way to the next community's fields, or whether there was a space in between that either could serve as common grazing land or was reserved for hunting.

In much of Mediterranean Europe and parts of the Balkans, transhumant pastoralism has been a significant economic factor in historical and recent times, and a number of authorities have argued that it was so also in prehistory.[53] Twenty-five years ago there was considerably more optimism about the possibilities for identifying such practices from faunal remains than is the case today, and it has been convincingly argued that it should indeed be possible to identify transhumance archaeologically.[54] On this basis, faunal remains should show complementary age profiles between upland and lowland sites, with younger animals being culled in the uplands and older in the lowlands. This is the pattern in Bronze Age samples from parts of Serbia.[55] On the other hand, it is clear that transhumance arises not merely from environmental conditions but rather from a particular set of social and political circumstances,[56] and a number of authors have argued that the archaeological and ecological evidence does not support the idea of Mediterranean transhumance as developed by members of the 'palaeoeconomy school' in the 1960s and 1970s.[57] In north-west Greece, for instance, Halstead denies that transhumance was occurring in prehistory, arguing that as flocks grew in size with the removal of forest cover, there was insufficient pasturage available to feed them all the year round without high mountain pastures being exploited for much of the year.

Flocks were in all probability quite small in the Mediterranean lands in the Bronze Age (excluding the palace societies of Greece), and forest cover still fairly extensive. It is hard to prove that there was either the need or the context for specialised pastoralism in most of these areas. Certainly there was exploitation of some upland locales, but it remains to be demonstrated in most cases that the upland and lowland sites are truly complementary.

[53] e.g. Kilian 1973; Barker 1975; 1985, 57ff.; Jarman *et al.* 1982.
[54] Greenfield 1991.
[55] Greenfield 1986, 256ff.
[56] Cleary and Delano-Smith 1990.
[57] Lewthwaite 1981; Halstead 1987; 1990.

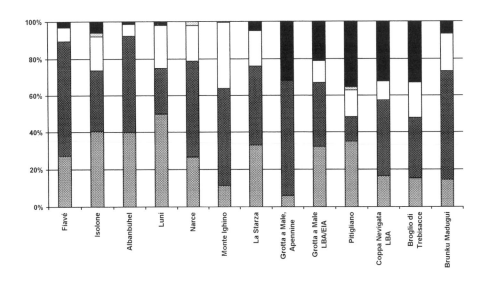

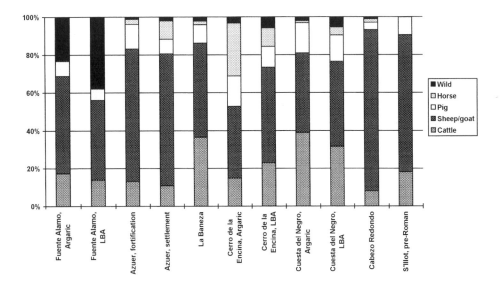

Fig. 4.7. Animal species at sites in Italy and Sardinia (*upper*); Spain and the Balearics (*lower*). In both graphs there is a strong dominance of caprines, though cattle are dominant at Luni and important elsewhere. Note the high proportion of wild species at central and southern Italian sites and at Fuente Alamo.

AREA SUMMARY (FIGS. 4.5–4.7)

Two large and one small faunal samples in the north-west show a massive preponderance of cattle,[58] but at other sites sheep/goat and pigs achieved equal importance in numerical terms (fig. 4.5, upper).[59] Clason characterises cattle-breeding as dominant at all periods since the Eneolithic in Holland.[60] During the Bronze Age, caprines increased in importance somewhat, which she interprets as evidence for a presumed new fashion of woollen clothing. In Scandinavia, a large group of bones from the early excavations at Voldtofte was studied many years ago, but samples studied by modern methods are all small. A recently studied Early Bronze Age group from Torslev demonstrated that all the normal domesticates were present except for horse, and that red deer and fish were also exploited.[61] There are likewise no large samples from Early Bronze Age Sweden, but in Scania at least the indications are that cattle were dominant.[62] A site on an islet off Gotland was dominated by seal bones, and fish are common on coastal sites.

In the Lausitz area of eastern Germany, cattle normally accounted for more than 50% of the total bones recovered in excavation, with pig sometimes achieving significant numbers (fig. 4.5, lower).[63] Only at Dresden-Coschütz were pigs close behind cattle in frequency.[64] Chicken were present at Wüste Kunersdorf (Seelow)[65] and the Bronze Age levels of the cult caves at Kyffhäuser (Bad Frankenhausen) (see p. 318), one of the earliest such records in northern Europe.[66] In Poland, large faunal samples are available from the fortified sites of the Late Bronze and Hallstatt periods. Early results from Biskupin indi-

---

[58] West Row Fen, Suffolk: over 30,000 bone fragments recovered (Olsen 1994); Bovenkarspel: over 17,400 bones recovered (Ijzereef 1981). The picture here compares well with that known from other Bronze Age sites in west Frisia, such as Hoogkarspel, which have a virtually identical species representation. Zwaagdijk: domesticated cattle were most important, with caprines in second place and pigs third (but only 350 identified bones: Clason 1964; 1965, 14f., table 10).

[59] Grimes Graves, Norfolk: Bronze Age midden material in two substantial deposits, the larger of the two – from Shaft X – comprising nearly 4000 identifiable bones (Legge 1992); the cattle bones in this assemblage are dominated by young specimens, in some cases very young: nearly half were killed before they were six months old, a practice which Legge interprets as indicating a predominantly milk-producing economy (Entwistle and Grant 1989 for a contrary opinion, *contra* Legge 1989); Runnymede: Done in Needham 1991.

[60] Clason 1965, 203f.; there is some evidence that in sandy dune areas cattle were less important, for instance at Vogelenzang (Clason 1965, 13f.).

[61] Nyegaard 1992–3.

[62] Kristensson *et al.* 1996.

[63] Kratzeburg and Gühlen-Glienecke: M. Teichert 1964; 1981; L. Teichert 1976; 1986; Ambros 1986; May 1996.

[64] Ambros 1986.

[65] M. Teichert 1968.

[66] The fauna in the 'cult caves' on the south slope of the Kyffhäuser hills included numerous wild species, birds, reptiles, amphibians and fish, as well as common domesticates. Most of these got there naturally, but some may have been connected with whatever cult practices the caves involved: M. Teichert 1978; 1981; M. Teichert and Lepiksaar 1977.

cated the importance of cattle in the overall economy,[67] and the same is true for other sites of the period.[68]

In east-central and south-east Europe the picture is quite variable.[69] Excavation of two pits at Dvory nad Žitavou produced an enormous preponderance of pig bones,[70] and the well at Gánovce also had a significant proportion of pig bones, but this may reflect a special purpose (ritual?) for the site (see p. 315).[71] In general on Hungarian tells, cattle account for around 30–50% of the bones found, with sheep/goat and pig vying for second place; there were sometimes significant numbers of wild animals (fig. 4.6, upper).[72] Some of the most extensive Bronze Age faunal samples available come from Romania, notably in sites of the Noua culture, where cattle are generally dominant (fig. 4.6, lower).[73] In Serbia, faunal samples studied by Greenfield show considerable variation in species representation, though cattle are typically present at 30–40% of the total bone number, with pig and sheep/goat varying in importance and sometimes with a significant number of wild animals.[74]

The extreme variety of Italian environments means that many different faunal spectra are present (fig. 4.7, upper). In Alpine regions, caprovines are

[67] Krysiak 1950.

[68] Ostoja-Zagórski 1974, 127; e.g. Smuszewo: over 19,000 bones recovered (Godynicki and Sobociński 1977), with cattle dominant at 40%, and pig at 33%.

[69] Bökönyi 1974.

[70] Ambros 1958.

[71] Ambros 1959. The presence of bear, beaver, hedgehog, birds and fish in this supposedly ritual well is of interest.

[72] At Békés-Városerdő wild animals accounted for 25% of the total bone assemblage and nearly 30% of the individual animals represented, with 80 wild pig, 89 red deer and 49 aurochsen being present which compare with 230 domestic pigs, 128 sheep/goat, and 273 cattle (Bökönyi 1974). Tószeg: cattle were dominant, but horses also accounted for a significant proportion of the total (Bökönyi 1952). Bökönyi (1952, 105) noted at Tószeg the increase of pig in direct relation as wild animals declined. He subsequently refined and elaborated this picture (1988). In meat weight, cattle were always most important, but at Berettyóújfalu-Szilhalom pig bones were the most numerous, and at other tells in the Berettyó valley they were of equal importance to caprids. More important is the finding that more than half the pigs were slaughtered young, that is for meat purposes, whereas cattle and sheep tended to live longer, and horses, which were uncommon, were mostly allowed to live into adulthood.

[73] At the Noua levels of Valea Lupului, Piatra Neamţ, Bîrlad and Gîrbovăţ the proportions of animal bones indicated that cattle occupied first place, but not overwhelmingly so: they were less than half the total individuals identified, with caprovines, horse and pig all making up a significant part of the whole: Florescu 1964, 165; Comşa 1988. Sixteen of the 22 sites investigated by Comşa had cattle dominant, regardless of period and province. At Piatra Neamţ, the proportion of wild animals reached 17%: Haimovici 1964. At Gîrbovăţ, a recent analysis reiterated the importance of cattle, with caprids in second place and pig in third; horse was present but with only 5% of the material: Haimovici 1991.

[74] Greenfield 1986. Ljuljaci: cattle, wild pig and domestic pig roughly equal at 20–25%, red deer at 15%, caprids insignificant, large number of wild animals. Livade: cattle dominant, pig at 25%, caprids and red deer at 10%. There is some variation between the representation in trenches, pits and features. Novačka Ćuprija: cattle typically around 35%, pigs and caprids each at around 20–25%, few deer.

dominant, as at Fiavé,[75] Albanbühel (south Tyrol),[76] or Ledro. On the Po plain and in parts of the Apennine foothills cattle are numerically as well as economically dominant.[77] But in the higher Apennines, the pattern was quite different, with cave sites showing significant numbers of caprines as well as cattle; the evidence has been interpreted as one where use of the cave by transhumant pastoral groups gave way to its use for permanent settlement as part of new pasturage strategies, perhaps in connection with the advent of more intensive cereal cultivation at Luni and Narce, and by extension elsewhere in southern Etruria and the central Apennines.[78] Finally, in the south and in Sardinia are sites where caprines were numerically dominant but cattle much the most important in terms of meat weight.[79]

In Spain and the Balearics, while some sites have cattle represented at over 30%, the dominant species are sheep and goat (fig. 4.7, lower).[80] On some sites, such as Moncín, extensive use was made of wild mammals, notably red deer but also smaller animals such as badger and rabbit.[81]

ANIMAL REMAINS: CONCLUSION

In spite of inadequate study and survival, a clear general picture of animal resources in Europe in the Bronze Age comes through. In almost all temperate areas studied, cattle were most important. When one allows for the much greater body and meat weight of cattle as compared to pigs and caprines, the preponderance becomes correspondingly greater. Bronze Age economies in temperate Europe were truly cattle-dependent. There is some divergence of opinion, and of evidence, as to whether the animals were primarily for meat

[75] 'Perhaps the largest and best preserved faunal sample from a Bronze Age settlement in the whole of Europe' (Gamble and Clark in Perini 1987), though in fact only selected contexts have been published. The pastoral economy at Fiavé was probably based on wool and milk production, with the additional aim of providing a guaranteed meat supply: Jarman 1975.

[76] Riedel and Rizzi 1995: caprines dominated the assemblage numerically, with cattle in second place and pig in third, but in terms of meat weight cattle would have accounted for nearly 70% of the total.

[77] Luni sul Mignone: cattle are present at up to 50% of the bone assemblage, with caprines at c. 25% and pigs at c. 20%: Gejvall 1967.

[78] Barker 1975; e.g. the Grotta a Male, Abruzzo: during the course of the Bronze Age there was a change from hunting and pastoralism based on caprines to an economy based on cattle and caprines together: in level 4, caprines were dominant over 60%, red and roe deer together c. 25%, and cattle a mere 6%, with no pig: Pannuti 1969. In later levels, deer were insignificant, cattle and caprines equal in numbers, and pigs between 8 and 18%. Pitigliano (Grosseto): de Grossi Mazzorin in Aranguren et al. 1985.

[79] Coppa Nevigata: Siracusano 1995. Of interest here was the increasing role of wild animals as time went on: by the latest Bronze Age levels, turtles and red deer were making up a significant proportion of the total meat provision on the site. Brunku Madugui, Genna Maria and Sant'Anastasia: Fonzo 1986.

[80] Cerro de la Virgen, Granada: von den Driesch 1972; El Azuer and Los Palacios, Ciudad Real (motillas): von den Driesch and Boessneck 1980; Fuente Álamo, Almería: von den Driesch et al. 1985; Cerro de la Encina, Monachil, Granada: Lauk 1976; Milz 1986; Friesch 1987; Son Ferrandell Oleza, Talayot 4, Mallorca: a large assemblage (10,000 bones) from this multiperiod site: Chapman and Grant 1997; S'Illot, San Lorenzo, Mallorca talayotic settlement: Uerpmann 1970.

[81] Harrison, Moreno Lopez and Legge 1994, 453ff.

or for dairying; they were surely used for both. Next in importance were caprines and pigs, their popularity increasing during the period. The benefits of pigs as omnivores, tolerant of a wide range of conditions and useful for land clearance by grubbing, would have been evident – apparently there were no taboos on the eating of pork. Caprines, as all-purpose animals, were both eaten and exploited for milk, wool, skin and horn, and in Mediterranean Europe were usually dominant; here issues of transhumant pastoralism assume an important role. Horses were always present, but not much exploited for food after the Beaker period. Wild animals played only a small part in most Bronze Age economies, though there were exceptions.

Plants

Although plant remains are commonly found, recovery techniques have frequently not been adequate to compose a satisfactory picture of the plant economy of the Bronze Age, and the lack of settlements in many areas and phases of the period also hinders research. Taphonomic studies have illustrated how far plant visibility is dependent on the amount of exposure to fire they receive during processing: thus glume wheats, which need to be parched, are most likely to be represented archaeologically, pulses least likely. Nevertheless, systematic work over the last two decades has enabled specialists to achieve much, particularly in central Europe.[82]

Throughout the Bronze Age, the main grain crops to be exploited were the wheats and barleys; this pattern continues in the Late Neolithic and Chalcolithic. In many areas, these were supplemented by pulses, peas and beans, and by other edible plants that were gathered wild rather than cultivated. A wide range of fruits and berries was also exploited, as the evidence from a number of well-preserved wet sites tells us. At certain times, other grains were also important, and oil plants usually played a role as well. A case has been made that vegetable tubers also played a significant role in prehistoric, including Bronze Age, economies.[83] In other words, a range of species was typically exploited, partly no doubt to provide variety in diet, but partly to maximise returns from a variety of growing environments.

A case has been made for seeing the economy of the Early Bronze Age as much less firmly based on cereal agriculture than is usually thought.[84] It has been argued that in southern Britain this period has none of the features indicating major arable activity (large-scale field systems, storage pits, the

---

[82] Surveys such as those by Hajnalová (1989), Hjelmqvist (1979), Klichowska (1984) and Körber-Grohne (1981) have placed the study of the plant economy on an altogether new footing. A series of regional essays (van Zeist *et al.* 1991) gives an unrivalled and up-to-date picture of the situation of each period including the Bronze Age in each country of Europe. The publication of important sites containing large quantities of macroscopic plant material, such as Hauterive-Champréveyres or Smuszewo, has also contributed greatly to the creation of an overall picture.

[83] Moffett 1991.

[84] Entwistle and Grant 1989.

regular finding of charred grain assemblages). At the same time, it is clear that cereals *were* present in the Early Bronze Age, and likely that field systems were developing at that stage. Although the scale of cereal agriculture was perhaps not large, cereals were part of a mixed system that goes back to the early Neolithic, as the plant evidence from Alpine lake sites shows.

In general, there was little change in this pattern of plant exploitation practice during the earlier half of the Bronze Age. Although the available information is far from complete, the picture is reasonably uniform when environmental factors are taken into account. Around the start of the Urnfield period, however, there was a very marked shift in practice, certainly in terms of species exploited, and probably also in intensity of cultivation. The systematic exploitation of a range of new species was begun, though previously utilised ones continued to be grown as well. Although small quantities of species other than the main grain crops were present earlier in some areas, notably in the Balkans in the Neolithic and Early Bronze Age, it is only around 1200 BC that they become abundant. Specifically, the introduction of regular cultivation of spelt wheat and millet, along with a much more intensive use of legumes and oil-bearing plants, can be demonstrated for many parts of Europe; the origins of the practice can be traced to the Near East.[85] Spelt, for instance, is rare before the Late Bronze Age.[86] There are large finds of millet at a number of sites in continental Europe;[87] in Britain there is possible evidence for the start of rye cultivation.[88] In terms of vegetables, the broad or Celtic bean becomes much more popular.[89] There are also many finds of oil-bearing plants (poppy, flax and *Camelina sativa* – gold of pleasure). *C. sativa* is not usually regarded as a food plant today, but like flax it is a good source of oil and is well attested archaeologically. At Smuszewo, 1950 cm^3 were found; at the Aggtelek cave in north-east Hungary, bread with *Camelina* seeds sprinkled on the crust was recovered.[90]

Explanations for these changes have tended to focus on environmental and demographic trends, and on the potential of particular plants to cope with new conditions. Millet is very hardy and fast-growing, and can tolerate a wide variety of soils and climates, including low rainfall and salt winds; only prolonged drought causes it to fail. It has a high protein content, and because of its very small seeds a low seed volume requirement – its returns are thus

[85] Nesbitt and Summers 1988.
[86] Helbaek 1952b; Jørgensen 1979; it occurs at Toos-Waldi in Switzerland (Behre 1990), at Bad Buchau and Langweiler in Germany (Knörzer 1972), and at Hallunda, Voldtofte and Bromölla in Scandinavia (Hjelmqvist 1979; Rowley-Conwy 1982–3).
[87] e.g. Černošice: Tempír 1985; Zürich-Mozartstrasse: Gross *et al.* 1987; Voldtofte: Rowley-Conwy 1982–3; Fort Harrouard: Bakels 1982–3; Smuszewo: Klichowska 1977; Hascherkeller: Wells 1983; Bornholm: Helbaek 1952a.
[88] Chambers and Jones 1984; Chambers 1989.
[89] Jäger 1965.
[90] Studies by Knörzer (1978) and Schultze-Motel (1979) have emphasised the importance of the plant, and listed many occurrences from Late Bronze Age and Early Iron Age contexts.

relatively large in relation to outlay. It has been used historically in a wide variety of foodstuffs, including porridges and fermented drinks, and was the standard food of Europe's poor in the Middle Ages. It is thus versatile and productive, and a good means of diversifying in crop exploitation. Horsebeans are easy to grow, even on heavy soils, and useful in crop rotation as nitrogen fixers. Their food value is extremely high (25% protein) and they are tasty both on their own, or made into a bean-meal for porridge. The much larger size of beans than peas and lentils means that harvesting is easier; young and tender pods can be eaten whole, and indeed in central Europe today the whole broad bean plant (successor to the Celtic bean) is harvested for animal feed.

Flax, on the other hand, may have been used not just for its oil but as a source of linen fibre, as came to be the case in the Iron Age and Roman periods. The discovery of what have been interpreted as flax-retting pits[91] at West Row Fen and Reading Business Park[92] seems to bear this out, and the numerous flax capsules found at Moncín were also interpreted as evidence for the utilisation of flax for linen production.[93]

I have argued that what is involved in this shift is an attempt to diversify in terms of growing characteristics and yield.[94] Whereas an economy based mainly on wheat, barley, cattle and sheep will usually be successful and productive, it utilises species that demand much the same conditions and are relatively intolerant of variation in those conditions. In such circumstances, millet could produce high yields when wheat and barley could not; beans are suitable in heavy soils and in rotation systems, being heavy croppers and highly nutritious. The shift to oil-bearing plants might indicate changes in cooking practice, or simply reflect changes in taste. Taken together, the evidence suggests a major change in practice at the start of the Late Bronze Age. Both climatic shifts and population expansion have been cited as possible causes; on the other hand, they might be thought of in purely technological terms, reflecting new ways of achieving old ends.

In arid or semi-arid environments, where rainfall was too slight or restricted to the winter months, successful plant agriculture required that irrigation was practised. This is particularly the case in parts of Spain, notably the southeast, and several authors have suggested that the emergence of complex societies was bound up with the creation of irrigation measures.[95] This idea, which would have profound consequences for both social and economic development, has not found universal favour, and a recent investigation appears to show that plant seed remains do not exhibit the characteristics which would

---

[91] Wet pit in which the fleshy part of the flax stem could be rotted off, leaving the fibrous element.
[92] Martin and Murphy 1988; Moore and Jennings 1992, 41ff., 108ff.
[93] Wetterstrom in Harrison *et al.* 1994.
[94] Harding 1989.
[95] Gilman 1976; Chapman 1990.

indicate the existence of artificial irrigation in the Copper and Bronze Ages, suggesting instead that natural conditions were sufficient for plant growth.[96]

AREA SUMMARY (FIGS. 4.8–4.9)[97]

In Bronze Age Britain, the main cereal crops were emmer and later spelt, with barley in some areas, notably in Scotland and also in Ireland, where it was the main crop. Bread wheat and naked barley declined in importance, while conversely spelt increased markedly. Flax was present and there is some evidence that rye began to be cultivated; oats, on the other hand, was at this time present only as a wild grass. Millet does not occur in Britain and Ireland at all.[98] In France a shift from naked to hulled barley is evident, and millet appears as a regular cultivar. A notable assemblage has been recovered from the recent re-excavation of Fort Harrouard.[99] In the Netherlands, a shift has been documented at Bovenkarspel from emmer and naked six-row barley to hulled barley, though elsewhere emmer remained important.[100] Flax and millet, along with a little oats, occur. At Bovenkarspel, large concentrations of carbonised grain were found inside small circular ditches, along with chaff and stem fragments and arable weed seeds. The ditches were interpreted as drainage for the area around corn-stacks.[101]

In Germany one sees strong representation of naked barley, emmer and millet as well as legumes. A mixed crop of einkorn and emmer was noted at Uhingen, spelt at Weisweiler and oats at Langweiler. An increase in weeds of cultivation has been attributed to the increased efficiency of bronze sickles, which could reap closer to the ground than flint ones. In Poland, the rich and prolific sites of the Late Bronze Age and Early Iron Age have produced great quantities of plant material. Barley and millet, with a single wheat species (varying from site to site), were the normal staples, along with legumes.[102] At Smuszewo, vegetable foods, notably peas, beans and lentils, occupied a sur-

---

[96] Araus et al. 1997.

[97] British Isles: Greig in van Zeist et al. 1991; western Europe: Bakels in van Zeist et al. 1991; central Europe: Knörzer, Wasylikowa et al. in van Zeist et al. 1991; Alpine sites: Küster in van Zeist et al. 1991; Scandinavia: Helbaek 1952a; 1952b; Jensen in van Zeist et al. 1991; Mediterranean sites: Hopf, Kroll in van Zeist et al. 1991.

[98] Runnymede: the main crops are emmer and spelt, barley and flax (Greig in Needham 1991, 259); Hallshill (East Woodburn, Northumberland): emmer and spelt wheat, six-row barley, flax, hazelnut and blackberry/raspberry were present. Van der Veen's analysis (1992, 29) suggests that Hallshill belongs, along with certain other slightly later sites in the same region, to a group of sites practising intensive, small-scale subsistence agriculture based on emmer.
     Wilsford shaft: a large collection of wild plant macrofossils, mostly representing species of arable fields, pasture, scrub and disturbed ground, was recovered (Robinson in Ashbee, Bell and Proudfoot 1989). Lofts Farm, Essex: the dominant cereal was emmer with some spelt and barley, and a few grains of oats; a single bean duplicates the finds from Springfield Lyons and Black Patch (Murphy in Brown 1988, 281ff.; Hinton in Drewett 1982, 382ff.).

[99] Bakels 1982–3; 1984.

[100] Buurman 1988.

[101] Buurman 1979.

[102] Wasylikowa in van Zeist et al. 1991.

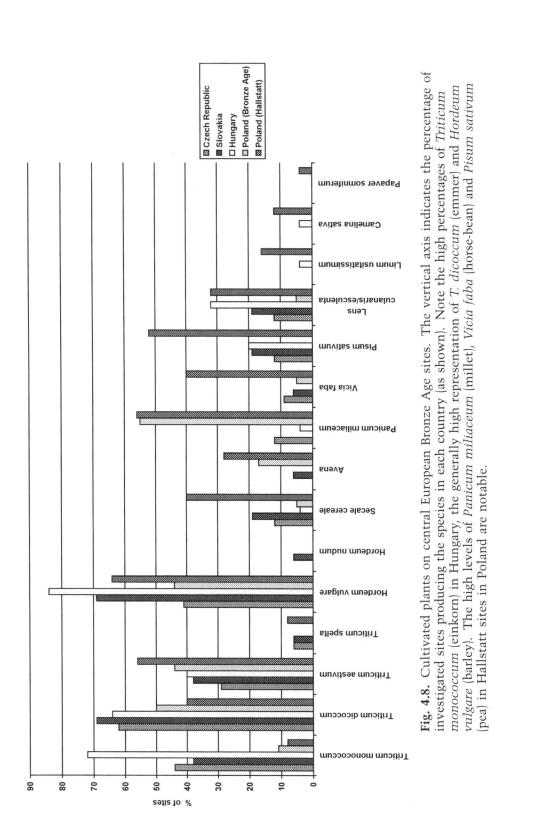

Fig. 4.8. Cultivated plants on central European Bronze Age sites. The vertical axis indicates the percentage of investigated sites producing the species in each country (as shown). Note the high percentages of *Triticum monococcum* (einkorn) in Hungary, the generally high representation of *T. dicoccum* (emmer) and *Hordeum vulgare* (barley). The high levels of *Panicum miliaceum* (millet), *Vicia faba* (horse-bean) and *Pisum sativum* (pea) in Hallstatt sites in Poland are notable.

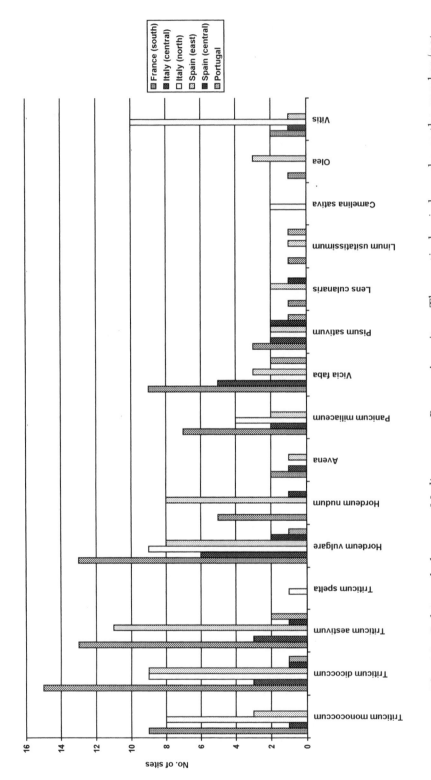

Fig. 4.9. Cultivated plants on Mediterranean Bronze Age sites. The vertical axis here shows the number (not the percentage) of investigated sites where each species is represented, and the low figures for some areas may thus indicate gaps in research rather than genuine absence. As well as the frequent occurrence of emmer, note the importance of *Triticum aestivum* (bread wheat) in southern France and eastern Spain.

prisingly large place in the 52 samples analysed. Very large numbers of seeds of *Camelina sativa* were found, no doubt for use in the preparation of oil. Of the grain crops, emmer was most abundant, but great quantities of millet were present.[103] There is evidence from a number of Danish sites which indicates that the changes found in central and southern Europe affected the north also, particularly as far as the presence of millet was concerned.[104] At Lindebjerg barley was more important than emmer, part of a trend that continued through the Neolithic into the Bronze Age.[105] At Egehøj bread wheat was present and being cultivated as a crop in its own right, along with naked six-row barley and emmer.[106]

A special place is occupied by sites in the sub-Alpine region of Europe by virtue of their excellent preservation of organic materials, including plant remains. Much attention has been paid to the sites on Lake Zürich, where some of the classic sites of Swiss lake research are situated, but also some of the most informative recently investigated sites.[107] Grain crops consisted of several sorts of wheat (emmer, einkorn, bread wheat and spelt), barley and three sorts of millet including broomcorn millet, the most usual variety. Then there were oil plants (poppy and flax), peas, beans and lentils, and perhaps most informative because not found on dry-land sites, wild fruits and berries: apples, raspberries, blackberries, strawberries, pears, sloes, rose-hips, elderberries and nuts (acorn, hazel and beech), as well as various other species which could have been eaten, though they are not primary food plants. A range of species similar to that of the Swiss sites is known from Fiavé, where pears, apples, cornelian cherries and various berries, along with hazelnuts and acorns, accompanied the usual range of grain crops and pulses.[108] Millet appears in the Late Bronze Age, and *Camelina sativa* is also present. Vines are attested regularly through the Bronze Age.

In Slovakia and Hungary, the dominant species were emmer, barley, field peas and lentils (fig. 4.8). Smaller amounts of einkorn, spelt and bread wheat occur; rye and oats are uncommon. Barley was grown as a separate crop. By the Hallstatt period, spelt and bread wheat were much more common, and beans, *C. sativa*, flax and millet had joined the main grain crops as regular finds.[109] In Romania, cereals are mainly barley and spelt, with some einkorn, emmer, rye and millet. Especially rich remains come from the Eneolithic–Bronze Age tell site of Sucidava-Celei (Olt), where in addition to the standard cereals – rye, spelt, *C. sativa* – there are also legumes, vines,

[103] Klichowska 1977.
[104] Helbaek 1952a; Voldtofte: Rowley-Conwy 1982–3.
[105] Rowley-Conwy 1978.
[106] Rowley-Conwy 1984.
[107] Heitz *et al.* 1981; Gross *et al.* 1987, 198ff.
[108] Greig, and Jones and Rowley-Conwy in Perini 1984.
[109] Hajnalová, Hartyányi in van Zeist *et al.* 1991.

acorns and flax.[110] Millet is attested from an early stage of the Bronze Age, though on most sites that have produced plant remains the standard cereal crops are present.[111] Further east, there is evidence from Moldavia and Ukraine of a standard set of crops on excavated sites.[112]

In general, the Bronze Age situation around the Mediterranean reflects the same changes that have been noted in temperate Europe (fig. 4.9). Spelt was grown instead of naked wheat, and in the east barley and a little rye were also grown. The Urnfield period sees a complete change, with two sorts of millet, several legumes, chestnuts and other species being intensively cultivated. The range of plants was surprisingly uniform in spite of the great variety of environments exploited. In Iberia, a broad range of plants is represented on Argaric sites, including several wheat species, two barleys, millet and flax.[113] Pulses are notable in Portugal. At Moncín in north-east Spain, the plant economy was dominated by wheat and barley, with a small contribution from edible wild plants and fruits.[114] Lentils were present, but only rarely. Flax was also found, but whether cultivated or not is not known. The sweet acorns from *Quercus ilex*, the Mediterranean holm-oak, were common, and unlike the tannin-rich products of *Q. robur* could have been eaten either uncooked or roasted; they may also have been mixed with wheat for bread.

Fields

As well as artefactual and biological sources of information, there are the locations where agriculture was carried out, that is, fields. This supposes that, in the Bronze Age, fields really did exist in other places as well as those well-known parts of Britain where they are exceptionally well preserved. Agriculture can be carried on without any formal divisions at all ('open field systems'), merely by changes in utilisation (one crop to another, or sown to fallow).

It is a moot point whether a field is an archaeological site at all. It is detectable not through the area that was exploited, but through the edges, where nothing actually happened. As one knows from the present day, these edges can take various forms: hedges, fences, walls, banks and ditches, or various combinations of these elements, ranging from substantial impediments to the flimsiest and most transitory of divisions. Archaeologically, it is the latest form of these boundaries that one detects. Farmers probably only devoted as much attention to their creation and maintenance as was necessary for the efficient use of the land (clearance of stone) or control of animals

---

[110] Cărciumaru in van Zeist *et al.* 1991.
[111] Sărata-Monteoru, Cîrlomăneşti, Oarţa de Sus: Cărciumaru 1996.
[112] Pashkevich, Yanushevich in van Zeist *et al.* 1991.
[113] Hopf in van Zeist *et al.* 1991.
[114] Wetterstrom in Harrison, Moreno Lopez and Legge 1994.

(creation of impenetrable barriers). Granted that there was no barbed wire in the Bronze Age, much use was probably made of its biological equivalents, the various kinds of thorn bush, wild roses, brambles and the like, which are extremely effective once they have achieved a certain size, and which would have formed hedges (as has been argued for the Neolithic).[115] If, as has been suggested, fields were originally created as strip-like forest clearings with a thin band of uncleared land left between each cleared element, many bushes and shrubs would have been present from the start, and with the increase in light resulting from the removal of trees they would have revelled in the more open conditions. What appears today as a modest bank or wall was probably a much more substantial barrier in prehistory.

In a few instances, it has been possible to discern the presence of fences, either as precursors to walls or as isolated elements of field boundaries. At Holne Moor, Dartmoor, Fleming found a stretch of fencing (represented by small post-holes) running parallel to a reave (stone wall),[116] while another team found that a reave on Shaugh Moor was preceded by a line of posts.[117] Under the great barrow of Lusehøj ran lines of brushwood fences and post-holes, running radially out from the phase 5 grave chamber and therefore presumably not agricultural in function;[118] but the presence of extensive ard-marks in phase 3 shows that the barrow was probably constructed on agricultural land, and the 'mortuary fences' were probably no different in form from agricultural ones. Fence lines were found under barrow mounds at Trelystan, Powys,[119] and Tumuli 14, 20 and 21 at Toterfout Halve Mijl, North Brabant (fig. 4.10).[120]

As mentioned above, the evidence for prehistoric field form comes almost exclusively from north and west Europe, and in a Bronze Age context there is no other country remotely so well endowed with relict fields as Britain. Parts of Scandinavia and the Low Countries have ancient fields, but many of these are Iron Age or even medieval in date. The reasons for this survival in Britain and disappearance elsewhere are not straightforward, but the single most important one is the prevalence of pastoral land use in so much of Britain, particularly the upland areas. Whereas large tracts of continental Europe are occupied either by forests or by arable land, in Britain large parts of both the elevated moorlands and the grass downlands of southern England remained unploughed into the present century, with field monuments experiencing a consequential benefit. The finding of field boundary systems in alluvial plains through air photography illustrates, however, that other factors are at work too. Even in areas where there has been regular flying for many

[115] Groenman-van Waateringe 1970–1.
[116] Fleming 1988, 89ff. fig. 56.
[117] Smith *et al.* 1981, 210, fig. 4.
[118] Thrane 1984, 79ff., figs. 68–9; 93ff., figs 89–94.
[119] Britnell 1982, 160f.
[120] Glasbergen 1954a, 64ff., 76ff., figs. 23, 29–30.

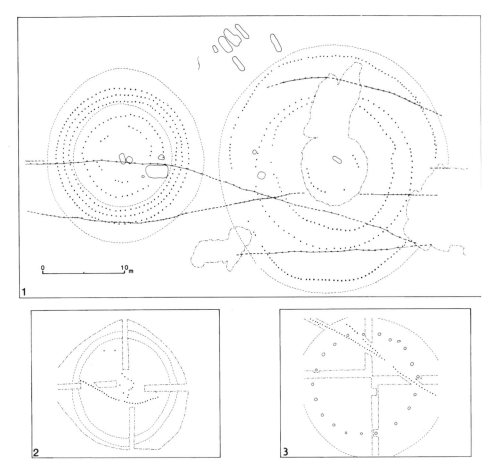

Fig. 4.10. Fence lines under barrows. 1. Trelystan, Powys (after Britnell 1982). 2–3. Toterfout Halve Mijl, barrows 21 and 14 (after Glasbergen 1954a).

years, such as parts of Bavaria or the northern French lowlands, prehistoric field systems have not generally been found, perhaps because deep ploughing has been in progress for so long or because enclosed fields did not exist. They may, however, have been more widespread than has been thought.[121] For instance, a study of Bronze Age development in southern Germany drew attention to various German and Swiss sites that have evidence for terracing and cultivation strips in close proximity to mounds of probable Middle Bronze Age date.[122]

It is common in British archaeology to refer to 'field systems', meaning

[121]   e.g. Bradley's recognition of such systems in northern France (1978), and the work of Brongers (1976) and others.
[122]   Balkwill 1976, 205ff.

agglomerations of fields, but implying that their layout betokened a plan to which they endeavoured to conform. Other authors have referred, with greater accuracy, to 'blocks' of fields, meaning areas covered by fields as opposed to the unenclosed land in between. In fact there is little indication that Bronze Age fields were ever laid out with any kind of master plan in mind.

In the British context, one must distinguish between upland and lowland fields. In lowland Britain, principally central southern England, are found the so-called 'Celtic' fields, so named at a time when most of them were assumed to date to around the time of the Roman Iron Age and to reflect 'native' agricultural practices. In fact there is now extensive evidence to show that these fields had their main period of creation and use in the Bronze Age. These fields are mostly square or rectangular, and as they are often on sloping ground are defined by banks – 'lynchets' – which prevented soil from moving down-slope. The fields seem to occur in small groups, typically a few hectares in extent, and to have been separated by areas without any division into fields. These intervening areas were presumably either woodland or communal pasture. Such a pattern can be seen very well in a number of parts of Wessex, for instance around the hillforts of Danebury,[123] Segsbury, Quarley and Sidbury (fig. 4.11).[124]

The fields probably grew up as a result of both social and technological considerations. Initially, it is suggested that land would be cleared and cultivated in broad strips; these would allow the plough-team an uninterrupted progression from one end to the other (a distance of perhaps 200 metres or more). Subsequently, the strips were divided into smaller, squarish units. This might have been to facilitate the separation of exploited land into different crops; or it might reflect different workers, as for instance when a father divides his land between his sons. In such a situation, there is a choice between expansion on to hitherto undivided land (extension of the field system), or intensification of what is already under cultivation – provided that the plots do not become too small for economic use.

Although these field systems are most easily studied in the Wessex area, where a combination of survival in the field and recognition from the air has enabled the largest body of evidence to be built up, there are many traces in other areas, though relatively few that form 'systems' in the Wessex sense. Fragments, small or larger, are known from Mucking and Lawford (Essex), Fengate (Cambridgeshire) and Fisherwick (Staffordshire), the last entirely (as far as is known) of Iron Age date.[125] It is quite evident from settlement patterns that there must have been intensive agriculture on many other areas of

---

[123] Palmer 1984, 65ff., 109ff.
[124] Fowler 1983, 99 fig. 40; Bradley *et al.* 1994.
[125] Smith 1979; Fowler 1981.

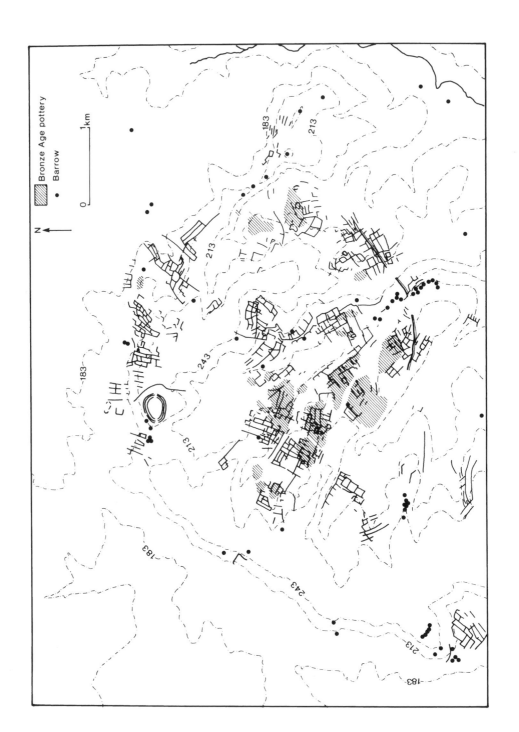

Bronze Age pottery

Barrow

N

0 1km

lowland Britain, for instance on alluvial gravels, but picking up the traces of fields, and more particularly field systems, has proved much more difficult.

This lowland pattern contrasts with a varied situation in the uplands, where many of the field systems are very hard to date. Here it does indeed seem to be the case that the process of field creation went on into the Roman period or beyond. The famous relict landscape near Grassington, West Yorkshire, for instance,[126] is associated with enclosures of Iron Age and Romano-British type, and a number of the upland systems termed 'coaxial' may be similarly late in date.[127] But there is no doubt about the antiquity of many instances of ancient field formation and agricultural activity, whether regular or not. The most famous, and best studied, of these is the extensive series of field systems on Dartmoor in south-west England.[128] There are in fact two types of field system on Dartmoor: small square or rectangular fields, not unlike those of Wessex, and dubbed 'arable' by Fleming; and long strip fields on the higher moors, presumed to have a pastoral function (fig. 4.12). The standard division was the wall of stone rubble, on Dartmoor given the local name of 'reave'. These walls form either long meandering lines running across miles of moorland at roughly the same height (the 'contour reaves') or multiple closely set parallel walls forming narrow strip fields. It has commonly been supposed that the major division walls reflect a situation in which changing patterns of land-holding enabled groups or individuals to parcel out not just a few hectares of land but vast tracts, sometimes termed (in a rather loaded terminology) estates. As with the Wessex systems, it is clear on Dartmoor that areas with fields were interspersed with areas without; the process of enclosure was not continuous across the landscape. Fleming has interpreted this pattern as indicating that groups occupying Dartmoor and adjacent lowlands in the Bronze Age ordered matters so as to ensure access to several different environmental (and thus economic) zones: lowland, moor sides and lower plateaux, and upland.

Although there is evidence from Dartmoor settlements for a significant arable component in the Bronze Age utilisation of the area, in the form of

[126] Raistrick 1938.
[127] Fleming 1987.
[128] Fleming 1988, summarising earlier reports.

Fig. 4.11. (opposite page) Field systems on the Marlborough Downs, Wiltshire, showing field systems (plotted from air photographs) and areas with pot scatters (after Gingell 1992). Note the areas between the field clusters where no fields have been found, which were probably wooded or open grazing land. Note too in the south of the area the line of a 'ranch boundary' cutting through the earlier fields. The ditched enclosure, centre top, is Barbury Castle.

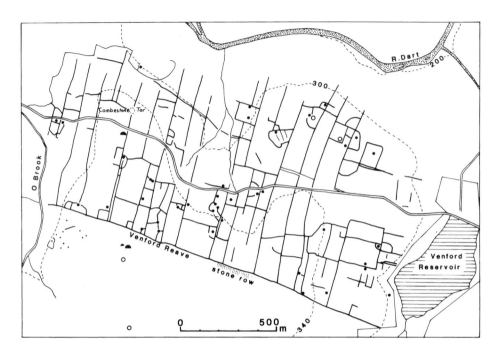

Fig. 4.12. Field system on Holne Moor, Dartmoor, showing coaxial fields and associated settlements (after Fleming 1988). Key: Large filled dots: houses; mound symbols: large cairns; small filled dots: small cairns; open circles: ring-cairns.

Fig. 4.13. (opposite) Animal hoofprints on Bronze Age sites. *Upper*: Horse hoofprints at Ullunda, Sweden. Photograph Gunnar Risberg, copyright Arkeologikonsult AB (courtesy N. Price); *lower*: Mixed hoofprints at Shaugh Moor, Dartmoor. Photograph copyright English Heritage (courtesy G. J. Wainwright and Plymouth City Museum and Art Gallery).

querns, cereal pollen and grain impressions on pottery, it seems unlikely (nor is there any evidence) that the strip fields defined by the stone reaves were used for grain-growing. This would surely have been the task of lower lying land. What, then, were these strip fields used for? The only clear and unambiguous evidence on this point comes from the excavation of a stretch of field and field wall on Shaugh Moor, where the hoofprints of a number of animals were recovered, mainly cattle and sheep but with some horses and a few badger prints (fig. 4.13, lower);[129] these are paralleled in situation if not in context by the horse-prints from Ullunda (fig. 4.13, upper).[130] If grazing was

[129] Smith *et al.* 1981, 214 pl. 14.
[130] Price 1995.

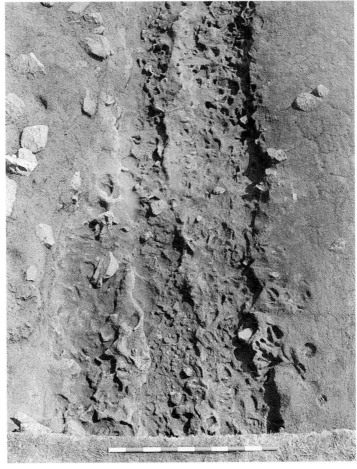

the main use of these moorlands, one might reasonably wonder why so much effort had been invested in the creation of the regular walled fields, when a policy of open grazing would do just as well. The open moor above the fields was, presumably, used in just this way. The main produce of the lower moor slopes, prior to the degradation of the soil that has prevented its economic use in medieval and modern times, must have been grass for use in animal foddering. One suggestion for the shape of the Dartmoor strip fields is that each reave served as a successive barrier in staged grazing, the animals moving gradually across the land in a managed grazing regime. One can see the same strategy today, where a field will be made available to animals strip by strip, a movable electric fence serving to keep them within the allotted area. Depending on growing conditions, any grass that is not then grazed can be cut and stored. This would not be possible if animals had free access to the whole area at the outset. The individual fields in the Dartmoor parallel systems seem typically to be from 5 to 15 ha in size, and their width from 80 m to around double that.[131] Considering the likely grass yield of land at the elevation of Dartmoor, this represents a reasonable amount of pasture for a moderate size of herd or flock to feed on by rotation.

This policy is therefore one of yield maximisation, and there is another factor which might be taken as tending to the same conclusion. One of the continuing and time-consuming tasks of the peasant farmer is the removal of stones from the ground surface. The extent to which this is necessary depends on the ground conditions, but is especially needed in upland areas, off alluvial or clay soils. Dartmoor would certainly have needed removal of stone if stretches of land where movement could be unimpeded were to be available. In some spots, this stone was heaped up into mounds, but in the reave sections it was placed in regular straight rows. Stone removal is by no means a complete and satisfying explanation for the existence of the coaxial reave systems, but it is certainly one factor in their creation. It does not in itself explain why regular straight walls should have been built, only that the stone which went into them had to be removed anyway.

Elsewhere, the situation was very varied but usually much less regular. If one takes the situation in the Derbyshire Peak District or the North York Moors, one finds two recurring elements: small irregular stretches of walling, interspersed with small mounds of stone. These cairns are now universally recognised as emanating from stone clearance activities, and the clusters have long been given the name of 'cairnfields'. They may vary in number from half a dozen to many hundreds, and the area they cover from less than a hectare to many hundreds or thousands of hectares. The stretches of walling that lie between the cairns cannot, for the most part, qualify for the term 'field system', as they are simply too irregular and fragmentary; probably they too, like

[131] Fleming 1988, 65 fig. 37.

the cairns, served as a means of heaping up unwanted stone that had been picked from the ground surface. Rather than continue to create more and more cairns, it would sometimes have been more economic of effort and less wasteful of space to create longer lines of stone, which appear as irregular walls.

Why clear the stone in the first place? And what were the cairnfields used for once the stone had been cleared? In the first place, clearance of stone would in many areas have been essential if any economic activity was to be carried out. There are many stretches of moorland today where the soil has been eroded away and an extraordinarily dense litter of stones results, only suitable for rough grazing (and where bracken has invaded, not even that). In such situations, not even grass can be effectively grown, and the grazing of anything but sheep, and then at a low density, would be difficult if not impossible. Secondly, it seems from the distribution of cairnfields that they may have served as the economic space of individual groups, probably families, much as the small groups of Celtic fields did in parts of Wessex. Each location would then have needed to maximise its returns from its own economic space if the entire demographic pattern was not to break down. As in Dartmoor, it is unlikely that the cairnfield areas were used for arable agriculture; rather for grass production, either for animals directly or for hay crops. Arable was practised, as querns and cereal pollen indicate to us, but probably in the intervening valleys or off the higher land altogether.

These themes can be illustrated from the recently investigated sites of Danby Rigg in North Yorkshire and Highlow Bank and elsewhere in Derbyshire. Danby Rigg is one of the largest known cairnfields in the country, extending for over a kilometre in one direction and over 500 m in the other, and comprising some 700 cairns.[132] In between the cairns are the small stretches of walling, with in one or two cases larger, more regular, walls that may be of later date. Interspersed with the cairns are ritual monuments (barrows and ring cairns) of the Early Bronze Age, and defensive earthworks (apparently medieval in date) cut the hill off from the higher land to the south. This is one of a number of large cairnfields in the northern part of the North York Moors, and may have served a special purpose, perhaps connected with ritual; the norm is a much smaller affair, including perhaps 10–20 cairns and extending over a hectare or two. This is also the pattern seen at Highlow Bank and other Derbyshire sites (fig. 4.14), where the cairnfields are interpreted as having a 'primary function as areas of agricultural activity', and developing in different ways according to local conditions.[133] Much has been written about cairnfields and their function in recent years, but the last word remains to be said about how they functioned in their landscape. The paucity

[132] Harding 1994.
[133] Barnatt 1987; 1991.

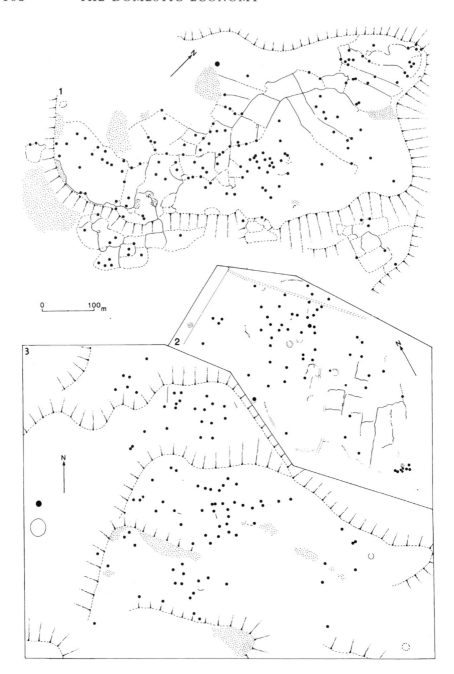

Fig. 4.14. Cairnfields and field systems in the Midlands and north of England. 1. Big Moor, Derbyshire (after Barnatt 1987). 2. Todlaw Pike, Northumberland (after Gates 1983). 3. Eyam Moor, Derbyshire (after Barnatt 1987). The 'fields' are represented by cairns (dots) and rudimentary wall lines; stipple shows areas of uncleared stone.

of evidence associated with them makes it hard to say much about dating and function, and uncertainties are likely to remain.

A further variant on the theme is seen in the enclosures, field banks and cairnfields of Northumberland, which have only been investigated in recent years and about which there is still relatively little information (fig. 4.14, 2). Small and medium-sized cairnfields, in close proximity to enclosures, areas of ridge cultivation and walls or banks, were commonplace; fields varied from 0.1 ha to 2.1 ha in size, with an average of 0.6 ha of enclosed land per house.[134] Individual settlements could have one field or several.[135] To add to the evidence for stone clearance and field formation, the recent discovery of cultivation marks in the form of narrow parallel ridges known as cord rig, as at Snear Hill, Northumberland, is of special interest, suggesting as it does that arable activities were important in these enclosed areas as well as the pastoralism that is widely assumed to have taken place over these northern uplands.[136] Although this narrow ridge cultivation is hard to date, its discoverers have suggested a start as early as the Late Bronze–Early Iron Age transition; it seems unlikely on present evidence to have been a mainstream Bronze Age practice or in use prior to the first millennium BC.

Fields in other areas

Although the best evidence for Bronze Age fields and field systems comes from Britain, other areas do possess them. The well-known Iron Age fields of the Netherlands had a Bronze Age ancestry, in particular at Vaassen, where two phases, labelled 'pre-Celtic field' and 'Celtic field', were identified, the change occurring in the middle of the first millennium BC.[137] On Bornholm, too, field systems are said to emerge during the earlier first millennium BC,[138] and the same is true for parts of southern and western Sweden (fig. 4.15).[139]

Fields: later developments

The story of field creation and use was not static, nor did fields stay in use indefinitely. While the dating of fields is invariably difficult, it is possible to see in some cases that an existing set of fields went out of use, because other features became superimposed on to them. This is the case in a number of instances in southern England in the later part of the Bronze Age. Blocks of

---

[134] Gates 1983, 111 fig. 5.
[135] As at Hazeltonrigg Hill 2 (one field); Linhope Burn, Hazeltonrigg Hill 1, Kidlandlee Dean 1, and others (several fields).
[136] Gates 1983, 114 fig. 11; Topping 1989.
[137] Brongers 1976. Brongers also refers to Bronze Age 'parcelling systems' from West Friesland (1976, 69), though it seems these are not systematically developed fields.
[138] Nielsen 1984.
[139] Windelhed 1984; Mascher 1993.

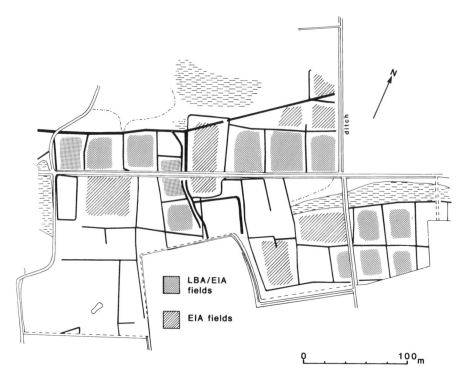

Fig. 4.15. Prehistoric fields at Vinarve, Rone parish, Gotland, showing fields established at the end of the Bronze Age and during the pre-Roman Iron Age (after Windelhed 1984).

fields are traversed by major boundary features, consisting of bank-and-ditch lines ('linear ditches'); sometimes these features continue for considerable distances across the landscape, and join up with defensive structures (hillforts), though in at least some instances they predate these. This process, which can be clearly seen in a number of areas of Dorset, Wiltshire and Hampshire, has been commonly assumed to represent a phase of development in which large 'estates' or 'ranches' were created over wide stretches of the Wessex landscape, probably in connection with a process of settlement nucleation, a move to central places (fig. 4.11).[140] These developments have been seen as representing a move away from arable towards pastoral agriculture, the linear ditches marking the edges of large-scale estates for the keeping of herds of animals.[141] In practice, it must be considered doubtful whether these linear

---

[140] Bowen 1978; especially clear at Quarley Hill but probably also present at Danebury and other East Hampshire sites (Palmer 1984, 65ff., 109ff.), at Uffington and elsewhere in Berkshire (Ford 1981–2; Bradley and Ellison 1975, 183ff., 196ff.), at Sidbury, Wiltshire (Fowler 1983, 99 fig. 40), and elsewhere; see Spratt 1989 for East Yorkshire, where the extensive dyke systems may go back as far as the Bronze Age.

[141] Bowen 1978; Fowler 1983, 189ff.; Bowen 1990.

divisions could ever have been effective for such a purpose, though it is true that by slicing through the lines of earlier fields they imply that the latter were obsolete. The changes that they represent seem more likely to be connected with social than with economic developments.

The field systems of Bronze Age Britain are an astonishing survival, both in scale and in complexity. The changes that they introduced to the Neolithic landscape were no less astonishing. Although discussion continues about the real extent and intensity of woodland clearance in both the Neolithic and Bronze Age, once field systems were in place there can be no doubt that substantial areas were permanently cleared. And the long-term effects were more dramatic than that. In upland areas clearance of woodland and subsequent cultivation meant that an irreversible change occurred in the nature of the land. The onset of podsolisation caused much of the British uplands to become useless for arable agriculture, and to stay like that for centuries. Bronze Age farmers can have had little idea of the permanent impact they would make on the landscape of Britain, if not of Europe as a whole.

Agriculture and food production: summary

It is highly likely that the Bronze Age landscape was divided up into manageable blocks from an early stage, and then subdivided into smaller units which served for the cultivation of particular crops, though these divisions need not necessarily have been marked by permanent or large-scale barriers as they were in Britain. But the evidence of the crops grown shows clearly that discrete areas must have been maintained for the cultivation of each species. Though one cannot impose the British pattern of Bronze Age agriculture on to continental situations, the evidence of tools, plant and animal remains, and vegetational history gives some indication of the importance of subsistence practices, which applied in all areas. It is to be hoped that the widespread adoption of air photography for archaeological purposes will now fill in some of the gaps that are present on the agricultural map of Bronze Age Europe.

CHAPTER 5

TRANSPORT AND CONTACT

If 'no man is an island', no group of people is an island either. Not only were contacts essential demographically for the maintenance of biological groups through provision of marriage partners, they were also a necessary element in the articulation of relationships between different members of the same community and between different communities. They served as channels for the movement of goods, and goods, i.e. artefacts, are the archaeologically concrete expression of relationships, as well as representing the supply of materials wanted for the maintenance of life.

What is being talked of here is trade, or more accurately exchange, since many, perhaps most, transactions that take place in pre-monetary societies cannot be considered commercial in the sense in which the term is understood today. Goods can move between different people, and between different groups or political units in a variety of ways, many of them not 'economic' at all. A range of commentators have shown how within the community most of these transactions are social in nature, depending on reciprocated giving ('balanced reciprocity') that reinforce particular relationships. On the other hand, exchange or procurement of goods outside the community might well witness the effects of bargain-hunting, the desire to get as good a deal as possible, perhaps at the expense of the exchange partner ('negative reciprocity'). Both these cases assume that goods entered communities from outside, that they were available on some kind of supply network, and passed from supply or production area to consumer destination. In order for this to happen, various technological hurdles had to be overcome, including those of transport.

Land transport

There are many forms of transport over land that do not involve wheeled vehicles, and some of these were assuredly used in the Bronze Age. The most basic form of transport is Shanks's pony, i.e. walking, and a variety of carrying devices are known ethnographically.[1] Simple precursors of wheeled vehi-

---

[1] Cole 1954; Fenton *et al.* 1973.

cles were sledges and slide-cars, though little is known of these in a European context.[2]

The wheel is first represented in Europe in the Copper Age, when solid wooden disc wheels appear in various parts of Europe from the Ukraine to Holland and Denmark. Such wheels were part of carts that must have been used for agricultural purposes: there are models of some of them from Hungary and Romania, with high sides or tilts (probably of wickerwork).[3] The earliest such wheels come from sites of the earlier third millennium BC,[4] but by the middle of the second millennium model wagons and disc wheels are found widely through the Carpathian Basin in contexts of the Early Bronze Age; for instance, one of the Romanian models comes from a site of the Wietenberg culture and is decorated in motifs that characterise pottery of that culture. A series of small clay wheels are often interpreted as belonging to model vehicles, though they may also be spindle-whorls.[5] Further west there is very little evidence, other than depictions, between the time of the Corded Ware and the Late Bronze Age, though since the technology existed and wagons were indeed utilised in east-central Europe this must be more a matter of preservation than any real prehistoric absence. In the Copper Age many of the wheels come from wet sites, notably in Switzerland and the Low Countries. For some reason such finds have been less common in Bronze Age contexts, though an exception is the find of four wheels from Glum near Oldenburg in Lower Saxony, which have been radiocarbon-dated to the mid-second millennium BC (fig. 5.1.4), and a find from Catoira (Pontevedra) in north-west Spain with a date at the very beginning of the Bronze Age.[6] Another example came from the Italian *terramara* site of Castione dei Marchesi,[7] and much the same form, though with lunate openings in the solid wood, is seen at Mercurago in Piedmont near Lake Maggiore (fig. 5.1, 1).[8] This same form occurs too in the latest part of the Bronze Age at the Wasserburg near Bad Buchau (fig. 5.1, 6)[9] and at Biskupin.[10] What used to be considered the only tripartite disc wheel from Britain, the ash wheel from a bog at Blair Drummond, Perthshire, has been dated to 1255–815 cal. BC, the later Bronze Age (fig. 5.1, 5).[11] Recently a tripartite disc wheel has been found at Flag Fen, 80 cm across and made of alder, with pegs of oak; this joins an axle found a few years earlier.[12]

[2] Piggott 1968.
[3] Bóna 1960; Bichir 1964; Piggott 1983, 44ff., 83ff.
[4] As with the recent find from Börzönce-Temetődülő, in a pit with pottery of the Chalcolithic Somogyvár-Vinkovci culture (Bondár 1990).
[5] Bóna 1960, 98; Bichir 1964, 12; recent find from Hungary (Bakonszeg-Kádárdomb): Máthé 1988, pl. 9,7.
[6] Hayen 1972; Chapman 1990, 122.
[7] Säflund 1939, 105 pl. 98, 4; Woytowitsch 1978, 26f. no. 1, pl. 2, 1a–b.
[8] Woytowitsch 1978, 27f. no. 2, pl. 1, 2a–b.
[9] Kimmig 1992, 71 pl. 58, 1.
[10] Kostrzewski 1936, 136 pl. 46, 7.
[11] Piggott 1957; *Archaeometry* 35, 1993, 154–5; Sheridan 1996.
[12] *British Archaeological News*, October 1994, 8.

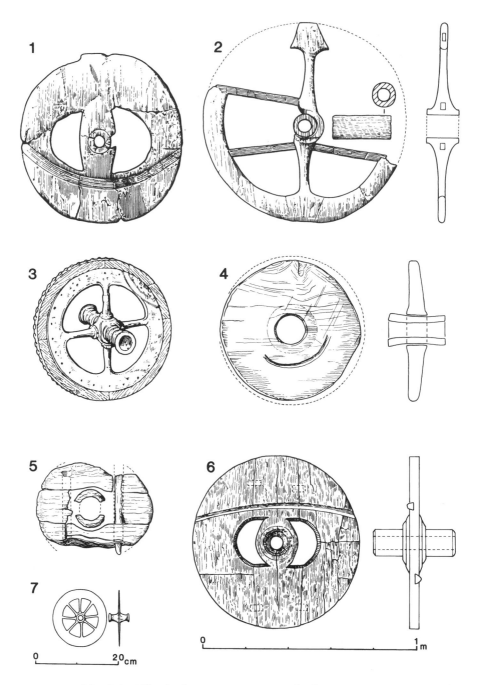

Fig. 5.1. Wheels from Bronze Age vehicles. 1–2. Mercurago (after Woytowitsch 1978). 3. Stade (after Pare 1992). 4. Glum (after Hayen 1972). 5. Blair Drummond (after Piggott 1957). 6. Bad Buchau, Wasserburg (after Kimmig 1992). 7. Strettweg, 'cult waggon' (after Egg 1996). 3 bronze on wood, 7 bronze, others wood.

Such vehicles must have been immensely heavy. If, as seems likely from the models and from surviving wheels, they contained around 1 m³ of oak wood, they must have weighed up to 700 kg.[13] Resting on wheel surfaces only a few centimetres across, they would all too easily become bogged down in mud, and it is unlikely that they travelled very far or very fast. Today, similar carts pulled by oxen move at a slow walking pace: 1.8–2.5 km an hour is quoted as normal, giving a daily figure of 20 ± 4 km,[14] assuming the existence of tracks and relatively dry and level ground.

The possible traces of paving and wheel-ruts have been found on a Middle Bronze Age site at Cham-Oberwil (Zug, Switzerland).[15] The 'paving' consisted of lines of heat-treated stones and potsherds, the wheel-ruts lying beneath them. A piece of paved road was recently excavated near Oxford, a causeway 35 m long and 5 m wide having limestone pieces carefully laid on its surface; timber posts running along the side might have formed a hand-rail.[16]

For faster travel, and for mobility in battle, the light chariot was developed. In Europe, this first appears in the Shaft Graves of Mycenae.[17] The first essential technical advance was the invention of the spoked wheel, or in some instances the cross-bar wheel (fig.5.1, 2).[18] Either way, the intention was to reduce the weight without materially affecting the strength. Early examples of what appear to be spoked wheels occur in the south Russian steppes of the Volga–Ural region,[19] and fine spoked-wheel vehicles are found in Georgia and Armenia in the second millennium BC.[20] Further west, the presence on certain Early Bronze Age sites in central Europe of what are often interpreted as model spoked wheels is important evidence for the spread of light vehicles, and wheel figures also occur on pottery; at Vel'ké Raškovce in eastern Slovakia they are shown as part of two-wheeled vehicles drawn by horses.[21] Such vehicles may be similar to well-known cult pieces such as the clay models from Dupljaja in the southern Banat.[22] These curious objects, the complete one a three-wheeler with bowl-like car and pair of shaft-poles terminating in birds' heads, have four-spoked wheels and presumably represent real vehicles of the period, in this case ritual carts. They do, however, indicate the existence of light two-wheeled vehicles capable of rapid travel in good conditions. Certainly vehicles with spoked wheels were present by the time of rock-art depictions in the Camonica valley, in central-southern Spain and at Frännarp

[13] Estimated by Piggott 1992, 17.
[14] Piggott 1983, 89; 1992, 18 gives 3.2 km per hour.
[15] Gnepf *et al.* 1996.
[16] *British Archaeology* 36, July 1998, 5.
[17] Pare 1992, 12ff.
[18] As known from Mercurago: Littauer and Crouwel 1977; Woytowitsch 1978, 28f. no. 3, pls. 2–3; Piggott 1983, 97ff. fig. 53.
[19] Piggott 1983, 91f.
[20] Piggott 1968; 1983, 95.
[21] Vizdal 1972.
[22] D. Garašanin 1951; Piggott 1983, 109.

Fig. 5.2. Cult vehicle from Strettweg, Austria. Source: Egg 1996.

and Kivik in Scania, but the problem here is that rock art is very difficult to date, and some of the Camonica depictions belong to the Iron Age.[23] Four-spoked and multi-spoked wheels are shown, and at least some of the multi-spoked examples are allegedly Bronze Age in date, even though there are no surviving examples.

In the Late Bronze Age, much of the surviving evidence comes from model vehicles, depicting cult wagons (fig. 5.2).[24] Whether these adequately reflect the real situation in everyday life is hard to say, but they at least indicate the extent to which the technology had progressed. The wheels are usually four-spoked, though fragments and depictions of multiple-spoked versions are known, and some are of solid bronze while others are of wood with a bronze casing. Other vehicle fittings are also found. The presence of vessels and bird

[23] Anati 1961, 142ff.; Woytowitsch 1978, 101ff.
[24] Pare 1992, 19ff.

heads on these vehicles is cultic in nature; the vessels rest on a rectangular chassis and in at least one case there is a pole projecting at the front, for fastening to a yoke or similar arrangement. An early Urnfield group, represented by finds such as those from Acholshausen or Milavče (Bohemia), has flattish solid bronze wheels; the more elaborate later group, sometimes called the Stade type after a famous find-spot in Lower Saxony (fig. 5.1, 3),[25] has bronze sheathing over wood. Fittings of other types indicate that there was considerable diversity of wagon and wheel form by the end of the Bronze Age.[26]

There are also fragments of wheel and vehicle fittings from Urnfield graves, the so-called pyre graves, of which the Bavarian site of Hart an der Alz is the most famous.[27] This was almost certainly a full-size vehicle on which the dead person was laid, the whole being burnt in the funeral pyre. Fragments of nave-sheathing, axle-caps and spoke-sheathing for spokes with expanded ends survive; the felloes were presumably of wood, and there is no indication of metal tyres. Such wheels, and the vehicles from which they emanated, may have been standard Urnfield equipment. They are relatively light – compared to the wooden agricultural carts discussed above – and high in draught. Drawn by horses, they must have been capable of a speed at least twice that of the ox-drawn wagons, though since higher speeds on rough ground would have reduced their lifespan considerably, they were probably used with circumspection. They were not sprung, had no means of reducing friction on the axle parts, no dishing of the wheels to counteract the outward thrust of the load, and without an independently swivelling front axle would have needed a large space in which to turn.

Another twist to the tale of spoked-wheel vehicles comes from the identification of a particular type of spoke which branches into a squarish or semicircular pattern just before it joins the felloe.[28] This design is seen both in depictions and on real examples,[29] and recurs on wheel-shaped pin-heads that are known from Italy and Greece in the Late Bronze Age. It has been convincingly demonstrated that this form was earlier in the Aegean and Cyprus than in continental Europe, and must represent an aspect of cultural transmission from the south-east northwards.

Harness and horsepower

As discussed in chapter 4, the horse appeared for the first time in Beaker and Early Bronze Age contexts in various parts of Europe. Initially, horses were

---

[25] More recently renamed the Coulon group after a new find from the centre of the distribution: Pare 1992, 30ff.

[26] Pare 1992.

[27] Müller-Karpe 1956.

[28] Pare 1987; see Winghart 1993 for further discussion of this and wheel reconstructions from the wagon-grave of Poing, Ldkr. Ebersberg, Bavaria.

[29] As in the case of the fittings for Hart an der Alz, or the complete wheel from Obišovce.

being used as a food source, but it was not long before they were harnessed for traction purposes. The stelae of the Shaft Graves at Mycenae depict animals harnessed to hunting chariots, but in continental Europe there is no such iconographic evidence. Instead, there are the parts of harness equipment, initially in the form of antler 'cheek-pieces' (the side parts of a bridle arrangement, fitting the side of the horse's head, with a leather strap running between them through the horse's mouth). Two main varieties existed: discs and bars, with a few intermediate pieces showing some features of both. The discoid cheek-pieces (Scheibenknebel) (fig. 5.3, 7–8) sometimes have projecting knobs or spikes on their flat surface, believed to be intended to produce a quicker reaction time from the horse by pressing into the sensitive skin at the side of the mouth; this form is not found further west than Romania, with simple perforated discs reaching Hungary. Bar cheek-pieces (Stangenknebel), which developed into the first bronze snaffle-bits, come in a variety of perforation patterns whose precise method of use has been the subject of considerable discussion over the years.[30] The earliest examples are from Hungary, where they date to the Early Bronze Age (fig. 5.3, 1–2, 6).[31] During the course of the Bronze Age similar pieces turn up throughout central Europe and in Italy (fig. 5.3, 5),[32] and (rather rarely) in Britain, as in the Heathery Burn cave find (fig. 5.3, 4).[33] By the end of the Bronze Age in western Europe, bronze hoards quite frequently contain fittings that are believed to have been part of harnessing arrangements.[34]

On the other hand, there is little or no evidence that horses were actually ridden at this stage. It is possible to ride a horse bareback, in which case only horse bones would survive, but it is much more effective to have a proper saddle and harness, including a pair of stirrups. Harness used for riding cannot be distinguished from that used for traction in this period, and the earliest metal stirrups in Europe do not appear until much later;[35] either they were not used prior to this, or they were made of rope or textiles which have not survived.

Pack animals

Beasts of burden must have played a crucial role in Bronze Age trade and transport. As well as the harnessing of horses, depictions on rock art show

---

[30] Mozsolics 1953; Hüttel 1981; etc.
[31] New examples were found recently at both Bakonszeg-Kádárdomb and Berettóújfalu-Szilhalom: Máthé 1988, 35 pl. 9, 3; 28, 1.
[32] Woytowitsch 1978, 117 pls. 52–4.
[33] Britnell 1976; Britton and Longworth 1968, nos. 27–8.
[34] Many such pieces are present in the Isleham hoard, for example (Britton 1960), and in hoards of the Ewart Park phase and its equivalents on the Continent, e.g. the Prairie des Mauves hoard (Briard 1965, 219ff.).
[35] Littauer 1981.

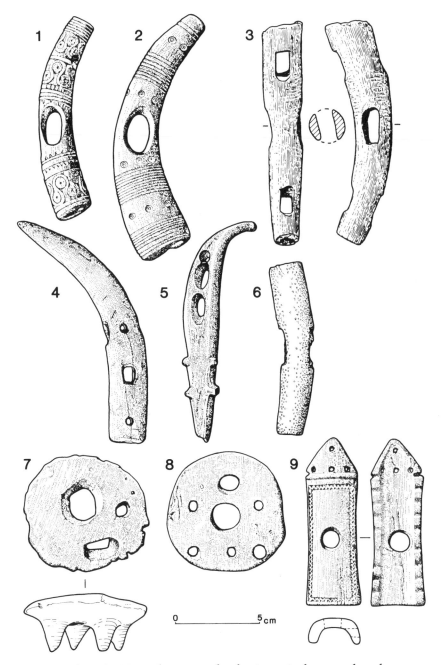

Fig. 5.3. Horse harness: cheek-pieces in bone and antler.
1. Nitriansky Hrádok. 2. Pákozdvár. 3. Bad Buchau, Wasserburg
(after Kimmig 1992). 4. Heathery Burn cave (after Britton and
Longworth 1968). 5. Castione dei Marchesi. 6. Tószeg.
7. Trakhtemirov. 8. Füzesabony. 9. Komarovka. 1–2, 5–9 after
Hüttel 1981.

ploughing scenes using oxen (more rarely horses). With oxen some kind of saddle or pack would have been necessary, probably of wood or leather, or else wagons and carts would have been pulled. Yoking arrangements are shown on models and in rock art (p. 128, fig. 4.2). Similarly, a 'swingletree' (a pivoted crossbar to the ends of which traces are fastened) from White Moss in Orkney gave the date range 1516–1253 cal BC.[36]

It is generally considered that splaying or asymmetry of the metapodial bones in cattle also indicates use of the animals for traction; some experimental work seems to support this.[37] Dimorphism or trimorphism in animal bone samples is usually interpreted in this way: at Bovenkarspel for instance, males, females and castrates are all present.[38] The castrates were presumably used for traction purposes.

Roads, tracks and waterways

The reconstruction of ancient roads in pre-Roman times depends largely on inference from other types of site. Actual roads in the form of wooden trackways occur only in, and were conditioned by the existence of, wet locations, and thus cannot represent the norm for transport possibilities in prehistoric periods. Instead, the location of sites in relation to each other and to natural features provides a guide to the reconstruction of transport routes in the Bronze Age, as in other periods.

Thus while there are no known paved roads in the Bronze Age, with the possible exception of the sites at Cham-Oberwil, Oxford (above) and certain Danish examples,[39] considerable numbers of short stretches of roadway in the form of wooden tracks crossing wet areas are preserved. These are concentrated in a few areas of north-west Europe, though it is becoming clear that there are many more than has previously been realised; there were far more marshy areas in prehistory than there are today (or were even in the Roman period), and they evidently needed to be traversed in certain situations. Thus recent work has shown that many marshy areas existed in east London, and has produced fragments of a number of wooden trackways.[40] The bulk of the evidence, however, comes from a few well-studied areas, of which the Somerset Levels,[41] the Irish Midlands,[42] the east Dutch *veen* near Emmen,[43] the north-west part of Lower Saxony,[44] and parts of Jutland are paramount.[45]

[36] Sheridan 1996.
[37] Bartosiewicz *et al.* 1993.
[38] Ijzereef 1981, 42ff.
[39] Schou Jørgensen 1993.
[40] Philp and Garrod 1994; Meddens 1993.
[41] Coles and Coles 1986.
[42] Lucas 1985; Raftery 1990; Moloney 1993a.
[43] Casparie 1984.
[44] Hayen 1957; 1987.
[45] Schou Jørgensen 1982.

Track-building in these areas took place over a long period, starting in Somerset in the Early Neolithic and continuing in several areas into the Iron Age. A variety of techniques were used; in Holland and Germany, the most usual one was that of laying parallel cross-timbers, corduroy style (fig. 5.4, 1), but in Somerset Tinney's A track was composed of bundles of brushwood, the Eclipse track was made of hurdles (fig. 5.4, 6), while the Meare Heath track consisted of paired planks running longitudinally on transverse bearers (fig. 5.4, 2).[46] In all cases various other timbers were rammed down vertically into the mud in an effort to stabilise the structure.

In most cases in the Somerset Levels, tracks led from one dry island to another, and seen on a wider scale connected the high ground to the south (the Polden Hills) to the Mendips (fig. 5.5). Almost all go north-east to south-west across the grain of the land, and it is therefore likely that they represent a small part of a larger transport route connecting inland areas with the coast. The flat lands of Holland are less flat than they appear to the untutored eye: slight raised sandbanks separate areas that would be wet if they were not effectively drained, and it is between these small dry islands that the tracks run. When one considers the construction methods of the Wasserburg or Biskupin, it seems highly likely that trackways were present in the vicinity of these sites but have not yet been discovered.

The existence of ridgeway routes has been presumed from the location of sites along them.[47] The case of the Berkshire Ridgeway is often mentioned in this connection, usually in an Iron Age context; but these hills had been used since the Neolithic (e.g. the chambered tomb of Wayland's Smithy), and the Bronze Age occupation of Ram's Hill also indicates that links along the Ridgeway must have gone back at least to this period. The antiquity of other ancient ways, such as the Icknield Way running from Norfolk to Wiltshire (the Berkshire Ridgeway forming part of it), could also go back as far as this; other examples are the so-called 'Jurassic Way' between Lincolnshire and Dorset and the 'Pilgrims' Way' on the North Downs of Kent and Surrey. The country around Hampshire hillforts, for instance the Danebury–Sidbury area, is a good example of a landscape where well-informed guesses may be made as to the routes passing through. Such work replaces completely the speculative surveys that were popular in earlier decades.[48]

Goldmann has put forward a case for reconstructing an extensive network of waterways in Europe, and particularly in Brandenburg and the Berlin (Spree drainage) area.[49] His theory that a number of prehistoric or medieval earthworks were built specifically to manipulate water flows is hard to prove in

[46] Coles and Orme 1976; Coles *et al.* 1982; Coles and Coles 1986, 117ff.
[47] Taylor 1979, 31ff.; Coles 1984.
[48] e.g. Hippisley Cox 1927/1944.
[49] Goldmann 1982a; 1982b; 1982c.

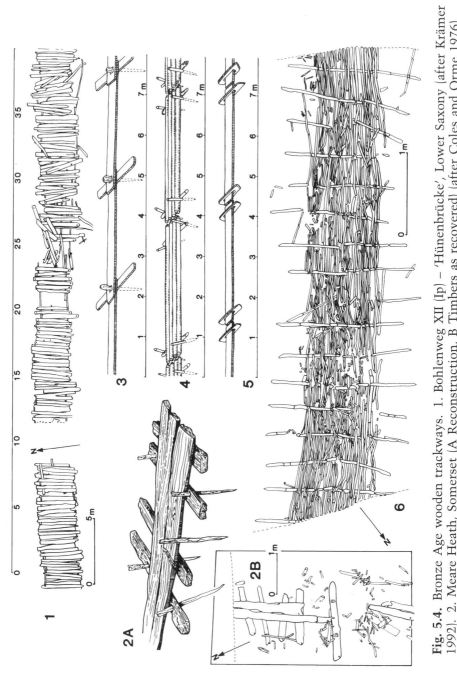

Fig. 5.4. Bronze Age wooden trackways. 1. Bohlenweg XII (Ip) – 'Hünenbrücke', Lower Saxony (after Krämer 1992). 2. Meare Heath, Somerset (A Reconstruction, B Timbers as recovered) (after Coles and Orme 1976). 3–5. Bou XVII, XVIII and XVI, Holland (after Casparie 1984). 6. Eclipse Track, Somerset (after Coles et al. 1982).

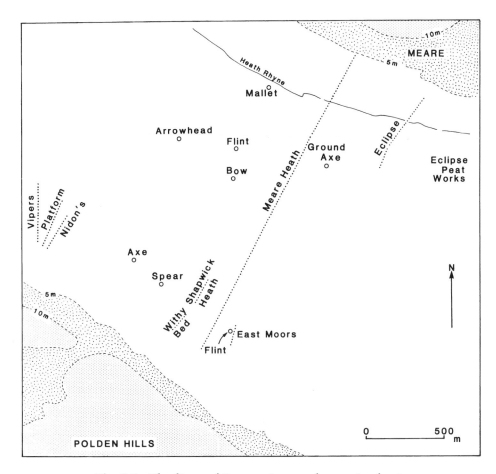

Fig. 5.5. The lines of Bronze Age trackways in the Somerset Levels (after Coles *et al.* 1982). Many of these run from the Polden Hills to the raised ground around Meare.

detail but plausible in general terms. On the European scale, it has been a matter of discussion since the work of Sprockhoff in the 1930s that natural routes existed along which people and major commodities passed (fig. 5.6).[50] The method adopted was to plot the distribution of finds (in Sprockhoff's case that of hoards or individual finds of imported bronzes) over a map of medieval trade routes, which themselves followed natural features such as mountain passes and rivers and have often been duplicated by modern transport links such as railway lines. Such an approach was also adopted by Navarro for the 'amber routes', though its shortcomings were tellingly analysed by Stjernquist.[51] Horst, working along the same lines, claimed to be able to

[50] Sprockhoff 1930, 145ff. pl. 45.
[51] Navarro 1925; Stjernquist 1967a; 1967b.

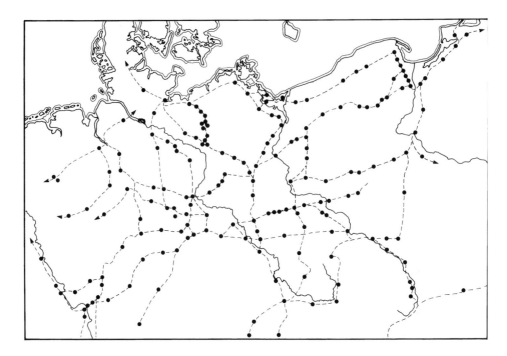

Fig. 5.6. Sprockhoff's attempt at representing Late Bronze Age trade routes in northern Germany and Poland. The circles are points where hoards or imported goods were found. Only major rivers are shown here (after Sprockhoff 1930).

identify a long-distance trade centre in the region of Brandenburg, where a cluster of imported objects is known along with what appear to be local copies (as with the pottery bowls with 'bosses' (circular depressions) in imitation of bronze vessels).[52]

Transport routes at the local level have been claimed in a number of areas. Damell's study of Södermanland (south-west of Stockholm) pointed to the existence of various natural routes, with proximity to water playing a key role (sea level was relatively over 15 m higher in this area in prehistory).[53] Cairns over 10 m in diameter are placed near the Bronze Age coast, and rock carvings and bronze artefacts also show a tendency to cluster along presumed transport routes.

Movement of goods by land: discussion

Wheeled vehicles in the Bronze Age had primarily a local role, either in agriculture or for use in battle. What they were not was the Bronze Age

[52] Horst 1986.
[53] Damell 1988.

equivalent of articulated lorries thundering through Europe on major arterial routes. Even in the Near East, depictions of vehicles for purposes other than warfare and display are relatively infrequent. One is that at Medinet Habu in Egyptian Thebes, where the adversaries of the Egyptians at the battle of the Delta in year 8 of the reign of Ramses III (c. 1186 BC) are shown with their camp followers, who have wagons with solid or wicker sides drawn by oxen. This intriguing picture raises all sorts of questions, many of which are equally relevant to barbarian Europe. What kind of surface did these vehicles travel on? Did they need paved surfaces or (more likely) would they be capable of travelling on dust tracks, at least outside the rainy season? How fast and far could they travel? Did they commonly convey the household possessions of a family? Could they be used to transport goods as well?

In Europe, dirt tracks were the norm and must have experienced considerable 'drift' in wet weather as travellers and convoys endeavoured to find firm ground. For this reason, wagons are unlikely to have been the main mode of transport for traded goods; instead, pack-animals must have played a crucial role. In the Near East, caravans of animals were responsible for moving the traded commodities of the great cities, including bulky and heavy material such as metal; so when bulky goods were moved around Europe, convoys of animals (oxen, horses) were probably used.

Water transport[54]

Although there are still a considerable number of Bronze Age boats of one sort or another in existence, and an enormous number of depictions, the great majority of these are not sea-going vessels but rather intended for use in rivers and creeks, or at most along coasts. Of the two sorts of boat known, the more common was the dug-out canoe (fig. 5.7).[55] These craft were made from half a tree-trunk, hollowed out in the middle and provided with certain additional features such as a detachable stern-board. They vary considerably in size, the largest being around 16 m long, the smallest under 3 m.[56] It is presumed that they would usually have been paddled or possibly poled, since they do not often incorporate facilities for fastening oars to the gunwales, and the objects that survive[57] are paddles rather than oars; they were present at Biskupin (fig. 5.8, 3–4),[58] and examples were recently found on the foreshore at North Ferriby, near the find-spot of the famous boats (below),[59] on the wetland

[54] Casson 1971; Johnstone 1980; McGrail 1987.
[55] McGrail 1978; 1987, 56ff.; Arnold 1985; Lanting and Brindley 1996.
[56] Ibid., 88, 325.
[57] Such as the find from the river Crouch at Canewdon, Essex: Heal in Wilkinson and Murphy 1995, 152ff.
[58] Slaski 1950, 167f. fig. 11.
[59] *British Archaeology* 3, 1995, 5.

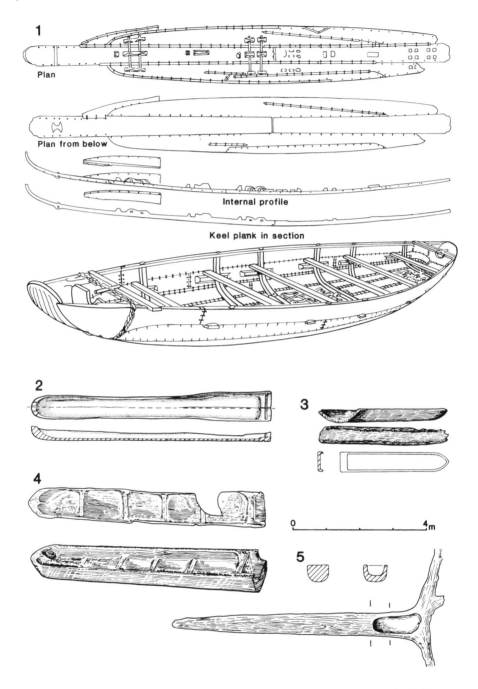

Fig. 5.7. Bronze Age boats. 1. North Ferriby, sewn plank boat (after Wright 1990). 2. Short Ferry, log boat (after McGrail 1978). 3. Mercurago, log boat (after Castiglioni 1967). 4. Twann, log canoe (after Ammann *et al.* 1977). 5. Untersberger Moor, Salzburg, unfinished log boat (after Hell 1913).

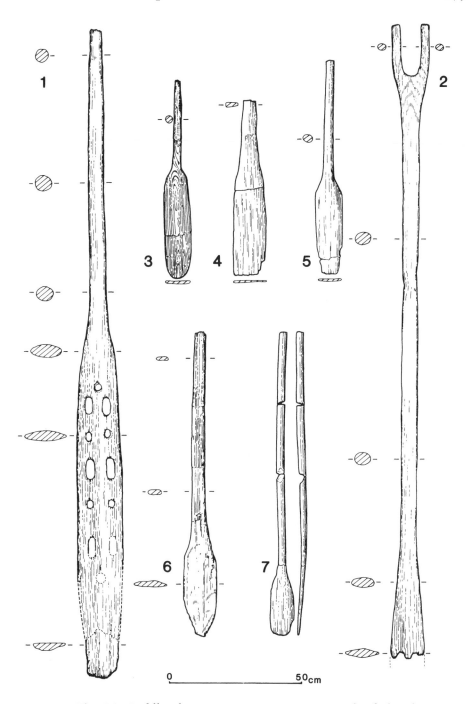

Fig. 5.8. Paddles from Bronze Age sites. 1–2. Clonfinlough, Co. Offaly (after Moloney 1993b). 3–4. Biskupin (after Slaski 1950). 5, 7. Bad Buchau, Wasserburg (after Kimmig 1992). 6. Steinhausen, Zug (after Gnepf and Hochuli 1996).

settlement of Clonfinlough, Co. Offaly (fig. 5.8, 1–2),[60] and in a pile site at Steinhausen (Zug, Switzerland), giving a Late Bronze Age radiocarbon date (fig. 5.8, 6).[61] In a very few instances, rowlocks or holes for thole-pins are present.

Such craft are inherently very unstable, largely because they do not have the beam (i.e. breadth) to compensate for their great weight relative to their narrowness, so that they would be liable to roll if they were not handled with great care, unless they were used in pairs lashed together (a number of finds have been made of two or more boats in the same locality, but in no Bronze Age example are they known to have been used in this manner). For this reason, it has usually been supposed that they would have been suitable only for movement in calm water, primarily lakes and rivers. Examples are known from several parts of inland Britain and Ireland (fig. 5.7, 2),[62] as well as from certain Alpine and sub-Alpine lakes,[63] for instance at Twann and Erlach-Heidenweg on the Bielersee (fig. 5.7, 4),[64] from the Federsee in Baden-Württemberg,[65] from Italy (fig. 5.7, 3),[66] as well as from Lower Saxony[67] and elsewhere. A canoe of this sort was discovered half-finished on the Untersberger Moor near Salzburg (fig. 5.7, 5);[68] the tree (a fir) had been felled, the roots left in place and hollowing-out of the interior had been started; another example came from Tündern, Kr. Hameln, in Lower Saxony.[69]

The other type of craft is known only from rare survivals in Britain, and consists of multiple piece boats, sewn together with withies and other fibres.[70] Examples of this type of boat have been known since the discovery of vessels either side of the river Humber, notably at North Ferriby on the north and at Brigg on the south side (fig. 5.7, 1),[71] though a recent (disputed) reassessment of the Brigg 'raft' sees it as a round-bilge boat with a bent frame, the earliest example of its kind.[72] These vessels were clearly used to undertake river crossings and exploitation of the creeks on either side of the river; it had not been thought that they would have been suitable for open sea crossings. Startling new light has, however, been shed on this type of boat by the discovery in 1992 in the area of the Roman waterfront in Dover of a well-preserved boat of this kind, presumed to be *c.* 15 m long (one part remains

---

[60] Moloney 1993b, 51ff.
[61] Gnepf and Hochuli 1996.
[62] McGrail 1978; Lanting and Brindley 1996; new finds from Co. Mayo: Robinson and Shimwell 1996.
[63] Arnold 1985.
[64] Ammann *et al.* 1977; Suter *et al.* 1993.
[65] Paret 1930.
[66] Castiglioni 1967; Castiglioni and Calegari 1978.
[67] Ellmers 1973.
[68] Hell 1913; Ellmers 1974.
[69] Ellmers 1973, 25ff.
[70] McGrail and Kentley 1985; McGrail 1987, 98ff.
[71] Wright and Wright 1947; Wright 1990; McGrail 1981.
[72] Roberts 1992; McGrail 1994.

in the ground) and up to 2.20 m wide.[73] It is hard to imagine what this boat would have been doing other than operating in the Channel. Its broad beam and flat base would have made it fairly stable in a moderate sea, though it cannot have travelled very fast (there is no indication of a mast for the attachment of a sail, so that like the dug-outs it must have been propelled entirely by paddling).

There is a considerable amount of evidence available on the vessels in use in the Mediterranean world for the transport of materials. The shipwrecks from Cape Gelidonya[74] and Ulu Burun[75] will not add greatly to knowledge of boats since hardly anything of the structures has survived, nor do vessels like the funerary boat of Cheops help since this was a special-purpose boat which, if it ever sailed, would have operated on the relatively calm water of the Nile.[76] Depictions in the Aegean area include those on the Miniature Fresco at Thera, where the boats are plainly plank-built affairs with masts and elaborate superstructures. Since Aegean goods were transported to the central and west Mediterranean, such vessels were probably used for the purpose. It is likely that long open sea crossings were avoided, and coast-hopping was the main type of movement; this would be relatively easy as far as Sardinia, and potentially beyond to southern France, the Balearics and Spain, possibly even beyond the Straits of Gibraltar. Since Bronze Age anchors of Mediterranean type, and ox-hide ingots, have been found off the Bulgarian coast,[77] clearly the Black Sea was also within range.

Hugging the coast was not always successful as is evident from the wreck sites that eloquently mark the places where ancient voyages came to a sudden and unforeseen end (fig. 5.9). These are commonest in the Mediterranean,[78] which is not surprising in view of that sea's known role in trade throughout the whole of antiquity, but they are also known from southern England,[79] southern France,[80] and Spain,[81] in addition to the famous Turkish Bronze Age wrecks mentioned above. The finding of Early Bronze Age pottery in the sea off Lipari in the Aeolian Islands is also suggestive,[82] and a Mycenaean stirrup jar was found off Capo Graziano.[83] Since the chances of finding other major trading stations in south Italy and Sicily must be declining, given the

[73] Parfitt 1993.
[74] Bass 1967.
[75] Bass *et al.* 1989.
[76] Lipke 1984.
[77] Frost 1970; McCaslin 1980; see also Harding 1984a, 49, 241.
[78] Parker 1992.
[79] Langdon Bay, by Dover Harbour, and Moor Sands near Poole: Muckelroy 1980; 1981.
[80] Rochelongues and Cap d'Agde, Hérault: Jully *et al.* 1978; Bouscaras 1971; Bouscaras and Hugues 1967 – the Cap d'Agde finds were made in isolation with no sign of a boat, but were very likely from a wreck – not listed in Parker 1992.
[81] Huelva: Albelda 1923; Almagro 1940; 1958; 1974; analyses in Junghans *et al.* 1974, 256ff., Rovira 1995; Ruiz-Galvez Priego 1995 for an alternative, ritual, interpretation.
[82] Ciabatti 1984.
[83] Bernabò Brea and Cavalier 1966, 171.

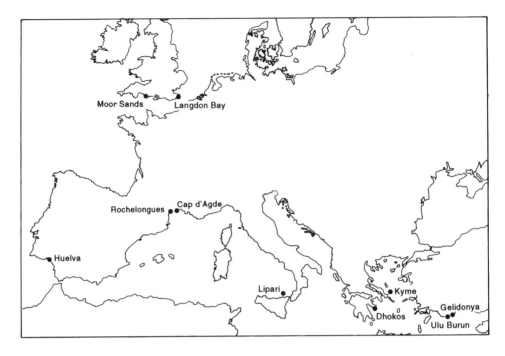

Fig. 5.9. Bronze Age wreck sites around European shores.

intensive use of the coastline at the present day, the best hope for a new find which will revolutionise understanding of the trade with Greece is a wreck site in the area around Sicily or Sardinia.

The discovery of cargoes and boats on the southern English coast raises the question of the nature of seafaring in the Channel in the Bronze Age. While it is not certain that the Langdon Bay finds emanate from a wreck, the metalwork is mostly of continental types that are not at home in Britain, and Northover's work has demonstrated how continental metal was in widespread use in north-west Europe, including Britain. McGrail has suggested that three routes across the Channel would have been in use from the second millennium BC: the Rhine to the Thames; the Seine to the Solent; and the Rance (St Malo) to Christchurch harbour (Poole).[84] Other routes, for instance the direct crossing at the shortest point and the westernmost route between western Brittany and Cornwall, along with coastal movement on both sides of the Channel, he sees as having come into operation in the first millennium. In practice, there is little evidence for the dates at which particular routes came to be utilised. Bronze Age finds at Mount Batten, for instance, might suggest

[84] McGrail 1993.

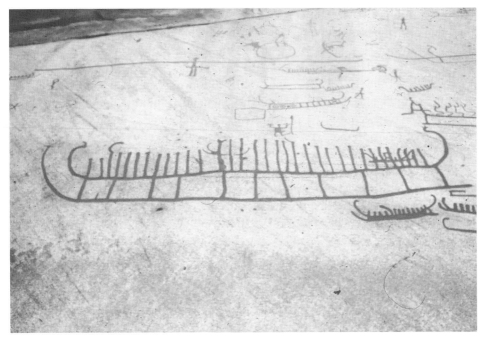

Fig. 5.10. Boats from a rock-art panel at Vitlycke, Bohuslän, western Sweden, showing the wooden framework, raised prow and stern, and vertical dashes on the deck, possibly indicating the crew. Photo: author.

an earlier use of this western route;[85] while the supposition that Christchurch harbour saw Bronze Age use is speculative in the absence of a significant Bronze Age presence in the area, for instance at Hengistbury Head.

Scandinavia

The decorated rock panels of Scandinavia represent one of the most prolific sources of information about Bronze Age boats, even though to date not a single *in corpore* find of a boat has been made (fig. 5.10). Tens of thousands of such depictions are known from all the countries of the North, and especially Sweden and Norway, and more are being discovered all the time. As well as depictions on rock art, those on bronzes provide another rich source of information, which number several hundred and, though no easier to interpret, are generally more distinct.[86]

Much debate has taken place about the precise form and method of con-

---

[85] Cunliffe 1988.
[86] Kaul 1995.

struction of the boats.[87] Since the engravings are not consistent in the way they depict the vessels, even at the same locality, this is not surprising. Thus different authorities have interpreted the depictions in radically different ways: as skin boats or as plank-built boats for instance. Although it has been pointed out that wood was the main building material in Bronze Age Scandinavia, and that the plank-built Hjortspring boat only post-dates the Bronze Age by a couple of centuries,[88] the fact that no single plank-built Bronze Age example has yet been found in Scandinavia seems to reduce the likelihood that they were the normal form. On the other hand, until the Dover boat was found in 1992, sewn boats as known from the Humber were thought to be suited only to riverine traffic, and a peculiarity of northern England. There is little or no information about seagoing vessels outside the Mediterranean in the Bronze Age.

In spite of these uncertainties, there are certain features of the boats of Scandinavia whose interpretation is not in doubt. They have such high prows and sterns that it is not always possible to tell which is which; sometimes they have a projection at the water-line in the manner of the beak known on many ships from antiquity, perhaps a safety device for preventing accidental damage when beaching or sailing close to rocky shores. The outlines of the vessels as shown presumably represent the outlines of real craft, but even here there are puzzling features. For instance, do the lines drawn inside the outline represent a wooden framework or are they decorative? And most curious of all, do the rows of dashes shown projecting above the gunwales represent the crew members (oarsmen) shown schematically? If so, there would appear to have been considerable variation in the number of crew present. On occasion there are structures shown on the decks of the vessels, but as these are often in conjunction with human figures clearly engaged in ritual activities (dances, horn-playing), these may well have been related to sacred practice rather than navigational necessity.

However one interprets the details depicted on these boats, there are certain implications for society and economy. Whatever their method of construction, they represent a considerable investment of time and resources for their owner or owners. Assuming that wooden parts represented a substantial proportion of the boat (certainly the frame, potentially also the walls of the boat), there are obvious time and skill inputs to consider. Even such a minimal wooden element would require a substantial amount of carpentry time; if skins were used for the hull, they would need curing and treating to ensure that they were watertight. Both these raw materials would have been plentiful. If Gilman is right to view the rise of elites in terms of the exploita-

[87] Marstrander 1963; 1976; Johnstone 1972; Hale 1980. The experimental reconstructions of a boat based on a design at Kalnes, Østfold, Norway, showed that they are reasonably manoeuvrable, stable and watertight.
[88] Randsborg 1995; Kaul 1995.

tion of those making long-term capital investments, one should regard the investment of time in the production of boats as of equal importance to that made on particular cultivation regimes or crops.[89] But to assess this possibility, one needs to consider what the boats were actually used for.

Although many boat depictions are today some way from the sea, it is evident that taking relative land uplift into consideration, many were positioned to face creeks and other bodies of water (fig. 5.11). Boats might have been used purely to get from place to place, or they could have served as fishing vessels. The dissected coastline of Norway and Sweden, and the presence of numerous peninsulas and small islands, makes movement along these coasts much more efficient by boat. Even today, many such areas have no roads, and even those roads that do exist involve long detours to avoid deep inlets and creeks. Curiously, fishing is hardly ever shown on the art panels. This might have been because it was so much an everyday practice that it had no special significance to the artists. It certainly seems inconceivable that fishing should not have taken place in such coastal areas, where land resources, notably arable land, are relatively scarce. These were coastal societies: boats represented not only capital investment but also the fundamental means of communication with neighbouring and more distant groups.

Other boats

There remain a small number of rather ambiguous finds or models which do not obviously fit into the categories outlined above. Some of these may be coracles.[90] The Caergwrle boat model, made of shale, may also represent a craft of this kind.[91] Such vessels are light and manoeuvrable, and quickly built, but suited mainly to river and estuarine journeys, with relatively small loads. A large group of sheet-gold objects from Nors in Denmark, with rounded bottoms and tapering to a point at each end, and with gunwales and ribs made of thin bronze wire, may also be boat models, but it is impossible to determine of what kind.[92] These, and the representations in rock art, may have been hide or skin boats which could have been capable of open sea voyages, not unlike Irish curraghs; but until a Bronze Age example is found, one cannot take these speculations further.

Contact and exchange

The technological matters discussed so far in this chapter relate only to a means, not an end in itself. Transport was for a purpose, that of maintaining

---

[89] Gilman 1981.
[90] Such as Watkins (1980) reconstructed – on rather flimsy evidence – for Barns Farm, Dalgety, Fife.
[91] Corcoran 1961; Denford and Farrell 1980; Green *et al.* 1980.
[92] Broholm 1952–3, 37, 63 no. 337.

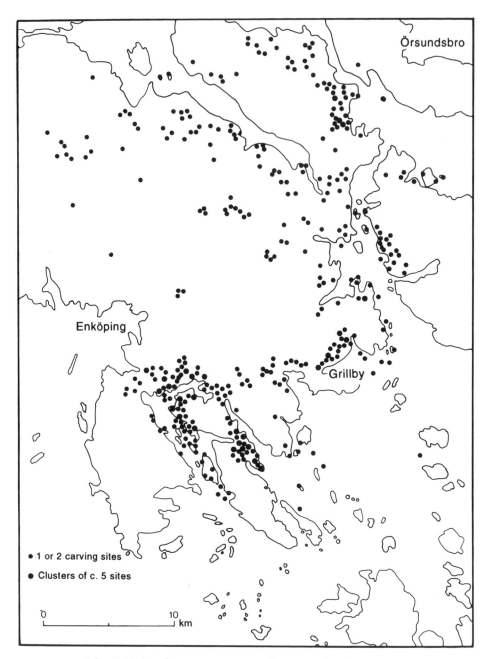

Fig. 5.11. Rock-art sites in southern Uppland in relation to a presumed Bronze Age shoreline 20 m higher than that of the present day. Some art was on small rocky islets in the bay (after Coles 1994).

contact with other people. Contact may have occurred for various reasons, some relating to kinship and social obligations, others to economic needs. The exchange of goods and materials could have fallen into either category. In the case of raw materials, especially metals, the economic need was probably paramount, but with finished objects or exotic materials other factors need to be considered.

Recent advances in provenancing techniques have enabled a wide range of materials to be sourced. In the context of Bronze Age Europe, the sourcing of metal ores and artefacts is perhaps the best known, but other materials, notably amber, were also important. Identifying where artefacts were manufactured is often more difficult because of the lack of knowledge about workshops. Amber, for instance, could have been transported in raw or finished state, and only workshop debris might be expected to answer the question.

Models for exchange

A number of authors have discussed the ways in which exchange might be practised.[93] In the context of Bronze Age Europe, where it is unlikely that the more sophisticated forms of trading took place, the most significant models would probably be those labelled 'down-the-line' and 'prestige-chain' exchange, though direct access to resources may have played its part. The social context in which exchange took place was very likely one in which reciprocity was all-important.

Usually when talking about exchange in a Bronze Age context one thinks of long-distance exchange, that is, movement of goods not merely beyond the frontiers of the local residential unit but far beyond it. Deciding which model is appropriate is, however, a matter of interpreting artefact distributions, since no other analytical tool is likely to be available. This is a form of archaeological interpretation that was very popular in the heyday of processual archaeology, when it was commonly believed that archaeological answers could be forthcoming from the appropriate analysis of artefacts; it is less popular today, though it is far from certain that a successor has been found. Today, more attention might be paid to the context in which goods occurred as an indicator of their significance, though in essence this is just a change of emphasis.

It is still reasonable to infer that declining abundance of a material or artefact from its source indicates that it was being passed down a line of communities, those nearest the source being most likely to have utilised it and benefited from it, those furthest away having poorest access to it. In cases where the distribution pattern shows discrete pockets of abundance, with

[93] Notably Renfrew 1972, 465ff.; 1975; 1977, who proposed a series of models to account for the known or reconstructible types of trade and exchange in the ancient world; see too Hansen 1995.

little correlation with distance from source, a type of movement based on limited access through social mechanisms might be in play, especially where there is reason to think that the goods were connected with prestige or display. Most difficult of all will be the determination of actors and access, whether materials were freely available to all and thus the object of individual enterprise, or whether they were controlled at source and handed down in strictly defined conditions.

Raw materials

Many raw materials must have been moved around Europe. Some materials were plentifully available over most of the continent, while others were scarce. In the context of a metal age, attention focuses on metal ores, but in fact the commonest materials in daily use were wood, clay, in some areas stone. Nothing is known about the movement of wood.[94] Even where wood is preserved on waterlogged sites, it will never be possible to demonstrate that it came from further afield than the immediate vicinity, say within a radius of a few kilometres. The case of clay is similar. Few parts of Europe lie far from clay sources, and for the everyday production of pottery, particularly coarse pottery, most of these would have sufficed. Fine wares, however, would have required clays that had particular properties, and these were less readily available. In general, it is unlikely that clays were moved other than in very special circumstances; on the other hand vessels, usually fine wares, certainly were moved. Chemical analysis cannot separate movement of clay from movement of pots, but petrographic analysis is helpful. In Mediterranean contexts, and with Roman ceramics, considerable success has attended attempts at pinning down the origin of clays and therefore the place of manufacture of pottery, particularly fine wares;[95] earlier work using optical emission spectrography and petrographic analysis is now supplemented by the use of neutron activation, ICPMS and other methods, with the problems of chemical characterisation being progressively reduced.[96] Elsewhere in Europe, however, the most successful work has used ceramic petrology[97] and neutron activation analysis.[98] Some success has also been achieved using diatom analysis, though in the Milfield Basin, Northumberland, most Late Neolithic/Early Bronze Age pottery was demonstrably made from local clays.[99] Local clay sources were also used for Early Bronze Age pottery in Spain.[100]

---

[94] The piece of unworked ebony on the Ulu Burun ship is an exception: Bass *et al.* 1989.
[95] Reviewed in Jones 1986; Pollard and Heron 1996, ch. 4.
[96] Mommsen *et al.* 1988; Neff 1992.
[97] Peacock 1969 for the movement of clays in Neolithic England.
[98] e.g. Barrett *et al.* 1978 for Middle Bronze Age Cranborne Chase; Topping 1986 for the demonstration that local clay sources were used in the later prehistoric Hebrides.
[99] Gibson 1986.
[100] Andres and Balcazar 1989.

Because metal ores are found sporadically in Europe, movement of raw metal (and of finished or half-finished metal products) must have taken place between metal-rich and metal-less areas. On this basis, metalliferous zones such as the Carpathians and Alps, the Harz Mountains and parts of Spain, Brittany and Ireland would have been the source of materials for neighbouring areas where no metals are found. It is indeed remarkable that some of the richest areas of Europe in terms of metal objects found are also those where non-ferrous metals do not occur naturally – such as Denmark or Hungary. In Hungary, metals would have been moved on to the plain from the mountains of the Carpathian ring to the east and north, no very large distance; in Denmark, metal must have been moved from the south (Harz, Alps) or the west (British Isles, Heligoland), a considerable distance. Hundt believed that all metal in the North was imported from southern sources – Alpine or Carpathian – and that the course of the Nordic Bronze Age reflected continual contact with the south, as shown in community of artefact forms.[101]

The movement of metals is usually studied by means of metal analysis, though problems in the interpretation of spectrographic data have delayed a definitive understanding. Lead isotope analysis holds out greater hope for the future, though so far this has mostly taken place in the context of Mediterranean ores and artefacts.[102] In some cases, analysis has been able to determine the presence of 'foreign' metal types, for instance Northover's metal types P, R and S in Middle and Late Bronze Age north-west Europe.[103] Especially for metal type S, an Alpine origin is likely – it is certainly not British, despite forming the backbone of the Wilburton metal industry (fig. 6.5).[104] It also found its way into many other areas, for instance Croatia.[105]

How did this metal move around? Water transport was one obvious possibility, though pack-animals and vehicles must also have been used. In view of the distances that were travelled, down-the-line movement is most unlikely for common metals, though it may have operated in the case of gold. Instead, one must probably envisage 'caravans' consisting of groups of animals, not unlike the situation somewhat earlier in the second millennium in the Near East, where donkeys and pack-asses were used. During the second millennium BC in central and western Europe horses became available, and horse transport seems intrinsically more likely than either vehicle transport (given their weight and the lack of paved roads) or oxen used as pack-animals (given their slowness).

The movement of amber is also instructive. Although there were some sources of amber in southern Europe, analysis of Greek, Yugoslav and Italian

[101] Hundt 1978.
[102] Review in Gale 1989b.
[103] Northover 1982a.
[104] Northover 1982b.
[105] Forenbaher 1995.

amber finds has shown that the great majority were of 'Baltic' amber, that is, from the sources of northern Europe, of Tertiary age and spread about by the Quaternary ice-sheets around and to the south of the Baltic Sea. Particularly in the case of Mycenaean Greece the implications of this movement are highly important.[106] Study of particular amber forms has shown that there is a specific connection between southern Greece and southern England, since the so-called amber spacer-plates of both areas were fashioned in identical ways; spacers in France and Germany, even where similar in design, were utilised in different ways. Amber spacer-plates in Greece are an intrusive, foreign form of north-western origin; they must have got there by long-distance exchange across the continent of Europe (a sea route, while not physically impossible, is probably less likely than a cross-continent land route). Many authors have pointed to the puzzling lack of intermediate finds between Greece and the Alps; though Italy started to receive quantities of amber in the late Urnfield period and more especially in the Iron Age, on the eastern side of the Adriatic finds remain few and far between.[107] The site of Frattesina near the mouth of the Po is especially important in this regard,[108] since amber-working took place on the site, and particular bead shapes may have been produced such as the Tiryns[109] and Allumiere types (fig. 5.12),[110] which turn up from Sardinia in the west to Switzerland in the north and Syria and the Ukraine in the east.[111]

Movement of finished goods

It used to be thought that other materials, notably glass and faience, were similarly moved across Europe, though in this instance from south to north. More recently, however, the local origin of a majority of faience finds in Early Bronze Age Europe has been analytically demonstrated,[112] though glass objects of the Early and Middle Bronze Age may well indicate an origin in the southeast (see chapter 7). It is, however, the technological implications which are important, since they imply the transfer of technology from one area to another.

The cases of amber and faience were exceptional. Much more usual is the situation where objects of bronze and gold were moved about over a defined distribution zone. For example, certain types of leg-guard with spiral terminals have very restricted distributions in Poland.[113] The Wierzbięcin type is

---

[106] Harding and Hughes-Brock 1974; Harding 1984a.
[107] Harding 1984a, 73ff.; Palavestra 1993; Forenbaher 1995, 275ff.
[108] Bietti Sestieri 1980; Arenoso Callipo and Bellintani 1994.
[109] Harding and Hughes-Brock 1974; Palavestra 1992.
[110] Steinhauser and Primas 1987.
[111] Lo Schiavo 1981; Todd 1985; Klochko, pers. comm.
[112] Harding and Warren 1973; Aspinall and Warren 1976.
[113] Blajer 1984, 59ff., pl. 78B.

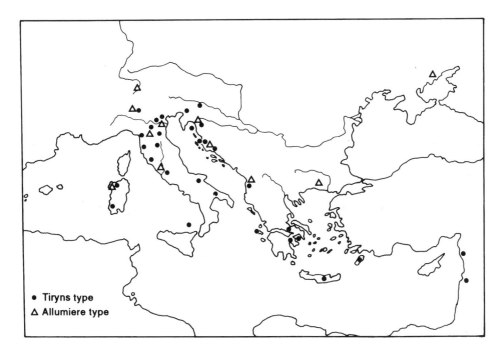

Fig. 5.12. Distribution of amber beads of the Tiryns and Allumiere types. While the main concentration is along Adriatic shores, note the finds in Sardinia, Greece, Syria and the Ukraine (after Palavestra 1992; Steinhauser and Primas 1987; and Lo Schiavo 1981).

mainly found near Szczecin, but there are outliers near Słupsk to the east, and on Møn in Jutland to the west. In the case of razors in western Europe, a number of comparable cases occur (fig. 5.13): the Ins/Serres type of lunate razor is mostly found in southern France west of Marseilles, but a couple of examples come from the Saône valley 400 km to the north; the Magny-Lambert type is found in Burgundy and the Jura but one example is known from Langenthal in the Swiss Midlands, and a very similar piece comes from Nin on the Dalmatian coast.[114]

These are objects of personal use or adornment which can plausibly be interpreted as indicating the movement of individuals from one place to another, without necessarily implying any more regular or deep-seated contact or exchange. With objects of an industrial nature, the situation is rather different. One can search in vain for evidence that sickles, to take one example, were regularly transported from one area to another – the case of the

---

[114] Jockenhövel 1980b, 182ff., pl. 57B; Weber 1996, no. 608.

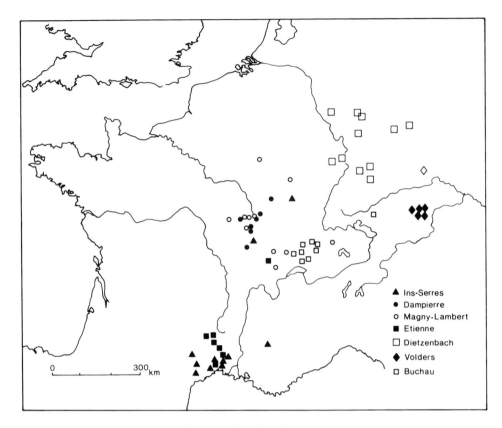

Fig. 5.13. Distribution of selected razor types in western Europe, showing discrete areas of currency of particular forms (after Jockenhövel 1980b).

Transylvanian sickle from the Slovakian hoard of Blatnica is an exception.[115] An interesting case-study is that of the bronze finds from the Montlingerberg hillfort in eastern Switzerland.[116] Consisting mainly of pins, knives, sickles and axes, the material was shown to fall into three main groups: pins and axes with southern connections, those with northern connections, and other forms foreign to the region entirely, having a place of origin in Italy, Slovenia, or still further afield.

The movement of weapons is different again. Since weapons probably reflect directly the movement of the individuals wielding them, or the paths along which exchange of prestige goods took place, their places of deposition are of unusual importance. Study of swords, for instance – which is the most developed field in terms of systematic publication of the main finds – indicates

[115] Furmánek 1995, 165.
[116] Primas 1977b.

that, while certain types were specially favoured in some areas, it was common for many forms to travel over considerable distances. The case of Mycenaean and Mycenaean-derived swords in Albania, Bulgaria, Macedonia and Kosovo is a case in point,[117] as is the Rixheim sword from the Rimavská Sobota hoard,[118] or the Alpine rod-tang swords from Salaš Noćajski in Serbia and the Moor Sands cargo,[119] and the continental antenna swords from the river Witham and Deeping Fen in Lincolnshire.[120] In all these cases, the area, if not the exact place, of manufacture can be pinned down quite closely, and in all of them it lies far from the place of deposition.

In addition to bronze objects of personal use, relatively small and easily carried, there were others, much larger, that appear to reflect the movement of prestige items over long distances. Among these may be mentioned metal vessels imported into Scandinavia from a production place in the Carpathian Basin (fig. 5.14),[121] and in a few instances objects of Scandinavian origin found in Hungary; a decorated belt-disc has even been suggested as exemplifying Nordic technology introduced to the Carpathian Basin.[122] Certain objects interpreted as cult items were also moved over long distances, such as the Balkåkra 'sun drum' and other similar objects found in Scandinavia, which show close similarities to cult vessels in central Europe.[123]

Trade across the English Channel represents an important source of information because of the implications for transport and presumably the intentionality involved.[124] Studies of specific artefact movements have been amplified by the finds from Langdon Bay.[125] This cargo (whether or not it was intended to arrive on English shores) consists mainly of continental forms, for instance sword fragments, median-winged axes and palstaves that would be most at home in France. The cargo from Moor Sands, Salcombe, also contained swords including a complete example of the Monza type,[126] itself a variant of a form found widely on the Continent but almost never in Britain.[127] Similarly, one can point to a considerable number of isolated objects which plainly crossed the Channel: a palstave from Horridge Common, Dartmoor,[128] Breton palstaves from various sites,[129] or, going in the opposite direction, Irish flat axes.[130]

---

[117] Kilian-Dirlmeier 1993; Harding 1995, 20ff.
[118] Furmánek 1995, 165.
[119] Harding 1995, 18.
[120] Burgess and Colquhoun 1988, 122, nos. 751–2.
[121] Thrane 1963; 1966; 1979.
[122] Szabó 1994–5.
[123] Olausson 1992, 263; Knape and Nordström 1994.
[124] Butler 1963; O'Connor 1980. General discussions: Brun 1993; Briard 1993.
[125] Muckelroy 1980; 1981; Needham and Dean 1987; Burgess and Colquhoun 1988, 14ff. pls. 137–43.
[126] Bianco Peroni 1970, 30.
[127] Burgess and Colquhoun 1988, 11ff.
[128] Fox and Britton 1969.
[129] Burgess 1969.
[130] Megaw and Hardy 1938.

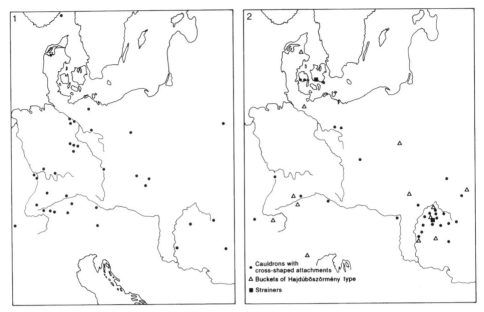

Fig. 5.14. Distribution of bronze vessel types: 'Fuchsstadt cups' (*left*); buckets, cauldrons and strainers (*right*) (after Thrane 1966). These vessels are mostly of central European manufacture, but their distribution into Scandinavia illustrates the way that fine metalwork could be moved far from its production area.

From these finds it would appear that during the course of the Bronze Age cross-Channel exchange developed significantly in extent and frequency. From an early stage, individual items were moved between communities on either side of the water. By the later stages, there is evidence for the extensive movement of metal, presumably in ingot form, and for the transport of finished items. Even if the two southern coastal cargoes do not represent intentional movement of metal and artefacts to Britain, there are enough objects of continental type known within Britain to indicate that there were mechanisms in place which facilitated the transport of such goods between users on both sides of the Channel. In much of the Continent, where no stretch of water larger than a river separated communities, such movement of goods must have been easier and more frequent.

A study by P. Brun has examined relations between the two cultural complexes of the 'Rhin-Suisse – France orientale' and 'Manche' cultures.[131] Study of Atlantic and North Alpine types in central France suggests the existence of a kind of buffer zone between the two distribution provinces, which developed during the Middle and Late Bronze Age, having been absent during the

[131] Brun 1993.

Early Bronze Age. The buffer zone is notable for containing hillforts, e.g. Fort Harrouard, which seem to be linked closely to the circulation and production of bronze objects, mainly prestige goods; artefacts from both provinces coexist in the forts. Concentration of prestige metal lies along stretches of river in the buffer zone. In the latest part of the Bronze Age, the situation changes, with forts and hoards much more widespread, indicating a change in socio-political relations (see chapter 8). The study relates the development of this trading network to social processes involving the position of chieftains, who could control supra-local networks.

Exchange in the Bronze Age economy

Discussions of the Bronze Age economy are forced to concentrate on the tangible evidence of subsistence and related practices which can be seen in the archaeological record, such as plant and animal remains. Such things were necessary to the people who used them, but they were not the only aspects of the economy which were of importance. This is not to say that one should adopt a 'formalist' or 'modernist' approach to the ancient economy. In the period under review, economic activity, including that involving commercial relations, was 'primitive' in the sense used by economic anthropologists. It was not formally structured, had no 'money' or markets, and can best be considered more a part of social life than a purely economic phenomenon. One cannot even presume that 'laws' of supply and demand applied, though no doubt in some instances something akin to them might have been seen.

From the evidence presented above, it is reasonable to view many Bronze Age communities as partaking in exchange on a local or regional level; some on an inter-regional level. Local exchange of foodstuffs was probably practised, either as a result of different growing conditions in different areas or as a consequence of specialisation by particular groups. Further afield, it is less likely that foodstuffs would (or could) have been moved very far, with the possible exception of special items such as spices, or conceivably dried or salted foods. It is possible to demonstrate, on the other hand, that certain raw materials – notably metals, in ore or ingot form – were moved on a regional and inter-regional level.

As well as this relatively mundane exchange, there were a number of instances of long-distance movement of special materials or goods occurred. Such is the case with amber and potentially with other items that travelled the long route between south and north, or vice versa, and with the movement of Aegean and East Mediterranean goods to the central and west Mediterranean.[132] There has been much debate in recent years about the

---

[132] Fully discussed in a previous work (Harding 1984a).

significance of such movement to the local economies involved. Such matters are best studied in the framework of a 'social' view of the economy.

The study of Bronze Age exchange in Europe has progressed enormously in recent years with the advent of new discoveries and new analytical techniques, coupled with the systematic publication of corpora of material. While one cannot predict what further new discoveries will be made, or in what ways new techniques of analysis will aid archaeology in the future, it is possible to look forward to the day when a more or less complete body of information (*sensu* artefact documentation) is at hand, on the basis of which the movement of goods can be followed with precision. Such work is tedious and unfashionable. I believe, however, that it represents an essential part of the process by which it will be possible to arrive at a fuller understanding of the processes which drove the exchange, to refine existing models and to develop new ones.

CHAPTER 6

METALS

Of the various materials and industries that were current during the Bronze Age, metals occupy a special place: not so much because they were especially important to the population of the period as a whole; more because of the association of the name with the assumed production of metal objects on a wide scale. During the 1500 years over which the Bronze Age lasted, metallurgical technology developed from the use of unalloyed copper and gold for simple objects that were hammered to shape or made in open moulds, to the creation of a large and varied repertory using a variety of metals. From the middle of the second millennium, very large numbers of objects were made, principally in tin-bronze but also in other alloys of copper, and in gold. Thanks to recent experimental and analytical work, most of the processes involved, and the places where they were conducted, are well understood. But many questions remain concerning the way in which metals were regarded and utilised in other than functional terms, how the objects into which they were made operated in the society and economy of the period, and what status was accorded those who carried out the work of procuring the materials and producing the objects.

A number of general accounts of metallurgical processes are available, though none is written purely from a Bronze Age point of view, or with the situation in Europe principally in mind. The works of R. F. Tylecote are commonly cited, but other valuable general accounts are those by Coghlan, Mohen, Ottaway and Craddock.[1]

The natural occurrence of metals

Distribution maps of ore sources for copper, tin, lead and gold, the metals mainly used in the Copper and Bronze Ages, are an essential preliminary to any enquiry about the methods and role of metallurgy in those periods. However, they present at best a partial picture since they cannot show the multiplicity of small surface sources which for early metalworkers would have represented the first port of call for ore supplies. Most such sources have

---

[1] Tylecote 1986; 1987; Mohen 1990; Ottaway 1994; Craddock 1995. In more specialist matters the works of Drescher, Hundt and Northover deserve special mention.

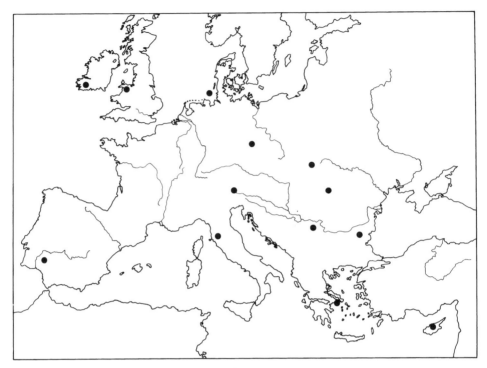

Fig. 6.1. Major sources of copper in Europe. The highly generalised picture presented here does not imply that these were the
only, or even the main, sources exploited in the Bronze Age.

disappeared, having been totally worked out or obliterated by much larger-
scale operations in the Roman and medieval periods.

Nevertheless, a map of raw material sources does have the merit of indicating some major options open to ancient metallurgists, assuming that they
possessed the necessary technology to tap these resources. Europe possesses
(or possessed) some major copper deposits, some of them exploited into historic times (or in rare cases to the present day) (fig. 6.1). Various parts of the
Balkan peninsula (Bulgaria, Serbia, Albania), the Carpathians (Transylvania,
Slovakia), the Alps (Austria), central Europe (the Harz and Ore Mountains of
Germany) and western Europe (France, Spain, Britain and Ireland, and also
Heligoland) have, or once had, significant deposits. Mention is sometimes
made of deposits in Sweden, where commercial exploitation occurred in the
last century, but there is no indication that these deposits were known and
exploited in ancient times.

The best way to determine which sources were used at different times and
for different groups should be through compositional analysis of ores and finished products. In spite of recent work it is still only possible to provide good
correlations of ores with objects in a limited number of instances, principally

in the Mediterranean area. Early attempts using spectrographic analysis represented pioneering efforts to solve the problem and are a major source of data for later workers, but have been found wanting in terms of the crucial link between source and product.[2] Thus, while it is possible to identify impurity patterns and alloy types, tying metals down to particular ore sources is another matter altogether. For this, more advanced (and expensive) techniques, notably that of lead isotope analysis, are necessary.[3]

In practice, it is likely that many small sources of copper were exploited in prehistory, which today are regarded as insignificant. In the Alpine valleys of Switzerland, Austria and the Trentino, for example, there are many such small deposits, their location often only discovered by chance since they are far too small to have been worth working commercially in recent centuries (fig. 6.2). In the region around Monte Bego in the Ligurian Alps, too, there are many deposits of both oxide and sulphide ores, and it has been suggested that their exploitation might have been a main reason for the presence of so much activity in the region, as seen in the rock art.[4] The same is probably true for south-east Spain, home to the Argaric Bronze Age.[5] Many deposits are listed for Slovakia.[6] Similarly, in upland parts of Britain and Ireland there are indications of small deposits, sometimes associated with other minerals, which have produced evidence of working in prehistoric times, but preserve no exploitable ore today – the Mount Gabriel-type mines in south-west Ireland are a good example of this. This presents something of a problem for the archaeologist seeking to understand the nature of ancient copper-working. In such circumstances, it is reasonable to concentrate on those areas where quantity and quality of information are fairly good, while exercising caution when attempting to transfer the results to other areas or types of working. In fact, the best available evidence for ancient copper-working in the Old World comes not from Europe but from Timna in southern Israel, where the long-term explorations of Rothenberg and his collaborators have shed light on the whole process of the mining, smelting and refining of copper, from the Chalcolithic to the Islamic periods;[7] by comparison, European results are meagre.

The case of gold is different.[8] Most Bronze Age gold was probably extracted through placer mining, for instance panning in gold-bearing streams. Ore extraction may have taken place at certain major sources, notably the Wicklow Mountains of eastern Ireland and the Munţii Metalici of western

[2] Pittioni 1957; Junghans, Sangmeister and Schröder 1960; 1968.
[3] There has been debate in recent years about the significance of lead isotope results (Budd *et al.* 1996 with further refs.; Gale forthcoming).
[4] Mohen and Eluère 1990–1.
[5] Montero Ruiz 1993.
[6] Bátora 1991, 106f.
[7] Rothenberg 1972; 1990.
[8] Lehrberger 1995.

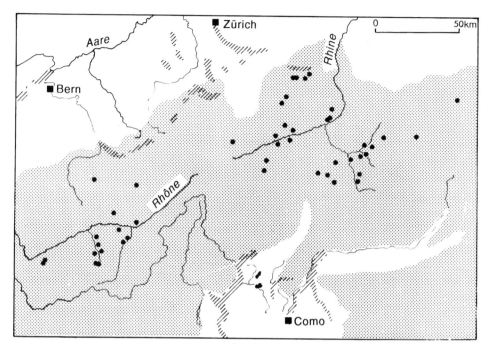

Fig. 6.2. Copper ore sources in the Swiss Alps (*Fahlerz* and sulphide ores) (after Bill 1980). Stippled area: land over 1500 m.

Transylvania. Spectrographic analysis by Hartmann has successfully characterised these two major gold sources, though not the host of smaller ones.[9] Small placer deposits were probably present in other areas, for instance in Cornwall, where alluvial gold occurs in small quantities along with tin. New analytical techniques show good results in identifying these alluvial deposits in terms of their elemental associations or 'fingerprints'.[10]

Tin sources in Europe are extremely few.[11] Cornwall was the largest, and certainly exploited by the Romans. That prehistoric exploitation is also probable is seen from the find of cassiterite pebbles from St Eval, Trevisker, and tin-smelting slag from the barrows at Caerloggas, St Austell.[12] The Wicklow Mountains of Ireland have been thought to have had tin deposits that could be recovered by placer working as there is some documentation of cassiterite in gold streams there, but it remains uncertain whether this could really reflect ancient tin extraction in the area.[13] Brittany, Iberia, Tuscany and

[9] Hartmann 1970.
[10] Taylor *et al.* 1996.
[11] Muhly 1973, 248ff.; Penhallurick 1986.
[12] ApSimon and Greenfield 1972, 309, 350; Shell n.d. [1980]; Tylecote in Miles 1975, 37–8.
[13] Budd *et al.* 1994 for a sceptical view.

Sardinia all have small quantities of tin, as do parts of western Serbia;[14] the Ore Mountains (Erzgebirge) in the Czech–German border area also have it, but it is disputed whether or not it could have been exploited with a Bronze Age technology.[15] What is not in doubt is that Bronze Age sites lie not far from the known tin sources, notably in the Elster valley.[16] Placer mining of tin may well have been carried on there, and this might have supplied the major central European bronze industries, for instance those in Germany, Poland, Bohemia and Austria; perhaps also those of Scandinavia. Whether they could also have supplied smiths further east, for instance in Hungary and Romania, is more doubtful.

Through much of Europe, it is unknown how the bronzesmiths who turned out such enormous quantities of bronzework, containing typically 5–10% of tin, acquired their supplies. Even if one supposes that the tin of the Erzgebirge was accessible, the distances involved were considerable. On the other hand, Cornwall – the only source for which good evidence for Bronze Age exploitation exists – cannot realistically have supplied smiths throughout continental Europe and Scandinavia. Claims have also been made for tin sources in Yugoslavia, which would have the merit of being well situated from the point of view of supply routes to either the Aegean or the Hungarian plain and northwards.[17] Much remains to be elucidated in this area, crucial both for technological understanding and for a realistic appreciation of the transport and exchange patterns. This puzzle applies also to the great cultures of the East Mediterranean, for instance Minoan and Mycenaean Greece, Egypt and the cities of the Levant, and is not definitively solved to this day.[18]

Lead is much more widely found, notably in the form of galena. It commonly contains significant amounts of silver, and the extraction of that silver by the technique of cupellation (raising argentiferous smelted lead to red heat in an open dish and blowing air across the surface) may have been a main reason for interest in lead, though it was also much used in its own right.[19]

---

[14] Durman 1997; Balkan sources are under-researched and could prove to be extremely important.

[15] Muhly 1973, 256; Taylor 1983; Waniczek 1986; Bouzek, Koutecký and Simon 1989.

[16] Bouzek *et al.* 1989, favoured also by Waniczek 1986.

[17] McGeehan-Liritzis and Taylor 1987.

[18] Texts from cities such as Mari (Middle Bronze Age) or Ugarit (Late Bronze Age) make frequent reference to a material, *annaku*, that was being moved from the east in great caravans, and the consensus has been that this represents tin. The discovery of a large amount of tin on the Ulu Burun ship confirms the hypothesis that tin was in circulation around the Mediterranean in the Late Bronze Age, though it does not in itself indicate where that tin had come from (Maddin 1989). Recent work has suggested the Taurus Mountains of southern Turkey (Yener and Özbal 1987; Yener and Vandiver 1993), the eastern desert of Egypt (Muhly 1985; 1993) and Afghanistan (Cleuziou and Berthoud 1982; Stech and Pigott 1986).

[19] This technique may have been used in the Rio Tinto mines in southern Spain (Blanco and Luzon 1969; Craddock *et al.* 1985/1992).

Metal types and alloys

Identifying metal types and the objects for which they were used is important because of the possibility of tying down the routes and processes by
which metals were moved around. The attribution to specific ore sources
must be distinguished from the identification of a particular metal composition, which will only rarely be attributable to an ore source. Such work usually depends on compositional analysis.[20] The question of metal types, in the
sense of ore compositions, is complicated by the fact that finished artefacts
were rarely, after the initial period of metal production, made of copper alone.
Other minerals were added, to facilitate casting, improve hardness or even to
bulk out the copper metal in order to make it go further. Alloying, by means
of the addition of arsenic, tin or lead to the copper, means that the composition of finished objects will be a further stage removed from that of the ore.
Where small amounts of a mineral were added, it can even lead to doubt as
to whether its presence was intentional or simply an impurity in the copper
ore.

In general, it is not in doubt that the metals used proceeded from pure copper through copper–arsenic and copper–tin alloys to copper–tin–lead during
the course of the Bronze Age.[21] Since tin and lead were usually added in substantial quantities (several per cent, or more in the case of some Late Bronze
Age lead-bronzes) it is not hard to detect their presence and to deduce that
the addition was for specific purposes. The addition of arsenic and/or antimony is a more difficult matter, however, since both minerals are naturally
present in many copper ores as impurities. Where, as is often the case with
Early Bronze Age objects, arsenic is present in quantities of 1% or more, the
consensus used to be that it was intentionally added to the metal during
smelting on the basis that it improves the hardness of the finished product
(fig. 6.3).[22] On the other hand, it has been persuasively contended that the
extraction and smelting of arsenical minerals in the Bronze Age is highly
unlikely, and that the presence of arsenic in copper objects reflects the use
of secondary copper ores containing arsenates, which can easily be reduced
to form copper–arsenic alloys.[23] But it has been shown in a variety of contexts that arsenic content varies according to artefact type, there usually being
more in objects with a cutting edge and less in axes and ornaments;[24] similarly, sickles from Late Bronze Age hoards in Slovenia have been shown to
have less tin (3–4%) than axes (6–7%), probably a deliberate alloying proce-

[20] Such as the enormous corpus of material assembled in the 1960s by the Stuttgart analysis
team (Junghans, Sangmeister and Schröder 1960; 1968, etc.).
[21] Tylecote 1986, 26; Northover 1980/1991.
[22] Charles 1967.
[23] Budd et al. 1992.
[24] Ottaway 1994, 134.

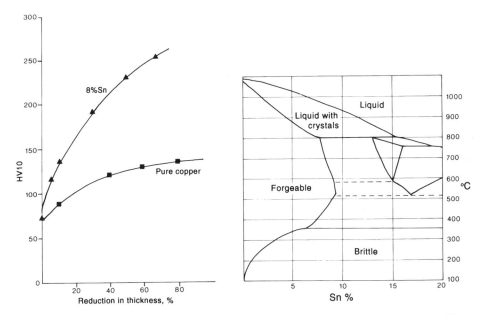

Fig. 6.3. *Left:* The effect on hardness after cold working of adding 8% tin to copper (after Tylecote 1987c); hardness on the vertical axis. Continued hammering to reduce thickness barely makes pure copper any harder after the initial stages, whereas the copper–tin alloy continues to increase in hardness. *Right:* 'Phase diagram' of a copper–tin alloy (stages through which the metal passes with increasing temperature, at different admixtures of tin). Although pure copper becomes forgeable very quickly, it does not become liquid until well over 1000° C is achieved. By contrast, the admixture of 10% tin does nothing for the forging qualities but reduces the melting temperature to around 800° C (after Mohen 1990).

dure to make the tools more malleable for frequent resharpening.[25] In fact, it has been claimed that most British–Irish ore sources would have produced more or less pure copper, so that metal objects with significant impurities represent the mixing of pure and impure metal sources, in other words a much more developed circulation system than has usually been considered likely.[26]

The interpretation of compositional analyses is fraught with difficulties,[27]

[25] Trampuž Orel *et al.* 1996.
[26] Ixer and Budd 1998.
[27] One of the more acute criticisms of the Stuttgart analyses has been that the results fly in the face of archaeological sense, largely because the statistical treatment utilised in the original publications does not take archaeological data into account: Waterbolk and Butler 1965; Härke 1978.

but sensible results can be obtained from this great corpus of information.[28] It has long been clear that a very pure copper (named E00) was prevalent in the earliest period of metalworking, another was commonly used for the production of ingot rings (C2 or 'Ösenring metal'), while a multi-impurity metal with high levels of nickel and antimony and moderate to high arsenic and silver was very widely found ('Singen metal').[29] More detailed applications can show how such metals were used at the site level. At Výčapy-Opatovce different metal types were used preferentially for specific artefact types, for instance 89% of the rings are of Singen metal, and 52% of the willow-leaf ornaments are of so-called VO metal.[30]

Northover has identified a series of impurity groups and alloy types in the artefacts of Bronze Age Britain and north-west Europe, seeing them moving within 'metal circulation zones'.[31] Initially the bulk of metalworking and metal emanated from Ireland, mainly for axes, with some coming in from the Continent in the form of daggers and halberds. This pattern then gave way, in the developed Early Bronze Age, to one in which local ores were exploited more intensively in Scotland and Wales, notably with metal types A, B and C (fig. 6.4). With the Acton Park phase (Middle Bronze Age I), there was a dramatic change: the north Welsh sources began to supply much of lowland Britain (copper with 9–12% tin and increasingly the addition of lead, the introduction of impurity groups M1 and M2). In the next, Taunton, phase (Middle Bronze Age II), the dominant composition group had a consistently high tin content (13–17%); at the end of the Middle Bronze Age (Penard phase), two new impurity patterns (P and R) appear, with tin alloys in the region of 8–11%. Such metal is widespread also in France and Germany, and seen also in the Langdon Bay wreck.[32]

The Late Bronze Age metal types are very different. Of particular importance was metal type S, with major impurities of arsenic, antimony, cobalt, nickel and silver, and in some areas – notably that of the Wilburton industry[33] – a high lead content indicating intentional alloying. Northover's analyses suggest that this S metal, which cannot be British because of its impurities, may be Alpine or Carpathian, certainly central European; it is

---

[28] e.g. Coles 1969 for Scotland; D. and M. Liversage 1989 for Denmark; 1990 for Slovakia; Liversage 1994 for the Carpathian Basin.

[29] Waterbolk and Butler 1965, 237ff. graphs 8–9; Krause 1988, 183ff.

[30] The discussion by D. and M. Liversage (1990) of the published analyses from the Výčapy-Opatovce cemetery (Točík 1979) shows that around 65% were of Singen metal, having the characteristic impurity patterns for antimony and nickel (> 0.75%), arsenic (0.14–1.4%), and silver (0.23–0.75%); 20% (38/169) were of another type (moderate arsenic, low antimony, silver and nickel), and a third group (10 analyses) was similar to Singen metal but with low arsenic. Ten other low-impurity objects do not fall into any group.

[31] Northover 1980a; 1982a.

[32] Muckelroy 1981.

[33] Northover 1982b. In addition to the dominant S group, Group H, with arsenic as the main impurity, occurs mainly in the later hoards (e.g. Selbourne) and in hoards of scrap metal such as the great Isleham hoard (Britton 1960).

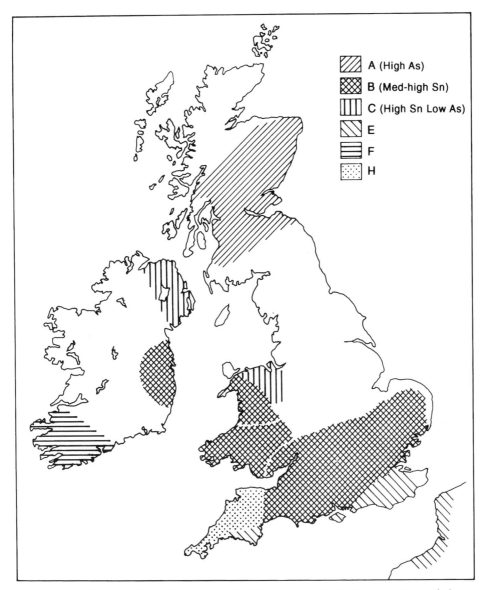

Fig. 6.4. Metal types in the 'Developed Early Bronze Age' of the British Isles, showing the way in which local ores were exploited in western regions (after Northover 1982a).

widely found in Europe at this time (fig. 6.5). It introduced a large amount of lead into circulation, which continued to have an effect into the following phases, including the Carp's Tongue metalwork phase.

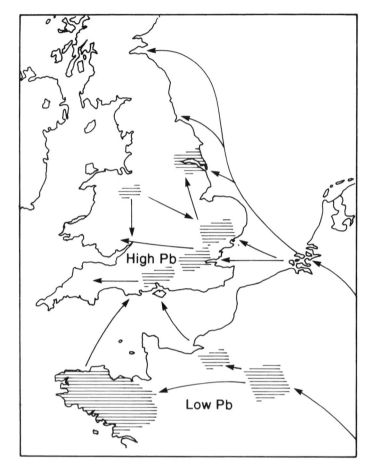

Fig. 6.5. Metal types in the Wilburton phase, showing the suggested movement of S metal from the Continent (Alps or Carpathians) into Britain, where lead was added in local industries. Hatched zones indicate concentrations of Wilburton metalwork (after Northover 1982a).

Ore to metal

The first step in the set of complex processes referred to as metallurgy was the location and extraction of the raw materials. In some parts, for instance at Ergani Maden in Turkey, gossans (iron oxides emanating from sulphide deposits) appear on the earth's surface, and would have acted as an indicator that other minerals were present lower down.[34] A knowledge of ore types and

---

[34] Tylecote 1976, 8. O'Brien points out that in the British Isles many copper mines were in areas that had already experienced millennia of hard rock extraction for axe production, so that prospectors would have had an intimate knowledge of the local rock types.

their attendant geology is necessary for understanding how ores may have been located and worked, but it does not answer all the questions that arise. In Europe many of the surface deposits which were the first target of Copper and Bronze Age miners have long since been worked out, and the extent to which deeper deposits were then exploited is controversial. So a reconstruction based on practices in other parts of the world, or on medieval European practice, may indicate likelihoods and possibilities, but it cannot be regarded as definitive.

It is generally assumed that copper ore bodies would initially be noted where they appear on the earth's surface in their oxidised form, that is as ores such as malachite or azurite, which have a brightly coloured appearance, or, in more southerly areas where glacial action has not been a factor, where the gossan lay above sulphidic copper ores. Sometimes the sulphur-bearing ores such as chalcopyrite, or the products of the enrichment zone between the oxide and sulphide ores (the best known being the *Fahlerz* grey ores), can appear in oxidised form on the surface, as is the case in parts of south-west Ireland. Although not coloured blue or green as the oxidised ores are, shiny grey or gold patches or chunks within the dull rock matrix, sometimes a centimetre or more across, indicate that the rock is of special interest. Many copper ores occur in polymetallic deposits, along with small quantities of other metals such as silver or nickel. Large quantities of iron are usually present within many of the ore bodies, and although separation of the iron from the copper was a primary concern, such iron was not suitable for the production of iron objects.

Direct traces of prehistoric exploitation are discernible in a tiny minority of known sources in Europe, almost all of them relating to copper. They are known and have been investigated in Russia,[35] Bulgaria,[36] Serbia,[37] Slovakia

[35] Recent work has shown that a vast mining area at Kargaly, in the south-western periphery of the Urals, was exploited in the Bronze Age (Chernykh 1996 and elsewhere). Although so far only relatively small areas have been investigated, the amount of recovered material is colossal. Chernykh estimates that the Kargaly mining area would have produced not less than 1.5–2 million tonnes of extracted mineral.

[36] Chernykh (1978a) located numerous copper sources in south-east Bulgaria; few have evidence for date. There is little indication of Bronze Age exploitation; a little Late Bronze Age pottery at the Eneolithic mines of Aibunar (Stara Zagora) (Chernykh 1978b) is paralleled at Gorno Aleksandrovo (Sliven), while there is Early to Middle Bronze Age pottery at Tymnjanka (Stara Zagora).

[37] North-east Serbia, particularly around Bor where the Rudna Glava mines have produced much evidence of Eneolithic working, is prolific; there are also extensive Roman and medieval workings, which have obliterated many of the traces of earlier work. There seems to be no direct evidence of Bronze Age exploitation (Jovanović 1982 with full bibliography).

(fig. 6.6),[38] Austria (see below), France,[39] Spain,[40] Britain[41] and Ireland;[42] the absence of the other sources listed above does not mean that they were not exploited, only that direct field evidence has not yet been forthcoming. Exploitation of all these sources was probably relatively small-scale in com-

[38] The mines at Špania Dolina, near Banska Bystrica, and Slovinky, district of Spišská Nová Ves, central Slovakia, have been investigated under rescue conditions (Točík and Bublová 1985; Točík and Žebrák 1989). Both oxides and sulphide ores are present. Rescue excavations recovered large numbers of waisted and other stone tools, along with pottery of Eneolithic character and a little attributable to the Lausitz culture.

[39] At Cabrières, Hérault (Vasseur 1911; Ambert et al. 1984; Ambert 1995; 1996), the veins of Pioch Farrus and Roque Fenestre were utilised in the Copper and Early Bronze Ages. The ores are varied; Fahlerz was abundant, along with malachite, and was probably used in preference to the sulphide ores present at greater depths.

[40] The province of Huelva, and especially the area inland from Huelva itself around Chinflon and the Rio Tinto, was one of the richest metal sources in classical antiquity, producing silver, copper and other metals. The copper is largely sulphidic, but there are indications that oxides must also have been present (Rothenberg and Blanco-Freijeiro 1981). Oxide ores would quickly have been worked out, and Bronze Age miners must then have found a way of penetrating the very hard gossan cap to the secondary enrichment zone underneath with its copper, silver and gold. Major working of these ores did not take place until the Early Iron Age, when numerous shafts and galleries were dug, but the presence of Late Bronze Age material indicates the possibility of an earlier start for some of this working.

Radiocarbon dates indicating mine-working in the Copper Age and earliest Bronze Age have also been recovered from the mines of El Aramo (Riosa) and El Milagro in northern Spain (Blas Cortina 1996 with full references).

[41] At the Great Orme's Head (Llandudno), Cwmystwyth, Dyfed, and other sites in north and central Wales a number of traces of Bronze Age mining have been found, those at the Great Orme's Head being the most extensive. Here excavation has revealed a complex set of workings that extended up to 27 m deep and more than 100 m long (James 1988; Lewis 1990; Dutton 1990; Jenkins and Lewis 1991; Dutton and Fasham 1994). The dolomitised limestone with interbedded mudstones contains crystals and thin veins of chalcopyrite, with oxidisation to form malachite at the surface. Stone tools, mainly in the form of mauls, have been found in some quantity, and were evidently used to smash the softer rock faces and drive the shafts back. In places where harder rock intervened, fire-setting was probably used. Radiocarbon dates on charcoal and bone taken from spoil indicate an Early to Middle Bronze Age date. At Cwmystwyth, where chalcopyrite is present, sectioning of waste tips in 1986 produced hammer stones and antler, and charcoal which also gave radiocarbon dates in the Early to Middle Bronze Age (Timberlake and Switsur 1988; Timberlake 1990b); comparable dates have been obtained from Parys Mountain on Anglesey, and Nantyreira north of Cwmystwyth (Timberlake 1990a; 1991).

At Alderley Edge, Cheshire (Craddock and D. Gale 1988; D. Gale 1990), malachite and azurite occur, and have been worked into relatively recent times. An early phase of extraction used a 'pitting' technique with stone hammers (many waisted); distinctive peck marks appear on the rock where such pits are present. Although there is no dating evidence for this phase of activity, a Bronze Age date has been suggested, based on parallels for the stone hammers and a radiocarbon date of 1888–1677 cal BC (1σ) on a wooden shovel from the mines (Garner et al. 1994).

[42] At Mount Gabriel, Co. Cork, Derrycarhoon, and other sites in south-west Ireland an extensive field research programme has been carried out (O'Brien 1994). There are two groups of prehistoric mines in Cork and Kerry: those located on sedimentary copper beds, like Mount Gabriel, and those working richer vein-style mineralisations, like Ross Island, Killarney (O'Brien 1995). At Mount Gabriel there are thirty-two workings (individual shafts or shaft systems), which were driven along mineralised copper-bearing strata; similar workings are present at other spots in the Mizen and Beara peninsulas. The ores are sulphide, mainly chalcocite, chalcopyrite and boerite, with surface oxidation to produce 'staining' in the form of malachite and azurite; there is no Fahlerz at Mount Gabriel. Radiocarbon dates for waterlogged wood and for charcoal removed from adjacent spoil tips confirm Bronze Age mining from c. 1700 to 1400 BC (Jackson 1968; 1980; 1984; O'Brien 1990; 1994, 178ff.). Recent excavations at Ross Island confirm the extraction of Fahlerz and chalcopyrite in the period 2400–1900 BC. The early production of arsenical copper in this site, linked to the users of Beaker pottery, continued into the earliest phase of insular tin-bronze production (O'Brien 1995).

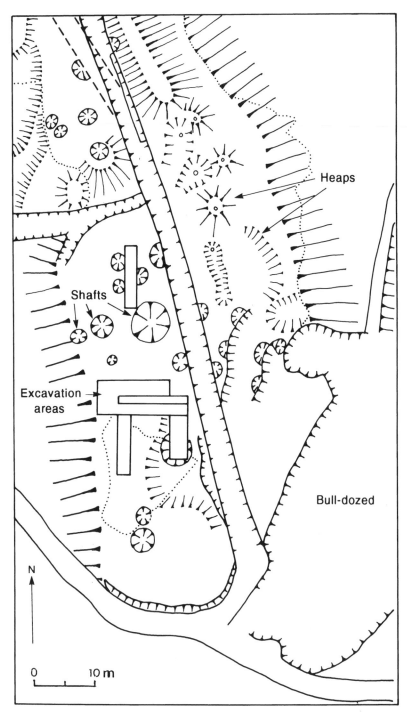

Fig. 6.6. Extraction area at Špania Dolina-Piesky, central Slovakia, showing shafts and waste heaps (after Točík and Bublová 1985).

parison with that of the major East Mediterranean sources: most notably Cyprus, but also Laurion in Attica and, further afield, Timna and parts of the eastern desert of Egypt. The evidence for the importance of Cypriot copper in the economies of the eastern Mediterranean is overwhelming, and finds its most dramatic representation in the Ulu Burun shipwreck, full of copper and tin ingots. The existence of major supplies of raw materials to the east was inevitably a factor for the inhabitants of Greece and therefore for other parts of Europe from which she might have obtained metal.

The lack of direct evidence of working, then, does not mean that sources were not worked. Particularly in the case of the Carpathians the conclusion (based on the distribution of metalwork products) seems unavoidable that pre-historic working took place; the absence of prehistoric mine shafts cannot be used as an *argumentum ex silentio*. Similarly, the Harz Mountains are com-monly cited as the nearest copper sources to Scandinavia, where the Bronze Age metal industries were rich. But direct evidence of their exploitation does not begin until the third century AD,[43] though finds of Bronze Age pottery near the Harzburg in the northern Harz has suggested Bronze Age interest in the area, and excavation of smelting sites has produced stone tools, hearths and furnaces very similar to those in the Austrian Alps.[44] Copper was cer-tainly being extracted on Heligoland in the medieval period, and could well have started much earlier.[45] No prehistoric workings are known, but the find-ing of flat copper disc-like ingots in shallow water south of the island, dated to the medieval period by radiocarbon determinations on charcoal inclusions in the discs, the proximity of the island to the German and Danish coast (the presence of Early Bronze Age sites on the island shows that it was in the cul-tural orbit of Schleswig-Holstein), and the fact that no other copper source lies so close to the north German/Scandinavian Bronze Age cultures, make this probable.[46]

By far the greatest volume of Bronze Age copper mine-working in Europe comes from the Austrian Alps, particularly the Mitterberg area west of Bischofshofen in the Salzach valley south of Salzburg, but also from several other parts of the north and east Tyrol; adjacent parts of Italy, Switzerland and Slovenia also have deposits and in some cases traces of mining.[47] Although no mines have yet been found in the Trentino, it is likely from the number of slag and other finds of metallurgical debris that they were (and perhaps still are) present.[48] The Libiola mines in Liguria are known to have been worked in the Chalcolithic, since a wooden axe haft from them has given a

[43] Klappauf *et al.* 1991; Kurzynski 1994.
[44] Nowothnig 1965; Preuschen 1965.
[45] Lorenzen 1965.
[46] Stühmer *et al.* 1978; Hänsel 1982.
[47] Teržan 1983; Drovenik 1987.
[48] Lunz 1981, 11ff.; Perini 1988.

radiocarbon date in this period.[49] At the Mitterberg, the work of the mining engineers K. Zschocke and E. Preuschen between the world wars uncovered numerous traces of prehistoric shafts and waste heaps in the course of modern exploitation of the copper that is still present.[50] Unfortunately, their work is familiar to most modern readers only through secondary sources, though it remains a classic of the mining literature.

The ore mainly represented at the Mitterberg is chalcopyrite, a sulphide. The veins of ore run for many kilometres through this mountainous region, the main lode 1–2 m thick, some others less than this. To extract the ore from the quartz matrix, fire-setting was used in conjunction with picks and hammers to create *Pingen*, large pit-like features up to 10 m across that in some cases turn into shafts or adits. These apparently reached considerable lengths – 100 m or more – and elaborate arrangements had to be made, by the use of pit-props, to stow the waste. Rows of *Pingen* run across the mountainside, sometimes with parallel rows in close proximity. Outside the shafts, a number of separating areas have been found, relying partly on hand separation and partly on water-dependent devices involving wooden constructions; remains of post-and-plank constructions were found during excavation together with sediments of various particle sizes, suggesting that water separation was used to concentrate ore or metal (fig. 6.7). Not far away, slag-heaps attest to the fact that smelting took place locally, usually a little lower down the mountain on more level ground, close to water. Analysis of this slag shows that much of it is fayalite with a very low copper content, attesting to an efficient extraction process. Datable artefacts and radiocarbon dates from the excavations indicate a lifespan for the Mitterberg mines throughout the Bronze Age, but so far no detailed chronology is available.

Estimates of the amount of copper extracted have been attempted on a number of occasions. Even allowing for orders of magnitude discrepancies, the quantities of copper obtained from the Mitterberg area alone are very large, amounting to many hundreds of tonnes. Zschocke and Preuschen calculated that over 18,000 tonnes of raw copper could have been produced in prehistory, assuming a concentration of copper in the quartz matrix of around 2.5%, a 10% loss in preparatory roasting, and a 25% loss in smelting. One cannot know that all this copper was produced in the Bronze Age, and even if it were, the time over which the mines were demonstrably worked – perhaps 1000 years – would produce a yearly average of only 18 tonnes. Zschocke and Preuschen further calculated that one team, consisting of 180 people, could produce 315 kg of smelted copper per day; at that rate, 18 tonnes could be produced in a mere 57 days. Even allowing for very great variability in extrac-

---

[49] Barfield 1996.
[50] Zschocke and Preuschen 1932; Pittioni 1951. Recent work (Eibner-Persy and Eibner 1970; Eibner 1972; 1974; Gstrein and Lippert 1987) has confirmed many of these findings.

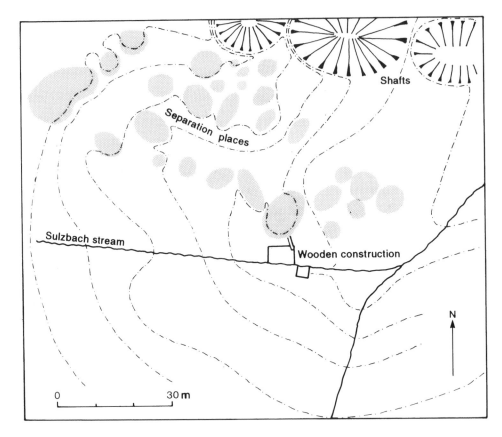

Fig. 6.7. Extraction shafts (*Pingen*) and adjacent processing areas at the Mitterberg (after Eibner-Persy and Eibner 1970).

tion rates across those 1000 years, there is nothing inherently unlikely in the figures suggested. Indeed, if two teams were working 6 days a week throughout the year, yearly extraction could have reached nearly 200 tonnes. In practice, the availability of wood might well have become a problem: each team would require an estimated 20 m³ of wood daily, a major constraint on the progress of the work, especially as it would have to be brought from progressively further away as time went on. Furthermore, winter conditions must have made extraction difficult if not impossible.

A number of features are common to all of these mines:

1. Assessment of value. To be worth working, the metal content of an ore source had to be sufficiently large for the labour expended in extracting it not to become excessive, or not to exceed that involved in exploiting other comparable sources or in obtaining metal by exchange from other areas. It also had to be present in a form that could actually be extracted using available technology. The main criterion must have been that the nodules or concentrations of metal should be large enough to be both easily visible and successfully separable from the parent rock by physical means. It is evident from what ancient miners left behind that there was a limit beyond which they did not go in this respect: the sites of many ancient mines exhibit rocks that contain small flecks of metal, large enough to see but too small to be successfully extracted.[51]

2. Extraction. For detaching large chunks of rock the technique of fire-setting was often used, depending on the depth and complexity of the workings. The lighting of a fire against a rock surface would, by means of the differential expansion of the crystals within the rock, cause cracks to form or to expand. If sudden cooling by means of quenching with water was also adopted, the effect would be still more marked. The remains of charcoal layers in mining waste suggest that fire was frequently used in this way, and the rounded undercutting of rock faces indicates the application of this technique, which has been reproduced experimentally.[52] After the fire had cooled, picks could be inserted into the cracks and leverage exerted on the blocks of stone. Stone hammers and mauls were also used, the waisted shape being particularly characteristic (fig. 6.8); on occasion the pock-marks can be seen on surviving rock surfaces in mine shafts, as at Alderley Edge.[53] By these means an opening would be formed in the rock, and if the metalliferous area continued downwards or inwards into a hillside, in time a shaft or tunnel would be formed. These were commonly no more than a metre or so across, suggesting that children must have been used to work the shafts.

Fire-setting would become progressively more laborious once the shaft had reached more than a certain distance from the surface, and the problems of smoke and lack of ventilation would hinder access to it for anything but initial kindling. For the same reason, quenching and other operations would be difficult. In spite of this, evidence for ancient fire-setting was found in the Mitterberg at considerable depths, and historical sources show that it can indeed be carried out at depths of 100 m or more. The cramped, dark, damp and dangerous conditions in which ancient mining for metals took place can only be imagined.

---

[51] A heap of silver ore (jarosite) in a Roman gallery at Rio Tinto was left unsmelted; the concentration is estimated at 120 ppm (0.012%). Ores containing more than 3000 ppm were available (Craddock *et al.* 1985, 207). Muhly (1993, 252) considers that the reported concentration of tin in the the Bolkardag ores of 3400 ppm (0.34%) would be too small for Early Bronze Age metallurgists even to detect, let alone utilise. The acceptable lower limits clearly vary with ore and matrix type, minerals involved and technology available.
[52] Pickin and Timberlake 1988; Timberlake 1990.
[53] Craddock 1986, 108.

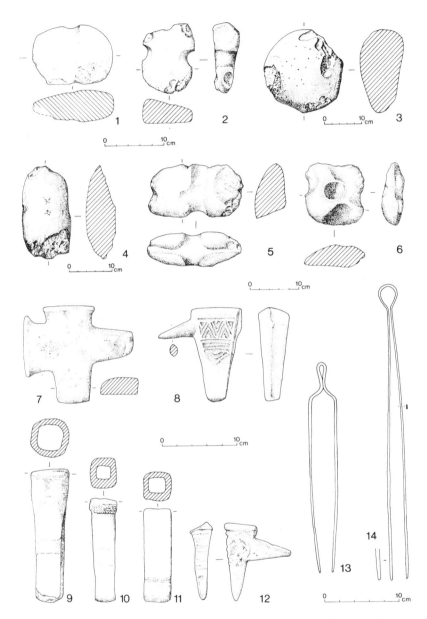

Fig. 6.8. 'Mining tools' from copper mines, and tongs, hammers and anvils from metalworking sites. 1. Rio Corumbel, Site 52C (after Rothenberg and Blanco-Freijeiro 1981) 2, 5–6. Špania Dolina-Piesky (after Točík and Bublová 1985); 3. Great Orme (after Dutton and Fasham 1994); 4. Cwmystwyth (after Timberlake 1990b); 7, 9–11. Bishopsland (after Eogan 1983); 8. Wollishofen (after Ehrenberg 1981); 12. Fresné-la-Mère (after Ehrenberg 1981); 13. Siniscola (after Lo Schiavo 1978); 14. Heathery Burn (after Britton and Longworth 1968).

3. *Lighting, ventilation and drainage.* In order to continue mining to greater depths, a variety of devices were necessary to facilitate the work. The lighting of fires may have served to draw in air, while light could have been provided by a bowl of fat or oil with a wick floating in it, or by pine splints (which have actually been found in a number of sites, including Mount Gabriel). In either case, smoke would have been a constant irritant, the light given off inconstant, and the danger of burning the operator considerable. Removal of water from the shaft end or bottom would also become a major consideration, depending on local conditions. By the very nature of the terrain where many mines are situated, rainfall and groundwater would have been abundant, and the digging of a hole in the ground likely to trap water. It is possible that mining took place mainly at times of the year when such problems would be minimised, but even so some shafts would very likely have had to be abandoned, at least temporarily, because water had collected in them.

The Austrian mines have produced a variety of wooden implements that seem to have served the needs of the Bronze Age miner, not only shovels but also pointed posts and planks (shaft lining or supports for stowage of waste), parts of carrying packs or buckets, troughs, pipes or channels, kindling sticks and notched poles that probably served as ladders. Considerable timber needs are implied (as also by the fire-setting technology) as well as labour to work and transport the wood. The recent finds of wood at Mount Gabriel and other sites give some idea of the wealth of information still to be recovered.

4. *Beneficiation.* Fire-setting, particularly where stone hammers are also used to pound the heated surfaces, tends to produce highly comminuted rock fragments, which would aid the manual concentration of mineralised rock outside the mine. Where larger rock pieces were produced, however, it had to be broken up into small lumps, or 'cobbed', using heavy stone hammers. Such hammers have been found on many sites and are often a prime indicator of 'primitive' working on a site (fig. 6.8).[54] In addition to hammers, a variety of pounders, mortars, millstones and anvils were used for breaking up and grinding the ore. At the Mitterberg, water-processing was used in addition to hand-sorting.

5. *Roasting and smelting.* Chemical knowledge in prehistory was purely empirical in nature and the technology built up on a trial-and-error basis; the majority of what survives in the archaeological record represents the successes, while the failures were destroyed by remelting. The first step would have been to break up the ore and convert sulphide to oxide by a simple roasting in an open bonfire. Ores from the surface oxidation zone would have

---

[54] Pickin 1990; D. Gale 1991; 1990.

needed this stage much less than those from deeper deposits, from which sulphur compounds as well as other undesirable elements had to be removed.

Smelting was the next stage, the process of producing a chemical alteration in the ore to concentrate the metal in one place by removing the unwanted elements. Molten metal does form, but it collects at the bottom of the furnace and cannot be poured. The difference between specific gravities of copper and waste products means that the former will sink to the bottom in the form of globules of pure copper, leaving the latter above; this waste can be tapped (allowed to run off), from a tap or valve in the furnace side solidifying to form the slag that characterises ancient smelting localities. The composition of the slag depends on the type of ore that was used in the first place: it is common for copper slags to be high in iron, reflecting the fact that sulphide ores commonly occur in a matrix of iron-bearing rock or have been fluxed with iron oxide. The flux (added material to facilitate the chemical reaction) was an important element in this process; its precise nature would have depended on the nature of the ore. Wood ash, which would have developed from the charcoal, is itself a fluxing agent, and in some cases the addition of anything else may not have been necessary.

Slag is the commonest indicator of ancient metallurgical activity, since it is produced at some stage in most ore-to-metal operations and is almost indestructible. In the Mitterberg area, for instance, there are many large slagheaps. The remains of slag on numerous Late Bronze Age settlements in southern Germany show that smelting took place on site, probably in crucibles, as is shown by large graphite or stone and clay containers.[55] On the other hand, there is no slag in the British Isles that demonstrably accompanies Early Bronze Age workings of the sort known at Mount Gabriel and elsewhere, and some attention has been paid to the question of how the ore reduction could have been carried out without slagging.[56] It has been suggested that early smelting would have taken place at low temperatures and concentrated on arsenate copper ores such as olivenate.[57] Such ores can look similar to copper carbonates and often occur in the same places. Unlike them, however, they can be smelted in a bonfire to produce a copper–arsenic alloy that might then have been melted in a crucible.

In order to raise temperatures to 1083°, the melting point of copper, an enclosed furnace would have been necessary, and a forced draught using bellows would have introduced oxygen. The form and attributes of such furnaces can be reconstructed since the technical requirements are well understood, but few installations from archaeological sites survive. A site

[55] Jockenhövel 1986, 219.
[56] Craddock 1986.
[57] Budd *et al.* 1992; Budd 1993. On the other hand, the recent work at Ross Island suggests that shallow pit furnaces were being used in Beaker times to smelt the sulphide and *Fahlerz* ores present on the site; there is no sign that the model suggested by Budd is correct for this site.

interpreted as a smelting furnace on Kythnos consisted of a series of small round stone structures; an excavated example contained a clay-lined bowl with fragments of slag and copper.[58] Numerous sites at Timna illustrate similar constructions, dating from various prehistoric and historic periods.[59]

Experiments based on recovered smelting ovens at Mühlbach in Salzburg province have suggested that the ovens were originally 1 m high, and that two batteries of ovens were used so that two ovens could be in operation simultaneously. Not far away lay a roasting bed, for the preliminary treatment of the sulphide ores that were commonest at the Mitterberg.[60] A smelting place was recently recovered at Bedollo in the Trentino, consisting of a series of six pits in line, with a stone wall providing a surround for them.[61]

The production of charcoal is an aspect of metalworking that is often ignored.[62] Charcoal was the ideal fuel for furnaces prior to the advent of coke because it promotes a strongly reducing atmosphere in the furnace, consisting as it does of almost pure carbon, and on burning creates an oxygen-starved atmosphere, essential if oxygen compounds are to be removed from the metal being worked. The forcing of air into an enclosed charcoal-burning furnace raises the temperature rapidly; charcoal has a calorific value about twice that of dried wood. To make charcoal, cut timber is ignited in a sealed heap or pit and allowed to smoulder; only sufficient oxygen is admitted at the start to get the fire going, after which the process continues without the addition of oxygen. By this means combustion is incomplete, no ash results, and almost everything except carbon is removed from the wood. Considerable quantities of timber would have been needed in the most prolific metal-production areas. It has been estimated that to produce 5 kg of copper metal one would need at least 100 kg of charcoal, which would in turn have required some 700 kg of timber, a considerable requirement in terms of labour.

Charcoal has been found in many mining and smelting areas, for instance at the Great Orme mines.[63] This is probably the end-product of fire-setting; it is possible that the process resulted in the production of charcoal which could then be used for smelting and metal production.

---

[58] Hadjianastasiou and MacGillivray 1988.
[59] Rothenberg 1972, 65ff.; 1985; 1990, 8ff. Furnace IV in Area C, Site 2, for instance, was a round bowl-shaped affair set in the ground with a thick layer of clay mortar forming its wall and bottom, holes set into it for the insertion of tuyères, and on the opposite side the slag tapping pit, a rectangular depression with a lining of large stone slabs; around the upper rim, large flat stones formed a working area for the smelters.
[60] Herdits 1993.
[61] Čierny *et al.* 1992. This find confirms a number of earlier finds of slag-heaps and smelting places in South Tyrol and the Trentino going back to the Chalcolithic (Dal Ri 1972; Perini 1988; Šebesta 1988/1989; Fasani 1988; Storti 1990–1).
[62] Horne 1982; Hillebrecht 1989.
[63] Dutton and Fasham 1994, 280f.

Ingots

The smelting operation produced copper in agglomerated, relatively pure form. This may have been in the form of 'prills' of copper (irregular elongated masses not unlike icicles, 'frozen' as the dripping metal cooled and solidified), which would be added direct to a crucible or, where simple bowl furnaces were used for smelting, the copper would have collected in a concave depression at the bottom of the furnace to form a lump of copper that was flat on top and curved underneath, the so-called plano-convex ingot. Many hoards of bronze in Europe contain whole or fragmentary ingots of this kind. Axe-shaped ingots were also used. In the Mediterranean in the Late Bronze Age, a specialised form was used, the 'ox-hide' ingot (so called supposedly because the shape resembles a hide, but more likely because the four handles that project from a basically rectangular block enabled easy porterage). Originally these ingots were thought to be exclusively an East Mediterranean phenomenon, occurring as they do in Crete and mainland Greece, in Cyprus and parts of the Levant, on the two ships wrecked at Cape Gelidonya and Ulu Burun off the south Turkish coast, and in miniature form or representations in Cyprus and Egypt.[64] There are also a number of such ingots, or fragments, in Sardinia and Sicily,[65] though in Italy, as elsewhere in Europe, the normal form was the plano-convex ingot. Fragments of an ox-hide ingot were recently identified in a hoard from Unterwilflingen-Oberwilflingen in southwest Germany (Ostalbkreis, Baden-Württemberg),[66] and a miniature example has recently been found on a settlement site in Romania. Only one production site is known, at Ras Ibn Hani in Syria, where a sandstone mould is set into the ground in a part of the palace devoted to industrial activities. It is highly likely, however, that such ingots were also made in Cyprus, where a number of sites (Enkomi, Kition, Athienou) have major metalworking installations. The presence of such ingots in Sardinia has, therefore, caused much interest and not a little controversy.[67] Most surprisingly, the Sardinian ox-hide ingots appear to be made of Cypriot copper (though other ingots and finished artefacts are most probably of local copper), a striking case of coals to Newcastle.

In Europe, an unusual kind of hoard appears, that containing objects which from their form are usually called 'loop neck-rings' (Ösenhalsringe) or sometimes just 'loop rings' (Ösenringe) after the loops or eyelets formed at each end of the ring, but they are better described as ring ingots.[68] A less commonly found form is the Rippenbarren or rib ingot. Both ingot forms occur

[64] Buchholz 1959; Bass 1967; N. Gale 1989.
[65] Lo Schiavo, Macnamara and Vagnetti 1985, 10ff.
[66] Primas 1997.
[67] Lo Schiavo 1989; N. Gale 1989, with refs.
[68] Bath-Bílková 1973; Menke 1978–9; Eckel 1992.

in such large numbers – sometimes several hundred in a single find – that it is highly unlikely that they really served a purpose as personal ornaments (except where they appear in graves).[69] Instead, it seems most likely that they represent a means of transporting metal about, their form intended for easy carrying by inserting a pole through the middle. No moulds for ring ingots are known, but they could readily have been cast into simple grooves in stone – perhaps even in living rock – and then hammered into their ring shape. They may well have been manufactured close to the smelting sites or else in valley settlements after transport of the pure copper in plano-convex form down from the mountain. The distribution of ingots northwards from the eastern Alps, with especially dense concentrations in southern Bavaria, Lower Austria and Moravia, is very striking and seems likely to be connected with the known production of copper in the Austrian mines.

Attempts have been made over many years to tie these objects down to ore sources.[70] Examination of the analyses of the copper carried out by the Stuttgart laboratory suggested that two main copper types were involved. One – accounting for over 75% of all analysed pieces – has relatively high impurities; the other is of very pure copper and accounts for around 15% of analysed pieces.[71] What cannot at present be demonstrated is any correlation between the two distinctive copper types and any particular source area. Indeed, a number of hoards contain metal of both types, made into identical objects. This may suggest that the two metal types relate rather to stages and methods of working than to different origins for the metal. The two different metals look different today and would have handled differently in the workshop; smiths cannot have failed to be aware of different properties resulting from different treatment during and after smelting.

Ingots were one form in which metal circulated, though even here there are stages which are not properly understood. For instance, breaking ingots up for use was no simple matter. Fragments are commonly found, indicating that ingots must have been heated to a high temperature first.[72] But as well as ingots, much scrap metal undoubtedly circulated. Hoards of broken objects are commonly supposed to represent such circulation (though ritual explanations have also been proposed: below, p. 361). Although much metal was consigned to the ground for good during the course of the Bronze Age, much must have been reused. The fact that metal objects can be melted down and made into new artefacts is, after all, one of the great advantages of a metal technology over a stone-based technology.

[69] It is necessary to record, however, that some authorities do indeed believe that the rings were in the process of being made into ring ornaments, and were not 'pure ingots': Butler n.d. [1980].
[70] Pittioni *et al.* (1957) identified the high impurity metal of the ingots, and believed that this represented copper that had been brought in from the east (*Ostkupfer*), meaning the Carpathian ring in general and Slovakia in particular.
[71] Butler n.d. [1980]; Harding 1983.
[72] Tylecote 1987b.

From metal to object

While smelting usually took place in the immediate vicinity of the mining sites, bronze-working could occur almost anywhere; there are indications from various settlements, for instance, of working being carried out on site. Working near ore sources would probably be that of 'primary' metal, while that on settlements might well include recycled metal, melted down from bronze scrap. The furnace would be constructed much as already described, though it would not need to be so large as a smelting furnace, nor would it need a tapping hole or pit, or a bowl-shaped base to collect the copper. Instead, pieces of copper would be put in a crucible and the crucible heated in a charcoal fire in a clay-lined furnace, with forced air being introduced to raise the temperature to the required point.

No archaeological finds of bellows or blowpipes seem to be known from Bronze Age Europe, but the majority would have been of organic materials and are thus unlikely to survive. Pot bellows, a broad open pottery vessel with a nozzle in the wall and a skin stretched over the top, might be a possibility, as is the case in the Near East,[73] but they have yet to be certainly identified. Experiments in both smelting and refining have demonstrated the efficiency of pot bellows, but conventional blacksmith's bellows deliver a higher air flow and would leave few, if any, non-organic parts in the archaeological record.[74]

Tuyères, clay nozzles through which the bellows were inserted into the furnace, are known from various sites and come in a large version believed to be for smelting furnaces[75] and a small, conical version, perhaps for the insertion of a blowpipe such as is shown on Egyptian tomb paintings, for melting furnaces (fig. 6.9).[76] These small conical tuyères are known from a number of finds in central and eastern Europe, for instance from Únětice and related Early Bronze Age groups, and from the Timber Grave culture grave at Kalinovka in south Russia (below, p. 239).[77] Tuyères can be straight or curving, in certain examples even turning a right angle. Many more examples are known from the Near East and Cyprus than Europe;[78] there a hemispherical 'small' tuyère (perforated lump of clay) is distinguished from a tubular, built-in tuyère, the latter always very fragmentary and therefore unlikely to survive in a European climate. In the Aegean area, the best example is that from the bronze workshop in the Unexplored Mansion at Knossos.[79]

[73] Davey 1979.
[74] Merkel 1983; 1990.
[75] e.g. Fort Harrouard: Mohen and Bailloud 1987, 128f. pl. 5, 15; pl. 98, 19; Velem St Vid: von Miske 1908; 1929.
[76] Hundt 1974, 172 fig. 27; 1988; Tylecote 1981; Jockenhövel 1985.
[77] Jockenhövel 1985.
[78] For instance the series studied at Timna by Rothenberg (1990, 29ff.); see Tylecote 1971.
[79] Catling in Popham 1984, 220 pl. 199, i; 207, 5; described as a 'bellows nozzle'.

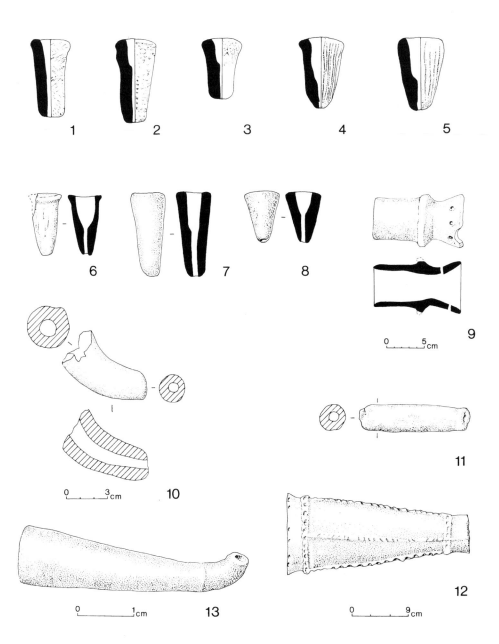

Fig. 6.9. Tuyères from Bronze Age metalworking sites.
1–3. Kalinovka; 4. Bogojeva; 5. Tószeg (after Hundt 1988);
6. Mierczyce; 7. Lago di Ledro; 8. Nowa Cerekwia (after
Jockenhövel 1985); 9. Knossos, Unexplored Mansion (after Catling
in Popham 1984); 10. Fort Harrouard (after Mohen and Bailloud
1987); 11. Ewanrigg (after Bewley *et al.* 1992); 12. Bad Buchau,
Wasserburg (after Kimmig 1992); 13. Löbsal (after Pietzsch 1971).

An interesting recent find was of a 'connecting rod' of clay from an Early Bronze Age cemetery at Ewanrigg, Cumbria (fig. 6.9, 11).[80] This clay tube, some 17 cm long and 3.7 cm in diameter with an irregular internal perforation 1.2 cm in diameter, is thought to have served as an intermediate piece between bellows and tuyère; its slightly rounded end would have connected somewhat flexibly with the tuyère, and its presence would have provided an additional means of preventing hot gas from the furnace being drawn back into the bellows, at the same time as representing an additional source of fresh cold air for the bellows.

An extensive range of tools was needed for casting and working the metal: crucibles, moulds, tongs, hammers, blocks, anvils and others.[81] These are found relatively rarely, though they must have been common enough in the smith's toolkit. Crucibles were commonly made of a coarse sand–clay mixture, less often of stone, and could be narrow and deep or shallow and broad, sometimes with a pouring lip. A suitable method of holding the crucible for lifting and pouring metal no doubt also presented problems: Egyptian paintings appear to illustrate pairs of staves being used for the purpose, but since even green wood would flame rapidly under such intense heat it may be that these are metal bars, or conceivably wood covered in metal sheet.

Metal tongs are known but occur infrequently (fig. 6.8, 13–14);[82] examples are found in Cyprus, Crete and the Levant but may have been rather for holding hot metal objects during hammering.[83]

Anvils are well known, especially in western Europe (fig. 6.8, 7, 8, 12).[84] The basic distinction is between simple, beaked and complex anvils (those with multiple spikes or 'beaks' and facets). Many of these tools are relatively small (less than 8 cm across) and could have been carried around; others, including large stones sometimes used for the purpose, must have been fixtures. Some have holes for hole-punching or swages (grooves) in which metal could be beaten into wire or thin bars, and there are two wire-drawing blocks in the Isleham (Cambridgeshire) hoard.[85] A small anvil from Lichfield, Staffordshire, contained particles of gold in its surface layer and was probably used for beating out gold sheet. It also includes a swage groove on one end, perhaps for creating bar bracelets.[86]

The counterpart to the anvil is the hammer, of which six different forms

[80] Bewley et al. 1992, 343ff., fig. 13.
[81] Coghlan 1975, 92ff.; Mohen 1984–5.
[82] e.g. Siniscola, Sardinia: Lo Schiavo 1978, 86–7 pl. 27, 2; Lo Schiavo, Macnamara and Vagnetti 1985, 23–5 fig. 9; Heathery Burn cave: Britton 1968.
[83] Catling 1964, 99 A1 fig. 11, 4 pl. 10a; Catling in Popham 1984, 206–7, 219f., pl. 199; Vagnetti 1984. Catling (in Popham 1984, 215) suggests that tweezers or pincers may also have been used to hold hot furnace materials.
[84] Ehrenberg 1981; examples from central Europe: Hralová and Hrala 1971, 19ff.
[85] Eluère and Mohen 1993, 20.
[86] Needham 1993; another stone with gold traces comes from a settlement at Choisy-au-Bec (Oise) (Eluère 1982, 176 fig. 164).

are known in central Europe.[87] Many occur in the large hoards of the early Urnfield period (fig. 6.8, 9–11),[88] on sites interpreted as locations for metal-working, such as the Breiddin, Powys, Wales,[89] and on Swiss lake sites, although metalworking installations have not been recovered there.[90] Socketed hammers are associated by Jockenhövel with the practice of beating metal sheet into objects such as vessels, helmets, shields and the like; they must have had predecessors in stone.[91] Used in conjunction with an anvil or swage block, thin sheet could be produced, decorated with delicate patterns. There must also have been larger anvils (probably of stone) and sledge-hammers for fashioning large objects where fineness of work was not a consideration, but these seem not to survive in continental Europe; examples are known from Cyprus and Sardinia.[92]

Bronze Age mould technology is reasonably well understood, though duplicating the results of ancient smiths is not always successful. In general there was a progression from simpler to more complex types, from open moulds cut on to the surface of a stone block to two-piece moulds, each half the mirror image of the other, and from stone to clay (depending on area). Multiple mould finds in stone illustrate something of the range which was possible: they are especially common in the north Pontic area, as in the great hoard of Majaki (Kotovsk, Odessa), with 13 moulds for spearheads, daggers, socketed axes, rings and pins;[93] the strange collection from Pobit Kamăk (Razgrad) in Bulgaria is even more remarkable, containing moulds for socketed and shaft-hole axes, for a large dagger and an extraordinary halberd with spirally curved blade, and a collection of small objects that may have been pommels or hilt attachments to swords, daggers or knives.[94] Both of these finds belong to the local Late Bronze Age. Somewhat earlier is the large find of 41 stone moulds from Soltvadkert (Kiskörös) east of the Danube in central Hungary.[95] As well as tools (socketed and flanged axes) there are pins, bracelets, pendants and beads represented in this find. The stone is sandstone, which must have come either from across the Danube in Transdanubia or from the Carpathians to the east. Another plentiful source of stone moulds is Sardinia.[96]

[87] Hralová and Hrala 1971; Jockenhövel 1982a; Lo Schiavo, Macnamara and Vagnetti 1985, 22f.
[88] Examples include those from Surbo (Apulia) (Macnamara 1970), Lengyeltóti, Hungary (Wanzek 1992) and Fresné-la-Mère (Calvados) (Coghlan 1975, 95ff. fig. 23; see too Larnaud, Jura: Chantre 1875–6, 110ff.; Vénat (St-Yrieix, Charente): Coffyn *et al.* 1981, 118f. pl. 22, 1–3, and other sites in the Charente basin (Gomez 1984) or Breton hoards (Briard 1984)). Sets of hammers, an anvil and other tools from the Bishopsland (Co. Kildare) hoard: Eogan 1983, 36, 226 fig. 10.
[89] Coombs in Musson 1991, 133f.
[90] Auvernier: Rychner 1979, pls. 125–6; 1987, 74 pl. 29, 5–8.
[91] Hundt 1975.
[92] Lo Schiavo *et al.* 1985, 22 fig. 7, 6–7. Catling (1964, 99) suggests that massive wooden mallets covered in metal sheet could have been used as sledge-hammers, or perhaps such hammers could have had metal inserts of some kind.
[93] Bočkarev and Leskov 1980, 15ff. pls. 4–7.
[94] Hänsel 1976, 39ff. pls. 1–3; Chernykh 1978a, 254ff. figs. 67–8.
[95] Mozsolics 1973, 80f. pls. 108–9; Gazdapusztai 1959; Kovacs 1986.
[96] Becker 1984.

In contrast to these stone mould finds, in the west of Europe there are large collections of fragmentary clay moulds, especially in the British Isles.[97] In the Swiss lake sites, stone moulds are commonest but clay ones do occur.[98] These moulds are fragmentary because they have to be broken after the metal has been poured in order to get the object out; they are intended for use once only, in contrast to moulds of stone or metal. They would have been made by pressing clay round a 'master' object or pattern, taking on the exact form of the pattern and enabling great homogeneity between different pieces to be achieved. Interestingly, wooden patterns for the production of clay moulds are known from Ireland.[99]

Clearly there was a balance to be struck between the labour of making clay moulds afresh each time a casting was required and the more time-consuming process of fashioning stone moulds for multiple usage. If suitable clay was available, this was the more appropriate material for mass production of objects and may have had desirable properties for successful castings. There does not seem to have been a functional difference between stone and clay, but clay had two intrinsic advantages: more complex forms could be cast and standardised manufacture was possible, since each clay mould was the negative of the same master and hence the bronze product was the clone of that master. On the other hand, at Dainton different clays were used in moulds for different object classes, though whether this is connected with metallurgical practice or with different episodes of work is impossible to say.

Moulds were also made of metal, on the face of it a curious practice. A number of studies of these have been made, and it has been demonstrated experimentally that they can be used for successful casting.[100] The inner surfaces of the mould would need to be coated in graphite or some similar medium onto in order to prevent the newly poured metal from adhering to the mould.

A variety of techniques were used to produce hollow castings, complex objects and other specialities. In some instances debris from these operations survives: cores, valves, chaplets or 'core-prints' (small rods to pin a core in position inside a mould) and other devices. Cores and gates are present among the mould debris at Jarlshof, Shetland.[101]

In the Late Bronze Age, a number of highly elaborate bronze objects were made using the technique of lost wax casting (cire perdue). The principle of

[97] Hodges 1954; Collins 1970; Mohen 1973: as at Dainton (Devon) (Needham 1980), Rathgall (Raftery 1971), Fort Harrouard (Mohen and Bailloud 1987, 130ff.); see too Peña Negra (Gonzalez Prats 1992).

[98] Rychner 1979, pl. 131, 5–6; 1987, pl. 33, 1–5, pl. 34, 2; Weidmann 1982.

[99] Hodges 1954, 64ff. fig. 3. A group of objects from a bog at Tobermore, Co. Derry, are of the form of Late Bronze Age bronzes (leaf-shaped spearheads and socketed axes). On certain bronzes the grain of the wooden model is still visible.

[100] Drescher 1957; Mohen 1978; Rychner 1979, pl. 137, 7; 1987, 78ff., pl. 35, 1; Tylecote 1986, 92; Voce in Coghlan 1975, 136ff.

[101] Curle 1933–4, 282ff.

this method is that a form or pattern is made in wax or wax around a clay core; fine details can be modelled in the soft material that are much harder to create on stone or even on clay. The form is then covered in clay and fired, during which the wax runs out, leaving a cavity. Molten metal can then be poured into the cavity and the outer clay walls broken away to reveal a metal version of the original wax form. Numerous objects were made by this technique, not only those with elaborately moulded appendages but also, it seems, those with intricate surface decoration. The highly regular spiral decoration on objects of Periods II and III in Scandinavia was executed by creating the design on wax rather than punching it onto finished objects.[102] Other objects for which this was true include the great ceremonial trumpets or *lurs* of Scandinavia, and the rather similar horns of Ireland. Detailed study of some of these has shown that lures are cast in lost-wax moulds in several separate pieces.[103] On some of the lures, slots or holes can be seen where core-supporters were present and have dropped out; such holes were probably filled with plugs of resin or wax, or had extra metal cast on. The sections were then joined with locking joints, of which the most interesting are the so-called maeander joints, made by incorporating a dove-tailed end to the base of each section. A further piece of lost-wax casting then enabled the sections to be joined together and the length to be adjusted so that each lure was exactly the same as its partner (they appear in pairs, the bells facing in opposite directions).[104] The mouthpiece and bell, with elaborately decorated plate or disc, were then cast on and the whole object polished to remove casting traces and other imperfections. In the case of the Irish horn, holes were usually cut into the wall of the instrument, great care being taken to achieve regularity both of diameter and of positioning so as to achieve the desired musical results.

A suggestion to account for the relative lack of moulds in some parts of Bronze Age Europe is that moulds were made from a special casting sand (sand with an admixture of gum, oil or fine clay to enable it to stick together).[105] To make a bivalve mould by this process, two hollowed-out pieces of wood – such as a tree-trunk or branch – would be needed. One would be filled with sand and the pattern pressed into it (after being dusted with graphite or a similar substance to prevent it sticking in the sand), the second placed on top and more sand inserted from a hole in the upper surface. Then the two parts would be separated, the shape of the pattern now imprinted in the sand. The addition of an end piece to retain the metal when it has been

---

[102] Rønne 1989a.
[103] Basic studies by Schmidt (1915), Broholm, Larsen and Skjerne (1949) and Oldeberg (1947) for the Nordic area, and Holmes (n.d. [1980]) for Ireland.
[104] On some lures a tubular ring was used to strengthen the joint. A locking device, consisting of a triangular projection that slotted under the ring-band to ensure that the sections did not come apart, also appears (Schmidt 1915, 103–4).
[105] Coghlan 1975, 50f.; Goldmann 1981.

poured completes the process. Such moulds can apparently be used without the need for channels for the escape of gas (the gas percolates through the sand) and do not need preheating. If this technique really was suitable for the casting of bronze objects, all that would be needed would be a supply of suitable sand and clay.

The technique of casting on, also known as 'running on' (in German *Überfangguss*), was used to fabricate objects made in more than one piece, to repair broken objects, or to add pieces on to existing objects (for example, the solid bronze hilt to a sword).[106] A separate mould would be made and the original cast object inserted into it and heated before the metal was poured. In spite of the technical difficulties, very many successful castings of this type were made, especially handles, hilts and other attachments. Evidence for its use is noted on Wilburton hoard material in Britain.[107] A striking case of casting on to effect a repair can be seen in two swords from Kosovo, where rapiers were remodelled into flange-hilted swords by the addition of cast-on hilts.[108] In like manner, casting faults could be repaired by skilful casting on to fill gaps, as with the circular additions to the blade of a solid-hilted sword from Kuhbier, Kr. Ost-Prignitz.[109]

Decoration and finishing

After the casting of an object and its successful extraction from its mould, it had to be finished. In the case of simple tools such as axes, this might consist of no more than the removal of the most intrusive evidence of the casting process, such as the flashes and projecting seams where the metal ran into the venting holes and the gap between the mould halves. This was presumably done by hammering, though filing or grinding with a stone may have been equally effective.[110] Hammering would have been carried out to increase the hardness of objects, and hot forging to sharpen cutting edges. After this, the surface would probably have been finished by using a stone for fine grinding and polishing, and a high sheen could have been imparted by a polisher of wool, initially with an abrasive agent such as fine sand, followed by oil or wax. Many bronzes retain their sheen to the present day: the arts of the Bronze Age smith were effective and durable.

At Hesselager, Gudme district (Funen), a grave contained a collection of stone objects that have been interpreted as polishers or grinders for metal-finishing.[111] These are similar to the collections from Ommerschans and

---

[106] Drescher 1958; Coghlan 1975, 64f.
[107] Northover 1982b, 94.
[108] Harding 1995, 21 pl. 4.
[109] Born and Hansen 1991.
[110] Coghlan 1975, 104ff.; bronze files would more likely have been used for working wood: e.g. Velem St Vid (von Miske 1908, 132).
[111] Randsborg 1984.

Lunteren in the Netherlands and seem to represent the portable equipment of a metal-finisher.[112] The Lunteren find includes a group of stones which may include touchstones for determining the purity of gold objects. The polishing stones are repeated in the find from Ordrup (north-west Zealand).[113]

The decoration of objects, for instance with line ornament, bosses or dots, could be achieved either through the casting (by creating the decoration on the mould) or through working the metal after casting by incision or punching on to the surface, or by pushing the thin metal into a wooden form (repoussée work). A range of punches, chisels, scribers and gravers are known which account adequately for most of the ornamentation seen.[114] The methods used to create decoration on the surface of bronze objects are of considerable interest. Bronze chisels and punches are of limited use on copper and of no use at all on bronze, as experiments have shown.[115] The possibility that iron punches were in use at least by the time of the Late Bronze Age has been raised, since marks of such tools on bronze objects have been recognised.[116] Bronze tools leave marks that are broad, shallow and rounded in the middle, while iron produces sharp, narrow and angular marks. The marks of iron punches can be recognised on bronzes of Ha A2 and B1, though not on those of Br D and only doubtfully on those of Ha A1. The finding of an iron punch on a Middle Bronze Age trackway in Holland is taken as corroborating evidence for the existence of such punches long before the start of the Iron Age.[117]

Tools such as these were not only used for creating new objects in the first place; they were also used to repair broken pieces. On a sword from Croatia, for instance, a broken blade was repaired by sawing through the midrib, filing off the rib and inserting a rivet which was then hammered down to fill the missing rib area. In spite of these attentions, the blade broke again a little further down.[118]

Drills must have been available for some of the fine work, and possible drill bits have been identified in the metalwork from the Unexplored Mansion.[119] No such examples are known from continental Europe, and punching or casting is considered to have been the standard method of

---

[112] Butler and Bakker 1961; Butler and van der Waals 1966, 63f.

[113] Rønne 1989b.

[114] Maryon 1937–8, 1938; Wyss 1971; Coghlan 1975, 98ff.; Bouzek 1978; Mohen 1984–5. The hoards from Larnaud (Jura), Génelard (Sâone-et-Loire) and Fresné-la-Mère (Calvados) include many of these tools, and other collections come from Swiss lake sites (Rychner 1979, pl. 126, 1–17; 1987, pl. 29, 9–10) and Ireland (Tylecote 1986, 103). The Génelard hoard has a curious set of what are believed to be moulds, though they look more like punches, for making buttons and ornaments with concentric circles (Eluère and Mohen 1993).

[115] Drescher 1956–8; Coghlan 1975, 99f.

[116] Bouzek 1978.

[117] Casparie 1984; Charles 1984. The small but slowly rising number of iron objects lends some weight to this notion (Harding 1993).

[118] Harding 1995, 34 pl. 11.

[119] Catling, in Popham 1984, 214; Deshayes 1960, i 46f., ii 10–11 pl. 2.

perforating bronzework.[120] Experiments showed that drill bits of bronze rapidly wear out; iron bits would have done the job but have not been found.
Holes needed to be bored in order to take rivets, a common joining technique
(seen, for instance, on buckets and cauldrons of the Late Bronze Age), and for
the insertion of wire, which is found in a number of hoards and other finds.
Riveting was a standard feature in the attachment of hafts and handles, for
instance the hilts of swords and daggers or the handles of sickles. A curious
feature of solid-hilted swords is that they often have skeuomorphic rivet
designs on the hilts, the appearance of a rivet where there was none. Smiths,
it seems, expected to provide rivets on sword hilts and carried on doing so
even when there was no need.

Other metals

Not much is known about silver in pre-Iron Age Europe.[121] Native silver is
rare and most silver must have been obtained by cupellation from lead, so it
is not surprising that silver objects are rare in Bronze Age Europe. The famous
sources in Greece (Siphnos, Laurion), Early Bronze Age artefacts in Egypt,
Crete and Troy[122] and Late Bronze Age objects in the Shaft Graves of Mycenae
find little echo in lands to the north; there are a few finds of Copper Age date
scattered through Europe.[123] Daggers from Usatovo belong to the Early Bronze
Age, parallel with early Troy, while the silver dagger, spearheads and pin from
the Borodino hoard also suggest Aegeo-Anatolian connections; its date is disputed, but must lie in the second millennium BC.[124] The famous hoard from
Perşinari (Ploieşti) contains, in addition to the well-known gold sword, four
silver axes,[125] and a silver dagger in the Hungarian National Museum presumably belongs to the same horizon. Silver pendants are present at the
Zimnicea cemetery (Teleorman) in southern Romania and other Romanian
sites.[126] Two silver rings were found in graves at Singen in southern
Germany.[127] Much the most spectacular, however, are the finds from the west,
notably the diadems, rings and beads of the Argaric Bronze Age in southern
Spain[128] and the silver cups from barrows at Saint-Adrien (Côtes-du-Nord) and

---

[120] Coghlan 1975, 104.
[121] Mozsolics 1965–6, 34ff.; Primas 1996.
[122] Branigan 1968; Gale and Stos-Gale 1981.
[123] e.g. spiral ornament from the megalithic grave MVI at Petit Chasseur, Sion, Switzerland
(Primas 1996), and a shaft-hole axe from the tumulus at Mala Gruda (Tivat, Montenegro)
(Parović-Pešikan and Trbuhović 1971).
[124] Harding 1984, 200ff.
[125] Mozsolics 1965–6, 5ff., 50.
[126] Alexandrescu 1974, 85; Oarţa de Sus in the Sălaj depression: Kacsó 1987, 69f., fig. 23.
[127] Krause 1988, 88f., fig. 46.
[128] Siret and Siret 1887, 147, 152ff., 223ff., 259ff., pls. 20, 27, 29–34, 36, 43–5, 63, 68; Hook *et
al.* 1987; Pingel 1992, 36ff.; Montero Ruiz 1993, 53ff.

Saint-Fiacre en Melrand (Morbihan).[129] A silver bead recently turned up on a destroyed burial mound in southern England, the first Bronze Age silver find from Britain.[130]

By contrast, gold finds are relatively common. From the time of the Varna cemetery, gold seems to have occupied an important place in the scheme of values prevalent in Europe – dangerous though it is to attempt judgements of value for remote periods of the past. A number of recent accounts of the development of gold-working in the Bronze Age are available, from which it is clear that the amounts of gold varied enormously from region to region and period to period, presumably a reflection of both availability and fashion, as well as (in the case of hoard finds of gold) factors other than utilitarian.[131]

The beaten sheet goldwork seen in the Early Bronze Age of the west on lunulae, discs and diadems was in technological terms the equivalent to the gold of Varna or other Eneolithic finds in eastern Europe. To make a lunula, a bar of gold metal was beaten out thin using stone or metal hammers, and decoration added by the repoussée technique. The trick of decorating dagger pommels in Wessex and Brittany with minute gold pins is also noteworthy.[132] But more complicated forms were also possible, as is shown by the group of sheet-gold vessels of Early Bronze Age date, the earliest probably a golden Beaker from Eschenz (Switzerland), soon followed by cups from Fritzdorf (Bonn) and Rillaton (Cornwall).[133] In the Carpathian Basin, too, there are gold cups, discs and small ornaments, but also a series of massive bracelets and shaft-hole axes, as seen in the finds from Ţufalău and Biia,[134] and gold came to be used for similar prestige objects in the German area (for instance in the Leubingen barrow). The Argaric Bronze Age of south-eastern Spain produced a range of mostly small gold objects,[135] both in sheet and in more solid form, and small objects were present in the west of Spain at the same period; an extraordinary hoard from Caldas de Reyes (Pontevedra) contains vessels, arm-rings and a diadem.[136]

In later stages of the Bronze Age, a bewildering variety of techniques was used to create the extraordinary range of magnificent showpieces that survive in the treasuries of European museums. Sheet gold-working continued, as can be seen from the Mold cape,[137] and from the large and varied repertoire of highly decorated cups and other vessels,[138] including the so-called

---

[129] Briard 1975; 1978; other silver finds from Brittany are ring-headed pins and spirally wound armrings: Gallay 1981, 87 table 53 (Pleudaniel), 93 table 56 (Quimperlé).
[130] Bradley 1997, 28.
[131] Hardmeyer 1976; Taylor 1980; Eluère 1982; Hartmann 1982; Pingel 1992; Eogan 1994.
[132] Taylor 1980, 47ff.; Eluère 1982, 45ff.
[133] Hardmeyer and Bürgi 1975.
[134] Mozsolics 1965–6.
[135] Including hilt-plates on swords: Almagro Gorbea 1972.
[136] Pingel 1992, 55ff.
[137] Powell 1953.
[138] Eogan 1981; Eluère 1982, 102ff.

'crowns' from Avanton, Ezelsdorf and Schifferstadt.[139] Such cups came to occupy a central place in the provision of 'service sets', such as the magnificent collections from Messingwerk near Eberswalde in Brandenburg,[140] or Mariesminde on Funen.[141] Many of these may have had ritual functions. Bar-working became extremely common after the Early Bronze Age, gold bars being hammered into various shapes (flat bands, bars that were square or round in cross-section, sometimes with raised flanges), where appropriate twisted, and then bent to the desired form. By this means, elaborate bracelets, earrings and neckrings were created. Gold sheet was also used to encase objects made of other materials, a technique that started in the Early Bronze Age but was revived later on. In the latest part of the Irish Bronze Age, new forms appear: 'lock-rings', gorgets, 'dress-fasteners' and 'sleeve-fasteners', bracelets with flaring terminals, and many other forms.[142] The extraordinary penannular lock-rings are made out of two circular pieces of gold plate or individual gold wires soldered together and are held together by binding strips round the edge.[143] The gorgets are large penannular ornaments decorated with ridges, bosses and rope patterns, with a disc terminal soldered to each end. The multitude of splendid ornaments produced in Ireland and other areas indicates both the proficiency of goldsmiths and the ready availability of gold. Unfortunately, little is known about the contexts in which this gold was used and deposited. Iberia also saw a rich development of gold-working, with the hoard of Villena-Rambla del Panadero (Alicante) containing elaborately decorated vessels, armrings and other objects.[144]

Lead was important for the bronze-worker, not only in its own right for making objects but also as an alloying material and as a material for fittings and repairs. Because of its weight and relative malleability, it was well suited for making small fittings and attachments on bronze and other objects, for instance in the attachment of hilt-plates and pommels to swords, and also for repairs and to remove imperfections in bronze.[145] It was used in the hafting of implements, for instance swords: the cavity in the grip of a number of solid-hilted swords (*Vollgriffschwerter*) was filled with the metal, no doubt to improve the balance of the sword which would otherwise be far too light for the size of the blade.[146] This practice remained somewhat unusual, however, and is not present on many of the examples investigated. Lead was used to fill spaces left by cores in casting.[147] At the *nuraghe* of Antigori in southern

[139] Schauer 1986; Gerloff 1995.
[140] Kossinna 1913; Schuchhardt 1914.
[141] Brøndsted 1962, 167ff., 298.
[142] Eogan 1994.
[143] Eogan 1969.
[144] Soler García 1965; Pingel 1992, 207ff. table 70.
[145] Schmidt 1915, 92ff.
[146] Wüstemann 1992.
[147] As with a double-looped palstave from Spain (Harrison and Craddock 1981).

Sardinia, lead rivets or clamps were used to mend both local nuragic and imported Mycenaean pottery.[148] It was also used to make small objects, for instance a block and a sword pommel at Runnymede,[149] and small irregular oblong beads, as in a unique find from Peeblesshire, southern Scotland.[150] At Auvernier there is a circular weight with a lifting loop,[151] and at Antigori a small double-axe was of lead, either votive or a toy.[152] Two lead earnings were found in grave 351 at Jelšovce, Slovakia, belonging to the Únětice-Mad'arovce phase. At present, this is the earliest known lead find from Europe.[153] Somewhat larger lead objects are also occasionally found, notably socketed axes,[154] and some of the Late Bronze Age Breton socketed axes have a high lead content.[155] As discussed in chapter 9, these axes may have had a votive function, though it has also been suggested that the addition of lead was a way of eking out copper in times of scarcity.

Inevitably, there was more lead metal in circulation than it is possible to reconstruct from the surviving material. Some of this was in the form of ingots, as from Fort Harrouard and sites in Brittany.[156] Something of the abundance of lead can be seen from a number of moulds that have either lead adhering to them or lead traces present on the surfaces. The former, along with the socketed axes, suggests that lead patterns may have been used in the production process, or even that casting by 'lost lead' may have been practised; the latter probably reflect the use of lead in alloyed copper rather than that of lead on its own.

Small objects of tin are also found, albeit rarely, for instance tin beads on a necklace at Odoorn (Drenthe) and Sutton Veney (Wiltshire) and tin pins on the dagger hilt from Bargeroosterveld (Drenthe) and the wooden vessels from Guldhøj in Jutland.[157] Its use as a decorative material on pottery in the north Alpine area and elsewhere recalls a similar use on Mycenaean pottery;[158] in the Swiss–German area, its presence does not seem to be related to any particular pottery production tradition or grave deposition pattern. An example is that on the pottery from sites on the Lac du Bourget (Savoie).

---

[148] Ferrarese Ceruti 1979, 248.
[149] Needham and Hook 1988.
[150] Hunter and Davis 1994.
[151] Rychner 1979, pl. 130, 11.
[152] Ferrarese Ceruti 1979, 248 pl. 1; reinterpreted as a boat model by Lo Schiavo 1986b.
[153] J. Bátora, pers. comm.
[154] Tylecote 1987c, 93.
[155] de Lisle 1881; Briard 1965.
[156] Briard 1990–1.
[157] Shell n.d. [1980]; Primas 1985.
[158] Primas 1985, 558; Fischer 1993; Immerwahr 1966.

Metalworking sites

One of the most frustrating aspects of the study of European Bronze Age metallurgy is the almost total lack of sites with satisfactory evidence for the processes of metalwork production. This is probably because furnaces were slight affairs, consisting of pits with clay lining and superstructure, all above-ground elements being destroyed at the end of the firing. Pits containing evidence of such firing may, therefore, be all that survives, and unless they contain specific indications that metallurgy took place in them (for example through the finding of slag or metal waste) they can easily be interpreted as something quite different. With modern excavation techniques, a number of sites have been shown to have hosted metallurgical operations, even without the survival of the furnace.

The remains of a furnace were found at Taltitz near Plauen in the Vogtland of Saxony.[159] In an area with many traces of Urnfield settlement, and with both copper and tin sources close at hand, a series of pit concentrations, each 50–100 m across, led up a small side valley of the river Elster. At the northernmost was found a pair of pits of sub-rectangular shape with flat floor and steeply sloping sides, about 50 cm long and 30 cm wide, connected by a flat channel; between the pits the floor was strongly reddened in a circular shape. A broadening of the channel in the middle exhibited particularly strong signs of heat, but there was no sign of slagging or sintering, which makes it likely that this was a casting and not a smelting furnace.[160]

A sizeable number of Danish Late Bronze Age settlements also produced mould and crucible fragments and bronze waste.[161] It has been suggested that Urnfield settlements can be divided into 'production' and 'user' sites in the context of metallurgy. Many did not practise metallurgy themselves but were dependent on neighbouring sites which did. In many others, only everyday items were produced, such as sickles, axes and small ornaments. Fortified sites played an especially important role in this, not only supplying themselves but also serving as regional recycling centres. If they also practised crucible smelting, almost all necessary processes could have happened on them.

Notable assemblages of metalworking debris, some with the remains of furnaces, come from many sites, such as Fort Harrouard (Sorel-Moussel,

---

[159] Simon 1992.

[160] Comparable remains have been found at other German sites, notably Parchim (Becker 1989) and Dresden-Coschütz (Pietzsch 1971), where bronze waste was found near the metalworking site, along with moulds, finished bronzes, bun ingots, scrap hoards and a chisel for surface bronze-working. Copper ore is present in the immediate vicinity of this site too; analysis of the slags on the site, however, ruled out the possibility that the ovens there were used for smelting ores rather than for secondary working of copper metal. The situation in the upper Saale valley and Orla basin in eastern Thuringia is similar, with workshop sites lying close to copper-bearing rocks (e.g. Pössneck-Schlettwein: Simon 1982).

[161] Levy 1991.

Eure-et-Loir)[162] and other sites in central France;[163] Auvernier and Hauterive-Champréveyres, Lake Neuchâtel, and a number of other sites on the Swiss lakes;[164] the Wasserburg at Bad Buchau, Württemberg;[165] Karlstein (Berchtesgaden, Bavaria);[166] Säckingen (Waldshut, southern Baden);[167] Nieder Neundorf (Niesky) and other fortified settlements of the Billendorf group in eastern Germany;[168] Velem St Vid in western Hungary;[169] Hallunda, Botkyrka, Södermanland, Sweden;[170] Fiavé and Ledro, north Italy;[171] and sites in Spain (for instance Cerro Virtud (Almeria),[172] El Ventorro, Madrid,[173] Peña Negra, Alicante[174] and sites of the Argaric Bronze Age[175]), Corsica and Sardinia (as at

[162] Mohen and Bailloud 1987, 126ff. Numerous locations on this important site had traces of metallurgical activity, both from the old, poorly recorded excavations and from the new work in the 1980s; most date to the Early and Middle Bronze Age. These concentrate on the periphery of the site, and some indicate specialisation in the production of particular forms: spearheads in 'locus 1', the 'smith's house'; daggers, bracelets, pins and axes elsewhere; swords in a large find made in 1984 (Mohen 1984). Fired clay structures found in both old and new excavations are interpreted as the bases of smithing furnaces; in at least one case, the tuyère slot was evident.

[163] Charente and adjacent areas: caves of Queroy at Chazelles and of Perrats at Agris (Bourhis and Gomez 1985), as well as the site at Bois-du-Roc at Vilhonneur (Coffyn *et al.* 1981, 29f.; Gomez 1984). At the latter was the base of a furnace with slag from bronze-casting, at the former clay tuyère and crucible fragments and moulds.

[164] Wyss 1971, 123; Rychner 1987; Rychner-Faraggi 1993.

[165] Moulds, hammers and a tuyère were found, but no sign of any metalworking location inside the settlement itself. This has led observers to suggest that such workshops must have lain outside the site, far enough away to avoid sparks from the furnace endangering the wooden buildings but near enough for workers to retreat inside the palisade in time of danger (Jockenhövel 1986; Kimmig 1992).

[166] Menke 1968. Three mould fragments, for flanged axe, ingot and dagger blade, were found with a fragment of a 'tongue' ingot (*Zungenbarren*), slag, clay fragments with slag adhering, and pieces of ore.

[167] Gersbach 1969, 38ff.; Jockenhövel 1986b, 223, 232: a large Urnfield settlement lies on an island in the Rhine, where industrial waste is spread over a wide area, including slag, ingot pieces, smelting crucibles, moulds, funnels and other metal waste.

[168] Buck 1982: of 12 stockades certainly belonging to the Billendorf group, five have produced evidence for bronze-working. At Nieder Neundorf a post-built house contained numerous clay mould fragments, and both inside and nearby were tuyères and crucibles. Also on the site were pins complete with runners and miscastings.

[169] von Miske 1908; 1929: this site lies near sources of copper, with malachite and azurite obtainable on the surface on the I'rottkö (Geschriebenstein) mountain, part of the Günsergebirge range that straddles the border. On the site were found numerous bronze-working implements, including stone hammers, crucibles, tuyères, bun ingots, moulds, a range of bronze hammers and chisels, a saw and various punches. Unfortunately, the excavation techniques of the time did not permit the recovery of working installations, which must undoubtedly have been present.

[170] Jaanusson 1981; Jaanusson and Vahlne 1975; Jaanusson, Löfstrand and Vahlne 1978: in Site 13 a large building (the 'workshop') contained the foundations of six furnaces, with a further six outside. Large furnaces were placed in a pit lined with stones, small ones rested directly on the ground. Fired, partly vitrified, clay floors and parts of the collapsed domes were present. In their vicinity were fragments of crucibles, clay moulds and a few bronze rods. Similar but less extensive evidence came from Sites 69 and 76.

[171] Metalworking equipment has been found in both these pile sites in north Italy, including crucibles, tuyères and moulds. At both sites, crucibles of clay with a socket for the insertion of a wooden handle were found (Perini 1987, 34ff.; Rageth 1974, 175ff. pls. 89–91).

[172] Delibes de Castro *et al.* 1996 (late Neolithic).

[173] Priego Fernández del Campo and Quero Castro 1992 (Beaker date).

[174] Gonzalez Prats 1992 (Late Bronze Age).

[175] El Argar: Siret and Siret 1887, 127f., pl. 27; Lull 1983; Montero Ruiz 1993.

Terrina IV (Aléria) and Monte d'Accoddi.[176] Sites in Britain and Ireland have also produced metalworking remains in recent years, though none has given such extensive evidence as the continental examples listed above. These include the Breiddin hillfort, Powys, Wales;[177] Mucking North Ring;[178] Dainton, Devon;[179] Grimes Graves;[180] Jarlshof;[181] Lough Gur;[182] Dun Aonghasa (Inis Mór, Aran Islands);[183] Rathgall, Co. Wicklow;[184] and Killymoon, Co. Tyrone.[185]

The organisation of metal production

All these metallurgical processes involve specialist knowledge, but also an input of labour. But metal production is not a 'public' operation like the erection of megalithic tombs or standing stones; for space reasons, most operations can have involved only a limited number of people. At the same time, the number of those involved in servicing the industry (woodmen, animal

---

[176] At Aléria crucibles, slag and tuyères, along with an awl of arsenical copper, were found; the copper may have come from the local source at Linguizetta (Lo Schiavo 1986, 232).

[177] Musson 1991, 57ff., 147ff. fig. 60: crucible and mould fragments, fragments of copper alloy melting slag and broken bronzes from Area B3-4-5 in the hillfort interior, from which were recovered hearths and a complex of pits, furnace bases and working-hollows of Late Bronze Age date.

[178] Needham in Bond 1988: clay mould fragments and part of a crucible, with a little bronze scrap, from the ditch of a Late Bronze Age circular enclosure. Similar material comes from Springfield Lyons, Essex (not yet published).

[179] Needham 1980: a large assemblage of metalworking debris in and around a pit beside mound 2. Crucible fragments, moulds for spearheads, swords and rings, and a little bronze waste, were represented. The crucibles, which were of two distinct classes and included legged varieties, gave evidence of use over a period of time because of relining and wall heightening.

[180] Needham in Longworth et al. 1991: a few crucible fragments and around 150 clay mould fragments were found in the Middle Bronze Age midden in the top of Shaft X. The moulds were all, where recognisable, for basal-looped spearheads and represent certain evidence that clay moulds were in use by the Middle Bronze Age.

[181] Curle 1933-4; Hamilton 1956, 21f., 28f.: one of the houses of the Late Bronze Age settlement produced in its last phase of use a crucible fragment, 200 mould fragments with 44 gate pieces, other valve and casing fragments, the core for a socketed knife and a knife into which it fitted.

[182] Ó Ríordáin 1954, 400-3, 420-2: clay and stone moulds and crucibles were found in House I, Site D, along with a few small bronzes; in Site F, a large collection of clay moulds and some bronze waste occurred in, and was possibly associated with, a stone-walled house. A crucible fragment and bronzes also occurred in Site C.

[183] Recent excavations produced settlement evidence as well as clay moulds for Late Bronze Age swords, spearheads, axes, pins, bracelets and other objects, and crucible fragments, in a hut whose walls extend under, and thus predate, the stone fortification wall, which is usually attributed to the Iron Age (Cotter 1994).

[184] Raftery 1971: more than 400 clay mould fragments, including those for swords, spearheads and tools, and lumps and bars of bronze, occurred in an area with nine large hearths near the round-house in the innermost area of the fort; a large mould fragment was found in one of the hearths.

[185] This consisted of an area of grey ashy soil deriving from three mounds full of baked clay and charcoal (Hurl 1995). Bronze and gold objects, spindle-whorls, polished stone axes, saddle querns, clay moulds and stone hammers and polishers were found, the datable objects belonging to the Dowris phase.

handlers and others) would have meant that the workforce was far from negligible. Estimates have been made of the number of workers who might have serviced the Mitterberg production, a figure of 180 allegedly accounting for all those needed for transport, haulage and timber erection as well as mining, in a 'mining-unit comprising three open-casts'; a figure of 500–600 was suggested for the whole Salzburg mining region.[186] Shennan uses ethnographic and historical sources, and an estimate of 10 tonnes output of copper per annum, to suggest that 270–400 people could have been involved in the production at the Mitterberg, making allowance for those not engaged in the activity and for time spent on other activities such as food production.[187] The figure compares well with his estimate of a population on the settlement site of the Klinglberg at St Veit near Bischofshofen of 40–100; the Klinglberg is one of three such sites in the area. It is certainly possible, however, in view of limitations on space in the mines themselves, that the numbers involved were smaller still. The mode of operation at Mount Gabriel was probably also distinctly limited. If, in contradiction of the inflated figures produced by Jackson, these mines were worked for around 200 years, producing as little as 15 kg of copper per annum (enough for around 46 bronze axes), the scale of production was potentially much smaller than would appear at first sight.[188]

Was the access to ore sources controlled? There is little or no sign that the maintenance of life was centralised, at least in the earlier stages of the Bronze Age, but one can argue that from an early stage there were defined notions of territoriality which would include control of resources, while the input of labour and energy involved in initiating mining was such that control would not have been relinquished lightly. By contrast, the 'direct access model' would envisage that human groups could have come to a mine and exploited it as and when they wanted, on a seasonal basis. It must be a task for Bronze Age research in the coming years to try to understand by what means decisions to undertake mining operations were taken, and how the procurement of a given quantity of ore then led to the production of a given number and type of axes or other products. What transactions occurred between the production of raw copper and the conversion into objects? Were the miners and the smiths one and the same?

Shennan has attempted to answer some of these questions as a consequence of his excavation of the settlement site of St Veit-Klinglberg in the Salzach valley of central Austria.[189] Analysis of metal waste ('casting cake') on the site, and of the slag temper in pottery, showed that more than one metal source was being exploited by the occupants of the Klinglberg, either through

[186] Zschocke and Preuschen 1932; Pittioni 1951.
[187] Shennan 1995, 300ff.
[188] O'Brien 1994, 195ff., 235ff.; Jackson n.d. [1979].
[189] Shennan 1995.

exchange with other neighbouring groups or by Klinglbergers spending time away from their home base. What is more, cereals found on the site suggest that foodstuffs were imported and therefore that productive workers were devoting their time to mining rather than agriculture. This fits a picture of rapid expansion of work in the Mitterberg mines, with deeper sulphide ores coming into use for the first time in the Early Bronze Age. By the Middle Bronze Age, settlement sites considerably larger than the Klinglberg are known, reflecting an increase in productive effort by a further order of magnitude.

If little is known about miners, there is not much more known about smiths, artefacts being the main source of evidence with which to reconstruct their mode of operation. Childe's model has been widely adopted, implicitly or explicitly, in many works dealing with the Bronze Age.[190] According to this model, the smith was an itinerant specialist, his skills restricted in distribution and therefore carefully guarded. As smithing was a full-time occupation, the rest of society provided for the smith in return for the products of his craft. He was itinerant – peripatetic would be a better description – in the sense that he travelled from village to village, setting up his workshop and casting his products in each place as he came to it; he did not operate from a central workshop.

There are a number of reasons why Childe and others adopted this model. First, there seemed to be no evidence for permanent workshops from which smiths might have operated. Bronze Age villages were invariably small-scale and dependent on agriculture, with no sign of an industrial component to their economies. Second, the relative scarcity of raw materials in many parts of Europe meant that special access to supplies had to be organised; for a peasant farmer it would be better to leave this in the hands of a specialist who could move between suppliers and users as required. Third, and most important, was the evidence of bronze hoard deposition, where hoards of broken or miscast bronze objects were collected together, apparently for remelting and recasting into new objects. Such finds were thought to be the stock-in-trade of a smith, travelling between communities and recovering his stock at each stop. Alternatively, the metal might have belonged not to the smith but to the village or community. In this case, the metal would not need to be transported about, but the failure to recover the stock is no less puzzling. The problem is that this model is rarely, if ever, supported by ethnographic evidence.[191] Although smiths could sometimes be peripatetic, their travels were determined not by free enterprise on their part but as part of a wider settlement system under the control of a local chief; other examples

---

[190] Childe 1930, 44f.
[191] Rowlands 1971.

show that smiths are resident within communities and practise their craft on a seasonal or part-time basis. Certainly there is nothing to suggest that the pattern of hoard deposition that is seen in the Bronze Age finds any reflection in recent practice in Africa or Asia.

Detailed analysis of individual bronze objects, in particular that relating to smithing traditions and 'industries', sheds some light on the matter. Ideally one would seek to show which products were made by which smith, and over what time-scale. Since that is probably too ambitious a task, one should perhaps settle for indications that a particular working tradition, in other words a workshop, was responsible for certain objects.

In the case of the Middle Bronze Age metalwork of southern England, the restricted distribution of bronze types suggests that production was local in nature and probably seasonal.[192] Some of the hoards of palstaves, for instance, contain large numbers of 'blanks' of the same sub-type, indicating that a single operation would have been responsible for the production of a large number of identical pieces. This, together with the evidence for fixed facilities for hot-working, suggests that permanent workshops were the norm. A study of the so-called Stogursey socketed axe (formerly known as the south Welsh axe), characterised by a decoration of three ribs, a simple moulding round the mouth, and a side loop that is placed high up on the axe, shows that they are found thinly scattered in southern England and rather more densely in south Wales.[193] Stone moulds for such axes occur on five widely separated sites between Cornwall and Surrey; two different sorts of stone have been used, one restricted to Cornwall, the other found in central southern England. Local production of these axes thus probably took place in Devon and Cornwall, in central Wessex and probably also in Somerset, but in south Wales, where axes are most prolific, there are no mould finds and thus no direct evidence for production.[194]

Attempts have been made to identify Hungarian workshops on the basis of objects coming from identical moulds and on similar decoration on different objects.[195] Two daggers from the Kelebia find, apparently from the same mould, the swords from Apa and Hajdúsámson, the decoration on the ends of disc-butted axes and many other examples make it highly likely that a single production location, and perhaps also a single artist, was responsible for their creation. Further, the finding of a number of hoards of unfinished objects together with objects from the same mould, such as the socketed axes in

---

[192] Rowlands 1976.
[193] Needham 1981a; 1990.
[194] At Petters Sports Field, a mould of this type was of non-local stone and perhaps introduced to the Thames Valley by a smith working in the Bulford–Helsbury tradition of central and south-western England.
[195] Mozsolics 1967, 102ff; 1973, 84ff.

the hoard from Drajna de Jos (Prahova, southern Romania), illustrates the point.[196]

Production centres of some sort clearly did exist. What may be questioned is the scale of the enterprise, along with the location of the activity. As shown above, most smithing operations seem, from the scanty traces which they left, to have been on an extremely modest scale, the furnaces and the crucibles being rather small and thus likely to have serviced very limited amounts of metal at one time. Where there are no traces of metalworking at all, one is forced to rely instead on the distribution patterns of the objects produced, the general principle being that the production workshop should lie in the centre of the distribution, or where it clusters most thickly. Particular tricks in the formation of the hilt suggest the existence of workshops for the production of Early Bronze Age swords in the Nordic area, centring on Denmark.[197] The distribution of solid-hilted antenna swords of the Tarquinia type is concentrated massively in north Italy, where the rich centres of the emerging Iron Age were able to commission and absorb large quantities of prestige metalwork;[198] it would be amazing if these particular swords had been produced anywhere other than Etruria. On the other hand, when one takes all the different sub-varieties of antenna sword into account, the picture is somewhat different: although Italy still looms large, other types are distinctly trans-Alpine in distribution, most notably the Zürich and Lipovka types.[199]

But bronze types of the same general form can have an extremely wide distribution, even if detailed sub-types are restricted to a narrow area. This raises the question of how such knowledge was transmitted from area to area; how smiths came to produce such closely similar objects in widely separated parts of Europe. Of many examples which could be examined, one of the most remarkable is the flange-hilted sword of the early Urnfield period.[200] Almost identical forms are found from the East Mediterranean, the Balkans, Italy, central Europe and western Europe. In part, the necessity of weapon modernisation may be responsible (one cannot afford to let one's armoury become obsolete, either in the Bronze Age or today), in that the warriors who actually wielded these swords presumably demanded weaponry that could compete with that of their rivals. But if one is to deny the existence of peripatetic smiths, as the discussion above has suggested, the knowledge of bronze forms in different areas must spread by movement of the actual objects. The currency of bronze swords and hanging bowls in Denmark showed very different amounts of wear or resharpening, which may be due in part to the length

---

[196] Petrescu-Dîmboviţa 1978, 111f., no. 103, pl. 66.
[197] Ottenjann 1969.
[198] Müller-Karpe 1961, pl. 101.
[199] Ibid. pl. 97.
[200] Harding 1984, 162ff.; Bouzek 1985, 119ff., both with full refs.

of time they were in circulation.[201] This differs in different parts of Denmark, suggesting that there was differential access to supplies according to the local conditions in various parts of the country.

The custom and community of bronze-smithing thus documented demands explanation. Whether, as has sometimes been suggested, smiths had a 'mental template' in their production processes which resulted in the remarkable standardisation of forms which is seen, whether the exchange of moulds or patterns was responsible, or whether the copying of metalwork seen elsewhere is involved, the end result was often extraordinary.

In all this, the position of the smith himself remains uncertain, and his identity and mode of functioning shadowy. The smith is in many traditional societies a valued, if feared, craftsman (almost all ethnographic examples are of men), essential for the well-being of a community in many spheres – warfare, agriculture, carpentry, as well as the production of 'non-essential' items such as jewellery or religious goods. In weapon and agricultural tool production, societies depended in a very direct way on his labours. When one attempts to understand these matters, it is ethnographic examples from recent or historical times, usually relating to iron-working, that provide the main source of evidence and, suggestive though these may be, there is no guarantee that they are at all relevant to the Bronze Age. The elements of skill and restricted knowledge that the smith's art involves, and the processes by which this knowledge could be passed on to others, have often been stressed.[202] Ethnography tends to indicate that this is usually done in the context of kin-based social structures and that, the more developed the level of social hierarchisation, the more likely it will be that craft specialisation will apply.

As an epitaph for the smith, we may recall those graves that contained pieces of equipment belonging to the metalworking process. A famous example comes from Kalinovka in south Russia, but there is a series of graves in central Europe with ore pieces, tuyères, crucibles, ingots or bars from Urnfield and early Hallstatt contexts.[203] At Kalinovka kurgans 8 and 55 (Dubovka, Volgograd), two kurgans (barrows) of the Poltavka phase of the earliest Timber Grave culture contained conical tuyères, crucibles, moulds and grindstones, apparently the graves of smiths.[204] The collection of stone polishers from a grave at Hesselager on Funen has already been mentioned.[205] The significance of these graves may indicate the occupation of the deceased and the intimate connection of smithing tools with particular individuals. Their presence may imply special status for the smith, or that aspects of the smithing process were connected with votive acts (see chapter 9). Given the important role

---

[201] Kristiansen 1977; 1978.
[202] e.g. Williamson 1990.
[203] Jockenhövel 1982b.
[204] Shilov 1959a; 1959b; Gimbutas 1965, 546ff.
[205] Randsborg 1984.

that the smith must have played, it would not be surprising to find special treatment accorded him in death, as perhaps in life.

Epilogue: the change to iron

During the later stages of the Bronze Age, increasing numbers of iron objects were being produced, especially in the eastern half of Europe but also in the south, where East Mediterranean influences have been suspected.[206] A few pieces in iron were indeed present much earlier, in the Early Bronze Age, as with the famous dagger from a well at Gánovce in Slovakia.[207] It is commonly supposed that this iron must have come from Anatolia, though nothing is known of the processes by which this could have occurred. Certainly there is no indication of a local iron-producing industry in Europe at this time. A case has, however, been made, based on the evidence of the finely incised lines on some Urnfield bronzework, that iron tools for decorating bronze were in use much earlier than has otherwise been supposed.[208] Since the earliest examples of a phenomenon are the hardest to recover archaeologically, there is nothing inherently unlikely in this argument.

By the late Urnfield period, there was a significant number of iron objects in use, both in eastern and southern Europe and also in the centre and north.[209] In Sweden, finds of iron slag on Late Bronze Age sites (from Period IV onwards) indicate local working, taken to mean that iron technology was adopted by local bronze-smelters, by means of contact and exchange of ideas with 'foreign metalworkers', clear indication that the preferred model for the introduction of iron-working is the 'immigrant' model of Alexander.[210] Iron in the north is here seen as a functional, not a prestige, metal from the start, being used for minor cutting tools. Its ready availability led to its widespread adoption and the falling-off of long-distance trade routes which had brought copper metal to parts of Europe distant from the mining areas.

The process of transition to a full iron-using technology was a gradual one, and there are few signs that iron had any great impact on Bronze Age economies. At the same time, it has been suggested that the main reason for the enormous number of bronze hoards of the latest, Ewart Park, phase in Britain was the introduction of iron, and the consequent dumping of bronze (see chapter 10).[211] Certainly by Ha C, iron became the dominant metal for everyday use and was also in use for weapons and some ornaments. The

[206] Pleiner 1980; 1981; Waldbaum 1980; Delpino 1993.
[207] Vlček and Hajek 1963; Taylor 1989.
[208] Bouzek 1978; Drescher (1956–8) used similar arguments.
[209] László 1977; Čović 1980; Bouzek 1978; 1985; Kimmig 1981; Furmánek 1988; Bukowski 1989; Hjärthner-Holdar 1993.
[210] Hjärthner-Holdar 1993; Alexander 1981; the other models are peaceful introduction and warlike introduction.
[211] Burgess 1979.

decline of bronze was only the most obvious of the many elements of material culture that underwent a major transformation in the eighth and seventh centuries BC, and which would naturally be the subject of a book describing the ensuing period, the Age of Iron.

CHAPTER 7

OTHER CRAFTS

Metal production was a major preoccupation in the Bronze Age but it was by no means the only one, nor for many people the most important one. Commoner materials were at hand for daily use. Far and away the commonest archaeological material from the period is pottery, though this reflects survival as well as original abundance. On the other hand, the material used in most areas for building construction was wood, though usually only the negative traces of its former existence survive, in the form of post-holes. In areas where stone was available, it was also used, usually in rough form, but for items such as querns and grinders, or for the production of high-quality display items such as mace-heads or battle-axes, it could be finely worked and highly polished to bring out the veining in the material. Leather, bone and antler working were important in most areas, though few detailed studies are available.

Other crafts were also important, notably textile manufacture and glass production. The production and distribution of salt is a crucial (though often forgotten) aspect of life in all societies, and it was no less important in the prehistoric world than in today's. These crafts and industries have left traces of varying extent in the archaeological record.

Potting

In spite of its abundance, little is known about the context of production of Bronze Age pottery. It is not known who made pots (male or female, higher or lower status individuals) or in what situations they were fired, transported around communities, or 'commoditised' (see p. 404). There is some ethnographic support for the suggestion that potting was usually carried out by women, but there is no means of knowing if this was the case in Bronze Age Europe. Certainly it was the case that in some areas great effort was expended on pottery, especially in terms of elaborate shapes or decoration: in Italy, for instance. The pottery of the Apennine culture exhibits a range of exotic forms and ornaments, though in other ways the material culture of these sites was not at an advanced technological level.[1] It is almost as if people were mak-

[1] Trump 1958.

ing up for the lack of other skills (e.g. metalworking) by pouring their art into their pottery.

Pottery on most Bronze Age sites naturally divides into several categories of fineness, ranging from the very coarse (for storage and cooking) to the very fine (high-quality tableware). In some cases, it appears that particular shapes and fabrics were made specifically for deposition in graves or 'ritual' deposits; it is common to find certain types in graves but not in settlements (this is undoubtedly a factor that has contributed to the difficulty of defining the settlement archaeology of many cultures). The elaborate wares seen in the graves of the Velatice culture, for instance, show forms that seem unlikely to have graced the tables of the period, even those of elites.

Pot-firing kilns have occasionally been found, though in practice it is hard to tell which installations were really for this purpose rather than for others. Excavations in the Lausitz fortified settlements of Poland, for instance, showed that many ovens and hearths were present, marked by their baked clay floors; one assumes that some had a domed upper part and were for bread-making or something similar, but some could have been connected with other firing activities. The remains of pottery kilns have turned up on a number of Bronze Age sites, for instance at Hascherkeller and Elchinger Kreuz in Bavaria;[2] and at Sévrier on Lake Annecy (Haute Savoie) and Hohlandsberg in Alsace.[3]

Hoards of pottery, which recur with some regularity in several parts of the Bronze Age world, have been interpreted in various ways. Some authors have seen these as newly fired pots awaiting distribution, while others have preferred a ritual interpretation (see p. 331). These considerations indicate that while pottery production played a major role in Bronze Age industrial activity, most of it remains a closed book in terms of context and situation. Detailed analysis of form and ornament by find-spot remains one possible avenue of research that could be explored, as it has been in the Neolithic.[4]

Wood-working[5]

Although wood survives relatively rarely in the archaeological record, in pre-history it was one of the most frequently utilised materials, and for building probably the *most* utilised material – certainly in those areas where no suitable stone was available. In practice, lamentably little information is available for study. There are notable exceptions, of which the sites of the Somerset Levels and of the Italian Alps are the most striking, but they serve to indicate the depth of ignorance about most wood-working in the Bronze Age. A

[2] Wells 1983, 40ff.; Pressmar 1979.
[3] Audouze and Büchsenschütz 1991, 138f.
[4] Richards and Thomas 1984.
[5] Schweingruber 1976; Taylor 1981; Perini 1988b; Noël and Bocquet 1987; Earwood 1993.

survey of 1978 found that almost 200 artefacts of wood had been recovered from nearly 200 sites in Britain and Ireland.[6] These included relatively large numbers of handles, hilts and weapons, and a substantial number of coffins and/or boats (see pp. 103ff.).[7] Only 18 sites had produced structural timbers from buildings, which indicates how much is lacking in terms of detailed evidence on wood-working in one of its major applications. The number of wooden tools, for instance for agriculture, is also extremely small, but in Alpine sites they are prolific: wooden ards, mattocks, shovels, rakes and various other tools come from Fiavé, for instance.[8] A two-pronged pitchfork of coppiced hazel was found at Skinner's Wood, Shapwick, in Somerset.[9] The marks of a spade or shovel from Gwithian, Cornwall, also deserve mention (see p. 125).[10] The majority of agricultural tools for tilling the soil would have been made of wood, and very few of them survive.

Artefacts such as containers (bowls, boxes and other forms) occur in various wet situations (fig. 7.1).[11] In the Wilsford Shaft, for instance, were staves, withies and discoid bases for stitched buckets as well as fragments of a turned wooden bowl from a single large piece of timber.[12] At Caldicot, Gwent, there was a bowl of alder wood, a ladle of birch, a stave of ash and a fragmentary trough of alder, as well as a variety of long-handled tools of uncertain function.[13] Two containers from Islay, western Scotland, a box and a tub, have been radiocarbon-dated to the Late Bronze Age.[14] At Fiavé there were a number of one-piece wooden cups and bowls, as well as larger composite containers made out of fir or spruce wood with spruce withies tying the base to the walls.[15]

Apart from portable artefacts, wood was the main element in the construction of houses, defensive installations, platforms and pile-sites in wet situations. Planks and other structural elements occur on Swiss and Italian Alpine sites such as the Padnal near Savognin, the Bürg at Spiez and the Cresta at Cazis,[16] as well as on the better-known waterlogged lake-side sites. These sites are of course most prolific in piles but also produce worked planks, beams, wedges, cross-ties and other structural members, often with mortice-holes and matching tenons (fig. 7.2).[17] Boards and planks with holes and notches, as well as pegs, points and other structural elements, were com-

[6] Coles, Heal and Orme 1978; many more finds have been made since.
[7] McGrail 1979.
[8] Perini 1987.
[9] Coles and Orme 1978.
[10] Thomas 1970; Harding 1976.
[11] Earwood 1993, 38ff.
[12] Ashbee *et al.* 1989, 51ff.
[13] Earwood in Nayling and Caseldine 1997, 204ff.
[14] C. Earwood, pers. comm.
[15] Perini 1987, 276ff., 293ff.
[16] Schweingruber 1976, 83f.
[17] Perini 1987; Marzatico 1988; Maise 1997.

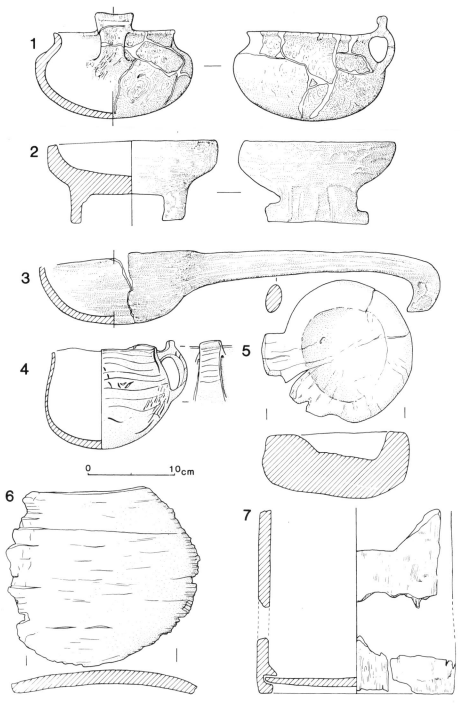

Fig. 7.1. Wooden containers. 1–3. Fiavé (after Perini 1987). 4–6. Ledro (after Rageth 1974). 7. Wilsford Shaft (after Ashbee *et al*. 1989).

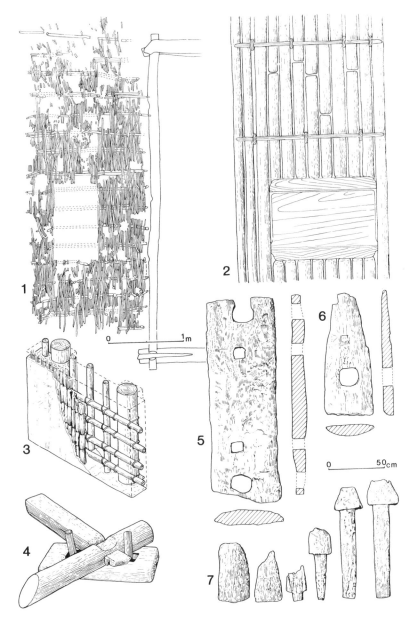

Fig. 7.2. Construction techniques on wooden trackways and pile sites. 1. Fallen wattle wall of hazel and ash, Greifensee-Böschen (after Eberschweiler *et al.* 1987). 2. Schematic reconstruction of a house wall and door from Swiss lake sites (after Maise 1997). 3. Reconstruction of a wattle and daub wall from Feudvar (after Hänsel and Medović 1991). 4. Detail of joint in the beams of a house at Greifensee-Böschen (after Eberschweiler *et al.* 1987). 5–7. Bargeroosterveld, elements of the 'sanctuary' (after Waterbolk and van Zeist 1961). 2, 3 and 4 not to scale.

monly found in the Somerset Levels trackways from sites of varying periods of the Neolithic and Bronze Age,[18] and large wood assemblages from wet sites are now known from several parts of Britain and Ireland.[19] Wooden objects also occur prolifically in mine sites, for instance in Austria (see above, p. 211).[20]

Wood was also invariably used in temperate Europe for palisades and box ramparts (earth and stones held in place by a rigid wooden framework) on those sites where defence was, or became, a major consideration. Many of the hillforts where early ramparts are present have such a box construction; stockade sites such as Biskupin also indicate the great importance of wood for defence (see p. 300).

But it is not only domestic architecture that needed wood. Where wood survives in tombs there are some remarkable finds, apart from the massive oak trunks hollowed out to form coffins. The chambers at Helmsdorf and Leubingen are the best-known examples (p. 97), though too little survives of them for study of the wood-working to be possible. The remarkable wooden cist at Pustopolje in the inland plateau near Kupres in Bosnia is a more recently excavated case, though the tribulations of that country since the excavation mean that the wood is not available for study; the cist was made of large elm planks and was fixed with wedges and other elements (fig. 7.3).[21] The curious timber structure at Bargeroosterveld (p. 309) used mortice-and-tenon joints for the split oak planks and posts from which it was made (fig. 7.2, 5–7).[22] It has often been stated that some of the technical tricks at Stonehenge are taken from carpentry,[23] for instance the mortice-and-tenon and tongue-and-groove joints seen on the sarsen uprights and lintels and a few of the bluestones.[24] It is easy to imagine that wooden versions of such circles, which are probably represented by pit circles as known from a number of localities in Britain, also utilised these arrangements for jointing the different members together. Some idea of the weight and volume of timber involved in large ritual constructions can be gauged from the reconstruction of the timber circle at Sarn-y-bryn-caled near Welshpool in east Wales.[25] The posts here were typically around 5 m long, the outer ring 30 cm in diameter, the inner five posts 66 cm in diameter, with estimated weights between one-third of a tonne and two tonnes.

[18] Orme and Coles 1983; 1985.
[19] e.g. Caldicot: Morgan in Nayling and Caseldine 1997, 194ff.; Blackwater area, Cos. Offaly, Roscommon and Galway: Moloney *et al.* 1995; Mountdillon Bogs, Co. Longford: Moloney in Raftery 1996.
[20] Ladders, troughs, etc.; see notched wooden ladders from Sutton Common, Flag Fen, Loft's Farm and elsewhere: *Proc. Prehist. Soc.* 63, 1997, 233.
[21] Benac 1986.
[22] Waterbolk and van Zeist 1961.
[23] e.g. Atkinson 1956, 25f.
[24] Notably bluestones 66 and 68: ibid., 44, pls. XVB, XVIII.
[25] Gibson 1994a; 1994b.

Fig. 7.3. Pustopolje tumulus 16, reconstruction of the wooden grave chamber. Source: Benac 1986.

The Somerset Levels work has shown clearly how woodland was managed throughout later prehistory.[26] Bronze Age oaks there averaged 30–50 cm in diameter, though Neolithic ones were larger; other tree species that were often used, mainly alder, birch, hazel, ash and willow, were smaller. Many timber pieces preserve the marks of cutting blows and secondary working, and numerous indications of primary and secondary splitting are present. The studies of Coles and Orme showed clearly that certain trees were favoured for certain trackways. Thus alder was the dominant species in the Abbot's Way, Tinney's, Godwin's and Stileway tracks; birch in Westhay, Viper's and Platform; oak at Meare Heath; and hazel in Eclipse, Tollgate and East Moors. At the latter hazel was the sole species used. Things are a little more complicated than this, however, because the construction of these trackways differed: East Moors, Eclipse and Stileway were hurdle tracks, the Abbot's Way was a corduroy track, Meare Heath a plank trackway, and Godwin's and Tinney's brushwood. All of the tree species were available locally, but the builders sometimes went out of their way to select a particular species for a particular construction. What is more, the history of the trackways shows that woodland management, notably coppicing, went back far into the Neolithic: hazel, for instance, is present in coppiced pieces on the Sweet Track as well as in Late Bronze Age tracks such as Tollgate.

[26] Orme and Coles 1983; 1985; see also Rackham 1977; 1979.

Salt Production

Salt production was in many parts of Europe an important industry, and its procurement an essential of everyday life.[27] A daily minimum intake of 3–7 g is usually provided by normal food consumption where this includes a large proportion of animal products, but its use as an additive in food preparation is culturally very important and may well reflect a biological preference for an intake of at least twice that minimum. Depending on diet, humans often like to add salt to food, especially meat, purely for taste, but it is also important as a preservative and in other types of food preparation such as cheese-making. Animals need salt too, but in many parts of the world they derive what they need from their natural diet, and because they enter the food web themselves, they pass on their salt content to humans. As a biological necessity, salt has achieved great importance as a commodity that is moved between production and consumption areas, both in historical times (notably in Africa) and in ancient times. Several studies have been devoted to the identification and significance of its movement.[28]

Salt can be obtained from salt water or from rock sources. In ethnographic situations it is also obtained from plants. The simplest way of procuring salt, at least in those areas with a sea coast, would have been to make use of salt water from the sea, from brine springs near the sea, or from salt lakes. To extract the salt, the water had to be evaporated, simple in principle but in temperate Europe unlikely to be possible purely through solar evaporation. On the other hand, the boiling of neat sea-water, in which the salt concentration is only around 2.6%, is enormously expensive in fuel. Instead, steps would be taken to collect materials in which the salt was already partly concentrated, such as seaweed, or through the products of small inland lagoons in summertime, where in hot dry spells concentration can be raised significantly, provided new water is kept out. The boiling that followed was done in troughs or pans raised on pedestals above a clay floor on which a fire would be lit. As the water was driven off, the salt crystals would be pressed into beakers or moulds and dried off to form a cake which could be easily transported. The archaeological remains of this process are the firing places (for instance the 'Red Hills' of the east coast of England) and the ceramic implements (pedestals, pans, beakers) or 'briquetage' that were used in the process (fig. 7.4). Such objects can be very characteristic when whole objects are represented, but where the material is fragmentary it is hard to recognise, especially as the clay used was often friable and poorly tempered, so that it must often have disintegrated and thus not been recognised archaeologically. It is likely that there are collections of material of many periods which include briquetage, but which cannot be identified for this reason. The classic studies

[27] Nenquin 1961.
[28] e.g. Alexander 1985; Jaanusson and Jaanusson 1988; Morris 1994.

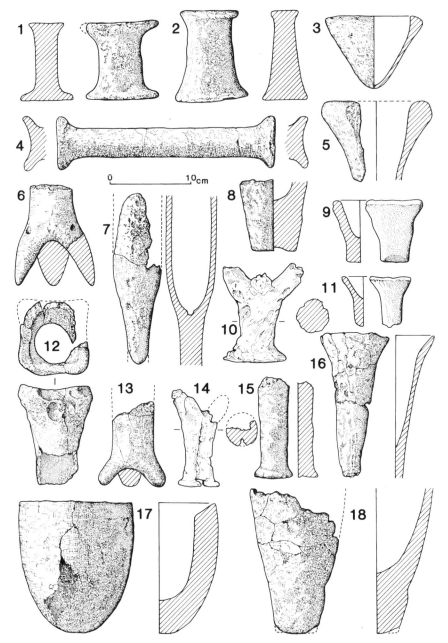

Fig. 7.4. Briquetage (Halle unless stated, after Matthias 1961).
1–2. Spool-shaped pedestals. 3, 5 Conical vessels. 4. Cylindrical
pedestal. 6, 13. Cylinder pedestal, splaying feet. 7. 'Chalice'.
8, 18. Goblets with long shafts. 10, 14. Brean Down, pedestals
(after Bell 1990) 9, 11, 16. Pointed chalices (9, 11 Boucaud,
Préfailles, Loire-Atlantique, after Tessier 1960). 15. Cylindrical
chalice foot. 17. 'Crucible'.

have identified the main forms as known from central Germany: chalice-like and conical vessels, pillar-shaped cylinders, crucible-shaped vessels, and basins or pans.[29]

Identification is not helped by the fact that briquetage cannot be shown unequivocally to have been specifically for salt production. In experiments it was found that better results were obtained simply by evaporating water in an ordinary storage or cooking vessel of the Lausitz culture than by using the chalice-like vessels for the purpose.[30] The coarse ceramic was inclined to crack with the heat, and a significant amount of salt seeped into the walls. Thus boiling in a normal pot recovered 46.58% of the salt content of 5 litres of brine, for the expenditure of 7 kg of wood; while with chalices only 24.61% of the salt in over 2 litres of brine was recovered, using much more wood.

Briquetage and firing sites tend to follow similar models in many different periods, so that it is often hard to date such material in the absence of characteristic finds of the relevant period. The great majority of early salt-working dates to the Early Iron Age and Roman periods, but in Germany, Poland and Romania there is extensive evidence for salt exploitation from the Neolithic.[31] The Bronze Age is the first period in which such material is found with any regularity; thereafter, it increased in frequency, especially from the Iron Age onwards. In a Bronze Age context, the best and most extensive evidence known at present comes from central Europe, and specifically from the area around Halle on the Saale in Sachsen-Anhalt, and the Salzkammergut in Upper Austria, but many other areas such as the important salt-producing areas in the Moselle basin, and specifically the valley of the river Seille south of Château-Salins, were early salt-producers and may have been exploited as early as the Bronze Age: the small pedestals in some of the Seille valley sites appear to date to the local *Bronze final*.[32] Ancient salt-working is also attested in west-central Germany.[33] In many areas, place-names indicate the importance of salt in the economy over the ages. In Greek, *hals* is salt and *hales* are saltworks (Halle, Hallein, Hallstatt); in Latin, *sal* is salt and *salinae* salt-works (as in Salzburg, Salins; Salinae was the Latin name for the Droitwich/Middlewich salt-production area of the English Midlands, and for Ocna Mureşului in western Transylvania).

In the Halle area, much evidence comes from sites in the suburb of Halle-Giebichenstein, where thousands of fragments of vessels and of pan supports – cylindrical, pointed, conical – were found.[34] In general, the evidence indicates that briquetage becomes common from Period IV onwards, but the so-

[29] Riehm 1954; 1961; 1962; Matthias 1961; 1976.
[30] Matthias 1961, 207f.
[31] Jodłowski 1971, 68ff.; Müller 1987; Ursulescu 1977.
[32] Riehm 1954; Poncelet 1966; Bertaux 1976.
[33] Leidinger 1983.
[34] Matthias 1961.

called 'oval columns' and pans, which are much less common in the Halle area than the other briquetage forms, were found with Aunjetitz pottery, and therefore date to the Early Bronze Age.[35] As well as the better-known briquetage from Halle, there is briquetage, partly of Bronze Age date, from several other areas in eastern Germany, for instance the Cottbus area,[36] while the lower Lausitz has also produced finds, and conical vessels with projecting finger-pinched carination below the rim are known from a number of sites between the Saale and the Neisse in eastern Germany.[37] As discussed above, they have often not been recognised for what they are: they have a coarsely formed outline, are usually only 5 cm high and truncated conical in shape, and are made of friable fabric with a sandy surface. Curiously, most of the lower Lausitz finds come from Late Bronze Age graves, as at Klein Jauer (Calau) and Saalhausen (Senftenberg). Given the 30,000 or more finds in the Halle region, however, the presence of a few pieces of briquetage elsewhere is hardly surprising. Finds published as crucibles or something similar may in some cases turn out to be briquetage.[38]

In Britain, Bronze Age briquetage is known from Mucking, Essex,[39] and Brean Down, where a substantial collection was found, consisting of pedestals and trays, the pedestals crudely made with triple tines forking off at the top.[40] Most came from inside the buildings, and covered a substantial timespan from Early to Late Bronze Age according to the radiocarbon dates. Few other sites in Britain can be firmly attributed to the Bronze Age;[41] exceptions are Northey near Peterborough,[42] Padholme Road, Fengate, Peterborough,[43] Billingborough and Tetney, Lincolnshire,[44] and a salt-production hearth in the Hullbridge basin.[45] Trade in characteristic vessels made specifically for salt transport cannot be demonstrated until the Early Iron Age.[46]

Perforated clay slabs were found at Lofts Farm, where their function was described as unknown.[47] Along with them were 'a few slabby fragments of unknown use' and some 'unremarkable lumps' of fired clay. Comparable perforated slabs are found on other Essex and Thames Valley sites, and at La

[35] Matthias 1976.
[36] Petzel 1987.
[37] Bönisch 1993.
[38] e.g. Šaldová 1981, 36 fig. 27, 1–4.
[39] Barford in Bond 1988.
[40] Foster in Bell 1990, 165ff.
[41] Barford 1990.
[42] Gurney 1980. Two types of fired clay object occurred: pedestals and fragments of large circular vessels, perhaps used in the later stages of the evaporation process.
[43] Pryor 1980, 18ff., 181.
[44] Chowne 1978; Palmer-Brown 1993. Briquetage in the form of a pedestal and other supports and various thin- and thick-walled vessels were found in the remains of a shallow pool at Tetney.
[45] Wilkinson and Murphy 1986, 187; 1995, 157ff.
[46] Morris 1985; 1994; such containers, emanating from the Droitwich area, complement the known production sites from this important inland salt area (see Woodiwiss 1992).
[47] Brown 1988, 280.

Panne in western Flanders.[48] They may have served as stands for the conical beakers or other salt-making vessels. Perforated lids are found in Lausitz culture contexts, but the perforations are usually much smaller and probably intended for the boiling of liquids in cooking.

Of the large number of salt-producing sites on the Breton coast, most are Iron Age or Roman, but a few seem to go back to the Bronze Age.[49] The small pedestals in some of the Seille valley sites appear to start in *Bronze final*.[50] Other authors have speculated on a greater antiquity for salt sites than commonly supposed for many coastal areas in north and west Europe – for instance the Skagerrak and Kattegat.[51] The waters of the Baltic are, however, brackish and unsuitable for salt extraction.

The Salzkammergut became a major producer in the Early Iron Age, and the importance of Hallstatt, the Dürrnberg near Hallein, and other sites is usually attributed to its place at the centre of the salt-producing industry based on mines, not springs. The saltworks at Hallstatt are the most famous but by no means the only ones. There, the Iron Age cemetery lies on a hillside which was exploited for massive salt extraction, the technique in Medieval times being that of elution and evaporation rather than direct mining of the rock. Exploitation began in the Late Bronze Age; detailed study of the form of the workings and of the objects from the mines has shown that there are three groups of working sites, called the Eastern, Northern and Western groups, and that the Eastern and Northern differ in character and in age.[52] Specifically, radiocarbon dates for the Northern group lie in the earlier first millennium bc, whereas those for the Eastern group lie between 700 and 200 bc.[53] The Northern group can therefore be assigned to the Bronze Age, and Barth has suggested that the wide, low tunnels seen there show a copper-mining technique that was applied to salt without adaptation.[54] Why the change to the Eastern zone was made, even though there was still plenty of salt in the Northern, is unknown.

It has been argued that large hoards and metalworking sites in Transylvania lie close to salt sources, which are very numerous and prolific: more than 300 rock-salt sources and 3000 salt springs are known from present-day Romania.[55] All the published evidence relates to exploitation in the Roman and Medieval periods, however, and nothing is certainly known from pre-Iron Age contexts, though at least in the case of Ocna Mureşului (Alba) exploita-

[48] Riehm 1962, 387.
[49] Curnic en Guissény: Giot *et al.* 1965; Pointe Saint-Gildas: Gouletquer 1969; 1970; Tessier 1960.
[50] Bertaux 1976.
[51] Jaanusson and Jaanusson 1988.
[52] Schauberger 1960; Barth 1973; 1982.
[53] Barth, Felber and Schauberger 1975.
[54] Barth 1982, 40.
[55] Rusu 1981, 381f.; Medeleţ 1995.

tion has been assumed since the Early Bronze Age on the basis of finds from the vicinity of the sources, and radiocarbon-dating of museum objects from at least one site has produced indications of Bronze Age date.[56]

It has been claimed that salt-moulding by the briquetage technique 'was a practice restricted to a specific group of people, the Urnfielders'.[57] Leaving aside the objection that no such 'people' existed, the theory that salt-working was specifically connected with a Late Bronze Age development takes too little account of the extensive earlier evidence from Halle and the sometimes equivocal evidence connecting salt evaporation to an Urnfield date. Salt springs were exploited early in many areas, with different technologies developing to meet different needs (for instance in the cases of the Hallstatt mines, where briquetage was not used). Equally, it is clear that much briquetage dates to later than the Urnfield period in France and Britain.

This review of salt-working indicates that salt production was a major industry in some areas by the Late Bronze Age, if not before. Salt was moved around in Africa in historic times in cakes that leave little or no archaeological trace, and the same may be true for prehistoric Europe. The identification of briquetage in more of the potential production sites would enable a clearer picture to be obtained.

Textiles

The study of Bronze Age textiles goes back to the 1930s when the first systematic publications of both Danish and Swiss finds appeared.[58] In the last ten years, further notable advances have been made.[59]

The presence of sheep in abundance in most periods of European prehistory had obvious potential for wool production. Apart from animal hide and skin, wool was a main resource available for making clothing. Some evidence for the importance of wool has also been seen in the abundance of sheep in faunal spectra, with a substantial number of individuals at many sites reaching an age of several years, certainly more than would indicate a solely meat-producing economy. It has been noticed that Danish woollen textiles utilised on the same piece both the soft inner wool and also coarser fibres, which came from the sheep's outer fleece. Nor was it only sheep's wool that was utilised: a strange textile found at Sheshader on the island of Lewis, western Scotland, in 1991 utilised in addition to woollen cord both horsehair and cattle fibre.[60]

By contrast, in south-central Europe, flax is the main material found: all

---

[56] Wollmann 1996, 405ff.
[57] Hopkinson 1975, 46.
[58] Broholm and Hald 1940; Vogt 1937; Schlabow 1937; Hald 1980.
[59] Bender Jørgensen 1986; 1992; Barber 1991.
[60] A. Sheridan, pers. comm.

the Neolithic textiles studied by Vogt were of flax,[61] and of the rather rare Bronze Age finds those from Ledro were all of flax, including a ball of linen thread and curious rings of other vegetable fibre.[62] It is not known, however, how representative of the original situation the archaeological finds might be: in the Alpine lakes vegetable materials are preserved but animal products are not; in the tree-trunk coffins of Denmark the situation is reversed. By comparison with the Neolithic, there are extraordinarily few textiles from the Alpine lakes in the Bronze Age, yet one can assume that all materials and technologies present in the earlier period were still available. The obvious conclusion is that textile manufacture in the Bronze Age switched to wool, perhaps because it was more reliably available and more predictable in its working qualities. Some textiles from Denmark were made of two materials, of which only the wool survives; the remainder was presumably made of vegetable fibres. This has been demonstrated on a textile from Unterteutschental, Saalkreis, to have been flax: the thin warp-threads were flax, and the thick wefts wool, the latter completely hiding the former.[63] Flax would have needed to be retted (subjected to bacterial agents to rot away all but the fibre, typically by the use of water or urine in pits), and pits found at West Row Fen (Suffolk) and Reading Business Park (Berkshire) containing flax capsules have been mentioned above (p. 145).

Apart from flax there is evidence for the use of other fibrous plants, such as the nettles found in the Bohøj at Voldtofte.[64] Hemp (*Cannabis sativa*) may also have been used, though at present the evidence suggests an introduction in the Iron Age.[65] Fragments of textile made from bast fibre, thought to be hemp, occurred in the St Andrews Late Bronze Age hoard.[66] In the Swiss lakes a variety of plant materials was used, notably tree-bast,[67] of which oak accounted for 45%, lime 35% and willow 8%.[68] A fine plain-weave textile from Zürich-Mythenquai, for instance, is of lime bast,[69] and the fibres forming cord which ran between the loops of many of the socketed axes in a hoard of Late Bronze Age metalwork from Beeston Regis, Norfolk, was of lime bast.[70]

A range of other plants were used for the manufacture of cord, thread and plaited materials. For instance, material from caves near Bad Frankenhausen in Thuringia included cords and woven material;[71] some of the cord was made of *Clematis vitalba* (wild clematis or old man's beard), a climbing plant whose

[61] Vogt 1937.
[62] Rageth 1974, pl. 121, 6–70.
[63] Schlabow 1959; 1976, 26f. fig. 3.
[64] Hald 1980, 126 fig. 117.
[65] Turner in Simmons and Tooley 1981, 269ff.
[66] Gabra-Sanders 1993 [1994].
[67] Rast-Eicher 1992a.
[68] Reinhard 1992.
[69] Rast-Eicher 1992b.
[70] Lawson 1980.
[71] Farke 1991.

tough fibrous stems are ideally suited for the purpose. Other plants, such as nettles, may well have been used in this way. On Neolithic sites, grasses and rushes were used to make plaited textiles,[72] and grasses and animal hair were used to tie bronze objects together in the St Andrews hoard.[73]

The technology of textiles revolves around the production of thread, usually by spinning, and its weaving into a fabric, using some form of loom. The two processes leave their respective archaeological remains. A recent find from the Horgen (late Neolithic) layers at Sipplingen-Osthafen was that of wooden spindles complete with whorls and spun thread.[74] Spindle-whorls are in general a common find in Bronze Age sites in all areas; for example, there is a rich collection of finds from Hungarian tells.[75] It is, however, not always possible to be sure that such objects, found in isolation, are really whorls rather than wheels such as are seen on model carts (see chapter 5). But one need be in no doubt that spinning with a whorl was a universal technology in the Bronze Age, as in other prehistoric periods; the implements needed are minimal and the skill is readily acquired.

It is usually assumed that prehistoric textiles were made on upright looms of the 'warp-weighted' variety, that is with a rigid frame composed of two vertical (or near-vertical) posts, a beam joining them at the top, and threads hanging down from the beam (the warp threads), weighted down by heavy weights which would typically be of clay.[76] Many pieces of surviving textile were probably made on such looms, but not all; where evidence for them, in the form of weights, is absent, a ground-loom, such as was used in Egypt, may have been used, though this is very uneconomical in terms of floor space and best suited to outdoor use. The principles of forming warp and weft are the same, but the loom lies horizontally instead of standing vertically. An alternative might have been an upright loom that did not require weights, such as a tubular loom. The special techniques used for starting, finishing and edging pieces of cloth give special information on the type of loom that could have been used, and in pieces from Trindhøj and Egtved the presence of closed warp loops at both ends means that an upright warp-weighted loom cannot have been used. Instead, some sort of tubular arrangement must have been used, though it is not yet known of precisely what sort.[77]

Looms themselves do not survive, even on wet sites (unless some of the wooden objects of unknown use are loom parts, for instance from Ledro).[78] What do survive are the weights that hung down from the vertical (warp) threads, and in a few cases the possible holes into which the vertical frame

---

[72] Schlichtherle 1990a, 124ff.
[73] Rast-Eicher 1992a.
[74] Ruoff and Suter 1990, 284 fig. 6.
[75] Bóna 1975, table 144: Vărşand.
[76] Hoffmann 1974.
[77] Hald 1980, 211ff. for the method; Bender Jørgensen 1986, 137ff.
[78] Rageth 1974, 192 pls. 102–3; some smaller objects may be shuttles.

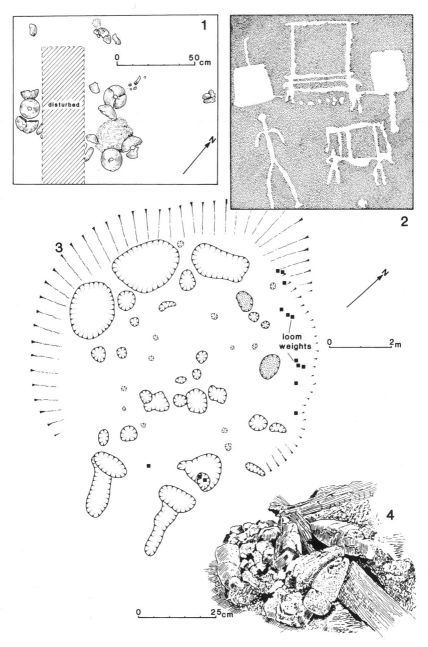

Fig. 7.5. Loom installations and depictions. 1. Tučapy (Vyškov, Moravia) (after Ludikovský 1958). 2. Naquane, Val Camonica, depiction of looms (after Anati 1960). 3. Black Patch, Sussex, plan of hut 3 on Hut Platform 4, showing position of loom-weights and possible loom installation (after Drewett 1982). 4. Biskupin, loom-weights lying in the street near house 50 (after Szafranski 1950).

members were inserted. Loom-weights of various shapes and sizes are common finds on sites in many areas, but one cannot necessarily be certain that such weights were really for looms; thatch on house roofs can also be secured by nets held down by large clay or stone weights. However, many clay weights are made of poorly fired clay that would not have survived very long if exposed to the rigours of the weather. Since loom-weights are common in the Neolithic, it is no surprise to find them in Hungary and the Czech lands in the earlier Bronze Age.[79] Two sorts of weight were present at Ledro, perhaps indicating two different types of loom.[80] A number of house sites in central southern England have produced such weights, of annular or cylindrical form.[81] In the Late Bronze Age on the Continent the standard form is a pyramidal, conical or sub-conical weight perforated near the thin end, such as is commonly found in Swiss lake sites[82] and at many other central European sites (fig. 7.6).[83] Some of the weights were quite modest in size (8–12 cm high being the norm at Fort Harrouard), but others are much larger, up to 20 cm and weighing nearly 3 kg. The size and weight employed will have varied with the thickness and strength of the thread being woven. On the other hand, loom-weights are absent from Denmark until the Early Iron Age, so that textiles must have been made on a loom that did not require them, either a ground-loom or an upright tubular loom.[84] The annular loom-weight from Jegstrup (Skive, central Jutland) is an exception, dating probably to Period V.[85]

Horst calculated that the span of the loom at Zedau was a minimum of 1 m, so that cloth up to 80 cm broad could be woven.[86] In one of the pits, a row of loom-weights lay in a line 59 cm long. Pits at Berlin-Buch and Lichterfelde also indicated looms of around this size; at Buch several of the pits held numbers of weights. An irregular pit at Wallwitz (Burg), the site dating to Period IV, contained a row of 27 loom-weights about 2 m long, with post-holes at either end, over 3 m apart.[87] The pit was assumed by the excavator to be to enable the cloth to be extended, presuming that the upper beam did not rotate, allowing the fabric to be wound in. No traces of a roofing structure were evident in the vicinity, although many hundreds of post-holes were identifiable on the site; but it hardly seems likely that weaving was

[79] Hradčany, Moravia: Barber 1991, 101, after Červinka; Tučapy, Moravia: Ludikovský 1958; Vărşand: Bóna 1975, tables 146–8.
[80] Rageth 1974, 178 pl. 93.
[81] For instance Black Patch (Drewett 1982, 371 fig. 34), Itford Hill (Burstow and Holleyman 1957, 200ff. fig. 25) and Shearplace Hill (Rahtz and ApSimon 1962, 321 fig. 22).
[82] Wyss 1971b, 136 fig. 15; Ruoff 1981, 254ff. figs. 6–7.
[83] Zedau: Horst 1985, 105 fig. 50 l–m; Sobiejuchy: Bukowski 1959–60, 213 pl. 49, 5–9; Biskupin: Szafranski 1950, etc.; Gadzowice-Kwiatoniów (Silesia): Macewicz and Wuszkan 1991; Fort Harrouard: Mohen and Bailloud 1987, 108 fig. 59; Staré Město: Hrubý 1968–9.
[84] Barber 1991, 253f.
[85] Davidsen 1982, 72 fig. 5, 11.
[86] Horst 1985, 105.
[87] Stahlhofen 1978.

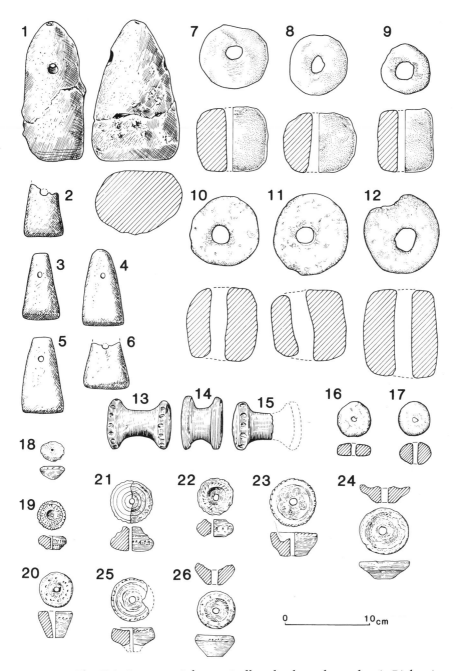

Fig. 7.6. Loom-weights, spindle-whorls and spools. 1. Biskupin (after Szafranski 1950). 2–6. Fort Harrouard (after Mohen and Bailloud 1987). 7–9. Fiavé (after Perini 1987). 10-12. Black Patch (after Drewett 1982). 13–15. Bad Buchau, Wasserburg (after Kimmig 1992). 16–17. Fiavé (after Perini 1987). 18–26. Bad Buchau, Wasserburg (after Kimmig 1992).

carried on in the open air at this latitude. Further south, a similar find came from Gars Thunau (Horn, Lower Austria), where the weights were flat clay discs perforated eccentrically.[88] A Ha B date is suggested by the pottery. An exhaustive series of experiments by this author with an upright loom and identical weights to those found attempted to determine what type of weaving had been practised at the moment of destruction. Although the possibility that the loom was in the counter-shed position for plain weave could not be excluded, it was considered more likely that twill was being woven (see below). Pits, post-holes and weights appear on other sites of similar age.[89] At Fort Harrouard similar groups were found, one being an oval pit containing 15 weights and a whorl. On the other hand, some of the Danish textiles indicate an original width of 3 m, which is large even by historical standards and must have needed several workers to operate the loom. Evidence that this was the case can be seen from the irregularities in some Danish fabrics, where the wefts cross over each other, indicating that two or three people were inserting the shuttles and passing them along to each other.[90]

Drewett assumed for Black Patch that where weights were found in the vicinity of a straight row of post-holes they indicated the foundations of a loom (fig. 7.5, 3).[91] In hut 3, this putative loom was situated opposite the door, so that a good light would be obtained. A distribution of loom-weights at Biskupin shows that only around half of all houses investigated produced such finds, and in a number of these cases they were restricted to one or two weights only.[92] On the other hand, in a few houses there were larger numbers, mostly represented by fragments. Perhaps most puzzling was the find of nine weights – the largest find of complete weights – at the end of street 2, apparently not in a house at all. Szafranski suggested that they came from a loom normally kept in house 37 and brought outside during a fine spell of weather (fig. 7.5, 4).[93] Looms were not an invariable component of Biskupin houses, suggesting an element of specialisation between different households.

Looms are depicted on the Grande Roccia at Naquane in the Val Camonica in northern Italy, apparently warp-weighted (fig. 7.5, 2); they are shown with their frame and upper beam, hanging weights, and two or three bars going across the body of the loom, representing the shed bar and one or more heddle bars.[94] According to Anati, they belong to phases IIIC–IV, or the Late Bronze Age and Early Iron Age.[95]

---

[88] Schierer 1987.
[89] e.g. Brno-Obřany, feature 29: Adámek 1961, 46 fig. 45, pl. 19; also pl. 89.
[90] Hald 1980, 152f. fig. 140.
[91] Drewett 1982, 339.
[92] Szafranski 1950, 156 fig. 24.
[93] A more likely explanation is provided by study of the plan of the finds (Szafranski 1950, figs. 13–15), which suggest strongly that the weights were actually in an unrecognised house in the area usually referred to as street 2.
[94] Anati 1960, 60ff.; Zimmermann 1988; Barber 1991, 82, 110f. for the terminology.
[95] Anati 1961, 138ff.; 1963.

Fig. 7.7. Textile from Ledro. Photo: Museo Tridentino di Scienze Naturali, Trento.

The fabrics (fig. 7.7)

All known fabrics from the first half of the Bronze Age were of plain weave, known as 'tabby', where the warps and wefts cross each other alternately (fig. 7.8, 5). It was, however, common for this to be disguised somewhat by the practice of making the warps more prominent than the wefts by using thicker thread for the former than the latter, effectively hiding the wefts ('warp-faced', 'ribbed' or 'repp') (fig. 7.8, 7). While the body of the fabrics was in this basic weave, a great variety of techniques was used for the starting and finishing borders and selvedges, often quite complex.

To complicate matters further, there were various conventions in the thread twisting used, as Bender Jørgensen has made clear. It is well known to textile specialists that thread can be twisted to the left or the right, giving the Z- and S-spun threads (fig. 7.8, 1–2). These can then themselves be plied into cord, which must be wound in the opposite direction to the threads, producing the so-called Zs and Sz plies (fig. 7.8, 3–4). Woven cloth consists of two sets of threads (warp and weft), which may be twisted differently; the simplest forms may then consist of s/s, s/z, z/s or z/z varieties (z/s indicat-

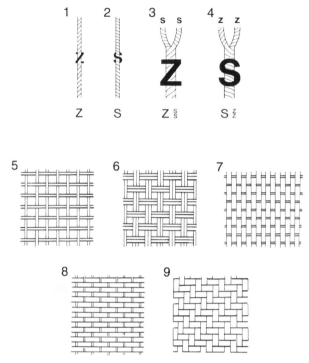

Fig. 7.8. Spin and weave types known from Bronze Age Europe.
1–2. Z and S spin; 3–4. Z/s and S/z plies (source: Bender Jørgensen
1986); 5. plain weave (tabby); 6. basket weave; 7. plain weave,
warp-faced; 8. plain weave, weft-faced; 9. twill.

ing left-spun on the warp and right-spun on the weft, and so on). The use of
differently spun thread was far from being a matter of chance or whimsy: special effects are created by the use of combinations of z- and s-spun yarns as
the light falls on the threads in different ways. This can be seen very clearly
from the belt in the Borum Eshøj grave, which was a plain warp-faced weave
but with S-spun threads forming a band at either side and Z-spun threads in
the middle, giving a clever banded effect.[96]

From Period II in Denmark, the first with a substantial quantity of surviving textiles, the majority (86 out of 118 pieces) were z/s-spun, only 19
being s/s-spun. What is more, the s/s-spun textiles were restricted to certain
parts of Denmark, mainly Jutland south of the Limfjord, and often found in
conjunction with other, z/s-spun, pieces. By contrast, in Period III over half
the 80 finds are s/s-spun, and only a third z/s-spun; there is no geographical
restriction on the appearance of either form.

There are too few finds in other parts of Europe in the earlier Bronze Age

[96] Barber 1991, 178f. fig. 6.7.

to be able to say that this pattern was repeated on a wider scale. In German Tumulus graves, the fabrics are s/s-spun, and a few of these are z-plied.[97] In Britain the fabrics were z-spun or z-plied, though s-ply is also found.[98] In Spain, z/z plain-weave fabrics are present in the Copper Age, as on a pair of tunics from Lorca (Murcia).[99]

In subsequent parts of the Bronze Age in Denmark, the change to cremation means that relatively little material is available for study, among which s/s and z/s spinning are both evident, s/s being the commoner. What is more important is the introduction of the new technique of twill weaving. Twills are those fabrics where the weft threads are passed under and over two or more of the warps; by shifting one warp thread sideways in each successive weft pass, diagonal patterns can be formed (fig. 7.8, 9). Twill fabrics are seen at Gerumsberg (Vester Götland, Sweden) and Haastrup on Funen in Denmark,[100] at the Ha B sites of Sublaines, Indre-et-Loire, Gevelinghausen, Kr. Meschede, Westphalia,[101] and also in the Late Bronze Age crannog site of Island MacHugh in Co. Tyrone, Ireland,[102] the sash from Cromaghs, Armoy, Co. Antrim, and in some of the finds from the salt mines of Early Iron Age Austria – which, it should be remembered, started production in the Late Bronze Age (see above).[103]

The pattern of spinning is no mere chance matter. Bender Jørgensen has been able to demonstrate in elegant fashion that the changes and variations which she has detected in thread pattern coincide with variations noticed in other parts of the archaeological record. The appearance of s/s-spun threads in Period II in Denmark, for instance, coincides with that in the western areas of south Scandinavia where Randsborg detected the early appearance of Period III types, such as the small fibula with cross-shaped head.[104] Similarly, the fabric from Voldtofte made from nettle fibres comes from a princely grave with a number of imported objects; it too might have arrived at Voldtofte as part of the imported collection. Finally, the Haastrup fabric is very similar to those from the Austrian salt mines, and could have been a southern import.

Yet in the case of the Early–Middle Bronze Age change from z/s to s/s fabrics there is no obvious technical reason why one fabric type should have been preferred over another. The subtleness of the change can plausibly be taken to reflect purely cultural concerns. The appearance of twill weaving is perhaps another matter, though the cloth that results is not qualitatively dif-

[97] Schlabow and Hundt in Feustel 1958, 28ff.
[98] Henshall 1950; Bender Jørgensen 1992.
[99] Alfaro 1992.
[100] Hald 1980, 189f.
[101] Hundt 1974a.
[102] Henshall 1950, 158.
[103] Hundt 1959, 1960.
[104] Randsborg 1968, 82, 131ff.

ferent in terms of wear or durability. What it did enable was ornamentation through an entirely new method: instead of having to add ornament to the surface of a fabric through embroidery or some similar technique, more interesting fabrics, often with elaborate inwoven motifs, could be produced at the initial weaving stage. The quantity of loom-weight finds from the Late Bronze Age probably reflects the renewed interest in and experimentation with weaving that these new techniques derive from.

As well as these more conventional weaving techniques, a great variety of special techniques is evident in Periods II and III in Denmark, in addition to the variety of borders and selvedges already mentioned. The plaiting technique known as 'sprang' can be seen in the hair-nets from Borum Eshøj and Skrydstrup, as can embroidery on the neck and sleeves of blouses from those graves. The men's caps from Muldbjerg, Trindhøj, Guldhøj and Borum Eshøj grave A (among others) are examples of piled fabrics, where hundreds of threads are sewn on the outside of the cap's material.[105] The cap from Muldbjerg is finished in button stitch. Lastly, the technique of the famous skirt from the Egtved burial deserves special mention. It is made of a warp-faced band at the waist, with a heavy cord formed by groups of twisted weft threads that were allowed to hang free and were then caught at the bottom by a spacing-cord, their ends being rolled into loops.

Bender Jørgensen's map of cloth-types in Europe (fig. 7.9) illustrates both the variety of fabrics, when taken on a European scale, but also the strength of local traditions in weaving matters.[106] Since these results reflect the situation only in those areas where textiles survive, and it is quite clear that flax was the favoured material in the southern half of continental Europe, it is evident that this picture is a very partial one; the notable absence of Swiss sites from the map indicates how incomplete the distribution must be. Nevertheless, it is evident that a number of local weaving traditions can be detected: Zs/Zs linen tabbies in southern Spain and Britain, Sz/Sz linen tabbies in central Europe, and s/s or s/z wool tabbies in northern Europe. Even in these areas there are exceptions to the norms outlined. It is reasonable to imagine that each area had very specific ways of carrying out its weaving. The presence of 'foreign' weaves could, if borne out by the developing evidence, indicate introductions of textiles from other areas, or even the movement of weavers (for instance women moving through marriage) from one area to another. Since these textiles were for the most part utilised on people's clothes, they represent a very personal statement about technology in daily life.

[105] Schlabow 1937, 60ff.
[106] Bender Jørgensen 1992, 117 fig. 140.

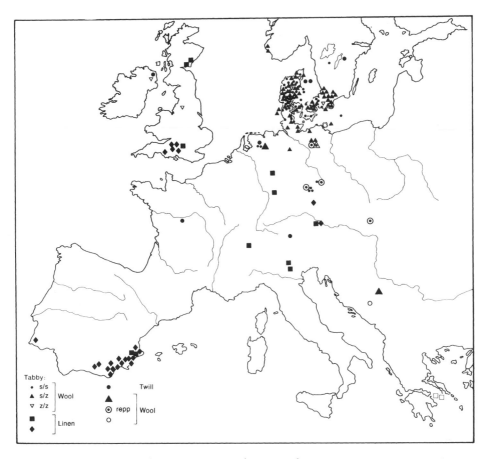

Fig. 7.9. The occurrence of spin and weave types in Bronze Age Europe (after Bender Jørgensen 1992).

Glass and faience

Production of vitreous materials was one of the inventions of the Bronze Age. Although the technology for the production of 'primitive glass' was not beyond what was available in the Copper Age, or even in the Late Neolithic, glassy materials only began to be made in the Near East in the third millennium BC, and in Europe during the second or towards the end of the third. 'Glass' was therefore truly an innovation of the period.

Glass and faience are essentially composed of the same raw materials, though in differing quantities.[107] The basic building block of all such substances is silica, usually derived from sand, though crushed quartz or other materials could also be used. To the sand are added small amounts of an alkali

---

[107] Harding 1984a, 88ff. for fuller account.

(to bind the sand or quartz grains together) and a lime (a fluxing agent, reducing the temperature at which chemical alteration takes place), along with a colouring agent. In glass, the chemical reactions go furthest, producing fusion of the silica crystals and thus vitrification; higher temperatures, but also subtle differences in the recipe used, brought this about. By contrast, 'faience' (in the sense used here – see below) is usually opaque and only slightly vitrified, or not vitrified at all. Lower firing temperatures were used, and the process also involved somewhat different admixtures for binding, fluxing and colouring than those used for glass.

The name 'faience' is the French form of Italian Faenza, the town in Emilia-Romagna where glazed majolica was produced from Renaissance times onwards. This is characterised by a white core and a glaze, applied after the core was already fired. The term was adopted by Egyptologists to describe certain products of ancient Egypt, and then by archaeologists elsewhere for substances that appeared similar. For many years it was assumed that the technology of Bronze Age faience was the same as, or similar to, that of Renaissance Italy, that is a two-stage process, but more recent work and experimental reconstructions have shown that faience can be produced in a single-stage process, and that the technology, while quite complex, was not the involved process it was once thought to be. Since all the materials are readily available, including copper as a colouring agent, and the firing temperature is no higher than that used in pottery manufacture or metallurgy, the production of faience was technically feasible from the start of the Bronze Age in much of Europe. Production of glass, on the other hand, required a rather more sophisticated set of ingredients and manufacturing instructions, though once these were mastered, there was no reason why the technology should not have become widely available.

Faience in this sense is found in the Near East from the fourth millennium BC, used for beads, pendants and the like; in the third millennium it reached Crete, probably as a result of Egyptian influence.[108] It does not occur in mainland Europe (including Greece), however, until the Early Bronze Age, in other words the centuries around 2000 cal BC. At that point, it is widely found in central Europe,[109] and also in France,[110] Spain[111] and the British Isles;[112] more isolated finds occur in Italy,[113] Malta, Denmark[114] and elsewhere. In Europe, all these finds are of small beads, suitable for stringing on necklaces. They are of simple rounded or ring forms, or take more unusual shapes: star-shaped,

[108] Beck and Stone 1936; Stone and Thomas 1956.
[109] Harding 1971; Venclová 1990, 35ff.
[110] Briard 1984b.
[111] Harrison *et al.* 1974.
[112] Beck and Stone 1936; Stone and Thomas 1956; Harding 1984a, 98ff.; Magee 1993.
[113] Barfield 1978.
[114] Becker 1954.

Fig. 7.10. Glass and faience beads. *Upper*: Košice, Slovakia (faience); *lower*: Blučina, Moravia (glass). Photos: author.

quoit-shaped, or segmented (like a series of rounded beads fused together). In central Europe, they often occur in very large numbers in Early Bronze Age graves (fig. 7.10, upper).

For many years, it was assumed that these beads were imported from the advanced cultures of the Near East or Egypt.[115] Nowadays, the perspective on this debate is rather different. While it is not in doubt that the technology for faience and glass manufacture ultimately originated in the Near East, analyses have shown that the majority of faience beads in central Europe and in Britain were in all likelihood made locally to local recipes using local materials.[116] The implications of this finding are that local communities in many parts of Europe had at their disposal both the materials and the technological knowledge to produce these objects, and did not have to be dependent on East Mediterranean civilisations for such manufactures. The spread of faience-making was very much a part of craft tradition in Bronze Age Europe.

With glass, the matter is more complex.[117] Until the Late Bronze Age in central Europe, when many small beads, usually blue or green, are found in Urnfield contexts (fig. 7.10, lower),[118] glass beads are extremely rare. Even then, areas other than central Europe have produced relatively little material earlier than the Iron Age. In the British Isles, for instance, a small number of glass beads have occurred in contexts that might indicate a Bronze Age date.[119] Perhaps the most striking instance is a plum-coloured bead from the Early Bronze Age grave Wilsford G42,[120] which seems to have a good context, and whose composition is unusual, falling outside the established European Bronze Age glass types.[121] Elsewhere, finds of glass beads earlier than the Late Bronze Age have been made in the Cioclovina hoard in Romania,[122] the Werteba cave near Bil'če Zolote (Borshchiv) in Podolia (Ukraine), a grave at Parkany (Odessa), and a few finds in central and western Europe.[123]

In the Late Bronze Age, two main glass types were being produced.[124] First there was a low-magnesium, high-potassium mixture, found especially at Rathgall and other sites in Ireland, Hauterive-Champréveyres on Lake Neuchâtel, and Frattesina in the Po valley. Then there was a high-magnesium mixture, known from analyses conducted on beads from Potterne in Wiltshire and a scatter of sites elsewhere in Britain and Europe; this composition resembles that found in the Mediterranean and has been considered to represent

---

[115] Stone and Thomas 1956.
[116] Newton and Renfrew 1970; Aspinall, Warren and Crummett 1972; Harding and Warren 1973; review of the debate in Harding 1984a, 98ff.
[117] Henderson 1988; 1989.
[118] Haevernick 1978; Venclová 1989 [1990]; 1990, 40ff.
[119] Guido 1978, 19ff.
[120] Guido et al. 1984.
[121] Henderson 1988.
[122] Comşa 1966.
[123] Harding 1984a, 102.
[124] Henderson 1988; Hartmann et al. 1997.

either the actual import of beads or their manufacture from imported raw glass. What is important is that there is clear evidence by the Late Bronze Age for local manufacture of this chemically complex material. The site of Frattesina, for instance, is a key locality in northern Italian prehistory, showing evidence for the working of bone, horn, ivory and amber as well as glass, and having imported Mycenaean sherds and ostrich eggshell.[125] The low-magnesium, high-potassium glass found there is quite different from contemporary products in the eastern Mediterranean and seems to be eloquent testimony to a major local industry.

In terms of ornamentation, the makers of beads in central Europe soon realised that decoration could be added through the way in which the thread of molten glass could be twisted into a spiral (as with the so-called *Pfahlbauperlen*, which are barrel-shaped and have an encircling spiral) or 'eyes' added through the addition of concentric rings of different coloured glass to a slight protrusion or boss.[126] There are also annular beads (*Ringchenperlen*), which as the name implies are torus-shaped. Variants on these themes appear in many of the areas of Urnfield Europe.[127]

The glass and faience industry in Bronze Age Europe thus represents the beginnings of a major new set of techniques for adding value and artistic merit to otherwise intrinsically 'worthless' materials. Just as the arrival of copper metallurgy enabled a whole new set of value objects to be created as it were out of nothing, so the adoption of glass-making produced commodities that seem, from the fact that they were initially used sparingly and were scarce, to have been items of value and prestige. Although it was to be many centuries before European glass-makers were able to make elaborate objects, representing the pinnacle of artistic achievement, nonetheless the technological seeds for the process were sown during the Bronze Age. In this sense, the invention and early development of glass and faience represent one of the most important aspects of craft or industrial production in the period.

Conclusion

Craft-workers in the Bronze Age practised a range of skills, many of them often overlooked. Potting, carpentry, salt-making, textile manufacture and glass-working were all everyday activities. One should not forget, however, that some aspects of craft or specialist skill are even less visible than these: musical accomplishments, for instance. The lures and horns of Scandinavia and Ireland have been mentioned above (p. 225); drums, pan-pipes and flutes

---

[125] Bietti Sestieri 1975; 1980, 28ff.
[126] The *Pfahlbaunoppenperlen* or *Augenperlen*: Haevernick 1978, though eye beads are mainly confined to the Iron Age.
[127] e.g. the Lausitz cemeteries of Poland and eastern Germany: Haevernick 1953; Durczewski and Olczak 1966; Alpine Urnfields: Neuninger and Pittioni 1959; other refs. in Guido 1978, 24.

are also known.[128] Though life must have been drudgery for many people much of the time, there were compensations. The pride that the finest craftspeople must have taken in their work can also count amongst these. Then as now, the human spirit could soar above the mundane preoccupations of daily life.

[128] Knape and Nordström 1994; Szydłowska 1972, 143ff.; Schöbel 1987.

CHAPTER 8

WARFARE

If Homer is to be believed, the Bronze Age Aegean was a world of heroes, whose eminence was measured less by their skills as diplomats than by their prowess on the battlefield. In terms of archaeological finds, this picture finds a reflection in the weaponry, armour and fortifications of the Late Bronze Age. It is a moot point whether one could have reconstructed the heroic age of Greece on the basis of such finds alone. In the barbarian world of Europe, where no literary aids are available, there is much to suggest a heroic era similar to that in Greece, even though the evidence differs in the two areas.

First and foremost, there are the weapons and armour of the period, which are comparable in quantity, if not in quality, to those of Mycenaean Greece. Next, there are the burials which contain such weaponry, usually seen as warriors' graves. And lastly, there are the fortifications of the period, whether built in stone (as in parts of the Mediterranean) or in earth with a wooden framework. The combination of these types of evidence leaves one in little doubt that group aggression, what may here be termed warfare, was a major preoccupation in Bronze Age life. Indeed, Treherne has suggested that the 'warrior grave' was the material residue of a 'heroic' mortuary ideology; the warrior hero can perhaps stand as a symbol of the age.[1] All these types of evidence combine in the rock art of Scandinavia to give an imposing picture of the Bronze Age warrior (fig. 8.1). Many rock-art 'scenes' appear to depict people engaging in 'fights', that is armed males facing each other with weapons – usually axes – raised as if to strike. The figures are often also depicted with a sheathed sword hanging at the waist. Sometimes they brandish spears. In a number of cases, the figures with these weapons are extra large, dominating the panel in which they appear. Usually such scenes depict only one or two individuals, but there are a few cases where larger numbers are present; a notable panel from Tegneby at Litsleby in northern Bohuslän shows warriors mounted on horses with spears raised above the head, apparently charging each other.[2]

In what way is one to interpret such scenes? Was fighting between individuals or groups so commonplace that it was depicted as a standard part of

---

[1] Treherne 1997.
[2] Coles 1990, 83.

Fig. 8.1. Ritual fighting with battle-axes: part of a rock-art panel at Fossum, Bohuslän. Photo: author.

everyday life? Do the scenes of combat depict specific encounters, or are they genre scenes, showing generalised fights that took place regularly?

The Bronze Age has long suffered from being viewed through eyes that romanticise its character, perhaps because of the Homeric associations that are commonly adduced. In such a society, war is considered glorious, and prowess in battle of enormous importance. For Homer's heroes, going to war was a natural consequence of the failure of other means to right the wrong done to Menelaus; even though the quarrel affected few other people directly, ties and obligations of kinship meant that both sides mustered substantial forces, who were prepared to leave behind hearth and home, allegedly for years, in order to vindicate the position of their kinsman.

We can survey such a scene from the comfort of our studies without having to stop to consider its sordidness and brutality. The various categories of evidence surveyed in this chapter provide a strong *prima facie* argument that fighting, in various forms, was prevalent. As with ritual life, economic organisation and industrial production, however, it may not be correct to enforce a rigid separation between aspects of warfare and the rest of daily life. Personal and group aggression was no doubt structured through the context of social relations as they existed in different areas and on different levels. While these cannot be experienced directly, consideration of what can be seen of the visible, artefactual, record may provide indicators of how those relations were organised.

Among the most important aspects of the artefactual record as it relates to warfare was the deposition of metalwork, whether singly or collectively in hoards. Consideration of this issue elsewhere suggests that much of this deposition was carefully structured, and related not to utilitarian issues such as the disposal of worn-out implements but to the provision of specialised items as part of a symbolic practice. A great number of these items are military in character. It is hard to avoid the conclusion that the symbolic provision of such military equipment was an expression of its importance in the maintenance of life. So it was not some unusual and undesirable aspect of the Bronze Age world but a recurrent and normal feature, however distasteful this may seem to modern sensibilities.

Warfare in tribal and chiefdom societies

The study of warfare in pre-state societies has long been of interest to all students of human social behaviour.[3] Debate has centred on the purposes of warfare in such societies, for instance whether it can be explained in functional terms, whether it is adaptive, or why some societies undertake it frequently but others do not.[4] Attempts have been made to see warfare in terms of human psychology, for instance as the result of innate aggression (most notably in the work of Konrad Lorenz), but critical consensus today does not take such views too seriously.

On the other hand, a small number of writers who bridge the anthropology/archaeology interface have drawn attention to the importance of warfare as a factor in the study of ancient, as well as recent, societies. Archaeologists frequently refer to warfare when discussing military sites and equipment, but rarely stop to consider the social, economic and political implications, perhaps because anthropologists are not in agreement themselves about the functions and causes of war.[5] A number of American anthropologists have addressed themselves specifically to this issue in the context of the Americas and the Pacific, where they have paid particular attention to the status of the societies concerned in terms of social evolution.[6]

From these studies, it is apparent that, while there may be some consensus on the immediate causes of warfare, its deeper significance remains a matter of dispute. Thus, one can point to such factors as the avenging of slights, insults, theft (especially of women), murder and other perceived wrongs as leading to armed conflict between groups. The blood-feud, common in the Balkans into the present century, is a case in point. In such cases, the conflict appears to have its own momentum, one act of aggression lead-

[3] e.g. Malinowski 1941.
[4] e.g. Fried, Harris and Murphy 1967; Ferguson in Haas 1990a.
[5] Exceptions to this have included Escalon de Fonton (1964), Behrens (1978) and Vencl (1983; 1984a; 1984b; 1984c) in European prehistoric studies, and Goldberg and Findlow (1984) in a Roman context.
[6] Notably Haas 1990b, Carneiro 1990 and Ferguson 1984; Ferguson and Whitehead 1992.

ing inevitably to another and needing no justification beyond that of revenge. But such instances seem to have little relevance to warlike societies such as (apparently) the Yanomamö, where acts of aggression are an endemic part of everyday life and every male is brought up to express aggression through play and other behaviour.[7] The net result is that around one-quarter of adult males are said to die violent deaths among the Yanomamö. It is hard to see such behaviour, which leads to a much less intensive occupation of the settlement space than could otherwise be the case, as promoting the welfare of the people practising it in any practical sense.[8]

This may be an extreme example, but it is possible to point to many cases, in the historical and ethnographic record of small-scale pre-state societies, of what appears to be aggression by groups against their neighbours, or to long-lasting feuds characterised by raiding, theft, murder and other features. In the context of the social groups believed to have occupied Europe in the Bronze Age, one is not talking about the institutionalised warfare that came to characterise early states and empires, but something on an altogether smaller scale. In such situations, small-scale raiding by parties numbering not more than a few score might well have been the prevailing mode of aggression, much along the lines suggested for the Anasazi.[9] But the role of the individual warrior should not be forgotten. Bravery and prowess in battle could lead to significant prestige and status in everyday life. There are good grounds for seeing such a situation in the Bronze Age world of Europe.

These matters are intimately bound up with the development of social systems, and specifically the evolution of chiefdoms. With the movement to a social organisation significantly more complex than that of tribes, and with the installation of single individuals of pre-eminent status at the head of such organisations, the size of territories dependent on a single central settlement, and therefore also of fighting units, probably increased, as in Fiji where hundreds, occasionally even thousands, of men might be assembled for warlike purposes.[10] Larger armies had implications for the conduct of war, so that the movement of men and material would be much more visible, the problems of supply much greater, and campaigns likely to last considerably longer. Whereas a band of men a few score strong can be mobilised, deployed and dispersed again in the space of two or three days, an army of several hundred would need several days to assemble, perhaps a minimum of two or three to organise and attack, and as much again to be wound down. With the advent of what may be termed an army, warfare ceased to be a quick opportunistic matter, in which little more than a rallying cry and a desire for glory were needed, and became a matter for bureaucrats and quartermasters.

[7] Chagnon 1967.
[8] This view of the Yanomamö has been challenged in recent years (Ferguson 1992).
[9] Haas and Creamer 1993.
[10] Carneiro 1990.

It is in this light that consideration of military equipment and installations in Bronze Age Europe should take place. The scale of political and probably also military organisation increased markedly during the course of the period, but even so much of what is found represents the concerns of individuals or at most small bands of warriors, reflecting small-scale political units akin to chiefdoms rather than states, relying on single heroes rather than regiments.

Arms and armour

The story of the Bronze Age is also to some extent the story of the inventions that occurred during it. High up on the list of these come the series of new weapons created during the period. The bow and arrow had existed since at least the Mesolithic, the dagger since the Neolithic. During the Early Bronze Age the halberd enjoyed a brief vogue, and there was an early appearance of the sword in the Carpathian Basin; the spear was also invented at this stage. During the course of the Middle Bronze Age the sword gained in popularity and by the Urnfield period was widespread, developing into several variant forms. Also during the Bronze Age sheet defensive armour was developed, perhaps starting in the Middle Bronze Age but culminating in the magnificent bronze parade armour of the Urnfield period, along with the less spectacular but undoubtedly more efficient and protective leather armour. Such armour was necessary because in the Bronze Age, for the first time, weapons were developed for the sole and specific purpose of killing humans rather than animals.

Most or all of these types had a functional (i.e. utilitarian) purpose, as well as in some cases a symbolic one. Presumably they were initially intended for real conflict, and some types never seem to have lost that function. But the battle-axe seems to have become merely a symbol of prestige and power rather than an effective weapon of war, and in other cases the degree of decoration on weapons, often in pristine condition, strongly suggests a symbolic role.

Daggers, stabbing weapons for offensive use at close quarters, were likely always to have been ancillary to longer range weapons, notably the bow. Depictions, on Copper Age stelae for instance, show warriors with a dagger at their waist; many burials from the Beaker period and Early Bronze Age were equipped with a dagger. The incidence of daggers in graves, which often leads analysts to imagine their bearers to have had special status, perhaps shows no more than that all those who could manage to acquire one did so; like other Bronze Age weapons, its purpose may have been mainly deterrent.

With the passage of time, the dagger became extended in length so that it could no longer be used for stabbing at very close quarters. The development of the dirk and the rapier (fig. 8.2, 1) by this means led to a weapon that could

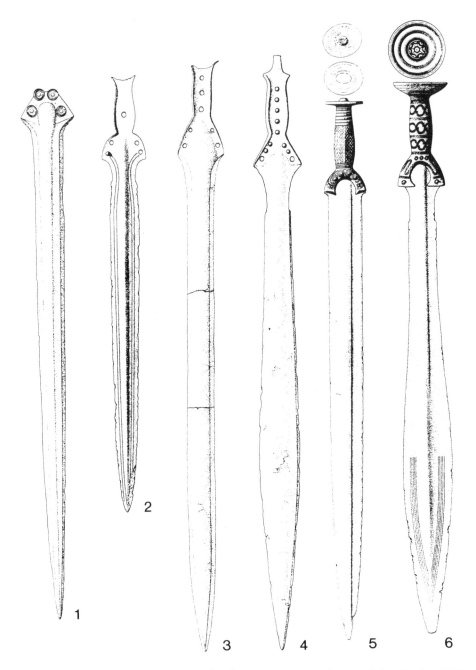

Fig. 8.2. Bronze swords: the progression of types (after Bader 1991; Schauer 1971; and Kemenczei 1991). 1. Rapier (separate grip, fastened by rivets). 2–4. Grip-tongue swords (*Griffzungenschwerter*), no. 4 with pommel tang. 5–6. Solid-hilted swords (*Vollgriffschwerter*): 5. Riegsee sword, 6. bowl-pommel sword (*Schalenknaufschwert*).

be used for thrusting, not stabbing or cutting. The popularity of such weapons was limited in time, mainly to the Middle Bronze Age, no doubt because they were not versatile enough in close combat, and in any case tended to come adrift from their hilts. The role of thrusting weapons came to be taken over by the spear, which had the great advantage that it could be mounted on a much longer shaft, enabling effective blows to be struck at greater distance and consequently less personal risk. The need for a weapon that could be used for fighting at close quarters was satisfied when the sword was developed, spelling the death-knell for the rapier.

It is difficult to be sure where the sword was invented. Traditional wisdom held that it was first developed in the Levant, and there are indeed early examples in that area; but the European series may have been separate, for two reasons. First, the parallelism between East Mediterranean and European events is currently under review, and there has been a significant pushing back of the European chronology; second, there is no sure indication that the Mediterranean sequence of weapons had any influence on the European at this early stage. The first swords in Europe, taking the criterion for a sword as being a weapon with a blade longer than 30 cm, appear in the Middle Bronze Age (Early Bronze Age in the Nordic area and terminology). Interestingly, from the start some were hafted in bronze (fig. 8.2, 5–6); some of these may have been parade weapons, but others surely saw combat. Initially this concerns a group of highly decorated swords found mainly in the Carpathian Basin but having outliers in north Germany and Scandinavia. These solid-hilted swords (*Vollgriffschwerter*) and swords of similar age that had organic hilt plates (*Griffzungenschwerter*, fig. 8.2, 2–4) were highly decorated with great technical proficiency in a spiral style that reached far across Europe. To this extent, they are unlikely to have been purely functional. On the other hand, the majority of them are significantly damaged, commonly with the hilt broken off, suggesting that they had seen at least some action. This early flowering of the sword-smith's art seems, however, to have been something of a flash in the pan, and it was not for another few centuries that the sword became standard equipment for the European warrior.

These first swords were relatively long and thin, suited still only to thrusting blows and therefore not versatile. For a while in the Middle Bronze Age combat seems to have been conducted along these lines, presumably a development of the earlier style of fighting with bow and arrow, and dagger. But this could not last. Swordsmen fighting at close quarters had to have more options open to them than merely that of thrusting; they had to be able to use their weapon to deliver blows from all kinds of angles, to cut, to parry and to thrust. For this reason, within a fairly short period (around 200 years) the new weapon with stouter blade and stronger hilt attachment was developed, the so-called cut-and-thrust sword (fig. 8.2, 2–4). To begin with, the

blade was parallel-sided and the whole weapon at around 60 cm in length relatively light, but before long the blade was expanded to form a leaf shape,
and being thickened down the centre it increased greatly in weight.
Surprisingly, the hilt often remained rather slight, leading to some lack of
balance; such swords do not feel comfortable to wield. Other refinements
include the provision of a ricasso (notched edges to the upper blade, to prevent damage to the hand if an opponent's sword slipped up the hilt in a clash
of weapons, and to provide additional grip by extending the forefinger to hold
it), grooves along the length of the blade (sometimes called blood channels,
but more likely a decorative feature), multiple rivets to improve the hilt
attachment, and the provision of a pommel (a disc, bowl or sphere forming
the termination of the hilt; fig. 8.2, 5–6). Pommels were not new – they were
present on daggers also – but they certainly became more elaborate; in the
latest stages of the Bronze Age bronzesmiths vied with each other to produce
more elaborate forms. The 'antenna sword' is so-called because the termination is represented by a flat plate across the top of the hilt, the ends coiled
into spirals and recalling the shape of an insect's antenna. What is not known
is how the pommel was fastened on to the hilt. One group of swords is provided with a 'pommel tang', a tongue-like projection at the end of the hilt
which was inserted into the pommel (fig. 8.2, 4); others have 'pommel ears',
small extensions of the flanges that flank the hilt and which likewise went
up into the pommel; but the majority have no clear indication of how the
attachment was achieved, suggesting that it was either glued on or integrated
with the hilt-plates. The function of the pommel was originally to stop the
hand sliding off the grip, and elaborate antenna pommels seem likely to have
represented an encumbrance rather than anything else: further evidence that
many swords were never intended for real fighting.

The interplay between grips made entirely of metal and those formed by
means of a thin plate of metal with side flanges to retain hilt-plates of organic
materials (bone or wood, to judge from surviving examples) is curious. The
overall form of the sword must have been the same, but these two quite distinct traditions emerged in the search to achieve an identical end-product.
Since organic hilt-plates could be decorated with metal pins and other elements to give an elaborate, even opulent appearance, show cannot have been
all there was to this divergence. There are in fact a number of differences
between the two traditions: the blade form of the solid-hilted swords is sometimes distinct, having a swelling rounded midrib; the attachment of blade and
grip is obviously quite different, with the two parts being cast separately and
then joined by over-casting; devices such as false rivets on the metal-hilted
version take the place of real rivets on the organic-hilted form. In spite of the
fact that metal-hilted swords are the better preserved, it seems likely that
there is a functional difference between the two, and that the organic-hilted
swords were intended for real fighting, and metal-hilted swords primarily for

display. The appearance of both forms in the same collective finds supports the idea of this functional difference.[11]

The sword was supplemented by a scabbard, which must usually have been of leather or wood. Many examples are known from the Nordic area of such finds, some remarkably well preserved. Further south, they do not survive, and one is left only with those few cases where metal scabbards, or fittings for them, occur. Complete metal scabbards were especially common in Early Iron Age Italy; metal chapes (the bottom of the scabbard) occur frequently in the latest part of the Bronze Age in the west of Europe (in hoards of the 'Carp's Tongue phase', for example). Occasionally they occur in great display ensembles, as with the magnificent find from Veliki Mošunj in Bosnia, complete with bronze chain pendants and other paraphernalia.

How were swords used? How many people possessed swords? The graves centred on Seddin in eastern Germany, for instance, possessed a modality in the deposition patterns of that area, with swords being restricted to a small number of rich graves.[12] In general in the Urnfield world, swords are exceptional finds in graves; the majority of Urnfield cemeteries do not contain them or any other weapons. Since this is to some extent a feature of the Urnfield deposition rite, one cannot necessarily rely on it as an indicator of sword frequency in particular areas. Examination of hoard finds shows that they must have been more common than graves would lead one to believe. The publication of many corpora of material enables one to put some figures on these speculations. Table 8.1 presents the crude figures for Late Bronze Age metal and organic hilted swords as presented for each country.

This picture, while by no means complete, gives some idea of the relative proportions of each type in each area. A number of points are clear. First, with the exception of Hungary, organic hilts are much commoner than metal ones, usually about three times as common but in Britain and Ireland overwhelmingly so. In Hungary, by contrast, the two traditions were equally prevalent. Second, the number and density of swords vary by area. Whereas in Italy and Yugoslavia there is on average less than one sword per 1000 square kilometres, and in Britain and north Germany between two and three swords, in central Europe (southern Germany, Austria, Switzerland, Hungary) the figure is much higher at 4.2–4.6 swords per 1000 km², while in the Nordic area it is 6.88 and in Ireland it reaches 7.61 per 1000 km², the highest of any region for which statistics are available. Again, this may relate in part to technology: the quantity of metalwork of all kinds is very high in Denmark, Hungary and Ireland, suggesting that these were areas where many skilled smiths were at work. Against this, one cannot rule out the possibility that fighting with

---

[11] e.g. Krasznokvajda (Borsod-Abaúj-Zemplén; Mozsolics 1972) or Velké Žernoseky (Litoměřice; Plesl 1961, 155 pl. 54).
[12] Wüstemann 1978.

Table 8.1. *Numbers of metal and organic-hilted swords in various countries of Europe*

	Organic	Metal	Area (1000 km²)	Density
Switzerland, Austria and south Germany[13]	672	489	275	4.22
Italy[14]	167	65	301	0.77
Romania[15]	273	80	238	1.48
Hungary[16]	226	202	93	4.60
Former Yugoslavia[17]	183	51	256	0.91
Denmark and north Germany[18]	604	641	181	6.88
Britain[19]	641	19	230	2.87
Ireland[20]	624	0	82	7.61

swords really was commoner in some areas than others. There may be yet other factors involved. The large number of finds in Britain, for instance, is influenced by the recovery of many from rivers and bogs, reflecting deposition for special reasons, whereas in Hungary a majority of the finds come from hoards of scrap metal. It would be reasonable to assume from this that swords, along with metalwork in general, played different roles in different areas.

Studies of wear on swords have shown how variable the amount of use as shown by resharpening on Danish swords was.[21] Some swords were pristine, others heavily resharpened, with all degrees of wear in between. There are two possible implications. On the one hand, the supply of bronze to south Scandinavia during the course of the Bronze Age may have varied, causing smiths in some areas continually to resharpen existing weapons rather than create new ones. On the other hand, the pattern may show that more fighting occurred at some times in some places than in others; the wear could simply be due to warriors' propensity for, and success at, impaling opponents in combat. Perhaps both factors were at work. Other studies have shown how prevalent damage to the edges of flange-hilted swords was, and how most features of swords were specifically related to achieving a successful combat weapon.[22] On the other hand, solid-hilted swords have consistently been shown to have little or no edge damage.

---

[13] Schauer 1971; Krämer 1985; von Quillfeldt 1995.
[14] Bianco Peroni 1970.
[15] Bader 1991.
[16] Kemenczei 1988; 1991.
[17] Harding 1995.
[18] Sprockhoff 1931; 1934; Ottenjann 1969.
[19] Burgess and Colquhoun 1988.
[20] Eogan 1965.
[21] Kristiansen 1984.
[22] Bridgford 1997.

Such studies bring home the fact that the Bronze Age sword was a weapon related to high status, restricted in distribution through society. Its role seems, therefore, to have been partly symbolic (the expression of warrior prowess), but also partly related to the real need for warriors to engage in combat when appropriate crises arose. More than anything else, the sword was the symbol of its age.

The spear (fig. 8.3) seems to have entered the world of Bronze Age Europe at the end of the Early Bronze Age, provided with a socket that could be fitted over the end of a wooden shaft. Earlier 'shoed' examples in Greece find a possible echo in a hoard from Kyhna in Saxony;[23] tanged weapons, as seen in the Sardinian finds from Ottana or the Arreton 'daggers' in Britain, may derive ultimately from Cypriot prototypes.[24] Pre-eminently a thrusting weapon, the spear must have superseded the dagger as a means of inflicting damage on an opponent without getting too close, and therefore represents a dramatic new development in fighting techniques. In addition, it is necessary to draw a distinction between spears that were held firm and used for thrusting, and those hurled through the air like a javelin. In some cases the socket seems too short for effective fastening to a shaft or for the hafting to remain undamaged on impact with a target. This has led some scholars to imagine that there was an intention that the head should separate from the shaft on hitting its target, on the principle of encumbrance, as seen also with the harpoon.[25] It is not easy to decide which function was served by which finds, though it is supposed that small spearheads would be suitable for throwing, large ones for thrusting.[26] There is an additional argument for this: a thrown weapon might well not be recovered (though presumably its counterpart would be received from the other side!), in which case not only the weapon but also a significant amount of bronze would be lost to its owner. Thus thrown weapons would be as small as possible, consistent with effectiveness in causing damage to the opponent.

Very few recent studies of the artefact class have appeared.[27] In the context of Mycenaean weaponry, where much greater variability in the size of spearheads is found, it is possible to discern patterns of deposition which suggest a changing use over time, perhaps under influence from the barbarian north.[28]

---

[23] Coblenz 1985; 1986.
[24] Lo Schiavo 1980.
[25] Bartlett and Hawkes 1965.
[26] The term 'lance' is often used to designate the thrusting spear, but this merely indicates the degree of confusion in the terminology since *lancer* in French means to hurl. Historically a lancer was a cavalryman armed with a long spear (lance) intended to impale an opponent during a charge. It is possible that some Bronze Age weapons were intended for use from a horse, but there seems little chance of identifying which. It is perhaps best to stick to the terms 'spear' and 'javelin', the former held and the latter thrown.
[27] Notably Jacob-Friesen 1967. Earlier works are still used: Greenwell and Brewis 1909; Evans 1933. More recent contributions: Burgess *et al.* 1972; Ehrenberg 1977; Needham 1979b; Briard and Mohen 1983. There are no *Prähistorische Bronzefunde* volumes except that for Greece (Avila 1983).
[28] Höckmann 1980.

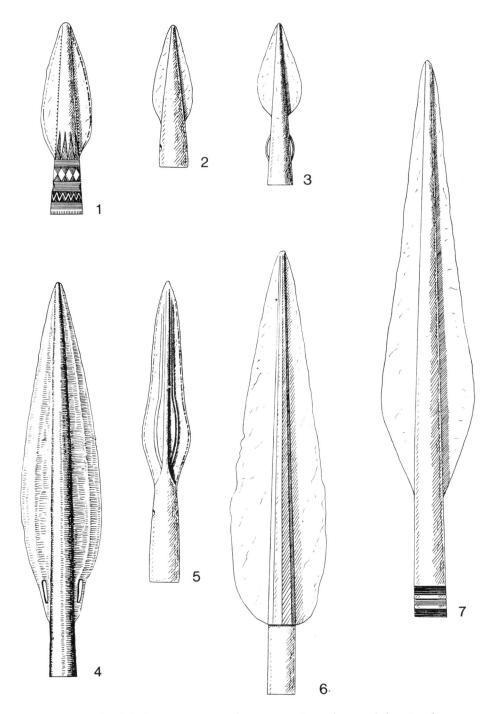

Fig. 8.3. Bronze spears: the progression of types (after Jacob-Friesen 1967). 1–3, 5. Javelin (lance) heads; 4, 6–7. Spearheads (4. basal-looped, 5. flame-shaped, 6. faceted).

Here too there are depictions which suggest strongly that certain long spears were used in chariot warfare and hunting, as a stela from Shaft Grave Circle A shows. In Europe as a whole, long spears are much less common than short ones. Nevertheless, long spearheads begin to appear as early as the Early Bronze Age in northern Europe,[29] though not until the Late Bronze Age in central Europe. There is no specific evidence to suggest that they were used from chariots as in Greece, though light vehicles of this sort were present from the Early Bronze Age onwards in central and eastern Europe. Bronze wheels of the Urnfield period are usually associated with cult or other special-purpose vehicles, and seem too large and unwieldy to have been fitted to light, fast-moving battle-chariots. Equally, the long spear could simply have been held by the foot-warrior and thrust at the opponent, or in the event of a charge held firm, as happened with phalanx warfare by hoplites in classical times.

The very large number of small spearheads is rather surprising in view of the foregoing, implying as it does that many spears were thrown. To judge from the quantity of finds in Europe, the first phase of combat may have consisted of the throwing of javelins from a distance, after which the combatants would have engaged in hand-to-hand combat. That distance is unlikely to have been more than 60–70 m, bearing in mind that the world record for throwing a precision-engineered modern javelin of 800 g was around 105 m (prior to the recent rule change). At that distance a javelin would be in the air for several seconds and one would think that avoiding it should not have been too difficult, unless there was such a crush of people that someone was likely to get hit, even if not the original target, or the rules of engagement dictated that one stood still, as in duelling. Perhaps more likely would be a distance of around 30 m, over which a well-thrown javelin should fly fast and low. Even so, it seems inevitable that it was the ensuing close combat that was really important in deciding the outcome of these encounters.

Recent studies in eastern Europe show how widespread the spearhead was in those areas (Ukraine, southern Russia), whereas the sword is rather rare.[30] Large numbers of spears are present in hoards, as moulds, as chance finds, and occasionally in graves. Arguably the steppelands saw the rise of squads of fighters not unlike the hoplite phalanx, rather than the sword-based warrior combat which the finds of central and western Europe suggest.

The weapon that was standard at the start of the Bronze Age was the bow and arrow. The frequent finding of chipped stone arrowheads in the Neolithic (and comparable projectile points much earlier) is strikingly confirmed by the discovery of a number of wooden bows in Neolithic and Bronze Age

---

[29] Jacob-Friesen's Typ Valsömagle: 1967, 117 pl. 27.
[30] Klochko 1993; 1995.

contexts.[31] Figured grave stelae of the Copper Age from Le Petit Chasseur at Sion in Switzerland also show warriors armed with bow and arrow.[32] Other iconographic evidence comes from the Italian rock art,[33] as well as (more commonly) from Sweden.[34] Sardinian bronze figurines often depict warriors bearing bows.[35] These depictions confirm the impression gained from the frequent finding of arrowheads that archery was common, and that it may in some circumstances have had a special meaning.[36] Such arrowheads were tanged and made of stone – typically flint – in the Early Bronze Age, but by the Middle Bronze Age were socketed and made of bronze.[37] In east-central Europe, the horizon that is thought to indicate the invasion or migration of iron-using peoples at the end of the Bronze Age (the 'Thraco-Cimmerians' or Scythians) is thought by some to be characterised by the finding of such arrowheads on destroyed stockades and forts;[38] on the Eurasian steppe the bow and arrow continued to develop right through the Bronze Age.[39]

While bow and arrow were no doubt regularly used for hunting throughout the Bronze Age (and beyond), it is not easy to know to what extent they were made use of in warfare. To begin with, the practices of the Neolithic and Chalcolithic must have continued, but presumably the advent of the sword, spear and armour indicates the adoption of a new mode of fighting which to some extent displaced these earlier practices. For long-distance fighting, however, there was no substitute – apart from slings and catapults – until the arrival of gunpowder and associated weapons in the late Medieval period, so that it is no surprise to find the bow and arrow a recurring element of Bronze Age armament throughout the period.

A recent attempt to determine the order of battle by means of analysis of weapon hoards deserves attention at this point.[40] This proceeds from the hypothesis that deposits of Bronze Age weaponry can yield significant meaning after the manner of the Hjortspring (Jutland) find of the Iron Age, where a case is made for identifying commanders and paddlers, the latter serving also as warriors. An interpretation of weapon hoards in terms of their utilitarian value is currently unpopular, which is not to say that it is impossible. Part of the analysis depends on an interpretation of axes and palstaves as

---

[31] Clark 1963; Sheridan 1992; 1996 (Scotland; see Switsur 1974); Switzerland: Bellwald 1992; Rageth 1974, 195f. fig. 13 (Ledro); see too the bow found with Ötzi the Ice Man (Egg 1992, 254ff.).
[32] Bocksberger 1978, 67 pl. 20.
[33] Anati 1961, 119.
[34] Coles 1990, 32ff. fig. 19d.
[35] Lilliu 1966, 58, 66ff.; Thimme 1980, 116ff., 280ff.
[36] e.g. the miniature antler bow from a Middle Bronze Age context at Isleham, Cambridgeshire: Gdaniec 1996.
[37] e.g. in the Tumulus Bronze Age: Stocký 1928, table 27, 2–9.
[38] Dušek 1964, 52ff.; 1971, 438; Bukowski 1977.
[39] Shishlina 1997.
[40] Randsborg 1995, 44ff.

weapons, which is itself doubtful. Further, in the Smørumovre hoard (the subject of the most detailed analysis) the scrap items and ingot have to be interpreted as currency and the light palstaves as tools perhaps used for payment; the number of palstaves then corresponds to the hypothetical number of warriors. The difficulties in the way of accepting this interpretation are not hard to see.

Defensive armour

To counter the constant improvements in offensive weaponry, Bronze Age warriors – or some of them – wore defensive armour. Such armour can take the form of items actually worn on the body (corslet, helmet, greaves) or carried (shield). Most of what survives is made of bronze, but there are good grounds for thinking that the majority of what would actually have been used in combat was made of leather or, in the case of shields, wood. The techniques of manufacture are similar in all cases, involving the manipulation of sheet metal or of skins and hides.

Presumably defensive armour had an initial phase which one cannot discern because at that stage it was made of organic materials which do not survive. In the Wessex culture grave in Bush Barrow near Stonehenge, for instance, fragments of wood were found intermixed with bronze rivets, which some have suggested could have been a shield.[41] It has sometimes been suggested that bronze buttons and discs found in isolation could have been attached to wooden shields. Until recently, this was an isolated example at such an early date, but a recently obtained radiocarbon date for the wooden shield mould from Kilmahamogue, Co. Antrim, was 3445 ± 70 BP (1950–1540 cal BC).[42] Perhaps the only surprising thing about this result is that it is still unique at so early a date. It appears to indicate that shields of organic materials *were* present in the Early Bronze Age, which need not in itself be surprising; its form – with concentric ribs interrupted by a V-shaped notch – is, however, otherwise only known in the Late Bronze Age (the Herzsprung type).[43] No one knows what this notch represents (it also appears in U-shaped form), but its distribution from Crete and Cyprus in the east to Iberia[44] (fig. 8.4) and Ireland in the west, and from Italy to Scandinavia, shows that it was widely known and to the Bronze Age smith a necessary part of shield creation. It was presumably skeuomorphic, or at least represents a feature that was in origin functional; it has been suggested that originally the design came from a fault on a famous 'ancestor' shield, thereafter copied in skeuomorphic form on all subsequent shields without any longer having any functional

---

[41] Though others have doubted if this was possible – Coles 1962, 172.
[42] Hedges *et al.* 1991, 128f.
[43] Sprockhoff 1930.
[44] Almagro 1966.

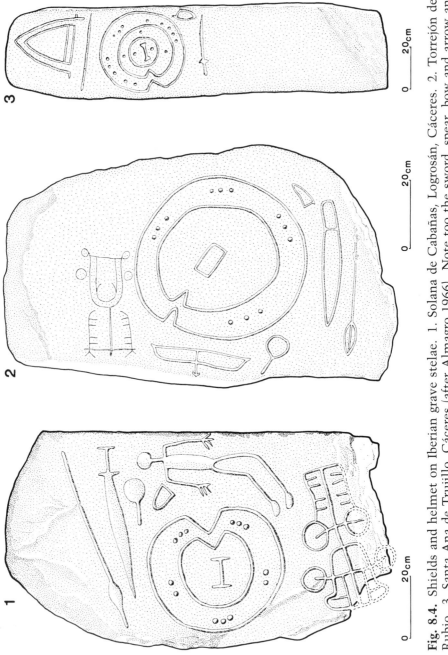

Fig. 8.4. Shields and helmet on Iberian grave stelae. 1. Solana de Cabañas, Logrosán, Cáceres. 2. Torrejón del Rubio. 3. Santa Ana de Trujillo, Cáceres (after Almagro 1966). Note too the sword, spear, bow and arrow and other (unidentified) objects; also the wagons on nos. 1 and 2.

meaning.[45] It is noticeable, however, that in most examples the notch and handle are aligned, which would mean that in normal use the notch would indicate which way up the shield was to be carried.

This find apart, the first certain shields are those from Hungarian hoards of the early Urnfield period,[46] and possibly also from a well-known but ambiguous find at Plzeň-Jíkalka,[47] which was allegedly found with a hoard dating to Br D. Since this piece is apparently of cast, not beaten, bronze and has an 'archaic' look to it, there is in principle no reason why it should not date to the start of the Urnfield period.

This is also the date of the first known body-armour, as in the rich grave at Čaka in western Slovakia, where fragments of bronze sheet were reconstructed to form a protective cape covering the shoulders and upper body.[48] Probably the origin of the gold 'cape' from Mold in north Wales lies in something similar,[49] which might again indicate an earlier date for the start of the tradition than commonly appreciated. With greaves, too, the earliest examples date to the early Urnfield period, as with the hoards from Cannes-Ecluse (Seine-et-Marne) and Rinyaszentkiraly (Somogy), as well as a number in the Sava valley of Croatia.[50] And the same story may also be told for helmets.[51] The indications are therefore clear that sheet-metal armour started its life with the Urnfield period and had an earlier history in organic materials.

Though it might seem as if it was a response to the new weapon types that also characterise this period, such an analysis is probably false. Experiments have demonstrated unequivocally that sheet-bronze shields are significantly less useful than leather or wooden examples; in a reconstruction, blows from a 'Bronze Age' sword were able to cut right through a beaten sheet-bronze shield, whereas they made little impression on one of hardened leather.[52] It is not known what the effect on a thicker, cast bronze shield might be; this could have been much more effective. The wooden shields from Ireland would have been heavy to carry but must have afforded very considerable protection against both slashing blows from a sword and piercing blows from a spear, arrow or rapier.

The clear implication is that the finds of beaten bronze metal armour were made not so much for defence as for display. Together with some of the more highly decorated weaponry, they offer significant clues to the understanding

---

[45] Undset, quoted by Sprockhoff (1930, 28f.).
[46] Patay 1968; Schauer 1980.
[47] Most recently Kytlicová (1986), who has provided strong arguments that two groups of finds were present at Jíkalka, the shield belonging to a later group that can be placed towards the end of the Bronze Age.
[48] Točík and Paulík 1960; Paulík 1968; Snodgrass 1971; Schauer 1978.
[49] Powell 1953.
[50] von Merhart 1956–7 [1958]; Schauer 1982. New find in Swabia: Krahe 1980.
[51] Oranienburg, Pass Lueg, Weissig: Hencken 1971, 37 fig. 13e; 179ff.
[52] Coles 1962.

of the position of the warrior in Bronze Age society. The mere sight of Achilles' armour, as worn by Patroclus in Book XVI of the *Iliad*, was enough to strike terror into Trojan hearts; added to the terrible war-cry that Achilles used in Book XVIII, the effect was complete. It is certainly not stretching

Fig. 8.5. Sheet-bronze cuirass from Marmesses. Photo: Réunion des Musées Nationaux, Paris. ©Photo RMN – Loïc Hamon.

imagination too far to see these finds representing something similar in the barbarian world of Europe.

In the more developed stages of the Urnfield period, some of these objects were technologically and artistically of the highest quality. The magnificent helmets from the 'ritual' hoard of Viksø (see below), for instance, or the corslet from Marmesses (fig. 8.5), indicate something of the expertise that was available to those with the status to command it. Curiously, however, no single find contains all the elements that might have been at the disposal of the Late Bronze Age warrior, and scholars have had to be content with reconstructions taken from several different sources in their attempts at viewing the complete outfit. Frustratingly, a number of finds of armour have come from poor contexts and not from graves, though some of the finds of corslets from Slovakia[53] and the eastern and western Alps,[54] or greaves like those from Ilijak on the Glasinac plateau in Bosnia or Torre Galli in north Italy,[55] are from graves that illustrate what items of military equipment might have been buried with a Late Bronze Age or Early Iron Age warrior in continental Europe.

A recent find from Sweden further illustrates the special attention paid to defensive armour. In what seems to be a clear foreshadowing of Iron Age practices (as seen for instance at Illerup in Jutland), at Fröslunda on the southern edge of Lake Vänern a series of 16 shields were recovered from land that is believed to be a silted-up creek.[56] The shields are of the Herzsprung type, that is round in shape with concentric circles of ribs and bosses raised on the bronze and U- or V-shaped 'notches' interrupting one or more of the ribs. Although one might interpret this find as connected with a local production centre for such armour, it is much more likely that it represents a votive deposit of the type studied by Levy and others,[57] especially as the bronze from which the shields were made is very thin. It joins a series of other shield finds from Scandinavia, for instance that from Taarup Mose on the Danish island of Falster, and from other areas, like those of the Nipperwiese type from Thorpe (Surrey) and Long Wittenham (Oxfordshire) in southern England,[58] or from Lough Gur (Co. Limerick) and Athenry (Co. Galway) in western Ireland.[59] The majority of shield finds in the west and north of Europe are from wet places; the majority of those from the centre and east from hoards. Certainly the wet finds reinforce the 'ritual' interpretation of beaten bronze body armour.

A comparable find was that made in 1942 in a peat bog in northern Zealand in the parish of Viksø of two bronze helmets made of beaten sheet metal

[53] Paulík 1968.
[54] von Merhart 1954.
[55] von Merhart 1956–7 [1958], 93f., 107ff.
[56] Hagberg 1988; 1994.
[57] Levy 1982.
[58] Needham 1979a.
[59] Coles 1962.

Fig. 8.6. The two bronze horned helmets from Viksø, Zealand.
Photo: National Museum, Copenhagen.

(fig. 8.6).[60] They were fashioned from two halves, riveted together, a heavy cross-shaped bronze fitting surmounting the peak, having space for a crest and terminating at the front in a beak-like hook. Either side of the beak are large bosses representing eyes, with curving rib-like features above for the

[60] Norling-Christensen 1946.

brows; large and small bosses decorate the rest of the cap. Most remarkable of all, two curving horns are attached to each helmet, made by lost-wax casting, with a biconical expansion near the tips.

Such helmets may have been worn in battle, but the artistic evidence that is most readily available, on rock surfaces and bronze figurines, suggests that it was in ritual performances that they were most at home. The rock panels from Hede near Kville in Bohuslän, for instance, depict several shields, and a number of figures have horns projecting from their schematically drawn heads, including lur-blowers from Kalleby in the same region. The performances seen in such images no doubt originated in real conflicts but seem here to be stylised and ritualised in nature. They do, nevertheless, speak for the importance accorded the warrior in the societies in question. More enigmatic are the small figurines of bronze, seen in Scandinavia and in Sardinia, some of which depict armed warriors. On a handle attachment from Grevensvænge, Næstved (Zealand) were a pair of men with horned helmets brandishing massive battle-axes; opinion has been divided as to whether these represent divinities or warriors in mid-performance.[61] In Sardinia a striking series of bronze figurines illustrate aspects of the warrior on that island (fig. 11.1).[62] These too may carry round shields, in this case with a central projecting spike, they wear horned helmets and wield massive swords or carry bows or spears. In some cases, a dagger or sword is slung on the chest. Although these Sardinian warriors did not apparently wear bronze armour, they did wear tunics, probably of leather, greaves, sometimes kilts bearing small roundels (perhaps bronze bosses), and bronze spiral neck and leg guards, much as occurred in central Europe in the Early and Middle Bronze Ages.[63] The appearance of shields and helmets in this context illustrates beyond doubt that such armour was available even in those areas where no *in corpore* examples survive. Perhaps the nearest to such a survival is seen in the statue-menhirs of neighbouring Corsica, especially those around the great site of Filitosa; some of these have holes in the head apparently for the insertion of horns, and many carry swords, daggers, or both.[64] Similar statues are present in Sardinia itself, but there is no evidence there for the representation of armour.[65]

Forts and fortifications

Sites with fortifications provide a prime source of evidence for inter-group conflict and aggression, but one must also consider sites with burning or with skeletal material lacking formal burial. These latter features are hard to

---

[61] Djupedal and Broholm 1952.
[62] e.g. Thimme 1980, 268ff.
[63] Lilliu 1966, 58ff. (greaves), 62 (shield and horned helmet), 75ff. (kilts).
[64] Grosjean 1966, 64ff.
[65] Atzeni 1978.

interpret and ambiguous in nature. Unwanted fires were a feature of daily life until relatively recent times, especially in settlements constructed mainly of wood.[66] Unless there are special grounds for doing so, it is dangerous to assume that the presence of charcoal or other carbonised material is necessarily anything to do with burning by an enemy. The first village of Biskupin was destroyed by burning, but given the close proximity of the houses to one another it would take no more than a strong wind and an errant spark to set the whole place alight. On the other hand, the fact that such a site was built at all suggests strongly that hostile action was responsible for its downfall. Similarly, the presence of human bone in pits and ditches does not automatically signify the slaughter of a site's inhabitants in an attack. On the one hand, the presence of numerous skeletons associated with material of the Velatice culture in the Cezavy hill at Blučina in Moravia has been taken, perhaps legitimately, as evidence of hostile attack; but on the other, the many instances of human remains in the ditches and pits of Velim, eastern Bohemia, are more likely an indication of special treatment of the dead (see p. 334).

In considering the origin and development of hillforts, it is usual to draw a distinction between settlements on hills and those with defensive installations (banks and ditches, ramparts, palisades). The positioning of settlements on low eminences was no doubt undertaken for practical reasons such as the need to avoid the damp conditions of valley floors; but the use of higher hill locations may reflect the desire to situate dwellings well away from potentially hostile neighbours. In such a situation, simply placing settlements on hills could act as a deterrent in itself; the provision of a fence or other slight surround could act in concert with the natural factors (slope, elevation) to deter hostile approach. If additional strength was required, the provision of a modest ditch and bank at certain weak spots might be all that was required – and indeed it can frequently be seen that 'defences' did not completely encircle sites, but were confined to small areas. The next logical step, that of providing a full set of defensive barriers, was one taken in the Late Bronze Age and more especially in the Early Iron Age, but it was more a question of degree than of different intention, perhaps also reflecting different modes of warfare and weaponry.

In several parts of central Europe, elevated sites were used for settlement throughout the Bronze Age.[67] A study of South Württemberg and adjoining areas listed several dozen sites where occupation of the Early and Middle Bronze Age could be demonstrated, in addition to those (sometimes the same ones) where settlement and defences of the Urnfield and Hallstatt periods were present (fig. 8.7).[68] Within the Early and Middle Bronze Ages, not all

---

[66] Cf. the fires that first damaged and later destroyed the reconstructed lake villages in Zürich in 1990: Ruoff 1992.
[67] Jockenhövel 1990.
[68] Biel 1980; 1987.

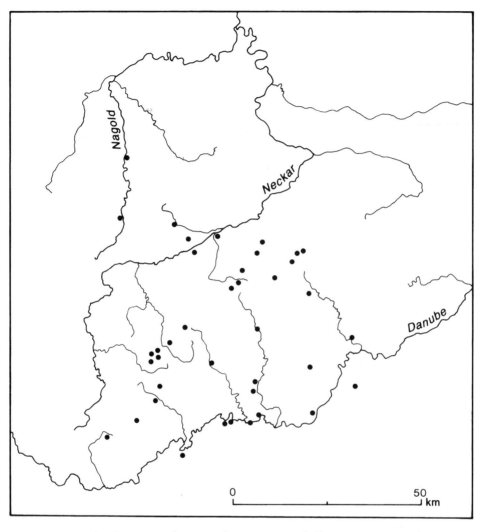

Fig. 8.7. Distribution of Bronze Age hilltop sites in southern Württemberg (after Biel 1980).

segments are equally well represented: occupation starts in Br A2 and not earlier, and sees a significant falling off during the course of the Tumulus period, except in certain areas (such as the upper Rhine valley in Switzerland). A site such as the Runder Berg at Urach (Reutlingen) has produced finds of Br A2 date and later;[69] a fortified site at Mörnsheim (Eichstätt, Bavaria) appears to have been occupied throughout the Bronze Age up to the early Urnfield period,[70] and a fair number of other sites with bank and ditch are known in

[69] Stadelmann 1980.
[70] Menke 1982.

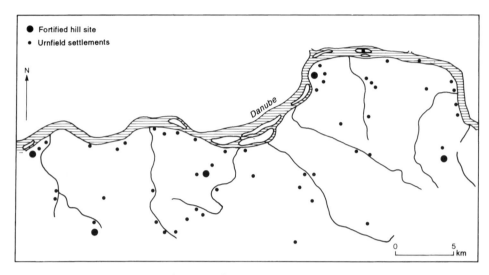

Fig. 8.8. Distribution of settlements and fortified hill-sites along the Danube in the Esztergom region of northern Hungary (after Bándi 1982).

central Europe from this period.

Further east, a number of Early Bronze Age sites in Slovakia and Poland have long been known to have had defences,[71] and in Moravia too a number of Early and Middle Bronze Age sites have surrounding ditches or defensible locations or both.[72] Of these, the best known is Spišský Štvrtok near Poprad in the hilly north-central part of the country, but other sites include Barca near Košice in the eastern lowlands. At Spišský, the excavator found various stone walls that apparently encircle the central part of the settlement, but the absence of any proper published plans and sections makes it hard to assess their true significance.[73] At Barca densely packed houses were surrounded by a ditch and wood-framed rampart.[74] Both these sites achieve additional significance from the fact that gold and bronze hoards were found on them, including heart-shaped pendants, amber beads, gold and bronze spirally wound and biconical beads, and at Barca a decorated dagger, at Spišský a gold armring.

Hilltop sites appear along with ordinary settlements along the Danube in Hungary (fig. 8.8).[75] Other sites on the fringes of the Hungarian plain were provided with surrounding ditches, but one must question whether these were all necessarily for defence against human attack rather than flood defences.

---

[71] Vladár 1973a, 273ff.; Gedl 1982; Točík 1982.
[72] Stuchlíková 1982.
[73] Vladár 1973a.
[74] Točík 1994 for the fortification sequence.
[75] Bándi 1982.

The case of Nitriansky Hrádok (Nové Zámky) in south-west Slovakia is often quoted, and certainly a ditch and rampart surrounded the domestic settlement on this site (fig. 2.16).[76] It lies, however, in the flood-plain of the river Nitra (today beside a tributary stream close to the confluence) in flat country. In a number of other cases on the Hungarian Plain, excavation around the tell has revealed a large ditch. This was present at Jászdózsa-Kápolnahalom,[77] and at a number of other sites on the Tisza flood-plain, as well as the 28 fortified Vatya culture sites of central Hungary.[78] An enclosure ditch surrounded the settlement at Aszod.[79] Equally, some sites were *not* surrounded by a ditch, for instance Füzesabony.[80] Whether such surrounding ditches were really defensive in nature is often doubtful in view of the fact that they are generally broad and shallow, with no clear indication of the nature of their accompanying ramparts; in a number of cases protection against flooding seems a better explanation.

In Transylvania, hilltop settlement was common. The type-site of Wietenberg near Sighişoara,[81] or the Otomani sites on the hills overlooking the edge of the Great Hungarian Plain,[82] are located on low hills, in some cases with a ditch and bank cutting off the easiest approach route. Only 14 Wietenberg sites were fortified in this way;[83] the rest were open.

In Alsace, such a site is situated on the Hohlandsberg near Wintzenheim (Haut-Rhin).[84] Although little is known about the structural evidence accompanying the numerous finds of Middle Bronze Age pottery in the areas investigated so far on this extensive hilltop 400 × 200 m across, it is certainly clear that such a hill, rising high above the Rhine valley below to a height of 640 m above sea level, would have been a major deterrent to hostile action; this is one of the most impressive hill settlements of the period prior to the Late Bronze Age (it continued to be occupied into that period). A site at Le Lébous in the Hérault represents a further example of a substantial fortified enclosure of the Copper and Early Bronze Age on the Mediterranean coast.[85]

There are signs already in the Middle Bronze Age in Britain that settlements were starting to be sited on hilltops; in the case of Rams Hill, Berkshire, an enclosure ditch was added to the pre-existing settlement towards the end of the Middle Bronze Age,[86] and other southern sites, such as Norton

---

[76] Točík 1981.
[77] Stanczik 1982, 384 fig. 7.
[78] Kovacs 1982; see also Bándi 1982.
[79] Tárnoki 1988.
[80] Szathmári 1992.
[81] Horedt and Seraphin 1971.
[82] Bader 1982.
[83] Three per cent of the total studied by Boroffka (1994, 76, 100).
[84] Bonnet 1973; Bonnet, Plouin and Lambach 1985.
[85] Arnal 1973.
[86] Needham and Ambers 1994.

Fitzwarren, Somerset, may show the same pattern.[87] At Mam Tor, Derbyshire, radiocarbon dates for settlement in the interior indicate a date range as early as 1578–1134 cal BC, though there is no evidence for the provision of fortifications at this time.[88] Yet in this early period there is little sign that there was any systematic network of sites in elevated positions; the observation that hilltops were increasingly used for settlement from the Early Bronze Age onwards cannot, in the present state of knowledge, be integrated into a more complete picture.

This situation clearly changed markedly in the ensuing centuries, when not only were hills provided with artificial defences but in some areas a network of sites was spaced more or less regularly along river valleys. Such a shift must relate to socio-political conditions, economic developments, technological changes leading to changes in warfare, or a combination of any or all of these. One suggestion is that there was a change in kinship relations, whereby a stronger emphasis was placed on the 'insider/outsider' distinction than had existed previously, perhaps as a result of agricultural intensification, leading to a stronger sense of 'property'.[89] The new forms of weaponry indicate new forms of warfare, as discussed above, and the hill sites were used as part of these new practices. On the one hand, personal combat between warriors was important; on the other, group security could principally be assured by placing non-combatants out of harm's way, even if that meant significant inconvenience and discomfort, for instance in the transport of water, food and other necessities.

It is the Late Bronze Age which sees the major development of forts and fortifications (fig. 8.9). This process took place through much of Europe, though the literature tends to give the impression that it happened mainly in central Europe. In fact, improved field evidence from many countries now indicates that fortifications were being erected in the Late Bronze Age wherever they have been systematically investigated – from Ireland and Portugal in the west to Romania and Ukraine in the east, from Scotland, Poland and Sweden in the north to Italy and Spain in the south.

Systematic studies of Bronze Age hillforts have been carried out in various parts of Europe, particularly in some areas of Germany.[90] It is clear from these studies that many of the forts that achieved greater prominence in the Iron Age were also occupied in the Urnfield period. Most of this evidence comes from chance surface finds or cuttings through the ramparts. Much information has thus been gathered about rampart form and construction method, especially in the Lausitz area of eastern Germany.[91] A variety of palisade and

---

[87] Ellis 1989.
[88] Coombs 1976; Coombs and Thompson 1979.
[89] Thomas 1997.
[90] e.g. Schubart 1961; Jockenhövel 1980a; 1982c; 1990; Biel 1980; Stadelmann 1980; Simon 1982b.
[91] Tackenberg 1949–50; Coblenz 1964; 1978; 1982, etc.; Herrmann 1969a.

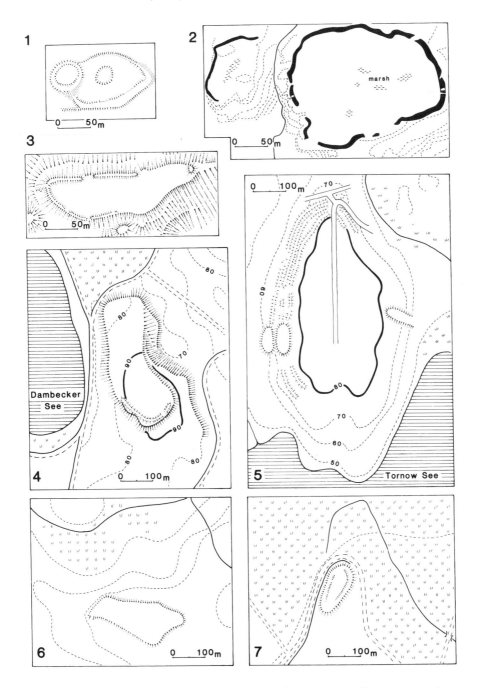

Fig. 8.9. Hillfort plans. 1. Nivize [Ajdovskigrad], Rupingrande (after Moretti 1978). 2. Predikstolen, Uppsala (after M. Olausson 1993). 3. Basedow, Malchin. 4. Kratzeburg, Neustrelitz. 5. Gühlen-Glienicke, Neuruppin. 6. Rühlow, Neubrandenburg. 7. Görne, Rathenow (3–7 after Horst 1982).

box rampart types were created, some using much more timber than others, some using dumps of earth, some using stone rubble as an infilling. At Nieder Neundorf (Niesky), for example, timbers were laid in alternate directions to form a rampart of more or less solid wood;[92] at the Schafberg near Löbau, what was basically a stone wall was anchored by wooden members passing through the rampart.[93] While the details of these rampart constructions provide fascinating material for excavators to puzzle over, what is important here is that already during the Urnfield period a highly structured method of enclosure was in place, with elaborate rampart building involving a lot of resources, both natural and human.

The rise of hillforts in Sweden has been seen as part of the same process that led to the emergence of a few very rich burials in the Late Bronze Age, as with the fort at Predikstolen near Uppsala (fig. 8.9, 2) and the nearby mound of Håga (see chapter 3), or a number of other Swedish sites that can be shown to have begun life at the start of the Late Bronze Age.[94] In the western part of Europe, too, there is now good and increasing evidence for a Bronze Age start to hillforts. At the Breiddin, Powys (mid-Wales), a substantial rampart was added to an area already settled since the Early Bronze Age; the associated dates fell in the range 1048–801 cal BC. Substantial occupation material, including a furnace and post-structures and four-posters, lay inside the rampart.[95] There are indications that other hillforts in this part of the Welsh Marches may also have Bronze Age beginnings.[96] Several Irish forts, for example Rathgall in Co. Wicklow, Mooghaun in Co. Clare and Dún Aonghasa on the Aran Islands (fig. 8.13), have all produced Late Bronze Age material, though it is uncertain to what extent this is to be associated with the fortified phases.[97]

Nor is it only sites on hilltops that were fortified: many lower lying sites came to be provided with defences. This is true of many of the sites of the north European plain, from Poland or south Russia to Germany and the Low Countries.[98] In Britain, too, sites such as Paddock Hill, Thwing (East Yorkshire), or Loft's Farm, Essex, were defended homesteads surrounded by a very considerable ditch and rampart.[99] As yet, however, there are still relatively few sites where the evidence is extensive enough to permit detailed appreciation of what Late Bronze Age forts were like, and none to rival the large-scale investigation of Iron Age sites such as Danebury or the Heuneburg. The great majority of sites have been investigated by no more than sections

[92] Coblenz 1963.
[93] Coblenz 1966.
[94] M. Olausson 1993.
[95] Musson *et al.* 1991, 20ff., 175ff.
[96] e.g. Moel y Gaer, Rhosesmor: Guilbert 1976.
[97] Raftery 1971; Cotter 1994; Grogan 1995.
[98] Buck 1982a; Horst 1982.
[99] Manby 1980; Brown 1988; Needham 1992, 52ff., 66 with list.

through the defences, coupled with the digging of small trenches in the interior in order to get some idea of the nature of internal constructions. The site that still has most extensive evidence is that of the Wittnauer Horn, Aargau, Switzerland.[100] Here the long narrow promontory was defended by cross-dykes, and two rows of building foundations were laid out along the promontory with an open space separating them. These foundations were principally visible as terrace-like steps cut into the bedrock; the complete absence of post-holes indicates a construction method based on sleeper beams. Bersu believed, from the depth of the occupation layer and the absence of burning, that there had been a long and unbroken period of use, though he was rightly puzzled by the absence of storage pits. Since the publication of this site in 1945 it has been accepted as the exemplar for Late Bronze Age fort interiors in central Europe. There has been little indication since then, however, that it was really typical of the situation in this area and period. Examination of the report suggests that other interpretations of the excavation evidence are possible. Bersu opened only narrow trenches (1 m wide), so that he was unable to recover the complete ground plan of any house, even in the few areas where these sondages were extended laterally. The edges of houses were defined as linear steps in the bedrock, and Bersu assumed that they continued through the unexplored areas, thus arriving at figures of around 35 houses in the north row, 30 in the south row, 4 in the interior and 1 at the east end, around 70 in total. While extensive occupation remains are certainly present, it is far from certain that there were so many, all occupied simultaneously. Confirmation that Bersu's dating is not completely reliable comes from the recent excavations on the site.[101]

A survey of the scene between Germany and Bulgaria shows that almost nowhere is anything like a full examination of any fort interior available for study.[102] In country after country, site after site, details of rampart date and construction method, based on section cuttings through the defences, are provided, while consideration of the nature of the occupation is almost absent. The main exception is formed by the stockade sites of the western part of Great Poland and north-eastern Germany, where there are indeed sites that have been investigated over extensive parts of the interior; many, perhaps all, belong to the Early Iron Age, with a Late Bronze Age phase present at some. One of the best-known examples is the Altes Schloss at Senftenberg, near Potsdam, where excavations earlier this century revealed an interior full of post-holes that can perhaps be joined up to form a series of buildings; a well and storage pits were also found. Around 30 buildings stood in rows separated

[100] Bersu 1945.
[101] Berger *et al.* 1996. This confirmed that there is Late Bronze Age occupation (through artefactual and radiocarbon evidence) but not that all the features Bersu assigned to the period really belonged to it, since the occupation stretches through to Ha D1; in particular the dating of the walled compound is completely uncertain.
[102] Beiträge 1982.

by 'streets' about 3 m wide, probably paved with wooden planks like the surrounding circuit road.[103] The most famous of these sites is Biskupin, but it appears to belong almost entirely to the Iron Age; not far away is the much bigger site of Sobiejuchy, which started life in the Late Bronze Age and largely falls earlier than Biskupin.[104] Here the whole interior was occupied – not necessarily simultaneously, but certainly all within a short time – while the surrounding rampart was modified on several occasions. That such sites were destroyed after a relatively short period of occupation shows that the system was structurally weak.

In many parts of the Mediterranean, stone is abundant and wood much less so. As a consequence, stone was used for the construction of defences and sites are correspondingly better preserved. Along the Adriatic, for instance, are the *castellieri* of the Trieste area and adjoining karst land, and the *gradine* of the Dalmatian coast and Bosnia.[105] One of these, Monkodonja in Istria, has spectacularly preserved stone walls and gateways and has been shown by recent excavation to date to the Middle Bronze Age (fig. 8.10).[106] On the tiny island of Pantelleria, south-west of Sicily, lies the fortified Early Bronze Age village of Mursia, surrounded by a vast stone wall with bastion-like projections on one side.[107] In northern Portugal there are the *castros*, the first phase of which falls in the Late Bronze Age.[108] Scores of such sites are known, though few have been extensively excavated. The surrounding walls are of stone rubble with little sign of built construction, and few interiors have been investigated in detail, but the elevated situations overlooking the coastal strip are often impressive.

A very special form of stone fort is that known from the western Mediterranean islands, principally Sardinia but also Corsica and the Balearics. The *nuraghi* of Sardinia are the most famous and the most impressive, though the *torre* of Corsica and the *talayots* of the Balearics are also noteworthy; the *motillas* of La Mancha in east-central Spain may be somewhat similar, if rather earlier.[109] These have been shown to be large permanent settlements with substantial fortification walls, and to be associated with arable agriculture; of a number of recently excavated examples, that of El Azuer stands out.[110] The *nuraghi* (conical towers) are built of masoned and coursed massive stone blocks, with staircases in the thickness of the walls and two, three or even more vaulted chambers one above the other (fig. 8.11).[111] Model

---

[103] Götze 1933; Herrmann 1969b.
[104] Bukowski 1959–60.
[105] Marchesetti 1903; Karoušková-Soper 1983; Čović 1965; Benac 1985.
[106] Teržan *et al.* 1998.
[107] Tozzi 1968; Tusa 1994, 139ff.
[108] Ferreira da Silva 1986.
[109] Martín *et al.* 1993; Fernández Castro 1995, 106ff.
[110] Molina *et al.* 1979.
[111] Lilliu 1962; 1987; Webster 1991; 1996.

Fig. 8.10. Two views of the Middle Bronze Age hillfort at Monkodonja, Istria, Croatia. *Upper*: Aerial view (photo: O. Braasch); *lower*: the massive masonry of the west gate. Photos by kind permission of the excavators, B. Hänsel and B. Teržan.

Fig. 8.11. A fortified tower on Sardinia: the Nuraghe Asoru, near
S. Priamo, southern Sardinia. Photo: author.

nuraghi show that, when complete, the towers had battlements and machico-
lation and were notably high in relation to their diameter. Starting as relatively simple constructions with interior corridors ('*protonuraghi*'), *nuraghi*
became more and more elaborate over time, with additional towers, curtain
walls, platforms and other features being added, but in a Bronze Age context
most of the sites were still relatively simply in layout. In terms of function,
nuraghi are usually assumed to represent fortified residences, an extreme form
of refuge-seeking, such as is often suggested for hillforts.[112] Once inside, access

[112] Webster 1991.

to the outside world would have depended on one's enemy not bothering to wait around; he, too, presumably lived in a *nuraghe* and had his own affairs to see to. If one is right to see Bronze Age warfare as involved above all with raiding, then the *nuraghi* must have provided the ideal answer.

On the other hand, it has recently been suggested that in view of the density of sites in some parts of Sardinia, these towers must have been intended primarily for display, as strongholds of single families.[113] Distribution analyses have often demonstrated how thickly *nuraghi* are concentrated in some parts of the island, with the north-west (west and south of Sassari) and the central southern area being particularly prolific (more than 0.6 per km²).[114] Some have assumed that this density reflects a sizeable population, but not all large populations in Bronze and Iron Age Europe engaged in such a wealth of monument erection. The cyclopean masonry and the elaborate layout of the towers would represent overkill if it were merely intended to be defensive; thus, although defence must have formed one purpose of the construction, the representation of power was certainly another. *Nuraghi* have reasonably been seen as a potent element in the process of increasing sociopolitical complexity, with claims to land and territory being backed up by the creation of alliances and hierarchical relationships between groups; certainly they represent an ideal laboratory for the study of emerging power structures.[115]

Studies in a number of areas of Europe have shown that forts can be linked to what may be termed 'territories'. The regular disposition of sites along river valleys in Baden-Württemberg, especially along the Danube and its tributaries, is a case in point.[116] If all these sites could be shown to be contemporary, the spacing would be as little as 3–4 km in some instances. Something of the same sort is visible in the forts of the Aran Islands (fig. 8.12). The small island of Inis Mór (Inishmore), for instance, a mere 14 km long and 3.25 km across at the widest point, contains no fewer than four forts, Inis Meáin (Inishmaan), 5 km long and 2.5 km wide, two forts. Of them only Dún Aonghasa (Dún Aengus) has actually produced material of Bronze Age date; this and other sites went on being occupied and used probably into the Medieval period. The multiplicity and spacing of forts suggest territories of only a few square kilometres, with the forts acting as the residence location for a population consisting of no more than a few families exploiting a minimal territory. A not dissimilar situation seems to have existed in those parts of Sardinia where *nuraghi* cluster most thickly, as for instance in the north-west part of the island, between Abbasanta and Sassari. The density of sites in parts of this area is higher than 0.6 per km², and in the part between

---

[113] Trump 1991.
[114] Lilliu 1962, 13, 62; 1987.
[115] Webster 1991; Bonzani 1992; Perra 1997.
[116] Biel 1980.

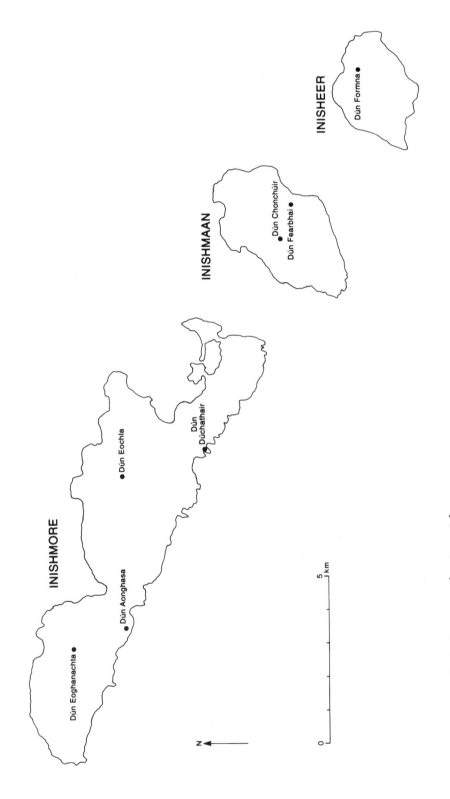

Fig. 8.12. Forts on the Aran Isles.

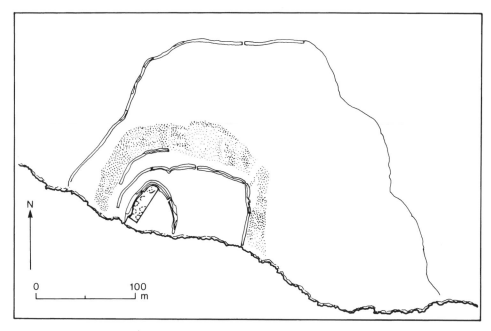

Fig. 8.13. Dún Aonghasa, plan showing excavated area with house outlines. Stippled area represents the *chevaux-de-frise*; sheer cliffs at southern edge of site (after Cotter 1994).

Macomer, Abbasanta and the west coast it can surpass 1 per km², an astonishingly high figure. Admittedly not all *nuraghi* are necessarily contemporary, and the number that can be shown to have started life in the Bronze Age is relatively small. Nevertheless, the conditions that they reflect in an Iron Age context are unlikely to have been much different from those preceding them. Here too territories must have been extremely small, little more in fact than the agricultural land to support the few dozen people who can have occupied one tower. The scale and nature of such territories is considered further in chapter 13.

It has been observed that on occasion the siting and form of forts were not chosen to best effect in terms of defensive capability. Certain southern English hillforts lie instead within a stretch of land that was already highly significant in terms of ritual monuments such as tumuli or henge-like enclosures.[117] This leads to the notion that earthwork sites may sometimes be constructed not for defence but for ritual or ceremonial purposes. Dún Aonghasa on Inis Mór is remarkable in many ways, not least for its situation, with its stone walls forming a semi-circle that ends without warning at the sheer cliffs rising

[117] Bowden and McOmish 1989.

nearly 100 m above the Atlantic (fig. 8.13).[118] Outside the walls is an extensive area of *chevaux de frise* (sharp upright stones), usually thought of as
intended to deter mounted attackers. The occupants and users of the site may
not have distinguished clearly between defence and ceremonial function.
Certainly it is hard to see the scale and nature of the defences overall as anything other than massively impregnable against attack from outside; equally,
the situation would appear to have been unnecessarily hazardous for the site's
occupants; in the event of a determined and prolonged attack, there seems to
have been only one way to go: downwards. An interpretation of Dún Aonghasa
as essentially ceremonial in origin is in many ways preferable to a defensive
interpretation.

Conclusion

Prestige weaponry was a major part of the panoply used to display rank in
Bronze Age society. Both the intricacies of decoration on weapons and the
differential wealth of weapon graves show that symbolic aspects were marked
by subtle differences in form and style. Symbolism can hardly have been the
only reason for weapon provision, however; weapons were undoubtedly used
as well as unconsciously understood.

Swords and spears are commonly found in graves of Periods II and III in
south Scandinavia, and their presence on rock art occasions no surprise.
Among all the encounters depicted on the panels, none certainly shows 'real'
combat in the sense that a person is actually struck or killed by a weapon.
The poses are threatening, but no more. Given that there are well-known
cases where the figures are standing in boats, it seems most probable that the
fights are of a ritual or ceremonial nature. In this respect, they provide an
interesting reflection of the sheet-bronze armour, also thought to be of a non-
utilitarian nature. The existence of combat scenes and the frequent depiction
of weaponry do, however, give a clear indication of the importance of these
aspects of Bronze Age life. What is more, the dominant position of some of
the individuals seems to fit in well with what may be deduced from studies
of weaponry from graves in various parts of Europe and leads to a reasonable
assumption that much of the Bronze Age world was dominated by high-
status individuals, who used these ceremonial combats – among other things
– as a means of maintaining that status. Combat, whether between individuals or between societal groups, was thus a natural and commonplace accompaniment to Bronze Age life. The parade, ceremonial and defensive aspects
of warrior equipment are all related features of the same general phenomenon. Although one cannot enter into the Bronze Age psyche, one can be left
in little doubt that real or simulated aggression was a structural part of Bronze

[118] Rynne 1992.

Age life. Apart from anything else, one can point to instances where wounds are visible on human bones.[119] In other cases, there are flint arrowheads embedded in bones, for instance in the Beaker period burial in the ditch at Stonehenge.[120] This is in addition to the instances of human bones that have been butchered (p. 334).

An interesting case has been made for seeing warrior equipment as part of a life-style involving the glorification of the warrior through both the ornamentation of his body and the provision of weaponry with which he could express his warrior role: 'For the Late Bronze Age warrior, an aesthetic of male beauty appears to have been central in life as well as death, the two states mutually constituting one another and together the individual's self-identity.'[121] In this analysis, the Bronze Age saw the rise of the warrior band that became so important in Germanic warfare, a form of combat that was only lost with the emergence of armies controlled by Medieval aristocrats.

Combat encounters were thus of great importance during the Bronze Age, a conclusion that is inevitable in view of the quantity of arms and armour manufactured in the period. Though a proportion of this weaponry was intended for parade and ritualised fighting rather than serious inter-group aggression, some of it clearly saw action. At the same time, there are good reasons for believing that a significant proportion of the weaponry was deposited for non-utilitarian reasons, as discussed in chapter 10; in other words it had a symbolic and ideological function rather than a practical one. In this sense, warfare was the hallmark of the age in Bronze Age Europe.

---

[119] A number of cases are recorded from Slovakia (Bátora 1991, 124f.), and trauma associated with spear-thrusts is attested from Dorchester, Oxfordshire, and Tormarton, Gloucestershire (Knight, Browne and Grinsell 1972).

[120] Evans *et al.* 1983.

[121] Treherne 1995.

CHAPTER 9

RELIGION AND RITUAL

Though the interpretation of spiritual matters in other societies is hard because of differences in culture and context, the facility for reflective thought and emotion is one of the features that distinguishes humans from animals, and shows every sign of having been an influential factor in all past societies. While it is impossible to enter into the psyche of prehistoric peoples or chart the psychological processes that led them to undertake particular spiritual journeys, one is justified in supposing that the processes existed, and that many aspects of material culture reflect these preoccupations.

It is common to refer these various processes and preoccupations to the catch-all terms 'religion' and 'ritual'. What is certain is that particular mental and psychological states can produce particular effects in terms of material behaviour – for instance the building of churches, synagogues or mosques, or artefacts bearing symbols of known significance such as the cross. These effects are visible among the material records available to Bronze Age archaeology as much as in any other period.

What appear to be symbolic manifestations are widely found in Bronze Age Europe, in portable objects, in decorative motifs and in the art carved on to rock outcrops. The locations for activities that may loosely be described as cultic or ritual are harder to identify. Such activities may have taken place almost anywhere; certainly they did not require a built construction, and could have utilised natural features such as hilltops, areas with curious rock formations, groves, marshes and bogs, pools and lakes, caves or rock fissures, and rivers or streams. The discovery of archaeological material in one of these places tends to lead scholars to assume a non-utilitarian function for the material. Many such features occur in the myths and legends of ancient civilisations.

A number of authors have written about the possibilities of identifying cult places and votive deposits or 'offerings' in the archaeological record.[1] In general, where a non-utilitarian function can be identified, deposition is assumed to belong to the symbolic, not the practical, sphere. Within this general scheme, however, there are numerous instances where a judgement is difficult, and the dangers of imposing on to the data a modern perspective of what is utilitarian are acute.

---

[1] Stjernquist 1962–3; Colpe 1970; Renfrew 1985.

The locations of ritual

For the Bronze Age, as for many other periods, there are very few 'sites', in the sense of constructions, that can be interpreted as having served as the location for religious or ritual practices. The great majority of material consists of art motifs that are found on rock panels or portable artefacts, and of deposits of material that is apparently 'votive' in nature. In a few instances, baffling arrangements of features on sites have also led to interpretations as cult centres or locations for ritual practices, but such evidence is invariably ambiguous and of uncertain significance.

Many sites have been claimed to represent installations for the special purposes of religious or ritual activities, usually for no other reason than that they appear to have unusual features that are not obviously domestic or funerary in nature. There are also many indications from places such as hilltops and caves that natural features were often seen as appropriate venues for activities connected with the spiritual.[2] A small number of sites seem to represent installations that were created in special ways, no doubt for special purposes. The elaborate wooden structure in the raised bog at Bargeroosterveld (Drenthe), for instance, is such a case (fig. 9.1, 3).[3] As reconstructed, the site consists of a square setting of upright posts, resting on two large parallel planks, with a superstructure of cross-beams terminating in curving ends that had been deliberately broken off, the whole thing fastened together by elaborate mortice and tenon joints. A ring of stones surrounded the structure. The horn-like appearance of the curving terminals, and the evidence for timber dressing using exceptionally broad-bladed axes, perhaps the 'ritual axes' that are known from northern Europe in this period, are especially suggestive.

Having much more of the character of a domestic building was the 'temple' at Sălacea on the edge of the Hungarian plain in western Romania.[4] This unique building, rectangular with an open porch, had two clay platforms or 'altars', one on each side. The finds included pyramidal clay objects said to be 'fire-dogs', curved stone knives and a cylindrical vase-support with cut-out sides. Elsewhere in the building were a hanging altar, figurines, miniature clay carts, model wheels, a clay model boat and various cult vessels. A supposed 'offering pit' lay outside, containing another cylindrical vase-support and the disarticulated bones of a child.

A rectangular structure at Sandagergård, Ferslev, northern Zealand, has also been interpreted as ritual in nature (fig. 9.1, 1).[5] Consisting of two rows of large rounded stones defining an area 18.5 m by 7.5 m in external dimensions, there were four engraved stones (decorated with the 'hand-and-arm

[2] See Schauer 1996.
[3] Waterbolk and van Zeist 1961.
[4] Ordentlich 1972; Coles and Harding 1979, 86f.
[5] Kaul 1985.

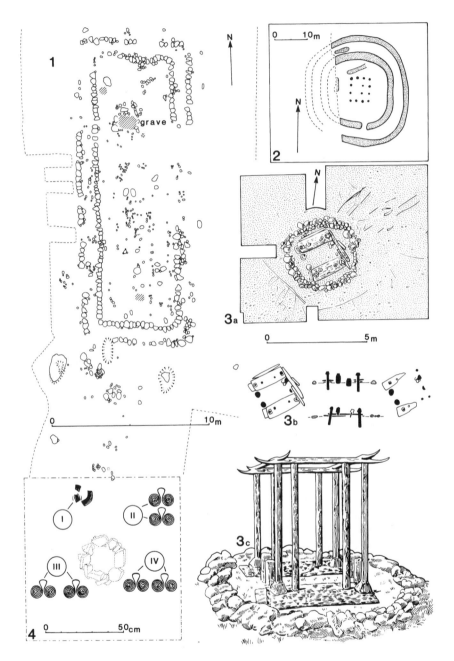

Fig. 9.1. Cult installations. 1. Sandagergård (after Kaul 1985).
2. Erlachhof, Bavaria (after Schauer 1996). 3. Bargeroosterveld
(after Waterbolk and van Zeist 1961) (3a general plan, 3b plans
and section of the wooden foundation elements; 3c reconstruction). 4. Tauberbischofsheim-Hochhausen, Baden-Württemberg
(after Wamser 1984).

motif') to its south, and standing stones flanking them. The structure, which was probably a building with wall material enclosed within the stone rows, contained pottery and mould and crucible fragments, but no flint; this marks it off from domestic buildings of the period (Period IV). There were also urn burials in the enclosed area, so that there was probably an overall connection with burial; this means it should be considered in the same bracket as the 'mortuary houses' at Grünhof-Tesperhude and Sottorf,[6] or Tofta Högar in Scania and other sites in Sweden (see p. 89).[7] Hand-and-arm carvings are found especially in Zealand,[8] but also occur in Østfold, Norway, while the standing stones recall the 'bauta stones' that are known from various parts of Sweden,[9] or the standing stones on or near barrows at Frejlev Skov, Lolland, Denmark. Standing stones are especially common in the British Isles and Brittany (see below).

More ambiguous remains, possibly indicative of a cult installation, have been found at Vadgård in north Jutland.[10] Among the post-holes and slot foundations of a village dated to Period II was found a curious collection of closely spaced post-holes in an arc surrounding a pit containing a large stone, on one face of which a stylised fish was carved, apparently with hooks embedded in it. In the vicinity were smaller stones that may have served as the footings for a small building.

Elements of structures that could be considered indicative of cult buildings have come from a number of other sites in central Europe, for instance the cross-shaped feature of stones with vases placed in the centre and at each arm termination from Černčín (Bučovice), or the curious platforms with bowl-like depressions and ox skulls and skeletons from the Middle Bronze Age site at Uherský Brod, Czech Republic.[11] 'Altars' and other comparable features come from a number of Czech sites,[12] while a couple of possible cult sites are known from Germany and France.[13] Here too are possible examples of defined deposition areas for votive objects, for example at Tauberbischofsheim (Main-Tauber-Kreis, south-west of Würzburg), where the excavator's reconstruction sees a wooden post serving as the centre for the deposition of four groups of bronzes, mainly spectacle spiral pendants (*Brillenspiralen*) (fig. 9.1, 4).[14]

A site that utilised and enhanced natural features to create what appears to have been a special installation for cultic purposes is Belverde di Cetona

[6] Kersten 1936.
[7] Kaul 1985, 50. Some think that other houses, such as that at Norddorf on the island of Amrum, should also be seen as mortuary structures, but this remains very uncertain (Struve 1954).
[8] Originally studied by Brøndsted 1941.
[9] Forssander 1940.
[10] Lomborg 1976, 424ff.
[11] Hrubý 1958.
[12] Coles and Harding 1979, 45.
[13] Hansen 1991, 185; Lambot 1993.
[14] Wamser 1984.

near Siena. Caves (the Antro della Noce, Antro del Poggetto and others) and rock crevices were used for the deposition of pots and human bone, and some of the rocky outcrops were artificially shaped, notably the area known as the 'Amphitheatre' with tiered seats on three sides.[15]

Sites interpreted as offering places and marked by burning have been noted in the Alpine area.[16] There is extensive burning at various sites in southern Germany, Switzerland and the eastern Alps,[17] with a great deal of animal bone; most of these sites date to the Urnfield or Hallstatt periods. A recently excavated example of the same thing is to be found at the Pillerhöhe in the upper Inn valley.[18] Caution should be exercised with this interpretation, however. It is hard to see that the sites in question are much different from the Irish *fulachta fiadh*, which are cooking sites, equivalent to the 'burnt mounds' in Britain or the 'heaps of fire-cracked stones' of Sweden.[19] Perhaps allied to these burning sites are middens, some of which have been interpreted – on the basis of their apparently structured and selective nature – as the remains of feasting. The site at East Chisenbury, Wiltshire, for instance, contained large quantities of pottery and animal bone, along with spindle-whorls, worked and decorated bone and stone, shale and a glass bead, and two skull fragments, all in a dark greasy matrix material.[20]

In the British Isles, many sites were created during the Late Neolithic and Early Bronze Age for which a ritual explanation is generally favoured: stone circles, alignments and standing stones.[21] Although some of these go back into the Neolithic, and many cannot be dated accurately (or at all), a significant number of those that can were used, if not constructed, in the Bronze Age.[22] The Druids' Circle at Penmaenmawr in north Wales, for instance, contained Early Bronze Age Food Vessels and cremation urns; Loanhead of Daviot in north-east Scotland contained Beakers and a pygmy cup as well as 'flat-rimmed ware' that may date late in the Bronze Age; Barbrook II in Derbyshire contained cremation urns,[23] and from this it is clear that one function of the sites was that of burial.

The ship settings of Scania have been mentioned above in connection with burials (p. 109, fig. 3.11),[24] and it is worth dwelling on the variety of forms that stone settings could take in Sweden, though a majority of them belong to the Iron Age rather than the Bronze Age. These include the curious trian-

[15] Calzoni 1933; 1954; Martini and Sarti 1990.
[16] Krämer 1966; Gleirscher 1996.
[17] e.g. Langacker, Reichenhall, Upper Bavaria, and 24 other sites.
[18] Tschurtschentaler and Wein 1996.
[19] Ó Ríordáin 1979, 84ff.; Buckley 1990; Larsson 1990.
[20] McOmish 1996.
[21] Burl 1976; Barnatt 1989; Thom, Thom and Burl 1990.
[22] Thom, Thom and Burl 1990, 380ff.
[23] Barnatt 1989, 161.
[24] Strömberg 1961.

gular or three-point stars and other unusual forms,[25] which were not used primarily for burial. They often contain charcoal, interpreted as evidence for ritual fires.

A powerful case has been made for seeing some of these megalithic sites, notably those in which linear alignments of stones are present, as connected with observation of the heavens, for instance the rising and setting of sun and moon at their maximum positions in the annual or lunar cycle.[26] Some of these are more convincing than others; the observation that most of the recumbent stone circles of north-east Scotland were orientated towards the south and specifically towards the moon during its travel through the sky at its maximum and minimum positions, is especially noteworthy.[27] If this theory is correct, the moon at its maximum (major standstill) would have been visible low in the southern sky grazing the top of the recumbent stone during its time in the night sky – which, at these latitudes, is brief. The other area where recumbent stone circles are present, in south-west Ireland, has also been examined for astronomical alignments,[28] and the case for accepting such a conclusion here, though less convincing, is still impressive.

The evidence of the various megalithic sites of the west shows that a variety of functions, part utilitarian and part symbolic, were served. Some sites suggest that astronomy was a major preoccupation; others came to be seen as appropriate locales for burial; all must have served a role in turning landscape into homescape by a process of interaction with the surrounding natural world.

Wells, pits and shafts (fig. 9.2)

A well-known feature of Celtic religion and of Iron Age archaeology was that of deep shafts, which served, among other things, as a means of communicating with the other world.[29] Shaft digging went back, in Britain at least, to the Neolithic. In a Bronze Age context, the most impressive find of this type is the Wilsford Shaft, near Stonehenge in Wiltshire.[30] At 30 m in depth, it is among the most impressive monuments of the Bronze Age, though entirely invisible on the ground surface. The finding at depths below 20 m of wooden objects (including containers), bone pins, amber beads and a shale ring, along with pottery, animal bones, rope pieces and other waterlogged material, indicates how the shaft must have been open to this depth for some considerable time. There has been some disagreement as to whether this site was simply a well or had ritual functions, but it is quite possible that both explanations

[25] Strömberg 1962–3.
[26] Burl 1983.
[27] Burl 1980.
[28] Barber 1973.
[29] Ross 1968; Piggott 1978; Ashbee, Bell and Proudfoot 1989, 134.
[30] Ashbee, Bell and Proudfoot 1989.

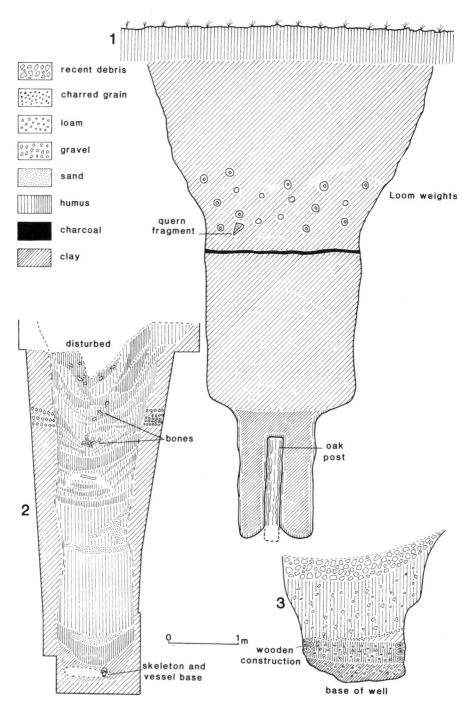

recent debris

charred grain

loam

gravel

sand

humus

charcoal

clay

1

Loom weights

quern
fragment

disturbed

bones

oak
post

2

0 ——— 1m

skeleton and
vessel base

3

wooden
construction

base of well

Fig. 9.2. Pits and shafts. 1. Swanwick, Hampshire (after Fox
1930). 2. Lossow, Frankfurt/Oder (after Griesa 1982). 3. Gánovce,
Poprad (after Vlček and Hajek 1963).

applied, and that wells (along with springs and other wet sites) formed the focus of particular cult activities. Also of interest is the pit from Swanwick, Hampshire, some 4.6 m in diameter at the surface, tapering to half that at the bottom of its main part, where it was 7.3 m deep (fig. 9.2, 1).[31] In the base was a narrow shaft containing an oak post, the walls lined with a brown matter that was interpreted as emanating from the burning of organic matter, perhaps blood. Some 20 cylindrical loom-weights of various sizes were found in the bottom of the tapering part of the shaft.

Features that seem to be wells are present in various German sites, notably at Berlin-Lichterfelde[32] and Senftenberg.[33] At the Lichterfelde site, two wood-lined wells were found outside the rather slight enclosure ditch, Well 2 being full of pottery, bone and other material. Some of the pottery was complete, suggesting that it had been placed deliberately and not thrown in with other rubbish. Complete pots were also present in the Senftenberg well. These features were initially used simply as wells but, with the silting and infilling which seems to have occurred during their lifetime, probably became useless for that purpose. Depositions of various kinds were then made, perhaps of a propitiatory nature. Other shafts, not apparently wells but claimed to be ritual in nature, are present on other sites, e.g. Lossow (Frankfurt/Oder), where human and animal skulls and other bones were found inside a stockade site (fig. 9.2, 2).[34]

The Budsene well on the island of Møn consisted of a hollowed-out alder trunk sunk into the ground, with stones packed round, and contained bronze hanging vessels, a belt ornament and three spiral armrings, along with animal bones (fig. 9.3, 1).[35] Another well that is thought to have had a ritual character comes from Gánovce (Poprad) in central Slovakia (fig. 9.2, 3).[36] Two metres deep and wood-lined, it contained various organic materials including a birch-bark vessel, animal and human bones, and an iron dagger. The claim of 'ritual cannibalism' for this site should perhaps be treated with the same caution as at other sites where cannibalism is claimed (see below). Another well or spring believed to be ritual in nature is that at St Moritz in the Oberengadin, Graubünden, Switzerland (fig. 9.3, 2).[37] Here a sunken double chamber of roundwood and plank construction surrounded two hollowed-out larch trunk sections; in the larger of the two were found two solid-hilted swords, half of a Rixheim sword, a dagger and a pin.

It was not merely in central and northern Europe that wells and springs had particular importance. Fifty or more springs on Sardinia are known to

[31] Fox 1928; 1930.
[32] von Müller 1964a, 19ff.
[33] Herrmann 1969b.
[34] Griesa 1982, 134.
[35] Nordmann 1920; Levy 1982, 17.
[36] Vlček and Hajek 1963.
[37] Heierli 1907; Wyss 1996.

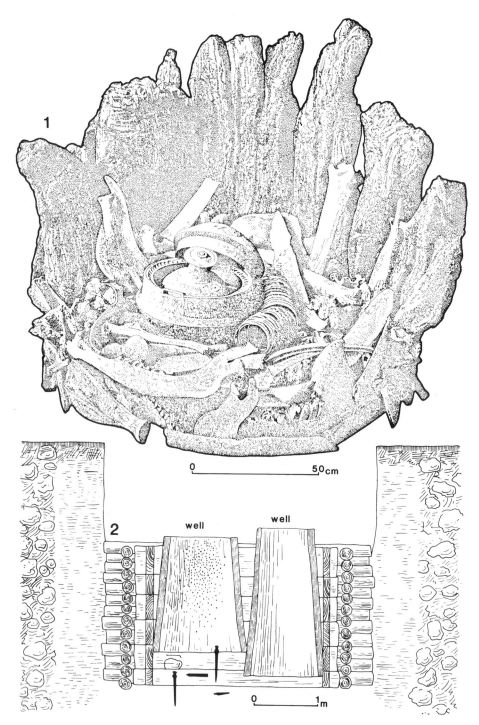

Fig. 9.3. Wells. 1. Budsene, Møn (after photo, National Museum, Copenhagen). 2. St Moritz, Graubünden (after Heierli 1907).

have been utilised as 'sacred wells' or water temples, Sant'Anastasia in Sardara being a prime example.[38] There, steps led down into a domed tholos some 4 m in diameter, with a central cistern. The extraordinary tholos of San Calogero on Lipari, where in the Capo Graziano period a domed cupola was built beside a thermal spring, also exploited water; perhaps, as in recent times, it was used for its healing and restorative powers.[39]

Caves

Caves and rock clefts, as dark and winding holes in the ground, are naturally impressive, even frightening; their use by predatory animals means that bones frequently occur in them; they are home to bats; they have special properties of sound and light. An association with the other-worldly is a commonplace in time and space. Their significance may have lain in their being perceived as openings to the underworld or homes to mythical and mystical beings, just as Aeneas found on his consultation with the Sibyl and subsequent journey to the underworld:

> Excisum Euboicae latus ingens rupis in antrum,
> quo lati ducunt aditus centum, ostia centum.

> 'There is a cleft in the Euboean rock forming a vast cavern.
> A hundred mouthways and a hundred broad tunnels lead into it'
> (Virgil, *Aeneid* VI, 42–3, trans. W. F. Jackson Knight).

> Spelunca alta fuit vastoque immanis hiatu,
> scrupea, tuta lacu nigro nemorumque tenebris.

> 'There was a deep rugged cave, stupendous and yawning wide,
> protected by a lake of black water and the glooming forest'
> (ibid., 237–8).

In an important article, Schauer has distinguished between sink-holes or rock clefts, some used for offerings of food and drink as well as human bodies, others for artefacts; caves used for the deposition of hoards; caves used for subterranean cult practices; and caves used for burials.[40] In practice, what this means is that one may find bones, articulated or disarticulated, and a variety of individual artefacts in caves. Burial in caves can perhaps be taken as suggesting that the deposition is symbolic in nature, but in fact such distinctions are more an artefact of the observer than a reflection of prehistoric reality. There is also evidence for domestic occupation in some instances, with no specific indication of a symbolic significance (see chapter 2); caves do, after all, provide shelter and in mountain areas where it might be imprac-

---

[38] Webster 1996, 147ff.
[39] Bernabò Brea and Cavalier 1990.
[40] Schauer 1981.

tical to construct built shelters would have provided instant refuge from the elements.

A remarkable example of non-utilitarian cave use is to be seen at the underground cavern of Mušja jama (Fliegenhöhle, 'Flies' Cave') in the karst region of Slovenia. Lying on the dissected limestone plateau that characterises this landscape, and entered from above, the cave produced large quantities of Urnfield period bronzes, some iron objects and much charcoal; many of the bronzes were damaged or melted together by fire, and burnt bone was present along with small quantities of unburnt human and animal bone.[41] Since the burning could not have taken place inside the cave, the excavator searched for such a spot outside the cave, but without success. Not far away was the Bone Cave, which contained large amounts of human and animal bone, some bronzes indicating an Urnfield date, and iron objects. These two caves were evidently used for specialised depositions in the Late Bronze and Early Iron Ages.

Caves further south, in Croatia, were similarly used for human bone deposition along with bronzes and pottery, the Bezdanjača cave (Vrhovina) being the most notable (fig. 9.4, 1).[42] This remarkable site contained an estimated 200 human burials, placed singly or arranged in groups. They were found along a 350 m stretch, mainly in the eastern arm of the cave. No special constructions were made to receive the burials, natural niches in between the stalagmites and other concretions being used instead; the burials were not covered with earth or stones and as a result have suffered much disturbance. Ochre was extensively used, perhaps to paint the face and hands of the dead; as well as considerable quantities of pottery and some bronzes, there were wooden spoons and poles with rounded, charred ends, perhaps used for spitting meat in connection with funeral feasts. Burnt areas were sometimes situated beside the body. Typology and radiocarbon determinations indicate a lifespan for this grave cult through much of the Middle and Late Bronze Age.

At the Grotta Pertosa in Campania large numbers of bronzes were found in a cave out of which emerges a powerful stream; other central Italian sites were utilised in a similar way.[43] In Britain, the Heathery Burn cave is the most famous, where human bones, including skulls, were found as well as quantities of bronze and worked bone (fig. 9.4, 3).[44] Many examples of such caves are known from Germany, most famously the caves in the Kyffhäusergebirge near Bad Frankenhausen in Thuringia,[45] but also in several

[41] Szombathy 1912.
[42] Drechsler-Bižić 1979–80.
[43] Rellini 1916; Bernabei and Grifoni Cremonesi 1995–6 – e.g. the Grotta dell'Orso (Sarteano) or the Grotta Misa (Ischia di Castro). For the connection with water, cf. the tholos construction of S. Calogero on Lipari (Bernabò Brea and Cavalier 1990).
[44] Greenwell 1894; Britton 1971. Much human bone was also found in the Sculptor's Cave, Covesea (Benton 1930–1; Shepherd 1995)
[45] Behm-Blancke 1958; 1976.

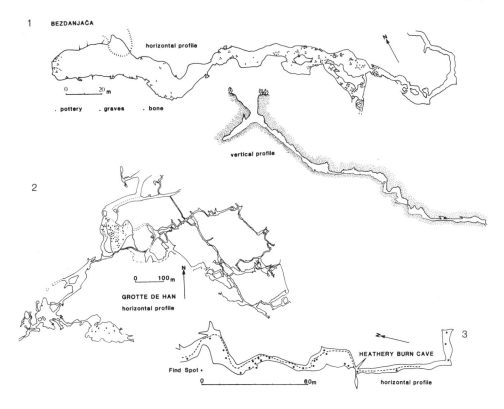

Fig. 9.4. Caves. 1. Bezdanjača, Croatia (after Drechsler-Bižić 1979–80). 2. Grotte de Han, Han-sur-Lesse (after Warmenbol 1996). 3. Heathery Burn, Co. Durham (after Britton 1971).

other parts of the country.[46] At Serlbach (Forchheim), 26 axes and four spearheads were found in a rock cleft in a sandstone quarry.[47] Late Bronze Age spearheads, knives and socketed hooks were found in a rock cleft at Pass Luftenstein in the Saalach valley of Austria,[48] and the well-known find of a parade bronze helmet came from high up in the Alps at Pass Lueg, also in Salzburg province. Recent excavations on the Pillerhöhe, high above the upper Inn valley in the North Tyrol, also produced bronzes and pottery in rock clefts, not far from a spot used for the deposition of burnt animal bone.[49]

Another cave site that saw important depositions during the Bronze Age was the Grotte (Trou) de Han at Han-sur-Lesse in the Ardennes south of Namur (fig. 9.4, 2).[50] This site, at the source of the river Lesse, consists of a

---

[46] Maier 1977; Buck 1979, 103 (Totenstein at Königshain, Kr. Görlitz); Flindt 1996 (Lichtensteinhöhle at Osterode am Harz); Schauer 1981.
[47] Hachmann 1957, 209 no. 477, pl. 53, 3–10.
[48] Hell 1939.
[49] Tschurtschentaler and Wein 1996.
[50] Mariën 1964; Mariën and Vanhaeke 1965; Warmenbol 1988; 1996.

huge underground chamber, from which (and from the river bed) have come large numbers of bronzes and a great deal of pottery, dating to *Bronze final* IIb and IIIa. The metalwork includes not only local types but also types with connections in distant places, such as gold discoid pendants with analogies in the Rheinland-Pfalz. Some objects, such as swords and bronze vessels, had apparently been deliberately thrown into the water.

Finds of pottery and other materials, though without burials or other signs of cult activity, are sometimes found in caves, for instance in the karst regions of Bohemia, Moravia and the northern Adriatic. Caves in the Bohemian karst south-west of Prague were especially commonly occupied in the Knovíz period, much less so in the Early to Middle Bronze Ages or Hallstatt Iron Age.[51] Most finds consist simply of a few sherds, but in some cases human bones also occurred in vertical rock clefts.[52] Comparable chronological differentiation was found in studies in other areas, e.g. the Bohemian Paradise in north-east Bohemia,[53] Moravia,[54] Slovakia,[55] Franconia/Thuringia[56] and Little Poland.[57] The caves around Trieste and adjacent parts of Slovenia were similarly utilised, perhaps over long periods. Examples include the cave of Veliki zjot by the Kupa river near Vinica in the extreme south of Slovenia,[58] and the upper levels of the Grotta Azzurra at Samatorza behind S. Croce near Trieste.[59] There is some evidence too for use of these caves for burial (as at the Grotta di S. Croce). The Baradla cave in the Aggtelek karst in north-east Hungary (Kom. Györ) produced material of many dates, including that of the Late Bronze and Early Iron Ages.[60]

Taken together, this evidence is strongly suggestive of a special role for caves and rock clefts in Bronze Age religion. While it is impossible to specify exactly what the significance of caves was, in other words why some caves were chosen for special depositions but not others, the sum of occurrences is impressive.

The locations of ritual thus surveyed cannot be categorised beyond the basic level of natural or artificial. Built structures existed, whose form and finds differed from those of domestic buildings; locations in the open air, and in naturally enclosed spots were also frequented. Only a contextual examination of each case can serve to further understanding; generalisations are impossible.

---

[51] Sklenář and Matoušek 1994.
[52] e.g. Bačín I, Sisyfova propast, both Beroun district.
[53] Filip 1947.
[54] Skutil 1965; Stuchlík 1981.
[55] Barta 1961; Furmánek *et al.* 1991, 174ff.
[56] Walter 1985.
[57] Rook 1980.
[58] Leben 1991.
[59] Cannarella and Cremonesi 1967.
[60] Tompa 1934–5 [1937].

Cult objects and symbols

Cult practice invariably brings with it certain paraphernalia with which to carry out the necessary actions and which provide references to the mythology and mental frameworks involved. Bronze Age cult practice was no exception. A variety of objects and symbols have been found, some specific to particular areas and periods, others transcending such boundaries.

One of the most important of these was the axe. Axes were vital tools in the carpenter's armoury, serving essential purposes for tree-felling and for the creation of shelter, transport, furniture and many other needs, including a role in battle. Axes apparently played a special role in the British Early Bronze Age,[61] as the evidence of deposited large axes and axes in rock clefts, on henges, and the depictions both at Stonehenge and at Ri Cruin in the important ritual centre of the Kilmartin valley of Argyll (south-west Scotland) attest. In Scandinavia, the axe was long-lived as a cult symbol, from Early through to Late Bronze Age;[62] oversize axes are known from a number of finds (e.g. Ekilstuna, Södermannland, Sweden), as well as being represented on art panels, notably at Simris and Kivik in southern Scania and Åby in Bohuslän.

Amulets (small objects, often occurring in groups, which do not appear to be ornaments or have any other utilitarian function) have been found in children's graves, and a notable increase in the Urnfield period has been charted (in the preceding Middle Bronze Age such objects appear patchily).[63] They included pendants (for instance wheel-shaped or crescentic), beads of various kinds (notably of amber but also of glass, clay, bone and antler), fossil stones, the shells of fish or snails, animal teeth and bones (astragali at Grünwald, for instance), small rings, and rattles of clay. The last-named can frequently be seen in Lausitz graves in Poland[64] and may represent toys rather than amulets. Miniature objects, for instance the halberd pendants seen in certain graves of the Wessex Early Bronze Age, or the 'wheel models' found in Slovakia, may also be toys and have no amuletic character whatsoever. One interpretation is that some objects have an apotropaic (warding off) character, such as animal teeth and fish vertebrae, or fossils, whereas pendants and beads have a close relationship to ornaments proper and may represent little more than charms. Most such amulets are perforated for wearing on a string; otherwise they may have been carried in a bag. The contents of the well-known grave at Hvidegård, Zealand, and some other Danish graves, are notable in this respect: the presence at Hvidegård of dried roots, bark, the tail of a grass-snake, the claw of a falcon, a squirrel's jaw in a leather case, and other curious objects perhaps indicate concerns with healing but may also have been talismans or had an apotropaic purpose.[65]

[61] Schmidt 1978–9.
[62] Jensen 1978.
[63] Kubach-Richter 1978–9.
[64] e.g. at Przeczyce: Szydłowska 1972, 148ff.; Laski: Ćwirko-Godycki and Wrzosek 1936–7.
[65] Glob 1974, 114ff.

Figurines are also usually taken as indicative of some kind of ritual intention. Deposits of figurines may be seen at Visegrád-Csemetekert, where pottery and animal figurines were present in a pit, dated typologically from Ha A2/B to Ha C/D.[66] Figurines can occur too on settlement sites, where they might have served equally as children's toys or for a cultic purpose.[67] A crude figurine in one of the ring of pits at Velim that was not otherwise notable for ritual material has been taken as confirming its ritual intention.

Wooden figurines are known from several sites in the British Isles and elsewhere (fig. 9.5), and radiocarbon dating has placed several of them, for instance that from Lagore crannog, in the Bronze Age.[68] There are comparable finds on the Continent, though the dating of curious pieces beside a trackway in Lower Saxony indicates that they belong in the later first millennium BC.[69] All the carvings are anthropomorphic and have almost all been found in wet places. An affinity of such pieces to known gods in later mythology is potentially a fruitful line of research.

Birds and animals also seem to have played a big part in the imagery and symbolism of Urnfield Europe.[70] A bewildering variety of forms and symbols are known, of which the most frequently recurring are anthropomorphic and zoomorphic figures and vessels (fig. 9.6, 3–6). Bird figures are especially common in the Urnfield world, being found frequently in clay but also in bronze, as terminals to various larger objects, little pendants or amulets, or as decoration on sheet bronze. The so-called 'bird boat' (Vogelbarke) seems to have played a special role in Urnfield symbolism[71] and may be connected with the funerary function of boats (see chapter 5). Boats themselves seem to have played an important role as symbols, especially in the Nordic area where they are abundant not only in rock art but also on bronze objects.[72] In some of these instances, especially on razors, the form is so heavily stylised that it can be unclear whether boats or birds are being depicted; there is an artistic ambiguity about the two forms which may reflect a psychological ambiguity. Other motifs found on pendants and in decorative elements include the wheel (or sun), the hour-glass (or double-axe), triangle, crescent, swallow-tail and various others. The snake also played a part in this symbolism, being found not only in the form of pendants but in stylised form on sheet bronzework.[73]

Especially in the Balkan–Danubian province, elaborately ornamented figures were created. Figurines or anthropomorphic vessels like those from

[66] Gróh 1984.
[67] e.g. Sobiejuchy and comparable sites in Poland: Bukowski 1959–60, 211, pl. 50, 14–17.
[68] B. Coles 1990.
[69] Hayen 1971.
[70] Kossack 1954b; Müller-Karpe 1978–9; Buck 1979, 104.
[71] Merhart 1952, 45ff.; Sprockhoff 1955.
[72] Coles 1993; Kaul 1995.
[73] Uenze 1993.

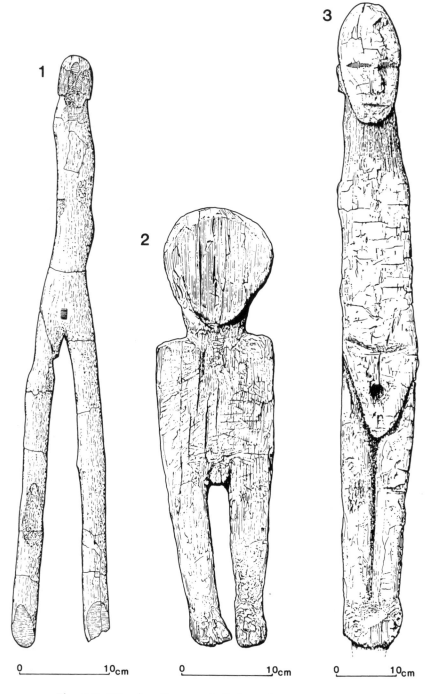

Fig. 9.5. Wooden figures. 1. Bad Buchau, Wasserburg (after Kimmig 1992). 2. Lagore crannog (after B. Coles 1990). 3. Ralaghan (after B. Coles 1990).

Kličevac and Dupljaja are justly famous, but they are only the most elaborate of a large series, decorated with spirals, concentric circles, pendant triangles and hatched bands, perhaps representing aspects of ornamentation applied to clothing or even body parts. The series of figurines from Cîrna in Oltenia show many of these features (fig. 9.6., 1–2).[74] From the cemetery came nine complete figurines and two fragments, varying between 13 and 25 cm in height. The head is highly stylised and shown as a simple knob-like protruberance, the upper body is a flattish disc, the waist shown drawn in and belted, and the lower body is bell-shaped and hollow. The rich impressed decoration indicates necklaces and other ornaments, elaborate coiffures, dress attachments and make-up (or perhaps tattoos). The excavator considered these figurines to represent a female divinity, the protectress of the graves, and sought parallels in Minoan–Mycenaean figurines. The Kličevac figurine is similar but even more elaborate.[75] The Dupljaja group consists of a stylised figure riding in a three-wheeled cart drawn by water-birds, all profusely decorated with concentric circles (sun symbols?).[76]

One can hardly believe that all figurines are 'ritual' in nature, in the sense that they assisted practices connected with belief systems and symbolism. On the other hand, deciding that they were toys or ornaments, or art for art's sake, is something that seems unlikely to command widespread agreement. A study of context in each instance must be undertaken, but even then one lacks the basic rules with which to adjudicate between rival explanations.

The importance of bird imagery in the Urnfield world has prompted speculation about where it might have originated, and whether there was any connection between objects decorated in this fashion in the Minoan–Mycenaean world and in central Europe and Italy.[77] Both areas possess an ancestry for such forms. Certainly by the late Mycenaean period there are indisputable connections between Greece and Italy, as is shown by various artefact types and decorative motifs.[78] In the context of bird images, the low bowl from a chamber tomb at Pylos with antithetically placed birds' heads is especially close to motifs seen on pottery of the Pianello group in central Italy.[79] Whether or not the bird had the same significance in both the Aegean and the Urnfield areas, it occurs in both with regularity and prompts speculation that the underlying symbolism is cognate.

---

[74] Dumitrescu 1961.
[75] Letica 1973.
[76] Kossack 1954b, 10ff.; D. Garašanin 1951; Bošković 1959; M. Garašanin 1983, 531f.; Pare 1989.
[77] e.g. Matthäus 1981; Pare 1989.
[78] Harding 1984a, 255ff.
[79] Ibid. 1984a, 205ff., 211 n. 55, with references.

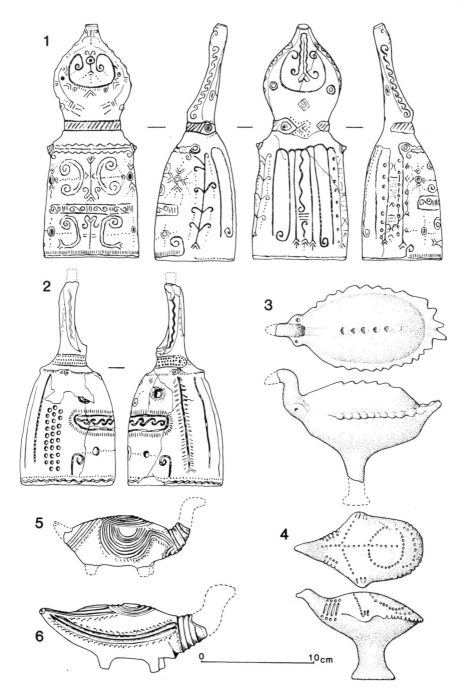

Fig. 9.6. Human and animal clay figurines. 1–2. Cîrna (after Dumitrescu 1961). 3. Przeczyce, Zawiercie (after Szydłowska 1968–72). 4. Topornica, Zamość (after Gedl 1996). 5–6. Bad Buchau, Wasserburg (after Kimmig 1992).

Votive deposits

The study of votive deposits is in many ways similar to that of hoards, which are considered more fully in chapter 10. At issue here are both single or isolated objects that appear to have been deposited for votive reasons and collective finds that do not have a utilitarian character. The potential scope of such an analysis is enormous, and it is necessary to restrict discussion to certain well-studied examples.

The work of Levy has come to occupy pride of place in the English-speaking world in the discussion of symbolic depositions.[80] It is the specific act of deposition that is of importance in the discussion of religion. To judge from rock art and other finds, such depositions and other symbolic acts were attended by a specific ceremonial involving parades, the blowing of horns or lures, ritualised combat and the like. The hoards are also seen as one means of contributing to the maintenance of social organisation since they involved specialised knowledge not available to the populace at large. Since religion and ritual are often used as a powerful means of social and political organisation, through the privileging of certain individuals at the expense of others, the evidence of the 'ritual' hoards is highly important. This work draws on, and is paralleled by, that carried out by Helms on Panamanian chiefdoms.[81]

Levy's operational criteria for distinguishing between ritual and non-ritual deposits concentrated on differences in location (wet or dry ground, depth of deposit, markers), special objects (dominance of ornaments and weapons or special forms, as opposed to a broad range of types), association with food or otherwise, and special arrangement of the objects.[82] Such criteria may be applied to a wide range of sites and finds. Jensen, for instance, has identified a fluctuating picture for the deposition of single 'votive' objects across the periods of the Late Bronze and Early Iron Age.[83] Armrings – presumptively female items – were usually deposited in wet places in collections of several different forms, but in Period VI the number of depositions with just a single type increases markedly. Does this reflect more than access to the products of a particular phase of production? Is it to be connected with the dress traits of particular women? Were they in any case exclusively used by women? Kubach showed that 'moor deposits' in the Rhine plain in south Hesse constitute a different category from finds on dry land or in rivers, suggesting that different mental concepts lay behind the different forms (fig. 9.7).[84] Pins far

---

[80] Levy 1982.
[81] Helms 1979.
[82] Levy 1982, 21f.
[83] Jensen 1972. The trend in deposition from swords in Period IV to swords, spearheads and neckrings in Period V, and thence to pins, neckrings and armrings in Period VI, is notable. It is particularly striking how spearheads abruptly stopped being deposited in Period VI, and how pins were virtually absent *before* this time.
[84] Kubach 1978–9.

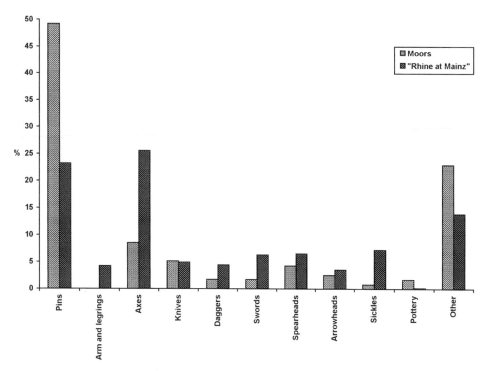

Fig. 9.7. The percentage representation of different categories of object from moorland and from the Rhine near Mainz (data from Kubach 1978–9). Note how pins are relatively more common on moorland, tools and weapons in the river.

outweigh other objects, and a number of these are foreign to the area.[85] Since such pins appear to be female in orientation, and since the number of male objects (axes) found on these moors is much smaller, might their presence be connected with specifically female places of offering?

The presence of numerous pins in this area recalls the large hoard from Villethierry (Yonne), where 913 objects were found in a large pottery container.[86] Of these, 488 were pins and 244 rings. Although this find was interpreted in the original publication as the stock-in-trade of a smith, the remarkable nature of its contents suggests that a votive explanation may be preferable.[87]

There are many instances of prestige objects – typically weaponry, armour or musical instruments – being deposited in wet places. Good examples of

[85] Notably the Binningen pins, which are most at home in and around the Swiss lakes, 300–400 km to the south.
[86] Mordant *et al.* 1976.
[87] Bradley (1990, 114ff.) has also argued for a votive interpretation of the find.

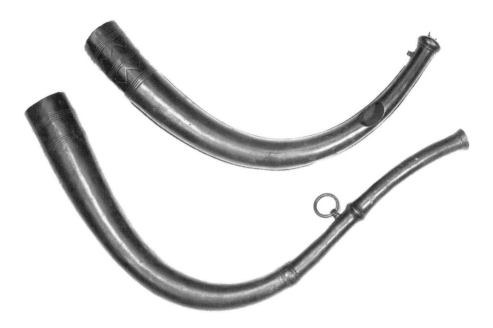

Fig. 9.8. Bronze horns from Drumbest, Co. Antrim. Photo: National Museum of Ireland.

this are shields,[88] horns,[89] lures[90] and drums.[91] Bronze shields, as discussed above (p. 285), were unlikely to have been functional, and much the same is probably true of other items of armour and for the musical instruments of Ireland (fig. 9.8) and Scandinavia. The horns of Ireland have been found in groups or pairs on a number of occasions, as with the 15–16 horns from a bog between Cork and Mallow, or the six from Chute Hall, Co. Kerry.[92] Lures almost always occur in matched pairs, which leads to a supposition that they were played together, simultaneously (or perhaps alternately, given the slight discrepancies between the paired instruments that would have led to slight differences in pitch). It does not seem likely that groups of Irish horns would have been played in orchestral fashion, even if the ingenuity of modern players can make this appear possible.[93]

The lures are even more elaborate in appearance than the Irish horns, though their musical capabilities were no more developed. A number of rock-

[88] Coles 1962.
[89] Coles 1963.
[90] Broholm *et al.* 1949; Maier 1997.
[91] Knape and Nordström 1994.
[92] Coles 1963, 351.
[93] Witness the skills of the group 'Reconciliation' who play horns of different sizes polyphonically, using the didgeridoo technique and circular breathing.

art panels depict lure-blowers in operation, in some cases standing in boats. Given the find circumstances of *in corpore* examples and the elaborateness of the objects, these instruments must surely have played a ceremonial role, perhaps to be used on special occasions and to impress rather than merely for musical appreciation, given the strictly limited possibilities for melodic and harmonic creation that they offered. The instruments cannot play any regular or recurring diatonic scale, western or other, relying instead on harmonics, and the discrepancies between instruments mean that particular effects of harmony must have been a matter of chance rather than intention. Nevertheless, if music is a human universal – and there are good grounds for believing that it is – one can ascribe as lively an interest in the sounds of a pair of lures to Bronze Age people as listeners today have in more recent musical creations, even if on a purely technical level the level of musical accomplishment was not by modern standards particularly high.

There are a number of important finds in Scandinavia which seem to fall in the category of special votive deposits.[94] In all these cases, special bronze forms occur, suggesting that they were made to be used in particular forms of display activity – not for real use in work or combat – and then deposited in situations that suggest a non-utilitarian function. The Fogdarp find, for instance, contained bronzes believed to be part of the accoutrements for horse display gear, the discs from the ends of lures, and other objects, deposited in a pit and covered by a stone on the side slope of a valley in central Scania.

There is another large category of finds to discuss here, those emanating from 'wet' locations such as rivers, bogs and lakes. In the vast majority of such cases, it is impossible to prove that the objects were deposited simultaneously, in a single act; they accumulated in a series of individual acts on the same spot, and, as discussed below in chapter 10, can with good reason be seen as entirely non-utilitarian in nature. The discussion of these depositions with no intent to recover is thus artificially divided between wet and dry – reflecting the apparently divided character of the material.

Since Torbrügge's seminal paper of 1970–1, where the significance of such deposition was systematically presented on a broad, European, scale for the first time,[95] there have been many studies of individual sites or rivers. Wegner, for instance, discussed in considerable detail the factors which might have been at work in the phenomenon of deposition of goods in the rivers Rhine and Main.[96] Broadly speaking, there is an even distribution of finds along the course of the Main,[97] but there are certain spots where unusually large

---

[94] Examples include the well at Budsene (above) and or the finds from Fogdarp (Larsson 1974), Viksø (Norling-Christensen 1946), Fröslunda (Hagberg 1988) and Grevensvænge (Djupedal and Broholm 1952).

[95] Torbrügge 1970–1.

[96] Wegner 1976.

[97] The study thus also serves as an object lesson in source criticism – see Kristiansen 1974; 1985.

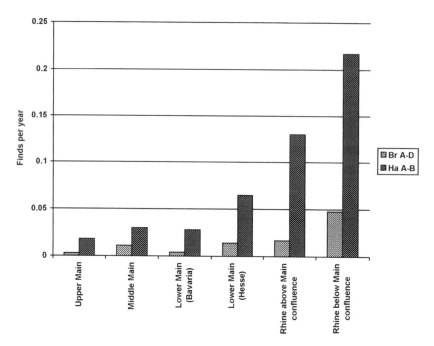

Fig. 9.9. The average numbers of finds per year (based on the presumed length of each period) in different parts of the Main and Rhine (data from Wegner 1976).

numbers of finds have been recovered (fig. 9.9). Does this relate to chance losses at river crossings or to intentional deposition at specific places? Since analysis of particular artefact classes suggests that selection was at work, a 'votive' explanation for these, and indeed for many dry-land hoards in Ha B3 as well, has been preferred. Similar conclusions have been achieved for Italy.[98] Other rivers, or parts of rivers, that have been examined include the Danube,[99] the Inn,[100] the Rhine,[101] the Elbe,[102] the Saône,[103] the Oise[104] and the Thames.[105] Although some authors have averred that such finds indicate the use of rivers for transport purposes, the overwhelming consensus now is that the objects were intentionally thrown in as votive deposits. The same is true for deposits in other wet places such as lakes, bogs and fens. On Late Bronze Age settle-

[98] Bianco Peroni 1978–9.
[99] Stroh 1955; Pollak 1986.
[100] Torbrügge 1960.
[101] Driehaus 1970.
[102] Zápotocký 1969.
[103] Armand-Calliat 1950.
[104] Blanchet *et al.* 1978.
[105] Ehrenberg 1980.

ments on the Swiss lakes, for instance, large quantities of metalwork are often found. In the past, these have been assumed to be the result of either the natural losses or disposals of everyday life or the suddenness of the flooding of the sites in question, which meant that people could not save their valuables. Some scholars nowadays consider it more likely that these bronzes were part of intentional depositions, either in contemporaneous hoards or as part of an ongoing deposition of objects on the same spot.[106]

A British example of such deposits may be seen at Flag Fen near Peterborough, where the use of metal detectors around the platform site revealed a remarkable series of metalwork objects – swords and rapiers, spearheads, chapes, knives, awls, razors, rings, pins, a gouge and an axe, and other small objects, as well as a smaller number of iron objects.[107] While many objects are complete, they show signs of wear and some are broken or damaged – though not to the extent that one sees in 'founders' hoards'. Pryor argues that objects were deliberately damaged and then dropped or tossed into water, or in a few cases buried in scoops. In certain instances, deliberate burial beneath timbers was noted. Furthermore, some objects appear to have been poorly made as if intended for such burial and not for real-life functions, just as with ceremonial bronzes such as shields and horns.

Another possible site type where votive depositions seem to have been made is on mountains and passes; these are known from all parts of the Alps and parts of Italy.[108] In some areas, cliffs seem also to have been used for such depositions.[109] Since different categories of object are differentially represented, and there is a marked decline in such finds in the latest stages of the Bronze Age, intentionality is assured.[110]

Deposits of pots are known from various contexts and locations in central and eastern Europe (fig. 9.10); some may represent food depositions, for instance at Zedau where chemical analysis of residues in pots indicated the presence of plant material and 'blood or organs'.[111] A pit found by chance in excavation in Plovdiv, central Bulgaria, contained six layers of complete pots, one above the other, with four layers of stones covering the find.[112] At Igrici (Borsod), 52 vessels were found on a hillslope where traces of more than 100 ovens or kilns have been noted. Most of these were high-quality tableware (high-handled cups, low conical bowls, amphoroid urns, jugs), and while it is possible that they were awaiting distribution after manufacture, it is equally

[106] Müller 1993.
[107] Pryor 1991; Coombs 1992.
[108] Mayer 1978–9; Bianco Peroni 1978–9; Wyss 1996.
[109] As with a group of 'stepped' armrings (Marquart 1993).
[110] Neubauer and Stöllner 1994.
[111] Horst 1977.
[112] Detev 1964.

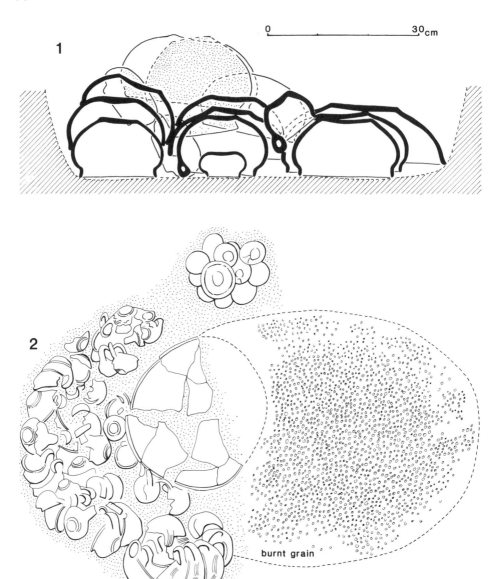

0 _____ 30 cm

1

2

burnt grain

N

0 _____ 5 m

Fig. 9.10. Pot deposits. 1. Hartmannsdorf, Nürnberg (after Schauer 1996). 2. Susani, Timiş (after Vulpe 1996).

likely that they were not intended for recovery at all.[113] Such deposits need not have been different in character or intention from the much better known metal finds, discussed above, for which an intentional motive for deposition has been argued.[114]

It was not only manufactured objects that may have possessed symbolic significance, especially where human burial was concerned. What have been taken to be ritual floral tributes have been identified at a number of monuments in Scotland, in the form of organic deposits containing the pollen of *Filipendula* (meadowsweet or dropwort).[115] While some instances, notably the find at Ashgrove, Fife,[116] containing a large amount of lime pollen, may be interpreted as a honey-based drink, in other cases a mat of flowers seems to have been laid beneath the body.

Human and animal sacrifice and cannibalism

Cannibalism, and the taboo on it, are cultural practices. In the vast majority of recorded societies cannibalism has been prohibited, but there are enough records of its occurrence under defined circumstances for it to occasion no surprise when it does turn up. Even in modern western society, one aspect of it is familiar: the symbolic eating of the divinity, as represented by the blood and body of Christ in Holy Communion, a practice found too in the ritual eating of animals or even humans that was part of the Dionysiac orgiastic cult in early Greece, representing the eating of the god himself.

Cannibalism as a practice has often been claimed in historical (e.g. the Aztecs) and ethnographic (e.g. New Guinea) situations, but reliable accounts of it occurring are in fact hard to come by. Homer's Cyclops was a cannibal;[117] for Herodotus, the distant and unknown Androphagi were 'man-eaters' by definition.[118] It is striking that many accounts of cannibalism repeat information at second or third hand, or are patently mythical; it never happens in any society from which the historian-ethnographer himself comes, and is usually attributed to other cultures on a 'lower' level of moral or social development. Although it has been claimed that institutionalised cannibalism has

---

[113] Hellebrandt 1990. The same may be true for a deposit of Gava urns from a pit on a site of uncertain character at Gyoma 133 in south-east Hungary (Genito and Kemenczei 1990), at Battonya (Kallay 1986) and at Schrattenberg in Lower Austria (Eibner 1969). A hoard of pottery was similarly found in the late Lausitz (Billendorf) site of Raddusch, Kr. Calau, and other sites in eastern and southern Germany (von Müller 1964b; Buck 1979, 103; Schauer 1996; Czyborra 1997).

[114] Horst argued this for the Lausitz culture, showing that special pot forms, made specially for the purpose with extra care, were used for such depositions. A majority occurred on or near Lausitz cemeteries, though outside the Lausitz area many were in isolated spots including moors and wet places.

[115] Tipping 1994.

[116] Dickson 1978.

[117] *Odyssey* IX, 287ff.

[118] *Histories* IV, 102–3.

never been securely attested,[119] there are enough reliable data available to show that, though rare, it has occurred in some societies in certain defined contexts. What is missing in the ethnographic literature is the study of those contexts as part of the overall social culture.[120] If true for ethnography, this is all the more true for archaeology. It would be mistaken to suppose that cannibalism was frequent in prehistory, but equally mistaken to suppose that it never happened.[121]

The treatment of humans and animals after death is usually quite different. Humans one expects to be laid out in inhumation graves or burnt in cremation pyres; one does not normally expect the bones to have been manipulated or damaged, except perhaps after a considerable period of time when they were already defleshed and circumstances necessitated some kind of clearing operation. With animals it is precisely the opposite: one expects to find their bones jointed or cut, and whole burials of meat-bearing animals are taken to indicate special treatment. These attitudes are culturally determined and need not have applied to any or all of the societies under examination. But where these roles are reversed, so that there is evidence for the jointing, cutting or smashing of human bones shortly after death, or the deposition of animals in contexts that indicate an interest other than as an economic resource, then one may be justified in seeking a cult or ritual explanation. Especially where such treatment of human bone is concerned, archaeologists are tempted to speculate that cannibalism was involved.

Examples of these practices have been found at a number of sites in central Europe belonging to the Tumulus, Velatice, Knovíz and Lausitz cultures.[122] Among the best known is that of Velim in eastern Bohemia, where a substantial number of human bones have cut marks.[123] In addition, there is considerable evidence for manipulation of the dead at various times after death, and for the deposition of the dead in many curious ways.[124] Late Bronze Age pit burials in central Europe sometimes provide evidence for dismemberment or partial burial, occasionally with different bones of the same individual in different pits.[125] Human bones also occur on settlement sites in

---

[119] Arens 1979.
[120] Brown and Tuzin 1983.
[121] Sagan (1974) has analysed some of the psychological forces that are supposed to underlie the practice.
[122] Lehmann 1929; Jelínek 1957; 1988; Malinowski 1970; Chudziakowa 1975; Salaš 1990.
[123] Dočkalová 1990.
[124] Other sites in central Europe where cannibalism and related practices have been claimed include Cezavy near Blučina (Salaš 1990), Hradisko and Rataj in the Czech Republic, Gánovce in Slovakia and, rather later, Biskupin in Poland.
[125] Bouzek and Koutecký 1980; Plesl 1988; Kytlicová 1988b. A recent article (*The Independent*, 19 September 1995) has reported the finding of dismembered human remains, including those of a child, in East Sussex, along with deliberately smashed pottery, cattle, sheep and pig bones, amber beads, horse harness pieces and bronze tools, several of them deliberately broken. The objects were apparently dropped into a marsh from a wooden platform.

eastern Germany, for instance at Lübbenau and Dresden-Coschütz.[126] At Ladenburg, north of Heidelberg, there was a large round funnel-shaped pit containing potsherds and broken pieces of bronze knife, and on its floor three large broken moon-shaped clay objects ('fire-dogs'), a complete bronze knife, and a human cranium.[127] Skulls are deposited in a number of sites in southern Germany in ways that may represent a skull cult.[128]

The burial of animals, either with or without humans, is also of interest. While never common, this recurs with sufficient frequency to suggest that it was a regular, if relatively uncommon, event in the life of Bronze Age communities. Deposits of animal bones have been found in eastern Germany, for instance at Neuendorf, Lübbenau and other sites.[129] At Berlin-Rahnsdorf, animal bones from a Late Bronze Age cremation cemetery were interpreted as at least in part symbolic in nature because meat-poor parts of the animals were deposited.[130] There are instances in Italy where there are unusual arrangements of animal bones, for instance at Toppo Daguzzo in the Basilicata, where a human skeleton lies over a layer of bones consisting of the heads and limbs of three cows.[131] On the same site were pits containing parts of animal skeletons. At Roca near Lecce ring-ditches contained much ash and cultural debris, and in one there was a dog skeleton together with the skull of a mature bovine. Whether such finds are really to be interpreted as cultic in nature is open to some doubt, but they certainly differ from normal domestic deposition.

Rock art

The carved rock panels of parts of Scandinavia, northern Italy/southern France, the British Isles and north-west Spain form one of the finest sources of evidence from which to gain an insight into the Bronze Age mind. While few, if any, such 'canvases' depict scenes of Bronze Age life in the sense of specific events, even a purely symbolic interpretation of the art provides a window on to practice and usage in a way that excavated site outlines or artefacts *tout court* cannot. Although rock art raises more questions than it

---

[126] Buck 1979, 103.
[127] Hansen 1991, 72.
[128] Schauer 1996. Vertebrae showing cut marks, interpreted as evidence of decapitation, were found in the Sculptor's Cave, Covesea, Morayshire (Benton 1930–1).
[129] Buck 1979, 103. Węgrzynowicz (1981) has drawn attention to this feature in Lausitz and Iron Age graves in Poland. Although the number of Lausitz cemeteries where the practice is attested is not large (40 out of over 3000 investigated cemeteries), wherever analysis of the cremated bones by an anthropologist has taken place the percentage has risen dramatically (22 out of 37 examples). Cattle dominate in such instances. Węgrzynowicz interprets these instances as examples of blood offerings, though they could also have been intended as edible accompaniments for the soul of the deceased in its journeyings after death.
[130] Müller 1989.
[131] Wilkens 1995.

answers, it remains a magnificent source of information, or at least hypotheses, on many aspects of Bronze Age life and death.[132]

It is generally considered that this art served a ritual purpose, but one should also consider whether any of it was created purely for 'artistic' purposes – as 'art for art's sake'. As with Palaeolithic cave art, such matters are notoriously difficult to resolve. One can respond to Palaeolithic art on a number of different levels. On the one hand, it is undeniably accomplished and many people would consider it 'beautiful', eliciting an emotional response in the viewer. On the other hand, it may well have been created not primarily as an artistic endeavour but for its symbolic or magical significance. Layton refers to the 'impossibility of learning much about prehistoric artists' intentions or values', a fact that applies to Bronze Age no less than to Palaeolithic art; similarly, concepts of 'beauty', including such matters as 'harmony, rhythm and proportion', are culturally conditioned.[133] Such attempts should not form part of one's aims, as they are almost certain to be fruitless; instead, one should look to place the art in its context, as far as this is possible. The 'art for art's sake' argument is often impossible to condemn out of hand but equally impossible to sustain as the main motivating force in Palaeolithic cave art. It is exactly the same with Bronze Age rock art, and for present purposes its purely artistic merit – if it were possible to agree on such a thing – will not be considered. Instead, its interest as a source of knowledge about Bronze Age spiritual and ceremonial life will be the main concern.

A distinction must be drawn between the art that is figurative and that which is purely symbolic. In some areas, only symbols are found; in other areas only figurative designs; in still others a mixture of the two. While it is easier to respond to the figurative art, this does not necessarily make it any easier to interpret. It is all too easy to be lulled into a false sense of security as far as one's understanding of the art is concerned, simply because one can say: 'That is a ship.' But why should that particular motif be chosen for depiction on rock art, and why was it so widely used?

Distribution and position

Bronze Age rock art is found principally in Scandinavia, the Alpine area, the British Isles and north-west Spain (fig. 9.11); a huge literature has built up, especially in Scandinavia.[134] For the Alpine area, the art of the Val Camonica

---

[132] A general account of Bronze Age rock art: Kühn 1956.
[133] Layton 1981, 3, 11ff.
[134] Older work by Baltzer, O. Almgren, Ekholm, Gjessing, Hallström, E. and P. Fett, Althin, and others; more recently Fredsjö *et al.* 1971 and other works, Marstrander 1963, Glob 1969, Capelle 1972, Burenhult 1973, 1980, Mandt Larsen 1972, Kjellén 1976, Nordbladh 1980, Malmer 1981, B. Almgren 1983/1987, Bertilsson 1987, Janson *et al.* 1989, Tilley 1991, and many others. Coles (1990; 1994) has provided brief up-to-date surveys of the material in Bohuslän and Uppland.

Fig. 9.11. The main rock-art provinces of Bronze Age Europe.

is the best known, but that of Mont (Monte) Bego is also important.[135] Only short accounts of rock art in Switzerland and Austria have appeared.[136] Prehistoric rock art is also present in Albania, Montenegro and Bulgaria,[137] where Iron Age or Medieval dates have sometimes been suggested. For Britain[138] and Ireland[139] there are both general accounts and county-based

---

[135] General accounts by Priuli 1983 and Pauli 1984, 170ff. Val Camonica: Anati 1960; 1961 (summarising account). Monte Bego: Bicknell 1913; Conti 1972; de Lumley and co-workers 1976; 1992. Other parts of the Alps: e.g. Rossi *et al.* 1989.

[136] Zindel 1968; Gallay *et al.* 1976; Austrian Alps: Burgstaller 1972; 1978.

[137] Korkuti 1968; Garašanin 1968; Mikov 1928–9; Georgiev 1978 with refs.; Hänsel 1973.

[138] Morris 1981; 1989 and other works; Beckensall e.g. 1986; Hedges 1986; Bradley 1997.

[139] Shee 1968; van Hoek 1987; 1988; O'Sullivan and Sheehan 1993; general account in O'Kelly 1989, 239ff.

surveys. For Galicia and northern Portugal, older work by Iberian scholars is now supplemented by new studies by R. Bradley and others.[140]

There are few factors which link together these different areas. The only universal is that there should be suitable rock surfaces on which to work. This means that glacial landscapes are most appropriate, in which the action of compressed ice has polished or smoothed rock surfaces, which are typically flat or inclined at only a gentle angle (usually less than 45°). In Bohuslän, north of Göteborg, the rocks are granite, in Uppland mostly gneiss, both very hard rocks which would have required long labour to carve. In the Val Camonica, the rock is mostly a hard Permian sandstone known as *verrucano lombardo*, with some schist. At Monte Bego most carvings are on polished schist surfaces. In Britain and Ireland a variety of rock types were utilised, commonly sandstones and mudstones, occasionally harder rocks such as millstone grit.

The hardness of the rocks involved means that a specialised set of tools and procedures would have been necessary to produce the carvings (by grinding and pecking rather than carving proper). There has been much speculation that fire and/or water may have been used to assist in the long process of grinding out the designs, but there is little hard evidence for this. A number of west Swedish art sites are traversed by springs and streams, which might have provided the required water, but in other areas this is not the case. The excavation at Hornnes in Norway was noteworthy in that the base of the decorated rock showed signs of burning; much broken pottery, burnt clay lumps and flint chips were found, but there were no chipping stones for working the rock face. All the finds were inside a line of stones forming an 'enclosure', running parallel with the rock face and thought to be the site of whatever ceremonies occurred – perhaps feasting followed by the smashing of pots against the rock.[141] This site may offer some indication of what went on once art panels had been created but it does not seem to shed light on how and when the motifs were originally carved.

The positioning of the art in the landscape is hard to appreciate today because of the difference in the relative heights of land and sea since the Bronze Age (fig. 5.11) and because of changes in vegetation and land use. In Uppland (east Sweden) the land was probably 20 m lower around 1800 BC than it is today, and in Bohuslän (west Sweden) 13 m lower at 1500 BC, so that the sea came much further inland; as a consequence, many of the carving sites were close to, or within sight of, creeks and inlets, if not the open sea.[142] During the 1000-year course of the Bronze Age, the land may have risen as much as 8 m, so that some art sites moved away from the sea, while

[140] Sobrino Buhigas 1935 (cited by Fett and Fett 1979); Santos Júnior 1942; Peña Santos and Vázquez Varela 1979; Bradley 1997.
[141] Johansen 1979.
[142] Coles 1994, 8ff., fig. 2A.

others were probably created near it. The ongoing effect of land uplift since prehistoric times means that almost all sites now appear to be well away from the shoreline. These factors may go some way towards explaining why ship depictions should appear in landscapes with no apparent access to water. At the same time, it has been shown that there is little relationship between the location of art sites in Norway and the economy of the society in question, so that the position of the art is of no value as far as interpretation is concerned.[143] Instead, carvings were made in areas where there was an abundance of desired resources, whatever they may have been.

Date

Since the art occurs on natural rock panels and usually has no association with any built monument or artefact to which a date can be assigned, dating is extremely difficult, though there are some grounds for optimism that new techniques will help.[144] In the case of Scandinavia and the Italian Alps, there are sufficient depictions of recognisable artefacts (boats, axes, daggers, swords) for a date in the Bronze Age to be assumed for much of the art.[145] In Austria, many of the sites had been extensively reused in medieval times, but the general character of the earliest designs appears to be prehistoric.[146] In the case of the British Isles and Spain, however, there is no help at hand from depicted artefacts, since the art is almost entirely symbolic in character or unspecific as to date (depictions of animals, for instance). This has led to debate about whether it is Neolithic or Bronze Age in date. In Ireland, it was originally thought that all rock art dated to the period of the megalithic art of the Boyne valley, until the different character of the art on living rock, especially that found in the south-west, was recognised.[147] Subsequently it was assumed that a Bronze Age date was likely for this 'Galician' type of art, though in the case of isolated panels there is no specific support for this – other than the supposition of contemporaneity with Scandinavia. Most recently Burgess has entered the debate by asserting that all such art is of Neolithic origin; this is now the subject of intense discussion.[148]

---

[143] Mandt 1978. Bertilsson demonstrated the relationship between art sites and the distribution of arable land in northern Bohuslän (1987, 174ff.). A comparable study by Johnston (1991) for Ireland suggests a good correlation between soils suitable for tillage and pasture and the distribution of rock-art sites.

[144] Bednarik 1992.

[145] e.g. Anati 1963; cf. Sognnes 1992, 162ff.

[146] Burgstaller 1972; 1978.

[147] MacWhite 1946.

[148] Burgess 1990. While on some sites cup-and-ring art seems to originate in Neolithic art, the assumption that the many unassociated panels must also have a Neolithic origin is unsupported by direct evidence; see MacKie and Davis 1988–9 (pro); Morris 1989–90 (hesitant); Waddington 1998. Most recently a cist grave with decorated cover from Witton Gilbert, Co. Durham, has produced a C-14 date in the Early Bronze Age.

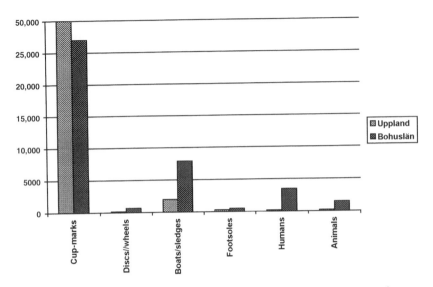

Fig. 9.12. The frequency of rock-art motifs in two parts of Scandinavia (data from Coles 1990; 1994).

Motifs

The range of motifs is considerable, though a small number account for the great bulk of those represented. The relative proportions of motifs vary from province to province, but in general it is true that in Scandinavia by far the commonest design was the cup-mark: on some panels hundreds of cups are found (fig. 9.12).[149] Of the figural motifs, much the commonest in Sweden and Norway (though not in Denmark) is the ship.[150] By comparison, human figures number some 3500 in northern Bohuslän but only 200 in Uppland. Of other abundant motifs, animals, discs or wheel signs, hands and feet (or soles), wheeled vehicles, ploughing scenes, trees and weapons are common; there is also a wide variety of other, rarer, images, often only interpretable as symbols. A number of scholars have used the variability in motif frequency to draw conclusions about the different character of the art in different provinces of Scandinavia, but it remains uncertain what the significance of this variation might be.[151]

In the Alpine area, the motifs are perhaps even more varied.[152] Animal and human figures are the commonest in this art, the animals either being hunted,

[149] Bertilsson 1989 and Coles 1994 give figures of around 27,000 cup-marks for northern Bohuslän and 30,000 for Uppland.
[150] Nearly 8000 known examples in northern Bohuslän and 2000 in Uppland (minimum figures as more sites are constantly being discovered).
[151] e.g. Burenhult 1980; Nordbladh 1980; Malmer 1981; Bertilsson 1987.
[152] Anati 1961.

ridden, or used for draught, the humans engaged in a great variety of activities – some apparently functional in nature, others symbolic. Some motifs are recognisably objects used in daily life – weapons, wagons, ards; others are part of a huge repertoire of motifs of symbolic character – wheels, footsoles, 'nets', 'paddles', 'buildings' and many geometric designs.

In the British Isles, by far the commonest motif is the cup-mark, or cup and ring.[153] It has been estimated that 80% of all sites with motifs more complex than simple cup-marks bear cup-and-ring motifs alone. There is here no certain figural art but instead a limited repertoire of geometric and abstract designs. Rings, concentric rings and spirals are the commonest of these;[154] there are a few crosses, triangles and footsoles. Although these motifs are limited by comparison with those in Scandinavia and Italy, the panels often make up in complexity for what they lack in variety. Particularly elaborate panels can be seen in Northumberland, where cup-marks are sometimes enclosed in surrounding sub-square 'enclosures', with lines connecting two or more such motifs and leading to the interpretation of the designs as simple maps of the ancient ritual landscape. In other provinces of Britain (e.g. Galloway, Argyll, Yorkshire) the designs are less complex but the composition of panels often extremely elaborate. At Greenland, Dunbartonshire, different parts of the same site have different preponderances of motifs.[155]

In Ireland, cup-and-rings are distributed rather thinly, but focus on the Cork–Kerry region of the south-west.[156] The art of Donegal has now been shown to be exceptionally rich in number and variety of motifs. The numbers of 'special' elements in the various provinces of the British Isles have been calculated in table 9.1.[157]

Table 9.1. *Special elements in art provinces of the British Isles*

Galloway	238
Northumberland	178
Donegal	123
Yorkshire	115
Argyll	90

This suggests that the first two areas engaged in a form of symbolic elaboration on a grand scale. In the most elaborate panels, such as High Banks in Galloway, Ormaig in Argyll, Ballochmyle in Strathclyde,[158] or Dod Law in

---

[153] Hadingham 1974; Morris 1989 and other works.
[154] van Hoek 1993.
[155] MacKie and Davis 1988–9.
[156] Shee 1968; Herity and Eogan 1977, fig. 54.
[157] van Hoek 1988, 41.
[158] Stevenson 1993.

Northumberland, scores of cup-marks and cup-and-rings occur on panels that clearly were intended as major foci of art even if they were not compositions as such. Equally, one can interpret large concentrations of art panels, as on Rombalds Moor in Yorkshire, as indicating special significance even though none of the panels by itself is especially impressive on a national scale.

In Galicia, cup-marks are again the commonest design but cup-and-rings are also common, sometimes elaborated into spirals, as well as animals (especially deer), weapons and axes.[159]

The art of Sils/Carschenna, high up at 1100 m above sea level near Thusis in the upper Rhine valley, has cup-marks, cup-and-rings with a line joining the centre to the outside, wheel or sun motifs, wavy lines and horsemen.[160]

Cup-marks occur widely through Europe,[161] in the west associated with chambered tombs (but also with the recumbent stone circles of north-east Scotland), but they are by no means restricted to the western and northern areas. They appear in the eastern Mediterranean in various contexts, at least some of them 'ritual' in nature.[162] They occur on Sardinian and Corsican statue-menhirs,[163] and on Portuguese cromlechs and menhirs.[164] *Schalensteine* are found in other areas of continental Europe, in southern Scandinavia as mentioned above but also in north Germany,[165] Brittany, Austria and Switzerland.[166] This shows that even areas with no other rock art of the Neolithic and Bronze Age have produced cup-marks. It is striking that similar symbolic worlds existed in widely separated parts of Europe in later prehistory; but the form is so generalised that it would be dangerous to read too much into this fact.

Recent fieldwork and analysis by Bradley and co-workers suggests that the apparently simple range of motifs and settings is deceptive, and that considerable elements of structure underlie the art of Galloway, as may also be the case in other art provinces in Britain.[167] Analysis of the landscape location in terms of view and visibility confirms earlier suggestions that the art is sited with particular views in mind, especially that of the sea.[168] What is more, there appear to be two broad types of art panel, simple and complex, each with particular design and setting characteristics. Those 'with four or fewer

[159] Sobrino Buhigas 1935 (cited Fett and Fett 1979, 74f.); Peña Santos and Vázquez Varela 1979; Peña Santos 1980.
[160] Zindel 1968; Sauter 1976, 111 pl. 48; fig. 18 shows other sites in the upper Rhine valley.
[161] Déchelette 1908, 615ff.; Hansen 1937; Röschmann 1962.
[162] Buchholz 1981.
[163] Lilliu 1967/1980, 136 pl. 12; Lilliu 1981, 17f., 74ff. (with discussion of occurrences in Italy, south France and Catalonia), pl. 9d, 26, 1.
[164] Pina 1976; Burgess 1990.
[165] Schwantes 1939, 255f.; Röschmann 1952; 1962; Wegewitz 1949, 138 fig. 162, table 36, 2; 1967; Nowothnig 1958; Capelle 1972, 229f.
[166] Déchelette 1908, 615ff.; Suter 1967; Liniger and Schilt 1976; Gallay *et al.* 1976; Pauli 1984, 170ff. 288 n. 99 with refs.
[167] Bradley *et al.* 1993; 1994.
[168] Bradley 1991.

concentric circles lack any additional features' and are generally small, whereas the more complex designs also have more elaborate circular motifs and are larger. There is also some evidence that the two design types had different widths and depths of view, which are interpreted as indicating a relationship to the likely audience for the art in terms of economic activities.

Art on portable rock

The great majority of art in Scandinavia is carved into 'living rock' (bedrock). In Denmark and north Germany, where the moraine landscape means that bedrock is not exposed, art is found instead on boulders or slabs.[169] In rare but significant instances in Sweden and Norway art is present in funerary contexts. The most famous of these is undoubtedly the great mound of Bredarör at Kivik in south-east Scania, where the cairn, 70–80 m in diameter, enclosed a stone cist formed of thin, roughly square, dressed slabs, four along one side and five along the other (when originally found in 1748 the stones were disturbed and their original position is uncertain).[170] Eight of the slabs are known to have been decorated, with designs that include boats, horses, spoked circles, axes and human figures. Most scholars have thought that opposing slabs were paired by subject matter, two with ships, two with spoked wheels (sun symbols?) and, most significant, two with processions of people: one with four men followed by a two-wheeled chariot pulled by two horses, with attendant animals and mourners, the other (very damaged) with rows of people including musicians and mourners. A recent re-examination of the Kivik cist and its art has confirmed earlier views which suggested that the decorated slabs were set up with the intention of creating a structured progression, with opposing slabs corresponding to each other in general subject matter.[171]

At the excavated barrow of Sagaholm (near Jönköping, north Småland), 15 of the incomplete ring of 45 slabs revetting the mound were decorated, these being mixed in with the undecorated.[172] The motifs, notably horses, with some ships, three human figures, and cup-marks on two slabs, form a very restricted selection from those normally available. Another burial monument with art is Mjeltehaugen on the island of Giske, in Sunnmøre, western Norway.[173] This included ships of a special 'square' kind, but also elaborate linear ornament which is difficult to parallel.[174]

---

[169] Glob 1969; Capelle 1972.

[170] Grinsell 1942; Nordén 1917/1926/1942.

[171] Verlaeckt 1993; Randsborg 1993, suggesting that the slabs have a shamanistic significance, perhaps related to the representation of a world view with the nether regions for the dead, the land of the living in the middle, and above them the heavens. For shamanism, see the well-known Period III grave from Hvidegård in Zealand (p. 321).

[172] Wihlborg 1977–8.

[173] Mandt 1983.

[174] See Marstrander 1978; Randsborg 1993, 72ff. Some of the best parallels are of Copper Age date in northern continental Europe.

Interpretation

The interpretation of rock art of any period is a matter from which archaeologists have traditionally shied away, beyond a generalised assumption that
the depictions are symbolic and their creation undertaken for reasons connected with the spiritual side of the human psyche. The art panels cannot be
called utilitarian, at least not in the sense of felling trees, tilling the land,
casting bronze, or erecting houses; they functioned in the human mind, in
thought processes, not directly in physical properties. But they could inspire
the human actors in the landscape to do these things, or at any rate to create a mental state in humans which led to these things getting done, and
therefore they can be reckoned to have had a role no less important than that
of many technological processes that are far more obvious in the archaeological record. Specialists in the study of art distinguish between instrumen-
tal and transcendental art.[175] On the one hand, the designs could serve a
specific purpose in people's minds, for instance in ensuring fertility or success in the hunt. On the other, the purely spiritual world of beliefs, for
instance in what happens at death or in the existence of deities, could engen-
der an art that is non-functional, purely symbolic in nature and content. For
the observer who is divorced from the context of creation, separating the two
will be difficult, if not impossible.

Interpretations of Scandinavian rock art fall into two broad categories: one
which views the art as an expression of particular rituals, and the scenes and
symbols as representations of mythological elements and ideas; the other ideological in nature, reflecting general principles of social structuring and 'world
view'. It has been suggested that the art reflected a general change in ideology that came about with the Bronze Age, so that depictions of warriors,
weaponry and prestige objects reflect 'conflicts and institutionalised rivalry
between and within regions'.[176] Others have seen the creation of art as a means
of asserting power through the representation of special activities that
reflected social prestige. In Bertilsson's view, ploughing scenes, instead of representing standard elements of a cult such as a fertility cult, should be seen
as 'elements and expressions of great general ideological importance for the
local society', that is for the maintenance of a social order and the legitima-
tion of a social elite. Thus ploughing was not a central but a marginal aspect
of the subsistence economy, and knowledge and control of it (for instance
through the ard) was restricted to elites. The products of such agriculture,
grain for instance, could have been used to make alcoholic drinks, which
could have played a role in ceremonies and ritual feasting that were used to
maintain and enhance these social divisions. In a similar way, it has been
proposed that symbols such as carts and ships represented items of special

---

[175] Coles 1994, 40ff.
[176] Bertilsson 1987; 1989, etc.

status, reflecting aspects of ownership and control in a ranked society.[177] Many art panels bear out the importance of rank and status, especially as shown by scenes of fighting, perhaps ritualised fighting.[178]

Much attention has been directed towards the interpretation of particular motifs or groups of motifs. The ship motif, for instance, can be connected with people's need to make and use the vehicles which enabled them both to acquire valuable economic resources, such as fish, and to maintain contact with neighbouring human groups along a rocky coastline where water transport was the simplest form of travel (see p. 183). Boats have also been connected by some commentators with a fertility god or with the sun as expressed by its passage through the sky; it can also be seen as a correlate of burial, the boat carrying off the body or spirit of the deceased.[179] Depictions of animals, wild or domestic, may reflect purely economic concerns. Scenes that show activities such as dancing or lure-blowing could on one level be taken as generic depictions of common acts. Depictions of purely symbolic motifs, however, have to be thought of in non-utilitarian terms.

At the same time, recent discussions have cast doubt on many interpretations previously accepted as standard. This has been particularly true in the case of the apparent lack of women in the art. Since many figures are depicted as phallic, and few have any clear indication of female attributes, it is usual to assume that most depictions are of men, while scenes of sexual intercourse are said to imply the presence of both male and female. The indicators of gender in the figures are much more ambiguous than commonly supposed, and at least some of the scenes may relate to homosexual intercourse;[180] the creators of the art were not necessarily making an explicit distinction but were intentionally ambiguous: one should not think of the images in terms of recent ideas of sexual identity and sexuality.[181] There is a marked discrepancy between the apparently male-dominated rock art and the plentiful evidence of female deposits and symbols in graves in Bronze Age Scandinavia, suggesting that many of the signs and symbols in the art are in fact representations of the female principle.[182]

In recent years the application of ideas from semiotics to the study of the art has come to enjoy a vogue. Art contains information, but the ability to comprehend that information depends on the ability to 'read' the language of the art; art is a form of visual communication, in which a variety of cultural

[177] Malmer 1981, 108; Harding 1984b.
[178] Nordbladh 1989.
[179] Almgren 1962; Grinsell 1941b.
[180] Yates 1990.
[181] Wood 1995.
[182] Mandt 1987.

conventions condition the means and mode of expression.[183] A study by Tilley, for instance, makes use of a variety of approaches derived from or allied to hermeneutics and semiotics to propose a set of interpretations of the art of Nämforsen in northern Sweden that stress the relational nature of the art, the idea that it represents a text which must be read according to the experience and world view of the creator and observer.[184] To do this he not only analyses the occurrence of motifs in relation to each other, he also deploys ethnohistoric data to illustrate the range of possibilities for understanding the context in which the art might have been created. The problem with the approach, as Tilley himself admits, is that of bringing about a generally acceptable interpretation of the art; the art could have had several meanings and each would be dependent on the context of the observer.[185]

As discussed above, recent research in Scotland suggests that the composition of some art panels, and their placing in the landscape, was not coincidental. The communities which created the art and whose purposes it served were territorial in nature (see chapter 14) and exploited particular socio-economic niches. On the other hand, Mandt's study of western Norway has suggested exactly the opposite conclusion,[186] which brings home the point that there are unlikely to be overriding rules that apply to all the rock art of the European Bronze Age. The art could have served a role both in local terms and also at regional and supra-regional levels. Large clusters of petroglyph sites are close to one another in Stjørdal (Trøndelag, northern Norway), suggesting they were made by sedentary groups, each with its own panel which would be added to at infrequent intervals (fig. 9.13).[187] Initially the petroglyphs were at four sites; and thence the practice of carving panels spread to the surrounding units. At the regional level, 'culture strongholds' controlled large hunting areas and the traffic along the Trondheim fjord. The replacement of 'Arctic' (i.e. hunting-based) art with 'Nordic' (i.e. farming-based) on the same panels is a reflection of this role. At the supra-regional level, the standardisation of the art over large areas of Scandinavia indicates a common culture in much the same way as bronzes were standardised in the Late Bronze Age. The position of Trøndelag, supposedly on the border between two zones, suggests that it played a role in the contact and interaction that is discernible over wide areas of Scandinavia.

The idea that the density of art sites is indicative of the social importance

---

[183] An excellent discussion to the background of such an approach: Layton 1981, 91ff. The discussion goes back to the original expression of the concept of the 'signifier' and the 'signified' developed for language by Saussure. Layton's analysis of the Narmer palette from Early Dynastic Egypt illustrates the point (ibid., 114ff.).

[184] Tilley 1991. Other examples: Nordbladh 1978; Yates 1990.

[185] Tilley 1991, 172ff.

[186] Mandt 1978.

[187] Sognnes 1992.

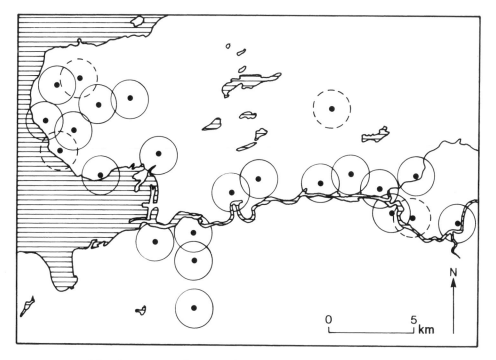

Fig. 9.13. Distribution of petroglyph clusters in Stjørdal, Nord-Trøndelag (after Sognnes 1992).

of particular areas has been suggested on a number of occasions.[188] Tables indicating the ranking order of sites show how certain localities in the parishes of Tanum and Kville had far more motifs and panels than other areas and must indicate special elaboration and status in the communities utilising them. The distribution of the art may thus represent a hierarchical social organisation, and the representation of warriors would also reflect aspects of a society in which status was intimately bound up with possession of status goods, with display and with competitive fighting, real or mock.

The progress of research has allowed significant advances to be made in understanding the role of rock art in Bronze Age society. It is widely appreciated that attempts at understanding individual symbols or groups of symbols are simplistic and can never be more than speculative; by contrast, viewing art in its totality, in terms of its socio-economic and ideological context, enables insights to be obtained that at least allow one to discern how the art may have operated.

[188] e.g. Bertilsson 1987, 91ff., 169ff.

Magicians and priests?

The role of the various individuals depicted on Bronze Age rock art might allow one to reconstruct both ceremonial scenes and also scenes of cult or ritual in which special persons, i.e. priests, officiated. Examples include a number from the Naquane rock in the Val Camonica where human figures are depicted wearing elaborate headdresses. Some of the objects which defy normal explanation in graves or other contexts may similarly relate to special equipment or clothing related to such priestly functions.

One such group of objects that has recently been interpreted, or reinterpreted, in this way is the set of gold cones of west-central Europe, from Schifferstadt in the Rheinland-Pfalz, Ezelsdorf in Bavaria, and Avanton (Vienne) in Poitou (fig. 9.14).[189] Although these curious and magnificent objects have sometimes been seen as gold covers for wooden posts, or something similar, both they and the gold bowls of Ireland and elsewhere might have served as ceremonial or ritual hats, presumably worn by special functionaries on ceremonial occasions. Parallels with depictions in Scandinavia, on the Kivik slabs and the Stockhult figurines, as well as with the pointed hats worn by Hittite gods in Anatolia, illustrate the point. If this was indeed the function of the cones, they would certainly have made an indelible impression on the observer. Such an impression would also have been made by the famous gold 'cape' from Mold in north Wales, which has likewise been associated with priestly or ceremonial functions.[190]

Nor should one forget the thesis that Britain in the period of the stone circles was allegedly a land of astronomer-priests in whose hands specialised knowledge was concentrated, particularly that relating to astronomical observation and its related activities.[191] Though the notion of a class of 'astronomer-priests' is perhaps overstated, it must certainly have been the case that the rites associated with standing stones and circles could have been the special preserve of a priestly class whose position was maintained by their access to specialised knowledge.

Ceremonial

Many aspects of ritual practice thus revolved around formalised presentations of various kinds, which may conveniently be grouped together under the term 'ceremonial'. Many aspects of the rock art suggest this; so do many of the specialised bronze and gold finds. Still other aspects may also fall into this category, for instance the ceremonial use of the chariot or wagon.[192] While

[189] Schauer 1986; Gerloff 1995.
[190] Powell 1953.
[191] MacKie 1977.
[192] Pare 1989.

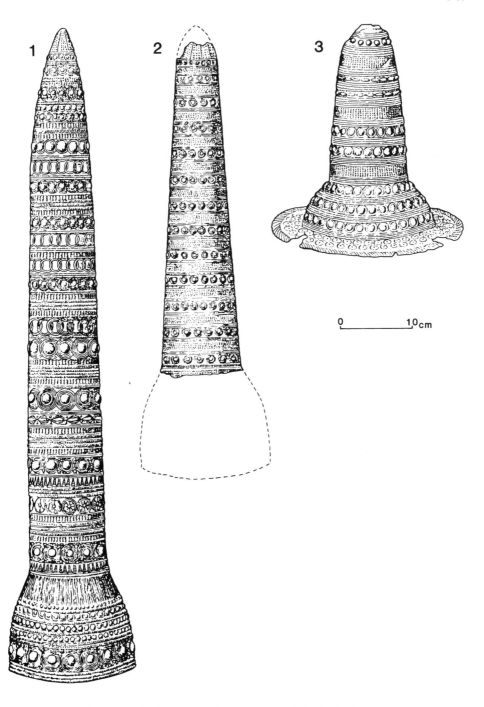

Fig. 9.14. Gold cones ('hats'). 1. Ezelsdorf. 2. Avanton.
3. Schifferstadt (after Gerloff 1995/Schauer 1986).

the knowledge of the spoked wheel is likely to have come to continental Europe from the south-east at the time of the Mycenaean Shaft Graves, the regular use of vehicles in graves and with cult associations does not start until the Urnfield period. At this time, the symbols discussed above became widespread, including for instance the use of the model wagon carrying a vessel or cauldron (*Kesselwagen*) or of the cart bearing birds on its pole (*Deichselwagen*).[193] Urnfield hoards not uncommonly include wagon parts or horse harness, sometimes indicating paired animals and often with female associations. The finding of real wagon and harness parts makes it highly likely that practices involving these items were a regular part of Bronze Age ritual.

The same is true of many of the other items that have been presented above, for instance the bronze musical instruments and drums (including for instance the famous drums from Balkåkra in southern Sweden and Hasfalva in western Hungary[194]), the sheet-metal weaponry, and the ritualised fighting and dancing depicted in the rock art. In many parts of Europe a highly formalised set of practices existed, ostensibly involving mainly men, but in fact including also many female associations.

Conclusion: the nature of Bronze Age religion

While it would be wrong to imagine that attitudes to cult and ritual were the same throughout Bronze Age Europe, a number of themes can be detected with applicability over a wide geographical area. There is extensive evidence for the use of natural features, notably wet places and caves, for the deposition of materials, and for supposing that deposition itself was a recurring element of Bronze Age practice. The frequent occurrence in central Europe and Italy of symbolic objects may suggest certain unifying forces in cultural terms, if one can assume that the reasons behind such objects were similar in different areas. If one may refer to the Christian cross as an element that symbolises an event central to the beliefs of the Christian church, or depictions of the Virgin Mary as both a reference to the genesis of the central figure of Christianity and a means of communicating with that figure, then the symbols seen in Bronze Age Europe – sun, birds, animals – can plausibly be taken to be comparable references.

At the same time as the maintenance of a cult-based sphere of activity, there was also a strong ceremonial element in much of the creation and deposition of art and artefacts in the Bronze Age. Parade bronzework of no practical use other than visual impact, the playing of musical instruments, the creation of locales to which meaning had been added by relatively discreet

---

[193] Maraszek 1997.
[194] Knape and Nordström 1994.

means – a standing stone in a grove, human bones in a cave – and where – if the rock art has been correctly interpreted – displays such as dancing took place: all these indicate a strong interest in the visual, in hieratically 'unnatural' poses and movements, perhaps too in audible and olfactory experiences. We may not be contextually able to understand the references thus created, but taken all in all we are not much worse off than are many ethnographers in their attempts to understand the symbolic referents of living or recently observed cultures, where even oral information has to be interpreted with reference to a context or world view. The progress of archaeological research is enabling that process of contextualisation to take place, in the Bronze Age as in other periods of the past.

CHAPTER 10

HOARDS AND HOARDING

One of the most remarkable things about the artefactual record of the European Bronze Age is the enormous quantity of metalwork which was consigned to the ground. This phenomenon, the deposition of 'hoards' of bronze (fig. 10.1), is one of the most discussed, though least understood, aspects of the Bronze Age. Whatever explanation one prefers, the vast amount of wasted raw material and encapsulated labour that these finds represent is by any standard extraordinary. If they were utilitarian in nature, how could the societies involved afford to lose so much material? If they were votive, why were they deposited on such a large scale? In view of the complexity of the issues, it is likely that no single explanation will account for more than a proportion of the finds.

Bronze hoards, that is collective finds of whole or fragmentary bronze implements or pieces of waste and uncast metal, vary greatly in size and constitution. This variability can be followed in both chronological and geographical dimensions; attempts at discerning regularities in this material are usually only valid for a restricted area and period. Conversely, when one looks at the picture over wider areas and across chronological divisions, any impression of neat patterning dissolves. But this very diversity has provided fertile ground for the germination of ideas on the nature and significance of the phenomenon. The literature is large and the difference in views between scholars treating identical material striking, ranging from the minutely detailed examination of particular collections of material, notably by German writers, to contextual treatments such as those of Bradley. Particularly in recent years, an enormous literature has developed on the subject, which makes a comprehensive overview impossible.[1]

The physical form of hoards

Strictly speaking, any collection of more than one object that was found together other than in a funerary or domestic situation can be called a hoard find. There are two implications in this statement: first, there is no minimum

---

[1] e.g. most recently Teržan 1995; Kultgeschehen 1996; A. and B. Hänsel 1997; Kadrow 1997; Maraszek 1998.

Fig. 10.1. Early Bronze Age hoard from Dieskau, Saalkreis. Photo: Landesmuseum für Vorgeschichte, Halle/Saale.

or maximum size for a hoard, merely that a hoard is not a single find; second, the context is important. Hoard finds are those that are demonstrably not grave-goods and not the *in situ* residue of a destroyed industrial or domestic site. In the case of finds deposited in wet places or on moors the nature of the patination is also considered to be important ('*Wasserpatina*', '*Moorpatina*' of German authors), enabling objects to be assigned to the same find or even to corroborate its find circumstances. These criteria are not always easy to fulfil. It is frequently far from certain that a given hoard find is complete, rather than part of a larger collection; and it is almost certainly false to separate collective finds from single finds in terms of the causes of deposition. The problem with single finds is that the possible causes for their appearance are so multifold that only large-scale patterning is likely to provide a convincing explanation for them. For the determination of context, the problems are even greater: while one may be reasonably certain that a given group of finds does not come from a grave, it is often impossible to say exactly what it does come from. A foundry site that had been disturbed by the plough, for instance, might well appear simply as a collection of bronze objects. Uncertainties resulting from recovery circumstances can only increase the difficulty of identifying the true context and nature of such finds.

Nevertheless, the vast material base available provides enough sets of circumstances for informed speculation about the nature of both context and role to be possible; the ensuing discussion assumes that a core of finds is sufficiently coherent for hypotheses to be developed.

Several broad categories or polarities in hoard contents can be distinguished: first, complete or perfect objects as against broken or miscast ones; second, hoards of one object type as against those with several or many types; third, differences in the types represented, for instance between ornaments, tools and weapons; fourth, hoards with objects said to have female associations as against those with male associations (this is itself a culturally conditioned judgement, which contrasts weaponry and razors with ornaments); fifth, hoards with a markedly industrial character such as those containing ingots or ingot fragments, metalworking tools, scrap metal, casting waste and the like, as opposed to those with what seems to be a votive character. These, however, are contextual judgements and need fuller discussion.

These indications of internal diversity would alone suggest that the phenomenon of hoarding was not a unitary one, and that no single explanation would suffice to account for all hoards. Scholars have, since the days of Worsaae and Sophus Müller, interpreted hoards as the product of a number of different processes. Broadly speaking, one may categorise these as *founders' hoards, traders' hoards, personal hoards or treasures, votive hoards* and *equipment for the afterlife*.[2] Thus founders' hoards would be those with scrap metal, ingots and casting debris; traders' hoards those consisting of multiple complete objects of one or a restricted number of types; personal hoards would consist of complete objects, with a few examples of a range of different types; votive hoards would also consist of complete objects, but here the context (for instance deposition in wet places) would suggest a special purpose; while equipment for the afterlife might consist of objects usually associated with grave deposition, for instance specialised eating or drinking equipment.

These categories may not account for all hoards, but they can be extended to embrace the great majority of finds. What is less certain is whether such categorisation actually assists in understanding the phenomenon. It is of course based on a modern, 'economic' view of the past, on a 'common-sense' interpretation of what past finds might have meant to their makers and owners. Thus, while foundry debris undoubtedly emanated from the industrial processes associated with bronze-casting, that does not in itself mean that a collection of such debris was necessarily placed in the ground for reasons connected with those industrial processes.

Traditionally, founders' hoards – those that contained broken or miscast objects not capable of functional use – have been seen as a direct consequence of the mode of operation of the Bronze Age smith. They are often extremely large and heavy; hoards of hundreds of objects are not uncommon, and some run into thousands. This bulk and weight means that it would be very

---

[2] See the useful review of the literature in Eogan 1983, 3.

unlikely that they were transported over any great distance, instead being kept in a single place for future use, the spot carefully guarded and its location kept secret. In this model, when the smith came on his rounds to a village where he had hidden a stock of metal, he would go to it to recover what he needed, reburying what was left over at the end of the operation. Motives of security have also been suggested for traders' and personal hoards, the objects being deposited for safekeeping, perhaps in times of unrest.

While this interpretation accounts for some of the observed facts, it falls short in a number of important respects, not least in the sheer unlikelihood that so many metal hoards of this kind – and they run into thousands – would have survived intact and unrecovered. It would mean that large numbers of smiths perished before they could return to their supplies, and since only they knew the location of the stock, it was destined to languish in the earth until the fortunes of discovery brought it to light in recent times.

The assumption that political unrest led to the practice of burying metal in the ground might be thought to derive support from the fact that hoards concentrate in particular periods. In Hungary, for instance, there is a clearly defined phase – the Koszider phase – coinciding with the end of many Early Bronze Age tell settlements, when hoards of a particular character were deposited. Throughout central and eastern Europe, the phase coeval with Ha A1 saw the deposition of many more hoards than any other period. By contrast, in the north and west of Europe there is a marked concentration on the last period of the Bronze Age. There are, therefore, regional and chronological trends in deposition. A connection has been suggested between hoard deposition and hillfort construction in the Urnfield period in southern Germany, as at the Bleibeskopf in the Taunus,[3] or the Bullenheimer Berg south-east of Würzburg in northern Bavaria.[4]

In other areas such connections are tenuous. In Britain and Ireland fort-building did begin during the Late Bronze Age, but such dating evidence as there is suggests that this was before, rather than contemporary with, the Ewart Park/Dowris phase when the greatest number of hoards was deposited. In central Europe there are some hilltop sites used during Ha A1, but relatively few compared to those occupied in later phases. One exception may be the Early Bronze Age forts of Slovakia, where there is some evidence to suggest that gold hoards accompanied the move to hilltops, as at Barca or Spišský Štvrtok.[5] On the other hand, the Middle Bronze Age example of Velim in eastern Bohemia, with its seven separate hoards or groups of gold and bronze finds, is certainly to be connected with ritual deposition, not with concerns for security.[6]

[3] Stein 1976, 106ff. Other examples are quoted by Janssen 1985.
[4] Diemer 1985.
[5] Vladár 1973a, 269ff.
[6] Hrala, Sedláček and Vávra 1992.

The varying number of bronze hoards may be related to the amount of bronze produced at different periods. The large number of hoards of the Ewart Park phase, and in particular of Carp's Tongue material, led to the suggestion that the introduction of large-scale iron-working to Britain 'caused the bottom to fall out of the bronze market'.[7] Iron is widely available in most areas of Britain, and its rapid adoption might have relegated bronze to a minor role, causing 'a massive flood of surplus bronze [to be] released onto the market', spelling catastrophe for traditional bronze-workers. Though this argument has its attractions, it is rendered weaker by applying only to a single period. Even in Britain, the theory would not account for the large number of hoards of the preceding Wilburton–Wallington phase, let alone the admittedly much smaller numbers of earlier hoards; but more significantly, in central Europe the high point of bronze hoard deposition was represented by Ha A1 and equivalent phases in areas further east. There can hardly be any question of iron replacing bronze at this stage of the Bronze Age: bronze continued as a major metal, and iron was still extremely scarce, even in Ha A2. The explanation for these massive quantities of deposited metal must be sought elsewhere.

One should not be in any doubt about the scale of these operations. When one looks at the standard corpora of bronze hoards for central and eastern Europe, the disproportionate numbers of hoards by period are instantly striking (table 10.1).[8]

Table 10.1. *Bronze hoards by period in northern Croatia, Hungary and Romania*[9]

Br B–C	34
Br C–D	168
Ha A1	265
Ha A2	70

As well as these crude figures for the absolute number of hoard finds, there are further remarkable features of the hoards. In northern Croatia, for instance, three-quarters of adequately documented hoards in Br D–Ha A1 contained more than 50 objects, in contrast with only one-quarter of those at all other periods. Some of the hoards are truly enormous: six large hoards in Transylvania contained around 10,000 objects, weighing an estimated 5 tonnes (fig. 10.2 for a breakdown of one of these hoards). The mismatch between these figures and those for other periods can only reflect special production and deposition circumstances. One can find other cases in other areas

[7] Burgess 1968; 1979, 275; see also Taylor 1993, 54ff.
[8] Vinski-Gasparini 1973; Petrescu-Dîmboviţa 1978; Moszolics 1973; 1985.
[9] Cf. the estimates given by Mozsolics (1985, 84): Aranyos horizon (Br D): 35–40 hoards; Kurd horizon (Ha A1): 300–320 hoards; Gyermely horizon (Ha A2): 100 hoards.

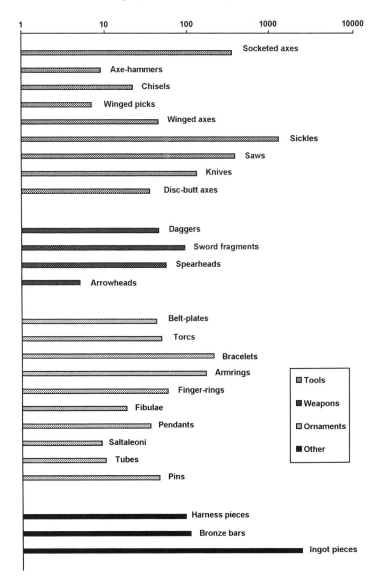

Fig. 10.2. The composition of the hoard from Uioara de Sus, Ocna Mureş, Alba county, Romania (data from Petrescu-Dîmboviţa 1978). Note logarithmic scale.

and periods, such as the massive hoard of over 6000 pieces from Isleham, Cambridgeshire, dating to the end of the Wilburton phase.[10]

What are the possible explanations for this remarkable mismatch between assumed metal in circulation and actual deposited finds? One can dismiss at

[10] Britton 1960.

the start any suggestion that the figures are in some way coincidental, i.e. that only the chances of discovery are responsible for the discrepancies, since the pattern repeats itself across wide tracts of territory. If differential amounts of metal were reaching the ground, either differential amounts of metal were in circulation, deposition practice varied at different times, or recovery rates varied.

1. *The supply of metal varied.* There is no evidence from the metal production areas that this was the case. The only artefactual evidence for dating at the main mining areas comes from isolated finds of pottery, which say nothing about the intensity of usage of the mines. In the British Isles, there is barely any dating evidence other than radiocarbon dates, which by their nature pinpoint individual episodes rather than occurrences of long duration. The other way that might measure metal circulation directly would be a study of the quantities and circulation times of metal items. In graves and settlements, it is not possible to see Ha A1 reflected as a phase that was more prolific than those that followed it, either in overall total of sites or in number of artefacts represented. In fact, as is evident from the demographic indicators for the Late Bronze Age, there are good reasons to suppose that the total human population, and therefore the amount of activity generally, increased throughout the period, not that it reached a maximum in Ha A1 and declined thereafter.

Measuring circulation times has been taken as an indicator of the abundance or otherwise of metal.[11] According to this view, the more worn objects are, the longer they have been in circulation and therefore the less new metal there is around to replace them (fig. 10.3). This argument has been applied both to swords and to hanging bowls (ornaments worn on the belt), and in a British context to ornaments, tools, weapons and other objects.[12] Unfortunately, in the case of swords it is not evident that extra wear really does indicate lack of fresh supplies rather than exceptional usage resulting from local political conditions. To achieve wear on a sword, one would have to use it a great deal in practice, perhaps combined with real fencing with enemies, and then resharpen it. Nor is it necessarily evident that wear on hanging bowls indicates a shortage of metal with which to replace old pieces. Kristiansen's analysis saw fluctuations between different areas of Denmark, but with most new metal in circulation in Periods II and V (i.e. at these times least wear is visible).[13] In Period III, north-west Jutland had virtually no new metal arriving, with the result that weapons show very heavy wear. In this period, too, some sword-hilts are so worn that their edges have been rubbed

---

[11] Kristiansen 1984.
[12] Taylor 1993, 58ff.
[13] Kristiansen 1977; 1984.

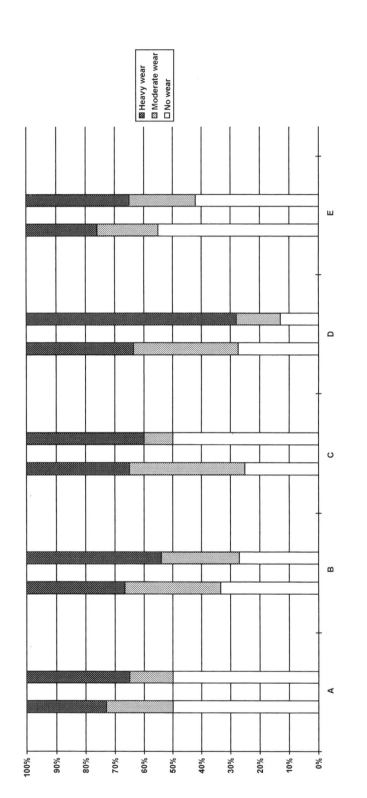

Fig. 10.3. Diagram showing the different representation of worn and unworn objects in different regions of Denmark in Periods II and III (data from Kristiansen 1977). Each left-hand column represents Period II, each right-hand column represents Period III. A: Zealand. B: East Jutland and Funen. C: NE Jutland. D: NW Jutland. E: West Jutland. Note that in general objects are more worn in Period III, especially in Zone D.

away. In Periods IV and V, the west of Denmark has plenty of graves but almost no metal, while in the north and east the percentage of very heavily worn objects decreases, that of moderately worn objects showing a corresponding increase. There is little in this to suggest that Period III/IV/Ha A1 was one of especially large quantities of metal in circulation, though it cannot be ruled out in view of the fact that the burial rite was changing in the Nordic area towards cremation, just as it did in central Europe, with a corresponding decline in surviving grave-goods. Similarly, in Britain it is clear that different artefact categories underwent different amounts of wear, interpreted as differential circulation times.[14]

2. *There was a change of practice in the deposition of metal in connection with smithing operations.* The main difficulty in accepting this explanation is the lack of any apparent technical rationale for it. Even if the level of smithing activity was significantly higher in Ha A1 than in Br D or Ha A2/B1/B3, smiths must have been extremely active in the latter periods to account for the large number of prestige bronzes that survive from contexts other than hoards. Scrap and raw metal may therefore not have been deposited in holes in the ground, instead staying above ground in structures such as workshops and storerooms where they were at hand for ready use. The implication of this might be, paradoxically, that the level of metallurgical activity was actually higher in periods when there is less metal in evidence in the form of hoards. In the case of Ha A2–B3 in central Europe this seems a reasonable view; in the case of Ewart Park, and specifically the Carp's Tongue complex, the prevalence of such hoards in wet places is a matter of interest in its own right.

3. *Recovery rates varied from period to period.* While this may have been the case, it is hard to think of any good reason why it should have been so, unless there was an element of intentionality about the loss of metal. Where there are grounds for thinking that hoard deposition was somehow 'ritual', the intention cannot be doubted; with founders' or scrap hoards, it is generally assumed that the intention was to recover. But need this necessarily have been so? If one can view the throwing of a collection of swords or bracelets into a river or bog as rational in the terms in which it was done by the thrower, there seems little in principle to distinguish this from the deposition of hoards containing some imperfect objects.

[14] Taylor 1993, 90. The predisposition of some artefacts to become worn is also recognised. Thus objects circulated for longer in the Wilburton period in East Anglia than they did in Wessex, and these circulation times remained long in the Ewart Park period though ornaments show less wear in that phase. For Taylor this represents the influence of external factors on supplies, interpretable as 'a restriction in the metal supply from the peripheries and through exchange' (1993, 67). One might equally as well suggest that internal structural problems and potentials created these effects.

Votive explanations

The view that hoards are votive in nature and intention has been advanced by many scholars over the years, but in recent years German scholars have led the way in propounding a votive explanation for almost all hoards, including many of those that might on the face of it appear utilitarian. Such explanations have to demonstrate why essentially industrial objects, such as ingots or fragments of them, should take on a votive role. The literature on this topic is now extensive.[15] But the basic question remains: were hoards hidden with the intention to recover, or were they thrown away deliberately? Or were they deposited for other reasons, for instance changes in burial practice in the Urnfield rite which showed a move from the deposition of grave-goods to *Totenschätze*, treasures provided for the dead in a funerary ritual?[16] These questions demand some consideration of a related category of material, that of metalwork found in rivers and bogs, an aspect which has traditionally been seen as inherently more likely to be involved with ritual (p. 329).

A number of authors have pointed out that in principle there is no difference between 'hoards' and single finds in terms of the reasons for their deposition. The problem is that single finds may appear thus for purely coincidental reasons. Is there in fact any difference between them and the 'one-piece hoards' of the south Scandinavian area, i.e. single finds that were deposited as such, and if not, what is the distinction between these and 'multiple hoards', which can themselves consist of one type or of many types ('mixed inventory')?[17] Since certain objects were regularly associated with hoards and not with graves, it is reasonable to assume that there were different rules for the selection of objects for hoards. Multiple hoards also show a chronological unity – they were not accumulated over time. Clearly a quite complex set of rules underpinned the selection and deposition of objects, which must relate also to the rules for grave deposition and to the division of goods by gender.

One of the ways forward in the study of this material must be a detailed source-critical analysis of the material, taking into account taphonomic factors and correlating content with context. In this connection, the work of

---

[15] Fundamental discussions have appeared at regular intervals, especially in the German literature: von Brunn (1968; 1980) and Kubach (1978–9; 1983; 1985) are basic; other important works: Hundt (1955), Aner (1956), Baudou (1960), Kolling (1968), Zimmermann (1970), Mandera (1972), Stein (1976), Menke (1978–9), Verron (1983), Eogan (1983), Willroth (1985a; 1985b), z. Erbach-Schönberg (1985), Schumacher-Matthäus (1985), Matthäus and Schumacher-Matthäus (1986), Moszolics (1987), Knapp, Muhly and Muhly (1988) and Hansen (1991). Some of these works present basic corpora of material (von Brunn, Stein, Menke, Eogan, Willroth) and then attempt interpretations; the others look for correlations and correspondences in the content of the hoards, or between content and context.
[16] As suggested by Hundt 1955.
[17] Willroth 1985a; 1985b.

Levy on the Scandinavian hoards and other deposits represents one of the clearest statements available, and has been widely quoted (p. 326).[18]

In trying to determine whether a votive or a utilitarian explanation is the more likely in particular instances, it is especially useful to compare the find circumstances of particular artefact types. A study of deposition in Urnfield Upper Austria, for instance, examined the relative occurrence of different artefact types in rivers, hoards, graves and isolated finds, paying especial attention to swords.[19] Not only were swords much more likely to end up in rivers or wet places than anywhere else in this area (61% of the total), they differed in this respect from other categories of metalwork, especially sickles (mainly in hoards), pins, arrowheads and knives (mainly in graves), and axes and spearheads (mainly isolated finds). The situation in Bavaria with swords is rather similar: there are more swords in graves there, but still many in rivers. By contrast, in other areas of Austria swords do not mainly come from rivers, and in Lower Austria and the Tyrol grave finds predominate. The find statistics across time are more complex but they do reinforce the finding that western Austria with Bavaria consistently saw more river finds than eastern Austria. The contrast was most marked in Br C, Ha B1 and Ha B3, when there were no river finds at all in the eastern areas. This analysis of a relatively small region compares with the situation across Europe as a whole, where some areas had many wet finds, others few; and within that general statement, some periods saw much more wetland deposition, and deposition of hoards generally, than others.

In the light of the shift in opinion discussed above, it is less surprising to find that some scholars view all, or almost all, hoards as having been deposited for ritual reasons. This was the view of Menke, for instance, for the hoards of ring ingots that are found north of the Alps, principally in Bavaria, Austria and Moravia;[20] it is the view of Hansen in a recent study;[21] it has also been propounded by Kubach and others.[22] Hoards in the Carpathian Basin concentrate in certain regions and consist there of particular groupings or selections of objects, including non-utilitarian objects, ingots and casting waste.[23] They are commoner in those areas where cremation was practised; in other words they reflect a deposition rite rather than a desire to hide for its own sake.

---

[18] Levy 1982.
[19] zu Erbach-Schönberg 1985.
[20] Menke 1978–9.
[21] Hansen 1991. Like Kolling (1968, 114), he points to the fact that hoards (other than scrap hoards) tend regularly to contain a *selection* of the available metalwork, thus indicating some kind of structuring principle. What is more, the contents of hoards that were deposited in wet places do not differ much from those placed in dry places. Any dichotomy between the two situations is thus a false one; the same principles should have operated in both cases. Granted that river finds cannot reasonably be seen as anything but votive in nature, the move towards identifying a large number of 'dry' finds as votive was irresistible.
[22] Kubach 1985.
[23] Schumacher-Matthäus 1985, 140ff.

The so-called ingot torcs, better called ring ingots, have a remarkable distribution northwards from the Alps, occurring in very large numbers in hoards that sometimes consist solely of this artefact type (see pp. 218f.).[24] Scholars have long supposed that these objects represent a form of ingot, a means of carrying metal around, perhaps on a pole – though the form may have originated in an ornament worn around the neck. The distribution strongly suggests that they emanated from the copper sources of the eastern Alps, and most previous writers have interpreted them as ingots. An interpretation of the hoards as votive, therefore, goes against received opinion. The grounds for believing this are various: they are unlikely to be metal stores because there is no evidence for on-site metalworking on Bavarian Early Bronze Age settlements, and by definition a metal store ought to lie close to the place of its working; the quantities of ore produced by the Alpine sources were very great and the potential demand for metal throughout the Bronze Age was enormous, so that there would be no point in burying it so close to source, especially in the Alpine foothills where metal was abundant; if they were simply deposits that their owner had failed to retrieve, one would expect a more or less even distribution in the hinterland of the sources, whereas there are more hoards in the Salzach valley than in other southern tributaries of the Danube; and if the hoards were deposited not by individuals but by communities, the failure to retrieve them would indicate depopulation, which is certainly not credible on other grounds in, for instance, the Straubing area of Bavaria. The apparent patterning of hoards, with a number of defined sets of objects present in them, suggests careful selection prior to deposition; and careful deposition in some cases.

While each of these arguments on its own seems convincing enough, one is left with a sense of unease at the interpretation of all these finds as votive. It is perfectly true that many hoards were carefully selected and carefully deposited, and their placing in the ground may well have had a significance that could not be separated in the minds of their owners from the symbolic side of things. But taking the distribution of ring ingots as a whole, the traditional explanation as raw material moving out from its place of extraction seems overall much more convincing. The absence of metalworking places on settlements is hardly an argument against this theory; such installations might well have been located away from domestic buildings, and in any case would often have left only fugitive traces.

Is it credible that all bronze hoards, or at least the great majority of them, were deposited for votive reasons? Several other authorities have not thought so, citing the vast number of finds and objects, for instance in the huge foundry hoards of Transylvania, as support for their view.[25] Although

---

[24] Bath-Bílková 1973; Butler 1978; Harding 1983b.
[25] Moszolics 1985, 84; Rusu 1981; *contra*: Petrescu-Dîmbovița 1971, 182.

relatively little attention has been paid to find circumstances in the eastern half of Europe, a glance at some of the main corpora of material quickly shows that the majority of finds were made during agricultural activities, usually ploughing, vineyard cultivation or ditch-digging.[26] Although the possibility that these relate to places that were once wet and are now dry (old river courses, for instance) cannot altogether be ruled out, the chances of any significant number being diverted in this way are rather small. Certainly there are wet finds in Hungary, for instance a significant number of bronzes from the Danube,[27] but in general these appear exceptional, and a far greater number of finds come from dry land.

In France, Britain and Ireland some authors have supposed that votive reasons were the principal ones involved, while others are reluctant to commit themselves to such a hypothesis.[28] In general, the debate in these lands has been more muted, and certainly there has been no activity comparable to that in Germany to investigate the correlations between hoard contents and other finds, or between different areas of this region: all the more surprising, given the fact that Celtic religion was later centred on these countries, with its well-known emphasis on deposition in wet places.[29] There has been general agreement in recent years that wet finds, such as weaponry and prestige bronzes from rivers and bogs, were votive in nature, but the idea that all hoards might be ritual in nature has been little considered in Britain and Ireland. Thus a recent interpretation of the Huelva river find, usually seen as a shipwreck, as ritual in nature or even a burial site, has found little resonance in these islands.[30]

But the arguments against accidental loss or inability to recover hidden stock are no less powerful, even if there is a higher proportion of founders' hoards, especially in southern England, than in central Europe. The phenomenon of hoarding is one that for all its regional and temporal variation represented the same set of activities in many different places. The great founders' hoards of southern England are different only in detail from those of Transylvania. Equally, a collection of perfect objects such as the Great Clare (Mooghaun) hoard is no different in kind from the hoards of perfect objects in Scandinavia.

A final explanation to be mentioned is that advanced by Sommerfeld, which sees some central European hoards, and specifically those containing large numbers of sickles, as being a primitive kind of 'coinage'.[31] According to this

[26] e.g. Moszolics 1985.
[27] Such as swords: Moszolics 1975.
[28] e.g. Eogan 1983.
[29] An exception is Taylor (1993). The otherwise excellent accounts of Burgess give the briefest of discussions (e.g. 1974, 210), while other general works on French, British and Irish prehistory have little more to say (Megaw and Simpson 1979, 297ff.; Gaucher 1988, 94ff.; Herity and Eogan 1977, 210; Parker Pearson 1993, 117).
[30] Ruiz-Gálvez Priego 1995.
[31] Sommerfeld 1994.

view, bronze sickles were not essential for harvesting, and certainly not in the quantities in which they appear. They almost all occur in hoards, and are complete and unused, following very specific design criteria and sometimes bearing 'marks'. In these respects they differ from most other artefact classes. The view that they represent value standards, like coinage, is intriguing and deserves examination in other contexts; it may have much to say about value systems and methods of exchange in the Bronze Age.

Hoarding was thus the most characteristic Bronze Age activity in much of Europe. In this connection it is necessary to glance at those areas where it did *not* occur to any great degree. One of these areas was Greece, where there is a startling mismatch between the quantities of metal known or assumed in the palatial societies of the Minoans and Mycenaeans and the number of hoards preserved in the ground. In this case it seems highly probable that structural reasons connected with the nature of the economy are responsible for the extraordinarily low representation of metal deposition. Virtually all the hoards known from mainland Greece in the Late Bronze Age are of tools and smithing debris. The metalwork from the Unexplored Mansion at Knossos was actually found in the ruins of a building and had certainly not been hidden far out of sight. In Cyprus, on the other hand, the indications are more ambiguous, and it has been argued that the hoards there are votive in nature, just like those in central Europe.[32] This argument has been fiercely criticised,[33] but in reality this debate is simply a re-run of that prevailing in central Europe, and there is no conceptual reason why the situation should be different in Cyprus from that in Europe generally. On the other hand, Cyprus had a special place in the East Mediterranean Bronze Age as a major copper producer. The association of deities with copper production (e.g. the Enkomi 'Ingot God', a figurine of the smiting god standing on an oxhide ingot) indicates the special position of bronze production on the island.[34] In this light, it could be argued that the context of bronze deposition was different on Cyprus from that in Europe.

Context

The study of hoard context has come to be recognised as a crucial element in Bronze Age metalwork studies. The approach taken by R. Bradley builds on earlier studies, stressing the changing role of finds such as swords in rivers and graves over time, and asking what the roles of complex grave-goods were.[35] Like many others before him, he is puzzled by the fact that 'utilitarian' hoards

---

[32] Matthäus and Schumacher-Matthäus 1986.
[33] Knapp, Muhly and Muhly 1988.
[34] Knapp 1986.
[35] Bradley 1990.

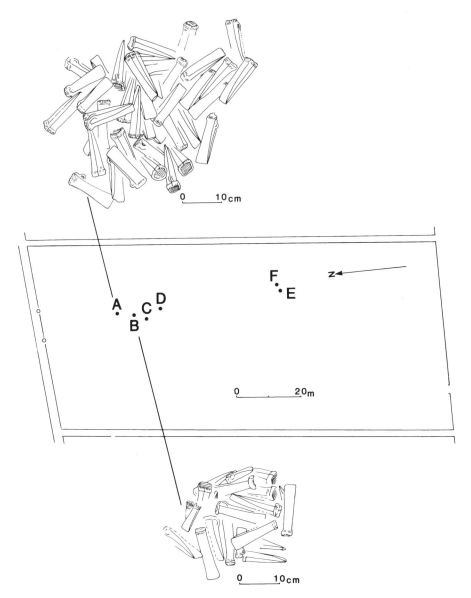

Fig. 10.4. Marchésieux (Manche). Field plan showing findspots of axe hoards, with details of Hoards A and B (after Verron 1983).

represented an enormous loss of bronze to the system, suggesting that 'different interest groups were competing for access to the same materials but using them in different ways'. The thrust of this discussion is thus to attempt to understand the overall context of the creation, use and deposition of bronzework in arriving at an interpretation of the phenomenon of hoarding. Were river depositions a new alternative to grave deposition? Were 'ritual' depositions of bronzes, such as the great find of bronzes (notably pins) deposited in a pot at Villethierry, Yonne (northern France), really different from 'smithing' or 'foundry' hoards? Detailed study of the types discovered in such finds suggests that the differences are less great than has sometimes been imagined. Furthermore, certain tool types (axes, sickles) appear to be 'over-represented', that is, present more often than would be expected simply from their assumed commonness in Bronze Age times. Did changes in other parts of the living system, for instance changes in settlement to encompass fortified sites, and the increasing role played by exotic objects that were perhaps part of a gift exchange system, correlate with increasing occurrence of hoard deposition?[36] River finds may have operated as funeral gifts but also as offerings to the supernatural, and as a means for mourners to 'stake a claim' by 'fixing status' and 'claim prestige associated with the deceased'. By this means, the Late Bronze Age in western Europe saw the establishment of a new system of metal deposits similar to that found in central Europe in the previous period, its adoption going hand in hand with 'the mobilisation of productive resources [new agricultural systems] and the adoption of defensive architecture'.[37]

On occasion, it has been possible to examine the deposition circumstances of hoards through excavation. In a recent French example, at Marchésieux (Manche) some 60 'Breton' socketed axes had been found in 1961, and a further source was discovered during agricultural operations in 1976 (fig. 10.4). Geophysical prospection carried out subsequently in the same field detected no fewer than six separate hoards in addition to the two already known.[38] The best preserved of these was hoard B, where the axes had been buried in a hole cut in the peat and a covering of branches and planks provided over the top. In total, well over 400 axes were found, and it is suggested that the separate hoards represent different groupings of axes of approximately equivalent value or status: hoards A, B and C numbering 150 axes, hoards D, E and F 153. It is further suggested that the distribution of the hoards in the field is significant, perhaps relating to a path crossing the bog.

Breton socketed axes have often been supposed to represent a form of currency, or to encapsulate metal for exchange,[39] but in the case of Marchésieux (the only one where detailed observations of the true disposition in the ground are available) the appearance is much more like that of the later Snettisham gold and silver torc hoards. It is ironic, therefore, that these magnificent collections have been interpreted not as votive but as treasure buried in time of

---

[36] 'The key to understanding the Later Bronze Age deposits in Western Europe probably lies with the interpretation of earlier grave-goods. These can be regarded, not necessarily as the property of the deceased, but as a specific set of gifts provided by the survivors' (ibid., 135).
[37] Ibid., 142.
[38] Verron 1983; Tabbagh and Verron 1983.
[39] Briard 1965, 242ff., 270f.

trouble.[40] It would appear from this that Iron Age scholarship has yet to run the debate over hoard deposition that the Bronze Age has already seen.

Conclusion

The sheer volume of bronze hoards dating to the Bronze Age, and especially to its second half, makes extended discussion of their function inevitable, if inconclusive. Minute examination of hoard composition and context in various geographical and chronological situations has demonstrated that there is good evidence for the existence of structuring principles in the process of deposition. Particular combinations of objects were deposited, some in specifically defined spots, whether on dry land or in wet places. Debate continues over the function of hoards, even those which appear to be unequivocally industrial in nature. Certainly it seems possible to say that some hoards appear to have no utilitarian function, at least on the primary level of metal production and distribution. They may have had such a function in the eyes of their makers and users, but if this was psychological in origin, it is not possible to specify exactly what it may have been.

Instead, one can point with some exactitude to the details of deposition in terms of archaeological context, associations and technology. While these cannot in themselves answer the higher order questions that need to be asked, they do provide an increasingly sophisticated means of specifying the parameters within which hoard deposition proceeded, in a period when, it would seem, 'everybody did it'.

[40] Stead 1991.

CHAPTER 11

PEOPLE

For all the apparent lack of personal information that is available on the people of the European Bronze Age, much can be said about their appearance and identity as expressed through dress and ornament. One of the most abundant categories of material to survive is human skeletal material; another is the depictions of people and the remains of their clothing and ornaments. This chapter considers some of the types of evidence that provide information on the human beings who lived in the period and whose handwork, homes and graves have been examined in previous chapters.

Appearance

In terms of physical build, skeletal material gives good information on stature and robustness, and some indication of morphological features such as head shape. With the exception of the Ice Man, the reconstruction of facial characteristics has not yet had any impact on the buried people of Copper and Bronze Age Europe other than in Greece, but this line of approach has obvious potential.[1]

Artistic depictions of people are of uncertain value, because naturalistic representation was frequently not the artist's aim. Thus one can no more imagine that all young men were the slender creatures seen in the Grevensvænge figurines than that people in the Camonica valley were stick figures. Where there is equipment for fastening on or attachment to the body, such as rings, bracelets, corslets or helmets, all the indications are that size and physical type were not greatly different from those of modern populations; certainly the degree of variation is unlikely to have been much different from what can be seen at the present day.

The figurines from Sardinia, Sweden and elsewhere (for instance the cult wagon from Strettweg) perhaps give the most vivid impression of Bronze Age people (fig. 11.1). Those from Sardinia, with their depictions of chieftains and warriors, shepherds and wrestlers, men and (much less commonly) women, are an especially interesting and unusual source of information on what the people of Nuragic Sardinia actually looked like. Equally, the curious acrobat

---

[1] Prag and Neave 1997.

Fig. 11.1. Sardinian bronze figurines (after Lilliu 1966).

Fig. 11.2. Dress in Bronze Age Denmark, male and female. *Left:* the Muldbjerg 'chieftain'; *right:* the Egtved girl. Photos: National Museum Copenhagen.

figurines of Scandinavia, apparently depicting people executing a back-flip (shown on the rock art happening in some cases in or beside boats), surely represent real Bronze Age people engaged in real activities, whether sport, leisure, or ceremonial.

The principal sources of information on Bronze Age clothing are surviving garments, mainly from Nordic coffin graves, the devices used to fasten clothing (fibulae, pins and buttons), and artistic depictions, in two or in three dimensions. An important accompaniment to the clothing was the ornaments that adorned parts of the body or the surface of the clothing; it is these items that constitute the largest single body of evidence available, since they were usually made of metal and therefore survived where clothing has not. The clothing from coffin graves, mainly in Denmark, has been the subject of intensive study over a long period (fig. 11.2).[2] Males in these coffins, which mostly belong to Period II, wear a kilt-like tunic, sometimes a loin-cloth, a cloak, cap and leather shoes consisting of an oblong or square piece of leather cut

[2] Glob 1974; Broholm and Hald 1935/1940; Broholm 1942.

into flaps at the toes, with the lace pulled through and round the foot. The Guldhøj barrow contained part of a cloth shoe with sewn-on leather sole. Females wear either a corded skirt and jacket (Egtved) or a blouse and long skirt, a belt with bronze disc, socks and leather shoes, and also a hair-band or hair-net. Much attention has been focused on the more unusual garments, for instance the skirt worn by the young woman in the Egtved mound, formed of a continuous twisted cord looped up and down and gathered at the bottom; it was short (well above knee length), but wound twice round the body – the wearer presumably compensated for chilliness of calves and knees brought about by the shortness of the mini-skirt by making sure her upper thighs were warm. An element of Scandinavian dress was formed by the bronze hanging-bowls that form a regular part of the grave-goods of Period IV. These have been seen as a means of gathering the folds of a dress on the back; the tutulus (disc with protruding knob) was used for a similar purpose at the front.[3]

The figurines give additional information about dress, mostly female.[4] The short corded skirt is shown a number of times: these individuals seem to have worn little else except ornaments, but it is likely that they are depictions of special people or special activities, not of everyday wear. These figures also indicate that the hair was elaborately coiffured and held in place with a band or net, just as has been found in the Borum Eshøj grave.[5] The figures from Cîrna and elsewhere on the lower Danube also imply an elaborate coiffure, though the stylised nature of the pieces makes its identification difficult (fig. 11.3).[6]

The depictions on rock art are much more vague about what people wore. Some of the figures from Bohuslän could be wearing tunics (for instance those that are shown with a square upper body), but really it is only their helmets and shields that are at all obvious, and the fact that most are phallic might imply they were naked or almost so. In the Camonica valley, most depictions show no certain clothing, but a few have apparently special items such as robes with projecting plumage. The dating of these is, however, very uncertain; they could be from well into the Iron Age.[7]

As is known now from the Ice Man find,[8] tattooing was practised in the Chalcolithic, and the Pazyryk finds show that it was also practised in the Scythian Iron Age; no doubt it was done at other places and periods also. Depictions on rock or other art may well be intended to represent body decoration of this kind, but *in corpore* Bronze Age examples do not seem to exist.

[3] Henning-Almgren 1952.
[4] Broholm and Hald 1935/1940, 152; Larsson 1974, 196.
[5] Broholm and Hald 1935/1940, 73f.
[6] Dumitrescu 1961.
[7] Anati 1961, 184–5, 190, 241.
[8] Spindler 1994, 167ff.

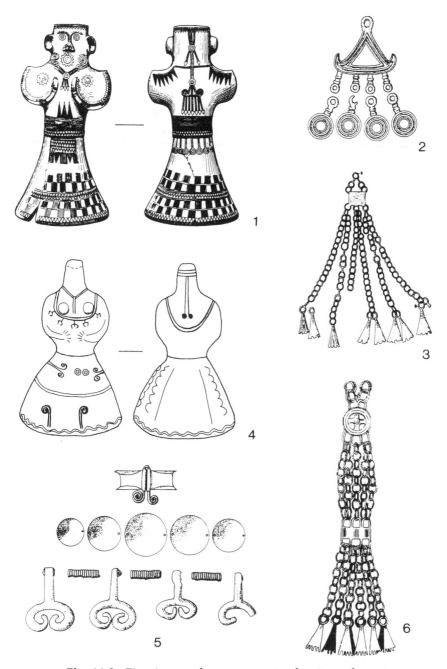

Fig. 11.3. Figurines and ornaments in the Carpathian Basin.
1. Kličevac, Smederevo (Serbia). 2. Gaj, Banat (Serbia), hoard.
3. Ciocaia, Săcueni (Romania), hoard. 4. Korbovo-Glamija, Zaječar
(Serbia). 5. Ornament set from Nagybátony, Nograd (Hungary),
grave 873. 6. Kemecse, Szabolcs-Szatmár (Hungary), hoard.
Source: Schumacher-Matthäus 1985.

There is, however, abundant information on the ornaments, mostly bronze, which people wore on their persons. Every cemetery, and a large proportion of the graves in those cemeteries, contains such information, though identifying regularities and associating them with specific practices and groups of people is another matter. Again, depictions sometimes provide a clear source of evidence: some of the Scandinavian figurines wear earrings and neckrings, while the Cîrna figures wear necklaces, pendants and other ornaments.[9]

It is important to know whether these ornaments were used randomly or in a structured fashion, for instance whether there were particular rules about which ornaments were appropriate to which people or circumstances. Specifically, were there particular sets or groupings of ornaments that went together and that were considered appropriate to particular circumstances? In Scandinavia, Levy demonstrated how 'sumptuary sets' were created and used, by the regular association of particular artefact types in graves and hoards; these probably marked social positions through their use as display items on the person.[10] Different sets marked out males from females, and the sets differed at different periods of the Bronze Age. In Period II, for instance, the association of the belt-plate with various other forms, singly or combined – dagger, tutulus, armring, neckring – formed such a set; in Period IV, the fibula and armring formed a commonly found set, or the hanging vessel with one or more of belt-plate, fibula, armring or neckring. Comparable data are available for other periods. Similarly, male and especially female clothing and ornament in Middle Bronze Age graves in the Lüneburg area exhibit regularities that probably derive from the use of such sets.[11]

These ornament sets are by no means confined to the Nordic world or the earlier Bronze Age. Kytlicová showed how specific ornament sets were placed in graves in the early Urnfield period, consisting of particular combinations of finger- and armring, bracelet, buttons and so on.[12] In the Urnfield and Hallstatt periods in Bavaria, it has been shown that what were formerly interpreted in cremation graves simply as bracelets can now be seen to have been worn in sets or in pairs, reflecting the wearing of one or several rings on each leg.[13] The number of rings worn appears to have chronological significance for the different areas, showing continuity from Ha B into Ha C, and probably also symbolic significance in that the wearing of sets of rings reflected more than mere fashion.

Interesting studies have also been conducted on the way in which ornament sets and types were specific to particular areas, so that when an example occurs outside its home area one may presume an intentional movement

[9] Schumacher-Matthäus 1985, 6ff.
[10] Levy 1982, 69ff.
[11] Laux 1981.
[12] Kytlicová 1981.
[13] Schopper 1993.

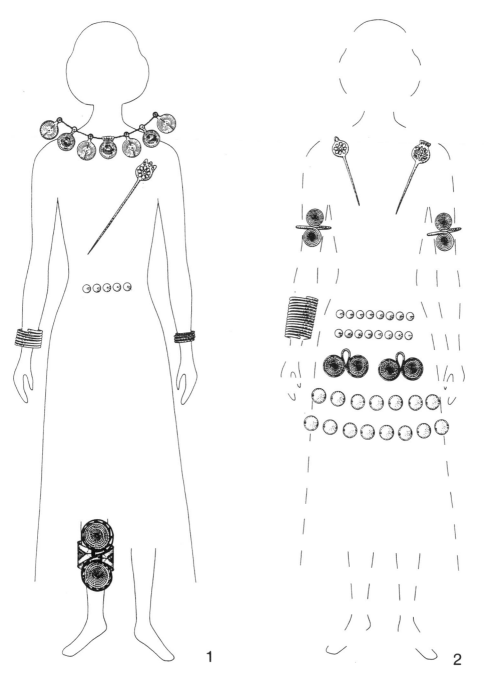

Fig. 11.4. Reconstructions of female ornament sets from graves of the Tumulus culture. 1. 'Rhine–Main grouping', with disc pendants (Bayerseich, Darmstadt, Hesse, tumulus 25 grave 1). 2. 'Fulda-Werra grouping', with spectacle spirals (Thundorf, Bad Kissingen, Bavaria). Source: Wels-Weyrauch 1989a.

of goods or people. The work of Wels-Weyrauch has been influential in this respect, determining the particular ornament styles of female graves in a series of Middle Bronze Age groups (fig. 11.4).[14] Regular associations of ornaments lead to the assumption that particular dress 'schemes' or rules are involved, consisting of pins, neck and chest ornaments, waist or hip ornaments, and arm-, finger- and leg-rings. Some adjacent groups practised very similar dress rules; others showed marked differences. What is not clear is the extent to which such differences are a matter of custom in given areas rather than the differentiation of particular individuals through wealth or other special status. The differences between graves with necklaces of pendants and those with long pins is a striking case in point. Jockenhövel has also made use of these data, assuming that the appearance of ornaments outside their home area reflects the movement of women in marriage between adjacent groups of people (p. 408).[15] The pattern of Middle Bronze Age ornament sets in the Carpathian Basin is also interesting (fig. 11.3).[16] They included diadems (forehead ornaments), pendants, head and back ornaments, neckrings, chest ornaments, leg-guards and spiral hand-guards. The latter seem to be male, some of the other ornaments (notably the diadems) female. The statistics provided give clear indications that particular sub-sets of this extensive range of equipment were used, frequently including one or two especially common items such as leg- or arm-guards and a selection from the rest.

Other studies have shown that Urnfield groups also adopted similar practices, though in general in a period where cremation was the norm detailed information of this sort is not to be expected. At Grundfeld (Lichtenfels, northern Bavaria) there were both inhumation and cremation burials, and a number of these were marked by especial attention to the head, grave 2/1983 being provided with a series of spirally wound wire ornaments that have been reconstructed to form a diadem (fig. 11.5).[17] Other graves possessed elaborate ornaments for the head, chest, neck or fingers. In a small cemetery like this it is impossible to say whether these individuals were out of the ordinary. These practices might represent local variations on a more general theme, and without more detailed information should be treated with some caution. What is certain is that in many phases of the Bronze Age, Early, Middle and Late, rules obtained through which individuals expressed their own and their group's identity.

[14] Wels-Weyrauch 1978; 1989a.
[15] Jockenhövel 1991.
[16] Schumacher-Matthäus 1985.
[17] Feger and Nadler 1985.

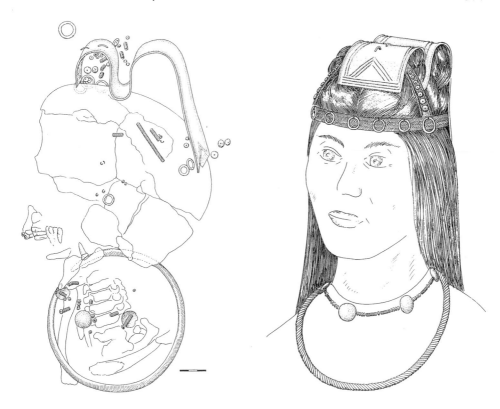

Fig. 11.5. Grave 2/1983 at Grundfeld, Bavaria: skull and ornaments as found (*left*) and reconstruction (*right*). Source: Feger and
Nadler 1985.

Mortality and health

A systematic modern study of Bronze Age populations from the point of view
of demography and mortality remains to be written, though a recent compilation includes much important material in this regard.[18] At present one can
only use studies of individual sites or groups of sites, though these suffer from
the fact that they frequently differ in methodology and deal with very small
numbers of people.

  As with most prehistoric populations, people in the Bronze Age did not live
long. Disease, whether chronic such as arthritis, or epidemic, such as viral
infections, must have been prevalent at all times and places. Mortality studies invariably show a pattern whereby perinatal and infant mortality was
extremely high and child mortality high; for those who survived into their
teens, the chances of making it into adulthood were quite good, but by the

---

[18] Rittershofer 1997.

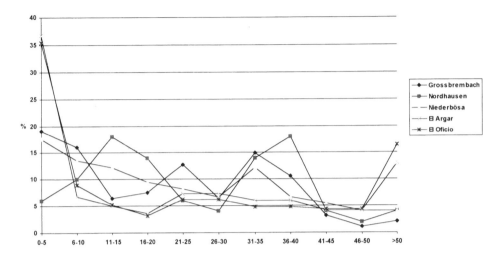

Fig. 11.6. Mortality curves for various Early Bronze Age populations. The percentage of individuals represented in the cemeteries
is recorded for a series of age groups. Note that the two Spanish
curves run closely in parallel, with a very high number of infant
deaths and around 15% of the population dying over the age of
50; at other ages there was a roughly even mortality. By contrast,
the three German sites have peaks of mortality at varying ages,
with most of the population dying by the age of 40. Age brackets
on x axis.

age of 35 the odds against further survival increased dramatically. People older
than 45 were unusual. This can be demonstrated from the analysis of El Argar,
where a large sample (563 individuals) was studied: life expectancy at birth
was 19.9 years, but at age 20 it was still a further 15.9 years;[19] the figures for
Grossbrembach and Velika Gruda are not dissimilar.[20] Brothwell estimated
an average lifespan for British Bronze Age males of 31.3 years and for females
of 29.9 years, with only 3.3% surviving beyond 50.[21]

Such information is concentrated in those areas and periods where burial
was by inhumation and in sizeable cemeteries (chapter 3), which rules out
large parts of the potential field of study. In practice, most studies have been
conducted on flat inhumation cemeteries of the Early Bronze Age in central
Europe, the principal area that satisfies the criteria, though the cemeteries of
the El Argar culture have also been studied.[22] Figure 11.6 illustrates mortality curves for a series of typical Early Bronze Age cemeteries, in which central European populations can be seen to have had a rather different age profile
from Iberian ones.

[19] Kunter 1990, 103.
[20] Ullrich 1972; Della Casa 1995; 1996a.
[21] Brothwell 1972, 83.
[22] Walker 1985; Kunter 1990.

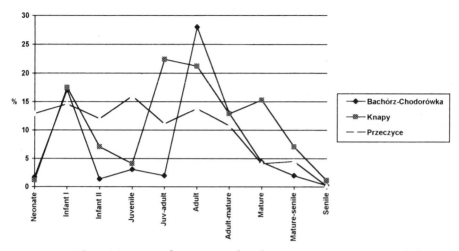

Fig. 11.7. Mortality curves for three Late Bronze Age Polish populations. The low number of infants represented at Bachórz and Knapy must indicate that infants were not buried in these cemeteries. Note too the steep decline in the curve from category 'adult' onwards, with hardly any people living beyond the age of 50.

By contrast, there are few Late Bronze Age cemeteries with anthropological determinations because of the prevalence of cremation in the period. In some cases, age and sex determination has been possible, but for the most part we depend on cemeteries where a sizeable part of the population was inhumed rather than cremated. One may question, therefore, to what extent the available data are representative. Figure 11.7 illustrates mortality curves for some Late Bronze Age populations; in these the low representation of infants is notable, suggesting that they were buried away from the adult cemetery.

Given the incidence of disease, the quality of life must in many cases have been poor. Those with chronic arthritis would have been in constant pain, and dependent on other members of the community for the maintenance of daily life. Even so 'minor' an affliction as tooth caries could have caused ongoing pain, while a tooth abscess could even have been life-threatening. Fourteen of the Grossbrembach adults had tooth caries, in some cases extensive. On Italian Bronze Age sites, the incidence varied from as little as 3.3% to as much as 19.7% of studied populations, and periodontal disease and dental hypoplasia were also found.[23] A large kidney-stone, 35 mm across and over 22 g in weight, was found in the pelvic area of a mature male from Csongrád-Felgyő.[24] No doubt people's tolerance of pain was higher than that of most

[23] Borgognini *et al.* 1995.
[24] Boross and Nemeskéri 1963.

people today; equally, there must also have been homely remedies and palliatives to ease the suffering. The contents of the purse carried by the man in the Hvidegård barrow have sometimes been seen as relevant in this context (see p. 321); the 'Ice Man' from the Hauslabjoch in the Tyrol carried a large mushroom on a string, believed to have healing properties.[25] A large range of herbal and homoeopathic remedies would have been available, some of which may have been quite effective. Hallucinogens and alcoholic drinks were probably used, then as now, to ease physical or mental pain. Surgery, in the form of trepanation (excision of a disc of bone from the skull), was practised frequently.[26] This was no doubt used to gain access to the brain and other internal cranial organs, perhaps in cases of severe pain or mental illness. It is hard to imagine that anyone actually profited from such an operation, undertaken without effective anaesthetics or infection control, but amazingly, some people survived it, since in some 'patients' the bone round the excision started to grow back. Such an operation was being conducted on a 30–year-old woman from grave 29 at Lauingen-'am Galgenberg', in order to treat an impression fracture from a violent blow to the skull, when the patient died on the operating table.[27]

Examples of pathological features deriving from chronic illness include spina bifida,[28] arthritis,[29] particularly of the vertebrae; inflammation-like changes in the bones of the hand;[30] and osteomyelitis.[31] An interesting interpretation is that relating to the incidence of Cribra orbitalia (spongy bone above the eye sockets);[32] it was present on 28% of 125 Italian Bronze Age individuals studied, and considered to be a reaction to parasitic infections that derive from animal breeding and in particular the consumption of untreated dairy products and cattle meat.[33] This feature was also present at El Argar and Gatas, where it is taken to be an indicator of blood iron deficiency, perhaps caused by malaria,[34] at Blučina in southern Moravia,[35] and at Franzhausen I, Gemeinlebarn F and Melk-Spielberg.[36]

---

[25] Spindler 1994, 113ff.
[26] Twice at Grossbrembach: Ullrich 1972. General discussions: Breitinger 1938; Piggott 1940; Jennbert 1991.
[27] Glowatzki and Schröter 1978.
[28] Grossbrembach: Ullrich 1972, 33.
[29] e.g. at Toppo Daguzzo: Borgognini et al. 1995; El Argar: Kunter 1990, 89; Gatas: Buikstra et al. 1995.
[30] Early Bronze Age skeleton from Ølmosehuse (Ringsted, Sorø): Bennike 1985, 199f.
[31] Toppo Daguzzo and other sites: Canci et al. 1991; 1992; Minozzi et al. 1994; Schöppingen: Trellisó Carreño 1996; Franzhausen I: Teschler-Nicola 1994.
[32] Hengen 1971.
[33] Minozzi et al. 1994; Borgognini et al. 1995.
[34] Kunter 1990, 88f.; Buikstra et al. 1995.
[35] Smrčka et al. 1988.
[36] Teschler-Nicola 1994.

Population estimates and demography

In general, it is not in doubt that Bronze Age communities were by today's standards small, as the extent of settlements and the size of cemeteries both testify. The methods for estimating population size are well established.[37] In the present context, the majority of information comes from cemetery studies. These give indications of group size and organisation. When one moves on to consider larger areas, such as tribal areas or quasi-political territories, estimates become much more speculative.

The Early Bronze Age cemetery of Singen is divided into distinct zones (fig. 3.3).[38] Assuming that each zone represented the burial area of a family or extended family, and with each zone containing 20 graves or so, a kin-based group numbering six could have provided sufficient deaths within 100 years. The radiocarbon dates for the Singen cemetery indicate a use life of some 200 years, so that the rate of deposition was not especially fast, reflecting rather the small population that was feeding into it. At Těšetice-Vinohrady the excavator suggested that with a duration for the cemetery of 30 years and a family of 3–4 people making 9–10 burials per 100 years, the cemetery might have been used by 19–20 families, each burying a couple of their members during the period.[39] In fact, 20 families of 4 people, each containing a male and female of reproductive age, would be likely to generate significantly more than 2 deaths in 30 years. Any adults alive at the beginning of the period would be dead at the end of it, and there would be progressively more chance of deaths occurring by the end of the period the nearer the start of it people were born.

Other inhumation cemeteries of the Early Bronze Age in central Europe have provided fruitful material for analysis. Thus the population reconstructed from the 714 graves (757 individuals) at Franzhausen I, assuming a use life of 300 years, would be 68.[40] At Gemeinlebarn F, the estimated population from the 258 buried individuals, assuming a cemetery life of 80 years, was at least 83,[41] or rather less if the cemetery life was longer; at Pitten it was 31.[42] Similar methods have been used at El Argar to arrive at figures of 40–60 for Phase A and 106–136 for Phase B;[43] and at Velika Gruda to suggest a living population of 28–35 individuals, or a village of 6 nuclear families of 5–6 individuals each.[44]

---

[37] Acsádi and Nemeskéri 1957; Welinder 1979; Hassan 1981.

[38] Krause 1988.

[39] Lorencová, Beneš and Podborský 1987. Such figures depend on an average life expectancy rather higher than is usually used for pre-modern societies, not least because children are severely under-represented.

[40] Berner 1997; 31 if a use life of 600 years is assumed. See too Teschler-Nicola and Prossinger 1997.

[41] Heinrich and Teschler-Nicola in Neugebauer 1991, 234.

[42] Teschler-Nicola 1982–5, 219.

[43] Kunter 1990, 116.

[44] Della Casa 1995; 1996a (the method applied also to other cemeteries in the Balkans).

In the late Lausitz cemetery at Sobiejuchy (site 2), central Poland, 745 individuals were recovered from some 518 graves; after allowing for destroyed
graves, children, and other factors, a total buried population of 1420 is arrived
at.[45] If the length of time over which the cemetery was used was 50 years
(probably too little), the living population might have numbered 600. The
nearby fortified site suggests that a short lifespan for the cemetery is likely,
and that a large population was resident (cf. p. 53). These figures, from the
end of the Bronze Age and start of the Iron Age, are of a different order from
those from earlier in the Bronze Age.

Turning to settlement data, Rageth estimated the population of Early Bronze
Age Padnal at 40–50, rising to 60–70 in the Early Middle Bronze Age and
80–90 in the Late Bronze Age.[46] Taking into account other settlements in the
immediate vicinity, a figure of 140–200 is arrived at for the population of the
Savognin region. Estimates for the population of Biskupin have ranged from
600–800 to 1000–1250.[47] Assuming that there were around 104 houses and
that a house served as the dwelling for a single family, such estimates seem
reasonable.

From this, it is evident that, at least in the Early and Middle Bronze Age
in central Europe, group size, that is the population of a single site, was typically a few tens or scores. In the agglomerated sites of south-east Spain, it
probably achieved a rather larger figure than this, certainly in the later stages
of the Argaric Bronze Age, and in central Europe at the end of the Bronze Age
group sizes of several hundred are likely.

A variety of methods have been used to arrive at population estimates for
larger-scale territories, for instance what one may interpret as tribal areas.
Atkinson's assumption of an average 3 burials per barrow was applied to the
area around Milton Keynes, but the population this produced was considered
far too low.[48] If we take instead a hypothetical figure of 10 persons per km^2
for each of the 350 km^2 in question, and assuming that only a certain proportion of the population were buried in barrows (1 in 44), there would have
been a barrow density of 3 per km^2, and they would have been constructed
at a rate of 1.44 per generation. These figures are highly speculative, and only
results from areas with better preservation will enable them to be tested.

Work on barrow densities in Sweden has made similar assumptions.[49]
Assuming the same original buried population of three individuals per barrow, and making various assumptions about the relationship of that buried
population and the contemporary living population, a range between 155 and
465 individuals for the 60 km^2 area around Ystad in southern Sweden is

[45] Ostoja-Zagórski and Strzałko 1984.
[46] Rageth 1997.
[47] Rajewski 1950; Ostoja-Zagórski 1974; Piotrowski 1995.
[48] Atkinson 1972; Green 1974.
[49] Olausson 1992, 260.

arrived at; if the settlement group size was 10, between 16 and 47 groups (individual farmsteads, such as at Fosie IV – p. 423) would have been present.

Brothwell suggests a population density for Britain in the Bronze Age of 5 persons per square mile and a total population range of 20,000–100,000.[50] Given what is now known about the extent of human interference with the environment in the period, in the form of both lowland and upland field systems, and the vast number of burial sites, even the upper of these two figures seems rather low. In Polish Pomerania a total population in the Late Bronze Age of 30,000 for the 5 analysed 'macroregions' has been suggested, using a figure of 3 persons per km², which translates into a living population at any one time of around 1200.[51] The total population of the Lausitz group (defined as the relevant parts of Germany and Poland), with a total area of 30,555 km², has been estimated as lying between 97,500 and 195,000.[52] Similar principles have been applied to the Terramara region of north Italy, where figures of some 18,000 in the MBA 2 period, rising to 29,000 in MBA 3, and at least 31,000 in the Late Bronze Age, have been arrived at.[53]

All of these are guesses, based on assumptions about population density at the level of the site and the number of sites co-existing at any one time. They do, nevertheless, provide a starting point from which to approach the problem. If it is right to imagine that the territory of Slovakia could have been occupied by around 200,000 people at the start of the Late Bronze Age, based on a growing population density from 1.3 to 3.5 people per km², then continental Europe as a whole must have been home to several million people. To take just Germany and France on this basis, the area of around 900,000 km² could have had a population of up to 3 million people in the Late Bronze Age, which might suggest 10 million or more in the continent as a whole as far east as the Bug – and that relates to only a single generation, or half century at most. It is therefore hardly surprising that sites and monuments of the Bronze Age are abundant, or that the remains of buried individuals from the period turn up with frequency.

Genetic origins

In earlier years, scholars were optimistic that the study of skeletal remains would yield information about the origins and development of the population in a given area, or indeed across the Old World. In the time-scale under review here, particular attention focused on the nature of the 'Beaker people', in other words the people who made and used Beaker pottery; major differences in skull type from previous Neolithic populations were commonly

---

[50] Brothwell 1972, 79.
[51] Ostoja-Zagórski 1982.
[52] Buck 1997.
[53] Cardarelli 1997; see too Furmánek 1997 for Slovakia.

interpreted as supporting the idea that 'Beaker people' were intrusive newcomers on the European scene.[54] Although more recently such interpretations have become rarer, it is still the case that many physical anthropologists assign skulls to broad groups depending on their shape (Nordic, Mediterranean, Armenoid, Palaeoeuropoid, Cromagnoid, etc.).[55] But most cemeteries produced a mixture of types, and nowadays the implications of these physical characteristics are regarded as very uncertain. A study of physical types in central Germany found that for most skull indices and measurements there were no significant differences between any of the prehistoric groups studied, from Early Neolithic to Early Bronze Age.[56] Only the Beaker individuals differed, and then only on two indices, which, it is argued, could have occurred through natural processes. Whereas Ullrich had argued that the Early Bronze Age population of Grossbrembach was markedly different from the local Copper Age groups and therefore had to be derived from the much more similar Únětician populations of Bohemia and Moravia,[57] it has now been shown convincingly that the Grossbrembach individuals are in fact statistically indistinguishable from most other populations and very close morphologically to local Corded Ware groups. This study indicates the unwisdom of attempting very much in the way of population genetics for European Bronze Age populations with traditional methods. A statistical treatment of a variety of index data has been attempted,[58] but such use of indices for statistical manipulation, and for the drawing of genetic conclusions, has been subjected to fierce criticism.[59] Whether more modern techniques, such as DNA analyses, will resolve such issues remains to be seen. Trace element analysis of bone may help studies of diet and nutrition, though hopes have been expressed that it could also be of use for more general issues in a Bronze Age context.[60]

Conclusion

The frustrations which are brought about by the general paucity of evidence on individuals in Bronze Age archaeology are mitigated both by the abundance of human skeletal material and by the extensive range of artefacts of a 'personal' nature. While study of the former still has a long way to go before conclusions of more than site-specific validity can be expected, advances in

---

[54] Notably Gerhardt 1953; supported too by data in Brothwell (1972, 81), and considered further in Brodie 1994.
[55] Examples of such work in a Bronze Age context include the studies by Jelínek 1959, Gerhardt 1964, Riquet 1970, Ullrich 1972, Miszkiewicz 1972 and Česnys 1991.
[56] Bach et al. 1972.
[57] H. Ullrich, unpublished dissertation (1962) cited by Bach et al. 1972.
[58] Schwidetzky and Rösing 1989.
[59] Walker 1985.
[60] Kaufmann 1996.

artefact studies mean that much can be inferred regarding the relationship between production, use and deposition by these prehistoric populations. It is ironic that one can sometimes tell the year, even the month, in which a Bronze Age person died, but not her/his name or what they looked like. Nevertheless, the materials for the physical study of Bronze Age people are extensive and show considerable potential for the future.

CHAPTER 12

SOCIAL ORGANISATION

In most of what has been presented in this book so far, the discussion has revolved around patterns of material culture and their relationship to various categories of human activity. This chapter, by contrast, is concerned with social inference; in other words, it seeks to elicit an interpretation of social aspects of the Bronze Age from the material culture. By 'social' aspects I mean the way society was structured, how power relations worked, how individuals operated within and reproduced the accepted norms of behaviour in their relations with others and with their residence or kin group, and how they expressed their identity in terms of gender, age and status. In the context of European Bronze Age archaeology, the sources of evidence for social organisation are few and capable of different interpretations. Despite the fact that material forms such as artefacts and sites cannot have occurred in a social vacuum, the reconstruction of a social past is inevitably based on the observer's subjective and experiential understanding of potential modes and means of organisation. In spite of the difficulties, it is therefore necessary to consider the implications involved in the creation of the material data, in terms of the articulation of society as a living entity.[1] Since the archaeological record consists of artefacts, it is the role of artefacts that forms the basis of the discussion that follows.

The reconstruction of a social past, for the Bronze Age as for other periods, has gone through a number of phases. In the first half of the twentieth century, when material culture was seen as all-important, a deep scepticism prevailed that social reconstruction was possible at all, at least in any form that could be related to the material evidence (as opposed to assumptions based on historical analogies). The oft-cited 'ladder of inference' of Hawkes exemplifies this position.[2] With the 1970s and the rise of processual archaeology came a belief that the collection and appropriate analysis of data would enable archaeologists to give answers to questions of social organisation, for instance the nature and extent of ranking, as revealed through the

---

[1] One attempt at writing a 'history of social structure' for prehistory and early history is by Steuer (1982); in that work, however, the account of Bronze Age social structure is little more than a backcloth against which the developments of the Merovingian and Carolingian periods can be viewed.
[2] Hawkes 1954.

differential provision of grave-goods in cemeteries. This standpoint assumes that such provision reflects wealth in life and therefore social standing; other correlates were also suggested.[3] More recently, doubts have been expressed that such procedures are relevant to the understanding of ancient societies. The point has been made that the study of mortuary variability as a reflection of the degree of organisational complexity of ancient society, a common procedure of processual archaeology, treats culture as if it were a static entity, taking a snapshot of it when what is really relevant is the nature of social reproduction, the means by which individuals acquire knowledge of what society is and reproduce it through their actions by engaging in a series of 'discourses' with their fellows.[4] The archaeologist interested in pursuing this line of enquiry will concentrate not on evidence purporting to indicate ranking or the reverse (e.g. differential provision of grave-goods) but on material that can be interpreted as indicating the structuring of behaviour within the various 'fields of discourse' (for instance the form, style and placing of artefacts).[5] Thus recent years have seen a return to the study of material culture for understanding past human behaviour, though the methods used have been very different from those of earlier generations.

A middle way has to be found between an approach based purely on artefacts and sites and one based on speculation derived primarily from a desire to be novel, interesting and 'relevant'. Likewise, a balance must be struck between the use of analogy for the reconstruction of the prehistoric past and the generation and interpretation of data directly from the sources under review. A number of complementary approaches will thus feed in to a successful interpretation of Bronze Age society: at the heart lies the archaeological record, the artefacts on which knowledge of the Bronze Age is based. This collection of artefacts is exploited initially by means of typology, that is, ordering the mass of data into usable categories. The study of material culture as text, of context, of higher-order divisions of the Bronze Age world (such as World Systems Theory: see chapter 13) and of analogy all draw on that central pool of artefactual data, while simultaneously providing the means to modify interpretations of it.

Social structure can thus be viewed at a number of different scales, ranging from the position of the individual to the nature of 'political' groupings. Most studies of the Bronze Age have related to the smaller scale of analysis, particularly where mortuary data are concerned, but a number of influential studies have been concerned with 'macroscopic' issues, the larger-scale units and the place of Bronze Age communities within them. The procedure to be adopted here will be to move from the 'macro' to the 'micro' level, from larger to smaller units.

---

[3] Peebles and Kus 1977.
[4] Barrett, Bradley and Green 1991, 120.
[5] Barrett 1988b.

Analogies in ethnography and history: types of early complex society

When the type of social and political organisation that obtained in the Bronze Age is being considered, the first port of call for many is the work of ethnographers on modern societies that are, or may be presumed to be, comparable in complexity to those of prehistory. In this the work of American anthropologists has been especially influential, notably Service with his distinction between band, tribe and chiefdom organisation,[6] but more recently Johnson and Earle, who distinguish between family-level groups, local groups (including acephalous groups and the 'Big Man collectivity') and regional polities, including chiefdoms and states.[7] These are based on a mixture of group size and social and economic complexity. It is not necessary to imagine that every facet that Service includes need have been present in any particular society in the past to see value in these categories. Empirically speaking, it seems that group size increased over time in the ancient past, and it is likely that social complexity grew correspondingly. This does not mean that tribe A was structurally the same as tribe B in the past any more than today, but the use of the term 'tribe' provides a convenient form of readily understood shorthand.

Thus, bands represent the smallest and culturally the most basic form of social organisation, based on hunting and foraging for wild food, organised on the basis of family groups and therefore numbering no more than tens or scores of individuals. They provide no evidence for economic or religious organisation transcending the local level: 'no special economic groups or special productive units such as guilds or factories, no specialized occupational groups, no economic institutions such as markets, no special consuming groups or classes . . . There is no separate political life and no government or legal system above the modest informal authority of family heads and ephemeral leaders. Likewise, there is no religious organization standing apart from family and band.' By contrast, a tribe consists of a larger number of 'economically self-sufficient residential groups which because of the absence of higher authority take unto themselves the private right to protect themselves . . . leadership is personal – charismatic – and for special purposes only . . . there are no political offices containing real power'.[8] Within this 'segmental' organisation there is an increase in specialisation in craft production and religious practice.

Chiefdoms, then, represent a somewhat more complex level of organisation.[9] A chiefdom is a 'polity that organises centrally a regional population in the thousands', more densely populated than simple segmented tribes, usu-

[6] Service 1962/1975.
[7] Johnson and Earle 1987.
[8] Service 1962/1975, 98.
[9] Ibid.; Sahlins 1968; Carneiro 1981; 1991; Earle 1987; 1991; 1997.

ally with evidence of inheritable social ranking and economic stratification, and central places 'which coordinate economic, social and religious activities'. Here, religious observance and control are major features of the maintenance of the status quo. The system is a hierarchical one that can be expressed in the form of a pyramid, with large numbers of labouring peasants or other workers at the base and a few powerful or rich individuals at the apex. The higher population is made possible through greater productivity associated with craft specialisation and redistribution. Developed chiefdoms are thus not unlike simple states, the last level of organisation postulated in the evolutionary hierarchy of social development, but in a European context there is no evidence that could be interpreted as reflecting a state level of organisation until the late pre-Roman Iron Age.

It will be evident from this that most Bronze Age groups would fall into the category of tribe, some of the simple segmented form, some more complex and qualifying for the label 'chiefdom'. Clearly they were larger and more complex than band societies. Equally clearly, they were not states; they fall somewhere in between. Some commentators have preferred to avoid terms like 'tribe', which carry superstructural connotations that may not be appropriate, or which are inadequate on other grounds.[10] Instead, they have found it safer to focus on the method by which authority was exercised and control organised. It is admittedly easier to envisage the exercise of control in a period such as the Neolithic or Copper Age, when the majority of the great megalithic and related monuments were erected. Such works self-evidently require a decision to erect them in the first place, and, once the construction is under way, they need regulating. But even though monument-building in this sense was a thing of the past by the time of the Bronze Age, it has usually been supposed that much the same organising principles would have applied, in other words society regulated itself through the mechanism of allowing certain individuals to achieve a special status and to use that status not only to obtain access to goods and valuables but also to act as leaders in decision-making, particularly where inter-group conflict was concerned. 'Chiefdoms' are the expression of this method of organisation. In other words, where there is evidence for ranking in the creation of artefacts and their provision in life or death, and where the economy can be shown to have been organised in such a way that there was differential access to goods, a chiefdom was probably the mode of social and political organisation. A further distinction suggested by Renfrew is between 'group-oriented' and 'individualising' chiefdoms.[11] The first were concerned with control in societies that undertook great communal enterprises such as megalith- or henge-building but which left few indications in the form of special burials with wealthy

[10] Such as the failure to consider language as a defining characteristic: Naroll 1964.
[11] Renfrew 1974.

grave-goods. The second, represented by the Bronze Age situation, saw the accumulation and display of wealth in the form of grave-goods, even though there is little in the way of communal monuments to reflect the power of those buried in this way.

How accurately do such labels reflect the apparent nature of Bronze Age society as it appears archaeologically? On the face of it, the chiefdom model appears to be a good way of describing the apparently hierarchical method of social organisation in Bronze Age Europe. Cemetery data often seem to reflect a situation where wealth was distributed unequally, with only a few graves containing the bulk of the valuables, and this is also reflected in the 'sumptuary' goods and hoards discussed above.[12] Prestige metalwork and other material objects were created, presumably for a 'rich' clientele; control of metal wealth has frequently been seen as intimately linked to social power.[13] In some areas, communal works were undertaken that would have required organisation and leadership. The rise of the elite and the aggrandisement of the few seem to be processes that are incontestably present in the period. But does that mean that society was organised as a chiefdom?

In recent years, this model has been increasingly criticised, both in general terms and in its applicability to later prehistory. The critique has centred on two main areas: on the one hand, the archaeological record does not always appear to illustrate the 'ideal' characteristics of chiefdoms as defined above; on the other, the methods by which chiefs would have acquired and maintained their elite status have been questioned. At the same time, the question of scale has been much discussed. How large were the areas over which chiefs had control? How constant did these areas stay? If in modern situations the scale can vary from the household level at the lowest to the 'interpolity' at the highest,[14] is it possible to generalise at all in the archaeological context? Could one actually distinguish between a regional chiefdom and a purely local one?

The 'ideal' chiefdom should have clear evidence of ranking, and this should presumably be expressed in both graves and settlement form. Yet the settlement record of Bronze Age Europe gives little or no indication that a hierarchical system was in operation. Settlements are very much like one another, and the houses on them are not generally differentiated in terms of size or richness of contents, nor does the subsistence evidence suggest marked differences in the way they functioned. Instead, one could be forgiven for believing that a system of small-scale settlement units, roughly equal to each other in size and resource availability, was the prevailing mode, similar to what has been described as characteristic of the tribal mode of organisation.

---

[12] Levy 1982, 69ff.
[13] e.g. most recently Earle 1997, 102 and elsewhere.
[14] Johnson and Earle 1987.

In answer to this, it has been suggested that what is in question is not a hierarchical system but a 'heterarchical' one, in which the system was either unranked or ranked in different ways.[15] So the organisation of society would not necessarily be ordered in a pyramidal structure, with a tribe composed of several villages, a village of several lineages, and a lineage of several households, each with its defined characteristics and spatial sphere of operation. Instead, an altogether more fluid mode of operation would be possible, with groups cross-cutting one another in a variety of different ways and on a variety of different levels. It is not altogether certain how such tendencies might manifest themselves in the archaeological record, other than that the evidence for ranking might not be consistently present, or that it might be evident in some areas and not in others.

If one accepts that ranked societies were a feature of European later prehistory, the question arises of how they were formed and how status distinctions were maintained. This matter has been much discussed in recent years.[16] Most authors have tended to view the rise of elites in functional terms, stressing the benefits they brought society at large. Thus decisions did need to be taken; wars did need to be waged and defence organised; the gods did need to be propitiated, or so people thought. For all these purposes, leaders were indispensable. But it is still unclear from such an analysis how individuals came to occupy positions of rank and authority in the first place. The distinction that has been drawn between the self-interest of elites and the needs of the community at large is a false one, since the interests of the masses need not have been at variance with the interests of the few. These interpretations recall those advanced for the origins of the state, one of which is the 'managerial', contending that leaders arose because of their decision-making role,[17] as opposed to the 'conflict' model in which higher-order socio-political groupings arose because of the demands of warfare and the need for defence.

It has been widely supposed that developing social complexity of this kind went hand in hand with developing technology and the resultant trend towards specialisation. Especially with the rise in importance of metals, a whole range of manufactured valuables became available that required the skill of a craftsman for their inherent value to be realised; they also provided a motor in the form of competition for resources.[18] Control of metal technology and control of the sources of metals may also have been factors in the process of elite emergence, as has often been suggested for phenomena such as the 'Wessex culture' of the southern English Early Bronze Age, though it has been questioned whether the scale of Bronze Age metal production in

[15] Crumley 1987; 1995; Levy 1995.
[16] e.g. Gilman 1981; 1991.
[17] Service 1962/1975; Wright 1977.
[18] See Shennan 1986.

Denmark would have been such as to provide the necessary stimulus towards hierarchisation.[19] Equally, developments in land use also have far-reaching social consequences, stretching from the first cultivation following tree clearance, through various intensification processes (manuring, double cropping, ploughing), to over-use and soil degradation, and eventually enclosure and division of land. The latter is as much a social as an economic effect, but it is uncertain which came first – or whether the two are actually separable.

In a much-cited work, Mann has detailed a number of pathways towards the creation of social power.[20] In particular, he has charted four 'sources and organizations of power': ideological, economic, military and political (IEMP), which in their different ways serve to transform groups of humans 'pursuing goals' into organisations dominated by power structures and powerful people. Although Mann has little to say about pre-state societies in Europe, his general approach is exemplified by his treatment of Stonehenge, which he recognises as representing the collective organisation of centralised authority, and as part of a cyclical process of fusion and fission among the social groups of prehistory.[21] Among essentially 'egalitarian' peoples, increasing intensity of interaction and population density can form larger settlement units with centralised, permanent authority; but if the persons in authority become 'overmighty, they are deposed. If they have acquired resources such that they cannot be deposed, the people turn their backs on them.'[22] This would indicate a large element of choice among prehistoric peoples, with social units able to create alternative networks and interactions.

It is debatable, even when using this relatively sophisticated model, whether one is really *explaining* the process of hierarchisation rather than *describing* it. In general terms there need be no doubt that the IEMP model is valid to describe the pathway from egalitarian societies in the hunter-gatherer (band) stage of social organisation to ranked societies (tribes and chiefdoms) in later prehistory. The four 'sources of power' and the interaction between them can in any analysis be anticipated. Effectively, one is free to speculate on which aspect played the more important role at each point along the route.

Certainly in recent years the tendency has been to play down the economic side of the argument and to stress instead the ideological (for instance the role of weaponry). The view that all social relations are founded in power has been pervasive, and it has become common for various aspects of prehistoric material culture to be interpreted as evidence of power relations. In this, control – of processes, of resources, of ritual – is all-important. It is interesting to note, however, that the simple statement and restatement of

[19] Levy 1991, *contra* Earle (1991; 1997).
[20] Mann 1986.
[21] Ibid., 63.
[22] Ibid., 68.

this fact is just as reductionist as most of the positions that it sought to criticise.

To conclude: assessing the status of Bronze Age societies in socio-political terms has been a preoccupation of many commentators over the last 50 years. Many of these assessments have been based on models advanced in ethnography, especially those emanating from the United States. Most scholars today agree that the band–tribe–chiefdom–state model is an oversimplification, though aspects of it, and particularly those pertaining to the chiefdom concept, are useful for an analysis of Bronze Age groups. Equally important is the analysis of the reasons for the rise to prominence of particular members of society, the 'sources of social power'. Here a combination of factors should be stressed, as in Mann's formulation. In spite of these theoretical advances, much remains to be understood, and in my opinion it is the study of material culture that will provide Bronze Age archaeology with the most important insights in the coming years.

Village, household and family: settlement evidence

Chapter 2 examined the various forms of settlement in Bronze Age Europe. This variability is presumed to reflect a real situation in prehistory, though there are considerable difficulties in interpreting the plans in social terms. The simple agricultural hamlets of Britain or Scandinavia offer very limited possibilities for social reconstruction. The size of these settlements alone indicates that in most cases only a single family group can have been involved. If Drewett's interpretation for Black Patch is accepted,[23] then individual round-houses may have served as residences for single individuals, a group of houses thus serving a family group. Differences in finds between houses might then indicate the different roles of different family members, for instance flint-knapping as opposed to spinning and weaving. In such instances, it is not special size or elaboration of the house structure itself that leads to inferences about chiefly dwellings.

In some of the cases where more extensive settlement plans are available (e.g. Lovčičky, p. 50), it is evident that large or elaborate structures were present. These were interpreted as long halls, perhaps for communal purposes, though some could also have served to differentiate households of differing social rank. Unfortunately, the published evidence on artefact distribution does not permit a judgement. The interpretation of separate units, small collections of houses arranged in oval groups with substantial open areas between the groups, strongly suggests a division of the site into socially or kinship-determined sub-units (always assuming that chronological differences are not responsible).

[23] Drewett 1979.

In enclosed and fortified sites, the evidence for social differentiation is little better. Both in lowland sites such as Biskupin or Senftenberg and in genuine hillforts such as the Wittnauer Horn house plans were undifferentiated.
Even the evidence from the Wasserburg at Bad Buchau, since its excavation
regarded as an indication of rank-based house differentiation, is hardly unambiguous; the slightly larger houses that Reinerth and others have interpreted
as chiefly can just as easily be interpreted in other, simpler, ways. Yet here
more than anywhere it would have been necessary for communal decisions
to be taken that would profoundly affect the whole community. Since the
period of hillforts is also one of increasing display in artefact terms (see below),
with a warrior society firmly in evidence, it seems clear that status distinctions were hardly, if at all, made manifest at the settlement level.

The identification of high-status settlements is not easy even in historical
periods. In Greek Bronze Age contexts it has been usual to identify 'palaces'
through their exceptional elaboration, but lower down the social scale differentiation is often controversial. On sites in Sicily and south Italy, where
some of the same conditions applied and where trade with the East
Mediterranean brought about marked social differences as seen in grave finds,
site plans are far from unambiguous in the social information they provide.
While the rectilinear features of Thapsos appear to echo grander buildings in
Greece, and may even contain elements of a palatial organisation (the site is
too eroded to be able to tell from the finds),[24] other Sicilian Bronze Age sites
offer little scope for such interpretations. A village like La Muculufa, for
instance (pp. 36f.), can have been little other than an agriculturally based ham-
let where those of higher rank expressed their position through means other
than house form or artefact accumulation. Even the 'anaktoron' at Pantalica,
sometimes regarded as a true palace, offers little real grounds for confidence
that the residence of elites has been found.[25]

The individual in society: the evidence of burial data

Burials represent the category of material most often considered suitable for
treatment in the quest for meaningful statements about ancient social systems, and the Bronze Age is no exception. They are the most prolific source
of material culture emanating from the period, and since cemeteries contain
the remains of actual people, they might be considered the preferred source
of evidence about how those people organised themselves in life, as in death.
In practice, burial data are rarely so unambiguous that interpretations of sites
and cultures are widely agreed, beyond the banal level of determining that

---

[24] Voza 1972; 1973.
[25] Orsi 1899; Bernabò Brea 1990.

wealth provision was not uniform. Many authors have provided general discussions of social ranking as deduced from burial data.[26]

The analysis of cemetery information has in recent years revolved around statistical treatment of graves and their accompanying grave-goods. Apart from questions of survival (post-depositional transformations), the problems with this approach are potentially threefold: incomplete representation of the living population in the cemetery, inadequate data on age and sex, and mismatch between status during life and provision of grave-goods, or grave form, in death. It is frequently evident that one or more of these problems are applicable to a cemetery: for instance when (as often happens) fewer infants and children are present than presumed mortality rates would predict, or when the artefactual record for a period indicates one thing and the burial record another. In spite of the gloomy assessments made by Ucko and some others,[27] the abundance of burial data cannot be ignored, and the current fashion for seeing material culture, in this case grave-goods, as text sheds an entirely new light on Bronze Age burial practice. Table 12.1 gives an overview of the situation regarding burial differentiation in different parts of the Bronze Age.

Table 12.1. *Burial differentiation by burial type*

	Artefact variety	Degree of differentiation
EBA flat cemeteries	Small	High
EBA barrows	Moderate	High
MBA barrows	Moderate	Moderate
LBA urnfields	Large	Low
LBA barrows	Large	High

It has been the clear expectation of many authors that the provision of grave-goods will show a pyramidal structure.[28] The inhumation cemeteries of Early Bronze Age central Europe and the barrows of Scandinavia provide the richest source material for this approach and have been intensively studied.[29] The cemetery at Brănc in Slovakia, for instance, with its 237 graves of the Nitra group,[30] provided enough clear-cut data for Shennan to carry out a detailed analysis.[31] Females were more richly provided for than males, and a few young females were unusually rich even by the standards of normal

[26] Saxe 1970; Binford 1971; Peebles and Kus 1977; Brown 1981; O'Shea 1984; 1996.
[27] Ucko 1969.
[28] e.g. Larsson 1986 for Scania, Lull 1983 for the Argaric Bronze Age.
[29] e.g. Randsborg 1974 for EBA Denmark, showing how 'wealth' as expressed in weight of bronze or gold was sparsely distributed and correlated with particular parts of Denmark; moreover, female wealth varied systematically with population density (as expressed by grave frequency).
[30] Vladár 1973b.
[31] Shennan 1975; 1982.

provision for females on the site. The interpretation offered, that male wealth could be shown through female display (women exhibiting not just their own but also their husband's status), may be applied to many other sites. An obvious alternative is that some power and wealth really were concentrated mainly in female hands, but this contradicts what is known from artistic depictions, from armour and from other warrior-like equipment with distinctively male connotations. Clearly such work depends on a number of assumptions, most notably (a) accurate age and sex data and (b) a complete and unrobbed set of graves. In the case of Branč doubts have been expressed on both counts. A considerable body of data now exists from several parts of central Europe, much of it unanalysed except in the crudest way. At Vyčapy-Opatovce, for instance, in spite of the fact that no analysis has been published, it is clear from the lists of grave-goods that more rich graves were female than male (p. 79).[32]

An exception to the above is represented by the work of Kadrow and O'Shea.[33] Kadrow analysed the distribution of 'wealth' in the Babia Góra cemetery of the Mierzanowice culture at Iwanowice near Kraków, and found that there was considerable differentiation between graves in terms of wealth, as well as gender-based differences. Nearly 60% of all graves had no grave-goods at all, while only some 2% of the total were 'rich'; of these, five were adult men and two were women. The next 2–3% were less well provided for, and included children and older people (fig. 12.1). The interpretation put forward is that only one 'rich' person would have been alive at one time, and that these were chiefs, manifesting their own wealth themselves, rather less commonly through their wives. In fact, the Babia Góra cemetery is one of the most poorly equipped sites of the period in the whole north Carpathian zone; at Mierzanowice, Kadrow showed that the range of wealth was several times greater than at Iwanowice, and in cemeteries of the Únětice and Mad'arovce cultures a considerably greater degree of differentiation is seen.[34]

The analysis of Mokrin in the Yugoslav Banat has been conducted on a number of levels.[35] The original publication provided a detailed catalogue of the graves and their contents, complete with osteological determinations, but it attempted little in the way of correlation analysis, let alone social interpretation. An analysis by Soroceanu was the first to introduce the concept of horizontal stratigraphy, a correlation table of grave-goods, and distribution of particular types across the cemetery.[36] On this basis it was suggested that

---

[32] Točík 1979.

[33] Kadrow 1994; Kadrow and Machnikowie 1992; O'Shea 1996.

[34] The analysis of Nitra culture cemeteries by Bátora (1991) arrives at similar conclusions, with a chiefly class represented by special grave constructions (wood-lined pits, surrounding ditches), special position of the body and grave, and special grave-goods (flint arrowheads, wristguards, boars' tusks, copper daggers and willow-leaf knives). Comparable differentiation is discernible in female graves.

[35] Girić 1971.

[36] Soroceanu 1975.

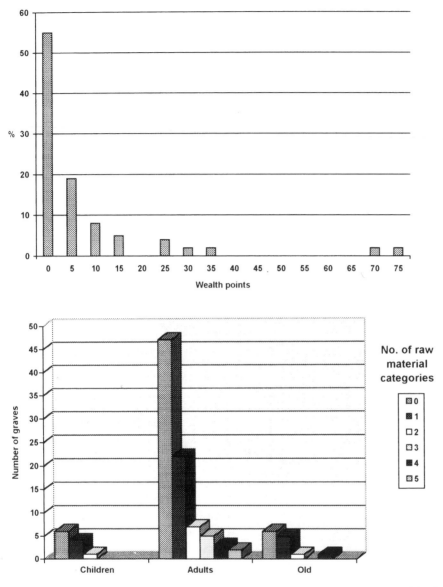

Fig. 12.1 Iwanowice, Babia Góra cemetery. *Upper*: Wealth distribution across all graves, expressed in terms of wealth points by percentage of graves; *lower*: wealth by age, expressed in terms of numbers of raw material categories (after Kadrow and Machnikowie 1992).

there were two major phases of development, with further subdivision of the later phase shown by the successive appearance of armrings, lockrings and daggers; in other words, the differences are chronological, not social in origin. Next, an analysis by Primas suggested that the cemetery could be divided

into zones of variable deposition density, with irregular rows separated by
narrow grave-free areas.[37] Some of these zones contain a single male grave
with an axe, perhaps the equipment of a leading personage. Stratigraphical
superpositioning showed that several parts of the cemetery were being used
simultaneously, presumably for family groups, rather than there being a linear progression across the site. Rich grave-goods could be found with either
male or female burials. In the most recent analysis, O'Shea has drawn these
varying views together into a full social analysis of all cemeteries of the Maros
group, into which Mokrin falls.[38] O'Shea distinguishes a 'normative' burial
mode (flexed inhumation, facing east), which represents the standard form
that a community member could expect on death, and a series of differentiated modes. Some of them, for instance weapons and certain head ornaments
with males and beaded sashes with females, are argued to be signs of hereditary social office, while other items, notably body ornaments, are seen as
representing 'associative' wealth, that is, wealth derived from membership of
a particular household by the person possessing it (fig. 12.2). Particular attention focuses on grave 10, an elderly male with an extensive set of equipment
usually found with females, regarded by O'Shea as an example of a compro-
mise to accommodate unique or unusual social circumstances.

The cemeteries of the Argaric Bronze Age of south-east Spain have been
the subject of much discussion.[39] Since early days, rich graves (as marked out
by, for instance, silver objects) have been distinguished, but recent analyses
have suggested there is much more structure in the record than this. Lull
identified a series of standardised vessel forms which appear to have been
used in a structured way in funerary contexts, as well as other objects which
served as status markers (daggers, halberds, diadems and other ornaments). A
further analysis then suggested that five ranked levels or groups were distin-
guishable according to the grave-goods included, the top two representative
of the 'dominant' class.[40] These included children's burials, thus suggesting
that wealth and status were hereditary or ascribed; what is more, the degree
of differentiation reached its maximum in the middle of the Argaric Bronze
Age. Given that these cemeteries are located near major agglomerated settlements, it is reasonable to suppose that political centralisation accompanied this trend towards hierarchisation in the burial record.

The picture thus obtained from these flat cemeteries is one where grave-
goods show clear signs of differentiation within individual cemeteries, which
can reasonably be interpreted as reflecting at least some of the divisions
within society. At this stage of the Bronze Age, as the overall artefactual
record shows, there was still a limited range of objects available with which

[37] Primas 1977a, 14ff.
[38] O'Shea 1996. This analysis is complex and cannot adequately be summarised.
[39] Lull 1983; Chapman 1990, 195ff.; Buikstra et al. 1995.
[40] Lull and Estévez 1986.

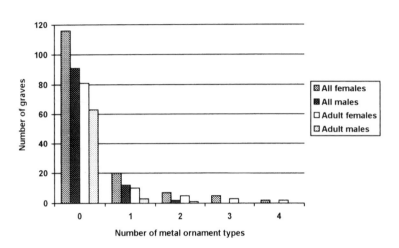

Mokrin

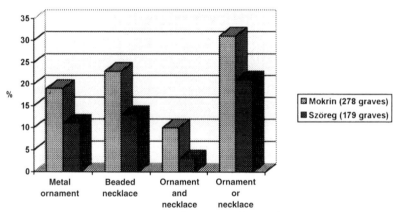

Exotic wealth markers in Maros cemeteries

Fig. 12.2. *Upper*: Mokrin, numbers of metal ornament types in male and female graves; *lower*: wealth markers at Mokrin and Szöreg (data from O'Shea 1996).

to display status distinctions, so that where marked differences are discernible their effect may be presumed to have been significant. Certainly by comparison with the situation in many Neolithic societies the burial record of the Early Bronze Age shows marked structure.

The Early Bronze Age barrows of central Europe represent special treatment for the dead (see p. 97). Although barrows are commoner than has often been asserted, they nevertheless occur much less frequently than do flat cemeteries. In the case of the well-known sites of Helmsdorf and Leubingen, where there were some rich grave-goods, it has been usual to view the sites as the resting-places of a local elite. Such an interpretation does not provide a full and satisfactory explanation for the phenomenon, however. While the size of these barrows certainly reflects an ability to mobilise labour forces, and their contents the ability to acquire both a large quantity and a high quality of grave-goods, it is uncertain how unusual such constructions were, taking Europe as a whole.

In the Middle Bronze Age Tumulus cultures, it is possible to point to individual rich graves, both male and female, which have often been interpreted as those of 'chieftains' and people from socially favoured groups.[41] While this interpretation is in general unobjectionable, it is rendered less than complete in view of the exceedingly poor information available on graves other than under tumuli in the Middle Bronze Age.

In the context of Urnfields, conclusions on social differentiation are rendered more difficult because the practice of cremating the dead along with their grave-goods tends to destroy evidence of age and sex along with much of the artefactual material. Nevertheless, in some instances it has been possible to make suggestions about social structure. A good example is an analysis of Bavarian and Tyrolean Urnfield cemeteries.[42] The Volders cemetery, where there is an almost complete cemetery plan, and other sites where at least part of the cemetery is fully known, suggest that much more of the original patterning is recoverable than was hitherto imagined. In the first place, a distinction is to be drawn between goods placed on the pyre with the corpse and goods placed unburnt in the grave, the latter group perhaps a less sumptuous version of the deceased's clothing and possessions. Among the fragmentary objects usually associated with the former group are occasional bronze objects – discs or buttons – with a gilded surface, and less frequently the remains of a sword or an object associated with a sword such as a double button, allegedly worn on the sword belt. Analysis of the chronology and grouping of the cemetery, in which four discrete areas are discernible, concluded that the separate areas were the burial places of different family groups, with two or three families using the areas in each generation, and with only one individual at a time in the entire site being the owner of a sword. Gilded discs, by contrast, could be present in the graves of several individuals in the same generation. The implications of this analysis are that communities, in this part of central Europe at least, and by implication also in other parts, were hierarchically organised, with a single individual able to acquire special importance through control of, or prowess in, weaponry – or at least the importance is articulated through the possession of weaponry that was denied to the rest of the community. Such individuals would, on this argument, be relatively numerous, one per community settled through the Urnfield world.

[41] Zeitler 1993, 84.
[42] Sperber 1992.

Even if one does not accept all the steps in the argument as outlined, there are enough elements to indicate that society in this north Alpine area was structured in sophisticated and subtle ways. The problems start when one looks further north, for instance to the Lausitz or Knovíz culture areas of Bohemia, Saxony and Poland, where the provision of swords in graves is extremely uncommon.[43] On the other hand, a strong case has been made that what is really important in Urnfield graves is not so much weaponry as drinking sets, in the form of cups or groups of bronze vessels, which are seen as reflecting ceremonials similar to those depicted on situla art of the Early Iron Age.[44] Particularly with those graves that include three or more vessels, such as Milavče, Hart an der Alz, Očkov or Osternienburg, it seems reasonable to suppose that only the highest status individuals or families were in a position to acquire the means of practising the ceremonials and then to destroy the objects.

It is easy to point to individual examples of 'rich' graves in various parts of the Urnfield world, even where the cremation rite has damaged or destroyed the grave-goods. From the earlier part of the period one can point to graves like that at Velatice in Moravia, with its sword, spearhead, beaten bronze cup, ornaments and other objects.[45] From the late part of the period, a grave such as that at Haunstetten near Augsburg in southern Bavaria illustrates the point.[46] This grave showed the remains of a pyre, and on it were various melted bronze objects including bracelets, pins, a belt ornament, a knife with elaborate ornamental grip, beads of glass, amber, jet and shell, tubular wire beads of gold, and other items.

An analysis of the area around Seddin (Perleberg, Brandenburg) in the Late Bronze Age clearly distinguished between the mass of simple urn graves and burials in carefully built cists. Within each of these categories distinctions were evident between those graves containing metal grave-goods and those (the great majority) without, differences which are interpreted as having social origins.[47] Furthermore, barrow graves are also present, themselves varying in elaborateness of construction (though this does not correlate with grave-goods or rite). In complete contrast to the urn graves, around half of the barrow graves contain metal grave-goods, but these are themselves differentiated, with small items such as rings and awls being more numerous than prestige weaponry such as swords, spears, socketed axes, decorated knives, harness items and metal vessels. These latter are in any case found exclusively in barrows. The barrow graves can then be divided further by means of their grave-goods, ranging from those with a sword (sometimes combined with a

---

[43] Kytlicová 1988a lists only 10 examples in the whole of Bohemia in the whole Urnfield period.
[44] Ibid.
[45] Říhovský 1958.
[46] Wirth 1991.
[47] Wüstemann 1974.

knife, a socketed axe, a razor or tweezers), those characterised by the presence of a knife, and a few which regularly contain socketed axe, spearhead,
harness items or bronze vessels. The spatial distribution of these graves gives
a strong indication that they form clusters, which are plausibly to be interpreted as correlating with the centres of territorial power, in other words with
local potentates. Similar conclusions have been reached with the small number of exceptionally rich graves from other parts of the northern Urnfield
world, as at Håga near Uppsala or Lusehøj on Funen.[48]

These instances are, however, exceptional in the context of the run of
Urnfield cemeteries. Much more common is a situation where few, if any,
graves contain 'rich' goods. There may be different numbers or types of objects
between graves, for instance pots, but it is arguable whether these reflect richness, rather than, for instance, number of people present at the funeral. At
Przeczyce, in Lower Silesia, the 'Urnfield' cemetery actually contains a distinct minority of cremation graves (132 out of 874), and fuller analysis has
therefore been possible.[49] Although considerable variability in grave-good provision is evident in this cemetery, the small range of goods provided, as compared with what one knows was available in the period, suggests that either
the people could not obtain the prestige goods or the provision of 'rich' goods
was not important to them. The number of pots varied with age and sex, the
most well provided for being adult males, where the commonest number was
four (for children, by contrast, the commonest number was zero) (fig. 12.3).
On the other hand, only one-third of the graves contained ornaments, and a
mere 37 contained tools and weapons. These can hardly be taken to indicate
wealth or status, at least not in terms of what one may find in hoards or ritual deposits, though sickles or axes could have taken on a special significance
when placed in graves.

It is evident from this discussion that the degree of social differentiation
displayed in graves is variable, depending on area and period. Certainly in the
Early Bronze Age there are ubiquitous signs that ranking was being marked
by differential provision of grave-goods, or (in the case of the west and north)
that some people were accorded burial in a barrow, while others were not.
Probably the same situation continued into the Middle Bronze Age Tumulus
cultures, though the situation is complicated by the lack of non-barrow burials. In the Late Bronze Age, there is an impression of extraordinary uniformity between graves on Urnfield cemeteries, which appear in very great
numbers and with minimal differentiation. Yet the few instances of richly
equipped burials, such as at Seddin, along with the evidence of the artefactual record which clearly shows that prestige bronzework was being created,
indicate that this situation is more apparent than real, and that society must

[48] Thrane 1981; 1984.
[49] Szydłowska 1968–72; Rysiewska 1980; Harding 1984b; 1987.

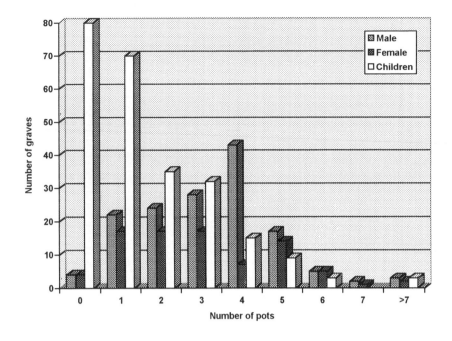

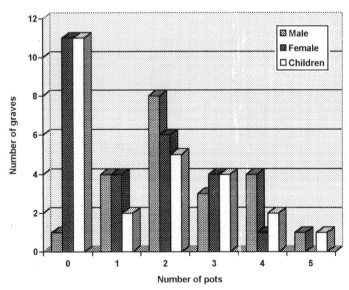

Fig. 12.3. Przeczyce, Lower Silesia, numbers of pots by age/sex category. *Upper*: Inhumations; *lower*: cremations. Note the strong tendency for children to have no or few pots, while most inhumed men have four; cremated adults of both sexes have two (data from Szydłowska 1972).

in fact have been proceeding fast along a path leading to the emergence of 'paramount chiefs' in the Early Iron Age.

The individual in society: the evidence of artefacts

While burial and settlement data are commonly regarded as fair game for the study of social reconstruction in the past, the evidence of artefacts in their own right is less often considered. Yet portable artefacts are the most abundant type of archaeological data and cannot be ignored. While they are often studied from the point of view of technology, typology, chronology, distribution and origin, their value as social documents is at least as important. They are the concrete expression of utilitarian needs, but also of psychological concerns, of pleasure, enjoyment and fear as well as comfort or practicality. As the central link between the ancients and ourselves, artefacts are crucial. The abundance of artefacts, their sensitivity to place and time, and the directness of their relationship with human activities make them a superb but underused and poorly understood source of information.

In a Bronze Age context artefacts play a major role in many areas of knowledge. They can be used to identify workshops and their distribution areas, and from this attempts have been made at specifying the size of Bronze Age socio-political groupings and the territories they occupied. Production of artefacts was important in terms of daily life, but it also served a role as an indicator of social and economic mechanisms. In this, bronzework occupies pride of place because of its relative abundance (in relation to goldwork or glass, for instance) and its specificity (in relation to pottery, whose forms are usually so general that it is impossible to make definite statements regarding production and range).

In recent years, much attention has focused on artefacts as a means of expressing human aspirations and concerns. One of these aspects is style, which reflects mental processes in those who create and determine it, and which has been considered one form of 'information exchange' between individuals and groups.[50] Another is the recognition that artefacts have a 'social life', in which they can develop new meanings and identities, switching from items of purely social value to 'commodities' and back again.[51]

The recognition that Bronze Age artefacts or artefact types can mean different things in different contexts has led to a variety of sophisticated accounts. Thus Larsson has charted the relationship between different artefact types in particular regions of Sweden, identifying a number of different production and distribution situations within an overall framework of non-egalitarian social relations.[52] The process by which materials became com-

---

[50] Wobst 1977; Conkey 1978; 1990.
[51] Appadurai 1986.
[52] Larsson 1986.

modities has also been explored by Shennan with specific reference to the circulation of metals in central Europe.[53]

The number of available forms into which bronze was made increased constantly through the period. Whereas in the Early Bronze Age these amounted to a mere dozen or so, mostly simple tools or ornaments, by the Late Bronze Age there were scores of possible ornaments and dozens of possible weapon types, quite apart from tools, which were available for the smith to produce and the individual to wear or possess. Social distinctions thus became, in theory, easier to express as time went on. In practice, things are not quite so straightforward since the full range of forms was not found in direct association with individuals, that is in their graves, in the Late Bronze Age. But in general, the enormous increase in quantity and range of metal goods leads one to speculate on the increased opportunities for consumption that were provided, and thereby the increased scope for a 'social life' for the artefacts of the Bronze Age. Some of these objects were 'commoditised', effectively entering the economic rather than merely the social sphere, but many were not. If the interpretation of hoards and many single finds as ritual is correct, it is reasonable to assume that metalwork frequently stayed outside the economic sphere altogether.

This social role for artefacts finds its most obvious reflection in the numerous objects identifiable as prestige in nature. Gold lunulae, for instance, were obviously items of personal adornment, intended for an individual to wear. Their clear similarity in shape and design to 'collier'-type necklaces formed of beads, including spacers of amber or jet, indicates that the currency of the form was wider than the distribution of metal lunulae alone would imply; and the fact that it only appears in these special materials indicates its particular significance. An even more extreme example is that of the extraordinary gold 'cape' from Mold, north Wales, which is unparalleled as to form, though some of the ornamental details are found on other objects. A great number of Late Bronze Age gold objects, such as bracelets, gorgets or lockrings, appear only rarely in graves but were widely available. Artefact production strongly suggests the emergence, maintenance and development of a prestige-good system, where warrior equipment was particularly important.[54]

In a Scandinavian context the amount of metal in ritual hoards is taken to reflect the wealth of families depositing it, and shows that the degree of inequality between families decreased over time, being significantly greater in Period II than in Periods IV–V.[55] Many of the ritual hoards consist of objects defined as 'sumptuary goods', that is goods reflecting 'sumptuary rules' which direct the way a society orders itself in matters of access to rank and author-

[53] Shennan 1993.
[54] See Hafner (1995) on solid-hilted daggers and spoon-shaped flanged axes in the Early Bronze Age.
[55] Levy 1982.

ity. Since the 'ritual hoards' consist largely of ornaments and weapons, especially suited for display and not for utilitarian purposes, and since they often
consist of a regulated set of ornaments, worn by a single person, a role in
social ordering is most likely.[56]

Gender

Of course some of this display was gender-related. In recent years much attention has been paid to the identification of gender-based manifestations in the
archaeological record.[57] In fact the existence of separable pieces and groups
of equipment attributable to women and to men has been well known for
many years; what is new is a conscious effort to look at the past through
other than male eyes, or at least by means of a perspective that is not overtly
androcentric. In this, one should not forget also the perspective of children,[58]
who made up a large proportion of the total of Bronze Age people and who
were often provided with special burial arrangements or equipment, such as
the so-called feeding bottles of the Urnfield period.[59]

   The discussion of funerary material showed that in many kinds of cemetery and burial there are graves that can be identified as female or male. This
is the case in flat cemeteries of the Early Bronze Age, where grave form and
orientation, as well as grave-goods, combine with skeletal analysis to show
distinct traditions. It is also the case in tumulus burials, famously so in
Denmark and the Nordic zone where male and female assemblages have long
been recognised in the great barrows of Jutland and Schleswig-Holstein, but
also in southern England where it is usual to identify male and female graves
on the basis of grave-goods with hardly any corroboration from physical
anthropology. Thus the Borum Eshøj barrow contained a young and an older
man, and a woman aged between 50 and 60 (old in Bronze Age terms).[60] Only
the woman was richly provided for, with bronze ornaments and personal items
as well as a dagger; both males were relatively 'poor' – the young man had a
dagger, a sword scabbard, a bone comb, a bark container and a wooden pin,
the old man only a wooden pin in addition to clothing. On the other hand,
the finds from Muldbjerg provide ample evidence that even in the Early Bronze
Age (Period II) males could also be richly equipped at death – this individual
is sometimes referred to as a chieftain in recognition of the fact that he possessed a sword with inlaid hilt and scabbard, and a fibula. Other items of
male equipment were tweezers, wound wire finger-rings, buttons, razors, arm
and wrist ornaments and (in Period III) knives and pins. Women could have

[56] These patterns were especially evident in Period V, where 21 set types could be arranged in
    five levels of complexity depending on the number of different ornament types in each set.
[57] e.g. Conkey and Spector 1984; Ehrenberg 1989; Gero and Conkey 1991; Stig Sørensen 1991.
[58] Sofaer Derevenski 1994.
[59] Eibner 1973; Siemoneit 1996.
[60] Glob 1974.

ornamental discs, collier-type neck-plates, and various other rings, buttons, fibulae and (in Period III) tutuli, knives and torcs.[61] Stig Sørensen believes that these costumes and accoutrements expressed easily read messages about gender, cultural position and social or marital status.[62] While some elements are clearly gender-associated, others are ambiguous or non-gendered; it was combinations of items of material culture that assigned gender to the person wearing them and, once assigned, the identity was permanent. Particular items of material culture, such as hair coverings or ornaments, probably served to mark out identity in specific fashion, whether ethnic, gender-related, age-related, status-related or a mixture of all or some of these.

Why should this separation of the sexes have been so marked in the Nordic area? In Britain the female graves of the Wessex culture, relatively rich by comparison with the undifferentiated burials of Deverel–Rimbury, have been explained by reference to the respective economic bases, the former being based on pastoralism, the latter on agriculture.[63] In many traditional societies, it can be seen that pastoralism promotes a more lavish display of wealth than arable agriculture, but paradoxically it is in the latter that women can achieve higher status. This argument could also apply to the heathy soils of Jutland. Are rich women's burials reflecting male wealth, as already suggested for Branč, or were there structural reasons within society which led to wealth accumulating in the hands of women?

In an Urnfield context, the cremation rite often means that satisfactory determination of sex is impossible, but there are a number of cases where good information is available. The cemetery at Grundfeld (Lichtenfels, Upper Franconia) was for the most part poor in grave-goods, but female graves with unusually rich goods, specifically for the adornment of the head and neck, did occur (above, p. 376, fig. 11.5).[64] There is no indication on this site that males could acquire such goods. As the cemetery used both inhumation and cremation, the criteria for according one rite rather than another might also be a relevant factor in gender-based differentiation.

The provision of marriage partners was inevitably a matter of concern in the Bronze Age, as in all other societies, ancient and modern. A fair number of graves, in several areas, contain a male and a female (sometimes one or more children as well), which has led to speculation that the pair were partners in life ('married');[65] such graves imply that the death of one partner was followed immediately by that of the other. Whatever the precise rules which govern marriage and similar alliances, the need for reproduction is a

---

[61] Struve 1971.
[62] Stig Sørensen 1991; 1997; see too Randsborg 1974 on the implications of female wealth in these graves.
[63] Ehrenberg 1989, 128.
[64] Feger and Nadler 1985.
[65] Müller-Karpe 1980, 474.

permanent and inescapable one. For this a supply of marriage partners has to be available, and this supply depends on the size, success and proximity of neighbouring communities. It is evident from their size that some Bronze Age settlements at the farmstead or even the village level were too small to be self-sustaining in reproductive terms. Families must have looked to neigh-bouring families, and wider groupings (phratries, for instance) to neighbour-ing groupings. The clear implication is that marriage partners must have been acquired from areas outside the home territory of most communities. In this connection, it is of interest that study of the Middle Bronze Age grave-goods in several parts of central Europe has identified 'foreign' elements, particu-larly ornaments, that may point to the presence of such marriage partners, especially women. These tumulus-using groups appear to have adopted a reg-ularly recurring set of equipment with which the dead, especially women, were provided. The rules for this provision were not absolute, and there is a considerable variation between very poor and very rich, which may be related to various factors in life (age and social position, for instance). The move-ment of goods is particularly clear between the Lüneburg heath in the north and Alsace in the south: recent studies have shown that each group of female dress ornaments has outliers in the territory of its neighbours.[66] The inter-pretation of this phenomenon as that of women moving residence to foreign parts upon marriage, 'fremde Frauen' (originally defined in the context of finds from Iron Age Manching), is an attractive one; it may also provide informa-tion on the scale of community groupings involved in the Middle Bronze Age. The concept has also been applied, in a modest way, to male equipment found outside its home area.[67]

Distribution maps as published in artefact studies, especially those that concern objects of personal adornment such as pins and bracelets, or toilet articles such as razors or tweezers, may well indicate more of this type of movement. For instance, razors of British–Irish type named the Feltwell and Dowris types occur in two Breton and one Belgian finds;[68] a south French razor type (St Etienne-du-Valdonnez) occurs in an example in the Jura, while a Burgundian type (Mauvilly) occurs in an example in the Hérault (fig. 5.13).[69] Since razors can plausibly be interpreted as the personal equipment of males, perhaps high-status males, their movement may well reflect the movement of those men across France or even across the Channel.

[66] Wels-Weyrauch 1989a; Jockenhövel 1991.
[67] Wels-Weyrauch 1989b.
[68] Jockenhövel 1980b, 64ff., table 50A.
[69] Ibid., 181ff., tables 57B, 58B.

Gender-related activities?

It was no doubt true that particular activities were the province of one sex or the other, but there is no sure guide to decide how to allocate the various tasks in the many cultural groups under review. Ethnographically, potting is frequently the domain of women, while metalworking is usually carried out by men; this does not of course mean that such an arrangement applied in prehistory, except in so far as certain tasks requiring particular muscle-power (this may include metallurgy) may perforce have been allocated to men. The presence of awls in graves on other grounds believed to be female at Singen may suggest that there at least leather-working was a female occupation. Where anthropological analysis of skeletal material has taken place, warrior equipment is usually associated with male burials, implying that aggressive and defensive relations with other groups were a male preserve – though some individuals identified as female were also provided with daggers. On the other hand, women were never buried with swords or armour, as far as is known.

In the light of the above, it is curious that the rich traditions of the Neolithic in terms of religious iconography did not find any continuation in the Bronze Age. For Gimbutas, the many female figurines that characterise the Balkan Neolithic indicated a matriarchal society and a pantheon of female gods. It does not necessarily follow that, because female figurines stopped being produced, matriarchy gave way to patriarchy in the later Neolithic and Bronze Age, though it is evident that symbolism related to females is rare throughout the European continent and specifically female-oriented ideologies are not found.[70] In fact, in the absence of figurines and other human depictions there are no clear indications either way. An exception is perhaps represented by the bell-like figurines of Cîrna in Oltenia and the comparable figurines in northern Yugoslavia (above, pp. 372f.), which plausibly indicate the importance of the female form in specific ritual acts carried out in this part of the Lower Danubian province.[71]

Does anything stand in the way of an interpretation of rich female barrow burials in the north as indications of a matriarchy? Here one might point to the evidence of the Nordic rock art. The overwhelming majority of figures where the sex is made clear are male, usually because they are depicted in priapic pose. A very few have primary female characteristics; many have no sexual characteristics at all, but it cannot be assumed from this that they are female. It is invariably men who are shown in situations where ritual activity, associated with dancing, wielding of axes and lures, and other forms of display, is depicted. Where fighting is shown, or extra-large individuals are present, these are again male. It is justified to conclude from this that men played a crucial role in ceremonial activities in Bronze Age Scandinavia. While

[70] Robb 1994 (Italy).
[71] Dumitrescu 1961; Letica 1973.

this may not have applied all over the Bronze Age world, there is no evidence to suggest that it did not, and the combination of cemetery, artefact and rock-art evidence may reasonably be taken to indicate that it did.

Conclusion: the emergence of complexity

In considering the nature of Bronze Age social organisation, it is inevitable that one concentrates on the members of society who stand out in some manner, those who appear from their material provision to have possessed elite status. But the obvious corollary of this is that the majority, those not so provided for, were of lesser status and were assigned a different role. Those who are most evident in the material culture are craftsmen and craftswomen, responsible for the creation of metalwork, pottery, woodwork and other productions. I have reviewed already the evidence that a certain number of men were by the time of the Late Bronze Age engaged in the acquisition and maintenance of prestige through combat. But however warlike a society may seem from its material remains, the fact remains that the fields had to be tilled, craft production maintained, the dead buried and rites and festivals duly observed. The constant reiteration in the literature that societies at this time were 'ranked' or 'stratified' tends to disguise the fact that most people probably never saw, let alone owned or wielded, parade armour or swords. The Bronze Age has been described as 'Europe's first golden age', but this represents a view of the past that contradicts the real character of the period for most people who lived in it. This 'grass-roots archaeology' may be less spectacular than the archaeology of the elite but it is no less truthful, and through it one is more likely to view the period as the great mass of the Bronze Age population experienced it. At the same time, it would be wrong to ignore the fact that some people did manage to acquire status, at least in terms of material possessions and probably too through warrior-related display. While there were many 'ordinary people', there were also 'big men' (fig. 12.4).

In general, communities were not large: most villages can never have housed more than a few hundred people at the most, and in very many cases – particularly in the earlier part of the period – they were merely farmsteads that can only have been home to a single family. In the later Bronze Age the size of communities and territorially organised groups increased markedly, but even in the largest sites a few hundred people, conceivably one thousand or so, is likely to have been the limit. Even then one cannot be sure that they lived in the same place for more than short periods at a time (for instance, whether early hillforts were permanently occupied or not). But however small individual settlement units were, they must have been linked to each other by ties of kinship and through the need for common social and economic activity; otherwise they were too small for viability. Individual farmsteads in an extended landscape can in many ways be thought of as a dispersed form

Fig. 12.4. Massive male figure holding a spear, from a rock-art panel at Litsleby, Bohuslän. Photo: author.

of village, with each family having frequent contact with its neighbours and everyone within a certain radius coming together for special purposes at regular intervals.

The role of artefacts, and specifically of imported artefacts, in such a society has been a source of fruitful speculation for many scholars. Their distribution through society was unequal; they would have served to reinforce social distinctions in both life and death. Hence the importance of commodities whose procurement can be seen to have entailed special labour or substantial distances. Almost any item which was moved from a distant source, and even some which were not, could have been treated in this way, but one thinks especially of the metals (notably gold), amber, and glass or faience.

But in many ways consideration of these items as filtering through society to those who could use them as a means of control is secondary to the whole question of how elite groups came into being and, once in being, how they maintained their position. The debate between those who favour an approach based on managerial considerations and those who prefer to deal through the medium of culture and its ideological implications has been briefly touched upon. There is undoubtedly also an economic dimension to this debate. The trajectories for social development in the Bronze Age depend crucially on the use of materials and the objects made from them to articulate the social structures evolving in the period.[72] The use of materials that were moved over considerable distances is an obvious case in point. One should also not forget the notion of 'social storage', propounded for the Aegean palace civilisations, in which foodstuffs might have been exchanged for other valuables in times of plenty, those valuables then serving as a buffer in times of scarcity.[73] Control of the valuables and of the trade in them could then serve to bolster the status of a few people, who might appear as highly ranked individuals.

This discussion has implied, though not explicitly discussed, the role of craft specialisation. Given the extent of craft production during the period, it is clear that specialisation was a key factor. Not only are differences within and between regions evident during the Bronze Age, there is good evidence for particular crafts being carried out in particular locations on individual sites (metalworking and weaving, for instance). This has been studied with greatest attention in Spain, but was equally important in other areas.[74] Taken in conjunction with the evidence for political centralisation and vertical differentiation within society, many of the elements for describing the evolution of Bronze Age society seem to be present.

It is striking how varied that evolution was across Europe. One would not expect developments in Scandinavia to mirror those in the Mediterranean, but in roughly comparable environments it might be thought that the processes of socio-political development would follow roughly comparable courses. The contrast between Sardinia and Spain is particularly striking. While in Spain there is extensive and early evidence for differentiation, seen in both settlements and burials, and a complex set of technological and economic conditions which relates to that differentiation, in Sardinia society remained non-hierarchical, the size of groups stayed small, and there was little or no movement towards increasing the scale of production or socio-political units. While in most of Europe the tendency was centripetal as the centuries passed, in Sardinia groups fissioned (or failed to coalesce). This can partly be ascribed to the relatively remote nature of the island; yet its extensive contacts with the eastern Mediterranean show that it was open to influences from more highly differentiated societies. Local conditions thus engendered a specific set of processes which give us the archaeological phenomena that are peculiar to the island. This suggests that social and political evolution must be studied afresh in each area; generalisations can only be simple and are unlikely to be powerful.

Social relations were not static. It is true that the study of process and 'culture change' ignores the whole area of social reproduction since each packet of archaeological data in essence represents the residue of a single event. But

---

[72] Proposed by, for instance, Shennan 1986.
[73] Halstead and O'Shea 1982.
[74] Chapman 1990; 1996.

that does not mean that they cannot be welded into a dynamic whole. The study of Scandinavian hoards provides a graphic illustration of the way in which artefact groups were viewed differently over time and therefore of one possible means by which social change can be documented and – even if through a glass darkly – the interpretation of ancient society expanded.

CHAPTER 13

THE BRONZE AGE WORLD: QUESTIONS OF SCALE AND INTERACTION

The attempt in the previous chapter to reconstruct aspects of social organisation was restricted to the individual, the group or the tribe, implying a geographically restricted area. Each tribal territory was, however, part of a wider continent. Though 'Europe' as a concept did not exist, the continent did: where no geographical barriers existed the inhabitants of one area had no reason not to be aware of their neighbours and of those neighbours' neighbours. Every person had a 'world' and a 'world view', but identifying the components of that view is not an easy matter. In particular, the identification of an overarching world that encompassed large parts of present-day Europe is something that has engendered intense debate.

Attempts at reconstructing a 'Bronze Age world view' can only ever be speculative in a Europe where the absence of literacy prevents mind-to-mind contact across the ages. Understanding is necessarily determined by familiarity with a variety of models relating to both past and present societies, derived from history and ethnography. Such models can provide several alternative views of the same society, though there may be others which are more appropriate though less well known (fig. 13.1).

Diffusion or local evolution?

Traditionally the European Bronze Age has been seen as some kind of appendage to the rich civilisations of the East Mediterranean. Most of the inventions which characterised the period were of Near Eastern origin, including metallurgy, wheeled transport, swords and body armour, and were thought of as spreading across Europe from the south-east, in classic diffusionist fashion. Even when it could be demonstrated that some of these elements had a local background, the case for seeing 'barbarian' Europe as somehow secondary to the Near East and East Mediterranean was dominant. This certainly applied to technology, and was reinforced by the situation with literacy, which was undoubtedly introduced to Europe under influence from the East Mediterranean, and iron-working, which is widely believed to have moved into Europe from Anatolia.

If the technological case is persuasive, that for other institutions is much

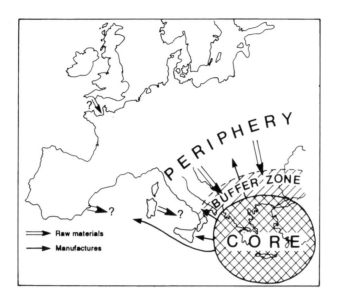

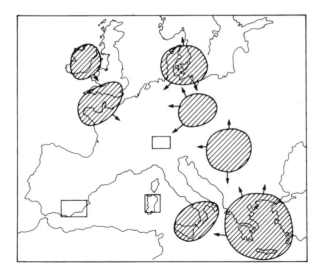

Fig. 13.1. Alternative models of the 'Bronze Age world'. *Upper*: Core–periphery model, the East Mediterranean representing the core and Europe the periphery; those parts nearest Greece, where Mycenaean trade is known to have taken place, are sometimes seen as a buffer zone. *Lower*: A model of Europe as a series of major centres or cores (hatched areas) and locally important zones (rectangles), all interacting with their neighbours and with other centres further afield.

more ambiguous. Of the characteristics which give the Bronze Age its special flavour, it is at least arguable that many were specifically European in
origin. The system of social organisation, in so far as it can be reconstructed,
depended on small local residential and power units. These were always based
on agriculture, initially in hamlets and later in larger villages. Only with the
creation of fortified centres did a nucleated pattern become visible, and even
then the extent of control and administration is arguable. This pattern is very
different from that prevailing in the East Mediterranean, certainly on the main
trade thoroughfares, and probably also in the more remote hinterland areas.
The existence of strong centralised political systems and highly developed
trading organisations cannot be certainly demonstrated before the Iron Age,
though elements of both may have been present in some Bronze Age contexts.

A minimalist view of the Bronze Age would be that of isolated small-scale
units with little or no interaction beyond that necessary for the adoption of
technologies and the maintenance of reproductive units. Elements of such a
view can be discerned in the trend, beginning in the 1960s and continuing in
some forms through the 1970s, of using radiocarbon dates to demonstrate
that there was no contact between the rich centres of the Aegean and East
Mediterranean and the cultures of central and western Europe.[1] Such a view-
point stressed the autonomy of various areas such as the Balkans in the
Copper Age.[2] Instead of an irradiation from the Near East, Europe was seen
as possessing most of the skills – latent or manifest – necessary for the development of the technologies and types that appeared to link the different areas.
In the best-known Bronze Age case-study, the divorcing of Mycenaean Greece
from the developments of the distant 'barbarian' world enabled Renfrew and
others to propose a model of temperate Europe in which processes inherent
in the cultures of the period could lead to an expansion of technology, a flowering of craftsmanship and an emergence of social diversity that is made manifest in the rich graves of the Early Bronze Age.[3] A more explicit set of
mechanisms for this process was laid out by Renfrew in the Greek context,
in which a systems approach to the modelling of cultural development was
used to show that Minoan and Mycenaean Greece could have emerged independently of influence from Egypt or the Near East through mechanisms such
as the 'multiplier effect' and internal feedback loops.[4] *Mutatis mutandis*, comparable processes could be regarded as applicable to other parts of Europe to
explain, or at any rate model, the way in which social and economic complexity came about.

A systems approach to archaeological culture is today less fashionable, and

[1] e.g. Renfrew 1968.
[2] Renfrew 1967.
[3] Renfrew 1968.
[4] Renfrew 1972.

to many people discredited, reflecting as it did the concerns of a positivist and scientistic age to solve the problems of the past as one would solve the problems of the present, by reducing them to their component parts and devising quasi-scientific tests and methods to answer specific questions about each one. However, it is not necessary to see such autonomy models solely in terms of systemic views of culture. Even accepting that no society could be completely closed in terms of exchange and kinship networks, it has nevertheless been common for individual cultures to be viewed as if they were independent entities. Indeed, the whole process of isolating separate 'cultures' is part of the archaeologist's aim at reducing the vast quantity of available artefactual data to manageable proportions so that they can be studied more readily. This process leads one to study them as if they really existed separately from what went on around them, even to think of them as independent of whatever else was going on in the Bronze Age world at the same time. In other words, what started off as a device of convenience ends up with a life of its own and an uncertain relationship to reality.

Reproduction and growth

For any small-scale society to continue to exist, the maintenance of links with the outside world is a *sine qua non*. Below a certain size, there are insufficient breeding partners to provide enough reproducing couples to maintain population, and opportunities for technological and economic change are limited. In much of the Bronze Age world, social groups were indeed small: the great majority of settlement sites known are of small agricultural hamlets. If these contained between 10 and 50 people, as seems often to have been the case, the problem of finding partners could easily become acute. Since low life expectancy meant that only a minority of people survived into mature adulthood, women would have had a maximum of perhaps 15 years for childbearing, in many cases probably less. If one allows one child per fertile year, and assumes that only one-quarter of those born survived into adulthood, a woman of child-bearing age might have produced three or four children capable of contributing to group continuance, assuming that partners were available and pregnancy was readily achieved. In practice, the number must often have been less as these conditions would not always have been fulfilled. In a group of 20, of which half were male and half female, only five women would have been capable of bearing children, and at the most only five men available for partnering. Such small numbers automatically carry with them the danger that insufficient breeding pairs will form stable and lasting bonds to allow a healthy supply of new group members. In such circumstances, inter-group contact would have been essential. If 10 such groups of 20 interacted, there would have been 50 males and females of breeding age, a much more viable number. From what can be seen of site size and proximity, such an assumption about group size seems reasonable. In all this, kinship connections with more distant groups remain possible, thus increasing the potentially available breeding stock exponentially.

Core–periphery models

The use of core–periphery models, or World Systems Theory, has had some influence on the thinking of some Bronze Age scholars in recent years.[5] This situation is curious in a number of respects, first because sociologists and economic historians do not now regard these theories as especially important, and second because the founder of this school of thought, Immanuel Wallerstein, denied that they were applicable to periods prior to AD 1450; indeed, he regarded them as an explicitly capitalist feature. Nevertheless, a series of authors have felt it worth while to apply these ideas to the more distant past, including the Bronze Age of Europe as far back as the third millennium BC (fig. 13.1, upper).

World Systems Theory was developed by economic historians as a model for understanding the transition to the capitalist economy of the 'modern' world.[6] It provided an overarching framework within which to set the states and economies of the early post-medieval world as they moved to create the political and economic structures that developed into the systems known from recent history. In particular, it placed in logical relationship to each other the central or core areas – in Wallerstein's formulation countries of Mediterranean and western Europe – and the peripheral areas from which they drew their resources, for instance parts of Africa, the Near and Middle East, or eastern Europe. Such definitions of cores and peripheries then become important for studying social and political developments within each area, since the relationship (expressed in terms of exploitation of resources or the movement of goods from one area to another) had effects on the local subsystems in all areas, for instance in the way society came to be structured, through the acquisition of prestige goods by local elites in the peripheral areas.

Since Wallerstein said nothing about the situation prior to AD 1450, it was left to others to consider whether there might have been a pre-capitalist World System.[7] The most daring in this respect has been the development economist G. A. Frank, who frequently refers to a '5000-year old World System' – not just any old ancient world system, but 'the *one* central world system', which has been dated to the mid-second millennium BC, or even earlier.[8] Frank sees 'an unbroken historical continuity between the central civilization/world system of the Bronze Age and our contemporary modern

[5] General discussions: Champion 1989.
[6] Wallerstein 1974/1980.
[7] Schneider 1977; Chase-Dunn and Hall 1991; Hall and Chase-Dunn 1993.
[8] Frank 1990; Wilkinson 1991; 1993; Gills and Frank 1993.

capitalist world system. It *is* the same system but it has not remained the same throughout its evolution.'[9] This implies the existence of such a system in the Bronze Age both of the Near East and of Europe.[10]

According to Frank, 'the criterion for identifying a single world system is that no part of this system would be as it is (or was) if other parts were not as they are (or were)'.[11] In other words, it is truly systemic in that it is an intricately interdependent construction, with events in one part of the system having effects on all the others. What is more, it has a centre, or core, and an outer part, or periphery. A core–periphery structure can be identified as an essential characteristic of early World Systems (according to Frank), as in modern Latin America. This means that one should be able to identify such a core and its peripheral areas. This is not just a geographical relationship. The core must be bound up with the periphery, perhaps even dependent on it, in terms of raw materials or other goods, and in turn the periphery must be linked to the core through bonds of trade or exchange, typically prestige goods that found their way specifically to elites within the local communities. It is easiest to envisage highly centralised political structures, such as empires, fulfilling this role, with political control being exercised throughout a given territory and either suppressing peripheral areas completely or incorporating them under the same system; but it is also possible to see what have been termed dendritic political economies functioning like this, with exchange between core and periphery but no overt political control.

For Wallerstein,

a world-economy is constituted by a cross-cutting network of interlinked productive processes which we may call 'commodity chains', such that for any production process in the chain there are a number of 'backward and forward linkages', on which the particular process (and the persons involved in it) are dependent. These various production processes usually require physical transportation of commodities between them, and frequently the transfers of 'rights' to commodities in a chain are made by autonomous organisations, in which case we talk of the existence of 'commerce'... Production for this cross-cutting set of integrated commodity chains is based on the capitalist principle of maximising capital accumulation.[12]

What reason is there to think that such a system has a prehistory that can be traced back into the Bronze Age? Some restrict the applicability of the concept to intersocietal systems with states and cities; others believe that smaller stateless and classless systems can also be studied.[13] For Frank, early state or city-state societies with abundant evidence of trade interests and

---

[9] Frank 1993, 387.
[10] Applications to the 'barbarian' world of Europe: Kristiansen 1987; 1994; Sherratt 1993a; 1993b. Critiques: Kohl 1987; Dietler 1995, with further refs.
[11] Frank 1993, 387.
[12] Wallerstein 1984, 2–3.
[13] Frank and Gills 1993; Chase-Dunn and Hall 1991.

connections would qualify for inclusion in the world system. According to him, one can discern cycles, or alternating phases of expansion and contraction, in the history of the 'world' from 3000 BC onwards. Such cycles are a key part of the argument that there was a World System in the Bronze Age, since if they could be shown to exist, it would suggest that there was an interlinked system that experienced phases of boom and bust, expansion and contraction, with happenings in one part affecting all the others. Other commentators have suggested that what is discernible in the Ancient Near East is not one world system but several smaller units.[14]

Sherratt's application of the model to Bronze Age Europe is much more subtle.[15] For a start, identifying core and peripheral areas in particular contexts is not necessarily the same as identifying a World System. For him the term 'periphery' can only be usefully applied to areas which underwent structural transformation as a result of regular exchanges of products; a technology gap between the two areas is not sufficient. He sees a shifting set of relationships, with Europe becoming 'marginal' to the Near East in different ways at different times, and in the Bronze and Iron Ages acting as a margin (his preferred term) which 'takes its place as the third element in what can now be described as a core/periphery/margin system'. The margin, it transpires, is dominated by time-lag phenomena – 'escapes' – rather than structural interdependence with the core, and such time-lag processes are allegedly responsible for many of the features which came to characterise the Bronze Age, including metal technology and usage, textiles, transport technology, and food and drink. So the margin (i.e. Europe) was transformed as a result of Near Eastern urbanisation, and in particular 'marginal' trade grew. Some support is adduced from the fact that many areas, and not just Europe, proceeded along much the same course; this envisages 'chains of regional economies (themselves with a limited degree of core/periphery differentiation) contributing specialised products into inter-regional networks that at certain periods traversed the whole breadth of the continent'. The amber trade, for instance, is envisaged as being especially important as a moulder of expectation and perhaps taste in northern elites.

Kristiansen has argued that 'southern Scandinavia was directly dependent for its social reproduction on its participation in the larger European network of bronze exchange. It follows that northern Scandinavia should be defined as a periphery from the point of view of its relationship to southern Scandinavia.'[16] More recently he has proposed that the inter-regional network depended on the local organisation of core–periphery relations for its maintenance, and that this explains the rise of rich centres, rock-carving clusters

---

[14] e.g. Kohl 1987.
[15] Sherratt 1993a; 1993b.
[16] Kristiansen 1987, 81.

and so on.[17] Core–periphery relations were thus an essential structural feature of Bronze Age society, forming a hierarchy from local to regional and inter-regional core–periphery structures and tending to direct surplus towards local and regional centres of strong chiefdoms in a system of unbalanced exchange. This whole process was integrated into an international network of core–periphery relations that linked the Mediterranean with central Europe and Scandinavia. After initially proposing that with the Iron Age the system collapsed, his perspective is now rather different, emphasising the cyclical transformations of Bronze and Iron Age societies and seeing an oscillation between two dominant types of social organisation: one based on sedentary centres of metal production and distribution controlled by an elite, the other on a more decentralised social and economic setting of warrior societies. The cycles of communal versus individual burial, and hilltop versus open settlement are then manifestations of this process.[18]

Whether these arguments really do indicate that it is legitimate to take the existence of World Systems (as opposed to world systems) so far back in time is debatable. Obviously it is possible to identify the movement of goods. In the Near East, abundant textual sources make this clear; in Europe, there is no shortage of surviving physical evidence for transported goods in the Bronze and Iron Ages. Demonstrating the existence of trade and exchange is not the same as proving dependency relations between two areas, however. Even with the perfectly reasonable assumption that traded goods had their main effect on elites, enabling them through the control of commodity flows to exercise relations of dominance, it still does not imply that the linkage between different areas was one of dependency, general or specific.

Another objection to dependency theory as an apposite model for understanding the Bronze Age world is that it is not appropriate to speak of the ancient world in modern terms, and in particular that the capitalist arena should be separated from the pre-capitalist one by virtue of differences in logistics, costs, technology (for transport, for example) and the nature of the division of labour and human relations. Furthermore, divorcing political from social and economic forces is not appropriate in the early societies under examination, where scales of values were not necessarily measured in economic terms and where social institutions played a major role in economic life. In other words, the context of interaction must be studied: the costs and benefits to each side have to be studied in local, not global, terms.

An example of this, largely ignored by World Systems theorists, but much more persuasive as an argument for overarching links between different areas of Europe, is the communality of artefact tradition and technology that existed

---

[17] Kristiansen 1998, incorporating features from a number of his papers published in the 1990s.
[18] On the other hand, his identification of regional centres on the basis of artefact types ('political catchment areas') represents little more than what traditionally would have been called 'cultures' or 'artefact clusters'!

across wide stretches of territory. A view of the 'world' at 1300 BC, for instance, would quickly see how closely similar a whole range of artefact types was through much of Europe, something which traditional artefact studies are unable to account for satisfactorily. In the sense that craft traditions converged and thereby reflected processes other than themselves, one can reasonably view what was happening as part of a system linking different political and production areas. One can call this a world system as long as one makes clear what sort of system one is talking about. The model I prefer to adopt is one of many small 'cores' or centres, each locally important and each interacting with its neighbours and sometimes with areas further afield. Some of these central areas may have really acted as cores in the World Systems sense; others were primarily of local significance (fig. 13.1, lower).

Questions of *context* and *scale* are thus crucial to the debate about the most appropriate means of conceptualising the Bronze Age 'world': context in that notions of capitalism and economy are inappropriate to ancient societies which one cannot experience even indirectly; scale in that the scale of most of the groups which can be studied in Bronze Age Europe was quite different from that of more modern examples. To understand them, other approaches must be adopted.

Territories and the scale of settlement

In much of Bronze Age Europe prior to its later stages, residence and burial units were extremely small, sometimes no more than a single family or reproductive unit, or at most an extended family grouping. This was the case throughout temperate Europe in the Early and Middle Bronze Ages, and seems only to have changed to something larger in the Late period. In such situations, archaeological attempts at defining unities that linked people together in groups (e.g. 'tribes') are unlikely to succeed unless there is strong corroborating evidence, supported perhaps by literary material; for instance, statements that particular artefact types were specifically associated with particular peoples. Since the European Bronze Age was pre-literate, such information is not available, though in rare instances such an interpretation might be imposed on the artefact data. Such small groups of people would have produced a multitude of small leaders (small in the sense that their constituency was small); generalised groupings would by comparison have been relatively weakly bonded together, at a more distant kinship level. How authority then passed to more important leaders is not known. The absence of communal works and the prevailing impression of a lack of larger scale communal planning in much of Bronze Age Europe suggests that rather few activities were conducted at the level of the tribe: phratry-based action might be the most that was involved. The geographical implications of this would be relatively small in scale, perhaps extending over areas no more than a few tens of kilometres in extent.

Some idea of the scale of communities in the Alpine valleys of Switzerland is gained from the settlement pattern of the upper Rhine, where sites lie on glacial knolls around 5 km apart, and no one site appears to be more important than any other.[19] The distribution of Late Bronze Age sites along the major lakes shows regular patterning, the sites lying between 1 and 5 km apart from each other (fig. 13.2).[20] Such an egalitarian settlement picture mirrors what has been outlined above. Thus a site such as the Padnal at Savognin, with a mere two or three houses in each phase of its existence, would have been occupied by only a couple of families, or a single extended family (above, pp. 39f.). Most of the work involved in creating and maintaining such sites in good condition, i.e. reasonably dry and with access to necessary economic resources, could have been undertaken at the family (or at most extended family) level. These actions (tree-felling and transport, house and pile renewal) would have had to be repeated over and over again, creating a vast number of timbers over an extended period, but in principle they could have been done by a few able-bodied people: only two people are needed to fell a tree and rig up its transport using oxen, and not many more to erect it on site. The tasks certainly do not require the armies of labourers who have sometimes been envisaged.

Another approach to the reconstruction of territories is that based on an analysis of archaeological landscapes in defined areas. The detailed and sophisticated settlement structure reconstructed from the excavations at Fosie IV, on the outskirts of Malmö, or surveys around Ystad on the south coast of Scania, are notable. There are two levels of analysis in this work, micro and macro. At Fosie IV, extensive open-area excavation showed the slowly changing pattern of settlement during later prehistory, with individual villages (groups of houses) lying 200–300 m from each other in the examined area, which was around 2 km long and 300 m wide.[21] At the local level one can reconstruct the total living system, with residential areas, burial sites, fields and areas of wetland or marsh (fig. 13.3); comparable exercises have been carried out for Lausitz sites and on the Danish islands.[22] On the other hand, study of barrow distribution suggests a larger picture: 'This pattern could be interpreted as if the concentrations of large burial mounds have had a social/political background and represents nuclear areas in the Bronze Age habitation. It could be suggested that the nuclear areas represent a territorial level of a clan or subclan in a tribal society' (fig. 13.4).[23] A reconstruction of

---

[19] Harding 1983.
[20] Arnold 1990, 124f.
[21] Björhem and Säfvestad 1993.
[22] Buck 1986; Stig Sørensen 1992.
[23] Björhem and Säfvestad 1993, 385; Säfvestad 1993. A similar approach is adopted by T. Larsson (1993).

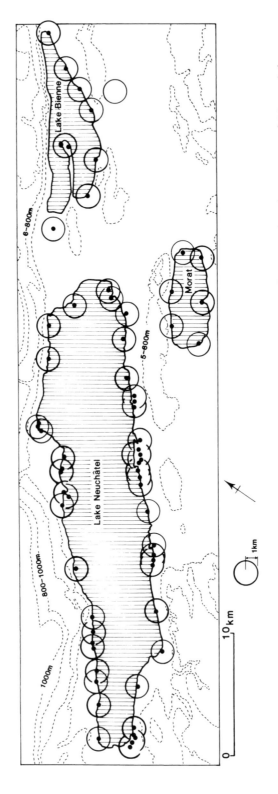

Fig. 13.2. Sites and site catchments in the Late Bronze Age on Lakes Neuchâtel, Bienne and Morat (after Arnold 1990).

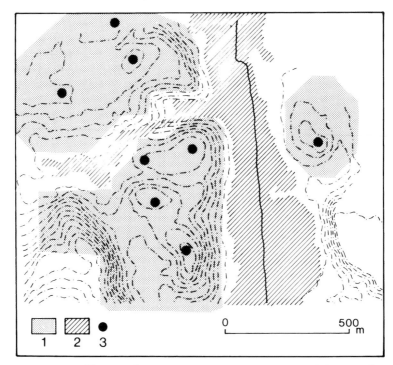

Fig. 13.3. Village and 'territory' at Fosie IV, Scania (after Björhem and Säfvestad 1993). 1. Fields. 2. Marshy areas. 3. Settlements.

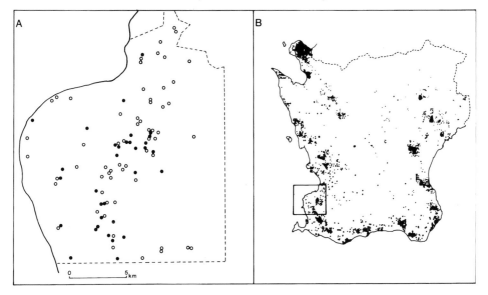

Fig. 13.4. Territorial patterning in the barrow distributions of Scania. A. Barrows in the Malmö area. Filled dots represent large barrows. B. Barrows in Scania. The clusters plausibly indicate the location of territorial centres (after Björhem and Säfvestad 1993).

the area west of Ystad suggests that primary settlement, as shown by barrow distribution, was in a 4-km-wide band along the coast.[24] These barrows continued to function as burial sites and potentially as territorial markers in the Late Bronze Age, with the addition of flat cemeteries near the sea. This coastal zone offers 'a gradient of natural zones', from light sandy soils near the coast, through clay till soils to the forests of the inland 'hummocky' landscape. Each settlement unit would have held rights to inland grazing as well as the intensively utilised resource zone on the coast, as was also suggested for Funen.[25] Something similar has been done to reconstruct settlement nuclei in the Netherlands (fig. 13.5).[26]

The distribution of grave finds, artefacts and rock art in north-east Scania has also been used as a means of identifying major settlement areas – effectively territories (fig. 13.6).[27] Thrane has attempted the reconstruction of territories on Funen in a similar manner,[28] while at Jyderup Skov in Odsherred parish (north-west Zealand) he reconstructed a permanently settled territory based on barrow distribution, in which the location of the domestic settlement might have moved about but the territory itself stayed the same.[29]

By contrast, in many parts of Late Bronze Age Europe there are clear signs of the rise of a hierarchical settlement structure. This is evidenced most clearly by the fortified sites, especially hillforts. As discussed in chapter 8, such sites can frequently be seen to have a fairly regular spacing across a given landscape, giving the clear impression of territoriality. In south Württemberg the spacing varies with the terrain, and no doubt also with the social and political conditions; inter-site distances can be as small as 3 km or as large as 20 km, but 5–10 km is most common, giving an area of between 20 and 80 km², with a population of several thousand.[30] This compares with a theoretical radius of about 50 km for groups based on artefact styles in the Tumulus Bronze Age (above, p. 408), which may, however, be connected with kinship affinities rather than political control. It would be dangerous to reconstruct territories from this, because not all sites were contemporaneously occupied, but the catchments would be large enough to include a variety of types of resource and a large number of subsidiary small-scale farming settlements. Such a pattern has been reconstructed in a number of comparable situations.[31]

Territories of this size, with forts of the complexity that characterises the period in much of central Europe, must represent the spatial dimension of

[24] Olausson 1992.
[25] Thrane 1984, 179.
[26] Ijzereef and van Regteren Altena 1991.
[27] Carlie 1994.
[28] Thrane 1989.
[29] Thrane 1991.
[30] Biel 1980.
[31] e.g. the Lausitz stockades of central Poland (Ostoja-Zagórski 1974; 1983).

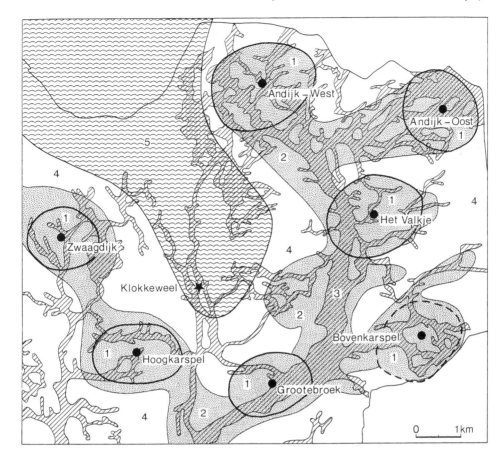

Fig. 13.5. Schematic reconstruction of settlement nuclei in north-eastern West Friesland, based on the distribution of surviving barrows. 1. Nuclei in the 'colonisation phase'. 2. Later extension of the inhabited areas. 3. Ridge. 4. Low-lying area, uninhabited. 5. Open water. Source: Ijzereef and van Regteren Altena 1991.

groups of people linked at more than a kinship level but less than a tribal level – depending on the size of tribe envisaged. In this connection it is worth glancing at the situation in one part of Europe where, in an Iron Age context, there is relatively early information regarding tribal territories, and numerous hillforts: the Dalmatian coastal area, and especially Albania, the homeland of the Illyrians.[32] While the Illyrians were an ethnically and linguistically homogeneous bloc, an 'ethnos' or people, they included in their number many smaller units best described as 'tribal' in character.[33] Few of these can be

[32] Wilkes 1992.
[33] Papazoglu 1978.

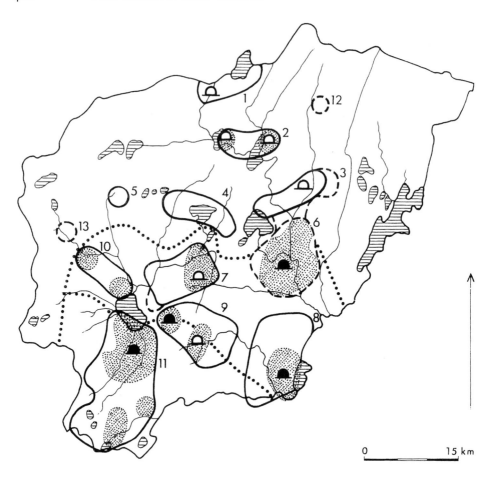

Fig. 13.6. Interpretative map of Bronze Age settlement areas in north-east Scania, based on the distribution of graves, rock-art sites and stone settings. Filled semicircles represent 3–4 barrows, open semicircles 1–2 barrows larger than 20 m in diameter; solid lines delimit settlement areas, dashed lines possible additional settlement areas. Stippled areas are those of major importance, notably area 6 which contains the Frännarp rock-art site and many other finds. Source: Carlie 1994.

localised with any confidence and, even where they can, there is only a presumption that sites which fall within their assumed territory were really settlements attributable to them. For instance, Thucydides speaks of the Taulantii who inhabited the hinterland of the city of Epidamnus (modern Durrës), describing them as 'barbarians, an Illyrian people'.[34] The location of ancient Epidamnus is not in doubt, but no site in its hinterland can be

[34] *Histories* I, 24.

specifically and unambiguously associated with the Taulantii.[35] Further north, near Zadar in Croatia, it proved very difficult to identify rural Bronze Age sites (other than cairns and field systems) which would complement the *gradine* (hillforts) that are highly visible in the area; but in this largely karst area, considerably removed from the zone of Greek influence, environmental and probably social and economic conditions were quite different from those further south.[36] Taking the evidence as it stands, the distribution of Illyrian 'tribes', as far as one can reconstruct them, suggests that named groups could occupy a territory as small as 50 km across, possibly even smaller in the area around Lake Shkodra, where a plethora of tribal names is known from the ancient sources. These names and this picture derive from the Iron Age, but some hillforts in Albania have produced Late Bronze Age finds, so it is likely that the Iron Age fort distribution pattern is not so different from that developing in the Bronze Age. Though the spacing of known major sites is not consistent, fortresses and 'proto-cities' that served tribal groupings were to be found at roughly 50 km intervals (depending on terrain), with subsidiary sites filling in some of the spaces, conceivably five or six to each urban centre.

The range of other 'territorial' approaches that have been adopted in recent years expands this material, so that the prospects for a refined understanding of territories in the Bronze Age are good.[37] This is not to say that uniformity can be expected across Europe: environments varied, and so did humans. But at least methodologies exist which offer fruitful possibilities.

Conclusion

The Bronze Age 'world' was, according to how you look at it, very large or very small. The general approach of this book, that of treating Europe as a whole, tends to give an impression that Europe was one large canvas on which a unified picture was being painted by the artists of the Bronze Age, but in fact this cannot have been so. The scale and size of settlements, and the territories inferred from them, show that the overwhelming majority of groupings in most periods before the latest part of the Bronze Age were small, numbering a few hundreds or thousands and extending over some tens or hundreds of square kilometres. Most people's perceived world would not have extended much beyond the land occupied by those linked to them in kinship bonds, or the local area over which the products of smiths and potters spread.

But there was another side to this. Some materials did penetrate the 'barbarian' world from afar, such as amber, glass and, in some instances, metals

---

[35] Between the rivers Shkumbi and Erzen there are Iron Age sites at Mlike and Dorëz, while Zgërdhesh (of the same date) lies some 30 km north of Tirana; to the south at Lleshan (near Elbasan) a fort goes back into the Late Bronze Age (Ceka 1985; 1986).
[36] Chapman, Shiel and Batović 1996.
[37] Harding 1997.

(notably gold). Though one cannot judge whether the ultimate origin of these items was known to the recipients, one can be sure they knew they were not locally available and came from far away. In this sense, they knew they were part of a 'world system', an interconnected network or set of networks that in some cases linked the inhabitants of the far north with those of the warm south. Opinions differ about the value of identifying all this as a World System or series of such systems. Whether or not one chooses to follow dependency theory, it seems doubtful that it can serve as a very useful guide to action in furthering the understanding of Bronze Age communities. For this, the study of scale and context, and of the 'social life' of these materials and artefacts, offers more fruitful possibilities, which are now being systematically and rapidly followed up. In twenty years' time, the Bronze Age 'world' may look radically different, as a series of 'worlds' in microcosm. The ripples created by a pebble dropped in water may eventually reach the furthest corners of the pool in some attenuated form, but they are felt most strongly close to the point of impact. In just this way, the understanding of production and distribution at the local level will, in my view, come to dominate the study of Bronze Age society.

CHAPTER 14

EPILOGUE

The preceding chapters have presented some aspects of the archaeological record for Bronze Age Europe, and no simple summary can do justice to them. It is evident, however, that a number of distinct spheres of activity may be recognised in Bronze Age research. Some of these are 'nuts-and-bolts' approaches (i.e. site- and artefact-based), while others are more theoretical in nature. While the trend is from the former to the latter, in many countries the study of cultures, for the purposes of ethnogenesis and culture history, still reigns supreme.[1]

- *Typology and artefact studies.* The enormous wealth of material culture in the Bronze Age naturally means that attention has focused on the products of the smith and the potter, sometimes to the exclusion of all other objects of study. Of the many examples which one could cite, the series Prähistorische Bronzefunde (PBF) is pre-eminent.[2] So far only one category of objects – swords – is even reasonably complete across Europe (and even there gaps remain), but others, such as metal vessels, are not far behind. There are, however, drawbacks to this approach. The objects, when drawn together on a page, lose their contextual information.[3] It is also misleading to present only finds of bronze, when identical objects might be made in wood, gold or iron, or other materials.
- *Corpora.* Among the best-known examples is the series Inventaria Archaeologica, sponsored by the Union Internationale des Sciences Pré- et Protohistoriques (UISPP), publishing associated finds of different types and periods.[4] An object lesson in the compilation and publication of corpora, in a Bronze Age or any other context, is the massive series *Die Funde der älteren Bronzezeit in Dänemark, Schleswig-Holstein und Niedersachsen*, edited by E. Aner and K.

[1] Ostoja-Zagórski (1996) has charted the reluctance of Polish Bronze Age specialists to move away from positivist and 'factographic' studies to model-building.
[2] The success of the PBF series has spawned imitators (Blažek and Smejtek 1993), and there are other comparable projects, e.g. the series published by the Société Préhistorique Française, *Typologie des objets de l'âge du bronze en France*.
[3] Quite apart from the fact that the redrawn objects in the uniform PBF style are often far removed from their actual appearance and condition.
[4] The coverage across Europe is very uneven. Some countries (Britain, for example) have published only a few fascicules and seem to have no intention of publishing more; others (for example Poland) continue to produce significant numbers. A rather similar enterprise, still in the early stages, is the British Museum's Associated Find Series entitled British Bronze Age Metalwork (BBAM).

Kersten. In progress since 1973, this will eventually publish all Early Bronze Age material from north-west Germany and Denmark in 25 volumes, of which at the time of writing 12 have been published and three are in preparation.[5] Volumes published by the Royal Commissions on Historical Monuments and the Victoria County History in Britain provide comparable data.[6]

- *Chronology.* Chronological studies have for many years represented a flourishing industry. Many journals – including influential ones – continue to publish detailed accounts of the chronology of small chunks of time in small geographical areas, based almost entirely on typological minutiae and stratigraphic indications from selected sites. Such articles are tedious to read, and today mostly unnecessary, since the means of obtaining absolute dates are available in most areas and periods. In the future, the emphasis will shift towards the creation of independent chronologies.
- *Settlement studies.* The excavation and surface recording of settlement sites has now achieved a general level of competence which enables fugitive and subtle house traces to be recovered. Where adequate survival enables the identification of individual houses, and even their internal fittings, more detailed analysis is possible. This is usually the case where stone was used for house construction, as in upland parts of north-west Europe or in the Mediterranean. Special problems occur in particular situations. In Hungary, for instance, where tells are the norm east of the Danube, few complete settlement plans exist. To excavate a multi-period tell satisfactorily requires a great deal of time and money.[7] But only with large-scale excavation will the dynamics of settlement change become apparent.
- *Landscape studies.* Settlements were only one part of a wider landscape, and the study of that landscape represents one of the most important and exciting developments in Bronze Age studies in recent years. This is especially the case in north and north-west Europe, where large tracts of unploughed land survive, either in the form of permanent pasture or as moorland. In Britain extensive agricultural landscapes have been recorded, in many cases together with the settlements that exploited them, and in areas such as the chalk downlands of southern England complex and subtle data have been successfully recorded and analysed.[8] The spread of the use of air photography will mean that such studies become commoner, especially in central and eastern Europe where aerial archaeology has hitherto been severely restricted.[9]
- *Palaeoenvironmental studies.* Faunal studies, plant macro studies and palaeobotany have all added greatly to understanding of eco-

---

[5] The finds are arranged by parish or district, and most space is devoted to the enormous number of grave mounds of the Early Bronze Age in the Nordic area; many of the finds are of great importance for Bronze Age studies, but published long ago or not at all.
[6] Grinsell 1957.
[7] Kovács 1988.
[8] e.g. Richards 1990; Woodward 1991.
[9] A good example of the advances emerging from this new work: Gojda 1997.

nomic processes in the Bronze Age. However, the evidence and its study is patchily distributed across Europe. The methodological advances which have brought biological specialists to prominence have not, perhaps, been as widely disseminated as they should be. To take a single example, when animal bone is among the most plentiful finds on many sites, why are there so few extensive and reliable bone reports for Bronze Age sites available?

- *Ethnogenesis*. The study of how nations formed, how languages and peoples arrived in the locations where they are to be found today or attested historically, is important in a Bronze Age context, for it was during this period that one can place much of the background development that led to the emergence of historical peoples into the light of day during the Iron Age. Other methods, for instance glottochronology, which attempts to determine time-scales for language evolution on the basis of rates of change in word and syntax development, also involve the Bronze Age since several languages are first attested during that period, and others shortly after it. Reviews of the Indo-European problem exemplify the approach.[10] While some countries have enthusiastically espoused an explicitly ethnohistoric approach (Albania is a good example), in western Europe there is more scepticism about the value of material evidence for the solution of ethnic problems, but also less need to do so since the main language blocs were in place from a relatively early period

- *Funerary studies*. Because the archaeological record is so biased towards human burials, there is an enormous mass of cemetery studies, which at their simplest present bare details of grave form and grave-goods. In fuller treatments, more sophisticated analyses can be provided, in which correspondences between position, age, sex and grave-goods may be presented. While the overall quantity of studies on individual cemeteries or groups of sites is extremely large, the number that move on to deal with more theoretical analyses of this kind is small; in the future this situation must change.

- *Social and political reconstruction*. Recent attempts at social reconstruction have gone far beyond what used to be considered possible in the days when Hawkes's 'ladder of inference' was the dominant methodological force. Positivist approaches adopted during the 1970s have now largely given way to those based on post-modern attitudes to data and theory. Nevertheless, a sizeable body of work dealing with social reconstruction, particularly the questions of ranking and organisation, has found wide acceptance. In recent years there has also been an increasing tendency to attempt the reconstruction of the Bronze Age in terms of overall world view and to identify quasi-political units in Bronze Age Europe based on the scale of regional groupings and settlement studies, particularly on fortified sites (potential 'central places'). The main problem with all these approaches is the lack of an agreed methodology.

- *Gender, identity and material culture*. Recent years have seen notable moves forward in this area, as scholars have come to realise the importance of artefacts as objects providing information on their

---

[10] e.g. Mallory 1989.

makers. In this there has been a move right away from typological studies towards the study of artefacts in context. Subtle distinctions in the form and positioning of objects, particularly those relating to the human body, have been examined and presented, with the result that much more is now known about how people in the Bronze Age presented themselves to the world around them.

The Bronze Age and its importance in world prehistory

The achievements of the European Bronze Age cannot be presented as a set of brief generalisations, but a number of factors stand out. Since at the start most areas were still in the process of developing from the mainly stone-using technologies of the Neolithic, with great communal enterprises in the megalithic province of the west, and by the end they were on the threshold of history, with developed tribal organisations, a high degree of political centralisation and powerful elites, it is obvious that much had happened in the intervening centuries. The processes that were under way were partly technological, partly cultural or ideological and partly social in nature. It is impossible to separate these three areas; they are all intimately interlinked.

Technological developments are perhaps the simplest to comprehend, and among them metallurgy takes pride of place. This places a heavy burden of responsibility on the craftworker, in particular the bronzesmith. Many authorities, since the days of Childe, have argued that craft specialisation played a crucial role in articulating social divisions, in propelling societies on to the trajectories that they followed. These workers created the products which enabled society to differentiate one person or group from another. Control of these resources and their distribution is usually seen as a mechanism by which social power was exercised.

Technology enabled social and economic developments but (depending on your point of view) it did not cause them. When we consider the nature of social, economic, ideological and political development in the Bronze Age, a number of trends are dominant. In most areas, social differentiation was a marked factor, though it is arguable whether it actually increased over the period. There was a strong move towards group coalescing, residence in larger units, and territorial patterning of fortified centres. Throughout the period, there is good evidence for the importance of non-utilitarian preoccupations, those aspects of ritual which arguably bolstered the authority of those who created and understood them.

Do these factors help us to understand what it was like to be a Bronze Age person? Yes and no. We can glimpse many aspects of the nature of the Bronze Age world (*sensu* living system); we understand how technology operated, how fields were tilled and how houses were erected. We are on less safe ground when we come to consider how social reproduction took place, what means were utilised to teach the denizens of the second and first millennia BC what their place in the world (physical and social) was. Much of the structure of the archaeological record may relate to precisely that point (though equally some of it may be incidental or contingent). We have seen a number of attempts at identifying the nature of the social environment in which Bronze Age people lived and worked. Ultimately, it is social reproduction that constitutes the very essence of the period, that defined for those who lived in it what they had to do and therefore what sort of remains they would (inadvertently) leave behind for archaeologists of the late twentieth century to interpret. The problem that faces us is the lack of a methodology that is sufficiently robust to persuade the archaeological world at large that it can ask the right questions and then answer them to the satisfaction of more than a self-perpetuating coterie.

The Bronze Age has until recently been the Cinderella of prehistoric studies, in that relatively few people have chosen to study it, and the approaches adopted have rarely been innovative. On the one hand, the volume of artefacts available from the Bronze Age has led to the intensive study and publication of numerous large and indigestible tomes detailing them, undoubtedly intimidating for the neophyte. On the other, there are in western Europe relatively few settlements by comparison with the situation in the Neolithic, so that the study of sites in their landscape has been less possible. There is the further problem that in areas where barrows are found many have been robbed and, even where there is a record of what was found in them, the information is rarely of sufficient quality for detailed study and comparison to be possible. There seems to be little that one can do to enhance such a poor database, at any rate where no new sites are available for study, which is the case for many of the areas in question.

Important though these factors may have been in discouraging study of the period, they need not be crucial. Perhaps the period suffers from having too much information available for highly speculative research but too little for that of a historical nature such as is being undertaken in the Iron Age. In fact, the resource base seems no less adequate, taken as a whole, than that for any prehistoric period, and it is considerably fuller than for some. In many ways the potential of the period remains untapped, which is frustrating for those trying to understand Bronze Age archaeology as it exists today but good news for the next generation of students, who have a rich source of research topics available for study.

REFERENCES

Abbreviations used in journal titles:

Antiqs	Antiquaries	Mitt.	Mitteilungen
Archaeol	Archaeological	Prehist.	Prehistoric
Archéol.	Archéologique	Proc.	Proceedings
Bull.	Bulletin, Bulletino	Soc.	Society, Société
Int.	International	Veröff.	Veröffentlichungen
J.	Journal		

Åberg, N. F. 1930–5. *Bronzezeitliche und früheisenzeitliche Chronologie.* Kungl. vitterhets historie och antikvitets Akademien. Stockholm: Verlag der Akademie.

Acsádi, G. and Nemeskéri, J. 1957. Paläodemographische Probleme am Beispiel des frühmittelalterlichen Gräberfeldes von Halimba-Cseres, Kom. Veszprém, *Homo* 8, 133–47.

Adámek, F. 1961. *Pravěké Hradisko u Obřan.* Brno: Krajské Nakladatelství.

Albelda, J. 1923. Bronzes de Huelva (Espagne), *Revue Archéol.* 5th series 18, 222–6.

Alcalde, G., Molist, M. and Toledo, A. 1994. *Procés d'occupació de la Bauma del Serrat del Pont (La Garrotxa) a partir del 1450 AC.* Publicacions Eventuals d'Arqueologia de la Garrotxa 1. Olot: Museu Comarcal de la Garrotxa.

Alexander, J. 1981. The coming of iron-using to Britain. In *Frühes Eisen in Europa. Festschrift Walter Ulrich Guyan zu seinem 70. Geburtstag*, ed. R. Pleiner, 57–67. Schaffhausen: Verlag Peter Meili.

  1985. The production of salt and salt trading networks of central and western Europe in 1st millennium BC. In *Studi di paletnologia in onore di Salvatore M. Puglisi*, 563–9. Rome: Università di Roma.

Alexandrescu, A. D. 1974. La nécropole du bronze ancien de Zimnicea (dép. de Teleorman), *Dacia* 18, 79–93.

Alfaro, C. 1992. Two Copper Age tunics from Lorca, Murcia (Spain). In *Archaeological Textiles in Northern Europe*, Tidens Tand 5, eds. L. Bender Jørgensen and E. Munksgaard, 20–30. Copenhagen

Allen, C. S. M., Harman, M. and Wheeler, H. 1987. Bronze Age cremation cemeteries in the East Midlands, *Proc. Prehist. Soc.* 53, 187–222.

Allen, M. J., Morris, M. and Clark, R. H. 1995. Food for the living: a reassessment of a Bronze Age barrow at Buckskin, Basingstoke, Hampshire, *Proc. Prehist. Soc.* 61, 157–89.

Almagro, M. 1940. El hallazgo de la ría de Huelva y el final de la edad del bronce en el Occidente de Europa, *Ampurias* 2, 85–143.

1958. *Depósito de la ría de Huelva. Inventaria archaeologica, España*, fasc. 1–4, E.1. Madrid: Instituto Español de Prehistoria.

1966. *Las estelas decoradas del suroeste peninsular.* Bibliotheca Praehistorica Hispana 8. Madrid: Instituto Español de Prehistoria/Universidad de Madrid.

1974. Depósito de bronces de la ría del Huelva. In *Huelva: preistoria y antiguedad,* 213–20. Madrid: Editora Nacional.

Almagro-Gorbea, M. 1972. La espada de Guadalajara y sus paralelos peninsulares, *Trabajos de Preistoria* 29, 55–82.

Almgren, B. 1962. Den osynliga gudomen. In *Proxima Thule. Sverige och Europa under forntid och medeltid. Hyllningsskrift till H. M. Konungen,* ed. G. Hamberg, 53–71. Svenska Arkeologiska Samfundet. Stockholm: P. A. Norstedt.

1983/1987. *Die Datierung bronzezeitlicher Felszeichnungen in Westschweden.* Uppsala: Universitets Museum för nordiska fornsaker Gustavianum.

Almgren, O. 1905. *'Kung Björns Hög' och andra fornlämningar vid Håga.* Arkeologiska Monografier 1. Stockholm: K. L. Beckmans Boktryckeri.

Ambert, P. 1995. Les mines préhistoriques de Cabrières (Hérault), quinze ans de recherche, état de la question, *Bull. Soc. Préhist. Française* 92, 499–508.

1996. Cabrières (France): mines et métallurgie au III° millenaire B.C. Apports de la métallurgie experimentale. In *XIII International Congress of Prehistoric and Protohistoric Sciences Forlì, Italy, 10: The Copper Age in the Near East and Europe. Colloquium XIX, Metallurgy: Origins and Technology,* 41–50. Forlì: ABACO Edizioni.

Ambert, P., Barge, H., Bourhis, J.-R., and Esperou, J.-L. 1984. Mines de cuivre préhistoriques de Cabrières (Hérault). Premiers résultats, *Bull. Soc. Préhist. Française* 81/3, 83–8.

Ambros, C. 1958. Zvieracie kosti z doby bronzovej z Dvorov nad Žitavou, *Slovenská Archeológia* 6/1, 66–81.

1959. Zvieracie zvyšky z doby bronzovej z Gánoviec, okr. Poprad, *Slovenská Archeológia* 7/1, 47–70.

1986. Tierreste von der Heidenschanze in Dresden-Coschütz, *Veröff. des Museums für Ur- und Frühgeschichte Potsdam* 20, 175–86.

Ammann, B., Furger, A. R., Joos, M. and Liese-Kleiber, H. 1977. *Die neolithischen Ufersiedlungen von Twann. III. Der bronzezeitliche Einbaum.* Bern: Staatliche Lehrmittelverlag.

Ampe, C., Bourgeois, J., Crombé, P., Fockedey, L., Langohr, R., Meganck, M., Semey, J., Van Strydonek, M., and Verlaeckt, K. 1996. The circular view. Aerial photography and the discovery of Bronze Age funerary monuments in East- and West-Flanders (Belgium), *Germania* 74, 45–94.

Anati, E. 1960. *La Grande Roche de Naquane.* Archives de l'Institut de paléontologie humaine, Mémoire 31. Paris: Masson and Cie.

1961. *Camonica Valley. A Depiction of Village Life in the Alps from Neolithic Times to the Birth of Christ as Revealed by Thousands of Newly Found Rock Carvings.* New York: Knopf.

1963. *La datazione dell'arte preistorica camuna.* Studi Camuni 2. Breno: Tipografia Camuna.

Andrea, Z. 1985. *Kultura ilire e tumave në pellgun e Korçës.* Tirana: Akademia e Shkencave e RPS të Shqipërisë.

Andres, A. M. de and Balcazar, J. L. 1989. Study of ceramic sherds of Early Bronze Age shelters (Peña Corva, Guadalajara, Spain). In *Archaeometry.*

Proceedings of the 25th International Symposium, ed. Y. Maniatis, 593–601. Amsterdam: Elsevier.

Aner, E. 1956. Grab und Hort, *Offa* 15, 31–42.

Aner, E. and Kersten, K. 1973–95. *Die Funde der älteren Bronzezeit des nordischen Kreises in Dänemark, Schleswig-Holstein und Niedersachsen, I–X, XVII–XVIII*. Copenhagen/Neumünster: Karl Wachholtz.

Angelucci, D. E. and Medici, T. 1994. Aspetti stratigrafici e culturali della terramara di Cavazzoli (Reggio Emilia). La campagna di scavo 1990, *Padusa* 30, 145–86.

Annable, F. K. and Simpson, D. D. A. 1964. *Guide Catalogue of the Neolithic and Bronze Age Collections in Devizes Museum*. Devizes: Wiltshire Archaeol. and Natural History Soc.

Anthony, D. W. 1996. V. G. Childe's world system and the daggers of the Early Bronze Age. In *Craft Specialization and Social Evolution: In Memory of V. Gordon Childe*, ed. B. Wailes, 47–66. University Museum Monograph 93. Philadelphia: University Museum, University of Pennsylvania.

Appadurai, A. (ed.) 1986. *The Social Life of Things. Commodities in Cultural Perspective*. Cambridge: Cambridge University Press.

ApSimon, A. M. and Greenfield, E. 1972. The excavation of Bronze Age and Iron Age settlements at Trevisker, St Eval, Cornwall, *Proc. Prehist. Soc.* 38, 302–81.

Aranguren, B. M., Pellegrini, E. and Perazzi, P. 1985. *L'insediamento protostorico di Pitigliano. Campagne di scavo 1982–83*. Pitigliano: Comunità Montana Zona 'S' Colline del Fiora.

Araus, J. L., Febrero, A., Buxó, R., Rodríguez-Ariza, M. O., Molina, F., Camalich, M. D., Martín, D. and Voltas, J. 1997. Identification of ancient irrigation practices based on the carbon isotope discrimination of plant seeds: a case study from the south-east Iberian peninsula, *J. Archaeol. Science* 24, 729–40.

Arenoso Callipo, C. M. S. and Bellintani, P. 1994. Dati archeologici e paleoambientali del territorio di Frattesina di Fratta Polesine (RO) tra la tarda età del bronzo e la prima età del ferro, *Padusa* 30, 7–65.

Arens, W. 1979. *The Man-Eating Myth: Anthropology and Anthropophagy*. New York: Oxford University Press.

Armand-Calliat, L. 1950. Quelques objets protohistoriques inédits trouvés dans le Saône aux abords de Chalon, *Revue Archéol. de l'Est et du Centre-Est* 1, 26–30.

Arnal, J. 1973. Le Lébous à Saint-Mathieu-de-Tréviers (Hérault). Ensemble du Chalcolithique au Gallo-Romain. I. Etude archéologique, *Gallia Préhistoire* 16, 131–93.

Arnold, B. 1977. Les deux villages immergés du Bronze final d'Auvernier: la station Brena et la station Nord, *Mitteilungsblatt der schweizerischen Gesellschaft für Ur- und Frühgeschichte* 8 (30/31), 46–57.

    1983. Les 24 maisons d'Auvernier-Nord (Bronze final), *Jahrbuch der schweizerischen Gesellschaft für Ur- und Frühgeschichte* 66, 87–104.

    1984. A propos de Cortaillod-Est (Bronze final): le pilotis, une source d'information trop souvent méconnue, *Archäologie der Schweiz* 7/2, 54–62.

    1985. Navigation et construction navale sur les lacs suisses au Bronze final, *Helvetia Archaeologica* 16, 91–117.

    1990. *Cortaillod-Est et les villages du lac de Neuchâtel au Bronze final*.

Structure de l'habitat et proto-urbanisme. Archéologie neuchâteloise 6.
Saint-Blaise: Editions du Ruau.

Arqueología en Catalunya 1983. *Arqueología en Catalunya, datos para una
síntesis.* Barcelona: Departament de Cultura de la Generalitat de
Catalunya.

Arribas Palau, A., Pareja Lopez, E., Molina Gonzalez, F., Arteaga Matute, O.
and Molina Fajardo, F. 1974. *Excavaciones en el poblado de la edad del
bronce 'Cerro de la Encina', Monachil (Granada) (El Corte Estratigrafico
no. 3).* Excavaciones Arqueologicas en España, 81 Madrid: Servicio de
Publicaciones del Ministerio de Educacion y Ciencia.

Ashbee, P. 1960. *The Bronze Age Round Barrow in Britain. An Introduction to
the Study of the Funerary Practice and Culture of the British and Irish
Single-Grave People of the Second Millennium BC.* London: Phoenix
House.

Ashbee, P., Bell, M. and Proudfoot, E. 1989. *Wilsford Shaft: Excavations
1960–62.* English Heritage Archaeological Report 11. London: Historic
Buildings and Monuments Commission for England.

Aspinall, A. and Warren, S. E. 1976. The provenance of British faience beads: a
study using neutron activation analysis. In *Applicazione dei metodi
nucleari nel campo delle opere d'arte*, 145–52. Atti dei Convegni Lincei 11.
Rome–Venice: Accademia dei Lincei.

Aspinall, A., Warren, S. E. and Crummett, J. G. 1972. Neutron activation
analysis of faience beads, *Archaeometry* 14, 27–40.

Atkinson, R. J. C. 1956. *Stonehenge.* London: Hamish Hamilton.
  1972. Burial and population in the British Bronze Age. In *Prehistoric Man in
  Wales and the West: Essays in Honour of Lily F. Chitty*, eds. F. Lynch and
  C. Burgess, 107–16. Bath: Adams and Dart.

Atzeni, E. 1978. Le 'statue-menhir' de Laconi. In *Sardegna centro-orientale dal
Neolitico alla fine del mondo antico*, 47–52. Sassari: Dessì.

Audouze, F. and Büchsenschütz, O. 1991. *Towns, Villages and Countryside of
Celtic Europe, from the Beginning of the Second Millennium to the End of
the First Century BC.* London: Batsford (translation of *Villes, villages et
campagnes de l'Europe celtique*, Paris: Hachette, 1989).

Avery, M. and Close-Brooks, J. 1969. Shearplace Hill, Sydling St Nicholas,
Dorset, House A: a suggested re-interpretation, *Proc. Prehist. Soc.* 35,
345–51.

Avila, R. A. J. 1983. *Bronzene Lanzen- und Pfeilspitzen der griechischen
Spätbronzezeit.* Prähistorische Bronzefunde V, 1. Munich: Beck.

Bach, A., Bach, H. and Simon, K. 1972. Anthropologische Aspekte der
Bevölkerungsentwicklung im westlichen Mitteldeutschland, *Jahresschrift
für mitteldeutsche Vorgeschichte* 56, 7–38.

Bader, T. 1982. Die befestigte bronzezeitlichen Siedlungen in
Nordwestrumänien. In *Beiträge zum bronzezeitlichen Burgenbau in
Mitteleuropa*, 47–70. Berlin: Zentralinstitut für Alte Geschichte und
Archäologie; Nitra: Archeologický Ústav Slovenskej Akadémie Vied.
  1991. *Die Schwerter in Rumänien.* Prähistorische Bronzefunde IV, 8.
  Stuttgart: Franz Steiner.

Baillie, M. G. L. 1989. Do Irish bog oaks date the Shang Dynasty? *Current
Archaeology* 117, 310–13.
  1995. *A Slice through Time. Dendrochronology and Precision Dating.*
  London: Batsford.

Bakels, C. C. 1982–3. Les graines carbonisées de Fort-Harrouard (Eure-et-Loir), *Antiquités Nationales* 14–15, 59–63.

    1984. Carbonized seeds from northern France, *Analecta Praehistorica Leidensia* 17, 1–27.

Balaam, N. D., Smith, K. and Wainwright, G. J. 1982. The Shaugh Moor project – environment, context and conclusion, *Proc. Prehist. Soc.* 48, 203–78.

Balkwill, C. J. 1976. The evidence of cemeteries for later prehistoric development in the upper Rhine valley, *Proc. Prehist. Soc.* 42, 187–213.

Bándi, G. 1982. Spätbronzezeitliche befestigte Höhensiedlungen in Westungarn. In *Beiträge zum bronzezeitlichen Burgenbau in Mitteleuropa*, 81–90. Berlin: Zentralinstitut für Alte Geschichte und Archäologie; Nitra: Archeologický Ústav Slovenskej Akadémie Vied.

Banner, J. and Bóna, I. 1974. *Mittelbronzezeitliche Tell-Siedlung bei Békés*. Fontes Archaeologici Hungariae. Budapest: Akadémiai Kiadó.

Banner, J., Bóna, I. and Márton, L. 1957. Die Ausgrabungen von L. Márton in Tószeg, *Acta Archaeologica* (Budapest) 10, 1–140.

Barber, E. J. W. 1991. *Prehistoric Textiles. The Development of Cloth in the Neolithic and Bronze Ages with Special Reference to the Aegean*. Princeton: Princeton University Press.

Barber, J. 1973. The orientation of the recumbent-stone circles of the south-west of Ireland, *J. Kerry Archaeol. Historical Soc.* 6, 26–39.

Barclay, G. J. 1983. Sites of the third millennium bc to the first millennium ad at North Mains, Strathallan, Perthshire, *Proc. Soc. Antiqs Scotland* 113, 122–281.

Barfield, L. 1971. *Northern Italy before Rome*. London: Thames and Hudson.

    1978. North Italian faience buttons, *Antiquity* 52, 150–3.

    1996. The Chalcolithic in Italy: considerations of metal typology and cultural interaction. In *XIII International Congress of Prehistoric and Protohistoric Sciences, Forlì, Italy, 10: The Copper Age in the Near East and Europe. Colloquium XIX, Metallurgy: Origins and Technology*, 65–74. Forlì: ABACO Edizioni.

Barford, P. 1990. Salt production in Essex before the Red Hills. Appendix 2 in A. J. Fawn, K. A. Evans, I. McMaster and G. M. R. Davies, *The Red Hills of Essex. Salt-Making in Antiquity*, 81–4. Colchester: Colchester Archaeological Group.

Barker, G. 1975. Prehistoric territories and economies in central Italy. In *Palaeoeconomy*, ed. E. S. Higgs, 111–75. Cambridge: Cambridge University Press.

    1985. *Prehistoric Farming in Europe*. Cambridge: Cambridge University Press.

Barnatt, J. 1987. Bronze Age settlement on the East Moors of the Peak District of Derbyshire and South Yorkshire, *Proc. Prehist. Soc.* 53, 393–418.

    1989. *Stone Circles of Britain. Taxonomic and Distributional Analyses and a Catalogue of Sites in England, Scotland and Wales*. Oxford: British Archaeological Reports 215.

    1991. The prehistoric cairnfield at Highlow Bank, Highlow, Derbyshire: a systematic survey of all remains and excavation of one of the cairns, *Derbyshire Archaeol. J.* 91, 5–30.

Barrett, J. C. 1988a. The living, the dead and the ancestors: Neolithic and Early Bronze Age mortuary practices. In *The Archaeology of Context in the Neolithic and Bronze Age: Recent Trends*, eds. J. C. Barrett and I. A.

Kinnes, 30–41. Sheffield: Department of Archaeology and Prehistory, University of Sheffield.

1988b. Fields of discourse – reconstituting a social archaeology, *Critique of Anthropology* 7/3, 5–16.

1994. Defining domestic space in the Bronze Age of southern Britain. In *Architecture and Order. Approaches to Social Space*, eds. M. Parker Pearson and C. Richards, 87–97. London: Routledge.

Barrett, J. C., Bradley, R., Cleal, R. and Pike, H. 1978. Characterisation of Deverel–Rimbury pottery from Cranborne Chase, *Proc. Prehist. Soc.* 44, 135–42.

Barrett, J. C., Bradley, R. and Green, M. 1991. *Landscape, Monuments and Society. The Prehistory of Cranborne Chase*. Cambridge: Cambridge University Press.

Barta, J. 1961. Zur Problematik der Höhlenbesiedlung in den slowakischen Karpaten, *Acta Archaeol. Carpathica* 2, 5–39.

Barth, F. E. 1973. Versuch einer typologischen Gliederung der prähistorischen Funde aus dem Hallstatter Salzberg, *Mitt. der anthropologischen Gesellschaft Wien* 102, 26–30.

1982. Prehistoric saltmining at Hallstatt, *Bull. Institute Archaeology London* 19, 31–43.

Barth, F. E., Felber, H. and Schauberger, O. 1975. Radiokohlenstoffdatierung der prähistorischen Baue in den Salzbergwerken Hallstatt und Dürrnberg-Hallein, *Mitt. der anthropologischen Gesellschaft Wien* 105, 45–52.

Bartlett, J. E. and Hawkes, C. F. C. 1965. A barbed bronze spearhead from North Ferriby, Yorkshire, England, *Proc. Prehist. Soc.* 31, 370–3.

Bartosiewicz, L. 1996. Bronze Age animal keeping in northwestern Transdanubia, Hungary, *Pápai Múzeum Értesítő* 6, 31–42.

Bartosiewicz, L., van Neer, W. and Lentacker, A. 1993. Metapodial asymmetry in draft cattle, *Int. J. Osteoarchaeology* 3, 69–75.

Bass, G. F. 1967. *Cape Gelidonya: a Bronze Age Shipwreck*. Transactions American Philosophical Soc., new series 57 part 8. Philadelphia.

Bass, G. F., Pulak, C., Collon, D. and Weinstein, J. 1989. The Bronze Age shipwreck at Ulu Burun: 1986 campaign, *American J. Archaeology* 93, 1–29.

Bath-Bílková, B. 1973. K problému původu hřiven, *Památky Archeologické* 64, 24–41.

Bátora, J. 1991. The reflection of economy and social structure in the cemeteries of the Chłopice–Veselé and Nitra cultures, *Slovenská Archeológia* 39, 91–142.

Batović, Š. 1983. Kasno brončanog doba na istočnom jadranskom primorju. In *Praistorija jugoslavenskih zemalja, IV, Bronzano doba*, ed. B. Čović, 271–373. Sarajevo: Akademija Nauka i Umjetnosti Bosne i Hercegovine, Centar za balkanološka ispitivanja.

Baudou, E. 1960. *Die regionale und chronologische Einteilung der jüngeren Bronzezeit im Nordischen Kreis*. Studies in North-European Archaeology 1. Stockholm: Almquist and Wiksell.

Beck, C. W. and Shennan, S. 1991. *Amber in Prehistoric Britain*. Oxford: Oxbow Monograph 8.

Beck, H. C. and Stone, J. F. S. 1936. Faience beads of the British Bronze Age, *Archaeologia* 85, 203–52.

Beckensall, S. 1986. *Rock Carvings of Northern Britain*. Princes Risborough: Shire Publications.

Becker, B., Billamboz, A., Egger, H., Gassmann, P., Orcel, A., Orcel, C. and Ruoff, U. 1985. *Dendrochronologie in der Ur- und Frühgeschichte. Die absolute Datierung von Pfahlbausiedlungen nördlich der Alpen im Jahrringkalender Mitteleuropas.* Antiqua 11. Basel: Verlag Schweizerische Gesellschaft für Ur- und Frühgeschichte.

Becker, B., Jäger, K.-D., Kaufmann, D. and Litt, T. 1989. Dendrochronologische Datierungen von Eichenhölzern aus den frühbronzezeitlichen Hügelgräbern bei Helmsdorf und Leubingen (Aunjetitzer Kultur) und an bronzezeitlichen Flusseichen bei Merseburg, *Jahresschrift für mitteldeutsche Vorgeschichte* 72, 299–312.

Becker, B., Krause, R. and Kromer, B. 1989. Zur absoluten Chronologie der frühen Bronzezeit, *Germania* 67/2, 421–42.

Becker, C. J. 1954. A segmented faience bead from Jutland. With notes on amber beads from Bronze Age Denmark, *Acta Archaeologica* (Copenhagen) 25, 241–52.

Becker, D. 1989. Bronzezeitliche Schmelzofenreste von der Gemarkung Parchim, *Ausgrabungen und Funde* 34, 129–32.

Becker, M. J. 1984. Sardinian stone moulds: an indirect means of evaluating Bronze Age metallurgical technology. In *Studies in Sardinian Archaeology*, eds. M. S. Balmuth and R. J. Rowland, 163–208. Ann Arbor: University of Michigan Press.

Bednarik, R. G. 1992. Developments in rock art dating, *Acta Archaeologica* (Copenhagen) 63, 141–55.

Beex, G. and Hulst, R. S. 1968. A Hilversum-culture settlement near Nijnsel, Municipality of St Oedenrode, North Brabant, *Berichten van de Rijksdienst voor het Oudheidkundig Bodemonderzoek* 18, 117–29.

Behm-Blancke, G. 1958. *Höhlen, Heiligtümer, Kannibalen. Archäologische Forschungen im Kyffhäuser.* Leipzig: F. A. Brockhaus.

   1976. Zur Funktion bronze- und früheisenzeitlicher Kulthöhlen im Mittelgebirgsraum, *Ausgrabungen und Funde* 21, 80–8.

Behre, K.-E. 1990. Getreidefund aus der bronzezeitlichen Höhensiedlung Toos-Waldi, Kanton Thurgau (Schweiz). In *Der Prähistorische Mensch und Seine Umwelt. Festschrift für U. Körber-Grohne zum 65. Geburtstag*, ed. H. Küster, 239–44. Forschungen und Berichte zur Vor- und Frühgeschichte in Baden-Württemberg 31. Stuttgart: Konrad Theiss.

Behrens, H. W. 1978. Der Kampf in der Steinzeit (ein Diskussionsbeitrag vom Aspekt des Prähistorikers), *Mitt. der Anthropologischen Gesellschaft Wien* 108, 1–7.

Bell, M. 1990. *Brean Down Excavations 1983–1987.* London: English Heritage Archaeological Report 15.

Bellwald, W. 1992. Drei spätneolithisch/frühbronzezeitliche Pfeilbogen aus dem Gletschereis am Lötschenpass, *Archäologie der Schweiz* 15/4, 166–71.

Beltran Martinez, A. 1984. Las casas del poblado de la I edad del hierro del cabezo de Monleón (Caspe), *Museo de Zaragoza Boletín* 3, 23–100.

Benac, A. 1985. *Utvrđena ilirska naselja (I). Delmatske gradine na Duvanjskom polju, Bučkom blatu, Livanjskom i Glamočkom polju.* Sarajevo: Akademija Nauka i Umjetnosti Bosne i Hercegovine, Monograph 60/Centar za balkanološka ispitivanja 4.

   1986. *Praistorijski tumuli na Kupreškom polju.* Sarajevo: Akademija Nauka i Umjetnosti Bosne i Hercegovine, Monograph. 64/Centar za balkanološka ispitivanja 5.

1990. Recently excavated Bronze Age tumuli in the Kupreško polje, Bosnia, Yugoslavia, *Antiquity* 64, 327–33.

Benac, A. and Čović, B. 1956. *Glasinac, I. Bronzezeit*. Katalog der vorgeschichtlichen Sammlung des Landesmuseums in Sarajevo 1. Sarajevo: Zemaljski Muzej.

Bender Jørgensen, L. 1986. *Forhistoriske textiler i Skandinavien (Prehistoric Scandinavian Textiles)*. Nordiske Fortidsminder series B, 9. Copenhagen: Kongelige Nordiske Oldskriftselskab.

1992. *North European Textiles until AD 1000*. Aarhus: Aarhus University Press.

Beninger, E. 1941. Die frühbronzezeitliche Dorfanlage von Grossmugl (Niederdonau), *Mitt. der Prähistorischen Kommission* 4, 3–4, 49–89.

Benkovsky-Pivovarová, Z. 1985. Das Bronzeinventar des mittelbronzezeitlichen Gräberfeldes von Pitten, Niederösterreich. In *Das mittelbronzezeitliche Gräberfeld von Pitten in Niederösterreich. Ergebnisse der Ausgrabungen des Niederösterreichischen Landesmuseums in den Jahren 1967 bis 1973. Mitt. der Prähistorischen Kommission der österreichischen Akademie der Wissenschaften* 19–20, eds. F. Hampl, F. Kerchler and Z. Benkovsky-Pivovarová, 23–125.

1987. Zur Hügelbestattung der Frühbronzezeit im mittleren Donauraum. In *Hügelbestattung in der Karpaten–Donau–Balkan Zone während der äneolithischen Periode* (Internationales Symposium Donji Milanovac 1985), eds. D. Srejović and N.Tasić, 167–71. Belgrade: Balkanološki Institut, posebna izdanja 29.

Bennike, P. 1985. *Palaeopathology of Danish Skeletons. A Comparative Study of Demography, Disease and Injury*. Copenhagen: Akademisk Forlag.

Bérenger, D. 1996. Archäologische Ausgrabungen zur Erforschung der Mittelbronzezeit im Kreis Paderborn (Ostwestfalen), *Die Kunde* 47, 127–42.

Benton, S. 1930–1. The excavation of the Sculptor's Cave, Covesea, Morayshire, *Proc. Soc. Antiqs Scotland* 65, 177–216.

Berger, L. *et al.* 1996. *Sondierungen auf dem Wittnauer Horn 1980–1982*. Basel: Basler Beiträge zur Ur- und Frühgeschichte 14.

Bergmann, J. 1982. *Ein Gräberfeld der jüngeren Bronze- und älteren Eisenzeit bei Vollmarshausen, Kr. Kassel. Zur Struktur und Geschichte einer vorgeschichtlichen Gemeinschaft im Spiegel ihres Gräberfeldes*. Kasseler Beiträge zur Vor- und Frühgeschichte 5. Marburg: N. G. Elwert Verlag.

1987. *Die metallzeitliche Revolution. Zur Entstehung von Herrschaft, Krieg und Umweltzerstörung*. Berlin: Reimer.

Bernabei, M. and Grifoni Cremonesi, R. 1995–6. I culti delle acque nella preistoria dell'Italia peninsulare, *Rivista di Scienze Preistoriche* 47, 331–66.

Bernabò Brea, L. 1990. *Pantalica. Ricerche intorno all'anáktoron*. Cahiers du Centre Jean Bérard, 14. Naples, Palazzolo Acreide: Centre Jean Bérard/Istituto Studi Acrensi.

Bernabò Brea, L. and Cavalier, M. 1966. Ricerche paletnologiche nell'isola di Filicudi (relazione preliminare), *Bull. Paletnologia Italiana* 75, 143–73.

1968. *Meligunìs-Lipára, III. Stazioni preistoriche delle isole Panarea, Salina e Stromboli*. Palermo: Flaccovio.

1980. *Meligunìs-Lipára, IV. L'acropoli di Lipari nella preistoria*. Palermo: Flaccovio.

1990. La tholos termale di San Calogero nell'isola di Lipari, *Studi Micenei ed Egeo-Anatolici* 28, 7–84.

Bernabò Brea, M., Cardarelli, A., Mutti, A., Bresciani, R., Bronzoni, L., Catarsi, M., Desantis, P., Labate, D., Macellari, R., Morico, G., Serges, A., Tirabassi, J., and Zanasi, C. 1991–2. Ambiti culturali e fasi cronologiche delle terramare emiliane in base alla revisione dei vecchi complessi e ai nuovi dati di scavo, *Rassegna di Archeologia* 10, 341–73.

Bernabò Brea, M. and Cremaschi, M. 1990. Les terramares dans la plaine du Pô. In *Colloque internationale de Lons-le-Saunier, 16–19 mai 1990*, 407–17.

  1996. Tredici anni di ricerche nella terramara Santa Rosa a Fodico di Poviglio (RE), *Pagine di Archeologia* (Reggio Emilia Musei Civici) 3, 1–47.

Berner, M. 1997. Demographie des frühbronzezeitlichen Gräberfeldes Franzhausen I, Niederösterreich. In *Demographie der Bronzezeit. Paläodemographie – Möglichkeiten und Grenzen*, ed. K.-F. Rittershofer, 35–42. Internationale Archäologie 36. Espelkamp: Verlag Marie Leidorf.

Bersu, G. 1945. *Das Wittnauer Horn*. Monographien zur Ur- und Frühgeschichte der Schweiz, IV. Basel: Birkhäuser.

Bertaux, J.-P. 1976. L'archéologie du sel en Lorraine, 'Le briquetage de la Seille' (état actuel des recherches). In *Livret-Guide de l'excursion A7, Champagne, Lorraine, Alsace, Franche-Comté*, eds. J.-P. Millotte, A. Thévenin and B. Chertier UISPP IXe congrès, Nice 1976, 64–79.

Bertemes, F. 1989. *Das frühbronzezeitliche Gräberfeld von Gemeinlebarn. Kulturhistorische und paläometallurgische Studien*. Saarbrückener Beiträge zur Altertumskunde 45. Bonn: Habelt.

Bertilsson, U. 1981. What do the cairns mean? Do monumental cairns in areas with many cairns have the same significance as cairns in areas with barrows? Bohuslän and Halland 1500–500 BC. In *Similar Finds? Similar Interpretations?*, ed. C.-A Moberg, C1–19. Gothenburg: University of Gothenburg, Department of Archaeology.

  1987. *The Rock Carvings of Northern Bohuslän. Spatial Structures and Social Symbols*. Stockholm Studies in Archaeology 7. Stockholm: Department of Archaeology, University of Stockholm.

  1989. Rock-carvings, ideology and society in the Bronze Age of western Sweden. In *Bronze Age Studies*, eds. H.-Å. Nordström and A. Knape, 101–9. Stockholm: Statens Historiska Museum, Studies 6.

Bewley, R. H., Longworth, I. H., Browne, S., Huntley, J. P. and Varndell, G. 1992. Excavation of a Bronze Age cemetery at Ewanrigg, Maryport, Cumbria, *Proc. Prehist. Soc.* 58, 325–54.

Bianco Peroni, V. 1970. *Die Schwerter in Italien / Le spade nell'Italia continentale*. Prähistorische Bronzefunde IV, 1. Munich: Beck.

  1978–9. Bronzene Gewässer- und Höhenfunde aus Italien, *Jahresbericht des Institutes für Vorgeschichte der Universität Frankfurt a.M.* 1978–9, 321–35.

Bichir, G. 1964. Autour du problème des plus anciens modèles de chariots découverts en Roumanie, *Dacia* 8, 67–86.

Bicknell, C. 1913. *A Guide to the Prehistoric Rock Engravings in the Italian Maritime Alps*. Bordighera: Bessone.

Biel, J. 1980. Die bronze- und urnenfelderzeitlichen Höhensiedlungen in Südwürttemberg, *Archäologisches Korrespondenzblatt* 10, 23–32.

  1987. *Vorgeschichtliche Höhensiedlungen in Südwurttemberg-Hohenzollern*. Forschungen und Berichte zur Vor- und Frühgeschichte in Baden-Württemberg 24. Stuttgart: Konrad Theiss.

Bietti Sestieri, A. M. 1975. Elementi per lo studio dell'abitato protostorico di Frattesina di Fratta Polesine (Rovigo), *Padusa* 11, 1–14.

1980. L'abitato di Frattesina. In *Este e la civiltà paleoveneta a cento anni dalle prime scoperte* (Atti dell'XI Convegno di Studi Etruschi e Italici, Este-Padova 1976), 23–37. Florence: L. S. Olschki.

Bill, J. 1980. Früh- und mittelbronzezeitliche Höhensiedlungen im Alpenrheintal im Lichte der Bronzeproduktion, *Archäologisches Korrespondenzblatt* 10, 17–21.

Billamboz, A., Keefer, E., Köninger, J. and Torke, W. 1989. La transition Bronze ancien–moyen dans le sud-ouest de l'Allemagne à l'exemple de deux stations de l'habitat lacustre (Station Forschner, Federsee) et littoral (Bodman-Schachen I, Bodensee). In *Dynamique du Bronze moyen en Europe occidentale*, Actes du 113ᵉ Congrès national des sociétés savantes, Strasbourg 1988, 51–78. Paris: Editions du CTHS.

Billig, G. 1958. *Die Aunjetitzer Kultur in Sachsen*. Leipzig: Veröffentl. des Landesmuseums für Vorgeschichte, 7.

Binford, L. R. 1971. Mortuary practices, their study and potential. In *Approaches to the Social Dimensions of Mortuary Practices*, ed. J. A. Brown, 6–29. Society for American Archaeology, Memoir 25.

Björhem, N. and Säfvestad, U. 1993. *Fosie IV. Bebyggelsen under brons- och järnålder*. Malmöfund 6. Malmö Museer.

Blajer, W. 1984. *Die Arm- und Beinbergen in Polen*. Prähistorische Bronzefunde X, 2. Munich: Beck.

Blajer, W. (ed.) 1997. *Beiträge zur Deutung der bronzezeitlichen Hort- und Grabfunde in Mitteleuropa*. Cracow: Oficyna Cracovia.

Blanchet, J.-C., Cornejo, A., Lambot, B. and Laurent, S. 1978. Dragages de l'Oise de 1973 à 1976 (deuxième partie), *Cahiers Archéologiques de Picardie* 5, 89–104.

Blanco, A. and Luzon, J. M. 1969. Pre-Roman silver miners at Riotinto, *Antiquity* 43, 124–31.

Blas Cortina, M. A. de 1996. La primera minería metálica del N. peninsular: las indicaciones del C-14 y la cronología prehistórica de las explotaciones cupríferas del Aramo y El Milagro. In Complutum Extra 6/1, *Homenaje al Professor Manuel Fernández-Miranda I*, eds. M. A. Querol and T. Chapa, 217–26. Madrid: Universidad Complutense.

Blažek, J. and Smejtek, L. 1993. *Die Bronzemesser in Nordwestböhmen*. Beiträge zur Ur- und Frühgeschichte Nordwestböhmens 1; Nordböhmische Bronzefunde 1, vol. 1. Prague: H. and H.

Blouet, V., Koenig, M.-P. and Vanmoerkerke, J. 1996. L'âge du bronze ancien en Lorraine. In *Cultures et sociétés du bronze ancien en Europe*, eds. C. Mordant and O. Gaiffe, 403–57. 117ᵉ Congrès national des sociétés historiques et scientifiques, Clermont Ferrand 1992. Paris: Editions du CTHS.

Boas, N. A. 1983. Egehøj, a settlement from the Early Bronze Age in east Jutland, *J. Danish Archaeology* 2, 90–101.

1989. Bronze Age houses at Hemmed Church, East Jutland, *J. Danish Archaeology* 8, 88–107.

Bočkarev, V. S. and Leskov, A. M. 1980. *Jung- und spätbronzezeitliche Gussformen im nördlichen Schwarzmeergebiet*. Prähistorische Bronzefunde XIX, 1 Munich: Beck.

Bocksberger, O. J. 1978. *Le Site préhistorique du Petit-Chasseur (Sion, Valais). 4. Horizon supérieur, secteur occidental et tombes Bronze ancien*. Cahiers d'archéologie romande 14. Geneva: Département d'Anthropologie, Université de Genève.

Bodegraven, N. van 1991. Nederzettingssporen uit de late bronstijd en de vroege ijzertijd op de Everse Akkers in St.-Oedenrode. In *Nederzettingen uit bronstijd en de vroege ijzertijd in de Lage Landen*, eds. H. Fokkens and N. Roymans, 129–40. Nederlandse Archeologische Rapporten 13. Amersfoort: Rijkdienst voor het Oudheidkundig Bodermonderzoek.

Bokelmann, K. 1977. Ein bronzezeitlicher Hausgrundriss bei Handewitt, Kreis Schleswig-Flensburg, *Offa* 34, 82–9.

Bökönyi, S. 1952. Die Wirbeltierfauna der Ausgrabungen in Tószeg vom Jahre 1948, *Acta Archaeologica* (Budapest) 2, 71–113.

   1974. *History of Domestic Mammals in Central and Eastern Europe*. Budapest: Akadémiai Kiadó.

   1988. Animal remains from Bronze Age tells in the Berettyó valley. In *Bronze Age Tell Settlements of the Great Hungarian Plain I*, eds. T. Kovacs and I. Stanczik, 123–35. Inventaria Praehistorica Hungariae. Budapest: Magyar Nemzeti Múzeum.

Bóna, I. 1960. Clay models of Bronze Age wagons and wheels, *Acta Archaeologica* (Budapest) 12, 83–111.

   1975. *Die mittlere Bronzezeit Ungarns und ihre südöstlichen Beziehungen*. Budapest: Akadémiai Kiadó.

   1992. Tószeg-Laposhalom. In *Bronzezeit in Ungarn*, 101–14.

Bond, D. 1988. *Excavation at the North Ring, Mucking, Essex: a Late Bronze Age Enclosure*. East Anglian Archaeology 43.

Bondár, M. 1990. Das frühbronzezeitliche Wagenmodell von Börzönce, *Communicationes Archaeologicae Hungariae 1990*, 77–91.

Bönisch, E. 1993. Briquetage aus bronzezeitlichen Gräbern der Niederlausitz, *Arbeits- und Forschungsberichte zur sächsischen Bodendenkmalpflege* 36, 67–84.

Bonnet, C. 1973. Une station d'altitude de l'époque des Champs d'urnes au sommet du Hohlandsberg, *Bull. Soc. Préhist. Française* 70, 455–77.

Bonnet, C., Plouin, S. and Lambach, F. 1981. Les tertres du Bronze moyen d'Appenwihr, forêt de Kastenwald (Haut-Rhin), *Bull. Soc. Préhist. Française* 78, 432–71.

   1985. Linsenbrunnen II, un nouveau secteur de la station d'altitude de Hohlandsberg (commune de Wintzenheim, Haut-Rhin), *Bull. Soc. Préhist. Française* 82, 449–509.

Bonzani, R. M. 1992. Territorial boundaries, buffer zones and sociopolitical complexity: a case study of the nuraghi on Sardinia. In *Sardinia in the Mediterranean: a Footprint in the Sea, Studies in Sardinian Archaeology Presented to Miriam S. Balmuth*, eds. R. H. Tykot and T. K. Andrews, 210–19. Sheffield: Sheffield Academic Press.

Borgognini, S. M., Canci, A., Minozzi, S., Repetto, E. and Scattarella, V. 1995. Skeletal and dental indicators of health conditions in Italian Bronze age samples. In *Proceedings of the IXth European Meeting of the Palaeopathology Association* (Barcelona 1992), 37–45. Barcelona: Museu d'Arqueologia de Catalunya.

Born, H. and Hansen, S. 1991. Antike Herstellungstechniken: ungewöhnliche Klingenreparaturen an einem spätbronzezeitlichen Vollgriffschwert, *Acta Praehistorica et Archaeologica* 23, 147–57.

Boroffka, N. G. O. 1994. *Die Wietenberg-Kultur. Ein Beitrag zur Erforschung der Bronzezeit in Südosteuropa*, 2 vols. Universitätsforschungen zur prähistorischen Archäologie 19. Bonn: Habelt.

Boross, M. M. and Nemeskéri, J. 1963. Ein bronzezeitliches Nierenstein aus Ungarn, *Homo* 14, 149–50.

Bošković, D. 1959. Quelques observations sur le char cultuel de Dupljaja, *Archaeologia Jugoslavica* 3, 41–5.

Bourhis, J. R. and Gomez, J. 1985. Déchets de fonderie de bronze des Grottes du Queroy à Chazelles et des Perrats à Agris (Charente). In *Paléometallurgie de la France Atlantique. Age du bronze (2)*, 111–17. Rennes: Travaux du Laboratoire anthropologie–préhistoire–protohistoire–quaternaire armoricains.

Bouscaras, A. 1971. L'épave des bronzes de Rochelongues, *Archeologia* 39, 68–73.

Bouscaras, A. and Hugues, C. 1967. La cargaison des bronzes de Rochelongues (Agde, Hérault), *Rivista di Studi Liguri* 33 (Omaggio a Fernand Benoit), 173–84.

Bouzek, J. 1978. Zu den Anfängen der Eisenzeit in Mitteleuropa, *Zeitschrift für Archäologie* 12, 9–14.

1985. K otázkám počátku doby železné ve střední Evropě, *Archeologické Rozhledy* 37, 83–92.

Bouzek, J. and Koutecký, D. 1964. Knovízské zásobní jámy, *Archeologické Rozhledy* 16, 28–43.

1980. Mohylové a knovízské kostrové 'pohřby' v jámách ze severozápadních Čech, *Památky Archeologické* 71, 360–432.

Bouzek, J., Koutecký, D. and Neustupný, E. 1966. *The Knovíz Settlement of North-West Bohemia*. Fontes Archaeologici Pragenses 10. Prague: National Museum.

Bouzek, J., Koutecký, D. and Simon, K. 1989. Tin and prehistoric mining in the Erzgebirge (Ore Mountains): some new evidence, *Oxford J. Archaeology* 8/2, 203–12.

Bowden, M. and McOmish, D. 1989. Little boxes: more about hillforts, *Scottish Archaeol. Review* 6, 12–16.

Bowen, H. C. 1978. 'Celtic ' fields and 'ranch' boundaries in Wessex. In *The Effect of Man on the Landscape: the Lowland Zone*, eds. S. Limbrey and J. G. Evans, 115–23. London: Council for British Archaeology, Research Report 21.

1990. *The Archaeology of Bokerley Dyke*. London: HMSO.

Boysen, Å. and Andersen, S. W. 1983. Trappendal, barrow and house from the Early Bronze Age, *J. Danish Archaeology* 2, 118–26.

Bradley, R. 1978. Prehistoric field systems in Britain and north-west Europe – a review of some recent work, *World Archaeology* 9/3, 265–80.

1990. *The Passage of Arms. An Archaeological Analysis of Prehistoric Hoards and Votive Deposits*. Cambridge: Cambridge University Press.

1991. Rock art and the perception of landscape, *Cambridge Archaeol. J.* 1/1, 77–101.

1994. Symbols and signposts – understanding the prehistoric petroglyphs of the British Isles. In *The Ancient Mind*, eds. C. Renfrew and E. Zubrow, 95–106. Cambridge: Cambridge University Press.

1997. *Rock Art and the Prehistory of Atlantic Europe: Signing the Land*. London: Routledge.

Bradley, R. and Ellison, A. 1975. *Rams Hill: a Bronze Age Defended Enclosure and its Landscape*. Oxford: British Archaeological Reports 19.

Bradley, R., Entwistle, R. and Raymond, F. 1994. *Prehistoric Land Divisions on*

Salisbury Plain. The Work of the Wessex Linear Ditches Project. London: English Heritage (Archaeological Report 2).

Bradley, R., Harding, J. and Mathews, M. 1993. The siting of prehistoric rock art in Galloway, south-west Scotland, *Proc. Prehist. Soc.* 59, 269–83.

Brady, N. D. K. 1990a. Early ard pieces in Finnish Museums, *Tools and Tillage* 6/3, 158–75.

1990b. A glimpse of early Irish agriculture, *Archaeology Ireland* 4/4, 18–19.

Branigan, K. 1968. Silver and lead in pre-palatial Crete, *American J. Archaeology* 72, 219–29.

Breddin, R. 1969. Der Aunjetitzer Bronzehortfund von Bresinchen, Kr. Guben, *Veröffent. des Museums für Ur- und Frühgeschichte Potsdam* 5, 15–56.

Breeze, D. J. 1974. Plough marks at Carrawburgh on Hadrian's Wall, *Tools and Tillage* 2/3, 188–90.

Breitinger, E. 1938. Zur Trepanation in der Frühbronzezeit. Zwei neue Fälle aus dem bayrischen Schwaben, *Anthropologischer Anzeiger* 15, 73–7.

Briard, J. 1965. *Les Dépôts bretons et l'âge du bronze atlantique*. Rennes: Travaux du Laboratoire d'anthropologie préhistorique.

1975. Nouvelles découvertes sur les tumulus armoricains, *Archaeologia Atlantica* 1, 17–32.

1978. Das Silbergefäss von Saint-Adrien, Côtes-du-Nord, *Archäologisches Korrespondenzblatt* 8, 13–20.

1983. La céramique des tumulus de l'âge du bronze du Morbihan, *Bull. Soc. Polymathique Morbihan* 110, 94–110.

1984a. L'outillage des fondeurs de l'âge du bronze en Armorique. In *Paléometallurgie de la France Atlantique. Age du bronze (1)*, 169–80. Rennes: Travaux du Laboratoire anthropologie–préhistoire–protohistoire–quaternaire armoricains.

1984b. Les perles en faïence du bronze ancien en Bretagne: méditerranéennes ou occidentales? *Revue Archéol. Ouest* 1, 55–62.

1984c. *Les Tumulus d'Armorique*. L'âge du bronze en France 3. Paris: Picard.

1990–91. Paléometallurgie armoricaine. Lingots en plomb du Bronze final et creusots protohistoriques, *Antiquités Nationales* 22–3, 37–42.

1993. Relations between Brittany and Great Britain during the Bronze Age. In *Trade and Exchange in Prehistoric Europe*, eds. C. Scarre and F. Healy, 183–90. Oxford: Oxbow Monograph 33.

Briard, J., Bourhis, J., Cabillic, H. and Onnée, Y. 1979. Tumulus et coffres à Plouhinec (Finistère). Les fouilles de Kergoglay, 1978, *Bull. Soc. Archéol. Finistère* 107, 33–54.

Briard, J. and Giot, P.-R. 1963. Fouille d'un tumulus de l'âge du bronze à Saint-Jude en Bourbriac (Côtes-du-Nord), *Annales de Bretagne* 70, 5–24.

Briard, J. and Mohen, J.-P. 1983. *Typologie des objets de l'âge du bronze en France. II: Poignards, hallebardes, pointes de lance, pointes de flèche, armement défensif*. Paris: Société préhistorique française.

Bridgford, S. 1997. Mightier than the pen? An edgewise look at Irish Bronze Age swords. In *Material Harm. Archaeological Studies of War and Violence*, ed. J. Carman, 95–115. Glasgow: Cruithne Press.

Brisson, A. and Hatt, J.-J. 1953. Les nécropoles hallstattiennes d'Aulnay-aux-Plances (Marne), *Revue Archéol. de l'Eest et du Centre-Est* 4, 193–233.

Britnell, W. J. 1976. Antler cheekpieces of the British Late Bronze Age, *Antiqs J.* 56, 24–34.

1982. The excavation of two round barrows at Trelystan, Powys, *Proc. Prehist. Soc.* 48, 133–201.

Britton, D. 1960. The Isleham hoard, Cambridgeshire, *Antiquity* 34, 279–82.

1971. The Heathery Burn cave revisited. An essay towards the reconstruction of a well-known archaeological discovery, *British Museum Quarterly* 35, 20–38.

Britton, D. and Longworth, I. H. 1968. *Late Bronze Age Finds in the Heathery Burn Cave, Co. Durham*. Inventaria Archaeologica, GB 55. London: British Museum.

Brøndsted, J. 1941. Danish arm-and-hand carvings, *Acta Archaeologica* 12, 119–25.

1962. *Nordische Vorzeit, 2. Bronzezeit in Dänemark*. Neumünster: Wachholtz (translation of *Danmarks Oldtid, 2. Bronzealderen*, Copenhagen 1958).

Brodie, N. 1994. *The Neolithic–Bronze Age Transition in Britain. A Critical Review of some Archaeological and Craniological Concepts*. British Archaeological Reports 208. Oxford: Tempus Reparatum.

Brogli, W. 1980. Die bronzezeitliche Fundstelle 'Uf Wigg' bei Zeiningen AG, *Jahrbuch der schweizerischen Gesellschaft für Ur- und Frühgeschichte* 63, 77–91.

Broholm, H. C. 1942. The Bronze Age people in Denmark, *Acta Archaeologica* (Copenhagen) 1–3, 100–49.

1944. *Danmarks Bronzealder. 1. Kultur og folk i den ældre Bronzealder*. Copenhagen: Nyt Nordisk Forlag/Arnold Busck.

1952–3. *Danske Oldsager. III. Aeldre Bronzealder. IV. Yngre Bronzealder*. Copenhagen: Gyldendalske Boghandel/Nordisk Forlag.

Broholm, H. C. and Hald, M. 1935/1940. *Danske Bronzealders Dragter* (Copenhagen: Nordiske Fortidsminder II, 5–6, 1935); = *Costumes of the Bronze Age in Denmark. Contributions to the Archaeology and Textile-History of the Bronze Age*. Copenhagen: Arnold Busck.

Broholm, H. C., Larsen, W. P. and Skjerne, G. 1949. *The Lures of the Bronze Age. An Archaeological, Technical and Musicological Investigation*. Copenhagen: Gyldendal.

Brongers, J. A. 1976. *Air Photography and Celtic Field Research in the Netherlands*. Nederlandse Oudheden 6. Amersfoort: Rijksdienst voor het Oudheidkundig Bodemonderzoek.

Bronzezeit in Ungarn 1992. *Bronzezeit in Ungarn. Forschungen in Tell-Siedlungen an Donau und Theiss*. Frankfurt am Main: Museum für Vor- und Frühgeschichte.

Brothwell, D. 1972. Palaeodemography and earlier British populations, *World Archaeology* 4, 75–87.

Brown, J. A. 1981. The search for rank in prehistoric burials. In *The Archaeology of Death*, eds. R. W. Chapman, I. Kinnes and K. Randsborg, 25–37. Cambridge: Cambridge University Press.

Brown, N. 1988. A Late Bronze Age enclosure at Lofts Farm, Essex, *Proc. Prehist. Soc.* 54, 249–302.

Brown, P. and Tuzin, D. F. (eds.) 1983. *The Ethnography of Cannibalism*. Washington DC: Society for Psychological Anthropology.

Brun, P. 1993. East–west relations in the Paris Basin during the Late Bronze Age. In *Trade and Exchange in Prehistoric Europe*, eds. C. Scarre and F. Healy, 171–82. Oxford: Oxbow Monograph 33.

Brunn, W. A. von 1968. *Mitteldeutsche Hortfunde der jüngeren Bronzezeit.* Röm.-Germ. Forschungen 29. Berlin: de Gruyter.

1980. Eine Deutung spätbronzezeitlicher Hortfunde zwischen Elbe und Weichsel, *Bericht der Römisch-Germanischen Kommission 61,* 91–150.

Bruzzi, G. F., Catarsi dall'Aglio, M. and dall'Aglio, P. L. 1989. Nuove ricerche geofisiche nella terramara di Colombare di Bersano (Piacenza), *Padusa 25,* 227–35.

Buchholz, H.-G. 1959. Keftiubarren und Erzhandel im zweiten vorchristlichen Jahrtausend, *Prähistorische Zeitschrift 37,* 1–40.

1981. 'Schalensteine' in Griechenland, Anatolien und Zypern. In *Studien zur Bronzezeit. Festschrift für Wilhelm Albert v. Brunn,* ed. H. Lorenz, 63–94. Mainz: v. Zabern.

Buck, D.-W. 1979. Die Billendorfer Gruppe, Part 2: Text, *Veröff. des Museums für Ur- und Frühgeschichte Potsdam 13.*

1982a. Befestigte Siedlungen der Lausitzer Kultur im Norden der DDR. In *Beiträge zum bronzezeitlichen Burgenbau in Mitteleuropa,* 97–118. Berlin: Zentralinstitut für Alte Geschichte und Archäologie; Nitra: Archeologický Ústav Slovenskej Akadémie Vied.

1982b. Zur Bronzemetallurgie bei den Stämmen der Billendorfer Gruppe, *Archeologia Polski 27/2,* 335–42.

1986. Siedlungswesen und sozialökonomische Verhältnisse bei den Stämmen der Lausitzer Gruppe, *Veröff. des Museums für Ur- und Frühgeschichte Potsdam 20,* 277–302.

1997. Bevölkerungszahl, Sozialstruktur und Bevölkerungsmobilität bei den Stämmen der Lausitzer Gruppe. In *Demographie der Bronzezeit. Paläodemographie – Möglichkeiten und Grenzen,* ed. K.-F. Rittershofer 137–54. Internationale Archäologie 36. Espelkamp: Verlag Marie Leidorf.

Buckley, V. (ed.) 1990. *Burnt Offerings. International Contributions to Burnt Mound Archaeology.* Dublin: Wordwell.

Budd, P. 1993. Recasting the Bronze Age, *New Scientist* 23 October 1993, 33–7.

Budd, P., Gale, D., Ixer, R. A. F. and Thomas, R. G. 1994. Tin sources for prehistoric bronze production in Ireland, *Antiquity 68,* 518–24.

Budd, P., Gale, D., Pollard, A. M., Thomas, R. G. and Williams, P. A. 1992. The early development of metallurgy in the British Isles, *Antiquity 66,* 677–85.

Budd, P., Haggerty, R., Pollard, A. M., Scaife, B. and Thomas, R. G. 1996. Rethinking the quest for provenance, *Antiquity 70,* 168–74.

Budinský-Krička, V. 1967. Vychodoslovenské mohyly, *Slovenská Archeológia 15/2,* 277–388.

Buikstra, J., Castro, P., Chapman, R., González Marcén, P., Hoshower, L., Lull, V., Micó, R., Picazo, M., Risch, R., Ruiz, M. and Sanahuja Yll, M. E. 1995. Approaches to class inequalities in the later prehistory of south-east Iberia: the Gatas project. In *The Origins of Complex Societies in Late Prehistoric Iberia,* ed. K. T. Lillios, 153–68. Ann Arbor: International Monographs in Prehistory, Archaeological Series 8.

Bukowski, Z. 1959–60. Łużyckie osiedle obronne w Sobiejuchach pow. Żnin, *Wiadomości Archeologiczne 26,* 194–224.

1977. *The Scythian Influence in the Area of Lusatian Culture.* Warsaw etc.: Ossolineum.

1989. Bemerkungen zur Problematik des frühen Eisens in Mittel- und Nordeuropa (Inga Serning in Memoriam), *Kungl. Vitterhets Historie och Antikvitets Akademiens Konferenser* 22, 115–41.

1990. Zum Stand der demographischen und siedlungsgeschichtlichen Forschung zur Lausitzer Kultur im Stromgebiet von Oder und Weichsel, *Acta Praehistorica et Archaeologica* 22, 85–119.

Burenhult, G. 1973. *The Rock Carvings of Götaland (Excluding Gothenburg County, Bohuslän and Dalsland). Part II, Illustrations.* Acta Archaeologica Lundensia, series in 4°, 8. Bonn: Habelt/Lund: Gleerup.

1980. *Götalands hällristningar, I (The Rock Carvings of Götaland, Part I).* Theses and Papers in North-European Archaeology 10. Stockholm: University of Stockholm, Institute of Archaeology.

Burgess, C. 1968. The later Bronze Age in the British Isles and north-western France, *Archaeol. J.* 125, 1–45.

1969. Breton palstaves from the British Isles, *Archaeol. J.* 126, 149–53.

1974. The Bronze Age. In *British Prehistory, a New Outline*, ed. C. Renfrew, 165–222. London: Duckworth.

1979. A find from Boyton, Suffolk, and the end of the Bronze Age in Britain and Ireland. In *Bronze Age Hoards, some Finds Old and New*, eds. C. Burgess and D. Coombs, 269–83. Oxford: British Archaeological Reports 67.

1980a. *The Age of Stonehenge.* London: Dent.

1980b. Excavations at Houseledge, Black Law, Northumberland, 1979, and their implications for earlier Bronze Age settlement in the Cheviots, *Northern Archaeology* 1/1, 5–12.

1984. The prehistoric settlement of Northumberland: a speculative survey. In *Between and Beyond the Walls: Essays in the Prehistory and History of Northern Britain in Honour of George Jobey*, eds. R. Miket and C. Burgess, 126–75. Edinburgh: John Donald.

1989. Volcanoes, catastrophe and the global crisis of the late second millennium BC, *Current Archaeology* 117, 325–9.

1990. The chronology of cup- and cup-and-ring marks in Atlantic Europe, *Revue Archéol. Ouest*, Supplement 2, 157–71.

Burgess, C. and Colquhoun, I. 1988. *The Swords of Britain.* Prähistorische Bronzefunde IV, 5. Munich: Beck.

Burgess, C. B., Coombs, D. and Davies, D. G. 1972. The Broadward complex and barbed spearheads. In *Prehistoric Man in Wales and the West*, eds. F. Lynch and C. B. Burgess, 211–83. Bath: Adams and Dart.

Burgstaller, E. 1972. *Felsbilder in Österreich.* Schriftenreihe des Institutes für Landeskunde von Oberösterreich 21. Linz: Landesinstitut für Volksbildung und Heimatpflege.

1978. Zur Zeitstellung der österreichischen Felsbilder. In *Acts of the International Symposium on Rock Art, Lectures at Hankø 1972*, ed. S. Marstrander, 238–46. Oslo: Universitetsforlaget.

Burl, A. 1976. *The Stone Circles of the British Isles.* London and New Haven: Yale University Press.

1980. Science or symbolism: problems of archaeo-astronomy, *Antiquity* 54, 191–200.

1983. *Prehistoric Astronomy and Ritual.* Princes Risborough: Shire Publications.

Burstow, G. P. and Holleyman, G. A. 1957. Late Bronze Age settlement on Itford Hill, Sussex, *Proc. Prehist. Soc.* 23, 167–212.

Butler, J. J. 1963. *Bronze Age Connections across the North Sea*
(= *Palaeohistoria* 9).

n.d. [1980]. Rings and ribs: the copper types of the 'ingot hoards' of the central European Early Bronze Age. In *The Origins of Metallurgy in Atlantic Europe* (Proc. Fifth Atlantic Colloquium, Dublin 1978), ed. M. Ryan, 345–62. Dublin: Stationery Office.

Butler, J. J. and Bakker, J. A. 1961. A forgotten Middle Bronze Age hoard with a Sicilian razor from Ommerschans, *Helinium* 1, 193–210.

Butler, J. J. and Schalk, E. 1984. Dömsöd: ein frühbronzezeitliches Urnengräberfeld in Ungarn, *Palaeohistoria* 26, 19–40.

Butler, J. J. and van der Waals, J. D. 1966. Bell Beakers and early metalworking in the Netherlands, *Palaeohistoria* 12, 41–139.

Buurman, J. 1979. Cereals in circles – crop processing activities in Bronze Age Bovenkarspel (the Netherlands). In *Festschrift Maria Hopf zum 65. Geburtstag*, ed. U. Körber-Grohne *(Archaeo-Physika* 8), 21–37. Cologne: Rheinland-Verlag (Bonn: Habelt).

1987. A Middle Bronze Age corn-stack at Twisk, province of North Holland, *Berichten van de Rijksdienst voor het Oudheidkundig Bodemonderzoek* 37, 7–37.

1988. Economy and environment in Bronze Age West-Friesland, Noord Holland (from wetland to wetland). In *The Exploitation of Wetlands*, eds. P. Murphy and C. French, 267–92. Symposia of the Association for Environmental Archaeology 7. Oxford: British Archaeological Reports 186.

Calzoni, U. 1933. L'abitato preistorico di Belverde sulla Montagna di Cetona, *Notizie degli Scavi* 6th series, 9, 45–102.

1954. *Le stazioni preistoriche della Montagna di Cetona. Belverde, I.* Istituto di Studi Etruschi e Italici, Quaderno 1. Florence: L. S. Olschki.

Canci, A., Borgognini Tarli, S. M. and Repetto, E. 1991. Osteomyelitis of probable haemotogenous origin in a Bronze Age child from Toppo Daguzzo (Basilicata, southern Italy), *Int. J. Osteoarchaeology* 1, 135–9.

Canci, A., Repetto, E. and Borgognini, S. M. 1992. Sellar pathology in a Middle Bronze Age skull from southern Italy, *Int. J. Osteoarchaeology* 2, 305–10.

Cannarella, D. and Cremonesi, G. 1967. Gli scavi nella Grotta Azzurra di Samatorza nel Carso triestino, *Rivista di Scienze Preistoriche* 22, 281–330.

Capelle, T. 1972. Felsbilder in Nordwestdeutschland. Eine Übersicht, *Acta Archaeologica* (Copenhagen) 43, 229–38.

1986. Schiffsetzungen, *Prähistorische Zeitschrift* 61, 1–63.

1991. Bronzezeitliche Hausbilder. In *Regions and Reflections. In Honour of Märta Strömberg*, eds. K. Jennberg, L. Larsson, R. Petré and B. Wyszomirska-Werbart, 129–33. Acta Archaeologica Lundensia, series in 8°, 20. Lund: Almqvist and Wiksell.

1995. Bronze-Age stone ships. In *The Ship as Symbol in Prehistoric and Medieval Scandinavia*, eds. O. Crumlin-Pedersen and B. Munch Thye, 71–5. Studies in Archaeology and History 1. Copenhagen: Danish National Museum.

Cărciumaru, M. 1996. *Paleoetnobotanica*. Studii în Preistoria şi Protoistoria României. Iasi: Editurii Glasul Bucovinei/Helios.

Cardarelli, A. 1997. The evolution of settlement and demography in the Terramara culture. In *Demographie der Bronzezeit, Paläodemographie – Möglichkeiten und Grenzen*, ed. K.-F. Rittershofer 230–7. Internationale Archäologie 36. Espelkamp: Verlag Marie Leidorf.

Carlie, A. 1994. *På arkeologins bakgård. En bebyggelsearkeologisk undersök-ning i norra Skånes inland baserad på synliga gravar.* Acta Archaeologica Lundensia, series in 8°, 22. Lund: Almqvist and Wiksell.

Carneiro, R. L. 1981. The chiefdom as precursor of the state. In *The Transition to Statehood in the New World*, eds. G. Jones and R. Kautz, 37–79. Cambridge: Cambridge University Press.

1990. Chiefdom-level warfare as exemplified in Fiji and the Cauca Valley. In *The Anthropology of War*, ed. J. Haas, 190–211. Cambridge: Cambridge University Press.

1991. The nature of the chiefdom as revealed by evidence from the Cauca Valley of Colombia. In *Profiles in Cultural Evolution. Papers from a Conference in Honor of Elman R. Service*, eds. A. T. Rambo and K. Gillogly, 167–90. Anthropological Papers 85. Ann Arbor: University of Michigan, Museum of Anthropology.

Casparie, W. A. 1984. The three Bronze Age footpaths XVI (Bou), XVII (Bou) and XVIII (Bou) in the raised bog of Southeast Drenthe (the Netherlands), *Palaeohistoria* 26, 41–94.

Casson, L. 1971. *Ships and Seamanship in the Ancient World*. Princeton: Princeton University Press.

Castiglioni, O. C. 1967. Le piroghe preistoriche italiane. Problematica ed inven-tario dei reperti, *Natura* (Milan) 58, 5–48.

Castiglioni, O. C. and Calegari, G. 1978. Le piroghi monossili italiane. Nuova tassonomia – aggiornamenti – iconografia, *Preistoria Alpina* 14, 163–72.

Castro Martínez, P. V., Gili Suriñach, S., González Marcén, P., Lull, V., Micó Pérez, R. and Rihuete Herrada, C. 1997. Radiocarbon dating and the prehis-tory of the Balearic Islands, *Proc. Prehist. Soc.* 63, 55–86.

Catling, H. W. 1964. *Cypriot Bronzework in the Mycenaean World*. Oxford: Oxford University Press.

Ceka, N. 1985. Fortifikimet parahistorike ilire, *Monumentet* 29/1, 27–58.

1986. Fortifikimet parahistorike ilire II, *Monumentet* 31/1, 49–84.

Česnys, G. 1991. The Neolithic and Bronze Age man in south-east Baltic area, 3. An essay on the genesis of craniological types, *Homo* 42, 232–43.

Chagnon, N. A. 1967. Yanamamö social organisation and warfare. In *War: the Anthropology of Armed Conflict and Aggression*, eds. M. Fried, M. Harris and R. Murphy, 109–59. New York: National History Press.

Chaix, L. 1996. L'exploitation de monde animal au bronze ancien et le prob-lème du cheval. In *Cultures et sociétés du Bronze ancien en Europe*, eds C. Mordant and O. Gaiffe, 181–88. 117ᵉ Congrès national des sociétés his-toriques et scientifiques, Clermont Ferrand 1992. Paris: Editions du CTHS.

Chambers, F. M. 1989. The evidence for early rye cultivation in north west Europe. In *The Beginnings of Agriculture*, eds. A. Milles, D. Williams and N. Gardner, 165–75. Oxford: British Archaeological Reports, Int. Series 496.

Chambers, F. M. and Jones, M. K. 1984. Antiquity of rye in Britain, *Antiquity* 58, 219–24.

Champion, T. C. 1989. Introduction. In *Centre and Periphery: Comparative Studies in Archaeology*, ed. T. C. Champion, 1–21. One World Archaeology, 11. London: Unwin Hyman.

Chantre, E. 1875–6. *Etude paléoethnologique dans le bassin du Rhône. Age du bronze. Recherches sur l'origine de la métallurgie en France, II. Gisements de l'âge du bronze.* Paris: Baudry.

Chapman, J. C. 1989/1991. The early Balkan village. In *Neolithic of*

Southeastern Europe and its Near Eastern Connections, International Conference 1987, Szolnok-Szeged, ed. P. Raczky, 33–53. Varia Archaeologica Hungarica 2. Budapest: Institute of Archaeology of the Hungarian Academy of Sciences (1989). Also in *Social Space: Human Spatial Behaviour in Dwellings and Settlements*, eds. O. Grøn, E. Engelstad and I. Lindblom, 79–99. Odense: Odense University Press (1991).

Chapman, J. C., Shiel, R. and Batović, Š. 1996. *The Changing Face of Dalmatia: Archaeological and Ecological Studies in a Mediterranean Landscape*. Soc. of Antiqs Research Report 54. London: Leicester University Press.

Chapman, R. W. 1990. *Emerging Complexity. The Later Prehistory of South-East Spain, Iberia and the west Mediterranean*. Cambridge: Cambridge University Press.

　1995. Urbanism in Copper and Bronze Age Iberia? In *Social Complexity and the Development of Towns in Iberia from the Copper Age to the Second Century AD (Proc. British Academy 86)*, 29–46.

　1996. 'Inventiveness and ingenuity'? Craft specialization, metallurgy and the west Mediterranean Bronze Age. In *Craft Specialization and Social Evolution: in Memory of V. Gordon Childe*, ed. B. Wailes, 73–83. Philadelphia: University of Pennsylvania Museum of Archaeology and Anthropology.

Chapman, R. W. and Grant, A. 1997. Prehistoric subsistence and monuments in Mallorca. In *Encounters and Transformations: the Archaeology of Iberia in Transition*, eds. M. S. Balmuth, A. Gilman and L. Prados-Torreira, 69–87. Sheffield: Sheffield Academic Press.

Chapman, R. W., Kinnes, I. and Randsborg, K. (eds.) 1981. *The Archaeology of Death*. Cambridge: Cambridge University Press.

Charles, J. A. 1967. Early arsenical bronzes: a metallurgical view, *American J. Archaeology* 71, 21–6.

　1984. The Middle Bronze Age iron punch of southeast Drenthe, *Palaeohistoria* 26, 95–9.

Chase-Dunn, C. and Hall, T. D. (eds.) 1991. *Core/Periphery Relations in Precapitalist Worlds*. Boulder: Westview Press.

Chernykh, E. N. 1978a. *Gornoe Delo i Metallurgija v Drevnejsej Bolgarii*. Sofia: Bulgarian Academy of Sciences.

　1978b. Aibunar, a Balkan copper mine of the fourth millennium BC, *Proc. Prehist. Soc.* 44, 203–17.

　1996. The dawn of mining and metallurgy in eastern Europe: new discoveries. In *XIII International Congress of Prehistoric and Protohistoric Sciences, Forlì, Italy, 10: The Copper Age in the Near East and Europe. Colloquium XIX, Metallurgy: Origins and Technology*, 85–93. Forlì: ABACO Edizioni.

Chertier, B. 1976. *Les nécropoles de la civilisation des Champs d'urnes dans la région des Marais de Saint-Gond (Marne)*. *Gallia Préhistoire*, Supplement 8.

Childe, V. G. 1930. *The Bronze Age*. Cambridge: Cambridge University Press.

Chleborád, M. 1963. Únětické hroby pod mohylami, *Archeologické Rozhledy* 15, 4–6.

Chowne, P. 1978. Billingborough Bronze Age settlement: an interim note, *Lincolnshire History and Archaeology* 13, 15–21.

Christlein, R. 1964. Beiträge zur Stufengliederung der frühbronzezeitlichen

Flachgräberfelder in Süddeutschland, *Bayerische Vorgeschichtsblätter* 29, 25–63.

Chronologie 1986. *Chronologie. Archäologische Daten der Schweiz*. Antiqua 15. Basle: Schweizerische Gesellschaft für Ur- und Frühgeschichte.

Chudziakowa, J. 1975. Ślady kanibalizmu odkryte na grodzisku kultury łużyckiej w Gzinie, pow. Chełmno, *Wiadomości Archeologiczne* 40, 291–7.

Ciabatti, E. 1984. Il relitto di Lipari, *Archeologia Viva* 3/4, 36–47.

Čierny, J., Weisgerber, G. and Perini, R. 1992. Ein spätbronzezeitlicher Hüttenplatz in Bedello/Trentino. In *Festschrift zum 50jährigen Bestehen des Institutes für Ur- und Frühgeschichte der Leopold-Franzens Universität Innsbruck*, eds. A. Lippert and K. Spindler, 97–105. Universitätsforschungen zur prähistorischen Archäologie, 8. Bonn: Habelt.

Ciugudean, H. 1995. The later Eneolithic/Early Bronze Age tumulus-burials in central and south-western Transylvania (I), *Apulum* 32, 13–32.

Clark, J. G. D. 1947. Sheep and swine in the husbandry of prehistoric Europe, *Antiquity* 21, 122–36.

  1963. Neolithic bows from Somerset, England, and the prehistory of archery in North-West Europe, *Proc. Prehist. Soc.* 29, 50–98.

Clarke, D. V., Cowie, T. G. and Foxon, A. 1985. *Symbols of Power at the Time of Stonehenge*. Edinburgh: HMSO.

Clason, A. 1964. The animal bones from the Bronze Age settlement of Zwaagdijk, Gem. Wervershoof, Prov. North Holland, *Berichten van de Rijksdienst voor het Oudheidkundig Bodemonderzoek* 14, 44–52.

  1965 (1967). *Animal and Man in Holland's Past*. Groningen (=*Palaeohistoria* 13A/13B).

Cleary, M. C. and Delano-Smith, C. 1990. Transhumance reviewed: past and present practices in France and Italy, *Rivista di Studi Liguri* A 66, 21–38 (Atti della Tavola Ronda Internazionale *Archeologia della pastorizia nell'Europa meridionale* I).

Cleuziou, S. and Berthoud, T. 1982. Early tin in the Near East. A reassessment in the light of new evidence from western Afghanistan, *Expedition* 25/1, 14–19.

Coblenz, W. 1963. Die Ausgrabungen auf dem Burgwall von Nieder-Neundorf (nach Unterlagen in den Städtischen Kunstsammlung Görlitz), *Arbeits- und Forschungsberichte zur sächsischen Bodendenkmalpflege* 11–12, 9–58.

  1964. Burgen der Lausitzer Kultur in Sachsen. In *Studien aus Alteuropa I*, eds. R. von Uslar and K. J. Narr, 189–204. Bonner Jahrbücher, Supplement 10/I. Cologne/Graz: Böhlau Verlag.

  1966. Die befestigte Siedlung der Lausitzer Kultur auf dem Schafberg bei Löbau, *Arbeits- und Forschungsberichte zur sächsischen Bodendenkmalpflege* 14–15, 95–132.

  1973. Eine Aunjetitzer Vorratsgrube mit Getreide aus Döbeln-Masten, *Ausgrabungen und Funde* 18, 70–80.

  1978. Zu den befestigten Siedlungen der Lausitzer Kultur in der DDR. In *Mitteleuropäische Bronzezeit. Beiträge zur Archäologie und Geschichte*, eds. W. Coblenz and F. Horst, 239–53. Berlin: Akademie-Verlag.

  1982. Zu den bronze- und früheisenzeitlichen Befestigungen der sächsisch-lausitzischen Gruppe. In *Beiträge zum bronzezeitlichen Burgenbau*, 149–57. Berlin: Zentralinstitut für Alte Geschichte und Archäologie; Nitra: Archeologický Ústav Slovenskej Akadémie Vied.

1985. Straubing und Aunjetitz. Bemerkungen zu einem neuen Depotfund aus Kyhna, Kreis Delitzsch, *Bayerische Vorgeschichtsblätter* 50, 113–26.

1986. Ein frühbronzezeitlicher Verwahrfund von Kyhna, Kr. Delitzsch, *Arbeits- und Forschungsberichte zur sächsischen Bodendenkmalpflege* 30, 37–88.

Coffyn, A., Gomez, J. and Mohen, J.-P. 1981. *L'Apogée de bronze atlantique: le dépot de Vénat*. L'âge du bronze en France, 1. Paris: Picard.

Coggins, D. and Fairless, K. J. 1984. The Bronze Age settlement site of Bracken Rigg, Upper Teesdale, Co. Durham, *Durham Archaeol. J.* 1, 5–21.

Coghlan, H. H. 1975. *Notes on the Prehistoric Metallurgy of Copper and Bronze in the Old World*. 2nd edition. Occasional Papers on Technology 4. Oxford: Pitt Rivers Museum.

Cogné, J. and Giot, P.-R. 1951. L'âge du bronze ancien en Bretagne, *L'Anthropologie* 55, 425–44.

Cole, S. M. 1954. Land transport without wheels. Roads and bridges. In *A History of Technology, I. From Early Times to the Fall of Ancient Empires,* eds. C. Singer, E. J. Holmyard and A. R. Hall, 704–15. Oxford: Clarendon Press.

Coles, B. 1990. Anthropomorphic wooden figures from Britain and Ireland, *Proc. Prehist. Soc.* 56, 315–33.

Coles, J. M. 1962. European Bronze Age shields, *Proc. Prehist. Soc.* 28, 156–90.

1963. Irish Bronze Age horns and their relations with northern Europe, *Proc. Prehist. Soc.* 29, 326–56.

1969. Metal analyses and the Scottish Early Bronze Age, *Proc. Prehist. Soc.* 35, 330–44.

1984. Prehistoric roads and trackways in Britain: problems and possibilities. In *Loads and Roads in Scotland and Beyond. Land Transport over 6000 Years*, eds. A. Fenton and G. Stell, 1–21. Edinburgh: J. Donald.

1990 (2nd edn 1994). *Images of the Past. A Guide to the Rock Carvings and Other Ancient Monuments of Northern Bohuslän*. Uddevalla: Bohusläns Museum.

1993. Boats on the rocks. In *A Spirit of Enquiry. Essays for Ted Wright*, eds. J. Coles, V. Fenwick and G. Hutchinson, 23–31. London: National Maritime Museum; Exeter: Ward.

1994. *Rock Carvings of Uppland. A Guide*. Department of Archaeology, Uppsala University: Occasional Papers in Archaeology 9. Uppsala: Societas Archaeologica Upsaliensis.

Coles, J. M., Caseldine, A. E. and Morgan, R. A. 1982. The Eclipse Track 1980, *Somerset Levels Papers* 8, 26–39.

Coles, J. M. and Coles, B. J. 1986. *Sweet Track to Glastonbury. The Somerset Levels in Prehistory*. London: Thames and Hudson.

Coles, J. M. and Harding, A. F. 1979. *The Bronze Age in Europe. An Introduction to the Prehistory of Europe c.2000–700 BC*. London: Methuen.

Coles, J. M., Heal, S. V. E. and Orme, B. J. 1978. The use and character of wood in prehistoric Britain and Ireland, *Proc. Prehist. Soc.* 44, 1–45.

Coles, J. M. and Orme, B. J. 1976. The Meare Heath trackway: excavation of a Bronze Age structure in the Somerset Levels, *Proc. Prehist. Soc.* 43, 293–318.

1978. Bronze Age implements from Skinner's Wood, *Somerset Levels Papers* 4, 114–23.

Collins, A. E. P. 1970. Bronze Age moulds in Ulster, *Ulster J. Archaeology* 33, 23–36.

Colpe, C. 1970. Theoretische Möglichkeiten zur Identifizierung von Heiligtümern und Interpretation von Opfern in ur- und parahistorischen Epochen. In *Vorgeschichtliche Heiligtümer und Opferplätze in Mittel- und Nordeuropa. Bericht über ein Symposium in Reinhausen bei Göttingen 1968*, ed. H. Jankuhn, 18–39. Abhandlungen der Akademie der Wissenschaften, Göttingen.

Comşa, E. 1966. Le dépôt en bronze de Cioclovina (Carpates Méridionales), *Acta Archaeologica Carpathica* 8, 169–74.

1988. Die Viehzucht im Bronzezeitalter auf rumänischem Gebiet, *Slovenská Archeológia* 36/1, 25–32.

Conkey, M. W. 1978. Style and information in cultural evolution: toward a predictive model for the Paleolithic. In *Social Archaeology*, eds. C. L. Redman et al., 61–85. New York: Academic Press.

1990. Experimenting with style in archaeology: some historical and theoretical issues. In *The Uses of Style in Archaeology*, eds. M. W. Conkey and C. A. Hastorf, 5–17. Cambridge: Cambridge University Press.

Conkey, M. W. and Spector, J. D. 1984. Archaeology and the study of gender. In *Advances in Archaeological Method and Theory* 7, 1–38.

Conti, C. 1972. *Corpus delle incisioni rupestri de Monte Bego*. Bordighera: Istituto Internazionale di Studi Liguri, Collezione di monografie preistorische ed. archeologiche 6, fasc. 1.

Contreras Cortés, F., Antonio Cámara Serrano, J., Lizcano Prestel, R., Pérez Bareas, C., Robledo Sanz, B. and Trancho Gallo, G. 1995. Enterramientos y diferenciacion social 1. El registro funerario del yacimiento de la edad del bronce de Peñalosa (Baños de la Encina, Jaén), *Trabajos de Prehistoria* 52/1, 87–108.

Coombs, D. G. 1976. Excavations at Mam Tor, Derbyshire 1965–1969. In *Hillforts. Later Prehistoric Earthworks in Britain and Ireland*, ed. D. W. Harding, 147–52. London: Academic Press.

1992. Flag Fen platform and Fengate Power Station post alignment – the metalwork, *Antiquity* 66, 504–17.

Coombs, D. G. and Thompson, F. H. 1979. Excavation of the hill fort of Mam Tor, Derbyshire, 1965–9, *Derbyshire Archaeol. J.* 49, 7–51.

Corcoran, J. X. W. P. 1961. The Caergwrle bowl: a contribution to the study of the Bronze Age. In *Bericht V. Internationales Kongress für Vor- und Frühgeschichte Hamburg 1958*, 200–3.

Cotter, C. 1994. Atlantic fortifications – the dúns of the Aran Islands, *Archaeology Ireland* 8/1, 24–8.

Courtin, J. 1976. Grottes de Baudinard, moyennes gorges du Verdon. In *Livret-Guide de l'excursion C2, Provence et Languedoc Méditerraneen. Sites paléolithiques et néolithiques* (IXᵉ Congrès UISPP), 18–29. Nice.

Čović, B. 1965. Uvod u stratifrafiju i kronologiju prahistorijskih gradinu u Bosni, *Glasnik Zemaljskog Muzea u Sarajevu* 20, 27–100.

1980. Počeci metalurgije željeza na sjeverozapadnom Balkanu, *Godišnjak* (Sarajevo) 18, 63–79.

Craddock, P. T. 1986. Bronze Age metallurgy in Britain, *Current Archaeology* 99, 106–9.

1989. The scientific investigation of early mining and metallurgy. In

Scientific Analysis in Archaeology, ed. J. Henderson, 178–212. Oxford: Oxford University Committee for Archaeology, Monograph 19.

1995. *Early Metal Mining and Production.* Edinburgh: Edinburgh University Press.

Craddock, P. T., Freestone, I. C., Gale, N. H., Meeks, N. D., Rothenberg, B. and Tite, M. S. 1985/1992. The investigation of a small heap of silver smelting debris from Rio Tinto, Huelva, Spain. In *Furnaces and Smelting Technology in Antiquity*, eds. P. T. Craddock and M. J. Hughes, 199–217. London: British Museum (Occasional Paper 48).

Craddock, P. T. and Gale, D. 1988. Evidence for early mining and extractive metallurgy in the British Isles: problems and potentials. In *Science and Archaeology, Glasgow 1987*, eds. E. A. Slater and J. O. Tate, 167–92. Oxford: British Archaeological Reports 196.

Crumley, C. 1987. A dialectical critique of heterarchy. In *Power Relations and State Formation*, eds. T. C. Patterson and C. W. Gailey, 155–9. Washington DC: American Anthropological Association.

1995. Heterarchy and the analysis of complex societies. In *Heterarchy and the Analysis of Complex Societies*, eds. R. M. Ehrenreich, C. L. Crumley and J. E. Levy, 1–5. Arlington: Archeological Papers of the American Anthropological Association, 6.

Csányi, M. and Stanczik, I. 1992. Tiszaug-Kéménytető. In *Bronzezeit in Ungarn*, 115–19.

Čujanová-Jílková, E. 1970. *Mittelbronzezeitliche Hügelgräberfelder in Westböhmen.* Archeologické Študijní Materiály, 8. Prague: Archaeological Institute.

1984. Rekonstrukce plánů mohylových pohřebišť' Milavče-Chrastavice, Lštění a Třebnice-Němčice, okres Domažlice, *Archeologické Rozhledy* 36, 411–22.

Cunliffe, B. 1988. *Mount Batten, Plymouth. A Prehistoric and Roman Port.* Oxford: Oxford University Committee for Archaeology Monograph 26.

Curle, A. O. 1933–4. An account of further excavations at Jarlshof, Sumburgh, Shetland, in 1932 and 1933, on behalf of HM Office of Works, *Proc. Soc. Antiqs Scotland* 68, 224–319.

Ćwirko-Godycki, M. and Wrzosek, A. 1936–7 (1938). Grzechotki z grobów cmentarzyska łużyckiego w Laskach w pow. kępińskim, *Światowit* 17, 171–254.

Czyborra, I. 1997. Gefässdeponierungen – Speise und Trank für Götter und Menschen. In *Gaben an die Götter. Schätze der Bronzezeit Europas*, eds. A. and B. Hänsel, 87–92. Berlin: Seminar für Ur- und Frühgeschichte der Freien Universität/Museum für Vor- und Frühgeschichte (Staatliche Museen zu Berlin – Preussischer Kulturbesitz).

Dal Ri, L. 1972. Spuren urgeschichtlicher Erzgewinnung in den Sarntaler Alpen, *Der Schlern* 46, 592–601.

Damell, D. 1981. Funderingar kring nordbottniska redskap och tidigt jordbruk i Norrbotten, *Fornvännen* 76, 169–77.

1988. Transport links in the Bronze Age landscape of Södermanland, Sweden. In *Trade and Exchange in Prehistory. Studies in Honour of Berta Stjernquist*, ed. B. Hardh, L. Larsson, D. Olausson and R. Petré, 113–17. Acta Archaeologica Lundensia, series in 8°, 16. Lund: Historiska Museum.

Davey, C. J. 1979. Some ancient Near Eastern pot bellows, *Levant* 11, 101–11.

Davidsen, K. 1982. Bronze Age houses at Jegstrup, near Skive, central Jutland, *J. Danish Archaeology* 1, 65–75.

De Lisle, P. 1881. Découvertes de haches en plomb (Bretagne), *Revue Archéol.* 42, 335–43.

De Lumley, H. 1992. *Le Mont Bégo. La Vallée des Merveilles et le val de Fontanalba.* Guides archéologiques de la France. Paris: Ministère de la Culture.

De Lumley, H., Fonvielle, M.-E. and Abelanet, J. (eds.) 1976. Vallée des Merveilles, *Livret-Guide de l'excursion C1* (IXe Congrès UISPP), Nice.

De Marinis, R., Rapi, M., Scandolo, M., Balista, C., Marziani, G., Iannone, A. and Camagni, B. M. 1992–93. La terramara dell'età del bronzo recente di Ca' de' Cessi (Sabbioneta, Mantova), *Sibrium* 22, 43–161.

Déchelette, J. 1908. *Manuel d'archéologie préhistorique, celtique et gallo-romaine. I. Archéologie préhistorique.* Paris: Picard.

Delibes de Castro, G., Montero Ruiz, I. and Rovira Llorens, S. 1996. The first use of metals in the Iberian peninsula. In *The Copper Age in the Near East and Europe*, eds. B. Bagolini and F. Lo Schiavo, 19–34. XIII International Congress of Prehistoric and Protohistoric Sciences, Forlì 1996, Series Colloquia vol. 10, Colloquium XIX – Metallurgy: Origins and Technology. Forlì: ABACO.

Della Casa, P. 1995. Zur sozialen Organisation bronzezeitlicher Nekropolen des 14. und 13. Jahrhunderts v. Chr. im dinarischen Raum. In *Trans Europam. Beiträge zur Bronze- und Eisenzeit zwischen Atlantik und Altai. Festschrift für Margarita Primas*, eds. B. Schmid-Sikimić and P. della Casa, 69–78. Antiquitas, series 3, 34. Bonn: Habelt.

1996a. Linking anthropological and archaeological evidence: notes on the demographic structure and social organisation of the Bronze Age necropolis Velika Gruda in Montenegro, *Arheološki Vestnik* 47, 135–43.

1996b. *Velika Gruda II. Die bronzezeitliche Nekropole Velika Gruda (opš. Kotor, Montenegro): Fundgruppen der mittleren und späten Bronzezeit zwischen Adria und Donau.* Universitätsforschungen zur prähistorischen Archäologie 33. Bonn: Habelt.

Delpino, F. 1993. Apporti egei nell'avvio di attività siderurgiche nell'Italia antica?, *Bull. Paletnologia Italiana* 84, 481–90.

Denford, G. T. and Farrell, A. W. 1980. The Caergwrle bowl – a possible prehistoric boat model, *Int. J. Nautical Archaeology* 9, 183–92.

Deshayes, J. 1960. *Les Outils de bronze de l'Indus au Danube (IVe au IIe millénaire)*, vols. 1–2. Paris: Geuthner.

Detev, P. 1964. Kolektivna nachodka ot glineni sǀdove v Plovdiv, *Arkheologiya* 6/4, 66–70.

Detev, P. and Macanova, V. 1977. Praistoričeskoto selišče pri selo Ognjanovo, *Izvestija na muzeite ot južna Bălgarija* 3, 45–86.

Dickson, J. H. 1978. Bronze Age mead, *Antiquity* 52, 108–13.

Diemer, G. 1985. Urnenfelderzeitliche Depotfunde und neue Grabungsbefunde vom Bullenheimer Berg: ein Vorbericht, *Archäologisches Korrespondenzblatt* 15, 55–65.

Dietler, M. 1995. The cup of Gyptis: rethinking the colonial encounter in Early-Iron-Age western Europe and the relevance of World-Systems models, *J. European Archaeology* 3/2, 89–111.

Dietrich, H. and Sorge, G. 1991. Eine urnenfelderzeitliche Siedlung bei Graben, *Das Archäologisches Jahr in Bayern 1991*, 75–6.

Dimbleby, G. W. 1962. *The Development of British Heathlands and their Soils.* Oxford Forestry Memoir 23. Oxford: Clarendon Press.

Djupedal, R. and Broholm, H. 1952. Marcus Schnabel og bronzealderfundet fra Grevensvaenge, *Aarbøger* 1952, 5–59.

Dočkalová, M. 1990. Characteristics of the Bronze Age osteological finds from the locality Velim near Kolín, *Anthropologie* 28/2–3, 197–202.

Drechsler-Bižić, R. 1979–80. Nekropola brončanog doba u pećini Bezdanjači kod Vrhovina, *Vjesnik Arheološkog Muzeja u Zagrebu* 3rd series 12–13, 27–85.

    1983. Japodska kulturna grupa. In *Praistorija jugoslavenskih zemalja, IV, Bronzano doba*, ed. B.Čović, 374–89. Sarajevo: Akademija Nauka i Umjetnosti Bosne i Hercegovine, Centar za balkanološka ispitivanja.

Drescher, H. 1956–8. Zur Verwendung von Bronzewerkzeugen in der älteren Bronzezeit, *Hammaburg* 5, 23–9.

    1957. Der Bronzeguss in Formen aus Bronze, *Die Kunde* 8, 52–75.

    1958. *Der Überfangguss. Ein Beitrag zur vorgeschichtlichen Metalltechnik.* Mainz: Verlag des Römisch-Germanischen Zentralmuseums.

Drewett, P. 1979. New evidence for the structure and function of Middle Bronze Age round houses in Sussex, *Archaeol. J.* 136, 3–11.

    1982. Later Bronze Age downland economy and excavations at Black Patch, East Sussex, *Proc. Prehist. Soc.* 48, 321–400.

Driehaus, J. 1970. Urgeschichtliche Opferfunde aus dem Mittel- und Niederrhein. In *Vorgeschichtliche Heiligtümer und Opferplätze in Mittel- und Nordeuropa. Bericht über ein Symposium in Reinhausen bei Göttingen 1968*, ed. H. Jankuhn, 40–54. Abhandlungen der Akademie der Wissenschaften, Göttingen.

Driesch, A. von den 1972. Osteoarchäologische Untersuchungen auf der Iberischen Halbinsel, *Studien über frühe Tierknochenfunde von der Iberischen Halbinsel* 3. Munich: University of Munich/Deutsches Archäologisches Institut, Abteilung Madrid.

Driesch, A. von den and Boessneck, J. 1980. Die Motillas von Azuer und Los Palacios (Prov. Ciudad Real): Untersuchung der Tierknochenfunde, *Studien über frühe Tierknochenfunde von der Iberischen Halbinsel* 7, 84–121. Munich: University of Munich/Deutsches Archäologisches Institut, Abteilung Madrid.

Driesch, A. von den, Boessneck, J., Kokabi, M. and Schäffer, J. 1985. Tierknochenfunde aus der bronzezeitlichen Höhensiedlung Fuente Álamo, Provinz Almería, *Studien über frühe Tierknochenfunde von der Iberischen Halbinsel* 9, 1–75. Munich: University of Munich/Deutsches Archäologisches Institut, Abteilung Madrid.

Drovenik, M. 1987. Bakrova nahajališča v Sloveniji/Copper ore deposits in Slovenia. In *Bronasta doba na Slovenskem 18.-8. st. pr. n. š*, 25–9. Ljubljana: Narodni Muzej.

Dumitrescu, V. 1961. *Necropola de incinerație din epoca bronzului de la Cîrna*. Biblioteca de Arheologie 4. Bucharest: Editura Academiei Republicii Populare Romîne.

Durczewski, D. and Olczak, J. 1966. Uwagi o technologii i pochodzeniu paciorków szklanych z grodziska kultury łużyckiej w Smuszewie, pow. Wągrowiec (Bemerkungen über die Technologie und Herkunft der Glasperlen aus dem Burgwall der Lausitzer Kultur in Smuszewo, Kr. Wągrowiec), *Fontes Archaeologici Posnanienses* 17, 55–64.

Durman, A. 1997. Tin in southeastern Europe? *Opuscula Archaeologica* 21, 7–14.

Dušek, M. 1964. Waren Skythen in Mitteleuropa und Deutschland? *Prähistorische Zeitschrift* 42, 49–76.

1969. *Bronzezeitliche Gräberfelder in der Südwestslowakei*. Archaeologica Slovaca – Catalogi 4. Bratislava: Verlag der Slowakischen Akademie der Wissenschaften.

1971. Slovensko v mladšej dobe halštatskej, *Slovenská Archeológia* 19/2, 423–59.

Dutton, A. 1990. Surface remains of early mining on the Great Orme. In *Early Mining in the British Isles*, eds. P. and S. Crew, 11–14. Proc. Early Mining Workshop 1989, Plas Tan y Bwlch Occasional Paper 1.

Dutton, A. and Fasham, P. J. 1994. Prehistoric copper mining on the Great Orme, Llandudno, Gwynedd, *Proc. Prehist. Soc.* 60, 245–86.

Džambazov, I. and Katinčarov, R. 1974. Raskopki v peščerata Magura prez 1971g., *Izvestija na archeologičeski institut* 34, 107–38.

Earle, T. K. 1987. Chiefdoms in archaeological and ethnohistorical perspective, *Annual Review of Anthropology* 16, 279–308.

1991. The evolution of chiefdoms. In *Chiefdoms: Power, Economy and Ideology*, ed. T. K. Earle, 1–15. Cambridge: Cambridge University Press.

1997. *How Chiefs Come to Power. The Political Economy in Prehistory*. Stanford: Stanford University Press.

Earwood, C. 1993. *Domestic Wooden Artefacts in Britain and Ireland from Neolithic to Viking Times*. Exeter: University of Exeter Press.

Eberschweiler, B., Riethmann, P. and Ruoff, U. 1987. Greifensee-Böschen ZH: ein spätbronzezeitliches Dorf. Ein Vorbericht, *Jahrbuch der schweizerischen Gesellschaft für Ur- und Frühgeschichte* 70, 77–100.

Eckel, F. 1992. *Studien zur Form- und Materialtypologie von Spangenbarren und Ösenringbarren, zugleich ein Beitrag zur Frage der Relation zwischen Kupferlagerstätten, Halbzeugproduktion und Fertigwarenhandel*. Saarbrücker Beiträge zur Altertumskunde 54. Bonn: Habelt.

Ecsedy, I. 1979. *The People of the Pit-Grave Kurgans in Eastern Hungary*. Budapest: Akadémiai Kiadó.

Egg, M. 1992. Zur Ausrüstung des Toten vom Hauslabjoch, Gem. Schmals (Südtirol). In *Der Mann im Eis I*, eds. F. Höpfel, W. Platzer and K. Spindler, 254–72. Veröffent. der Universität Innsbruck 187. Innsbruck: University of Innsbruck.

1996. *Das hallstattzeitliche Fürstengrab von Strettweg bei Judenburg in der Obersteiermark*. Römisch-Germanisches Zentralmuseum, Monograph 37. Mainz: Verlag des Römisch-Germanischen Zentralmuseums.

Ehrenberg, M. 1977. *Bronze Age Spearheads from Berkshire, Buckinghamshire and Oxfordshire*. Oxford: British Archaeological Reports 34.

1980. The occurrence of Bronze Age metalwork in the Thames: an investigation, *Transactions London and Middlesex Archaeol. Soc.* 31, 1–15.

1981. The anvils of Bronze Age Europe, *Antiqs J.* 61/1, 13–28.

1989. *Women in Prehistory*. London: British Museum Publications.

Ehrich, P. 1949. Die vorgeschichtlichen Totenhäuser und der Hausgedanke im Bestattungsbrauch, *Hammaburg* 1, 200–16.

Eibner, C. 1969. Ein mittelbronzezeitlicher Gefässverwahrfund von Schrattenberg, p. B. Mistelbach, NÖ. Zur Interpretation der sogenannten Töpfereiwarenlager, *Archaeologia Austriaca* 46, 19–52.

1972. Mitterberg-Grabung 1971, *Der Anschnitt* 24/2, 3–15.

1973. Die urnenfelderzeitlichen Sauggefässe. Ein Beitrag zur morphologischen und ergologischen Umschreibung, *Prähistorische Zeitschrift* 48, 144–99.

1974. Mitterberg-Grabung 1972, *Der Anschnitt* 26/2, 14–22.

Eibner-Persy, A. and Eibner, C. 1970. Erste Grossgrabung auf dem bronzezeitlichen Bergbaugelände von Mitterberg, *Der Anschnitt* 22/5, 12–19.

Eiroa, J. J. 1979. *La cueva del Asno, Los Rabanos (Soria), campañas 1976–1977.* Excavaciones Arqueologicas en España 107. Madrid: Ministerio de Cultura.

Elgee, H. W. and F. 1949. An Early Bronze Age burial in a boat-shaped wooden coffin from north-east Yorkshire, *Proc. Prehist. Soc.* 15, 87–106.

Ellis, P. 1989. Norton Fitzwarren hillfort: a report on the excavations by Nancy and Philip Langmaid between 1968 and 1971, *Somerset Archaeology and Natural History* 133, 1–74.

Ellison, A. B. 1981. Towards a socio-economic model for the Middle Bronze Age in southern England. In *Pattern of the Past*, eds. I. Hodder, G. Isaac and N. Hammond, 413–38. Cambridge: Cambridge University Press.

1987. The Bronze Age settlement at Thorny Down: pots, post-holes and patterning, *Proc. Prehist. Soc.* 53, 385–92.

Ellison, A. B. and Rahtz, P. A. 1987. Excavations at Hog Cliff Hill, Maiden Newton, Dorset, *Proc. Prehist. Soc.* 53, 223–69.

Ellmers, D. 1973. Kultbarken, Fähren, Fischerboote – Vorgeschichtliche Einbäume in Niedersachsen, *Die Kunde* 24, 23–62.

1974. Vor- und frühgeschichtliche Schiffahrt am Nordrand der Alpen, *Helvetia Archaeologica* 5, 94–104.

Eluère, C. 1982. *Les Ors préhistoriques. L'âge du bronze en France*, 2. Paris: Picard.

Eluère, C. and Mohen, J.-P. 1993. Problèmes des enclumes et matrices en bronze de l'âge du bronze en Europe occidentale. In *Outils et ateliers d'orfèvres de temps anciens*, ed. C. Eluère, 13–22. Antiquités nationales, Memoir 2. Saint-Germain-en-Laye: Société des amis du musée des antiquités nationales.

Entwistle, R. and Grant, A. 1989. The evidence for cereal cultivation and animal husbandry in the southern British Neolithic and Bronze Age. In *The Beginnings of Agriculture*, eds. A. Milles, D. Williams and N. Gardner, 203–15. Oxford: British Archaeological Reports, Int. Series 496.

Eogan, G. 1965. *Catalogue of Irish Bronze Swords*. Dublin: National Museum of Ireland.

1969. 'Lock-rings' of the Late Bronze Age, *Proc. Royal Irish Academy* 67C, 93–148.

1981. The gold vessels of the Bronze Age in Ireland and beyond, *Proc. Royal Irish Academy* 81C, 345–82.

1983. *Hoards of the Irish Later Bronze Age*. Dublin: University College.

1994. *The Accomplished Art. Gold and Gold-Working in Britain and Ireland during the Bronze Age*. Oxford: Oxbow Monograph 42.

Erbach-Schönberg, M.-C. zu 1985. Bemerkungen zu urnenfelderzeitlichen Deponierungen in Oberösterreich, *Archäologisches Korrespondenzblatt* 15, 163–78.

Escalon de Fonton, M. 1964. Naissance de la guerre en Occident aux temps préhistoriques, *Archeologia* (Paris) 1, 30–4.

Ethelberg, P. 1986. Early Bronze Age houses at Højgård, southern Jutland, *J. Danish Archaeology* 5, 152–67.

Evans, E. 1933. The bronze spearhead in Great Britain and Ireland, *Archaeologia* 83, 187–202.

Evans, J. G. *et al.* 1983. Stonehenge – the environment in the late Neolithic and Early Bronze Age and a Beaker Age burial, *Wilts. Archaeol. Magazine* 78, 7–30.

Farke, H. 1991. Schnüre, Geflechte und Leder aus Höhlen bei Bad Frankenhausen, *Alt-Thüringen* 26, 123–40.

Fasani, L. 1988. La sepoltura e il forno di fusione de La Vela di Valbusa (Trento), *Preistoria Alpina* 24, 165–81.

Feger, R. and Nadler, M. 1985. Beobachtungen zur urnenfelderzeitlichen Frauentracht. Vorbericht zur Ausgrabung 1983/84 in Grundfeld, Ldkr. Lichtenfels, Oberfranken, *Germania* 63, 1–16.

Fenton, A. 1972/1986. Early yoke types in Britain, *A Magyar Mezögazdasági Múzeum Közleményei* (1971–72) 69–75. Reprinted with additions in *The Shape of the Past 2. Essays in Scottish Ethnology*, 34–46. Edinburgh: J. Donald.

Fenton, A., Podolák, J. and Rasmussen, H. 1973. *Land Transport in Europe.* Folkelivs studier 4. Copenhagen: Nationalmuseet.

Ferguson, R. B. (ed.) 1984. *Warfare, Culture and Environment. Studies in Anthropology.* Orlando: Academic Press.

  1992. A savage encounter: Western contact and the Yanomami war complex. In *War in the Tribal Zone: Expanding States and Indigenous Warfare,* eds. R. B. Ferguson and N. L. Whitehead 199–227. Santa Fe: School of American Research Press.

Ferguson, R. B. and Whitehead, N. L. (eds.) 1992. *War in the Tribal Zone. Expanding States and Indigenous Warfare.* Santa Fe: School of American Research Press.

Fernández Castro, M. C. 1995. *Iberia in Prehistory.* Oxford: Blackwell.

Ferrarese Ceruti, M. L. 1979. Ceramica micenea in Sardegna (notizia preliminare), *Rivista di Scienze Preistoriche* 34, 243–53.

Ferreira da Silva, A. C. 1986. *A cultura castreja no noroeste de Portugal.* Paços de Ferreira: Museu Arqueológico da Citania de Sanfins.

Fett, E. N. and P. 1979. Relations west Norway–western Europe documented in petroglyphs, *Norwegian Archaeol. Review* 12, 65–92.

Feustel, R. 1958. *Bronzezeitliche Hügelgräberkultur im Gebiet von Schwarza (Südthüringen).* Veröffent. des Museums für Ur- und Frühgeschichte Thüringens 1. Weimar: H. Böhlaus Nachfolger.

Filip, J. 1947. *Dějinné počátky Českého ráje.* Prague: Státní archeologický ústav.

Fischer, C. 1993. Zinnachweis auf Keramik der Spätbronzezeit, *Archäologie der Schweiz* 16/1, 17–24.

Fischer, F. 1971. *Die frühbronzeitliche Ansiedlung in der Bleiche bei Arbon TG.* Schriften zur Ur- und Frühgeschichte der Schweiz 17. Basel: Schweizerische Gesellschaft für Ur- und Frühgeschichte.

Fleming, A. 1971. Territorial patterns in Bronze Age Wessex, *Proc. Prehist. Soc.* 27, 138–66.

  1987. Coaxial field systems: some questions of time and space, *Antiquity* 61, 188–202.

  1988. *The Dartmoor Reaves. Investigating Prehistoric Land Divisions.* London: Batsford.

Fletcher, R. 1977. Settlement studies (micro and semi-micro). In *Spatial Archaeology*, ed. D. L. Clarke, 47–162. London: Academic Press.

1981. People and space: a case study on material behaviour. In *Pattern of the Past: Studies in Honour of David Clarke*, eds. I. Hodder, G. Isaac and N. Hammond, 97–128. Cambridge: Cambridge University Press.

1984. Identifying spatial disorder: a case study of a Mongol fort. In *Intrasite Spatial Analysis in Archaeology*, ed. H. J. Hietala, 196–223. Cambridge: Cambridge University Press.

1995. *The Limits of Settlement Growth. A Theoretical Outline.* Cambridge: Cambridge University Press.

Flindt, S. 1996. Die Lichtensteinhöhle bei Osterode, Landkreis Osterode am Harz. Eine Opferhöhle der jüngeren Bronzezeit im Gipskarst des südwestlichen Harzrandes, *Die Kunde* 47, 435–66.

Florescu, A. C. 1964. Contribuţii la cunoasterea culturii Noua, *Arheologia Moldavei* 2–3, 143–216.

Fokkens, H. 1991. Nederzettingen uit de bronstijd en de vroege ijzertijd in Oss-Ussen, wijk Mikkeldonk. In *Nederzettingen uit de bronstijd en de vroege ijzertijd in de Lage Landen*, eds. H. Fokkens and N. Roymans 93–109. Nederlandse Archeologische Rapporten 13. Amersfoort: Rijksdienst voor het Oudheidkundig Bodemonderzoek.

Fokkens, H. and Roymans, N. (eds.) 1991. *Nederzettingen uit de bronstijd en de vroege ijzertijd in de Lage Landen.* Nederlandse Archeologische Rapporten 13. Amersfoort: Rijksdienst voor het Oudheidkundig Bodemonderzoek.

Fonzo, O. 1986. Reperti faunistici in Marmilla e Campidano nell'età del bronzo e nella prima età del ferro. In *La Sardegna nel Mediterraneo tra il secondo e il primo millennio a.C.* (Atti del II Convegno di studi 'Un millennio di relazioni fra la Sardegna e i Paesi del Mediterraneo', Selargius-Cagliari 1986), 233–42. Cagliari: Amministrazione Provinciale, Assessorato alla Cultura.

Ford, S. 1981–2. Linear earthworks on the Berkshire Downs, *Berkshire Archaeol. J.* 71, 1–20.

Forenbaher, S. 1995. Trade and exchange in Late Bronze and Early Iron Age Croatia. In *Handel, Tausch und Verkehr im bronze – und früheisenzeitlichen Südosteuropa*, ed. B. Hänsel, 269–82. Südosteuropa-Schriften 17/Prähistorische Archäologie in Südosteuropa 11. Munich/Berlin: Südosteuropa-Gesellschaft/Seminar für Ur- und Frühgeschichte der Freien Universität Berlin.

Forssander, J. E. 1940. Bautastenar från bronsåldern, *Årsberättelse 1939–1940*, 95–105, 129 (*Meddelanden från Lunds Universitets Historiska Museum* 51–61, 85).

Foster, S. M. 1989. Analysis of spatial patterns in buildings (access analysis) as an insight into social structure: examples from the Scottish Atlantic Iron Age, *Antiquity* 63, 40–50.

Fowler, P. 1981. Wildscape to landscape: 'enclosure' in prehistoric Britain. In *Farming Practice in British Prehistory*, ed. R. Mercer, 9–54. Edinburgh: Edinburgh University Press.

1983. *The Farming of Prehistoric Britain.* Cambridge: Cambridge University Press (= 'Later Prehistory' in *The Agrarian History of England and Wales*, I,1, 1981).

Fox, A. and Britton, D. 1969. A continental palstave from the ancient field system on Horridge Common, Dartmoor, England, *Proc. Prehist. Soc.* 35, 220–8.

Fox, C. 1939. The socketed bronze sickles of the British Isles, *Proc. Prehist. Soc.* 5, 222–48.

Fox, C. F. 1928. A Bronze Age refuse pit at Swanwick, Hants, *Antiqs J.* 8, 331–6.

1930. The Bronze Age pit at Swanwick, Hants: further finds, *Antiqs J.* 10, 30–3.

1941. The non-socketed sickles of Britain, *Archaeologia Cambrensis* 96, 136–62.

Frank, G. A. 1990. A theoretical introduction to 5000 years of world-system history, *Review* 14, 155–248.

1993. Bronze Age world system cycles, *Current Anthropology* 34/4, 383–429.

Frank, G. A. and Gills, B. K. (eds.) 1993. *The World System: Five Hundred Years or Five Thousand?* London: Routledge.

Fredsjö, Å, Nordbladh, J. and Rosvall, J. 1971. *Hällristningar i Kville härad i Bohuslän. Svenneby socken*. Studier i nordisk arkeologi 7. Göteborg: Göteborgs och Bohusläns Fornminnesforening i samarbete med Göteborgs Arkeologiska Museum.

Fried, M., Harris, M. and Murphy, R. (eds) 1967. *War: the Anthropology of Armed Conflict and Aggression*. New York: Natural History Press.

Friesch, K. 1987. Die Tierknochenfunde von Cerro de la Encina bei Monachil, Provinz Granada (Grabungen 1977–1984), *Studien über frühe Tierknochenfunde von der Iberischen Halbinsel 11.*

Frost, H. 1970. Bronze Age stone-anchors from the eastern Mediterranean, *The Mariner's Mirror* 56, 377–94.

Furmánek, V. 1988. Eisen während der Bronzezeit in der Slowakei, *Zeitschrift für Archäologie* 23, 183–9.

1995. Tausch und Verkehr im Spiegel bronzezeitlicher Horte der Slowakei. In *Handel, Tausch und Verkehr im bronze- und früheisenzeitlichen Südosteuropa*, ed. B. Hänsel, 1961–72. Südosteuropa-Schriften 17/Prähistorische Archäologie in Südosteuropa 11. Munich/Berlin: Südosteuropa-Gesellschaft/Seminar für Ur- und Frühgeschichte der Freien Universität Berlin.

1997. Stand der demographischen Erforschung der Bronzezeit in der Slowakei. In *Demographie der Bronzezeit. Paläodemographie – Möglichkeiten und Grenzen*, ed. K.-F. Rittershofer, 74–8. Internationale Archäologie 36. Espelkamp: Verlag Marie Leidorf.

Furmánek, V., Veliačik, L., and Vladár, J. 1991. *Slovensko v dobe bronzovej*. Bratislava: Veda.

Gabra-Sanders, T. 1993 [1994]. Textiles and fibres from the Late Bronze Age hoard from St Andrews, Fife, Scotland – a preliminary report. In *Archäologische Textilfunde – Archaeological Textiles. Textilsymposium Neumünster 1993* (NESAT 5), 34–42. Neumünster: Textilmuseum.

Gaffney, V. and Tingle, M. 1989. *The Maddle Farm Project: an Integrated Survey of Prehistoric and Roman Landscapes on the Berkshire Downs*. Oxford: British Archaeological Reports 200.

Gale, D. 1990. Prehistoric stone mining tools from Alderley Edge. In *Early Mining in the British Isles*, eds. P. and S. Crew, 47–8. Proc. Early Mining Workshop 1989, Plas Tan y Bwlch Occasional Paper 1.

1991. The surface artefact assemblage for a prehistoric copper mine,

Austria. In *Archaeological Sciences 1989*, eds. P. Budd, B. Chapman, C. Jackson, R. Janaway and B. Ottaway, 143–50. Oxford: Oxbow Monograph 9.

Gale, N. H. 1989a. Archaeometallurgical studies of Late Bronze Age ox-hide copper ingots from the Mediterranean region. In *Archäometallurgie der Alten Welt/Old World Archaeometallurgy*, Proc. Int. Symposium Heidelberg 1987, 247–68. Bochum: Deutsches Bergbau-Museum [= *Der Anschnitt*, Supplement 7].

1989b. Lead isotope analyses applied to provenance studies – a brief review. In *Archaeometry. Proceedings of the 25th International Symposium*, ed. Y. Maniatis, 469–502. Amsterdam: Elsevier.

Gale, N. H. and Stos-Gale, Z. A. 1981. Ancient Egyptian silver, *J. Egyptian Archaeology* 67, 103–15.

Gallay, A., Favre, S. and Blain, A. 1976. Stèles et roches gravées des Alpes suisses, in *UISPP IXᵉ Congrès, Nice 1976, Colloque XXVII, Les gravures protohistoriques dans les Alpes*, ed. E. Anati, 52–8.

Gallay, G. 1972. Beigaben der Frühbronzezeit Süddeutschlands in ihrer Verteilung auf Männer- und Frauengräber, *Homo* 23, 50–73.

1981. *Die kupfer- und altbronzezeitlichen Dolche und Stabdolche in Frankreich*. Prähistorische Bronzefunde VI, 5. Munich: Beck.

Gallus, S. and Horváth, T. 1939. *Un peuple cavalier préscythique en Hongrie. Trouvailles archéologiques du premier âge du fer et leurs relations avec l'Eurasie*. Dissertationes Pannonicae, Series II, 9. Budapest: Institut de Numismatique et d'Archéologie de l'Université Pierre Pázmány.

Garašanin, D. 1951. Prilog proučavanju dupljajskih kolica, *Starinar* new series 2, 270–2.

Garašanin, M. V. 1968. Neue prähistorische Felsbilder an der adriatischen Küste der Crna Gora (Montenegro), *Germania* 46, 213–24.

1983. Dubovačko-žutobrdska grupa. In *Praistorija jugoslavenskih zemalja IV, Bronzano doba*, 520–35. Sarajevo: Akademija Nauka i Umjetnosti Bosne i Hercegovine.

Garašanin, M. V. and D. 1956. Neue Hügelgräberforschung in Westserbien, *Archaeologia Iugoslavica* 2, 11–18.

Garner, A., Prag, J. and Housley, R. 1994. The Alderley Edge shovel. An epic in three acts, *Current Archaeology* 137, 172–5.

Garwood, P. 1991. Ritual tradition and the reconstitution of society. In *Sacred and Profane. Proceedings of a Conference on Archaeology, Ritual and Religion, Oxford 1989*, eds. P. Garwood, D. Jennings, R. Skeates and J. Toms, 10–32. Oxford: Oxford University Committee for Archaeology, Monograph 32.

Gates, T. 1983. Unenclosed settlements in Northumberland. In *Settlement in North Britain 1000 BC – AD 1000*, eds. J. C. Chapman and H. C. Mytum, 103–48. Oxford: British Archaeological Reports 118.

Gaucher, G. 1976. Les civilisations de l'âge du bronze dans le bassin parisien et le nord de la France. In *La Préhistoire française. II. Civilisations néolithiques et protohistoriques*, ed. J. Guilaine, 575–84. Paris: Editions du CNRS.

1988. *Peuples du bronze. Anthropologie de la France à l'âge du bronze*. Paris: Hachette.

Gazdapusztai, G. 1959. Der Gussformfund von Soltvadkert, *Acta Archaeologica* (Budapest) 9, 265–88.

Gdaniec, K. 1996. A miniature antler bow from a Middle Bronze Age site at
    Isleham (Cambridgeshire), England, *Antiquity* 70, 652–7.
Gedl, M. 1982. Frühbronzezeitliche Burgen in Polen. In *Beiträge zum
    bronzezeitlichen Burgenbau in Mitteleuropa*, 189–207. Berlin:
    Zentralinstitut für Alte Geschichte und Archäologie; Nitra: Archeologický
    Ústav Slovenskej Akadémie Vied.
    1996. Symbolgut, Opferplätze und Deponierungsfunde in Süd- und Ostpolen.
    In *Archäologische Forschungen zum Kultgeschehen in der jüngeren
    Bronzezeit und frühen Eisenzeit Alteuropas*, ed. C. Huth, 349–60.
    Regensburger Beiträge zur prähistorischen Archäologie, 2. Regensburg:
    Universitätsverlag (Bonn: Habelt).
Gejvall, N.-G. 1967. Esame preliminare del materiale osseo reperito negli scavi
    effettuati a Luni. Appendix I in C. E. Östenberg, *Luni sul Mignone e prob-
    lemi della preistoria d'Italia*, 261–76. Skrifter utgivna av Svenska Institutet
    i Rom, 4°, 25. Lund: Gleerup.
Genito, B. and Kemenczei, T. 1990. The Late Bronze Age vessels from Gyoma
    133, S.E. Hungary, *Communicationes Archaeologicae Hungariae* 1990,
    113–25.
Georgiev, G. I. 1978. Forschungsstand der alten Felskunst in Bulgarien. In *Acts
    of the International Symposium on Rock Art, Lectures at Hankø 1972*, ed.
    S. Marstrander, 68–84. Oslo: Universitetsforlaget.
Georgiev, G. I., Merpert, N. J., Katinčarov, R. V. and Dimitrov, D. G. 1979.
    Ezero, rannobronzovoto selišče. Sofia: Bulgarian Academy of Sciences.
Gergov, V. 1979. Praistoričeski nachodki ot peščerata pri s. Muselievo, pleven-
    ski okrug, *Izvestija muzeite severozapadna Bălgarija* 3, 35–55.
Gerhardt, K. 1953. *Die Glockenbecherleute in Mittel- und Westdeutschland.
    Ein Beitrag zur Paläoanthropologie Eurafrikas*. Stuttgart: E. Schweizerbart.
    1964. *Schädel- und Skelettreste der frühen Bronzezeit von
    Singen/Hohentwiel (Ldkrs. Konstanz)*. Badische Fundberichte, Special
    Supplement 5.
Gerloff, S. 1975. *The Early Bronze Age Daggers in Great Britain, and a
    Reconsideration of the Wessex Culture*. Prähistorische Bronzefunde VI, 2.
    Munich: Beck.
    1993. Zu Fragen mittelmeerländischer Kontakte und absoluter Chronologie
    der Frühbronzezeit in Mittel- und Westeuropa, *Prähistorische Zeitschrift*
    68, 58–102.
    1995. Bronzezeitliche Goldblechkronen aus Westeuropa. Betrachtungen zur
    Funktion der Goldblechkegel vom Typ Schifferstadt und der atlantischen
    'Goldschalen' der Form Devil's Bit und Atroxi. In *Festschrift für Hermann
    Müller-Karpe zum 70. Geburtstag*, ed. A. Jockenhövel, 153–94. Bonn:
    Habelt.
    1996. Wessex, Mycenae and related matters: the chronology of the British
    Bronze Age in its European setting. In *The Bronze Age in Europe and the
    Mediterranean, Colloquium XX: Absolute, Relative and Comparative
    Chronological Sequences*, 11–19. XIII International Congress of Prehistoric
    and Protohistoric Sciences, Forlì 1996, Section 11. Forlì: ABACO Edizioni.
Gero, J. M. and Conkey, M. W. (eds.) 1991. *Engendering Archaeology. Women
    and Prehistory*. Oxford: Basil Blackwell.
Gersbach, E. 1969. *Urgeschichte des Hochrheins (Funde und Fundstelle in den
    Landkreisen Säckingen und Landshut)*. Badische Fundberichte, Special
    Supplement 11. Freiburg im Breisgau.

Gibson, A. M. 1986. Diatom analysis of clays and late Neolithic pottery from the Milfield basin, Northumberland, *Proc. Prehist. Soc.* 52, 89–103.

1994a. The timber circle at Sarn-y-bryn-caled: an exercise in reconstruction. In *Les sites de reconstitutions archéologiques. Actes du colloque d'Aubechies 1993*, 47–52. [Place not stated]: Ministère de la région wallonne, division du patrimoine.

1994b. Excavations at the Sarn-y-bryn-caled cursus complex, Welshpool, Powys, and the timber circles of Great Britain and Ireland, *Proc. Prehist. Soc.* 60, 143–223.

Gilks, J. A. 1973. The Neolithic and Early Bronze Age pottery from Elbolton cave, Wharfedale, *Yorkshire Archaeol. J.* 45, 41–54.

Gills, B. K. and Frank, G. A. 1993. World system cycles, crises, and hegemonic shifts, 1700 BC to 1700 AD. In *The World System: Five Hundred Years or Five Thousand?*, ed. G. A. Frank and B. K. Gills , 143–99. London: Routledge.

Gilman, A. 1976. Bronze Age dynamics in south-east Spain, *Dialectical Anthropology* 1, 307–19.

1981. The development of social stratification in Bronze Age Europe, *Current Anthropology* 22/1, 1–23.

1991. Trajectories towards social complexity in the later prehistory of the Mediterranean. In *Chiefdoms: Power, Economy and Ideology*, ed. T. K. Earle, 146–68. Cambridge: Cambridge University Press.

Gimbutas, M. 1965. *Bronze Age Cultures in Central and Eastern Europe*. The Hague: Mouton.

Gingell, C. 1992. *The Marlborough Downs: a Later Bronze Age Landscape and its Origins*. Wiltshire Archaeol. and Natural History Soc. Monograph 1. Devizes.

Giot, P.-R., L'Helgouach, J. and Briard, J. 1965. Le site du Curnic en Guissény, *Annales de Bretagne* 72, 49–70.

Girić, M. 1971. *Mokrin, nekropola ranog bronzanog doba/Mokrin, the Early Bronze Age Necropolis*. Dissertationes et Monographiae 11. Washington: Smithsonian Institution/Kikinda: Narodni muzej/Belgrade: Arheološko Društvo Jugoslavije.

1987. Die Erforschung der äneolithischen Hügelgräber im nördlichen Banat. In *Hügelbestattung in der Karpaten–Donau–Balkan Zone während der äneolithischen Periode*, eds. D. Srejović and N. Tasić, 71–6. Belgrade: Balkanološki Institut, posebna izdanja 29.

Glasbergen, W. 1954a. Barrow excavations in the Eight Beatitudes. The Bronze Age cemetery between Toterfout and Halve Mijl, North Brabant, I. The excavations, *Palaeohistoria* 2, 1–134.

1954b. Barrow excavations in the Eight Beatitudes. The Bronze Age cemetery between Toterfout and Halve Mijl, North Brabant, II. The implications, *Palaeohistoria* 3, 1–204.

Gleirscher, P. 1996. Brandopferplätze, Depotfunde und Symbolgut im Ostalpenraum während der Spätbronze- und Früheisenzeit. In *Archäologische Forschungen zum Kultgeschehen in der jüngeren Bronzezeit und frühen Eisenzeit Alteuropas*, ed. C. Huth, 429–49. Regensburger Beiträge zur prähistorischen Archäologie, 2. Regensburg: Universitätsverlag (Bonn: Habelt).

Glob, P. V. 1951. *Ard og plov i Nordens Oldtid*. Jysk Arkaeologisk Selskabs Skrifter 1. Aarhus: Universitetsforlaget.

1969. *Helleristninger i Danmark*. Aarhus: Jutland Archaeological Society.

1974. *The Mound People. Danish Bronze-Age Man Preserved*. London: Faber and Faber.

Glowatzki, G. and Schröter, P. 1978. Versorgte Impressionsfraktur eines Schädels aus der frühen Bronzezeit in Bayern, *Homo* 29, 250–9.

Gnepf, U. and Hochuli, S. 1996. Steinhausen ZG, Cosmetochem, GBP 1267, *Jahrbuch der schweizerischen Gesellschaft für Ur- und Frühgeschichte* 79, 237.

Gnepf, U., Moser, P. and Weiss, J. 1996. Morastige Wege und stattliche Häuser im mittelbronzezeitlichen Cham, *Archäologie der Schweiz* 19/2, 64–7.

Godynicki, S. and Sobociński, M. 1977. Zwierzęce szczątki kostne z grodziska kultury łużyckiej w Smuszewie, woj. pilskie, *Fontes Archaeologici Posnanienses* 28, 3–35.

Gojda, M. 1997: *Letecká archeologie v Čechách/Aerial Archaeology in Bohemia*. Prague: Institute of Archaeology.

Goldberg, N. and Findlow, F. 1984. A quantitative analysis of Roman military aggression in Britain, circa AD 43–238. In *Warfare, Culture and Environment*, ed. B. Ferguson, 359–85. Orlando: Academic Press.

Goldmann, K. 1981. Guss in verlorener Sandform – das Hauptverfahren alteuropäischer Bronzegiesser? *Archäologisches Korrespondenzblatt* 11, 109–16.

1982a. Märkische Kulturlandschaft – das Erbe bronzezeitlicher Kolonisation? *Ausgrabungen in Berlin* 6, 5–50.

1982b. Die Lage der Burgen im Verkehrswegenetz. In *Beiträge zum bronzezeitlichen Burgenbau in Mitteleuropa*, 209–20. Berlin: Zentralinstitut für Alte Geschichte und Archäologie; Nitra: Archeologický Ústav Slovenskej Akadémie Vied.

1982c. Die Lausitzer Kultur der mitteleuropäischen Bronzezeit, *Berliner Museen* 24, 11–12.

Gomez, J. 1973. La grotte sépulchrale des Duffaits (La Rochette, Charente). Etude archéologique, *Bull. Soc. Préhist. Française* 70, 401–44.

1984. Materiel de fondeur de l'âge du bronze dans le bassin de la Charente. In *Paléométallurgie de la France Atlantique. Age du bronze (1)*, 169–80. Rennes: Travaux du Laboratoire anthropologie–préhistoire–protohistoire–quaternaire armoricains.

González Marcén, P., Lull, V. and Risch, R. 1992. *Arqueología de Europa, 2250–1200 A.C. Una introducción a la 'edad del bronce'*. Historia Universal 6, Prehistoria. Madrid: Editorial Síntesis.

Gonzalez Prats, A. 1992. Una vivienda metalurgica en la Peña Negra (Crevellente-Alicante). Aportación al conocimiento del Bronce atlántico en la península ibérica, *Trabajos de Prehistoria* 49, 243–57.

Götze, A. 1933. Die Ausgrabung des Burgwalles von Senftenberg, Kr. Calau, *Nachrichtenblatt für deutsche Vorzeit* 9, 35–9.

Gouletquer, P.-L. 1969. Etudes sur les briquetages, IV, *Annales de Bretagne* 76, 119–47.

1970. *Les Briquetages armoricains. Technologie protohistorique du sel en Armorique*. Rennes: Travaux du Laboratoire d'anthropologie préhistorique, faculté des sciences.

Govedarica, B. 1987. Einige Fragen der Chronologie und Herkunft der ältesten Tumuli mit Steinkistengräbern im ostadriatischen Gebiet. In

Hügelbestattung in der Karpaten–Donau–Balkan Zone während der äneolithischen Periode, eds. D. Srejović and N. Tasić, 57–70. Belgrade: Balkanološki Institut, posebna izdanja 29.

Green, C. and Rollo-Smith, S. 1984. The excavation of eighteen round barrows near Shrewton, Wiltshire, *Proc. Prehist. Soc.* 50, 255–318.

Green, H.S. 1974. Early Bronze Age burial, territory and population in Milton Keynes, Buckinghamshire, and the Great Ouse valley, *Archaeol. J.* 131, 75–139.

  1980. *The Flint Arrowheads of the British Isles*. Oxford: British Archaeological Reports 75.

  1987. The Disgwylfa Fawr round barrow, Ceredigion, Dyfed, *Archaeologia Cambrensis* 136, 43–50.

Green, H. S., Smith, A. H. V., Young, B. R. and Harrison, R. K. 1980. Caergwrle bowl: its composition, geological source and archaeological significance, *Report Institute Geological Sciences* 80/1, 26–30.

Greenfield, H. J. 1986. *The Palaeoeconomy of the Central Balkans (Serbia): a Zooarchaeological Perspective on the Late Neolithic and Bronze Age (4500–1000 BC)*. Oxford: British Archaeological Reports, Int. Series 304.

  1991. Fauna from the Late Neolithic of the central Balkans: issues in subsistence and land use, *J. Field Archaeology* 18, 161–86.

Greenwell, W. 1894. Antiquities of the Bronze Age found in the Heathery Burn cave, County Durham, *Archaeologia* 54, 87–114.

Greenwell, W. and Brewis, P. 1909. The origin, evolution and classification of the bronze spearhead in Great Britain and Ireland, *Archaeologia* 61, 439–72.

Griesa, S. 1982. Die Göritzer Gruppe, *Veröff. des Museums für Ur- und Frühgeschichte Potsdam* 16.

Grimes, W. F. 1938. A barrow on Breach Farm, Llanbleddian, Glamorgan, *Proc. Prehist. Soc.* 4, 107–21.

Grinsell, L. V. 1941a. The Bronze Age barrows of Wessex, *Proc. Prehist. Soc.* 7, 73–113.

  1941b. The boat of the dead in the Bronze Age, *Antiquity* 15, 360–70.

  1942. The Kivik cairn, Scania, *Antiquity* 16, 160–74.

  1957. Archaeological gazetteer. In *A History of Wiltshire, I part 1*, ed. R. B. Pugh. The Victoria County History of the Counties of England. London: University of London, Institute of Historical Research.

  1959. *Dorset Barrows*. Dorchester: Dorset Natural History and Archaeol. Soc.

  1974. Disc barrows, *Proc. Prehist. Soc.* 40, 79–112.

  1982. *Dorset Barrows Supplement*. Dorchester: Dorset Natural History and Archaeol. Soc.

  n.d. *The Stonehenge Barrow Groups*. Salisbury: Salisbury and South Wiltshire Museum.

Grøn, O. 1991. A method for reconstruction of social structure in prehistoric societies and examples of practical application. In *Social Space. Human Spatial Behaviour in Dwellings and Settlements*, eds. O. Grøn, E. Engelstad and I. Lindblom, 100–17. Odense University Studies in History and Social Sciences, 147. Odense: Odense University Press.

Groenman-van Waateringe, W. 1970–1. Hecken im westeuropäischen Frühneolithikum, *Berichten van de Rijksdienst Oudheidkundig Bodemonderzoek* 20–1, 295–9.

Grogan, E. 1995. North Munster project, *Discovery Programme Reports 2, Project Reports 1993*, 45–61. Dublin: Royal Irish Academy/Discovery Programme.

Gróh, D. 1984. Előzetes jelentés a Visegrád-Csemetekert lelőhelyen végzett későbronzkori és koravaskori feltárásról, *Communicationes Archaeologicae Hungariae 1984*, 53–66.

Grosjean, R. 1966. *La Corse avant l'histoire. Monuments et art de la civilisation mégalithique insulaire du début du IIIe à la fin du IIe millénaire avant notre ère*. Paris: Editions Klincksieck.

Gross, E. *et al.* 1987. *Zürich 'Mozartstrasse'. Neolithische und bronzezeitliche Ufersiedlungen, I*. Berichte der Zürcher Denkmalpflege, Monographien 4. Zurich: Orell Füssli.

Gross-Klee, E. and Maise, C. 1997. Sonne, Vulkane und Seeufersiedlungen, *Jahrbuch der schweizerischen Gesellschaft für Ur- und Frühgeschichte 80*, 85–94.

Gstrein, P. and Lippert, A. 1987. Untersuchung bronzezeitlicher Pingen am Hochmoos bei Bischofshofen, Salzburg, *Archaeologia Austriaca 71*, 89–100.

Guido, M. 1978. *The Glass Beads of the Prehistoric and Roman Periods in Britain and Ireland*. London: Soc. of Antiqs Research Report 35.

Guido, M., Henderson, J., Cable, M., Bayley, J. and Biek, L. 1984. A Bronze Age glass bead from Wilsford, Wiltshire: Barrow G42 in the Lake group, *Proc. Prehist. Soc. 50*, 245–54.

Guilaine, J. (ed.) 1976. *La Préhistoire française. II. Les Civilisations néolithiques et protohistoriques de la France*. Paris: Editions du CNRS.

Guilbert, G. 1976. Moel y Gaer (Rhosesmor) 1972–1973: an area excavation in the interior. In *Hillforts. Later Prehistoric Earthworks in Britain and Ireland*, ed. D. W. Harding, 303–17. London: Academic Press.

Gurney, D. 1980. Evidence of Bronze Age salt-production at Northey, Peterborough, *Northants Archaeology 15*, 1–11.

Haas, J. (ed.) 1990a. *The Anthropology of War*. Cambridge: Cambridge University Press.

  1990b. Warfare and the evolution of tribal polities in the prehistoric Southwest. In *The Anthropology of War*, ed. J. Haas, 171–89. Cambridge: Cambridge University Press.

Haas, J. and Creamer, W. 1993. *Stress and Warfare among the Kayenta Anasazi of the Thirteenth Century A.D. Fieldiana*, Anthropology, new series 21. Chicago: Field Museum of Natural History.

Hachmann, R. 1957. *Die frühe Bronzezeit im westlichen Ostseegebiet und ihre mittel- und südosteuropäischen Beziehungen. Chronologische Untersuchungen*. Atlas der Urgeschichte, Supplement 6. Hamburg: Flemmings Verlag.

Hadingham, E. 1974. *Ancient Carvings in Britain: a Mystery*. London: Garnstone Press.

Hadjianastasiou, O. and MacGillivray, J. A. 1988. An Early Bronze Age copper smelting site on the Aegean island of Kythnos II: archaeological evidence. In *Aspects of Ancient Mining and Metallurgy, Acta of a British School at Athens Centenary Conference, Bangor 1986*, ed. J. Ellis Jones, 31–4.

Haevernick, T. E. 1953. Einige Glasperlen der Lausitzer Kultur in Sachsen, *Arbeits- und Forschungsberichte zur sächsischen Bodendenkmalpflege 3*, 52–6.

1978. Urnenfelderzeitliche Glasperlen, *Zeitschrift für schweizerische Archäologie und Kunstgeschichte* 35, 145–57.

Hafner, A. 1995. 'Vollgriffdolch und Löffelbeil', Statussymbole der Frühbronzezeit, *Archäologie der Schweiz* 18/4, 134–41.

Hagberg, U. E. 1988. The bronze shields from Fröslunda near Lake Vänern, west Sweden. In *Trade and Exchange in Prehistory. Studies in Honour of Berta Stjernquist*, eds. B. Hardh, L. Larsson, D. Olausson and R. Petré, 119–26. Acta Archaeologica Lundensia, series in 8°, 16. Lund: Historiska Museum.

1994. Fröslundsköldarna – ett ovanligt depåfynd från Västsverige, *Fynske minder 1994, Fra Luristan til Lusehoj (Festskrift til Henrik Thrane)*, 93–7.

Haimovici, S. 1964. Studiu asupra resturilor de fauna descoperte in asezarile apartinînd culturii Noua de la Bîrlad şi Piatra Neamţ, *Arheologia Moldavei* 2–3, 217–36.

1991. Materialul faunistic de la Gîrbovăţ. Studiu arheozoologic, *Arheologia Moldavei* 14, 153–66.

Hajek, L. 1961. Zur relativen Chronologie des Äneolithikums und der Bronzezeit in der Ostslowakei. In *Kommission für das Äneolithikum und die ältere Bronzezeit, Nitra 1958*, 59–76. Bratislava: Verlag der Slowakischen Akademie der Wissenschaften.

Hajnalová, E. 1989. Katalóg zvyškov semien a plodov v archeologických nálezoch na Slovensku, *Acta Interdisciplinaria Archaeologica* 6 (*Súčasné poznatky z archeobotaniky na Slovensku*), 3–192.

Hald, M. 1980. *Ancient Danish Textiles from Bogs and Burials. A Comparative Study of Costume and Iron Age Textiles*. Copenhagen: Publications of the National Museum, Archaeological-Historical Series 21 (2nd edition of *Olddanske Tekstiler*, 1950).

Hale, J. R. 1980. Plank built in the Bronze Age, *Antiquity* 54, 118–27.

Hall, T. D. and Chase-Dunn, C. 1993. The world-systems perspective and archaeology: forward into the past, *J. Archaeol. Research* 1/2, 121–37.

Halliday, S. 1985. Unenclosed upland settlement in the east and south-east of Scotland. In *Upland Settlement in Britain. The Second Millennium BC and After*, eds. D. Spratt and C. Burgess, 231–51. Oxford: British Archaeological Reports 143.

Halstead, P. 1987. Traditional and ancient rural economy in Mediterranean Europe: plus ça change? *J. Hellenic Studies* 107, 77–87.

1990. Present to past in the Pindhos: diversification and specialisation in mountain economies, *Rivista di Studi Liguri* A 66, 61–80 (Atti della Tavola Ronda Internazionale *Archeologia della pastorizia nell'Europa meridionale* I).

Halstead, P. and O'Shea, J. 1982. A friend in need is a friend indeed: social storage and the origins of social ranking. In *Ranking, Resource and Exchange. Aspects of the Archaeology of Early European Society*, eds. C. Renfrew and S. Shennan, 92–9. Cambridge: Cambridge University Press.

Hamilton, J. R. C. 1956. *Excavations at Jarlshof, Shetland*. Ministry of Works, Archaeological Report 1. Edinburgh: HMSO.

Hammond, N. G. L. 1967. Tumulus burial in Albania, the Grave Circles of Mycenae, and the Indo-Europeans, *Annual British School Athens* 62, 77–105.

1974. The tumulus burials of Leucas and their connections in the Balkans and northern Greece, *Annual British School Athens* 69, 129–44.

Hampl, F., Kerchler, F. and Benkovsky-Pivovarová, Z. 1981/1985. *Das mittel-*

bronzezeitliche Gräberfeld von Pitten in Niederösterreich. Ergebnisse der Ausgrabungen des Niederösterreichischen Landesmuseums in den Jahren 1967 bis 1973. Mitt. der Prähistorischen Kommission der österreichischen Akademie der Wissenschaften 19–20 (vol. 1: Fundbericht und Tafeln); 21–2 (vol. 2: Auswertung, Section 1).

Hänsel, A. and B. 1997. *Gaben an die Götter. Schätze der Bronzezeit Europas.* Berlin: Seminar für Ur- und Frühgeschichte der Freien Universität/Museum für Vor- und Frühgeschichte (Staatliche Museen zu Berlin – Preussischer Kulturbesitz).

Hänsel, B. 1968. *Beiträge zur Chronologie der mittleren Bronzezeit im Karpatenbecken.* Bonn: Habelt.

1973. Höhlen- und Felsmalereien an der unteren Donau und ihre Bedeutung für die Hallstattkunst Mitteleuropas. In *Actes du VIIIᵉ Congrès international des sciences préhistoriques et Protohistoriques, Beograd, 9–15 septembre 1971,* eds. M. Garašanin, A. Benac and N. Tasić, III, 112–19.

1976. *Beiträge zur regionalen und chronologischen Gliederung der älteren Hallstattzeit an der unteren Donau.* Bonn: Habelt.

1982. Frühe Kupferverhüttung auf Helgoland, *Archeologia Polski* 27/2, 319–22.

(ed.) 1995. *Handel, Tausch und Verkehr im bronze- und früheisenzeitlichen Südosteuropa.* Südosteuropa-Schriften 17/Prähistorische Archäologie in Südosteuropa 11. Munich/Berlin: Südosteuropa-Gesellschaft/Seminar für Ur- und Frühgeschichte der Freien Universität Berlin.

Hänsel, B. and Medović, P. 1991. Vorbericht über die jugoslawisch-deutschen Ausgrabungen in der Siedlung von Feudvar bei Mošorin (Gem. Titel, Vojvodina) von 1986–1990, *Bericht der Römisch-Germanischen Kommission* 72, 45–204.

Hansen, S. 1991. *Studien zu den Metalldeponierungen während der Urnenfelderzeit im Rhein-Main-Gebiet.* Universitätsforschungen zur prähistorischen Archäologie 5. Bonn: Habelt.

1995. Aspekte des Gabentausches und Handels während der Urnenfelderzeit in Mittel- und Nordeuropa im Lichte der Fundüberlieferung. In *Handel, Tausch und Verkehr im bronze – und früheisenzeitlichen Südosteuropa,* ed. B. Hänsel, 67–80. Südosteuropa-Schriften 17/Prähistorische Archäologie in Südosteuropa 11. Munich/Berlin: Südosteuropa-Gesellschaft/Seminar für Ur- und Frühgeschichte der Freien Universität Berlin.

Hansen, W. 1937. Verbreitung und Bedeutung der Schalensteine im Glauben und Brauch der Vorzeit. Hamburg (Inaugural Dissertation Hamburg 1929).

Harding, A. F. 1971. The earliest glass in Europe, *Archeologické Rozhledy* 23, 188–200.

1976. Bronze agricultural implements in Bronze Age Europe. In *Problems in Economic and Social Archaeology,* eds. G. de G. Sieveking, I. H. Longworth and K. Wilson, 513–22. London: Duckworth.

1980. Radiocarbon calibration and the chronology of the European Bronze Age, *Archeologické Rozhledy* 32, 178–86.

(ed.) 1983a. *Climatic Change in Later Prehistory.* Edinburgh: Edinburgh University Press.

1983b. The Bronze Age in central and eastern Europe: advances and prospects, *Advances in World Archaeology* 2, 1–50.

1984a. *The Mycenaeans and Europe.* London: Academic Press.

1984b. Aspects of social evolution in the Bronze Age. In *European Social Evolution: Archaeological Perspectives*, ed. J. L. Bintliff, 135–45. Bradford: University of Bradford.

1987. Social and economic factors in the origin and development of the Urnfield cultures. In *Die Urnenfelderkulturen Mitteleuropas. Symposium Liblice 1985*, eds. E. Plesl and J. Hrala, 37–41. Prague: Archäologisches Institut der Tschechoslowakischen Akademie der Wissenschaften.

1989. Interpreting the evidence for agricultural change in the Late Bronze Age in northern Europe. In *Bronze Age Studies*, eds. H.-Å. Nordström and A. Knape, 173–81. Stockholm: Statens Historiska Museum.

1993. Europe and the Mediterranean in the Bronze Age: cores and peripheries. In *Trade and Exchange in Prehistoric Europe*, eds. C. Scarre and F. Healy, 153–60. Oxford: Oxbow Monograph 33.

1994. Prehistoric and early medieval activity on Danby Rigg, North Yorkshire, *Archaeol. J.* 151, 16–97.

1995. *Die Schwerter im ehemaligen Jugoslawien*. Prähistorische Bronzefunde IV, 14. Stuttgart: Franz Steiner.

1997. Wie gross waren die Gruppenverbände der bronzezeitlicher Welt? In *Χρόνος. Beiträge zur prähistorischen Archäologie zwischen Nord- und Südeuropa. Festschrift für Bernhard Hänsel*, eds. C. Becker *et al.*, 443–51. Internationale Archäologie, Studia Honoraria 1. Espelkamp: Verlag Marie Leidorf.

Harding, A. F. and Hughes-Brock, H. 1974. Amber in the Mycenaean world, *Annual British School Athens* 69, 145–72.

Harding, A. F. and Ostoja-Zagórski, J. 1984. Excavations at Sobiejuchy, west-central Poland, *Archaeological Reports for 1983* [Universities of Durham and Newcastle upon Tyne], 17–23.

1989. Survey and excavation in the Sobiejuchy microregion, Central Poland, 1988, *Archaeological Reports for 1988* [Universities of Durham and Newcastle upon Tyne], 12–20.

Harding, A. F. and Warren, S. E. 1973. Early Bronze Age faience beads from central Europe, *Antiquity* 47, 64–6.

Hardmeyer, B. 1976. *Prähistorisches Gold Europas im 3. und 2. Jahrtausend vor Christus*. Privately published (Switzerland).

Hardmeyer, B. and Bürgi, J. 1975. Der Goldbecher von Eschenz, *Zeitschrift für Schweizerischen Archäologie und Kunstgeschichte* 32, 109–20.

Härke, H. 1978. Probleme der optischen Emissionsspektroanalyse in der Urgeschichtsforschung. Technische Möglichkeiten und methodische Fragestellungen, *Prähistorische Zeitschrift* 53, 165–276.

Harrison, R. J. 1988. *Spain at the Dawn of History*. London: Thames and Hudson.

Harrison, R. J. and Craddock, P. T. 1981. A study of the Bronze Age metalwork from the Iberian peninsula in the British Museum, *Institut de Prehistoria i Arqueologia Barcelona*, Monograph 64, 113–79.

Harrison, R. J., Jusmet, F. M. and Giró, P. 1974. Faience beads and Atlantic bronzes in Catalonia, *Madrider Mitt.* 15, 95–107.

Harrison, R., Moreno Lopez, G. and Legge, A. J. 1994. *Moncín. Un poblado de la edad del bronce en Aragón*. Serie Arqueología Aragonesa. Zaragoza: Cometa.

Hartmann, A. 1970. *Prähistorische Goldfunde aus Europa*. Studien zu den Anfängen der Metallurgie 3. Berlin: Mann.

1982. *Prähistorische Goldfunde aus Europa, II*. Studien zu den Anfängen der Metallurgie, Band 5. Berlin: Mann.

Hartmann, G., Kappel, I., Grote, K. and Arndt, B. 1997. Chemistry and technology of prehistoric glass from Lower Saxony and Hesse, *J. Archaeol. Science* 24, 547–59.

Haselgrove, C. C. and Gwilt, A. (eds.) 1998. *Reconstructing Iron Age Societies*. Oxford: Oxbow Monograph 71.

Hassan, F. A. 1981. *Demographic Archaeology*. New York: Academic Press.

Häusler, A. 1974. *Die Gräber der älteren Ockergrabkultur zwischen Ural und Dnepr*. Berlin: Akademie-Verlag.

1976. *Die Gräber der älteren Ockergrabkultur zwischen Dnepr und Karpaten*. Berlin: Akademie-Verlag.

1977. Die Bestattungssitten der frühen Bronzezeit zwischen Rhein und oberer Wolga, ihre Voraussetzungen und ihre Beziehungen, *Zeitschrift für Archäologie* 11, 13–48.

1994. Grab- und Bestattungssitten des Neolithikums und der frühen Bronzezeit in Mitteleuropa, *Zeitschrift für Archäologie* 28, 23–61.

1996. Totenorientierung und geographischer Raum. In *Terra et Praehistoria. Festschrift für Klaus-Dieter Jäger*, eds. S. Ostritz and R. Einicke, 61–92. Beiträge zur Ur- und Frühgeschichte Mitteleuropas 9. Wilkau-Hasslau: Beier and Beran.

Hawkes, C. F. C. 1954. Archaeological theory and method: some suggestions from the Old World, *American Anthropologist* 56, 155–68.

Hawley, W. 1909–10. Notes on barrows in South Wilts., *Wilts. Archaeol. Magazine* 36, 615–28.

Hayen, H. 1957. Der bronzezeitliche Bohlendamm VII. Einige Ergebnisse der Ausgrabung im Herbst 1956 aus dem Ipwegermoor, *Nordwest-Heimat* 4/57 (Supplement 40 der *Nordwest-Zeitung*, Oldenburg).

1971. Hölzerne Kultfiguren am Bohlenweg XLII (Ip) im Wittemoor (Gemeinde Berne, Landkreis Wesermarsch) (Vorläufiger Bericht), *Die Kunde* 22, 88–123.

1972. Vier Scheibenräder aus dem Vehnemoor bei Glum (Gemeinde Wardenburg, Landkreis Oldenburg), *Die Kunde* 23, 62–86.

1987. Peatbog archaeology in Lower Saxony, West Germany. In *European Wetlands in Prehistory*, eds. J. M. Coles and A. J. Lawson, 117–36. Oxford: Clarendon Press.

Hebert, B. 1991. Hörbing-Forstgarten: eine bronzezeitliche Siedlung am Stadtrand von Deutschlandsberg, *Archäologie Österreichs* 2/2, 41.

Hedges, J. D. (ed.) 1986. *The Carved Rocks on Rombalds Moor. A Gazetteer of the Prehistoric Rock Carvings on Rombalds Moor, West Yorkshire*. Wakefield: West Yorkshire Archaeology Service/Ilkley Archaeology Group.

Hedges, J. W. 1986. Bronze Age structures at Tongs, Burra Isle, Shetland, *Glasgow Archaeol. J.* 13, 1–43.

Hedges, R. E. M., Housley, R. A., Bronk, C. R. and van Klinken, G. J. 1991. Radiocarbon dates from the Oxford AMS system, *Archaeometry* 33, 121–34.

Heierli, J. 1907. Die bronzezeitliche Quellfassung von St Moritz, *Anzeiger für schweizerische Altertumskunde*, new series 9, 265–78.

Heitz, A., Jacomet, S. and Zoller, H. 1981. Vegetation, Sammelwirtschaft und

Ackerbau um Zürichseegebiet zur Zeit der neolithischen und spät-bronzezeitlichen Ufersiedlungen, *Helvetia Archaeologica* 45–8, 139–52.

Helbaek, H. 1952a. Preserved apples and *Panicum* in the prehistoric site at Nørre Sandegaard in Bornholm, *Acta Archaeologica* (Copenhagen) 23, 107–15.

1952b. Spelt (*Triticum spelta* L.) in Bronze Age Denmark, *Acta Archaeologica* (Copenhagen) 23, 93–107.

Hell, M. 1913. Ein Baumtrogfund in Untersberger Moor bei Salzburg, *Sitzungsbericht der Anthropologischen Gesellschaft Wien* 1912/13 (Anhang zu *Mitt. Anthropologischen Gesellschaft Wien* 43, 1913), 47–9.

1939. Ein Passfund der Urnenfelderkultur aus dem Gau Salzburg, *Wiener Prähistorischer Zeitschrift* 26, 148–56.

Hellebrandt, M. B. 1990. Az igrici kerámiadepot, *Communicationes Archaeologicae Hungariae 1990*, 93–111.

Helms, M. 1979. *Ancient Panama: Chiefs in Search of Power*. Austin: University of Texas Press.

Hencken, H. 1942. Ballinderry crannog no. 2, *Proc. Royal Irish Academy* 47C, 1–77.

1971. *The Earliest European Helmets, Bronze Age and Early Iron Age*. Cambridge (Mass.): American School of Prehistoric Research/Peabody Museum.

Henderson, J. 1988. Glass production and Bronze Age Europe, *Antiquity* 62, 435–51.

1989. The earliest glass in Britain and Ireland. In *Le Verre préromain en Europe occidentale*, ed. M. Feugère, 19–28. Montagnac: Editions Monique Mergoil.

Henderson, J. C. 1998. Islets through time: the definition, dating and distribution of Scottish crannogs, *Oxford J. Archaeology* 17/2, 227–44.

Hengen, O. H. 1971. Cribra orbitalia: pathogenesis and probable etiology, *Homo* 22, 57–76.

Henning-Almgren, I. 1952. Hängkärl och bronsåldersdräkt, *Tor* 1949–51, 46–50.

Henshall, A. 1950. Textiles and weaving appliances in prehistoric Britain, *Proc. Prehist. Soc.* 16, 130–62.

Herdits, H. 1993. Zum Beginn experimentalarchäologischer Untersuchungen einer bronzezeitlichen Kupferverhüttungslage in Mühlbach, Salzburg, *Archaeologia Austriaca* 77, 31–8.

Herity, M. and Eogan, G. 1977. *Ireland in Prehistory*. London: Routledge and Kegan Paul.

Herrmann, F.-R. 1975. Hausgrundrisse aus einer urnenfelderzeitlichen Siedlung von Künzing (Niederbayern). In *Ausgrabungen in Deutschland gefördert von der Deutschen Forschungsgemeinschaft 1950–1975*, ed. K. Böhner, 155–70. Mainz: Römisch-Germanisches Zentralmuseum Mainz, Forschungsinstitut für Vor- und Frühgeschichte, Monograph I,I.

Herrmann, J. 1969a. Burgen und befestigte Siedlungen der jüngeren Bronze- und frühen Eisenzeit in Mitteleuropa. In *Siedlung, Burg und Stadt: Studien zu ihren Anfängen*, eds K.-H. Otto and J. Herrmann, 56–94. Berlin: Akademie-Verlag.

1969b. Die früheisenzeitlichen Burgen von Podrosche, Kr. Weisswasser, und Senftenberg in der Niederlausitz, *Veröff. des Museums für Ur- und Frühgeschichte Potsdam* 5, 87–108.

Hessing, W. 1991. Bewoningssporen uit de midden-bronstijd en do vroege ijzertijd op 'De Horden' te Wijk bij Duurstede. In *Nederzettingen uit det bronstijd en de vroege ijzertijd in de Lage Landen*, eds. H. Fokkens and N. Roymans, 41–52. Nederlandse Archeologische Rapporten 13. Amersfoort: Rijkdienst voor het Oudheidkundig Bodemonderzoek.

Hillebrecht, M.-L. 1989. Untersuchungen an Holzkohlen aus frühen Schmelzplätzen. In *Archäometallurgie der Alten Welt/Old World Archaeometallurgy*, Proc. Int. Symposium Heidelberg 1987, 203–12. Bochum: Deutsches Bergbau-Museum [= *Der Anschnitt* Supplement 7].

Hillier, B. and Hanson, J. 1984. *The Social Logic of Space*. Cambridge: Cambridge University Press.

Hippisley Cox, R. 1927/1944. *The Green Roads of England*. London: Methuen.

Hjärthner-Holdar, E. 1993. *Järnets och järnmetallurgins introduktion i Sverige*. Aun 16. Uppsala: Societas Archaeologica Upsaliensis.

Hjelmqvist, H. 1979. Beiträge zur Kenntnis der prähistorischen Nutzpflanzen in Schweden, *Opera Botanica* 47, 1–58.

Höckmann, O. 1980. Lanze und Speer im spätminoischen und mykenischen Griechenland, *Jahrbuch des Römisch-Germanischen Zentralmuseums Mainz* 27, 13–158.

Hodder, M. A. and Barfield, L. H. (eds.) 1991. *Burnt Mounds and Hot Stone Technology. Papers from the Second International Burnt Mound Conference, Sandwell 1990*. West Bromwich: Sandwell Metropolitan Borough Council.

Hodges, H. W. M. 1954. Studies in the Late Bronze Age: 1. Stone and clay moulds, and wooden models for bronze implements, *Ulster J. Archaeology* 17, 62–80.

1958. A hunting camp at Cullyhanna Lough near Newtown Hamilton, County Armagh, *Ulster J. Archaeology* 21, 7–13.

Hoffmann, M. 1974. *The Warp-Weighted Loom. Studies in the History and Technology of an Ancient Implement*. Oslo: Universitetsforlaget.

Holmes, P. n.d. [1980]. The manufacturing technology of the Irish Bronze Age horns. In *The Origins of Metallurgy in Atlantic Europe* (Proc. Fifth Atlantic Colloquium, Dublin 1978), ed. M. Ryan, 165–88. Dublin: Stationery Office.

Honti, S. 1996. Ein spätbronzezeitliches Hügelgrab in Sávoly-Babócsa, *Pápai Múzeum Értesitő* 6, 235–48.

Hook, D. R., Arribas Palau, A., Craddock, P. T., Molina, F., and Rothenberg, B. 1987. Copper and silver in Bronze Age Spain. In *Bell Beakers of the Western Mediterranean. Definition, Interpretation, Theory and New Site Data. The Oxford International Conference 1986*, eds. W. H. Waldren and R. C. Kennard, 147–72. Oxford: British Archaeological Reports, Int. Series 331 (i).

Hopkinson, B. 1975. Archaeological evidence of saltmoulding at important European saltsites and its relationship to the distribution of Urnfielders, *J. Indo-European Studies* 3, 1–52.

Horedt, K. and Seraphin, C. 1971. *Die prähistorische Ansiedlung auf dem Wietenberg bei Sighişoara-Schässburg*. Antiquitas, series 3, 10. Bonn: Habelt.

Horne, L. 1982. Fuel for the metal worker. The role of charcoal and charcoal production in ancient metallurgy, *Expedition* 25/1, 6–13.

Horst, F. 1977. Bronzezeitliche Speiseopfer in Gefässen. In *Geneza kultury łużyckiej na terenie nadodrza*, eds. B. Gediga *et al.*, 109–48. Wrocław: Polish Academy of Sciences.

1982. Die jungbronzezeitlichen Burgen im nordwestlichen Teil der DDR. In *Beiträge zum bronzezeitlichen Burgenbau in Mitteleuropa*, 243–52. Berlin: Zentralinstitut für Alte Geschichte und Archäologie; Nitra: Archeologický Ústav Slovenskej Akadémie Vied.

1985. *Zedau, eine jungbronze- und eisenzeitliche Siedlung in der Altmark*. Berlin: Akademie Verlag.

1986. Ein jungbronzezeitliches Fernhandelszentrum im Gebiet von Brandenburg/Havel, *Veröff. des Museums für Ur- und Frühgeschichte Potsdam* 20, 267–75.

Hrala, J., Sedláček, Z. and Vávra, M. 1992. Velim: a hilltop site of the Middle Bronze Age in Bohemia. Report on the excavations 1984–90, *Památky Archeologické* 83, 288–308.

Hralová, J. and Hrala, J. 1971. Hromadný nález bronzů z Březovic u Chrudimi (s úvahou o mlado- a pozdně bronzových kladivech), *Archeologické Rozhledy* 23, 3–26.

Hrubý, V. 1958. Kultovní objekty lidstva středodunajské kultury mohylové na Moravě, *Památky Archeologické* 49/1, 40–57.

1968–9. Nález tkanin z mladší doby bronzové ve Starém Městě, *Časopis Moravského Muzea* 53/4, 51–8.

Hügelbestattung 1987. *Hügelbestattung in der Karpaten-Donau-Balkan Zone während der äneolithischen Periode* (Internationales Symposium Donji Milanovac 1985), eds. D. Srejović and N. Tasić. Beograd: Balkanološki Institut, posebna izdanja 29.

Hulst, R. S. 1973. A contribution to the study of Bronze Age and Iron Age house-plans: Zijderveld, *Berichten van de Rijksdienst voor het Oudheidkundig Bodemonderzoek* 23, 103–7.

1991. Nederzettingen uit de midden-bronstijd in het rivierengebied: Zijderveld en Dodewaard. In *Nederzettingen uit de bronstijd en de vroege ijzertijd in de Lage Landen*, eds. H. Fokkens and N. Roymans, 53–9. Nederlandse Archeologische Rapporten 13. Amersfoort: Rijkdienst voor het Oudheidkundig Bodemonderzoek.

Hundt, H.-J. 1955. Versuch zur Deutung der Depotfunde der nordischen jüngeren Bronzezeit, unter besonderer Berücksichtigung Mecklenburgs, *Jahrbuch des Römisch-Germanischen Zentralmuseums Mainz* 2, 95–140.

1959. Vorgeschichtliche Gewebe aus dem Hallstätter Salzberg, *Jahrbuch des Römisch-Germanischen Zentralmuseums Mainz* 6, 66–100.

1960. Vorgeschichtliche Gewebe aus dem Hallstätter Salzberg, *Jahrbuch des Römisch-Germanischen Zentralmuseums Mainz* 7, 126–50.

1974a. Die Gewebereste von Gevelinghausen. Appendix 1 in A. Jockenhövel, Eine Bronzeamphore des 8. Jahrhunderts v. Chr. von Gevelinghausen, Kr. Meschede (Sauerland), *Germania* 52, 16–54.

1974b. Donauländische Einflüsse in der frühen Bronzezeit Norditaliens, *Preistoria Alpina* 10, 143–78.

1975. Steinerne und kupferne Hämmer der frühen Bronzezeit, *Archäologisches Korrespondenzblatt* 5, 115–20.

1978. Die Rohstoffquellen der europäischen Nordens und ihr Einfluss auf die Entwicklung des nordischen Stils, *Bonner Jahrbücher* 178, 125–62.

1988. Einige Bemerkungen zu den älterbronzezeitlichen Tondüsen, *Slovenská Archeológia* 36/1, 99–104.

Hunter, F. and Davis, M. 1994. Early Bronze Age lead – a unique necklace from southeast Scotland, *Antiquity* 68, 824–30.

Hurl, D. 1995. Killymoon – new light on the Late Bronze Age, *Archaeology Ireland* 9/4, 24–7.

Hüttel, H.-G. 1981. *Bronzezeitliche Trensen in Mittel- und Osteuropa. Grundzüge ihrer Entwicklung*. Prähistorische Bronzefunde XVI, 2. Munich: Beck.

Hyenstrand, Å. 1967–8. Skärvstenshögar och bronsåldersmiljöer. Preliminär översikt över undersökningar i Mälarområdet, *Tor* 1967–8, 61–77.

Ijzereef, G. F. 1981. *Bronze Age Animal Bones from Bovenkarspel: the Excavations at Het Valkje*. Nederlandse Oudheden 10; Project Noord-Holland 1. Amersfoort: Rijksdienst voor het Oudheidkundig Bodemonderzoek.

Ijzereef, G.F. and Regteren Altena, J.F. van 1991. Nederzettingen uit de midden- en late bronstijd bij Andijk en Bovenkarspel. In *Nederzettingen uit de bronstijd en de vroege ijzertijd in de Lage Landen*, eds. H. Fokkens and N. Roymans, 61–82. Nederlandse Archeologische Rapporten 13. Amersfoort: Rijkdienst voor het Oudheidkundig Bodemonderzoek.

Immerwahr, S. 1966. The use of tin on Mycenaean vases, *Hesperia* 35, 381–96.

Ixer, R. A. and Budd, P. 1998. The mineralogy of Bronze Age copper ores from the British Isles: implications for the composition of early metalwork, *Oxford J. Archaeology* 17/1, 15–41.

Jaanusson, H. 1981. *Hallunda. A Study of Pottery from a Late Bronze Age Settlement in Central Sweden*. Stockholm: State Historical Museum.

Jaanusson, H. and V. 1988. Sea-salt as a commodity of barter in Bronze Age trade of northern Europe. In *Trade and Exchange in Prehistory. Studies in Honour of Berta Stjernquist*, eds. B. Hardh, L. Larsson, D. Olausson and R. Petré, 107–12. Acta Archaeologica Lundensia, series in 8º, 16. Lund: Historiska Museum.

Jaanusson, H., Löfstrand, L. and Vahlne, G. 1978. *Fornlämning 69, boplats Hallunda, Botkyrka sn, Södermanland, Del III, Arkeologisk undersökning 1969–71*. Riksantikvarieämbetet och Statens Historiska Museer Rapport, Uppdragsvertsamheten 1978: 11. Stockholm.

Jaanusson, H. and Vahlne, G. 1975. *Arkeologisk Undersökning 1969–71, Hallunda, Botkyrka sn, Södermanland, Del II: Fornlämning 13, boplats*. Riksantikvarieämbetet Rapport B64. Stockholm.

Jackson, J. S. 1968. Bronze Age copper mines on Mount Gabriel, West County Cork, Ireland, *Archaeologia Austriaca* 43, 92–114.

n.d. [1980]. Metallic ores in Irish prehistory: copper and tin. In *The Origins of Metallurgy in Atlantic Europe* (Proc. Fifth Atlantic Colloquium, Dublin 1978), ed. M. Ryan, 107–25. Dublin: Stationery Office.

1980. Bronze Age copper mining in Counties Cork and Kerry, Ireland. In *Scientific Studies in Early Mining and Extractive Metallurgy*, ed. P. T. Craddock, 9–30. London: British Museum (Occasional Paper 20).

1984. The age of the primitive copper mines on Mount Gabriel, West County Cork, *J. Irish Archaeology* 2, 41–50.

Jacob-Friesen, G. 1967. *Bronzezeitliche Lanzenspitzen Norddeutschlands und Skandinaviens*. Veröff. der urgeschichtlichen Sammlungen des Landesmuseums zu Hannover 17. Hildesheim: August Lax.

Jäger, K.-D. 1965. Verkohlte Samen aus einem bronzezeitlichen Grabgefäss von Tornow, Kr. Calau – Ein Beitrag zur Anbaugeschichte der Ackerbohne (*Vicia faba* L.) in Mitteleuropa, *Ausgrabungen und Funde* 10, 131–8.

James, D. 1988. Prehistoric copper mining on the Great Orme Head, Llandudno, Gwynedd. In *Aspects of Ancient Mining and Metallurgy, Proc. British School Athens Centenary Conference on Ancient Mining and Metallurgy*, ed. J. Ellis-Jones, 115–21. Bangor: University College of North Wales.

Janin, T. 1996. Pratiques funéraires et sociétés protohistoriques en France méridionale: les nécropoles du Bronze final IIIB mailhacien, approche préliminaire et premiers resultats, *Revista d'Arqueologia de Ponent* 6, 7–34.

Janson, S., Lundberg, E. B., and Bertilsson, U. (eds.) 1989. *Hällristningar och hällmålningar i Sverige*. Stockholm: Forum.

Janssen, W. 1985. Hortfunde der jüngeren Bronzezeit aus Nordbayern. Einführung in die Problematik, *Archäologisches Korrespondenzblatt* 15, 45–54.

Jarman, M. 1975. The fauna and economy of Fiavé, *Preistoria Alpina* 11, 65–73.

Jarman, M. R., Bailey, G. N. and Jarman, H. N. (eds.) 1982. *Early European Agriculture: its Foundations and Development*. Cambridge: Cambridge University Press.

Jelínek, J. 1957. Antropofagie a pohřební ritus doby bronzové na podkladě nálezů z Moravy a z okolních území, *Časopis Moravského Muzea v Brně, vědy přírodní* 42, 85–134.

  1959. *Anthropologie der Bronzezeit in Mähren*. Anthropos 10. Brno: Moravské Muzeum.

  1988. Lidské oběti, antropofagie a studium rituálů bronzové a železné doby. Současný stav. In *Antropofagie a pohřební ritus doby bronzové*, ed. M. Dočkalová, 1–16. Brno: Moravské Muzeum – Ústav Anthropos.

Jenkins, D. A. and Lewis, C. A. 1991. Prehistoric mining for copper in the Great Orme, Llandudno. In *Archaeological Sciences 1989*, ed. P. Budd *et al.*, 151–61. Oxford: Oxbow.

Jennbert, K. 1991. Trepanation from Stone Age to medieval period from a Scandinavian perspective. In *Regions and Reflections. In Honour of Märta Strömberg*, eds. K. Jennbert, L. Larsson, R. Petré and B. Wysomirska-Werbart, 357–78. Lund: Almqvist and Wiksell.

Jensen, J. 1972. Ein neues Hallstattschwert aus Dänemark. Beitrag zur Problematik der jungbronzezeitlichen Votivfunde, *Acta Archaeologica* (Copenhagen) 43, 115–64.

  1978. Kultøkser fra bronzealderen, *Nationalmuseets Arbejdsmark* 1978, 17–26.

Jørgensen, G. 1979. A new contribution concerning the cultivation of spelt, *Triticum spelta* L., in prehistoric Denmark. In *Festschrift Maria Hopf zum 65. Geburtstag*, ed. U. Körber-Grohne (*Archaeo-Physika* 8), 135–45. Cologne: Rheinland-Verlag (Bonn: Habelt).

Jobey, G. 1978. Unenclosed platforms and settlements of the later second millennium BC in northern Britain, *Scottish Archaeol. Forum* 10, 12–26.

  1978–80. Green Knowe unenclosed platform settlement and Harehope cairn, Peeblesshire, *Proc. Soc. Antiqs Scotland* 110, 72–113.

  1983. Excavation of an unenclosed settlement on Standrop Rigg, Northumberland, and some problems relating to similar settlements between Tyne and Forth, *Archaeologia Aeliana* 5th series 11, 1–21.

1985. The unenclosed settlements of Tyne–Forth: a summary. In *Upland Settlement in Britain. The Second Millennium BC and After*, eds. D. Spratt and C. Burgess, 177–94. Oxford: British Archaeological Reports 143.

Jockenhövel, A. 1969–70. Die frühbronzezeitlichen Gräber [in Vorgeschichtliche Funde aus Hofheim (Main-Taunus-Kreis)], *Fundberichte aus Hessen* 9–10, 56–68.

1980a. Bronzezeitliche Höhensiedlungen in Hessen, *Archäologisches Korrespondenzblatt* 10, 39–47.

1980b. *Die Rasiermesser in Westeuropa*. Prähistorische Bronzefunde, Abteilung VIII, 3. Munich: Beck.

1982a. Zu den ältesten Tüllenhämmern aus Bronze, *Germania* 60, 459–67.

1982b. Zeugnisse der primären Metallurgie in Gräbern der Bronze- und Alteisenzeit Mitteleuropas, *Archeologia Polski* 27/2, 293–301.

1982c. Jungbronzezeitlicher Burgenbau in Süddeutschland. In *Beiträge zum bronzezeitlichen Burgenbau in Mitteleuropa*, 253–72. Berlin: Zentralinstitut für Alte Geschichte und Archäologie; Nitra: Archeologický Ústav Slovenskej Akadémie Vied.

1985. Bemerkungen zur Verbreitung der älterbronzezeitlichen Tondüsen in Mitteleuropa. In *Frühbronzezeitliche befestigte Siedlungen in Mitteleuropa, Materialien der Internationalen Arbeitstagung, Kraków 1983*, 196–205. Archaeologia Interregionalis. Warsaw: Wydawnictwa Uniwersytetu Warszawskiego.

1986a. Bemerkungen zur Frage der Metallverarbeitung in der 'Wasserburg' Buchau, *Germania* 64, 565–72.

1986b. Struktur und Organisation der Metallverarbeitung in urnen-felderzeitlichen Siedlungen Süddeutschlands, *Veröff. des Museums für Ur- und Frühgeschichte Potsdam* 20, 213–34.

1990. Bronzezeitlicher Burgenbau in Mitteleuropa. Untersuchungen zur Struktur frühmetallzeitlicher Gesellschaften. In *Orientalisch-Ägäische Einflüsse in der europäischen Bronzezeit*, Monographien des Römisch-Germanischen Zentralmuseums Mainz 15, 209–28.

1991. Räumliche Mobilität von Personen in der mittleren Bronzezeit des westlichen Mitteleuropa, *Germania* 69, 49–62.

Jodłowski, A. 1971. *Eksploatacja sóli na terenie Małopolski w pradziejach i we wczesnym średniowieczu*. Studia i materiały do dziejów żup sólnych w Polsce 4. Wieliczka: Muzeum Żup Krakowskich.

Johansen, Ø. 1979. New results in the investigation of the Bronze Age rock carvings, *Norwegian Archaeol. Review* 12/2, 108–14.

Johnson, A. W. and Earle, T. 1987. *The Evolution of Human Societies: from Foraging Group to Agrarian State*. Stanford: Stanford University Press.

Johnston, S. 1991. Distributional aspects of prehistoric Irish petroglyphs. In *Rock Art and Prehistory. Papers Presented to Symposium G of the AURA Congress, Darwin 1988*, eds. P. Bahn and A. Rosenfeld, Oxford: Oxbow Monograph 10, 86–95.

Johnstone, P. 1972. Bronze Age sea trial, *Antiquity* 46, 269–74.

1980. *The Sea-Craft of Prehistory*. London: Routledge and Kegan Paul.

Jones, R. E. 1986. *Greek and Cypriot Pottery: a Review of Scientific Studies*. Fitch Laboratory Occasional Paper 1. Athens: British School of Archaeology.

Jovanović, B. 1975. Tumuli stepske kulture grobova jama u Podunavlju, *Starinar* 26, 9–24.

1982. *Rudna Glava, najstarije rudarstvo bakra na Centralnom Balkanu.* Belgrade: Arheološki Institut/Bor: Muzej rudarstva i metalurgije.

Jully, J.-J., Fonquerle, D., Aris, R. and Adgé, M. 1978. *Agde antique. Fouilles sub-aquatiques et terrestres.* Etudes sur Pézenas et l'Hérault, numéro spécial. Pézenas: Les Amis de Pézenas.

Junghans, S., Sangmeister, E. and Schröder, M. 1960. *Kupferzeitliche und frühbronzezeitliche Bodenfunde aus Europa.* Studien zu den Anfängen der Metallurgie 1. Berlin: Gebr. Mann Verlag.

1968. *Kupfer und Bronze in der frühen Metallzeit Europas.* Studien zu den Anfängen der Metallurgie 2. Berlin: Gebr. Mann Verlag.

1974. *Kupfer und Bronze in der frühen Metallzeit Europas.* Studien zu den Anfängen der Metallurgie 2, 4. Berlin: Mann.

Kabát, J. 1955. Otomanská osada v Barci u Košic, *Archeologické Rozhledy* 7, 594–600, 611–13; cf. 742–6.

Kacsó, C. 1987. Beiträge zur Kenntnis des Verbreitungsgebietes und der Chronologie der Suciu de Sus-Kultur, *Dacia* 31, 51–75.

Kadrow, S. 1991a. *Iwanowice, stanowisko Babia Góra, cz. 1. Rozwój przestrzenny osady z wczesnego okresu epoki brązu.* Kraków: Instytut Kultury Materialnej Polskiej Akademii Nauk.

1991b. Iwanowice, Babia Góra site: spatial evolution of an Early Bronze Age Mierzanowice Culture settlement (2300–1600 BC), *Antiquity* 65, 640–50.

1994. Social structures and social evolution among Early Bronze Age communities in south-eastern Poland, *J. European Archaeology* 2/2, 229–48.

Kadrow, S. and Machnikowie, A. and J. 1992. *Iwanowice, Stanowisko Babia Góra. II. Cmentarzysko z wczesnego okresu epoki brązu.* Kraków: Instytut Archeologii i Etnologii Polskiej Akademii Nauk.

Kaliff, A. 1994. Skärvstenshögar och kremeringsplatser. Exempel och experiment med utgångspunkt från en utgrävning i Ringeby, Kvillinge sn, Östergötland, *Tor* 26, 35–55.

1997. *Grav och kultplats. Eskatologiska föreställningar under yngre bronsålder och äldre järnålder i Östergötland.* Aun 24. Uppsala: Uppsala University.

Kallay, A. Sz. 1986. Késő bronzkori edénydepot Battonya határában, *Archaeologiai Értesítő* 113, 159–65.

Karlenby, L. 1994. The Bronze Age house in central Sweden. An evaluation of two recent excavations, *Tor* 26, 5–33.

Karoušková-Soper, V. 1983. *The Castellieri of Venezia-Giulia, North-eastern Italy (2nd-1st Millennium BC).* Oxford: British Archaeol. Reports, Int. 192.

Katinčarov, R. 1972. Habitations de l'âge du bronze moyen du tell de Nova Zagora (Bulgarie du Sud), *Thracia* 1, 43–55. Primus Congressus Studiorum Thracicorum, eds. V. I. Georgiev, V. Tărkova-Zaimova and V. Velkov. Sofia: Bulgarian Academy of Sciences.

Kaufmann, B. 1996. Spurenelementuntersuchungen. Eine methodische Hilfe zur Bevölkerungsrekonstruktion der Bronzezeit in der Schweiz, *Archäologie der Schweiz* 19/4, 150–2.

Kaul, F. 1985. Sandagergård. A Late Bronze Age cultic building with rock engravings and menhirs from northern Zealand, Denmark, *Acta Archaeologica* 56, 31–54.

1995. Ships on bronzes. In *The Ship as Symbol in Prehistoric and Medieval*

Scandinavia, eds. O. Crumlin-Pedersen and B. Munch Thye, 59–70. Studies in Archaeology and History 1. Copenhagen: Danish National Museum.

Keefer, E. 1990. Die 'Siedlung Forschner' am Federsee und ihre mittel-bronzezeitlichen Funde, *Bericht der Römisch-Germanischen Kommission* 71, 38–51.

Keller, E. 1980. Ein Dorf der Urnenfelderzeit in Unterhaching, Landkreis München, Oberbayern, *Das Archäologisches Jahr in Bayern 1980*, 72–3.

Kemenczei, T. 1988. *Die Schwerter in Ungarn I (Griffplatten-, Griffangel- und Griffzungenschwerter)*. Prähistorische Bronzefunde IV, 6. Munich: Beck.

1991. *Die Schwerter in Ungarn II (Vollgriffschwerter)*. Prähistorische Bronzefunde IV, 9. Stuttgart: Franz Steiner.

Kent, S. 1990. A cross-cultural study of segmentation, architecture, and the use of space. In *Domestic Architecture and the Use of Space. An Interdisciplinary Cross-Cultural Study*, ed. S. Kent, 127–52. Cambridge: Cambridge University Press.

Kersten, K. 1936. Das Totenhaus von Grünhof-Tesperhude, Kreis Herzogtum Lauenburg, *Offa* 1, 56–87.

Kersten, W. 1948. Die niederrheinische Grabhügelkultur, *Bonner Jahrbücher* 148, 5–81.

Kiekebusch, A. 1923. *Die Ausgrabung des bronzezeitlichen Dorfes Buch bei Berlin*. Deutsche Urzeit 1. Berlin: Dietrich Reimer Verlag.

1928. *Das Königsgrab von Seddin*. Führer zur Urgeschichte 1. Augsburg: Benno Filser.

Kilian, K. 1973. Zur eisenzeitlichen Transhumanz in Nordgriechenland, *Archäologisches Korrespondenzblatt* 3, 431–5.

Kilian-Dirlmeier, I. 1993. *Die Schwerter in Griechenland (ausserhalb der Peloponnes), Bulgarien und Albanien*. Prähistorische Bronzefunde IV, 12. Stuttgart: Franz Steiner.

Kimmig, W. 1981. Ein Grabfund der jüngeren Urnenfelderzeit mit Eisenschwert von Singen am Hohentwiel, *Fundberichte aus Baden-Württemberg 6*, 93–120.

1992. *Die 'Wasserburg Buchau' – eine spätbronzezeitliche Siedlung. Forschungsgeschichte – Kleinfunde*. Materialhefte zur Vor- und Frühgeschichte in Baden-Württemberg 16. Stuttgart: Konrad Theiss.

Kjellén, E. 1976. *Upplands hällristningar*. Stockholm: Kungl. Vitterhets historie och antikvitets Akademien.

Klappauf, L., Linke, F.-A., Brockner, W., Heimbruch, G. and Koerfer, S. 1991. Early mining and smelting in the Harz region. In *Archaeometry 1990*, eds. E. Pernicka and G. A. Wagner, 77–86. Basle: Birkhäuser.

Klichowska, M. 1977. Rośliny uprawne i dziko rosnace z grodziska ludności kultury łużyckiej w Smuszewie, woj. pilskie, *Fontes Archaeologici Posnanienses* 28, 36–44.

1984. Struktury uprawne w epoce brązu i we wczesnej epoce żelaza na ziemach polskich w świetle badań archeobotanicznych, *Archeologia Polski* 29, 69–108.

Klochko, V. I. 1993. *Weapons of the Tribes of the Northern Pontic Zone in the 16th–10th Centuries B.C.* Baltic-Pontic Studies, 1. Poznań: Adam Mickiewicz University.

1995. Zur bronzezeitlichen Bewaffnung in der Ukraine. Die Metallwaffen des 17.-10. Jhs. v. Chr., *Eurasia Antiqua* 1, 81–163.

Knape, A. and Nordström, H.-Å. 1994. *Der Kultgegenstand von Balkåkra*.

Museum of National Antiquities, Stockholm, Monograph 3. Stockholm: Statens Historiska Museum.

Knapp, A. B. 1986. *Copper Production and Divine Protection: Archaeology, Ideology and Social Complexity on Bronze Age Cyprus*. Studies in Mediterranean Archaeology, Pocket Book 42. Göteborg: Paul Åströms Förlag.

Knapp, A. B., Muhly, J. D. and Muhly, P. M. 1988. To hoard is human: Late Bronze Age metal deposits in Cyprus and the Aegean, *Report Department of Antiquities, Cyprus* 1988/1, 233–62.

Knight, R. W., Browne, C. and Grinsell, L. V. 1972. Prehistoric skeletons from Tormarton, *Transactions Bristol and Gloucester Archaeol. Soc.* 91, 14–17.

Knörzer, K.-H. 1972. Subfossile Pflanzenfunde aus der bandkeramische Siedlung Langweiler 3 und 6, Kr. Jülich, und ein urnenfelderzeitlicher Getreidefund innerhalb dieser Siedlung, *Bonner Jahrbücher* 172, 395–403.

1978. Entwicklung und Ausbreitung des Leindotters (*Camelina sativa* s.L.), *Bericht der deutschen botanischen Gesellschaft* 91, 187–95.

Kohl, P. 1987. The use and abuse of World Systems Theory: the case of the 'pristine' West Asian state, *Advances in Archaeological Method and Theory* 11, 1–35 (also in *Archaeological Thought in America*, ed. C. C. Lamberg-Karlovsky, 218–40. Cambridge: Cambridge University Press).

Kolling, A. 1968. *Späte Bronzezeit am Saar und Mosel*. Saarbrücken: Saarbrücker Beiträge zur Altertumskunde 6. Bonn: Habelt.

Kooi, P. B. 1979. *Pre-Roman Urnfields in the North of the Netherlands*. Groningen: Wolters-Noordhoff/Bouma's Boekhuis.

1982. *De Urnenvelden in Drenthe*. Museumfonds Publicatie 7. Assen: Provinciaal Museum van Drenthe.

Körber-Grohne, U. 1981. Pflanzliche Abdrücke in eisenzeitlicher Keramik – Spiegelbild damaliger Nutzpflanzen? *Fundberichte aus Baden-Württemberg* 6, 165–211.

Korkuti, M. 1968. Le pitture rupestri di Treni (Albania), *Bolletino del Centro Camuno di Studi Preistorici* 4, 89–97.

Kosorić, M. 1976. *Kulturni, etnički i hronološki problemi ilirskih nekropola podrinja*. Tuzla: Muzej istočne Bosne.

Kossack, G. 1954a. Pferdegeschirr aus Gräbern der älteren Hallstattzeit Bayerns, *Jahrbuch des Römisch-Germanischen Zentralmuseums Mainz* 1, 111–78.

1954b. *Studien zum Symbolgut der Urnenfelder- und Hallstattzeit Mitteleuropas*. Römisch-Germanische Forschungen 20. Berlin: de Gruyter.

1913. *Der germanische Goldreichtum in der Bronzezeit, I. Der Goldfund von Messingwerk bei Eberswalde und die goldenen Kultgefässe der Germanen*. Würzburg: Kabitzsch.

Kostrzewski, J. 1936. Osada bagienna w Biskupinie, w pow. żnińskim, *Przegląd Archeologiczny* 5, 121–40.

(ed.) 1950. *III Sprawozdanie z prac wykopaliskowych w grodzie kultury łużyckiej w Biskupinie w powiecie żnińskim za lata 1938–1939 i 1946–1948*. Poznań: Polski Towarzystwo Prehistoryczny.

Kovács, T. 1977. *The Bronze Age in Hungary*. Budapest: Corvina Press.

1982. Befestigungsanlagen um die Mitte des 2. Jahrtausends v. u. Z. in Mittelungarn. In *Beiträge zum bronzezeitlichen Burgenbau in Mitteleuropa*, 279–92. Berlin: Zentralinstitut für Alte Geschichte und Archäologie; Nitra: Archeologický Ústav Slovenskej Akadémie Vied.

1986. Jungbronzezeitliche Gussformen und Giessereien in Ungarn, *Veröff. des Museums für Ur- und Frühgeschichte Potsdam* 20, 189–96.

1988. Review of the Bronze Age settlement research during the past one and a half centuries in Hungary. In *Bronze Age Tell Settlements of the Great Hungarian Plain I*. Inventaria Praehistorica Hungariae 17–25. Budapest, Magyar Nemzeti Múzeum.

Krahe, G. 1980. Beinschiene der Urnenfelderzeit von Schäfstall, Stadt Donauwörth, Landkreis Donau-Ries, Schwaben, *Das Archäologisches Jahr in Bayern 1980*, 76–7.

Krämer, R. 1992. Die 'Notgrabung' am Bohlenweg XII (Ip) aus dem Jahre 713 v. Chr. im Ipweger Moor, Ldkr. Wesermarsch, *Archäologische Mitt. aus Nordwestdeutschland* 15, 101–14.

Krämer, W. 1966. Prähistorische Brandopferplätze. In *Helvetia Antiqua. Festschrift Emil Vogt*, eds. R. Degen, W. Drack and R. Wyss, 111–22. Zurich: Schweizerisches Landesmuseum.

1985. *Die Vollgriffschwerter in Österreich und der Schweiz*. Prähistorische Bronzefunde IV, 10. Munich: Beck.

Krause, R. 1988. *Die endneolithischen und frühbronzezeitlichen Grabfunde auf der Nordstadtterrasse von Singen am Hohentwiel*. Forschungen und Berichte zur Vor- und Frühgeschichte in Baden-Württemberg 32. Stuttgart: Konrad Theiss Verlag.

Kristensson, A., Olson, C. and Welinder, S. 1996. Ecofacts indicating Late Neolithic and Early Bronze Age farming in Sweden, *Tor* 28, 53–67.

Kristiansen, K. 1974. En kildekritisk analyse af depotfund fra Danmarks yngre bronzealder (periode IV-V). Et bidrag til den arkaeologiske kildekritik, *Aarbøger* 1974, 119–60.

1977. The circulation of ornaments and weapons in Bronze Age Denmark, *Archaeologica Baltica* 2, 77–91.

1978. The consumption of wealth in Bronze Age Denmark. A study in the dynamics of economic processes in tribal societies. In *New Directions in Scandinavian Archaeology*, eds K. Kristiansen and C. Paludan-Müller, 158–90. Studies in Scandinavian Prehistory and Early History, 1. Copenhagen: National Museum of Denmark.

1984. Krieger und Häuptlinge in der Bronzezeit Dänemarks. Ein Beitrag zur Geschichte des bronzezeitlichen Schwertes, *Jahrbuch des Römisch-Germanischen Zentralmuseums* 31, 187–208.

1985. Bronze hoards from the late Neolithic and Early Bronze Age. In *Archaeological Formation Processes. The Representativity of Archaeological Remains from Danish Prehistory*, ed. K. Kristiansen, 129–41. Copenhagen: Nationalmuseet.

1987. Center and periphery in Bronze Age Scandinavia. In *Centre and Periphery in the Ancient World*, eds. M. Rowlands, M. T. Larsen and K. Kristiansen, 74–85. Cambridge: Cambridge University Press.

1994. The emergence of the European World System in the Bronze Age: divergence, convergence and social evolution during the first and second millennia BC in Europe. *Europe in the First Millennium BC*, eds K. Kristiansen and J. Jensen, 7–30. Sheffield Archaeological Monograph, 6. Sheffield: J. R. Collis Publications.

1998. *Europe before History*. Cambridge: Cambridge University Press.

Krysiak, K. 1950. Szczątki zwierzęce z Biskupina wydobyte z warstw kultury łużyckiej w sezonie wykopaliskowym 1948 r. In *III Sprawozdanie z prac wykopaliskowych w grodzie kultury łużyckiej w Biskupinie w powiecie żnińskim za lata 1938–1939 i 1946–1948*, ed. J. Kostrzewski, 39–71. Poznań: Polski Towarzystwo Prehistoryczny.

Kubach, W. 1978–9. Deponierungen in Mooren der südhessischen Oberrheinebene, *Jahresbericht des Institutes für Vorgeschichte der Universität Frankfurt a.M.* 1978–9, 189–310.

1983. Bronzezeitliche Deponierungen im Nordhessischen sowie im Weser- und Leinebergland, *Jahrbuch des Römisch-Germanischen Zentralmuseums Mainz* 30, 113–59.

1985. Einzel- und Mehrstückdeponierungen und ihre Fundplätze, *Archäologisches Korrespondenzblatt* 15, 179–85.

Kubach-Richter, I. 1978–9. Amulettbeigaben in bronzezeitlichen Kindergräbern, *Jahresbericht des Institutes für Vorgeschichte der Universität Frankfurt a.M.* 1978–9, 127–78.

Kühn, H. 1956. *The Rock Pictures of Europe.* London: Sidgwick and Jackson.

Kultgeschehen 1996. *Archäologische Forschungen zum Kultgeschehen in der jüngeren Bronzezeit und frühen Eisenzeit Alteuropas*, ed. C. Huth. Regensburger Beiträge zur prähistorischen Archäologie, 2. Regensburg: Universitätsverlag (Bonn: Habelt).

Kunter, M. 1990. *Menschliche Skelettreste aus Siedlungen der El Argar-Kultur. Ein Beitrag der prähistorischen Anthropologie zur Kenntnis bronzezeitlicher Bevölkerung Südostspaniens.* Madrider Beiträge 18. Mainz: v. Zabern.

Kurzynski, K. von (ed.) 1994. *Schätze des Harzes. Archäologische Untersuchungen zum Bergbau und Hüttenwesen des 3. bis 13. Jahrhunderts n. Chr.* Begleithefte zu Ausstellungen der Abteilung Urgeschichte des Niedersächsischen Landesmuseums Hannover 4. Oldenburg: Isensee Verlag.

Kytlicová, O. 1981. Ein Beitrag zu den Schmuckgarnituren des böhmischen Knovíz-Milavečer Bereichs. In *Studien zur Bronzezeit. Festschrift für Wilhelm Albert v. Brunn*, ed. H. Lorenz, 213–49. Mainz: v. Zabern.

1986. Der Schild und der Depotfund aus Plzeň-Jíkalka, *Památky Archeologické* 77, 413–54.

1988a. K sociální struktuře kultury popelnicových polí, *Památky Archeologické* 79, 342–89.

1988b. Rituální kostrové hroby na popelnicovém pohřebišti v Brdě u Manětína, okr. Plzeň-sever. In *Antropofagie a pohřební ritus doby bronzové*, ed. M. Dočkalová, 201–9. Brno: Moravské Muzeum – Ústav Anthropos.

Lamb, R. C. and Rees, S. E. 1981. Ard cultivation at Sumburgh, Shetland, *Tools and Tillage* 4/2, 117–21.

Lambot, B. 1993. Les sanctuaires du Bronze final d'Acy-Romance (Ardennes) et du nord-est de la France, *Archaeologia Mosellana* 2, 201–32.

Lanting, J. N. and Brindley, A. L. 1996. Irish logboats and their European context, *J. Irish Archaeology* 7, 85–95.

Larsson, L. 1974. The Fogdarp find. A hoard from the Late Bronze Age, *Meddelanden från Lunds Universitets Historiska Museum* 1973–4, 169–238.

1993a. *Bronsålderns gravhögar. Rapport från ett symposium i Lund 15.XI–16.XI 1991.* University of Lund, Institute of Archaeology Report Series 48.

1993b. Relationer till ett röse – några aspekter på Kiviksgraven. In *Bronsålderns gravhögar. Rapport från ett symposium i Lund 15.XI–16.XI 1991*, ed. L. Larsson, 135–49. University of Lund, Institute of Archaeology Report Series 48.

Larsson, T. B. 1985. Soziale Veränderung im Übergang von Bronzezeit zu Eisenzeit. Eine Analyse der Bestattungsdaten des Fiskeby Gräberfeldes in Östergötland. In *In Honorem Evert Baudou*, 415–24. Archaeology and Environment 4. Umeå: Umeå University.

1986. *The Bronze Age Metalwork in Southern Sweden. Aspects of Social and Spatial Organization 1800–500 BC*. Archaeology and Environment 6. Umeå: Department of Archaeology, University of Umeå.

1990. Skärvstenshögar – the burnt mounds of Sweden. In *Burnt Offerings. International Contributions to Burnt Mound Archaeology*, ed. V. Buckley, 142–53. Dublin: Wordwell.

1993. Storhögar i södra Sverige. Kring några utbredningskartor. In *Bronsålderns gravhögar. Rapport från ett symposium i Lund 15.XI–16.XI 1991*, ed. L. Larsson, 47–57. University of Lund, Institute of Archaeology Report Series 48.

Lasak, I. 1982. Pochówki w trumnach drewnianych jako forma obrządku grzebalnego we wczesnym okresie epoki brązu w świetle badań w Przecławicach, woj. Wrocław, *Silesia Antiqua* 24, 89–108.

1988. *Cmentarzysko ludności kultury unietyckiej w Przecławicach*. University of Wrocław, Studia Archeologiczne 18. Warsaw/Wrocław: Panstwowe Wydawnictwo Naukowe.

László, A. 1977. Anfänge der Benützung und der Bearbeitung des Eisens auf dem Gebiete Rumäniens, *Acta Archaeologica* (Budapest) 29, 53–75.

Lauermann, E. 1995. *Ein frühbronzezeitliches Gräberfeld aus Unterhautzenthal, NÖ. I. Archäologie*. Stockerau: Österreichische Gesellschaft für Ur- und Frühgeschichte.

Lauk, H. D. 1976. Tierknochenfunde aus bronzezeitlichen Siedlungen bei Monachil und Purullena (Provinz Granada), *Studien über frühe Tierknochenfunde von der Iberischen Halbinsel* 6. Munich: University of Munich/Deutsches Archäologisches Institut, Abteilung Madrid.

Laux, F. 1981. Bemerkungen zu den mittelbronzezeitlichen Lüneburger Frauentrachten vom Typ Deutsch Evern. In *Studien zur Bronzezeit. Festschrift für Wilhelm Albert v. Brunn*, ed. H. Lorenz, 251–75. Mainz: v. Zabern.

1996. Zur gesellschaftlichen und sozialen Gliederung der bronzezeitlichen Gruppen in Niedersachsen. In *Leben-Glauben-Sterben vor 3000 Jahren. Bronzezeit in Niedersachsen. Eine niedersächsische Ausstellung zur Bronzezeit-Kampagne des Europarates*, ed. G. Wegner, 147–65. Hanover: Niedersächsisches Landesmuseum.

Lawson, A. J. 1980. A Late Bronze Age hoard from Beeston Regis, Norfolk, *Antiquity* 54, 217–19.

Lawson, A. J., Martin, E. A. and Priddy, D. 1981. *The Barrows of East Anglia* (= *East Anglian Archaeology* 12).

Layton, R. 1981. *The Anthropology of Art*. London: Granada Publishing (Paul Elek).

Leben, F. 1991. Veliki zjot, bakreno- in bronastodobno jamsko bivališče v Beli Krajini, *Poročilo o raziskovanju paleolita, neolita in eneolita v Sloveniji* 19, 169–91.

Legge, A. J. 1989. Milking the evidence: a reply to Entwistle and Grant. In *The Beginnings of Agriculture*, eds. A. Milles, D. Williams and N. Gardner, 217–42. Oxford: British Archaeological Reports Int. 496.

　1992. *Excavations at Grimes Graves, Norfolk, 1972–1976. Fascicule 4. Animals, Environment and the Bronze Age Economy*. London: British Museum.

Lehmann, E. 1929. Knowiser Kultur in Thüringen und vorgeschichtlicher Kannibalismus, *Mannus*, Supplementary vol. 7, 107–22.

Lehrberger, G. 1995. The gold sources of Europe: an overview of the possible metal sources for prehistoric gold objects. In *Prehistoric Gold in Europe. Mines, Metallurgy and Manufacture*, eds. G. Morteani and J. P. Northover, 115–44. NATO ASI Series, E (Applied Sciences) 280. Dordrecht/Boston/London: Kluwer Academic.

Leidinger, W. 1983. Frühe Salzgewinnung in Werl, Kreis Soest, Westfalen, *Archäologisches Korrespondenzblatt* 13, 269–74.

Leighton, R. 1986. Paolo Orsi (1859–1935) and the prehistory of Sicily, *Antiquity* 60, 15–20.

Lerche, G. 1977. Double paddle-spades in prehistoric contexts in Denmark, *Tools and Tillage* 3/2, 111–24.

Letica, Z. 1973. *Antropomorfne figurine bronzanog doba u Jugoslaviji*. Dissertationes et Monografiae 16. Belgrade: Savez arheoloških društava Jugoslavije.

Levy, J. E. 1982. *Social and Religious Organization in Bronze Age Denmark. The Analysis of Ritual Hoard Finds*. Oxford: British Archaeological Reports, Int. Series 124.

　1991. Metalworking technology and craft specialization in Bronze Age Denmark, *Archeomaterials* 5, 55–74.

　1995. Heterarchy in Bronze Age Denmark: settlement pattern, gender and ritual. In *Heterarchy and the Analysis of Complex Societies*, eds. R. M. Ehrenreich, C. L. Crumley and J. E. Levy, 41–54. Arlington: Archeological Papers of the American Anthropological Association 6.

Lewis, A. 1990. Underground exploration of the Great Orme copper mines. In *Early Mining in the British Isles*, eds. P. and S. Crew, 5–10. Proc. Early Mining Workshop 1989, Plas Tan y Bwlch Occasional Paper 1.

Lewthwaite, J. 1981. Plains tails from the hills: transhumance in Mediterranean archaeology. In *Economic Archaeology: towards an Integration of Ecological and Social Approaches*, eds. A. Sheridan and G. Bailey, 57–66. Oxford: British Archaeological Reports, Int. Series 96.

Lilliu, G. 1962. *I nuraghi, torri preistoriche di Sardegna*. Cagliari: Edizioni 'La Zattera'.

　1966. *Sculture della Sardegna nuragica*. Cagliari: Edizioni 'La Zattera'.

　1967/1980. *La civiltà dei Sardi dal Neolitico all'età dei nuraghi*. Turin: ERI.

　1981. *Monumenti antichi barbaricini*. Ministero dei Beni Culturali e Ambientali, Sassari/Nuoro, Quaderni 10. Sassari: Dessì.

　1987. *La civiltà nuragica*. Sardegna Archeologica, Studi e Monumenti 1. Sassari: Carlo Delfino Editore.

Liniger, H. and Schilt, H. 1976. Der astronomisch geortete Schalenstein ob Tüscherz (Biel), *Jahrbuch der schweizerischen Gesellschaft für Ur- und Frühgeschichte* 59, 215–29.

Lipke, P. 1984. *The Royal Ship of Cheops*. National Maritime Museum, Archaeological Series 9. Oxford: British Archaeological Reports Int. 225.

Littauer, M. A. 1981. Early stirrups, *Antiquity* 55, 99–105.

Littauer, M. A. and Crouwel, J. 1977. The origin and diffusion of the cross-bar wheel? *Antiquity* 51, 95–105.

Liversage, D. 1994. Interpreting composition patterns in ancient bronze: the Carpathian Basin, *Acta Archaeologica* (Copenhagen) 65, 57–134.

Liversage, D. and M. 1989. A method for the study of the composition of early copper and bronze artefacts. An example from Denmark, *Helinium* 28/1, 42–76.

  1990. On distinguishing Materialgruppen in Early Bronze Age copper – the case of Vyčapy-Opatovce, *Památky Archeologické* 81/2, 466–75.

Lo Porto, F. G. 1963. Leporano (Taranto) – la stazione protostorica di Porto Perone, *Notizie degli Scavi di Antichità*, 8th series, 17, 280–380.

Lo Schiavo, F. 1978. Armi e utensili di Siniscola, *Sardegna centro-orientale dal Neolitico alla fine del mondo antico*, 85–7. Sassari: Dessì.

  1980. Wessex, Sardegna, Cipro: nuovi elementi di discussione, *Atti della XXII Riunione Scientifica dell'Istituto Italiano di Preistoria e Protostoria* (1978), 341–58.

  1981. Ambra in Sardegna. In *Studi in onore di F. Rittatore Vonwiller*, I, 3–22. Como.

  1986a. Sardinian metallurgy: the archaeological background. In *Studies in Sardinian Archaeology II, Sardinia in the Mediterranean*, ed. M. Balmuth, 231–50. Ann Arbor: University of Michigan Press.

  1986b. Una reinterpretazione: modellino di nave in piombo da Antigori (Sarroch, Cagliari). In *Traffici Micenei nel Mediterraneo. Problemi storici e documentazione archeologica* (Atti del Convegno di Palermo, 1984), eds. M. Marazzi, S. Tusa and L. Vagnetti, 193–97. Taranto: Istituto per la storia de l'Archeologia della Magna Grecia.

  1989. Early metallurgy in Sardinia. Copper ox-hide ingots. In *Archäometallurgie der Alten Welt/Old World Archaeometallurgy*, Proc. Int. Symposium Heidelberg 1987, 33–8. Bochum: Deutsches Bergbau-Museum [= *Der Anschnitt* Supplement 7].

Lo Schiavo, F., Macnamara, E. and Vagnetti, L. 1985. Late Cypriot imports to Italy and their influence on local bronzework, *Papers British School Rome* 53, 1–71.

Løken, T. 1989. Rogalands bronsealderboplasser – sett i lys av områdets kulturelle kontakter. In *Regionale forhold i Nordisk Bronzealder. 5. Nordiske Symposium for Bronzealderforskning på Sandbjerg Slot 1987*, ed. J. Poulsen, 141–8. Jysk Arkaeologisk Selskabs Skrifter 24.

Lomborg, E. 1976. Vadgård. Ein Dorf mit Häusern und einer Kultstätte aus der älteren nordischen Bronzezeit. In *Festschrift für Richard Pittioni zum siebzigsten Geburtstag. I. Urgeschichte*, eds. H. Mitscha-Märheim, H. Friesinger and H. Kerchler, 414–32. Vienna: Deuticke.

Longley, D. 1980. *Runnymede Bridge 1976: Excavations on the Site of a Late Bronze Age Settlement*. Surrey Archaeol. Soc., Research Volume 6. Guildford: Surrey Archaeol. Soc.

Longworth, I. H., Herne, A., Varndell, G. and Needham, S. 1991. *Excavations at Grimes Graves, Norfolk, 1972–1976. Fascicule 3. Shaft X: Bronze Age Flint, Chalk and Metal Working*. London: British Museum.

Lorencová, A., Beneš, J. and Podborský, V. 1987. *Těšetice-Kyjovice 3. Únětické pohřebiště v Těšeticích-Vinohradech*. Brno: Universita J. E. Purkyně.

Lorenzen, W. 1965. *Helgoland und das früheste Kupfer des Nordens. Ein*

Beitrag zur Aufhellung der Anfänge der Metallurgie in Europa.
Otterndorf/Niederelbe: Niederelbe-Verlag / Otterndorfer Verlagsdruckerei
H. Huster.

Lucas, A. T. 1985. Toghers or causeways: some evidence from archaeological,
literary, historical and place-name sources, *Proc. Royal Irish Academy* 85C,
37–60.

Ludikovský, K. 1958. Pravěké tkalcovský stav v Tučapech u Vyškova, *Přehled
Výzkumů* 1958, 28–9.

Lull, V. 1983. *La 'cultura' de El Argar. Un modelo para el estudio de las for-
maciones económico-sociales prehistóricas.* Madrid: Akal Editor.

Lull, V. and Estévez, J. 1986. Propuesta metodológica para el estudio de las
necrópolis argáricos. In *Homenaje a Luis Siret (1934–1984)*, 441–52. Seville:
Consejeria de Cultura de la Junta de Andalucia, Direccion General de
Bellas Artes.

Lundqvist, L. 1991. Undersökta skärvstenshögar i Västsverige. In *Arkeologi i
Sverige* new series 1, 43–60.

Lunz, R. 1981. *Archäologie Südtirols.* Archäologische-Historische Forschungen
in Tirol 7. Bozen: Lunz.

Lynch, F. 1993. *Excavations in the Brenig Valley. A Mesolithic and Bronze Age
Landscape in North Wales.* Cambrian Archaeological Monographs 5.
Bangor: Cambrian Archaeological Association.

Lynn, C. J. 1983. Some 'early' ring-forts and crannogs, *J. Irish Archaeology* 1,
47–58.

McCaslin, D. E. 1980. *Stone Anchors in Antiquity: Coastal Settlements and
Maritime Trade-Routes in the Eastern Mediterranean ca. 1600–1050 BC.*
Studies in Mediterranean Archaeology 61. Göteborg: Paul Åström.

McConnell, B. E. 1992. The Early Bronze Age village of La Muculufa and prehistoric hut architecture in Sicily, *American J. Archaeology* 96, 23–44.

Macewicz, K. and Wuszkan, S. 1991. Ciężarki tkackie z osady ludności kultury
łużyckiej w Gadzowicach-Kwiatoniowie, woj. Opole, *Silesia Antiqua* 33–4,
25–54.

McGeehan-Liritzis, V. and Taylor, J. W. 1987. Yugoslavian tin deposits and the
Early Bronze Age industries of the Aegean region, *Oxford J. Archaeology* 6,
287–300.

McGrail, S. 1978. *Logboats of England and Wales.* National Maritime
Museum, Archaeological Series 2; Oxford: British Archaeological Reports
51.

1979. Prehistoric boats, timber and woodworking technology, *Proc. Prehist.
Soc.* 45, 159–63.

(ed.) 1981. *The Brigg 'Raft' and her Prehistoric Environment.* National
Maritime Museum, Archaeological Series 6; Oxford: British Archaeological
Reports 89.

1987. *Ancient Boats in N.W. Europe. The Archaeology of Water Transport to
AD 1500.* London: Longman.

1993. Prehistoric seafaring in the Channel. In *Trade and Exchange in
Prehistoric Europe*, eds. C. Scarre and F. Healy, 199–210. Oxford: Oxbow
Monograph 33.

1994. The Brigg 'raft': a flat-bottomed boat, *Int. J. Nautical Archaeology*
23/4, 283–8.

McGrail, S. and Kentley, E. (eds.) 1985. *Sewn Plank Boats. Archaeological and
Ethnographic Papers Based on Those Presented to a Conference at*

Greenwich in November 1984. National Maritime Museum, Archaeological Series 10. Oxford: British Archaeological Reports, Int. Series 276.

MacKie, E. W. 1977. *Science and Society in Prehistoric Britain.* London: Paul Elek.

MacKie, E. W. and Davis, A. 1988–9. New light on Neolithic rock carving. The petroglyphs at Greenland (Auchentorlie), Dunbartonshire, *Glasgow Archaeol. J.* 15, 125–55.

McKinley, J. 1997. Bronze Age 'barrows' and funerary rites and rituals of cremation, *Proc. Prehist. Soc.* 63, 129–45.

Macnamara, E. 1970. A group of bronzes from Surbo: new evidence for Aegean contacts with Apulia during Mycenaean III B and C, *Proc. Prehist. Soc.* 36, 241–60.

McOmish, D. 1996. East Chisenbury: ritual and rubbish at the British Bronze Age–Iron Age transition, *Antiquity* 70, 68–76.

MacWhite, E. 1946. A new view on Irish Bronze Age rock-scribings, *J. Royal Soc. Antiqs Ireland* 86, 59–80.

Maddin, R. 1989. The copper and tin ingots from the Kaş shipwreck. In *Archäometallurgie der Alten Welt/Old World Archaeometallurgy,* Proc. Int. Symposium Heidelberg 1987, 99–105. Bochum: Deutsches Bergbau-Museum [= *Der Anschnitt* Supplement 7].

Madsen, T. 1979. Earthen long barrows and timber structures: aspects of the Early Neolithic mortuary practice in Denmark, *Proc. Prehist. Soc.* 45, 301–20.

Magee, R. W. 1993. Faience beads of the Irish Bronze Age, *Archeomaterials* 7/1, 115–25.

Maier, R. 1996. Siedlungs- und Grabfunde der Aunjetitzer Kultur aus dem Braunkohlentagebau Schöningen, Ldkr. Helmstedt, *Die Kunde* 47, 111–25.

Maier, R. A. 1977. Urgeschichtliche Opferreste aus einer Felsspalte und einer Schachthöhle der Fränkischen Alb, *Germania* 55, 21–32.

Maier, S. 1997. Klingenden Zeugen der Bronzezeit. Die ältesten spielbaren Blechinstrumente aus den Opfermooren Nordeuropas. In *Gaben an die Götter. Schätze der Bronzezeit Europas,* eds. A. and B. Hänsel, 77–81. Berlin: Seminar für Ur- und Frühgeschichte der Freien Universität/Museum für Vor- und Frühgeschichte (Staatliche Museen zu Berlin – Preussischer Kulturbesitz).

Maise, C. 1997. Elemente spätbronzezeitlicher Holzbautechnik, *Jahrbuch der schweizerischen Gesellschaft für Ur- und Frühgeschichte* 80, 192–5.

Malinowski, B. 1941. An anthropological analysis of war, *American J. Sociology* 46, 521–50.

Malinowski, T. 1970. Problème du cannibalisme parmi la population de la civilisation lusacienne en Pologne, *Actes du VIIᵉ Congrès international des sciences préhistoriques et protohistoriques, Prague, 21–27 août 1966,* I, 722–6.

Mallory, J. P. 1989. *In Search of the Indo-Europeans. Language, Archaeology and Myth.* London: Thames and Hudson.

Malmer, M. 1981. *A Chorological Study of North European Rock Art.* Stockholm: Almqvist and Wiksell.

Manby, T. G. 1980. Bronze Age settlement in eastern Yorkshire. In *Settlement and Society in the British Later Bronze Age,* eds. J. Barrett and R. Bradley, 307–70. Oxford: British Archaeological Reports 83.

Mandera, H.-E. 1972. Zur Deutung der späturnenfelderzeitlichen Hortfunde in Hessen, *Fundberichte aus Hessen* 12, 97–103.

Mandt Larsen, G. 1972. *Bergbilder i Hordaland. En undersøkelse av bildenes sammensetning, deres naturmiljø og kulturmiljø.* Årbok for Universitetet i Bergen, Humanistisk Serie 1970 no. 2. Bergen: Norwegian Universities Press.

Mandt, G. 1978. Is the location of rock pictures an interpretative element? In *Acts of the International Symposium on Rock Art, Lectures at Hankø 1972*, ed. S. Marstrander, 170–84. Oslo: Universitetsforlaget.

1983. Tradition and diffusion in West-Norwegian rock art. Mjeltehaugen revisited, *Norwegian Archaeol. Review* 16/1, 14–32.

1987. Female symbolism in rock art. In *Were They All Men? An Examination of Sex Roles in Prehistoric Society*, eds. R. Bertelsen, A. Lillehammer and J.-R. Næss, 35–52. Stavanger: Arkeologisk Museum.

Manley, J. 1985. Fields, cairns and enclosures on Ffridd Brynhelen, Clwyd. In *Upland Settlement in Britain. The Second Millennium BC and After*, eds. D. Spratt and C. Burgess, 317–49. Oxford: British Archaeological Reports 143.

1990. A Late Bronze Age landscape on the Denbigh Moors, northeast Wales, *Antiquity* 64, 514–26.

Mann, M. 1986. *The Sources of Social Power I. A History of Power from the Beginning to AD 1760.* Cambridge: Cambridge University Press.

Maraszek, R. 1997. Kultgerät im mittleren Oderraum: die Deichselwagen. In *Gaben an die Götter. Schätze der Bronzezeit Europas*, eds. A. and B. Hänsel, 71–5. Berlin: Seminar für Ur- und Frühgeschichte der Freien Universität/Museum für Vor- und Frühgeschichte (Staatliche Museen zu Berlin – Preussischer Kulturbesitz).

1998. *Spätbronzezeitliche Hortfunde entlang der Oder.* Universitätsforschungen zur prähistorischen Archäologie 49. Bonn: Habelt.

Marchesetti, C. 1903. I castellieri preistorichi di Trieste e della regione Giulia, *Atti Museo Civico di Storia Naturale* (Trieste) 4, 1–206.

Mariën, M. E. 1964. *Découvertes à la Grotte de Han.* Brussels: Musées royaux d'art et d'histoire.

Mariën, M. E. and Vanhaeke, L. 1965. *Nouvelles découvertes à la Grotte de Han.* Brussels: Musées royaux d'art et d'histoire.

Marović, I. 1991. Istraživanja kamenih gomila cetinske kulture u srednjoj Dalmaciji, *Vjesnik za arheologiju i historiju dalmatinsku* 84, 15–214.

Marquart, M. 1993. Zwei neue Bronzefunde vom bayerischen Untermain, *Acta Praehistorica et Archaeologica* 25, 111–16.

Marstrander, S. 1963. *Østfolds jordbruksristninger. Skjeberg.* Oslo/Trondheim: Universitetsforlaget.

1976. Building a hide boat. An archaeological experiment, *Int. J. Nautical Archaeology* 5, 13–22.

1978. The problem of European impulses in the Nordic area of agrarian rock art. In *Acts of the International Symposium on Rock Art, Lectures at Hankø 1972*, ed. S. Marstrander, 45–67. Oslo: Universitetsforlaget.

Martín, C., Fernández-Miranda, M., Fernández-Posse, M. D. and Gilman, A. 1993. The Bronze Age of La Mancha, *Antiquity* 67, 23–45.

Martin, E. and Murphy, P. 1988. West Row Fen, Suffolk: a Bronze Age fen-edge settlement site, *Antiquity* 62, 353–8.

Martini, F. and Sarti, L. 1990. *La preistoria del Monte Cetona.* Florence: Edizioni all'Insegna del Giglio.

Maryon, H. 1937–8. The technical methods of the Irish smiths in the Bronze and Early Iron Ages, *Proc. Royal Irish Academy* 44C, 181–228.

1938. Some prehistoric metalworkers' tools, *Antiqs J.* 18, 243–50.

Marzatico, F. 1988. I carpentieri di Fiavé. In *Archeologia del Legno. Documenti dell'età del bronzo dall'area sudalpina*, ed. R. Perini 35–50. Quaderni della Sezione Archeologica, Museo Provinciale d'Arte. Trento: Servizio Beni Culturali.

Mascher, C. 1993. *Förhistoriska markindelningar och röjningsröseområden i Västsveriges skogsbygder*. Kulturgeografisk Seminarium 2/93. Stockholm: Department of Human Geography, Stockholm University.

Mason, E. J. 1968. Ogof yr Esgyrn and Dan yr Ogof caves 1938–50, *Archaeologia Cambrensis* 117, 18–71.

Máthé, M. Sz. 1988. Bronze Age tells in the Berettyó valley. In *Bronze Age Tell Settlements of the Great Hungarian Plain I* 27–122. Inventaria Praehistorica Hungariae, Budapest: Magyar Nemzeti Múzeum.

Matoušek, V. 1982. Pohřební ritus rané únětické kultury v Čechách, *Varia Archaeologica* 3 (Praehistorica 10), 33–52.

Matter, A. 1992. Die spätbronzezeitlichen Brandgräber von Regensdorf-Adlikon. In *Bronzezeitliche Landsiedlungen und Gräber*, eds. A. Siegfried and C. Hauser, 287–336. Berichte der Zürcher Denkmalpflege, Archäologische Monographien 11. Egg: Fotorotar AG.

Matthäus, H. 1981. Κύκνοι δὲ ἦσαν τὸ ἅρμα. Spätmykenische und urnen-felderzeitliche Vogelplastik. In *Studien zur Bronzezeit. Festschrift für Wilhelm Albert v. Brunn*, ed. H. Lorenz, 277–98. Mainz: v. Zabern.

Matthäus, H. and Schumacher-Matthäus, G. 1986. Zyprische Hortfunde: Kult und Metallhandwerk in der späten Bronzezeit. In *Gedenkschrift für Gero von Merhart*, eds. O.-H. Frey, H. Roth and C. Dobiat, Marburger Studien zur Vor- und Frühgeschichte 7, 129–91. Marburg: Hitzeroth.

Matthias, W. 1961. Das mitteldeutsche Briquetage – Formen, Verbreitung und Verwendung, *Jahresschrift für mitteldeutsche Vorgeschichte* 45, 119–225.

1976. Die Salzproduktion – ein bedeutender Faktor in der Wirtschaft der frühbronzezeitlichen Bevölkerung an der mittleren Saale, *Jahresschrift für mitteldeutsche Vorgeschichte* 60, 373–94.

May, E. 1996. Tierknochenfunde aus der jungbronzezeitlichen Siedlung an der Walkemühle bei Göttingen, *Die Kunde* 47, 71–110.

Maya, J. L. 1992. Calcolítico y edad del bronce en Cataluña. In *Aragón/Litoral mediterráneo: intercambios culturales durante la prehistoria. En homenaje a Juan Maluquer de Motes*, ed. P. Utrilla Miranda, 515–54. Zaragoza: Institución Fernando el Católico.

Mayer, E. F. 1978–79. Bronzezeitliche Passfunde im Alpenraum, *Jahresbericht des Institutes für Vorgeschichte der Universität Frankfurt a.M.* 1978–9, 179–87.

Mays, S. 1989. Marxist perspectives on social organization in the central European Early Bronze Age. In *Domination and Resistance*, eds. D. Miller, M. Rowlands and C. Tilley, 215–26. One World Archaeology 3. London: Unwin Hyman.

Meddens, F. 1993. A trackway at Beckton, East London, *NewsWARP* 14, 34–5.

Medeleţ, F. 1995. Über das Salz in Dakien, *Archäologie Österreichs* 6/2, 53–7.

Medović, P. 1993. Raonik (lemeš) rala sa Bordjoša kod Novog Bečeja (Banat), *Rad Vojvodanskih Muzeja* 35, 33–40.

Megaw, B. R. S. and Hardy, E. M. 1938. British decorated axes and their diffusion during the earlier part of the Bronze Age, *Proc. Prehist. Soc.* 4, 272–307.

Megaw, J. V. S. and Simpson, D. D. A. 1979. *Introduction to British Prehistory, from the Arrival of* Homo sapiens *to the Claudian Invasion.* Leicester: Leicester University Press.

Menke, M. 1968. Frühbronzezeitliche Gussformen aus Karlstein, Ldkr. Berchtesgaden (Oberbayern), *Jahrbuch des Römisch-Germanischen Zentralmuseums Mainz* 15, 69–74.

   1978–9 [1982]. Studien zu den frühbronzezeitlichen Metalldepots Bayerns, *Jahresber. der bayerischen Bodendenkmalpflege* 19–20, 5–305.

   1982. Eine Befestigung der älteren Bronzezeit Süddeutschlands (Stand der Forschung). In *Beiträge zum bronzezeitlichen Burgenbau in Mitteleuropa*, 293–310. Berlin: Zentralinstitut für Alte Geschichte und Archäologie; Nitra: Archeologický Ústav Slovenskej Akadémie Vied.

Mercer, R. J. 1970. The excavation of a Bronze Age hut-circle settlement, Stannon Down, St Breward, *Cornish Archaeology* 9, 17–46.

   1985. Second millennium BC settlement in northern Scotland. In *Upland Settlement in Britain. The Second Millennium BC and After*, eds. D. Spratt and C. Burgess, 253–72. Oxford: British Archaeological Reports 143.

Merhart, G. von 1952. Studien über einige Gattungen von Bronzegefässen. In *Festschrift des Römisch-Germanischen Zentralmuseums Mainz zur Feier seines hundertjährigen Bestehens*, II, 1–71.

   1954. Panzer-Studie. In *Origines. Raccolta de scritti in onore di Mons. Giovanni Baserga*, Como, 33–61; reprinted in *Hallstatt und Italien*, Mainz: Verlag des Römisch-Germanischen Zentralmuseums, 149–71.

   1956–7. Geschnürte Schienen, *Bericht der Römisch-Germanischen Kommission* 37–8, 91–147; reprinted in *Hallstatt und Italien*, Mainz: Verlag des Römisch-Germanischen Zentralmuseums, 172–226.

Merkel, J. F. 1983. Summary of experimental results for Late Bronze Age copper smelting and refining, *MASCA J.* 2/6, 173–8.

   1990. Experimental reconstruction of Bronze Age copper smelting based on archaeological evidence from Timna. In *The Ancient Metallurgy of Copper. Archaeology-Experiment-Theory* (Researches in the Arabah 1959–1984, 2), ed. B. Rothenberg, 78–122. London: Institute for Archaeo-Metallurgical Studies.

Mikov, V. 1928–9. Skalni izobraženija ot' Bălgarija, *Izvestija na bălgarskija arkheologičeskija Institut* 5, 291–308.

Mikov, V. and Džambazov, I. 1960. *Devetaškata peščera.* Sofia: Bulgarian Academy of Sciences.

Miles, H. 1975. Barrows on the St Austell granite, Cornwall, *Cornish Archaeology* 14, 5–81.

Milz, H. 1986. Die Tierknochenfunde aus drei argarzeitlichen Siedlungen in der Provinz Granada (Spanien), *Studien über frühe Tierknochenfunde von der Iberischen Halbinsel* 10.

Minozzi, S., Canci, A., Borgognini Tarli, S. M. and Repetto, E. 1994. Stresi e stato di salute in serie scheletriche dell'età del bronzo, *Bull. Paletnologia Italiana* 85, 333–48.

Miske, K. von 1908. *Die prähistorische Ansiedelung Velem St. Vid.* Vienna: Carl Konegen.

   1929. Bergbau, Verhüttung und Metallbearbeitungswerkzeuge aus Velem St. Veit (Westungarn), *Wiener Prähistorische Zeitschrift* 16, 81–94.

Miszkiewicz, B. 1972. Die Aunjetitzer Bevölkerung aus Tomice, Kr. Dzierżoniów, *Homo* 23, 135–43.

Mizoguchi, K. 1992. A historiography of a linear barrow cemetery: a structurationist's point of view, *Archaeol. Review from Cambridge* 11, 39–49.

Moberg, C.-A. 1975. *Kivik. Bredarör och andra fornminnen*. Svenska fornminnesplatser 1. [Stockholm]: Riksantikvarieämbetet.

Modderman, P. J. R. 1964. Middle Bronze Age graves and settlement traces at Zwaagdijk, Gemeente Wervershoof, Prov. North Holland, *Berichten van de Rijksdienst voor het Oudheidkundig Bodemonderzoek* 14, 27–36.

Modena, 1989. *Modena dalle origini all'anno Mille. Studi di archeologia e storia, I–II.* Modena: Edizioni Panini.

Moffett, L. 1991. Pignut tubers from a Bronze Age cremation at Barrow Hills, Oxfordshire, and the importance of vegetable tubers in the prehistoric period, *J. Archaeol. Science* 18, 187–91.

Mohen, J.-P. 1973. Les moules en terre cuite des bronziers préhistoriques, *Antiquités Nationales* 5, 33–44.

   1978. Moules en bronze de l'âge du bronze, *Antiquités Nationales* 10, 23–32.

   1984–5. Les outils des métallurgistes de l'âge du bronze en France, *Antiquités Nationales* 16–17, 89–96.

   1990. *Métallurgie préhistorique. Introduction à la paléométallurgie.* Paris: Masson.

Mohen, J.-P. and Bailloud, G. 1987. *La Vie quotidienne. Les fouilles du Fort-Harrouard. L'âge du bronze en France, 4.* Paris: Picard.

Mohen, J.-P. and Eluère, C. 1990–1. Le rôle du métal dans le site du Mont Bégo, *Antiquités Nationales* 22–3, 27–36.

Molina, F., Nájera, T. and Aguayo, P. 1979. La motilla del Azuer (Daimiel, Ciudad Real): campaña de 1979, *Cuadernos de Prehistoria e la Universidad de Granada* 4, 265–94.

Moloney, A. 1993a. *Survey of the Raised Bogs of County Longford.* Irish Archaeological Wetland Unit, Transactions 1. Dublin: Office of Public Works/University College.

   1993b. *Excavations at Clonfinlough, Co. Offaly.* Irish Archaeological Wetland Unit, Transactions 2. Dublin: Office of Public Works/University College.

Moloney, A., Bermingham, N., Jennings, D., Keane, M., McDermott, C. and O Carroll, E. 1995. *Blackwater Survey and Excavations. Artefact Deterioration in Peatlands. Lough More, Co. Mayo.* Irish Archaeological Wetland Unit, Transactions, 4. Dublin: Crannóg Publication (Department of Archaeology, University College).

Mommsen, H., Kreuser, A. and Weber, J. 1988. A method for grouping pottery by chemical composition, *Archaeometry* 30/1, 47–57.

Montelius, O. 1986 (1885). *Dating in the Bronze Age, with Special Reference to Scandinavia* (translation of *Om tidsbestämning inom bronsåldern med särskildt afseende på Scandinavien*, Kungl. Vitterhets Historie och Antiqvitets Akademien Handlingar 30). Stockholm: Royal Academy of Letters, History and Antiquities.

Montero Ruiz, I. 1993. Bronze Age metallurgy in southeast Spain, *Antiquity* 67, 46–57.

Moore, J. and Jennings, D. 1992. *Reading Business Park. A Bronze Age Landscape* (Thames Valley Landscapes: The Kennet Valley 1). Oxford: Oxford Archaeological Unit.

Moore, M. J. 1995. A Bronze Age settlement and ritual centre in the Monavullagh Mountains, County Waterford, Ireland, *Proc. Prehist. Soc.* 61, 191–243.

Mordant, C., Mordant, D. and Prampart, J.-Y. 1976. *Le Dépôt de bronze de Villethierry (Yonne). Gallia Préhistoire*, Supplement 9. Paris: CNRS.

Moretti, M. 1978. Complessi dei castellieri di Nivize e Monte Grisa. In *I castellieri di Nivize – Monte Grisa – Ponte S. Quirino, complessi dell'età del bronzo*, 9–64. Atti dei Civici Musei di Storia ed Arte di Trieste, Monografie di Preistoria 2. Trieste: Electa Editrice.

Morris, E. L. 1985. Prehistoric salt distributions: two case studies from western Britain, *Bull. Board of Celtic Studies* 32, 336–79.

    1994. Production and distribution of pottery and salt in Iron Age Britain: a review, *Proc. Prehist. Soc.* 60, 371–94.

Morris, M. 1992. The rise and fall of Bronze Age studies in England 1840–1960, *Antiquity* 66, 419–26.

Morris, R. W. B. 1981. *The Prehistoric Rock Art of Southern Scotland*. Oxford: British Archaeological Reports 86.

    1989. The prehistoric rock art of Great Britain: a survey of all sites bearing motifs more complex than simple cup-marks, *Proc. Prehist. Soc.* 55, 45–88.

    1989–90. Cup-and-ring mark dating, *Glasgow Archaeol. J.* 16, 85–6.

Morrison, A. 1979. A Bronze Age burial site near South Mound, Houston, Renfrewshire, *Glasgow Archaeol. J.* 6, 20–45.

Morrison, I. 1985. *Landscape with Lake Dwellings. The Crannogs of Scotland*. Edinburgh: Edinburgh University Press.

Motyková, K. 1973. Sídliště lidu popelnicových polí u Sobčic, *Památky Archeologické* 64, 235–71.

Moucha, V. 1961. *Funde der Úněticer Kultur in der Gegend von Lovosice*. Fontes Archaeologici Pragenses 4. Prague: National Museum.

    1963. Die Periodisierung der Úněticer Kultur in Böhmen, *Sborník československé společnosti archeologické* 3, 9–60.

Mozsolics, A. 1942. *A kisapostagi korabronzkori urnatemető/Der frühbronzezeitliche Urnenfriedhof von Kisapostag*. Archaeologia Hungarica 26. Budapest: Magyar Történeti Múzeum.

    1952. Die Ausgrabungen in Tószeg im Jahre 1948, *Acta Archaeologica* (Budapest) 2, 34–69.

    1953. Mors en bois de cerf sur le territoire du bassin des Carpathes, *Acta Archaeologica* (Budapest) 3, 69–109.

    1965–6. Goldfunde des Depotfundhorizontes von Hajdúsámson, *Bericht der Römisch-Germanischen Kommission* 46–7, 1–76.

    1967. *Bronzefunde des Karpatenbeckens. Depotfundhorizonte von Hajdúsámson und Kosziderpadlás*. Budapest: Akadémiai Kiadó.

    1972. Újabb kardleletek a Magyar Nemzeti Múzeumban II, *Archaeologiai Értesítő* 99, 188–205.

    1973. *Bronze- und Goldfunde des Karpatenbeckens. Depotfundhorizonte von Forró und Ópályi*. Budapest: Akadémiai Kiadó.

    1975. Bronzkori kardok folyókból, *Archaeologiai Értesítő* 102, 3–24.

    1985. *Bronzefunde aus Ungarn. Depotfundhorizonte von Aranyos, Kurd und Gyermely*. Budapest: Akadémiai Kiadó.

    1987. Verwahr- oder Opferfunde? *Acta Archaeologica* (Budapest) 39, 93–8.

Muckelroy, K. 1980. Two Bronze Age cargoes in British waters, *Antiquity* 54, 100–9.

1981. Middle Bronze Age trade between Britain and Europe: a maritime perspective, *Proc. Prehist. Soc.* 47, 275–97.

Muhly, J. D. 1973. Copper and tin. The distribution of mineral resources and the nature of the metals trade in the Bronze Age, *Transactions Connecticut Academy of Arts and Sciences* 43, 155–535 (with Supplement, vol. 46, 1976, 77–136).

1985. Sources of tin and the beginnings of bronze metallurgy, *American J. Archaeology* 89, 275–91.

1993. Early Bronze Age tin and the Taurus, *American J. Archaeology* 97, 239–53.

Müller, A. von 1964a/1975. *Die jungbronzezeitliche Siedlung von Berlin-Lichterfelde.* Berliner Beiträge zur Vor- und Frühgeschichte 9. Berlin: Hessling.

1964b. Der jungbronzezeitliche Keramikfund von Raddusch, Kr. Kalau/Brandenburg, *Berliner Jahrbuch für Vor- und Frühgeschichte* 4, 155–74.

Müller, D. W. 1987. Neolithisches Briquetage von der mittleren Saale, *Jahresschrift für mitteldeutsche Vorgeschichte* 70, 135–52.

Müller, F. 1993. Argumente zu einer Deutung von 'Pfahlbaubronzen', *Jahrbuch der schweizerischen Gesellschaft für Ur- und Frühgeschichte* 76, 71–92.

Müller, H.-H. 1989. Tierreste aus Leichenbränden der jungbronzezeitlichen Gräberfeldes von Berlin-Rahnsdorf, *Zeitschrift für Archäologie* 23, 237–48.

1993a. Pferde der Bronzezeit in Mitteleuropa, *Zeitschrift für Archäologie* 27, 131–50.

1993b. Horse skeletons of the Bronze Age in central Europe. In *Skeletons in her Cupboard. Festschrift for Juliet Clutton-Brock*, eds. A. Clason, S. Payne and H.-P. Uerpmann, 143–50. Oxford: Oxbow Monograph 34.

Müller, U. 1986. *Studien zu den Gebäuden der späten Bronzezeit und der Urnenfelderzeit im erweiterten Mitteleuropa.* Berlin: privately published doctoral dissertation, Freie Universität.

Müller-Karpe, H. 1956. Das urnenfelderzeitliche Wagengrab von Hart a.d. Alz, *Bayerische Vorgeschichtsblätter* 21, 46–75.

1959. *Beiträge zur Chronologie der Urnenfelderzeit nördlich und südlich der Alpen.* Römisch-Germanische Forschungen 22. Berlin: de Gruyter.

1961. *Die Vollgriffschwerter der Urnenfelderzeit aus Bayern.* Munich: C. H. Beck.

1974/1981. *Handbuch der Vorgeschichte. III. Kupferzeit; IV. Bronzezeit.* Munich: Beck.

1978–9. Bronzezeitliche Heilszeichen, *Jahresbericht des Institutes für Vorgeschichte der Universität Frankfurt a.M.* 1978–9, 9–28.

Müller-Wille, M. 1968–9. Bestattung im Boot. Studien zu einer nordeuropäischen Grabsitte, *Offa* 25–26, 7–203.

Musson C. R., with Britnell, W. J. and Smith, A. G. 1991. *The Breiddin Hillfort. A Later Prehistoric Settlement in the Welsh Marches.* London: Council for British Archaeology Research Report 76.

Naroll, R. 1964. On ethnic unit classification, *Current Anthropology* 5, 283–312.

Navarro, J. M. de 1925. Prehistoric routes between northern Europe and Italy defined by the amber trade, *Geographical J.* 66, 481–504.

Nayling, N. and Caseldine, A. 1997. *Excavations at Caldicot, Gwent: Bronze Age Palaeochannels in the Lower Nedern Valley.* Council for British Archaeology Research Report 108. York: Council for British Archaeology.

Needham, S. P. 1979a. Two recent British shield finds and their continental
parallels, *Proc. Prehist. Soc.* 45, 111–34.

   1979b. A pair of Early Bronze Age spearheads from Lightwater, Surrey. In
   Bronze Age Hoards. Some Finds Old and New, eds. C. Burgess and D.
   Coombs, 1–39. Oxford: British Archaeological Reports 67.

   1980. An assemblage of Late Bronze Age metalworking debris from Dainton,
   Devon, *Proc. Prehist. Soc.* 46, 177–215.

   1981. *The Bulsford–Helsbury Manufacturing Tradition. The Production of
   Stogursey Socketed Axes during the Later Bronze Age in Southern Britain.*
   London: British Museum Occasional Paper 13.

   1990. *The Petters Late Bronze Age Metalwork. An Analytical Study of
   Thames Valley Metalworking in its Settlement Context.* London: British
   Museum Occasional Paper 70.

   1991. *Excavation and Salvage at Runnymede Bridge, 1978: the Late Bronze
   Age Waterfront Site.* London: British Museum.

   1992. The structure of settlement and ritual in the Late Bronze Age of south-
   east Britain. In *L'Habitat et l'occupation du sol à l'âge du bronze en
   Europe*, eds. C. Mordant and A. Richard, 49–69. Actes du colloque de Lons-
   le-Saunier, 1990. Documents préhistoriques 4. Paris: Comité des travaux
   historiques et scientifiques.

   1993. A Bronze Age goldworking anvil from Lichfield, Staffordshire, *Antiqs
   J.* 73, 125–32.

Needham, S. P. and Ambers, J. 1994. Redating Rams Hill and reconsidering
Bronze Age enclosure, *Proc. Prehist. Soc.* 60, 225–44.

Needham, S. P., Bronk Ramsey, C., Coombs, D., Cartwright, C. and Pettitt, P.
1997. An independent chronology for British Bronze Age metalwork: the
results of the Oxford radiocarbon accelerator programme, *Archaeol. J.* 154,
55–107.

Needham, S. P. and Dean, M. 1987. La cargaison de Langdon Bay à douvres
(Grande Bretagne) – la signification pour les échanges a travers la
Manche. In *Les Relations entre le Continent et les îles britanniques à l'
âge du bronze*, 119–24. Amiens: Revue Archéologique de Picardie,
Supplement.

Needham, S. P. and Hook, D. R. 1988. Lead and lead alloys in the Bronze Age –
recent finds from Runnymede Bridge. In *Science and Archaeology, Glasgow
1987*, eds. E. A. Slater and J. O. Tate, 259–274. Oxford: British
Archaeological Reports 196.

Neff, H. (ed.) 1992. *Chemical Characterization of Ceramic Pastes in
Archaeology.* Monographs in World Archaeology 7. Madison: Prehistory
Press.

Nekvasil, J. 1978. Mohylníky lužické kultury na Moravě, *Památky
Archeologické* 69, 52–116.

   1982. *Pohřebiště lužické kultury v Moravičanech.* Fontes Archaeologiae
   Moravicae, 14/1–2. Brno: Archeologický Ústav ČSAV.

Nenquin, J. 1961. *Salt. A Study in Economic Prehistory.* Ghent: Dissertationes
Archaeologicae Gandenses 6.

Nesbitt, M. and Summers, G. D. 1988. Some recent discoveries of millet
(*Panicum miliaceum* L. and *Setaria italica* (L.) P. Beav.) at excavations in
Turkey and Iran, *Anatolian Studies* 38, 85–97.

Neubauer, W. and Stöllner, T. 1994. Überlegungen zu bronzezeitlichen
Höhenfunden anhand eines kürzlich in der Ostschweiz gefundenen

Vollgriffmessers, *Jahrbuch des Römisch-Germanischen Zentralmuseums* 41, 95–144.

Neugebauer, J.-W. 1991. *Die Nekropole F. von Gemeinlebarn, Niederösterreich. Untersuchungen zu den Bestattungssitten und zum Grabraub in der ausgehenden Frühbronzezeit in Niederösterreich südlich der Donau zwischen Enns und Wienerwald.* Römisch-Germanische Forschungen 49. Mainz: v. Zabern.

    1994. *Bronzezeit in Ostösterreich.* Wissenschaftliche Schriftenreihe Niederösterreich, 98–101. St Pölten–Vienna: Verlag Niederösterreichisches Pressehaus.

Neuninger, H. and Pittioni, R. 1959. Woher stammen die blauen Glasperlen der Urnenfelderkultur? *Archaeologia Austriaca* 6, 52–66.

Newall, R. S. 1930–32. Barrow 85 Amesbury [Goddard's list], *Wiltshire Archaeol. Magazine* 45, 432–58.

Newton, R. G. and Renfrew, A. C. 1970. British faience beads reconsidered, *Antiquity* 44, 199–206.

Nielsen, V. 1984. Prehistoric field boundaries in eastern Denmark, *J. Danish Archaeology* 3, 135–63.

Nikolov, B. 1976. Mogilni pogrebeniya ot rannobronzovata epocha pri Tărnava i Kneža, Vračanski okrăg, *Arkheologiya* 18/3, 38–51.

Nikolova, Ja and Angelov, N. 1961. Razkopki na emenskata peščera (Les fouilles de la grotte Emen), *Izvestiya na archeologičeskiya institut* 24, 297–316.

Noël, M. and Bocquet, A. 1987. *Les Hommes et le bois. Histoire et technologie du bois de la préhistoire à nos jours.* Paris: Hachette.

Nordbladh, J. 1978. Images as messages in society. Prolegomena to the study of Scandinavian petroglyphs and semiotics. In *New Directions in Scandinavian Archaeology*, eds. K. Kristiansen and C. Paludan-Müller, 63–78. Copenhagen: National Museum.

    1980. *Glyfer och rum. Kring hällristningar i Kville.* Göteborg: University of Göteborg, Department of Archaeology.

    1989. Armour and fighting in the south Scandinavian Bronze Age, especially in view of rock art representations. In *Approaches to Swedish Prehistory: a Spectrum of Problems and Perspectives in Contemporary Research*, eds T. B. Larsson and H. Lundmark, 323–33. Oxford: British Archaeological Reports, Int. Series 500.

Nordén, A. 1917/1926/1942. *Kiviksgraven och andra fornminnen i Kivikstrakten.* Svenska Fornminnesplatser 1. Stockholm: Wahlström and Widstrand.

Nordmann, C. A. 1920. Offerbrunnen från Budsene, *Aarbøger* 1920, 63–87.

Norling-Christensen, H. 1946. The Viksø helmets. A Bronze Age votive find from Zealand, *Acta Archaeologica* (Copenhagen) 17, 99–115.

Northover, J. P. 1980a. The analysis of Welsh Bronze Age metalwork. In H. N. Savory, *Guide Catalogue of the Bronze Age Collections*, 229–43. Cardiff: National Museum of Wales.

    1980b/1991. Bronze in the British Bronze Age. In *Aspects of Early Metallurgy*, ed. W. A. Oddy, 63–70. British Museum Occasional Paper 17.

    1982a. The exploration of the long-distance movement of bronze in Bronze and Early Iron Age Europe, *Bull. Inst. Archaeology London* 19, 45–72.

    1982b. The metallurgy of the Wilburton hoards, *Oxford J. Archaeology* 1, 69–109.

Novikova, L. A. and Shilov, Ju. A. 1989. Pogrebeniya s licevymi nakladkami epokhi bronzy (Khersonskaja oblast'), *Sovietskaya Arkheologiya* 1989/2, 127–35.

Nowothnig, W. 1958. Der Teufelstein von Restrup, Gde Bippen, Kr. Bersenbrück, *Germania* 36, 181.

1965. Neue Ergebnisse der Bergbauforschung im Oberharz, *Neue Ausgrabungen und Forschungen in Niedersachsen* 2, 236–49.

Nyegaard, G. 1992–93. Animal bones from an Early Bronze Age midden layer at Torslev, northern Jutland, *J. Danish Archaeology* 11, 108–10.

O'Brien, W. F. 1990. Prehistoric copper mining in south-west Ireland: the Mount Gabriel-type mines, *Proc. Prehist. Soc.* 56, 269–90.

1994. *Mount Gabriel. Bronze Age Mining in Ireland.* Galway: Galway University Press.

1995. Ross Island – the beginning, *Archaeology Ireland* 9/1, 24–7.

O'Connor, B. 1980. *Cross-Channel Relations in the Later Bronze Age. Relations between Britain, North-Eastern France and the Low Countries during the Later Bronze Age and the Early Iron Age, with Particular Reference to the Metalwork.* Oxford: British Archaeological Reports 91.

O'Kelly, M. J. 1989. *Early Ireland. An Introduction to Irish Prehistory.* Cambridge: Cambridge University Press.

Olausson, D. 1986. Piledal and Svarte. A comparison between two Late Bronze Age cemeteries in Scania, *Acta Archaeologica* (Copenhagen) 57, 121–52.

1992. The archaeology of the Bronze Age cultural landscape – research goals, methods and results. In *The Archaeology of the Cultural Landscape. Field Work and Research in a South Swedish Rural Region*, eds. L. Larsson, J. Callmer and B. Stjernquist, 251–82. Acta Archaeologica Lundensia, series in 4°, 19. Stockholm: Almqvist and Wiksell.

1993. The Bronze Age barrow as a symbol. In *Bronsålderns gravhögar. Rapport från ett symposium i Lund 15.XI–16.XI 1991*, ed. L. Larsson, 91–113. University of Lund, Institute of Archaeology Report Series 48.

Olausson, M. 1993. Predikstolen – a Bronze Age hillfort in eastern central Sweden. In *Sources and Resources. Studies in Honour of Birgit Arrhenius*, PACT 38, 65–92.

Oldeberg, A. 1947. A contribution to the history of the Scandinavian bronze lur in the Bronze and Iron Ages, *Acta Archaeologica* (Copenhagen) 18, 1–91.

Olexa, L. 1982. Siedlungen und Gräberfelder aus der Bronzezeit von Nižná Myšl'a in der Ostslowakei. In *Südosteuropa zwischen 1600 und 1000 v. Chr.*, 387–97. Prähistorische Archäologie in Südosteuropa 1. Berlin: Moreland.

1992. Náleziská z doby bronzovej v Nižnej Myšli. Predbežná správa o vysled-koch vyskumu opevnenych sídlisk a pohrebiska otomanskej kultúry, *Slovenská Archeológia* 40, 189–204.

Olsen, S. L. 1994. Exploitation of mammals at the Early Bronze Age site of West Row Fen (Mildenhall 165), Suffolk, England, *Annals of Carnegie Museum* 63/2, 115–53.

Ondráček, J. 1962. Únětické pohřebiště u Rebešovic na Moravě, *Sborník československé společnosti archeologické* 2, 5–100.

Ó Nualláin, S. 1972. A Neolithic house at Ballyglass near Ballycastle, Co. Mayo, *J. Royal Soc. Antiqs Ireland* 102, 49–57.

Ordentlich, I. 1972. Contribuţia săpăturilor arheologice de pe 'Dealul Vida' (com. Sălacea, judeţul Bihor) la cunoaşterea culturii Otomani, *Satu Mare – Studii şi Comunicări* 1972, 63–84.

Ó Ríordáin, S. P. 1954. Lough Gur excavations: Neolithic and Bronze Age houses on Knockadoon, *Proc. Royal Irish Academy* 56C, 297–459.

1979. *Antiquities of the Irish Countryside*, 5th edition. London: Methuen.

Orlandini, P. 1962. *Il villaggio preistorico di Manfria presso Gela*. Palermo: Banco di Sicilia, Fondazione 'Ignazio Mormino', Publication 2.

Orme, B. J. and Coles, J. M. 1983. Prehistoric woodworking from the Somerset Levels: 1. Timber, *Somerset Levels Papers* 9, 19–43.

1985. Prehistoric woodworking from the Somerset Levels: 2. Species selection and prehistoric woodlands, *Somerset Levels Papers* 11, 7–24.

Orsi, P. 1899. Pantalica e Cassibile, *Monumenti Antichi* 9, fasc. 2, 33–146.

1911. Due villaggi del primo periodo siculo, *Bull. Paletnologia Italiana* 36, 158–93.

1926. Villaggio e sepolcreto siculo alle Sante Croci presso Comiso (Siracusa), *Bull. Paletnologia Italiana* 46, 5–17.

O'Shea, J. M. 1984. *Mortuary Variability: an Archaeological Investigation*. New York: Academic Press.

1996. *Villagers of the Maros. A Portrait of an Early Bronze Age Society*. New York/London: Plenum Press.

Ostoja-Zagórski, J. 1974. From studies on the economic structure at the decline of the Bronze Age and the Hallstatt period in the north and west zone of the Odra and Vistula basins, *Przegląd Archeologiczny* 22, 123–50.

1982. *Przemiany osadnicze, demograficzne i gospodarcze w okresie halsztackim na Pomorzu*. Wrocław etc.: Ossolineum.

1983. Aspekte der Siedlungskunde, Demographie und Wirtschaft hallstattzeitlicher Burgen vom Biskupin-Typ, *Prähistorische Zeitschrift* 58, 173–210.

1996. Bronze and Early Iron Age research in Poland, *World Archaeol. Bull.* 8, 216–23.

Ostoja-Zagórski, J. and Strzałko, J. 1984. Biologic–cultural changes in the Hallstatt period in the microregion of Sobiejuchy near Żnin, Bydgoszcz voivodship, *Archaeologia Polona* 23, 23–48.

O'Sullivan, A. 1995. Marshlanders, *Archaeology Ireland* 9/1, 8–11.

O'Sullivan, A. and Sheehan, J. 1993. Prospection and outlook: aspects of rock art on the Iveragh peninsula, Co. Kerry. In *Past Perceptions: the Prehistoric Archaeology of South-West Ireland*, eds. E. Shee Twohig and M. Ronayne, 75–84. Cork: Cork University Press.

Ottaway, B. S. 1994. *Prähistorische Archäometallurgie*. Espelkamp: Leidorf.

Ottenjann, H. 1969. *Die nordischen Vollgriffschwerter der älteren und mittleren Bronzezeit*. Römisch-Germanische Forschungen 30. Berlin: de Gruyter.

Pader, E.-J. 1982. *Symbolism, Social Relations and the Interpretation of Mortuary Remains*. Oxford: British Archaeological Reports, Int. Series 130.

Palavestra, A. 1992. Amber beads of the Tiryns type, *Balcanica* 23, 381–91.

1993. *Praistorijski ćilibar na centralnom i zapadnom Balkanu*. Belgrade: Srpska Akademija Nauka i Umetnosti, Balkanološki Institut, posebna izdanja 52.

Palmer, R. 1984. *Danebury, an Iron Age Hillfort in Hampshire. An Aerial Photographic Interpretation of its Environs*. London: Royal Commission on Historical Monuments (England), Supplementary Series 6.

Palmer-Brown, C. 1993. Bronze Age salt production at Tetney, *Current Archaeology* 136, 143–5.

Panayotov, I. and Dergachov, V. 1984. Die Ockergrabkultur in Bulgarien, Darstellung des Problems, *Studia Praehistorica* 7, 99–116.

Pannuti, S. 1969. Gli scavi di Grotta a Male presso l'Aquila, *Bull. Paletnologia Italiana* 78, new series 20, 147–67.

Papazoglu, F. 1978. *The Central Balkan Tribes in Pre-Roman Times: Triballi, Autariatae, Dardanians, Scordisci and Moesians*. Amsterdam: Adolf Hakkert.

Pare, C. F. E. 1987. Wheels with thickened spokes, and the problem of cultural contact between the Aegean world and Europe in the Late Bronze Age, *Oxford J. Archaeology* 6, 43–61.
    1989. From Dupljaja to Delphi: the ceremonial use of the wagon in later pre-history, *Antiquity* 63, 80–100.
    1992. *Wagons and Wagon-Graves of the Early Iron Age in Central Europe*. Oxford: Oxford University Committee for Archaeology, Monograph 35.

Paret, O. 1930. Die Einbäume im Federseeried und im übrigen Europa, *Prähistorische Zeitschrift* 21, 76–116.

Parfitt, K. 1993. The Dover boat, *Current Archaeology* 133, 4–8.

Parker, A. J. 1992. *Ancient Shipwrecks of the Mediterranean and the Roman Provinces*. Oxford: British Archaeological Reports, Int. Series 580.

Parker Pearson, M. 1993. *Bronze Age Britain*. London: Batsford/English Heritage.
    1996. Food, fertility and front doors in the first millennium BC. In *The Iron Age in Britain and Ireland: Recent Trends*, eds. T. C. Champion and J. R. Collis, 117–32. Sheffield: J. R. Collis Publications.

Parker Pearson, M. and Richards, C. 1994a. Ordering the world: perceptions of architecture, space and time. In *Architecture and Order. Approaches to Social Space*, eds. M. Parker Pearson and C. Richards, 1–37. London: Routledge.
    1994b. Architecture and order: spatial representation and archaeology. In *Architecture and Order. Approaches to Social Space*, eds. M. Parker Pearson and C. Richards, 38–72. London: Routledge.

Parović-Pešikan, M. 1977–8. Archeološka istraživanja u Boki Kotorskoj, *Starinar* 28–9, 19–67.

Parović-Pešikan, M. and Trbuhović, V. 1971. Iskopavanja tumula ranog bronz-anog doba u Tivatskom polju, *Starinar* 22, 129–44.

Patay, P. von 1938. *Frühbronzezeitliche Kulturen in Ungarn*. Dissertationes Pannonicae, series 2, 13. Budapest: Institut für Münzkunde und Archäologie der Péter Pázmány-Universität.
    1968. Urnenfelderzeitliche Bronzeschilde im Karpatenbecken, *Germania* 46, 241–8.

Patek, E. 1968. *Die Urnenfelderkultur in Transdanubien*. Budapest: Akadémiai Kiadó.

Pattison, P. and Fletcher, M. 1994. Grimspound, one hundred years on, *Proc. Devon Archaeol. Soc.* 52, 21–34 (*The Archaeology of Dartmoor. Perspectives from the 1990s*).

Pätzold, J. 1960. Rituelles Pflügen beim vorgeschichtlichen Totenkult – ein alter indogermanischer Bestattungsbrauch? *Prähistorische Zeitschrift* 38, 189–239.

Pauli, L. 1984. *The Alps. Archaeology and Early History*. London: Thames and Hudson.

Paulík, J. 1960. K problematike mladšej doby bronzovej na juhozápadnom Slovensku, *Archeologické Rozhledy* 12, 408–27.

1962. Der Velatice-Baierdorfer Hügelgrab in Očkov, *Slovenská Archeológia* 10, 5–96.

1966. Mohyla čakanskej kultúry v Kolte, *Slovenská Archeológia* 14, 357–96.

1968. Panzer der jüngeren Bronzezeit aus der Slowakei, *Bericht der Römisch-Germanischen Kommission* 49, 41–61.

1974. K významu mohýl z mladšej doby bronzovej v pravekom vývoji Slovenska, *Slovenská Archeológia* 22, 73–8.

1983. Mohyla čačianskej kultúry v Dedinke, okres Nové Zámky, *Zborník Slovenského Národného Múzea (História)* 77, 31–61.

1984. Čačianska mohyla v Dedinke, okres Nové Zámky (II), *Zborník Slovenského Národného Múzea (História)* 78, 27–48.

Peacock, D. P. S. 1969. Neolithic pottery production in Cornwall, *Antiquity* 43, 145–9.

Pedersen, J.-Å. 1986. A new Early Bronze Age house-site under a barrow at Hyllerup, western Zealand, *J. Danish Archaeology* 5, 168–76.

Peebles, C. S. and Kus, S. M. 1977. Some archaeological correlates of ranked societies, *American Antiquity* 42, 421–48.

Pellegrini, E. 1992. Le età dei metalli nell'Italia meridionale e in Sicilia. In *Italia preistorica*, eds. A. Guidi and M. Piperno, 471–516. Rome–Bari: Editori Laterza (Manuali Laterza 34).

Penhallurick, R. D. 1986. *Tin in Antiquity*. London: Institute of Metals.

Peña Santos, A. de la 1980. Las representaciones de alabardas en los grabados rupestros gallegos, *Zephyrus* 30–1, 115–29.

Peña Santos, A. de la and Vázquez Varela, J. M. 1979. *Los petroglifos gallegos: grabados rupestres prehistoricos al aire libre en Galicia*. La Coruña: Edic. do Castro.

Pericot García, L. 1972. *The Balearic Islands*. London: Thames and Hudson.

Perini, R. 1983. Der frühbronzezeitliche Pflug von Lavagnone, *Archäologisches Korrespondenzblatt* 13/2, 187–95.

1984. *Scavi archeologici nella zona palafitticola di Fiavé-Carera. I. Campagne 1969–1976. Situazione dei depositi e dei resti strutturali.* Patrimonio storico e artistico del Trentino 8. Trento: Servizio Beni Culturali della Provincia Autonoma di Trento.

1987. *Scavi archeologici nella zona palafitticola di Fiavé-Carera II, Campagne 1969–1976. Resti della cultura materiale, metallo – osso – litica – legno.* Patrimonio Storico e Artistico del Trentino 9. Trento: Servizio Beni Culturali della Provincia Autonoma di Trento.

1988a. Evidence of metallurgical activity in Trentino from Chalcolithic times to the end of the Bronze Age. In *Archeometallurgia, ricerche e prospettive* (Atti del Colloquio Internazionale di Archeometallurgia, Bologna 1988), ed. E. Antonacci Sampolo, 53–80. Bologna: Editrice CLUEB.

(ed.) 1988b. *Archeologia del legno. Documenti dell'età del bronzo dall'area sudalpina*. Quaderni della Sezione Archeologica, Museo Provinciale d'Arte. Trento: Servizio Beni Culturali.

Perra, M. 1997. From deserted ruins: an interpretation of nuraghic Sardinia, *Europaea* 3/2, 49–76.

Petersen, F. 1972. Traditions of multiple burial in later Neolithic and Early Bronze Age England, *Archaeol. J.* 129, 22–55.

1981. *The Excavation of a Bronze Age Cemetery on Knighton Heath, Dorset.* Oxford: British Archaeological Reports 98.

Pétrequin, P. 1985. *La Grotte des Planches près Arbois (Jura).* Paris: Maison des sciences de l'homme.

Petrescu-Dîmboviţa, M. 1971. Les dépôts tardifs de bronzes sur le territoire de la Roumanie (de Bronze D au Hallstatt B inclusivement), *Actes du VIIIe Congrès International des Sciences Préhistoriques et Protohistoriques* (Belgrade 1971), I, 175–92.

1978. *Die Sicheln in Rumänien (mit Corpus der jung- und spät-bronzezeitlichen Horte Rumäniens).* Prähistorische Bronzefunde XVIII, 1. Munich: Beck.

Petzel, M. 1987. Briquetage-Funde im Bezirk Cottbus, *Ausgrabungen und Funde* 32, 62–6.

Philp, B. and Garrod, D. 1994. A prehistoric wooden trackway at Greenwich, *Kent Archaeol. Review* 117, 147–68.

Pickin, J. 1990. Stone tools and early metal mining in England and Wales. In *Early Mining in the British Isles*, eds. P. and S. Crew, 39–42. Proc. Early Mining Workshop 1989, Plas Tan y Bwlch Occasional Paper 1.

Pickin, J. and Timberlake, S. 1988. Stone hammers and fire-setting: a preliminary experiment at Cwmystwyth mine, Dyfed, *Bull. Peak District Mines Historical Soc.* 10/3, 165–7.

Pieczyński, Z. 1969. Sprawozdanie z prac wykopaliskowych na osadzie z II okresu epoki brązu w Bruszczewie, pow. Kościan, stan. 5, *Fontes Archaeologici Posnanienses* 20, 268–71.

Pietzsch, A. 1971. Bronzeschmelzstätten auf der Heidenschanze in Dresden-Coschütz, *Arbeits- und Forschungsberichte zur sächsischen Bodendenkmalpflege* 19, 35–68.

Piggott, C. M. 1942. Five Late Bronze Age enclosures in north Wiltshire, *Proc. Prehist. Soc.* 8, 48–61.

1943. Excavation of fifteen barrows in the New Forest 1941–2, *Proc. Prehist. Soc.* 9, 1–27.

1952–3. Milton Loch crannog 1. A native house of the 2nd century AD in Kirkudbrightshire, *Proc. Soc. Antiqs Scotland* 87, 134–52.

Piggott, S. 1938. The Early Bronze Age in Wessex, *Proc. Prehist. Soc.* 4, 52–106.

1940. A trepanned skull of the Beaker period from Dorset and the practice of trepanning in prehistoric Europe, *Proc. Prehist. Soc.* 6, 112–32.

1957. A tripartite disc wheel from Blair Drummond, Perthshire, *Proc. Soc. Antiqs Scotland* 90, 238–41.

1968. The earliest wheeled vehicles and the Caucasian evidence, *Proc. Prehist. Soc.* 34, 266–318.

1973. The Wessex culture of the Early Bronze Age, Victoria County History, *Wiltshire* I (ii), 352–75. London: University of London, Institute of Historical Research.

1978. Nemeton, temenos, bothros: sanctuaries of the ancient Celts. In *I Celti e la loro cultura nell'epoca pre-romana e romana nella Britannia*, 37–54. Problemi attuali di scienza e di cultura, quaderno 237. Rome: Accademia Nazionale dei Lincei.

1983. *The Earliest Wheeled Transport, from the Atlantic Coast to the Caspian Sea.* London: Thames and Hudson.

1992. *Wagon, Chariot and Carriage. Symbol and Status in the History of Transport.* London: Thames and Hudson.

Pina, H. L. 1976. Cromlechs und Menhire bei Évora in Portugal, *Madrider Mitt.* 17, 9–20.

Pingel, V. 1992. *Die vorgeschichtlichen Goldfunde der Iberischen Halbinsel. Eine archäologiche Untersuchung zur Auswertung der Spektralanalysen.* Madrider Forschungen 17. Berlin: de Gruyter.

Piotrowski, W. 1995. Biskupin – the fortified settlement from the first millennium BC, *Quaternary Studies in Poland* 13, 89–99.

Pitt Rivers, [A. H.] 1888. *Excavations in Cranborne Chase near Rushmore on the Borders of Dorset and Wilts 1880–1888, II.* Printed privately.

Pittioni, R. 1951. Prehistoric copper-mining in Austria: problems and facts, *University of London Institute of Archaeology 7th Annual Report,* 16–43.

   1957. *Urzeitliche Bergbau auf Kupfererz und Spurenanalyse.* Archaeologia Austriaca, Supplement 1.

Pivovarová, Z. 1965. K problematike mohýl v lužickej kultúre na Slovensku, *Slovenská Archeológia* 13, 107–62.

Pleiner, R. 1980. Early iron metallurgy in Europe. In *The Coming of the Age of Iron,* eds. T. A. Wertime and J. D. Muhly, 375–416. New Haven and London: Yale University Press.

   1981. Die Wege des Eisens nach Europa. In *Frühes Eisen in Europa. Festschrift Walter Ulrich Guyan zu seinem 70. Geburtstag,* ed. R. Pleiner, 115–28. Schaffhausen: Verlag Peter Meili.

Pleinerová, I. 1960a. Únětické pohřby v rakvích, *Archeologické Rozhledy* 12, 49–50.

   1960b. Únětické pohřebiště a osada v Blšanech u Loun, *Památky Archeologické* 51, 488–526.

   1966. Únětická kultura v oblasti Krušnych hor a jejím sousedství I, *Památky Archeologické* 57, 339–458.

   1981. Zu einigen Sonderformen der Mehrbestattungen in der Aunjetitzer Kultur. In *Studien zur Bronzezeit. Festschrift für Wilhelm Albert v. Brunn,* ed. H. Lorenz, 349–62. Mainz: v. Zabern.

   1990. Les habitats et les maisons du bronze ancien en Bohème du nord-ouest. In *Colloque international de Lons-le-Saunier, 16–19 mai 1990,* 383–90.

Pleinerová, I. and Hrala, J. 1988. *Březno. Osada lidu knovízské kultury v severozápadních Čechách.* Louny: Okresní Muzeum.

Plesl, E. 1961. *Lužická kultura v severozápadních Čechách.* Prague: Czech Academy of Sciences.

   1988. K otázce kostrových pohřbů v období popelnicových polí. In *Antropofagie a pohřební ritus doby bronzové,* ed. M. Dočkalová, 211–19. Brno: Moravské Muzeum – Ústav Anthropos.

Polla, B. 1960. Birituelle Füzesabonyer Begräbnisstätte in Streda nad Bodrogom. In *Gräberfelder aus der älteren Bronzezeit in der Slowakei, I,* eds. B. Chropovský, M. Dušek. and B. Polla, 299–386. Archaeologica Slovaca Fontes 3. Bratislava: Academy of Sciences.

Pollak, M. 1986. Flussfunde aus der Donau bei Grein und den oberösterreichischen Zuflüssen der Donau, *Archaeologia Austriaca* 70, 1–85.

Pollard, A. M. and Heron, C. 1996. *Archaeological Chemistry.* Cambridge: Royal Society of Chemistry.

Poncelet, L. 1966. Le briquetage de la Seille, *Bull. Association des Amis de l'Archéologie Mosellane* 1966/4, 1–15.

Popham, M. R. 1984. *The Minoan Unexplored Mansion at Knossos.* London: British School of Archaeology at Athens/Thames and Hudson.

Powell, T. G. E. 1953. The gold ornament from Mold, Flintshire, north Wales, *Proc. Prehist. Soc.* 19, 161–79.

Prag, J. and Neave, R. 1997. *Making Faces: Using Forensic and Archaeological Evidence.* London: British Museum Press.

Pressmar, E. 1979. *Elchinger Kreuz, Ldkr. Ulm. Siedlungsgrabung mit urnenfelderzeitlichem Töpferofen.* Kataloge der Prähistorischen Staatssammlung 19. Kallmünz/Opf.: Lassleben.

Preuschen, E. 1965. Zum Problem früher Kupfererzverhüttung im Oberharz, *Neue Ausgrabungen und Forschungen in Niedersachsen* 2, 250–2.

Price, N. 1995. Houses and horses in the Swedish Bronze Age: recent excavations in the Mälar valley, *PAST* 20, 10–12.

Priego Fernandez del Campo, C. and Quero Castro, S. 1992. *El Ventorro, un poblado prehistorico de los albores de la metalurgica.* Estudios de Prehistoria y Arqueologia Madrileñas 8. Madrid: Museos Municipales del Ayuntamiento de Madrid.

Primas, M. 1977a. Untersuchungen zu den Bestattungssitten der ausgehenden Kupfer- und frühen Bronzezeit. Grabbau, Bestattungsformen und Beigabensitten im südlichen Mitteleuropa, *Bericht der Römisch-Germanischen Kommission* 58, 1–160.

    1977b. Die Bronzefunde vom Montlingerberg (Kanton St Gallen) – ein Beitrag zur Frage des prähistorischen Verkehrs. In *Festschrift zum 50jährigen Bestehen des Vorgeschichtlichen Seminars Marburg*, ed. O.-H. Frey, 107–27. Marburger Studien zur Vor- und Frühgeschichte 1. Gladenbach: Verlag Kempkes.

    1981. Erntemesser der jüngeren und späten Bronzezeit. In *Studien zur Bronzezeit. Festschrift für Wilhelm Albert v. Brunn*, ed. H. Lorenz, 363–74. Mainz: v. Zabern.

    1985. Tin objects in Bronze Age Europe. In *Studi di paletnologia in onore de Salvatore M. Puglisi*, 555–62. Rome: Università di Roma 'La Sapienza'.

    1986. *Die Sicheln in Mitteleuropa I (Österreich, Schweiz, Süddeutschland).* Prähistorische Bronzefunde XVIII, 2. Munich: Beck.

    1992. Velika Gruda, ein Grabhügel des 3. und 2. Jahrtausends v. Chr. in Montenegro, *Archäologisches Korrespondenzblatt* 22, 47–55.

    1996a. Frühes Silber. In *Studien zur Metallindustrie im Karpatenbecken und den benachbarten Regionen. Festschrift für Amália Mozsolics zum 85. Geburtstag*, 55–9. Budapest: Magyar Nemzeti Múzeum.

    1996b. *Velika Gruda I. Hügelgräber des frühen 3. Jahrtausends v. Chr. im Adriagebiet – Velika Gruda, Mala Gruda und ihr Kontext.* Universitätsforschungen zur prähistorischen Archäologie 32. Bonn: Habelt.

    1997. Bronze Age economy and ideology: central Europe in focus, *J. European Archaeology* 5/1, 115–30.

Priuli, A. 1983. *Incisioni rupestri nelle Alpi.* Ivrea: Priuli and Verlucca.

Pryor, F. 1980. *Excavation at Fengate, Peterborough, England: the Third Report.* Northants Archaeol. Soc., Monograph 1/Royal Ontario Museum, Archaeol. Monograph 6.

    1991. *Flag Fen: Prehistoric Fenland Centre.* London: Batsford/English Heritage.

Quast, D. 1992. Zwei Grabhügel der späten Urnenfelderzeit aus Illingen, Enzkreis, *Fundberichte aus Baden-Württemberg* 17/1, 307–26.

Quillfeldt, I. von 1995. *Die Vollgriffschwerter in Österreich und der Schweiz.* Prähistorische Bronzefunde IV, 11. Stuttgart: Franz Steiner.

Rackham, O. 1977. Neolithic woodland management in the Somerset Levels: Garvin's, Walton Heath and Rowland's Tracks, *Somerset Levels Papers 3*, 65–72.

1979. Neolithic woodland management in the Somerset Levels: Sweet Track, *Somerset Levels Papers 5*, 43–64.

Raddatz, K. 1978. Zum Grabraub in der frühen Bronzezeit und in der römischen Kaiserzeit. In *Zum Grabfrevel in vor- und frühgeschichtlicher Zeit. Untersuchungen zu Grabraub und 'Haugbrot' in Mittel- und Nordeuropa*, eds. H. Jankuhn, H. Nehlsen and H. Roth, 48–52. Abhandlungen der Akademie der Wissenschaften in Göttingen, Phil.-Hist. Klasse, 3rd series 113. Göttingen: Vandenhoeck and Ruprecht.

Raftery, B. 1971. Rathgall, Co. Wicklow; 1970 excavations, *Antiquity 45*, 296–8.

1990. *Trackways through Time*. Dublin: Headline Publishing.

1996. *Trackway Excavations in the Mountdillon Bogs, Co. Longford, 1985–1991*. Irish Archaeological Wetland Unit, Transactions 3. Dublin: Crannóg Publication (Department of Archaeology, University College).

Raftery, J. 1942. Knocknalappa crannóg, Co. Clare, *North Munster Antiqs. J. 3*, 53–72.

Rageth, J. 1974. Der Lago di Ledro im Trentino und seine Beziehungen zu den alpinen und mitteleuropäische Kulturen, *Bericht der Römisch-Germanischen Kommission 55*, 73–259.

1986. Die wichtigsten Resultate der Ausgrabungen in der bronzezeitlichen Siedlung auf dem Padnal bei Savognin (Oberhalbstein, GR), *Jahrbuch der schweizerischen Gesellschaft für Ur- und Frühgeschichte 69*, 63–103.

1997. Zur Bevölkerungszahl in der bronzezeitlichen Siedlung auf dem Padnal bei Savognin (Oberhalbstein, Graubünden). In *Demographie der Bronzezeit. Paläodemographie–Möglichkeiten und Grenzen*, ed. K.-F. Rittershofer, 97–104. Internationale Archäologie, 36. Espelkamp: Verlag Marie Leidorf.

Rahtz, P. and ApSimon, A. M. 1962. Excavations at Shearplace Hill, Sydling St Nicholas, Dorset, England, *Proc. Prehist. Soc. 28*, 289–328.

Raistrick, A. 1938. Prehistoric cultivations at Grassington, West Yorkshire, *Yorkshire Archaeol. J. 33*, 166–74.

Rajewski, Z. A. 1950. Budowle grodów kultury łużyckiej na półwyspie jeziora biskupińskiego w powiecie żnińskim (Les constructions des deux enceintes fortifées de civilisation lusacienne). In *III Sprawozdanie z prac wykopaliskowych w grodzie kultury łużyckiej w Biskupinie w powiecie żnińskim za lata 1938–1939 i 1946–1948*. ed. J. Kostrzewski, 239–85. Poznań: Polski Towarzystwo Prehistoryczny.

Randsborg, K. 1968. Von Periode II zu III, *Acta Archaeologica* (Copenhagen) 39, 1–142.

1974. Prehistoric populations and social regulation: the case of Early Bronze Age Denmark, *Homo 25*, 59–67.

1984 [1986]. A Bronze Age grave on Funen containing a metal worker's tools, *Acta Archaeologica* (Copenhagen) 55, 185–9.

1991. Historical implications. Chronological studies in European archaeology *c.* 2000–500 BC, *Acta Archaeologica* (Copenhagen) 62, 89–108.

1993. Kivik. Archaeology and iconography, *Acta Archaeologica* (Copenhagen) 64 /1, 1–147.

1995. *Hjortspring. Warfare and Sacrifice in Early Europe*. Aarhus: Aarhus University Press.

(ed.) 1996. *Absolute Chronology: Archaeological Europe 2500–500 BC. Acta Archaeologica* (Copenhagen) 67 (= *Acta Archaeologica Supplementa* 1). Copenhagen: Munksgaard.

Randsborg, K. and Nybo, C. 1984 [1986]. The coffin and the sun. Demography and ideology in Scandinavian prehistory, *Acta Archaeologica* (Copenhagen) 55, 161–84.

Rasmussen, M. 1992–3. Settlement structure and economic variation in the Early Bronze Age, *J. Danish Archaeology* 11, 87–107.

Rasmussen, M. and Adamsen, C. 1993. [The Bronze Age.] Settlement. In *Digging into the Past. 25 Years of Archaeology in Denmark*, eds. S. Hvass and B. Storgaard, 136–41. Aarhus: Royal Society of Northern Antiquaries/Jutland Archaeological Society.

Rast-Eicher, A. 1992a. Neolithische Textilien im Raum Zürich. In *Archaeological Textiles in Northern Europe*, Tidens Tand 5, eds. L. Bender Jørgensen and E. Munksgaard, Copenhagen, 9–19.

1992b. Die Entwicklung der Webstühle vom Neolithikum bis zum Mittelalter, *Helvetia Archaeologica* 23, 56–70.

RCHME 1975. *An Inventory of the Historical Monuments in the County of Dorset. 5. East Dorset*. London: HMSO.

Rees, S. E. 1979a. *Agricultural Implements in Prehistoric and Roman Britain*. Oxford: British Archaeological Reports 69.

1979b. Stone ard points from Orkney and Shetland, *Tools and Tillage* 3/4, 249–54.

Reinerth, H. 1928. *Die Wasserburg Buchau. Eine befestigte Inselsiedlung aus der Zeit 1100–800 v. Chr.* Führer zur Urgeschichte 6. Augsburg: Benno Filser.

Reinhard, J. 1992. Etoffes cordées et métiers à pierres, *Helvetia Archaeologica* 23, 51–5.

Reisenhauer, H. 1976. *Bronze- und urnenfelderzeitliche Siedlungsstellen im unteren Pegnitztal*. Abhandlungen der Naturhistorischen Gesellschaft Nürnberg 36.

Relations 1987. *Les Relations entre le Continent et les îles britanniques à l'âge du bronze. Actes du colloque de Lille*. Amiens: Revue Archéologique de Picardie, Supplement.

Rellini, U. 1916. La caverna di Latronico e il culto delle acque salutari nell'età del bronzo, *Monumenti Antichi* 24, 461–616.

Renfrew, A. C. 1967. The autonomy of the south-east European Copper Age, *Proc. Prehist. Soc.* 35, 12–47.

1968. Wessex without Mycenae, *Annual British School Athens* 63, 277–85.

1972. *The Emergence of Civilisation. The Cyclades and the Aegean in the Third Millennium BC*. London: Methuen.

1974. Beyond a subsistence economy: the evolution of social organisation in prehistoric Europe. In *Reconstructing Complex Societies: an Archaeological Colloquium*, ed. C. B. Moore, 69–95. Bull. American Schools of Oriental Research, Supplement 20.

1975. Trade as action at a distance: questions of integration and communication. In *Ancient Civilisation and Trade*, eds. J. A. Sabloff and C. C. Lamberg-Karlovsky, 1–60. Albuquerque: University of New Mexico Press.

1977. Alternative models for exchange and spatial distribution. In *Exchange Systems in Prehistory*, eds. T. K. Earle and J. E. Ericson, 71–90. London/Orlando: Academic Press.

1985. *The Archaeology of Cult. The Sanctuary at Phylakopi*. British School of Archaeology at Athens, Supplementary Volume 18. London: Thames and Hudson.

Reynolds, P. 1981. Deadstock and livestock. In *Farming Practice in British Prehistory*, ed. R. Mercer, 97–122. Edinburgh: Edinburgh University Press.

Richards, C. and Thomas, J. 1984. Ritual activity and structured deposition in later Neolithic Wessex. In *Neolithic Studies: a Review of some Current Research*, eds. R. Bradley and J. Gardiner, 189–218. Oxford: British Archaeological Reports 133.

Richards, J. 1990. *The Stonehenge Environs Project*. London: English Heritage Archaeological Report 16.

Riedel, A. and Rizzi, J. 1995. The Middle Bronze Age fauna of Albanbühel, *Padusa Quaderni* 1 (Atti del I° Convegno Nazionale di Archeozoologia, Rovigo 1993), 171–83.

Riehm, K. 1954. Vorgeschichtliche Salzgewinnung an Saale und Seille, *Jahresschrift für mitteldeutsche Vorgeschichte* 38, 112–56.

1961. Prehistoric salt-boiling, *Antiquity* 35, 181–91.

1962. Werkanlagen und Arbeitsgeräte urgeschichtlicher Salzsieder, *Germania* 40, 360–400.

Říhovský, J. 1958. Žárový hrob z Velatic I a jeho postavení ve vývoji velatické kultury, *Památky Archeologické* 49/1, 67–118.

1982. Hospodářský a společenský život velatické osady v Lovčičkách, *Památky Archeologické* 73, 5–56 (also published as *Lovčičky, jung-bronzezeitliche Siedlung in Mähren*. Materialien zur Allgemeinen und Vergleichenden Archäologie 15. Munich: Beck).

Riquet, R. 1970. *Anthropologie du Néolithique et du Bronze ancien*. Poitiers: SFIL/Texier.

Rittershofer, K.-F. 1987. Grabraub in der Bronzezeit, *Bericht der Römisch-Germanischen Kommission* 68, 5–23.

(ed.) 1997. *Demographie der Bronzezeit. Paläodemographie – Möglichkeiten und Grenzen*. Internationale Archäologie 36. Espelkamp: Verlag Marie Leidorf.

Rønne, P. 1989a. Early Bronze Age spiral ornament – the technical background, *J. Danish Archaeology* 8, 126–43.

1989b. Fund auf aeldre bronzealders keramik og smedevaerktøj fra Ordrup i Nordvestsjaelland, *Aarbøger* 1989, 99–114.

Robb, J. 1994. Gender contradictions, moral coalitions and inequality in prehistoric Italy, *J. European Archaeology* 2/1, 20–49.

Roberts, O. T. P. 1992. The Brigg 'raft' reassessed as a round bilge Bronze Age boat, *Int. J. Nautical Archaeology* 21/3, 245–58.

Robinson, M. and Shimwell, D. 1996. Boating in the Bronze Age – two logboats from Co. Mayo, *Archaeology Ireland* 10/1, 12–13.

Rodanés Vicente, J. M. 1992. Del Calcolítico al Bronce final en Aragón. Problemas y perspectivas. In *Aragón/Litoral mediterráneo: intercambios culturales durante la prehistoria. En Homenaje a Juan Maluquer de Motes*, ed. P. Utrilla Miranda, 491–513. Zaragoza: Institución Fernando el Católico.

Rook, E. 1980. Osadnictwo neolityczne w jaskiniach Wyżyny Krakowsko-Częstochowskiej, *Materialy Archeologiczne* 20, 5–130.

Röschmann, J. 1952. Zwei Schalensteine in der Gemarkung Deutsch-Nienhof, Kr. Rendsburg, *Offa* 11, 1–2.

1962. Schalensteine, *Offa* 19, 133–8.

Ross, A. 1968. Shafts, pits and wells – sanctuaries of the Belgic Britons? In *Studies in Ancient Europe. Essays in Honour of Stuart Piggott*, eds. J. M. Coles and D. D. A. Simpson, 255–85. Leicester: Leicester University Press.

Rossi, M., Gattiglia, A., di Maio, M., Peradotto, M. and Vaschetti, L. 1989. I petroglifi della bassa Valleorco tra Salto (Cuorgné) e Santa Maria di Doblazio (Pont Canavese), *Antropologia Alpina Annual Report* 1, 27–220.

Rothenberg, B. 1972. *Timna, Valley of the Biblical Copper Mines*. London: Thames and Hudson.

　1985. Copper smelting furnaces in the Arabah, Israel: the archaeological evidence. In *Furnaces and Smelting Technology in Antiquity*, eds. P. T. Craddock and M. J. Hughes, 123–50. London: British Museum Occasional Paper 48.

　(ed.) 1990. *The Ancient Metallurgy of Copper: Archaeology – Experiment – Theory*. Researches in the Arabah 1959–1984, 2. London: Institute for Archaeo-Metallurgical Studies/Institute of Archaeology.

Rothenberg, B. and Blanco-Freijeiro, A. 1981. *Studies in Ancient Mining and Metallurgy in South-West Spain. Explorations and Excavations in the Province of Huelva*. Metal in History 1. London: Institute for Archaeo-Metallurgical Studies.

Roudil, J.-L. and Soulier, M. 1976. La grotte du Hasard à Tharaux (Gard). I. La salle sépulchrale IG et le commerce de l'ambre en Languedoc-oriental, *Gallia Préhistoire* 19/1, 173–200.

Rovira, S. 1995. Estudio arqueometalurgico del deposito de la ría de Huelva. In *Ritos de paso y puntos de paso. La ría de Huelva en el mundo del Bronce final europeo*, ed. M. Ruiz-Gálvez Priego, 33–57. Complutum Extra, 5. Madrid: Universidad Complutense.

Rowlands, M. 1971. The archaeological interpretation of prehistoric metalworking, *World Archaeology* 3/2, 210–24.

　1976. *The Production and Distribution of Metalwork in the Middle Bronze Age in Southern Britain*. Oxford: British Archaeological Reports 31.

Rowlands, M., Larsen M. T. and Kristiansen, K. (eds.) 1987. *Centre and Periphery in the Ancient World*. Cambridge: Cambridge University Press.

Rowley-Conwy, P. 1978 [1979]. Forkullet korn fra Lindebjerg. En boplats fra aeldre bronzealder, *Kuml* 1978, 159–71.

　1982–3 [1984]. Bronzealderkorn fra Voldtofte, *Kuml* 1982–3, 139–52.

　1984. The Egehøj cereals. Bread wheat (*Triticum aestivum* s.L.) in the Danish Early Bronze Age, *J. Danish Archaeology* 3, 104–10.

　1987. The interpretation of ard-marks, *Antiquity* 61, 263–6.

Ruckdeschel, W. 1968. Geschlechtsdifferenzierte Bestattungssitten in frühbronzezeitlichen Gräbern Südbayerns, *Bayerische Vorgeschichtsblätter* 33, 18–44.

　1978. *Die frühbronzezeitlichen Gräber Südbayerns. Ein Beitrag zur Kenntnis der Straubinger Kultur*. Antiquitas ser. 2, 11. Bonn: Habelt.

Ruiz-Gálvez Priego, M. 1995. El significado de la ría de Huelva en el contexto de las relaciones de intercambio y de las transformaciones producidas en la transicion Bronce final/edad del hierro. In *Ritos de paso y puntos de paso. La ría de Huelva en el mundo del Bronce final europeo*, ed. M. Ruiz-Gálvez Priego, 129–55. Complutum Extra, 5. Madrid: Universidad Complutense.

Ruoff, E. 1981. Stein- und bronzezeitliche Textilfunde aus dem Kanton Zürich, *Helvetia Archaeologica* 12, 252–64.

Ruoff, U. 1984. Zug-'Im Sumpf' und Greifensee-'Böschen': Zwei Siedlungen mit Blockbaukonstruktionen, *Helvetia Archaeologica* 15 (57–60/2), 77–82.

1987. Die frühbronzezeitliche Ufersiedlung in Meilen-Schellen, Kanton Zürich. Tauchausgrabungen 1985, *Jahrbuch der schweizerischen Gesellschaft für Ur- und Frühgeschichte* 70, 51–64.

1992. The *Pfahlbauland* exhibition, Zurich 1990. In *The Wetland Revolution in Prehistory*, ed. B. Coles, 135–46. WARP Occasional Paper 6. Exeter: Prehistoric Society and WARP.

Ruoff, U. and Suter, P. 1990. Erste Tauchsondierungen in der Ufersiedlung Sipplingen-Osthafen am Überlinger See (Kr. Konstanz). In *Siedlungsarchäologie im Alpenvorland II*, 279–94. Stuttgart: Theiss.

Russell, M. 1996. Problems of phasing: a reconstruction of the Black Patch Middle Bronze Age 'nucleated village', *Oxford J. Archaeology* 15/1, 33–8.

Rusu, M. 1981. Bemerkungen zu den grossen Werkstätten- und Giessereifunden aus Siebenbürgen. In *Studien zur Bronzezeit. Festschrift für Wilhelm Albert v. Brunn*, ed. H. Lorenz, 375–402. Mainz: v. Zabern.

Rychner, V. 1979. *Auvernier 1–2. L'âge du bronze final à Auvernier. Typologie et chronologie des anciennes collections conservées en Suisse*. Cahiers d'archéologie romande 15–16. Lausanne: Bibliothèque historique vaudoise.

1987. *Auvernier 6. Auvernier 1968–1975: le mobilier métallique du Bronze final. Formes et techniques*. Cahiers d'archéologie romande 37. Lausanne: Bibliothèque historique vaudoise.

Rychner-Faraggi, A.-M. 1993. *Hauterive-Champréveyres. 9. Métal et parure au Bronze final*. Archéologie neuchâteloise 17. Neuchâtel: Musée cantonal d'archéologie.

Rynne, E. 1992. Dún Aengus and some similar ceremonial centres. In *Decantations. A Tribute to Maurice Craig*, ed. A. Bernelle, 196–207. Dublin: Lilliput.

Rysiewska, T. 1980. La structure patriarchale des clans comme type hypothétique de la structure sociale des groupes humains dans la culture lusacienne. Essai de vérification de l'hypothèse d'après la nécropole de Przeczyce, *Archaeologia Polona* 19, 7–48.

Säflund, G. 1939. *Le Terremare delle Provincie di Modena, Reggio Emilia, Parma, Piacenza*. Skrifter utgivna av Svenska Institutet i Rom, 7. Lund: Gleerup / Leipzig: Harrassowitz.

Säfvestad, U. 1993. Högen och bygden – territoriell organisation i skånsk bronsålder. In *Bronsålderns gravhögar. Rapport från ett sympósium i Lund 15.XI–16.XI 1991*, ed. L. Larsson, 161–9. University of Lund, Institute of Archaeology Report Series 48.

Sagan, E. 1974. *Cannibalism: Human Aggression and Cultural Form*. New York: Harper and Row.

Sahlins, M. D. 1968. *Tribesmen*. Englewood Cliffs: Prentice-Hall.

Salaš, M. 1990. To the problem of human skeletal remains from the Late Bronze Age in Cézavy near Blučina, *Anthropologie* 28/2–3, 221–9.

Šaldová, V. 1981. *Westböhmen in der Spätbronzezeit. Befestigte Höhensiedlungen Okrouhlé Hradiště*. Prague: Archaeological Institute.

Sandars, N. K. 1957. *Bronze Age Cultures in France. The Later Phases from the Thirteenth to the Seventh Century BC*. Cambridge: Cambridge University Press.

Sandberg, B. 1973. 15:130 Arendal Göteborg, röse bronsålder, *Fynd Rapporter 1973*, 239–57.

Santos Júnior, J. R. dos 1942. *Arte rupestre. Comunicação apresentada ao i Congreso do Mundo Portugues*. Oporto [no publisher stated].

Sarnowska, W. 1969. *Kultura unietycka w Polsce, I*. Wrocław: Muzeum Archeologiczne.

Sauter, M.-R. 1976. *Switzerland from Earliest Times to the Roman Conquest*. London: Thames and Hudson.

Saxe, A. A 1970. Social dimensions of mortuary practices. Unpublished Ph.D. dissertation, Ann Arbor, University of Michigan.

Schaeffer, C. F. A. 1926. *Les Tertres funéraires préhistoriques dans la forêt de Haguenau. I. Les Tumulus de l'âge du bronze*. Haguenau: Imprimerie de la Ville.

Schauberger, O. 1960. *Ein Rekonstruktionsversuch der prähistorischen Grubenbaue im Hallstätter Salzberg*. Prähistorische Forschungen 5. Vienna: Anthropologische Gesellschaft.

Schauer, P. 1971. *Die Schwerter in Süddeutschland, Österreich und der Schweiz I (Griffplatten-, Griffangel- und Griffzungenschwerter)*. Prähistorische Bronzefunde IV, 2. Munich: Beck.

    1978. Der urnenfelderzeitlichen Bronzepanzer von Fillinges, Dép. Haute-Savoie, Frankreich, *Jahrbuch des Römisch-Germanischen Zentralmuseums Mainz* 25, 92–130.

    1980. Der Rundschild der Bronze- und frühen Eisenzeit, *Jahrbuch des römisch-germanischen Zentralmuseums Mainz* 27, 196–248.

    1981. Urnenfelderzeitliche Opferplätze in Höhlen und Felsspalten. In *Studien zur Bronzezeit. Festschrift für Wilhelm Albert v. Brunn*, ed. H. Lorenz, 403–18. Mainz: v. Zabern.

    1982. Die Beinschienen der späten Bronze- und frühen Eisenzeit, *Jahrbuch des Römisch-Germanischen Zentralmuseums Mainz* 29, 100–55.

    1986. *Die Goldblechkegel der Bronzezeit. Ein Beitrag zur Kulturverbindung zwischen Orient und Mitteleuropa*. Römisch-Germanisches Zentralmuseum Mainz, Monograph 8. Bonn: Habelt.

    1996. Naturheilige Plätze, Opferstätten, Deponierungsfunde und Symbolgut der jüngeren Bronzezeit Süddeutschlands. In *Archäologische Forschungen zum Kultgeschehen in der jüngeren Bronzezeit und frühen Eisenzeit Alteuropas*, ed. C. Huth, 381–416. Regensburger Beiträge zur prähistorischen Archäologie 2. Regensburg: Universitätsverlag (Bonn: Habelt).

Schierer, I. 1987. Ein Webstuhlbefund aus Gars-Thunau. Rekonstruktionsversuch und Funktionsanalyse, *Archaeologia Austriaca* 71, 29–87.

Schlabow, K. 1937. *Germanische Tuchmacher der Bronzezeit*. Neumünster: Wachholtz.

    1959. Beiträge zur Erforschung der jungsteinzeitlichen und bronzezeitlichen Gewebetechnik Mitteldeutschlands, *Jahresschrift für mitteldeutsche Vorgeschichte* 43, 101–26.

    1976. *Textilfunde der Eisenzeit in Norddeutschland*. Neumünster: Wachholtz.

Schlichtherle, H. 1990. Die Sondagen 1973–1978 in den Ufersiedlungen Hornstaad-Hörnle I. Befunde und Funde zum frühen Jungneolithikum am westlichen Bodensee. *Siedlungsarchäologie im Alpenvorland I. Die Sondagen 1973–1978 in den Ufersiedlungen Hornstaad-Hörnle I.* Forschungen und Berichte zur Vor- und Frühgeschichte in Baden-Württemberg, 36. Stuttgart: K. Theiss.

Schmidt, H. 1915. Die Luren von Daberkow, Kr. Demmin. Ein Beitrag zur

Geschichte von Formen und Technik in der Bronzezeit, *Prähistorische Zeitschrift* 7, 85–105.

Schmidt, P. K. 1978–9. Beile als Ritualobjekte in der Altbronzezeit der Britischen Inseln, *Jahresbericht des Institutes für Vorgeschichte der Universität Frankfurt a.M.* 1978–9, 311–20.

Schneider, J. 1977. Was there a pre-capitalist world system? *Peasant Studies* 6, 20–29 (also in C. Chase-Dunn and T. D. Hall (eds.) 1991, *Core/Periphery Relations in Precapitalist Worlds*, 45–66. Boulder: Westview Press).

Schöbel, G. S. 1987. Ein Flötenfragment aus der spätbronzezeitlichen Siedlung Hagnau-Burg, Bodenseekreis, *Archäologische Nachrichten aus Baden* 38–9, 84–7.

Schönbäck, B. 1952. Bronsåldershus i Uppland, *Tor* 2 (1949–51), 23–45.

Schopper, F. 1993. Zur Frage der Trachtkontinuität von der späten Urnenfelder- zur Hallstattzeit in Bayern am Beispiel der Schaukelringe, *Acta Praehistorica et Archaeologica* 25, 137–52.

Schou Jørgensen, M. 1982. To jyske bronzealderveje – og en ny metode til arkæologisk opmåling, *Nationalmuseets Arbejdsmark* 1982, 142–52.
    1993. [The Bronze Age] Roads. In *Digging into the Past. 25 Years of Archaeology in Denmark*, eds. S. Hvass and B. Storgaard, 144. Aarhus: Royal Society of Northern Antiquaries/Jutland Archaeological Society.

Schubart, H. 1961. Jungbronzezeitliche Burgwälle in Mecklenburg, *Prähistorische Zeitschrift* 34, 143–75.

Schuchhardt, C. 1914. *Der Goldfund von Messingwerk bei Eberswalde.* Berlin: Verlag für Kunstwissenschaft.

Schultze-Motel, J. 1979. Die Anbaugeschichte des Leindotters, *Camelina sativa* (L.) Crantz. In *Festschrift Maria Hopf zum 65. Geburtstag*, ed. U. Körber-Grohne *(Archaeo-Physika 8)*, 267–81. Cologne: Rheinland-Verlag (Bonn: Habelt).

Schumacher-Matthäus, G. 1985. *Studien zu bronzezeitlichen Schmucktrachten im Karpatenbecken. Ein Beitrag zur Deutung der Hortfunde im Karpatenbecken.* Marburger Studien zur Vor- und Frühgeschichte 6. Mainz: Zabern.

Schwantes, G. 1939. *Die Vorgeschichte Schleswig-Holsteins (Stein- und Bronzezeit).* Neumünster: Wachholtz.

Schwarz, W. 1996. Bronzezeitliche Hausgrundrisse von Hesel im Landkreis Leer, *Die Kunde* 47, 21–50.

Schweingruber, F. H. 1976. *Prähistorisches Holz: die Bedeutung von Holzfunden aus Mitteleuropa für die Lösung archäologischer und vegeta-tionskundlicher Probleme.* Academia Helvetica 2. Bern: Haupt.

Schwidetzky, I. and Rösing, F.W. 1989. Vergleichend-statistische Untersuchungen zur Anthropologie von Neolithikum und Bronzezeit, *Homo* 40, 4–45.

Šebesta, G. 1988/1989. La via del rame, *Economia Trentina* 37/1, 43–94; 37/4, 43–91; 38/2, 58–103.

Service, E. R. 1962/1975. *Primitive Social Organization, an Evolutionary Perspective.* New York: Random House.

Shee, E. A. 1968. Some examples of rock-art from Co. Cork, *J. Cork Historical and Archaeol. Soc.* 73, 144–51.

Shell, C. n.d. [1980]. The early exploitation of tin deposits in south-west England. In *The Origins of Metallurgy in Atlantic Europe* (Proc. Fifth Atlantic Colloquium, Dublin 1978), ed. M. Ryan, 251–63.

Shennan, S. 1975. The social organisation at Branč, *Antiquity* 49, 279–88.

1982. From minimal to moderate ranking. In *Ranking, Resource and Exchange. Aspects of the Archaeology of Early European Society*, eds. C. Renfrew and S. Shennan, 27–32. Cambridge: Cambridge University Press.

Shennan, S. J. 1986. Central Europe in the third millennium BC: an evolutionary trajectory for the beginning of the European Bronze Age, *J. Anthropological Archaeology* 5, 115–46.

1993. Commodities, transactions and growth in the central European Early Bronze Age, *J. European Archaeology* 1/2, 59–72; also in *Festschrift zum 50 jährigen Bestehen des Institutes für Ur- und Frühgeschichte der Leopold-Franzen Universität Innsbruck*, eds. A. Lippert and K. Spindler, 535–42. Universitätsforschungen zur prähistorischen Archäologie 8 (1992). Bonn: Habelt.

1995. *Bronze Age Copper Producers of the Eastern Alps. Excavations at St Veit-Klinglberg*. Universitätsforschungen zur prähistorischen Archäologie 27. Bonn: Habelt.

Shepherd, I. A. G. 1995. The Sculptor's Cave, Covesea, Moray: from Bronze Age ossuary to Pictish shrine? *Proc. Soc. Antiqs Scotland* 125, 1194–5.

Sheridan, A. 1992. A longbow from Rotten Bottom, Dumfriesshire, Scotland, *NewsWARP* 12, 13–15.

1996. The oldest bow ... and other objects, *Current Archaeology* 149, 188–90.

Sherratt, A. G. 1993a. What would a Bronze Age world system look like? Relations between temperate Europe and the Mediterranean in later prehistory, *J. European Archaeology* 1/2, 1–57.

1993b. 'Who are you calling peripheral?' Dependence and independence in European prehistory. In *Trade and Exchange in Prehistoric Europe*, eds. C. Scarre and F. Healy, 245–55. Oxford: Oxbow Monograph 33.

Shilov, V. P. 1959a. O drevney metallurgii i metalloobrabotke v nizhnem povolzh'e, *Materialy i issledovaniya po Arkheologii SSSR* 60 (*Pamyatniki nizhnego povolzh'ya 1. Itogi rabot Stalingradskoy arkheologicheskoy ekspedicii*, ed. E. I. Krupnov), 11–38.

1959b. Kalinovskij kurganniy mogil'nik, *Materialy i issledovaniya po Arkheologii SSSR* 60 (*Pamyatniki nizhnego povolzh'ya 1. Itogi rabot Stalingradskoy arkheologicheskoy ekspedicii*, ed. E. I. Krupnov), 323–523.

Shishlina, N. I. 1997. The bow and arrow of the Eurasian steppe Bronze Age nomads, *J. European Archaeology* 5/2, 53–66.

Shramko, B. A. 1964. Drevniy derevyanniy plug iz sergeevskogo torfyanika, *Sovietskaya Arkheologiya* 1964/4, 84–100.

1971. Der Hakenpflug der Bronzezeit in der Ukraine, *Tools and Tillage* 1/4, 223–4.

1992. Tilling implements of south eastern Europe in the Bronze Age and Early Iron Age, *Tools and Tillage* 7/1, 48–64.

Siemoneit, B. 1996. Das Kind in der Bronzezeit. Archäologische und anthropologische Befunde aus Niedersachsen, *Die Kunde* 47, 341–71.

Simek, R. 1993. *Dictionary of Northern Mythology*. Cambridge: D. S. Brewer.

Simmons, I. and Tooley, M. (eds.) 1981. *The Environment in British Prehistory*. London: Duckworth.

Simon, K. 1982. Zum urnenfelder- und hallstattzeitlichen Burgenbau in Thüringen. In *Beiträge zum bronzezeitlichen Burgenbau in Mitteleuropa*, 355–62. Berlin: Zentralinstitut für Alte Geschichte und Archäologie; Nitra: Archeologický Ústav Slovenskej Akadémie Vied.

1992. Ein Schmelzofen der späten Bronzezeit aus dem sächsischen Vogtland, *Arbeits- und Forschungsberichte zur sächsischen Bodendenkmalpflege* 35, 51–82.

Simpson, W. G. 1976. A barrow cemetery of the second millennium BC at Tallington, Lincolnshire, *Proc. Prehist. Soc.* 42, 215–39.

Siracusano, G. 1995. La fauna del Bronzo tardo del sito stratificato di Coppa Nevigata, *Padusa Quaderni* 1 (Atti del I° Convegno Nazionale di Archeozoologia, Rovigo 1993), 185–91.

Siret, H. and L. 1887. *Les Premiers Ages du métal dans le sud-est de l'Espagne.* Antwerp: privately published (translated as *Las primeras edades del metal en el sudeste de España*, Barcelona 1890).

Skeates, R. and Whitehouse, R. (eds) 1994. *Radiocarbon Dating and Italian Prehistory.* Accordia Specialist Studies on Italy, 3/Archaeological Monographs of the British School at Rome, 8. London: British School at Rome / Accordia Research Centre.

Skjöldebrand, M. 1995. On variations in Bronze Age social and economic structure in a homogeneous area, *J. European Archaeology* 3/1, 91–104.

Sklenář, K. and Matoušek, K. 1994. *Die Höhlenbesiedlung des Böhmischen Karstes, vom Neolithikum bis zum Mittelalter.* Fontes Archaeologici Pragenses 20. Prague: National Museum.

Skutil, J. 1965. Vorgeschichtliche und jüngere Höhlenbesiedlung im Mährischen Karst, *Die Höhle* 16, 33–8.

Slaski, J. 1950. Łużyckie wyroby drewniane z Biskupina. In *III Sprawozdanie z prac wykopaliskowych w grodzie kultury łużyckiej w Biskupinie w powiecie żnińskim za lata 1938–1939 i 1946–1948.* ed. J. Kostrzewski, 160–71. Poznań: Polski Towarzystwo Prehistoryczny.

Smith, C. (ed.) 1979. *Fisherwick. The Reconstruction of an Iron Age Landscape.* Oxford: British Archaeological Reports 61.

Smith, K., Coppen, J., Wainwright, G. J. and Beckett, S. 1981. The Shaugh Moor project: third report – settlement and environmental investigations, *Proc. Prehist. Soc.* 47, 205–73.

Smrčka, V., Horn, V., Salaš, M. and Loosová, J. 1988. Známky antropofagie a anémie na Blučině (Jižní Morava) ve starší době bronzové (předběžné sdělení). In *Antropofagie a pohřební ritus doby bronzové*, ed. M. Dočkalová, 51–9. Brno: Moravské Muzeum – Ústav Anthropos.

Snagge, T. W. 1873. Some account of ancient oaken coffins discovered on the lands adjoining Featherstone Castle, near Haltwhistle, Northumberland, *Archaeologia* 44, 8–16.

Snodgrass, A. 1971. The first European body-armour. In *The European Community in Later Prehistory*, eds. J. Boardman, M. A. Brown and T. G. E. Powell, 31–50. London: Routledge and Kegan Paul.

Sobrino Buhigas, R. 1935. *Corpus Petroglyphorum Gallaeciae.* Santiago/Madrid: Seminario de Estudios Galegos.

Sofaer Derevenski, J. 1994. Where are the children? Accessing children in the past, *Archaeol. Review from Cambridge* 13/2, 7–20.

Sognnes, K. 1992. The role of rock art in the Bronze Age and Early Iron Age in Trøndelag, Norway, *Acta Archaeologica* (Copenhagen) 63, 157–88.

Soler García, J. M. 1965. *El tesoro de Villena.* Excavaciones Arqueológicas en España 36. Madrid: Ministerio de Educacion Nacional.

Sommerfeld, C 1994. *Gerätegeld Sichel. Studien zur monetären Struktur bronzezeitlicher Horte im nördlichen Mitteleuropa.* Vorgeschichtliche Forschungen, 19. Berlin/New York: de Gruyter.

Soroceanu, T. 1975. Die Bedeutung des Gräberfeldes von Mokrin für die relative Chronologie der frühen Bronzezeit im Banat, *Prähistorische Zeitschrift* 50, 161–79.

Soudský, B. 1953. Únětická osada v Postoloprtech, *Archeologické Rozhledy* 5, 308–18.

Speck, J. 1954. Die Ausgrabungen in der spätbronzezeitlichen Siedlung Zug-Sumpf. In *Das Pfahlbauproblem*, 275–334. Schaffhausen: Schweizerische Gesellschaft für Urgeschichte.

Speitel, E. 1991. Das bronzezeitliche Hügelgräberfeld von Solberg bei Auleben, Kr. Nordhausen, *Alt-Thüringen* 26, 59–121.

Sperber, L. 1987. *Untersuchungen zur Chronologie der Urnenfelderkultur im nördlichen Alpenvorland von der Schweiz bis Oberösterreich.* Antiquitas ser. 3, 29. Bonn: Habelt.

1992. Bemerkungen zur sozialen Bewertung von goldenem Trachtschmuck und Schwert in der Urnenfelderkultur, *Archäologisches Korrespondenzblatt* 22, 63–77.

Spindler, K. 1994. *The Man in the Ice. The Preserved Body of a Neolithic Man Reveals the Secrets of the Stone Age.* London: Phoenix.

Spratt, D. A. 1989. *Linear Earthworks of the Tabular Hills, Northeast Yorkshire.* Sheffield: Department of Archaeology and Prehistory.

(ed.) 1993. *Prehistoric and Roman Archaeology of North-East Yorkshire.* Oxford: British Archaeological Reports 104/York: Council for British Archaeology Research Report 87.

Sprockhoff, E. 1930. *Zur Handelsgeschichte der germanischen Bronzezeit.* Vorgeschichtliche Forschungen 7. Berlin: de Gruyter.

1931. *Die germanischen Griffzungenschwerter.* Römisch-Germanische Forschungen 5. Berlin/Leipzig: de Gruyter.

1934. *Die germanischen Vollgriffschwerter der jüngeren Bronzezeit.* Römisch-Germanische Forschungen 9. Berlin/Leipzig: de Gruyter.

1955. Das bronzene Zierband von Kronshagen bei Kiel. Eine Ornamentstudie zur Vorgeschichte der Vogelsonnenbarke, *Offa* 14.

Stadelmann, J. 1980. Der Runde Berg bei Urach, eine bronze- und urnen-felderzeitliche Höhensiedlung, *Archäologisches Korrespondenzblatt* 10, 33–8.

Stahlhofen, H. 1978. Eine spätbronzezeitliche Webstuhlgrube in Wallwitz, Kr. Burg, *Ausgrabungen und Funde* 23, 179–83.

Stanczik, I. 1980. Az 1973–74. évi Tószegi ásatások / Die Ausgrabungen von Tószeg in der Jahren 1973–74, *A Szolnok Megyei Múzeumok Évkönyve* 1979–80, 63–81.

1982. Befestigungs- und Siedlungssystem von Jászdózsa-Kápolnahalom in der Periode der Hatvan-Kultur. In *Beiträge zum bronzezeitlichen Burgenbau in Mitteleuropa*, 377–88. Berlin: Zentralinstitut für Alte Geschichte und Archäologie; Nitra: Archeologický Ústav Slovenskej Akadémie Vied.

Stanczik, I. and Tárnoki, J. 1992. Jászdózsa-Kápolnahalom. In *Bronzezeit in Ungarn*, 120–7.

Stauffer-Isenring, L. 1983. *Die Siedlungsreste von Scuol-Munt Baselgia (Unterengadin GR). Ein Beitrag zur inneralpinen Bronze- und Eisenzeit.* Antiqua 9. Basel: Schweizerische Gesellschaft für Ur- und Frühgeschichte.

Stead, I. M. 1991. The Snettisham Treasure: excavations in 1990, *Antiquity* 65, 447–64.

Stech, T. and Pigott, V. C. 1986. The metals trade in southwest Asia in the third millennium BC, *Iraq* 48, 39–64.

Steensberg, A. 1943. *Ancient Harvesting Implements. A Study in Archaeology and Human Geography*. Copenhagen: Bianco Lunos Bogtrykkeri.

Stein, F. 1968. Beobachtungen zu Tracht- und Bestattungssitten der früh-bronzezeitlichen Bevölkerung von Gemeinlebarn, *Bericht der Römisch-Germanischen Kommission* 49, 1–40.

  1976. *Bronzezeitliche Hortfunde in Süddeutschland. Beiträge zur Interpretation einer Quellengattung*. Saarbrücker Beiträge zur Altertumskunde 23. Bonn: Habelt.

Steinhauser, R. and Primas, M. 1987. Der Bernsteinfund vom Montlingerberg (Kt. St. Gallen, Schweiz), *Germania* 65, 203–14.

Stenberger, M. 1977. *Vorgeschichte Schwedens*. Nordische Vorzeit, IV. Neumünster: Karl Wachholtz.

Steuer, H. 1982. *Frühgeschichtliche Sozialstrukturen in Mitteleuropa. Eine Analyse der Auswertungsmethoden des archäologischen Quellenmaterials*. Abhandlungen der Akademie der Wissenschaften in Göttingen, Phil.-Hist. Klasse, 3rd series 128. Göttingen: Vandenhoeck and Ruprecht.

Stevenson, J. B. 1993. Cup-and-ring markings at Ballochmyle, Ayrshire, *Glasgow Archaeol. J.* 18, 33–40.

Stig Sørensen, M. L. 1991. The construction of gender through appearance. In *The Archaeology of Gender*, eds. D. Walde and N. D. Willows, 121–9. Chacmool: Archaeol. Assoc. University Calgary.

  1992. Landscape attitudes in the Bronze Age: the Als project, *Cambridge Archaeol. J.* 2/1, 130–6.

  1997. Reading dress: the construction of social categories and identities in Bronze Age Europe, *J. European Archaeology* 5/1, 93–114.

Stjernquist, B. 1961. *Simris II. Bronze Age Problems in the Light of the Simris Excavation*. Acta Archaeologica Lundensia, series in 4°, 5. Bonn: Habelt/Lund: Gleerup.

  1962–3. Präliminarien zu einer Untersuchung von Opferfunden. Begriffsbestimmung und Theoriebildung, *Meddelanden från Lunds Universitets Historiska Museum* 1962–3, 5–64.

  1967a. *Ciste a cordoni (Rippenzisten). Produktion – Funktion – Diffusion*. Acta Archaeologica Lundensia, series in 4°, 6. Bonn: Habelt/Lund: Gleerup.

  1967b. *Models of Commercial Diffusion in Prehistoric Times*. Scripta Minora 1965–6, 2. Lund: Gleerup.

  1969. *Beiträge zum Studium von bronzezeitlichen Siedlungen*. Acta Archaeologica Lundensia, series in 8°, 8. Bonn: Habelt/Lund: Gleerup.

Stocker, E. 1976. *Die grosse Zeit der Buchauer Ausgrabungen*. Bad Buchau: Verlag A. Sandmeier.

Stocký, A. 1928. *Čechy v době bronzové*. Prague: Jan Štenc.

Stone, J. F. S. 1941. The Deverel–Rimbury settlement on Thorny Down, Winterbourne Gummer, south Wilts., *Proc. Prehist. Soc.* 7, 114–33.

Stone, J. F. S. and Thomas, L. C. 1956. The use and distribution of faience in the ancient East and prehistoric Europe, *Proc. Prehist. Soc.* 22, 37–84.

Storti, C. 1990–1. Esame delle scorie del forno di fusione de 'La Vela' di Valbusa (Trentino), *Sibrium* 21, 349–61.

Stroh, A. 1955. Neue Baggerfunde aus der Donau bei Regensburg, *Germania* 33, 407–10.

1988. Hausdarstellungen auf Gefässen aus dem vorgeschichtlichen Gräberfeld Schirndorf, *Bayerische Vorgeschichtsblätter* 53, 263–7.

Strömberg, M. 1954. Bronzezeitliche Wohnplätze in Schonen, *Meddelanden från Lunds Universitets Historiska Museum* 1954, 295–380.

1961. Die bronzezeitlichen Schiffssetzungen im Norden, *Meddelanden från Lunds Universitets Historiska Museum* 1961, 82–106.

1962–3. Kultische Steinsetzungen in Schonen, *Meddelanden från Lunds Universitets Historiska Museum* 1962–3, 148–85.

1973–4. Untersuchungen zur Bronzezeit in Südostschonen. Probleme um die Besiedlung, *Meddelanden från Lunds Universitets Historiska Museum* 1973–74, 101–68.

1975. *Studien zu einem Gräberfeld in Löderup (Jungneolithikum bis römische Kaiserzeit). Grabsitte – Kontinuität – Sozialstruktur.* Acta Archaeologica Lundensia, Series in 8°, 10. Bonn: Habelt/Lund: Gleerup.

Struve, K. W. 1954. Der erste Grundriss eines bronzezeitlichen Hauses von Norddorf auf Amrum, *Offa* 13, 35–40.

1971. *Die Bronzezeit, Periode I–III.* Geschichte Schleswig-Holsteins, vol. 2. Part 1. Lieferung. Neumünster: Karl Wachholtz.

Stuchlík, S. 1981. *Osídlení jeskyň ve starší a střední době bronzové na Moravě.* Studie Archeologického Ústavu ČSAV v Brně 9/2. Prague: Academia.

1987. *Únětické pohřebiště v Mušově.* Studie Archeologického Ústavu ČSAV v Brně 14/2. Prague: Academia.

Stuchlík, S. and Stuchlíková, J. 1996. *Pravěké pohřebiště v Moravské Nové Vsi – Hruškách.* Studie Archeologického Ústavu Akademie Věd ČR v Brně 16/1. Brno: Archeologický Ústav.

Stuchlíková, J. 1982. Zur Problematik der Burgwälle der älteren Bronzezeit in Mähren. In *Beiträge zum bronzezeitlichen Burgenbau in Mitteleuropa,* 389–403. Berlin: Zentralinstitut für Alte Geschichte und Archäologie; Nitra: Archeologický Ústav Slovenskej Akadémie Vied.

Stühmer, H. H., Schulz, H. D., Willkomm, H. and Hänsel, B. 1978. Rohkupferfunde von Helgoland; Kupferverhüttung auf Helgoland; C14–Datierung der Kupferfunde von Helgoland; zur Bedeutung des Rohkupferfundes von Helgoland, *Offa* 35, 11–35.

Sulimirski, T. 1968. *Corded Ware and Globular Amphorae North-East of the Carpathians.* London: Athlone Press.

1970. *Prehistoric Russia: an Outline.* London: Baker.

Suter, H. 1967. Über einige Schalensteine in den Kantonen Waadt, Wallis und Graubünden, *Ur-Schweiz* 31, 4–14.

Suter, P. J., Francuz, J. and Verhoeven, P. 1993. Der bronzezeitliche Einbaum von Erlach-Heidenweg, *Archäologie der Schweiz* 16/2, 53–5.

Switsur, R. 1974. The prehistoric longbow from Denny, Scotland, *Antiquity* 48, 56–8.

Szabó, G. 1994–5. Északi bronztárgyak – vagy északi technológia a Kárpátmedencében? *Archaeológiai Értesítő* 121–2, 79–87.

Szafranski, W. 1950. Ciezarki tkackie i prześliki z grodu kultury łużyckiej w Biskupinie. In *III Sprawozdanie z prac wykopaliskowych w grodzie kultury łużyckiej w Biskupinie w powiecie żnińskim za lata 1938–1939 i*

1946–1948. ed. J. Kostrzewski, 132–60. Poznań: Polski Towarzystwo Prehistoryczny.

Szathmári, I. 1992. Füzesabony-Öregdomb. In *Bronzezeit in Ungarn. Forschungen in Tell-Siedlungen an Donau und Theiss*, 134–40. Frankfurt am Main: Museum für Vor- und Frühgeschichte.

Szombathy, J. 1912. Altertumsfunde aus Höhlen bei St. Kanzian im österreichischen Küstenlande, *Mitt. der Prähistorischen Kommission* 2/2, 127–90.

Szydłowska, E. 1968–72. *Cmentarzysko kultury łużyckiej w Przeczycach, pow. Zawiercie.* Rocznik Muzeum Górnośląskiego w Bytomiu, Archeologia, 5, 8, 9.

    1972. Cmentarzysko kultury łużyckiej w Przeczycach, pow. Zawiercie; omówienie materiałów. Bytom: Muzeum Górnośląskie.

Tabbagh, A. and Verron, G. 1983. Etude par prospection électromagnétique de trois sites à dépôts de l'âge du bronze, *Bull. Soc. Préhist. Française* 80, 375–89.

Tackenberg, K. 1949–50. Die Burgen der Lausitzer Kultur, *Prähistorische Zeitschrift* 34–5, 18–32.

Tákacs, L. 1982. Grubbing by swine as a means of preparing the soil on swampy ground, *Tools and Tillage* 4/3, 155–7.

Tárnoki, J. 1988. The settlement and cemetery of the Hatvan culture at Aszód. In *Bronze Age Tell Settlements of the Great Hungarian Plain I*, 137–69. Inventaria Praehistorica Hungariae 1. Budapest: Hungarian National Museum.

    1992. Törökszentmiklós-Terehalom. In *Bronzezeit in Ungarn. Forschungen in Tell-Siedhungen an Donau und Theiss*, 128–30. Frankfurt am Main: Museum für Vor- und Frühgeschichte.

    1979. *Roads and Tracks of Britain.* London: Dent.

Taylor, J. J. 1980. *Bronze Age Goldwork of the British Isles.* Cambridge: Cambridge University Press.

Taylor, J. J., Watling, R.J., Shell, C. A., Ixer, R.A., Chapman, R. J., Warner, R. B. and Cahill, M. 1996. From gold ores to artifacts in the British Isles: a preliminary study of a new LA-ICP-MS analytical approach, *Archaeological Sciences 1995: Proceedings of a Conference on the Application of Scientific Techniques to the Study of Archaeology*, eds. A. J. Sinclair, E. A. Slater and J. A. J. Gowlett, 144–54. Oxford: Oxbow Monograph 64.

Taylor, J. W. 1983. Erzgebirge tin: a closer look, *Oxford J. Archaeology* 2, 295–8.

Taylor, M. 1981. *Wood in Archaeology.* Princes Risborough: Shire Books.

Taylor, R. J. 1993. *Hoards of the Bronze Age in Southern Britain. Analysis and Interpretation.* British Archaeological Reports 228. Oxford: Tempus Reparatum.

Taylor, T. 1989. Iron and Iron Age in the Carpatho-Balkan region: aspects of social and technological change 1700–1400 BC. In *The Bronze Age–Iron Age Transition in Europe. Aspects of Continuity and Change in European Societies c.1200 to 500 BC*, eds. M. L. Stig Sørensen and R. Thomas, 68–92. Oxford: British Archaeological Reports, Int. Series 483 (i).

Teichert, L. 1976. Die Tierreste aus den Siedlungen der späten Lausitzer Kultur bei Lübben-Steinkirchen und Lübbenau, Kr. Calau, *Veröff. des Museums für Ur- und Frühgeschichte Potsdam* 10, 107–30.

    1986. Tierknochenuntersuchung der spätbronzezeitlichen Siedlung Zitz, Lkr.

Brandenburg, im Vergleich zu Ergebnissen einiger zeitgleicher Fundorte, *Veröff. des Museums für Ur- und Frühgeschichte Potsdam* 20, 163–73.

Teichert, M. 1964. Die Tierreste von den jungbronzezeitlichen Burgwällen Kratzeburg und Gühlen-Glienicke, *Prähistorische Zeitschrift* 42, 107–42.

1968. Die Tierreste der germanischen Siedlung Wüste Kunersdorf, Kr. Seelow, *Veröff. des Museums für Ur- und Frühgeschichte Potsdam* 4, 101–25.

1978. Die Katzenknochen aus den urgeschichtlichen Kulthöhlen des Kyffhäusergebirges, *Alt-Thüringen* 15, 32–67.

1981. Fauna und Landschaft am Südhang der Kyffhäusergebirges in der Bronzezeit, *Ethnographisch-Archäologische Zeitschrift* 22, 649–55.

Teichert, M. and Lepiksaar, J. 1977. Die Vogelknochen aus den urgeschichtlichen Kulthöhlen des Kyffhäusergebirges, *Alt-Thüringen* 14, 108–44.

Tempír, Z. 1985. Rozbor rostlinných zbytků z Černošic, *Archeologické Rozhledy* 37, 14–15.

Teržan, B. 1983. Das Pohorje – ein vorgeschichtliches Erzrevier? *Arheološki Vestnik* 34, 51–84.

(ed.) 1995. *Depojske in posamezne kovinske najdbe bakrene in bronaste dobe na Slovenskem / Hoards and Individual Metal Finds from the Eneolithic and Bronze Ages in Slovenia*. Catalogi et Monographiae, 29. Ljubljana: Narodni Muzej.

Teržan, B., Mihovilić, K. and Hänsel, B. 1998. Eine älterbronzezeitliche befestigte Siedlung von Monkodonja bei Rovinj in Istrien. In *Archäologische Forschungen in urgeschichtlichen Siedlungslandschaften, Festschrift für Georg Kossack zum 75. Geburtstag*, eds. H. Küster, A. Lang and P. Schauer, 155–84. Regensburg: Universitätsverlag / Bonn: Habelt.

Tesch, S. 1992. House, farm and village in the Köpinge area from Early Neolithic to the Early Middle Ages. In *The Archaeology of the Cultural Landscape. Field Work and Research in a South Swedish Rural Region*, eds. L. Larsson, J. Callmer and B. Stjernquist, 283–344. Acta Archaeologica Lundensia, series in 4°, 19. Stockholm: Almqvist and Wiksell.

Teschler-Nicola, M. 1982–85. Die Körper- und Brandbestattungen des mittelbronzezeitlichen Gräberfeldes von Pitten, Niederösterreich, demographische und anthropologische Analyse, *Mitt. der prähistorischen Kommission der österreichischen Akademie der Wissenschaften* 21-2, 127–272.

1994. Bevölkerungsbiologische Aspekte der frühen und mittleren Bronzezeit. In J.-W. Neugebauer, *Bronzezeit in Ostösterreich*. Wissenschaftliche Schriftenreihe Niederösterreich, 98–101, 167–88. St Pölten–Vienna: Verlag Niederösterreichisches Pressehaus.

Teschler-Nicola, M. and Prossinger, H. 1997. Aspekte der Paläodemographie anhand der frühbronzezeitlichen Friedhöfe des Unteren Traisentales (Franzhausen I, Franzhausen II, Gemeinlebarn F und Pottenbrunn-Ratzersdorf). In *Demographie der Bronzezeit. Paläodemographie – Möglichkeiten und Grenzen*, ed. K.-F. Rittershofer, 43–57. Internationale Archäologie 36. Espelkamp: Verlag Marie Leidorf.

Tessier, M. 1960. Découverte de gisements préhistoriques aux environs de la Pointe-Saint-Gildas, *Bull. Soc. Préhist. Française* 57, 428–34.

Thimme, J. (ed.) 1980. *Kunst und Kultur Sardiniens vom Neolithikum bis zum Ende der Nuraghenzeit*. Karlsruhe: C. F. Müller.

Thom, A., Thom A. S. and Burl, H. A. W. 1990. *Stone Rows and Standing*

Stones: Britain, Ireland and Brittany. Oxford: British Archaeological Reports, Int. Series 560.

Thomas, C. 1970. Bronze Age spade marks at Gwithian, Cornwall. In *The Spade in Northern and Atlantic Europe*, eds. A. Gailey and A. Fenton, 10–17. Belfast: Ulster Folk Museum.

Thomas, N. and Thomas, C. 1955. Excavations at Snail Down, Everleigh: 1953, 1955. An interim report, *Wiltshire Archaeol. Magazine* 56, 127–48.

Thomas, R. 1997. Land, kinship relations and the rise of enclosed settlement in first millennium BC Britain, *Oxford J. Archaeology* 16/2, 211–18.

Thomas, R., Robinson, M., Barrett, J. and Wilson, B. 1986. A Late Bronze Age riverside settlement at Wallingford, Oxon, *Archaeol. J.* 143, 174–200.

Thorneycroft, W. 1932–3. Observations on hut-circles near the eastern border of Perthshire, north of Blairgowrie, *Proc. Soc. Antiqs Scotland* 67, 187–208.

Thrane, H. 1963. The earliest bronze vessels in Denmark's Bronze Age, *Acta Archaeologica* (Copenhagen) 33, 109–63.

1966. Dänische Funde fremder Bronzegefässe der jüngeren Bronzezeit (Periode IV), *Acta Archaeologica* (Copenhagen) 36, 157–207.

1979. Fremde Bronzegefässe in südskandinavischen Funden aus der jüngeren Bronzezeit (Periode V), *Acta Archaeologica* (Copenhagen) 49, 1–35.

1981. Late Bronze Age graves in Denmark seen as expressions of social ranking – an initial report. In *Studien zur Bronzezeit. Festschrift für Wilhelm Albert v. Brunn*, ed. H. Lorenz, 475–88. Mainz: v. Zabern.

1984. *Lusehøj ved Voldtofte – en sydvestfynsk storhøj fra yngre broncealder.* Fynske Studier 13. Odense: Bys Museer.

1985. Bronze Age settlements. In *Archaeological Formation Processes. The Representativity of Archaeological Remains from Danish Prehistory*, ed. K. Kristiansen, 142–51. Copenhagen: National Museum.

1989. Regionale aspekter af bronzealderbebyggelse på Fyn. In *Regionale forhold i Nordisk Bronzealder. 5. Nordiske Symposium for Bronzealderforskning på Sandbjerg Slot 1987*, ed. J. Poulsen, 101–6. Jysk Arkaeologisk Selskabs Skrifter 24.

1990. Bronzezeitlicher Ackerbau – Beispiel Dänemark. In *Beiträge zur Geschichte und Kultur der mitteleuropäischen Bronzezeit*, 483–93. Berlin/Nitra: Zentralinstitut für Alte Geschichte und Archäologie der Akademie der Wissenschaften der DDR/Archeologický Ústav Slovenskej Akadémie Vied.

1991. Territoriality in a Bronze Age landscape (Odsherred). In *Regions and Reflections. In Honour of Märta Strömberg*, eds. K. Jennberg, L. Larsson, R. Petré and B. Wyszomirska-Werbart, 119–28. Acta Archaeologica Lundensia, Series in 8°, 20. Lund: Almqvist and Wiksell.

1993. From mini to maxi: Bronze Age barrows from Funen as illustrations of variation and structure. In *Bronsålderns gravhögar, Rapport från ett symposium i Lund 15.XI–16.XI 1991.*, ed. L. Larsson, 79–90. University of Lund, Institute of Archaeology Report Series 48.

Tihelka, K. 1953. Moravská únětická pohřebiště, *Památky Archeologické* 44, 229–328.

1960. Moravské únětické pohřby v dřevěných rakvích, *Archeologické Rozhledy* 12, 748–9.

Tilley, C. 1991. *Material Culture and Text. The Art of Ambiguity.* London: Routledge.

Timberlake, S. 1990a. Excavations at Parys Mountain and Nantyreira. In *Early Mining in the British Isles*, eds. P. and S. Crew, 15–21. Proc. Early Mining Workshop 1989, Plas Tan y Bwlch Occasional Paper 1.

1990b. Excavations and fieldwork on Copa Hill, Cwmystwyth, 1989. In *Early Mining in the British Isles*, eds. P. and S. Crew, 22–9. Proc. Early Mining Workshop 1989, Plas Tan y Bwlch Occasional Paper 1.

1990c. Firesetting and primitive mining experiments, Cwmystwyth, 1989. In *Early Mining in the British Isles*, eds. P. and S. Crew, 53–4. Proc. Early Mining Workshop 1989, Plas Tan y Bwlch Occasional Paper 1.

1991. New evidence for early prehistoric mining in Wales – problems and potentials. In *Archaeological Sciences 1989*, 179–93. Oxford: Oxbow.

Timberlake, S. and Switsur, R. 1988. An archaeological investigation of early mineworkings on Copa Hill, Cwmystwyth: new evidence for prehistoric mining, *Proc. Prehist. Soc.* 54, 329–33.

Tinsley, H. and Grigson, C. 1981. The Bronze Age. In *The Environment in British Prehistory*, eds. I. Simmons and M. Tooley, 210–49. London: Duckworth.

Tipping, R. 1994. Ritual floral tributes in the Scottish Bronze Age – palynological studies, *J. Archaeol. Science* 21, 133–9.

Točík, A. 1964. *Die Gräberfelder der karpatenländischen Hügelgräberkultur*. Fontes Archaeologici Pragenses 7. Prague: National Museum.

1979. *Vyčapy-Opatovce und weitere altbronzezeitliche Gräberfelder in der Südwestslowakei*. Materialia Archaeologica Slovaca, 1. Nitra: Archeologický Ústav Slovenskej Akadémie Vied.

1981. *Nitriansky Hrádok – Zámeček, bronzezeitliche befestigte Ansiedlung der Mad'arovce-Kultur*. Materialia Archaeologica Slovaca 3. Nitra: Archeologický Ústav Slovenskej Akadémie Vied.

1982. Beitrag zur Problematik befestigter Siedlungen in der Südwestslowakei während der älteren und zu Beginn der mittleren Bronzezeit. In *Beiträge zum bronzezeitlichen Burgenbau in Mitteleuropa*, 405–16. Berlin: Zentralinstitut für Alte Geschichte und Archäologie; Nitra: Archeologický Ústav Slovenskej Akadémie Vied.

1994. Poznámky k problematike opevneného sídliska otomanskej kultúry v Barci pri Košiciach, *Študijné Zvesti* 30, 59–65.

Točík, A. and Bublová, H. 1985. Príspevok k výskumu zaniknutej ťažby medi na Slovensku, *Študijné Zvesti* 21, 47–135.

Točík, A. and Paulík, J. 1960. Výskum mohyly v Čake v rokoch 1950–51, *Slovenská Archeológia* 8, 59–124.

Točík, A. and Žebrák, P. 1989. Ausgrabungen in Špania Dolina-Piesky. In *Archäometallurgie der Alten Welt/Old World Archaeometallurgy*, Proc. Int. Symposium Heidelberg 1987, 71–8. Bochum: Deutsches Bergbau-Museum [= *Der Anschnitt* Supplement 7].

Todd, J. M. 1985. Baltic amber in the Ancient Near East: a preliminary investigation, *J. Baltic Studies* 16/3, 292–301.

Tompa, F. 1934–35 (1937). 25 Jahre Urgeschichtsforschung in Ungarn, *Bericht der Römisch-Germanischen Kommission* 24–5, 27–127.

Topping, P. 1989. Early cultivation in Northumberland and the Borders, *Proc. Prehist. Soc.* 55, 161–79.

1990–1 [1993]. The excavation of an unenclosed settlement, field system and cord rig cultivation at Linhope Burn, Northumberland, 1989, *Northern Archaeology* 11, 1–42.

Topping, P. G. 1986. Neutron activation analysis of later prehistoric pottery from the Western Isles of Scotland, *Proc. Prehist. Soc.* 52, 105–29.

Torbrügge, W. 1960. Die bayerischen Inn-Funde, *Bayerische Vorgeschichtsblätter* 25, 16–69.

1970–1. Vor- und frühgeschichtliche Flussfunde. Zur Ordnung und Bestimmung einer Denkmälergruppe, *Bericht der Römisch-Germanischen Kommission* 51–2, 1–146.

Torke, W. 1990. Abschlussbericht zu den Ausgrabungen in der 'Siedlung Forschner' und Ergebnisse der Bauholzuntersuchung, *Bericht der Römisch-Germanischen Kommission* 71, 52–7.

Tozzi, C. 1968. Relazione preliminare sulla I e II campagna di scavi effettuati a Pantelleria, *Rivista di Scienze Preistoriche* 23, 315–88.

Trampuž Orel, N., Doberšek, M., Heath, D. J. and Hudnik, V. 1996. Archäometallurgische Untersuchungen an Sicheln aus spätbronzezeitlichen Hortfunden Sloweniens, *Prähistorische Zeitschrift* 71, 176–93.

Treherne, P. 1995. The warrior's beauty: the masculine body and self-identity in Bronze Age Europe, *J. European Archaeology* 3/1, 105–44.

1997. Reclaiming heroism for the Bronze Age, *British Archaeology* 26, 7.

Trellisó Carreño, L. 1996. Anthropologische Auswertung der Leichenbrände aus Schöppingen, Kreis Broken, Westfalen, *Die Kunde* 47, 177–96.

Trump, D. 1958. The Apennine culture of Italy, *Proc. Prehist. Soc.* 24, 165–200.

1991. The nuraghi of Sardinia, territory and power: the evidence from the commune of Mara, Sassari. In *Papers of the Fourth Conference of Italian Archaeology. 1. The Archaeology of Power. Part 1*, eds. E. Herring, R. Whitehouse and J. Wilkins, 43–4. London: Accordia Research Centre.

Tschurtschentaler, M. and Wein, U. 1996. Kontinuität und Wandel einer alpinen Heiligtums im Laufe seiner 1800–jährigen Geschichte, *Archäologie Österreichs* 7/1, 14–28.

Turková, D. and Kuna, M. 1987. Zur Mikrostruktur der bronzezeitlichen Siedlungen. In *Die Urnenfelderkulturen Mitteleuropas. Symposium Liblice 21.–25.10.1985*, 217–29. Prague: Archaeological Institute, Czechoslovak Academy of Sciences.

Tusa, S. 1994. *Sicilia preistorica*. Palermo: Dario Flaccovio Editore.

Tylecote, R.F. 1971. Observations on Cypriot copper smelting, *Report Department of Antiquities Cyprus 1971*, 53–8.

1976. *A History of Metallurgy*. London: The Metals Society.

1981. From pot-bellows to tuyères, *Levant* 13, 107–18.

1986. *The Prehistory of Metallurgy in the British Isles*. London: Institute of Metals.

1987a. *The Early History of Metallurgy*. London: Longman.

1987b. Commentary on the metallurgy session. In *Studies in Sardinian Archaeology III. Nuragic Sardinia and the Mycenaean World*, ed. M. S. Balmuth, 223–4. Oxford: British Archaeological Reports, Int. Series 387.

1987c. *The Prehistory of Metallurgy in the British Isles*. London: Institute of Metals.

Ucko, P. J. 1969. Ethnography and archaeological interpretation of funerary remains, *World Archaeology* 1, 262–80.

Uenze, H. P. 1993. Die Schlange, ein Kultsymbol der Urnenfelder- und Hallstattzeit, *Acta Praehistorica et Archaeologica* 25, 132–6.

Uerpmann, H.-P. 1970. Die Tierknochenfunde aus der Talayot-Siedlung von S'Illot (San Lorenzo/Mallorca), *Studien über frühe Tierknochenfunde von der Iberischen Halbinsel* 2. Munich: University of Munich/Deutsches Archäologisches Institut, Abteilung Madrid.

Ullén, I. 1994. The power of case studies. Interpretation of a Late Bronze Age settlement in central Sweden, *J. European Archaeology* 2/2, 249–62.

Ullrich, H. 1972. *Das Aunjetitzer Gräberfeld von Grossbrembach. I. Anthropologische Untersuchungen zur Frage nach Entstehung und Verwandschaft der thüringischen, böhmischen und mährischen Aunjetitzer*. Weimar: Hermann Böhlaus Nachfolger.

Ursulescu, N. 1977. Exploatarea sării din saramura în neoliticul timpuriu în lumina descoperirilor de la Solca (jud. Suceava), *Studii şi cercetări de istoria veche* 28, 307–17.

Vagnetti, L. 1984. Testimonianze di metallurgia minoica dalla zona di Nerokourou (Kydonias), *Studi Micenei ed. Egeo-Anatolici* 25, 155–71.

van der Veen, M. 1992. *Crop Husbandry Regimes. An Archaeobotanical Study of Farming in Northern England 1000 BC – AD 500*. Sheffield Archaeological Monographs 3. Sheffield: University of Sheffield.

van der Veen, M. and Lanting, J. N. 1989. A group of tumuli on the 'Hooghalen' estate near Hijken (municipality of Beilen, province of Drenthe, the Netherlands), *Palaeohistoria* 31, 191–234.

van Giffen, A.E. 1930. *Die Bauart der Einzelgräber. Beitrag zur Kenntnis der älteren individuellen Grabhügelstrukturen in den Niederlanden*. Mannus-Bibliothek 44–5. Leipzig: Curt Rabitzsch.

van Hoek, M. A. M. 1987. The prehistoric rock art of County Donegal (Part I), *Ulster J. Archaeology* 50, 23–46.

1988. The prehistoric rock art of County Donegal (Part II), *Ulster J. Archaeology* 51, 21–47.

1993. The spiral in British and Irish Neolithic rock art, *Glasgow Archaeol. J.* 18, 11–32.

van Zeist, W., Wasylikowa, K. and Behre, K.-E. (eds.) 1991. *Progress in Old World Palaeoethnobotany. A Retrospective View on the Occasion of 20 Years of the International Work Group for Palaeoethnobotany*. Rotterdam/Brookfield: A. A. Balkema.

Vasseur, G. 1911. Une mine de cuivre exploitée à l'âge du bronze dans les garrigues de l'Hérault (environs de Cabrières), *L'Anthropologie* 22, 413–20.

Vatcher, F. de M. and H. L. 1976. The excavation of a round barrow at Poor's Heath, Risby, Suffolk, *Proc. Prehist. Soc.* 42, 263–92.

Vencl, S. 1983. K problematice fortifikaci v archeologii, *Archeologické Rozhledy* 35, 284–315.

1984a. Stopy zranění zbraněmi jako archeologický pramen poznání vojenství, *Archeologické Rozhledy* 36, 528–45.

1984b. *Problémy poznání vojenství v archeologii*. Archeologické Študijní Materiály 14. Prague: Archeologický Ústav ČSAV.

1984c. War and warfare in archaeology, *J. Anthropological Archaeology* 3, 116–32.

Venclová, N. 1989 [1990]. Sklo mladší a pozdní doby bronzové a doby halštatské a interregionální kontakty v Evropě. In *Problemy kultury łużyckiej na Pomorzu*, ed. T. Małinowski, 227–37. Słupsk: Wyższa Szkola Pedagogiczna.

1990. *Prehistoric Glass in Bohemia*. Prague: Archaeological Institute.

Veny, C. 1974. Anotaciones sobre la cronología de las navetas de Menorca, *Trabajos de Prehistoria* 31, 101–42.

Verlaeckt, K. 1993. The Kivik petroglyphs. A reassessment of different opinions, *Germania* 71, 1–29.

Verron, G. 1976. Les civilisations de l'âge du bronze en Normandie. In *La Préhistoire française. II. Civilisations néolithiques et protohistoriques*, ed. J. Guilaine, 585–600. Paris: Editions du CNRS.

  1983. L'interprétation des dépôts de l'âge du bronze à la lumière de prospections et de fouilles récentes. In *Enclos funéraires et structures d'habitat en Europe du nord-ouest. Table Ronde du CNRS, Rennes 1981*, 263–81. Rennes: Travaux du Laboratoire anthropologie–préhistoire–protohistoire–quaternaire armoricains.

Verwers, G. J. 1966. Non-circular monuments in the southern Dutch urnfields, *Analecta Praehistorica Leidensia* 2, 49–57.

  1972. *Das Kamps Veld in Haps in Neolithikum, Bronzezeit und Eisenzeit*. Leiden: Universitaire Pers (*Analecta Praehistorica Leidensia* 5).

Vinski-Gasparini, K. 1973. *Kultura polja sa žarama u sjevernoj Hrvatskoj*. Zadar: Filozofski Fakultet.

Vizdal, J. 1972. Erste bildliche Darstellung eines zweirädrigen Wagens vom Ende der mittleren Bronzezeit in der Slowakei, *Slovenská Archeológia* 20, 223–31.

Vladár, J. 1973a. Osteuropäische und mediterrane Einflüsse im Gebiet der Slowakei während der Bronzezeit, *Slovenská Archeológia* 21, 253–357.

  1973b. *Pohrebiská zo staršej doby bronzovej v Brančí*. Archaeologica Slovaca – Fontes, 12. Bratislava: Slovak Academy of Sciences.

Vlček, E. and Hajek, L. 1963. A ritual well and the find of an Early Bronze Age iron dagger at Gánovce near Poprad (Czechoslovakia). In *A Pedro Bosch-Gimpera en el septuagésimo aniversario de su naciamento*, ed. S. Genovés, 427–39. Mexico City: Instituto Nacional de Antropología e Historia.

Vogt, E. 1937. *Geflechte und Gewebe der Steinzeit*. Monographien zur Ur- und Frühgeschichte der Schweiz 1. Basle: Birkhäuser.

  1954. Pfahlbaustudien. In *Das Pfahlbauproblem*, 119–219. Schaffhausen: Schweizerische Gesellschaft für Urgeschichte.

Voigt, T. 1955. *Das frühbronzezeitliche Gräberfeld von Wahlitz, Kreis Burg*. Veröffent. des Landesmuseums für Vorgeschichte in Halle 14. Halle (Saale): Max Niemeyer.

Voza, G. 1972. Thapsos, primi resultati delle più recente ricerche, *Atti della XIV Riunione Scientifica dell'Istituto Italiano di Preistoria e Protostoria (Puglia 1970)*, 175–205.

  1973. Thapsos: resoconto sulle campagne di scavo del 1970–71, *Atti della XV Riunione Scientifica dell'Istituto Italiano di Preistoria e Protostoria (Verona-Trento 1972)*, 133–57.

Vulpe, A. 1996. Deponierungen, Opferstätten und Symbolgut im Karpatengebiet. In *Archäologische Forschungen zum Kultgeschehen in der jüngeren Bronzezeit und frühen Eisenzeit Alteuropas*, ed. C. Huth, 517–33. Regensburger Beiträge zur prähistorischen Archäologie, 2. Regensburg: Universitätsverlag (Bonn: Habelt).

Waddell, J. n.d. [1990]. *The Bronze Age Burials of Ireland*. Galway: Galway University Press.

Waddington, C. 1998. Cup and ring marks in context, *Cambridge Archaeol. J.* 8/1, 29–54.

Währen, M. 1984. Brot und Getreidebrei von Twann aus dem 4. Jahrtausend vor Christus, *Archäologie der Schweiz* 7, 2–6.

1987. Das Brot in der Bronzezeit und älteren vorrömischen Eisenzeit nördlich der Alpen unter besonderer Berücksichtigung von Brotfunden aus Kreisgrabenfriedhöfen des Münsterlandes. Eine Skizze zum Forschungsstand, *Ausgrabungen und Funde in Westfalen-Lippe* 5, 23–71.

1989a. Identifizierung von gesäuertem Brot in Knochenasche-Kristallen einer urnenfelderzeitlichen Bestattung in Bellenberg, Ldkr. Neu-Ulm. In E. Pressmar, *Bellenberg, Lkr. Neu-Ulm, Die Grabungen 1983–1987. Kataloge der Prähistorischen Staatssammlung München* 23, 59–65.

1989b. Brot und Gebäck von der Jungsteinzeit bis zur Römerzeit, *Helvetia Archaeologica* 20, 82–110.

Wainwright, G. J. and Smith, K. 1980. The Shaugh Moor project: second report – the enclosure, *Proc. Prehist. Soc.* 46, 65–122.

Waldbaum, J. C. 1980. The first archaeological appearance of iron and the transition to the Iron Age. In *The Coming of the Age of Iron*, eds. T. A. Wertime and J. D. Muhly, 69–98. New Haven and London: Yale University Press.

Walker, M. J. 1985. *Characterising Local Southeastern Spanish Populations of 3000–1500 BC*. Oxford: British Archaeological Reports, Int. Series 263.

Wallerstein, I. 1974/1980. *The Modern World-System*, vols. 1–2. New York: Academic Press.

1984. *The Politics of the World-Economy*. Cambridge: Cambridge University Press.

Walter, D. 1985. *Thüringer Höhlen und ihre holozänen Bodenaltertümer*. Weimarer Monographien zur Ur- und Frühgeschichte 14. Weimar: Museum für Ur- und Frühgeschichte Thüringens.

1990a. Siedlungshinterlassenschaften der Aunjetitzer Kultur bei Sundhausen, Kr. Nordhausen, *Alt-Thüringen* 25, 31–60.

1990b. Zum Übergang von der frühen zur mittleren Bronzezeit im Gebiet zwischen Thüringer Wald und Harz. In *Beiträge zur Geschichte und Kultur der mitteleuropäischen Bronzezeit*, 515–35. Berlin/Nitra: Zentralinstitut für Alte Geschichte und Archäologie der Akademie der Wissenschaften der DDR/Archeologický Ústav Slovenskej Akadémie Vied.

Wamser, L. 1984. Ein bemerkenswerter Hortfund der Spätbronzezeit von Tauberbischofsheim-Hochhausen, Main-Tauber-Kreis, *Fundberichte aus Baden-Württemberg* 9, 23–40.

Waniczek, K. 1986. Ein Beitrag zur Zinnmetallurgie der Bronzezeit, *Alt-Thüringen* 21, 112–35.

Wanzek, B. 1992. Der älterurnenfelderzeitliche Hortfund von Lengyeltóti ('Lengyeltóti II'), Komitat Somogy, Ungarn. Eine Vorlage, *Acta Praehistorica et Archaeologica* 24, 249–88.

Ward, A. H. 1987. Early agriculture on Rhossili Down, Gower, West Glamorgan, *Bull. Board of Celtic Studies* 34, 220–7.

1989. Land allotment of possible prehistoric date on Mynydd Llangynderyn, south-east Dyfed, *Archaeologia Cambrensis* 138, 46–58.

Warmenbol, E. 1988. Le groupe Rhin–Suisse–France orientale et les grottes sépulchrales du Bronze Final en Haute Belgique. In *Le Groupe Rhin–Suisse–France orientale et la notion de civilisation des Champs d'urnes. Actes du colloque international de Nemours 1986*, eds. P. Brun and C. Mordant, 153–63. Nemours: Mémoires du Musée de préhistoire d'Île-de-France 1.

1996. L'or, la mort et les Hyperboréens. La bouche des Enfers ou le Trou de

Han à Han-sur-Lesse. In *Archäologische Forschungen zum Kultgeschehen in der jüngeren Bronzezeit und frühen Eisenzeit Alteuropas*, ed. C. Huth, 203–34. Regensburger Beiträge zur prähistorischen Archäologie 2. Regensburg: Universitätsverlag (Bonn: Habelt).

Warrilow, W., Owen, G. and Gibson, A. M. 1986. Eight ring-ditches at Four Crosses, Llandysilio, Powys, 1981–85, *Proc. Prehist. Soc.* 52, 53–87.

Waterbolk, H. T. and Butler, J. J. 1965. Comments on the use of metallurgical analysis in prehistoric studies, *Helinium* 5, 227–51.

Waterbolk, H. T. and van Zeist, W. 1961. A Bronze Age sanctuary in the raised bog at Bargeroosterveld (DR.), *Helinium* 1, 5–19.

Watkins, T. 1980. A prehistoric coracle in Fife, *Int. J. Nautical Archaeology* 9/4, 277–86.

Weber, C. 1996. *Die Rasiermesser in Südosteuropa (Albanien, Bosnien-Herzegowina, Bulgarien, Griechenland, Kroatien, Rumänien, Serbien, Slowenien und Ungarn)*. Prähistorische Bronzefunde,VIII, 5. Stuttgart: Franz Steiner.

Webster, G. S. 1991. The functions and social significance of nuraghi. In *Arte militare e architettura nuragica, Nuragic Architecture in its Military, Territorial and Socio-economic Context*, ed. B. S. Frizell, 169–85. Stockholm: Skrifter utgivna av Svenska Institutet i Rom, series in 4°, 48.

1996. *A Prehistory of Sardinia 2300–500 BC*. Sheffield: Sheffield Academic Press.

Wegewitz, W. 1941. Totenhäuser und andere Grabformen der älteren Bronzezeit im Niederelbegebiet, *Die Kunde* 9, 75–82.

1949. *Die Gräber der Stein- und Bronzezeit im Gebiet der Niederelbe*. Hildesheim: August Lax.

1967. Der Schalenstein aus Putensen. In *Hamburg-Harburg, Sachsenwald, Nördliche Lüneburger Heide*, Führer zu den vor- und frühgeschichtlichen Denkmälern 7, Mainz: Zabern, 116–17.

Wegner, G. 1976. *Die vorgeschichtlichen Flussfunde aus dem Main und aus dem Rhein bei Mainz*. Materialhefte zur bayerischen Vorgeschichte 30. Kallmünz/Opf.: Lassleben.

Węgrzynowicz, T. 1981. Tierbestattungen und tierische Überreste als Beweise eines Kultwandels in der Bronze- und Eisenzeit Polens. In *Studien zur Bronzezeit. Festschrift für Wilhelm Albert v. Brunn*, ed. H. Lorenz, 499–507. Mainz: v. Zabern.

Weidmann, T. 1982. Keramische Gussformen aus der spätbronzezeitlichen Seerandsiedlung Zug 'Sumpf', *Jahrbuch der schweizerischen Gesellschaft für Ur- und Frühgeschichte* 65, 69–81.

Welinder, S. 1979. *Prehistoric Demography*. Acta Archaeologica Lundensia, Series in 8° Minore, 8. Bonn: Habelt/Lund: Gleerup.

Wells, P. S. 1983. *Rural Economy in the Early Iron Age. Excavations at Hascherkeller, 1978–1981*. Bull. American School of Prehistoric Research 36. Cambridge (Mass.): Peabody Museum.

Wels-Weyrauch, U. 1978. *Die Anhänger und Halsringe in Südwestdeutschland und Nordbayern*. Prähistorische Bronzefunde XI,1. Munich: Beck.

1989a. Mittelbronzezeitliche Frauentrachten in Süddeutschland (Beziehungen zur Hagenauer Gruppierung). In *Dynamique du Bronze moyen en Europe occidentale*, Actes du 113ᵉ Congrès National des Sociétés Savantes, Strasbourg 1988, 117–34. Paris: Editions du CTHS.

1989b. 'Fremder Mann', *Germania* 67, 162–7.

Wesselkamp, G. 1980. *Die neolithischen Ufersiedlungen von Twann, 5. Die organischen Reste der Cortaillod-Schichten.* Bern: Staatliche Lehrmittelverlag.

White, D. A. 1982. *The Bronze Age Cremation Cemeteries at Simons Ground, Dorset.* Dorset Natural History and Archaeol. Soc. Monograph 3. Dorchester.

Wihlborg, A. 1977–8. Sagaholm. A Bronze Age barrow with rock-carvings, *Meddelanden från Lunds Universitets Historiska Museum* new series 2, 111–28.

Wilhelm, M., Gerlach, T. and Simon, K. 1990. Aunjetitzer Bestattung mit 'indirekter Leichenverbrennung' von Jessnitz, Kr. Bautzen, *Ausgrabungen und Funde* 35, 21–29.

Wilhelmi, K. 1974. Siedlungs- und Bestattungsplätze der Bronzezeit und Eisenzeit bei Telgte, Kr. Münster, *Archäologisches Korrespondenzblatt* 4, 213–22.

   1981. *Zwei bronzezeitliche Kreisgrabenfriedhöfe bei Telgte, Kr. Warendorf.* Bodenaltertümer Westfalens 17. Münster: Aschendorff.

Wilkens, B. 1995. Animali da contesti rituali nella preistoria dell'Italia centromeridionale, *Padusa Quaderni* 1 (Atti del I° Convegno Nazionale di Archeozoologia, Rovigo 1993), 201–8.

Wilkes, J. 1992. *The Illyrians.* Oxford: Blackwell.

Wilkinson, D. 1991. Cores, peripheries and civilizations. In *Core/Periphery Relations in Precapitalist Worlds,* eds. C. Chase-Dunn and T. D. Hall, 113–66. Boulder: Westview Press.

   1993. Civilizations, cores, world economies, and oikumenes. In *The World System: Five Hundred Years or Five Thousand?* eds. G. A. Frank and B. K. Gills, 221–46. London: Routledge.

Wilkinson, T. J. and Murphy, P. 1986. Archaeological survey of an intertidal zone: the submerged landscape of the Essex coast, England, *J. Field Archaeology* 13, 177–94.

   1995. *The Archaeology of the Essex Coast, I: The Hullbridge Survey.* East Anglian Archaeology 71. Chelmsford: Essex County Council (Archaeology Section).

Williamson, D. 1990. The role and status of the Bronze Age smith and the organisation of metallurgy. Unpublished MA thesis, University of Durham.

Williamson, W. C. 1872. *Description of the Tumulus Opened at Gristhorpe, near Scarborough with Engravings of the Coffin, Weapons, etc.* Scarborough: S. W. Theakston (reprinted by Prehistory Research Section, Yorkshire Archaeological Society, 1976).

Willroth, K.-H. 1985a. Aspekte älterbronzezeitlicher Deponierungen im südlichen Skandinavien, *Germania* 63/2, 361–400.

   1985b. *Die Hortfunde der älteren Bronzezeit in Südschweden und auf den dänischen Inseln.* Neumünster: Wachholtz.

Willvonseder, K. 1937. *Die mittlere Bronzezeit in Österreich.* Vienna: Schroll.

Windelhed, B. 1984. 'Celtic fields' and prehistoric agrarian landscapes. In *Settlement and Economy in Later Scandinavian Prehistory,* ed. K. Kristiansen, 85–110. Oxford: British Archaeological Reports, Int. Series 211.

Winghart, S. 1993. Überlegungen zur Bauweise hölzerner Speichenräder der Bronze- und Urnenfelderzeit, *Acta Praehistorica et Archaeologica* 25, 153–67.

Wirth, S. 1991. Ein reiches Grabfund der späten Urnenfelderzeit von Haunstetten, *Das Archäologisches Jahr in Bayern 1991*, 77–8.

Wobst, H. M. 1977. Stylistic behavior and information exchange. In *For the Director: Research Essays in Honor of James B. Griffin*, ed. C. E. Cleland, 317–42. Museum of Anthropology Anthropological Paper 61. Ann Arbor: University of Michigan.

Wollmann, V. 1996. *Mineritul metalifer, extragerea sării şi carierele de piatră în Dacia Romană/Der Erzbergbau, die Salzgewinnung und die Steinbrüche im Römischen Dakien*. Bibliotheca Musei Napocensis 13 / Veröff. aus dem Deutschen Bergbau-Museum Bochum 63. Cluj-Napoca: Muzeul Naţional de Istorie a Transilvaniei.

Woltering, P. J. 1991. Nederzettingen uit de bronstijd en de vroege ijzertijd bij Den Burg, Texel. In *Nederzettingen uit de bronstijd en de vroege ijzertijd in de Lage Landen*, eds. H. Fokkens and N. Roymans, 83–92. Nederlandse Archeologische Rapporten 13. Amersfoort: Rijkdienst voor het Oudheidkundig Bodemonderzoek.

Wood, J. 1995. An archaeology of sexuality, focusing on the rock engravings of Bronze Age Scandinavia. Unpublished dissertation, University of Durham.

Wood-Martin, W. G. 1886. *The Lake Dwellings of Ireland*. Dublin: Hodges, Figgis and Co./ London: Longman, Green and Co.

Woodiwiss, S. (ed.) 1992. *Iron Age and Roman Salt Production and the Medieval Town of Droitwich*. Council for British Archaeology Research Report 81.

Woodward, A. B. and P. J. 1996. The topography of some barrow cemeteries in Bronze Age Wessex, *Proc. Prehist. Soc.* 62, 275–91.

Woodward, P. J. 1991. *The South Dorset Ridgeway. Survey and Excavations 1977–84*. Dorset Natural History and Archaeological Society, Monograph Series 8. Dorchester.

Woytowitsch, E. 1978. *Die Wagen der Bronze- und frühen Eisenzeit in Italien*. Prähistorische Bronzefunde XVII, 1. Munich: Beck.

Wright, E. V. 1990. *The Ferriby Boats. Seacraft of the Bronze Age*. London: Routledge.

Wright, E. V. and C. V. 1947. Prehistoric boats from North Ferriby, E Yorks, *Proc. Prehist. Soc.* 13, 114–38.

Wright, H. T. 1977. Recent research on the origin of the state, *Annual Review of Anthropology* 6, 379–97.

Wüstemann, H. 1974. Zur Sozialstruktur im Seddiner Kulturgebiet, *Zeitschrift für Archäologie* 8, 67–107.

  1978. Zur Sozialentwicklung während der Bronzezeit im Norden der DDR. In *Mitteleuropäische Bronzezeit. Beiträge zur Archäologie und Geschichte*, eds. W. Coblenz and F. Horst, 195–209. Berlin: Akademie-Verlag.

  1992. Jungbronzezeitliche 'Vollgriffschwerter' mit Bleifüllung, *Arbeits- und Forschungsberichte zur sächsischen Bodendenkmalpflege* 35, 39–49.

Wyss, R. 1971a. Siedlungswesen und Verkehrswege. In *Ur- und frühgeschichtliche Archäologie der Schweiz, III. Die Bronzezeit*, ed. W. Drack, 103–22. Basel: Verlag Schweizerische Gesellschaft für Ur- und Frühgeschichte.

  1971b. Technik, Wirtschaft und Handel. In *Ur- und frühgeschichtliche Archäologie der Schweiz, III. Die Bronzezeit*, 123–44. ed. W. Drack, Basel: Verlag Schweizerische Gesellschaft für Ur- und Frühgeschichte.

  1996. Funde aus Pässen, Höhen, aus Quellen und Gewässern der Zentral- und Westalpen. In *Archäologische Forschungen zum Kultgeschehen in der jüngeren Bronzezeit und frühen Eisenzeit Alteuropas*, ed. C. Huth, 417–28.

Regensburger Beiträge zur prähistorischen Archäologie 2. Regensburg: Universitätsverlag (Bonn: Habelt).

Yates, T. 1990. Archaeology through the looking glass. In *Archaeology after Structuralism*, eds. I. Bapty and T. Yates, 153–202. London: Routledge.

Yener, K. A. and Özbal, H. 1987. Tin in the Turkish Taurus Mountains: the Bolkardag mining district, *Antiquity* 61, 220–6.

Yener, K. A. and Vandiver, P. J. 1993. Tin processing at Göltepe, an Early Bronze Age site in Anatolia, *American J. Archaeology* 97, 207–38.

Yudin, A. I. and Lopatin, V. A. 1989. Pogrebenie mastera epokhi bronzy v stepnom Zavolz'e, *Sovietskaya Arkheologiya* 1989/3, 131–40.

Zápotocký, M. 1969. K vyznamu Labe jako spojovací a dopravní cesty (Zur Bedeutung der Elbe als Verbindungs- und Transportweg), *Památky Archeologické* 60, 277–366.

Zeitler, J. P. 1993. Mykenische Burgen in Süddeutschland. Gedanken zu einem Phänomen bronzezeitlicher Siedlungsarchäologie, *Acta Praehistorica et Archaeologica* 25, 77–86.

Ziegert, H. 1963. *Zur Chronologie und Gruppengliederung der westlichen Hügelgräberkultur*. Berlin: de Gruyter.

Zimmermann, W. H. 1970. Urgeschichtliche Opferfunde aus Flüssen, Mooren, Quellen und Brunnen Südwestdeutschlands. Ein Beitrag zu den Opferfunden vorherrschenden Fundkategorien, *Neue Ausgrabungen und Forschungen in Niedersachsen* 6, 53–92.

  1988. Frühe Darstellungen vom Gewichtswebstuhl auf Felszeichnungen in der Val Camonica, Lombardei. In *Archaeological Textiles, Report from the 2nd NESAT Symposium*, 26–38. Arkaeologiske Skrifter 2. Copenhagen: University of Copenhagen.

Zindel, C. 1968. Felszeichnungen auf Carschenna, Gde Sils im Domleschg, *Ur-Schweiz* 32, 1–5.

Zotović, M. 1985. *Arheološki i etnički problemi bronzanog i gvozdenog doba zapadne Srbije*. Dissertationes et Monographiae XXVI. Belgrade: Savez Arheoloških Društava Jugoslavije.

Zschocke, K. and Preuschen, E. 1932. *Das urzeitliche Bergbaugebiet von Mühlbach-Bischofshofen*. Materialien zur Urgeschichte Österreichs 6. Vienna: Anthropologische Gesellschaft in Wien.

INDEX

Italics indicate figures.

Aaby, 321
Aalestrup, 125n
Abbot's Way, 248
Access analysis, 27
Achilles, 288
Acholshausen, 169
Acorns, 132, 149, 150
Acton Park, hoard and phase, *15*, 18, 204
Adriatic Sea, 71n, 101, 190, *191*, 300, 320
Aegean, 9, 14, *16*, 169, 181, 195, 201, 220, 228, 271, 324, 412, 416
Aeneid, 317
Aeolian Islands, *16*, 36, 37, 61, 181
Aggtelek cave and karst, 132, 144, 320
Agriculture, arable, 124, 134, 146n, 150, 155, 159, 161, 162, 163, 176, 185, 236, 239, 244, 296, 300, 339n, 344, 387, 394, 407, 416, 426, 432
Aibunar, 207n
Air photography, 86n, 93, 118, 151, 153, 163, 432
Aisne valley, 85
Albanbühel, *139*, 142
Albania, 7, 77, 101, *102*, 193, 198, 337, 427, 429, 433
Alder, 165, 244, 248, 315
Alderley Edge, Cheshire, 208n, 213
Aléria, Terrina IV, 234
Alkalis, 265
Alloys, 197, 199, 202–5, 230, 231, 234n
Allumiere, 190, *191*
Alpha-analysis, 26
Alps, Alpine zone, 14, 19, 23, 38, 39, 40, 52, 118, 130, 132, 141, 144, 146n, 149, 180, 189, 190, 193, 198, 199, *200*, 204, *206*, 210, 219, 231, 243, 244, 255, 269n, 289, 312, 319, 331, 336, 337n, 339, 340, 362, 363, 401, 423
Alsace, 97, 295, 408
Altars, 309, 311
Amber, 91, 92, 108, 175, 187, 189, 190, *191*, 195, 269, 294, 313, 321, 334n, 401, 405, 411, 420, 429
Amesbury, barrow G.85, 92
Amulets, 321, 322
Analogy, 387, 388

Analysis, scientific, 189, 198, 199, 200, 203, 268, 384
Anasazi, 274
Anatolia, 228, 240, 348, 414
Ancestor rituals, 74
Anchors, 181
Androphagi, 333
Aner, E. and Kersten, K., 95, 105, 431
Animal motifs, 322
Animal sacrifice, 333–5
Animals, 28, 45, 56, 58, 60, 65, 69, 124, 128, 133–43, 156, 158, 159, 162, 170, 195, 249, 254, 256, 275, 333, 334, 335, 339, 340, 342, 345, 350
Animals, wild, 136, *137, 139*, 140n, 141, 143
Annaku, 201n
Anthropology, 273, 335n, 388, 406, 409
Anthropology, physical, 369, 379, 384
Anthropomorphic vessels, 322
Antigori, 230, 231
Antimony, 202, 204
Antler, 92, 170, *171*, 208n, 242, 284n, 321
Anvils, *214*, 215, 222, 223
Apa, 237
Apalle, 28, *29*
Apennine Bronze Age, Apennine culture, *16*, 18, 36, 242
Apennine mountains, 55, 142
Apples, 149
Aran Islands, 234, 298, 303, *304*
Aranyos horizon, 356n
Arbon, Bleiche site, 42n
Archery, 284
Ard-marks, 125, 126, *133*, 151
Ardennes, 319
Ards, 124, 125, 126, *127*, 128, 244, 341, 344
Argaric Bronze Age, 7, 18, 150, 199, 228, 229, 233, 382, 395n, 398
Argyll, 341
Arilje, Davidovića Cair, *102*
Arm-spirals, 80
Armenia, 167
Armies, 274
Armour, 100, 271, 275, 284, 285–91, 306, 327, 328, 396, 409, 410, 414
Armrings, 80, 229, 230, 294, 315, 326, 331n, *357*, 374, 376, 397